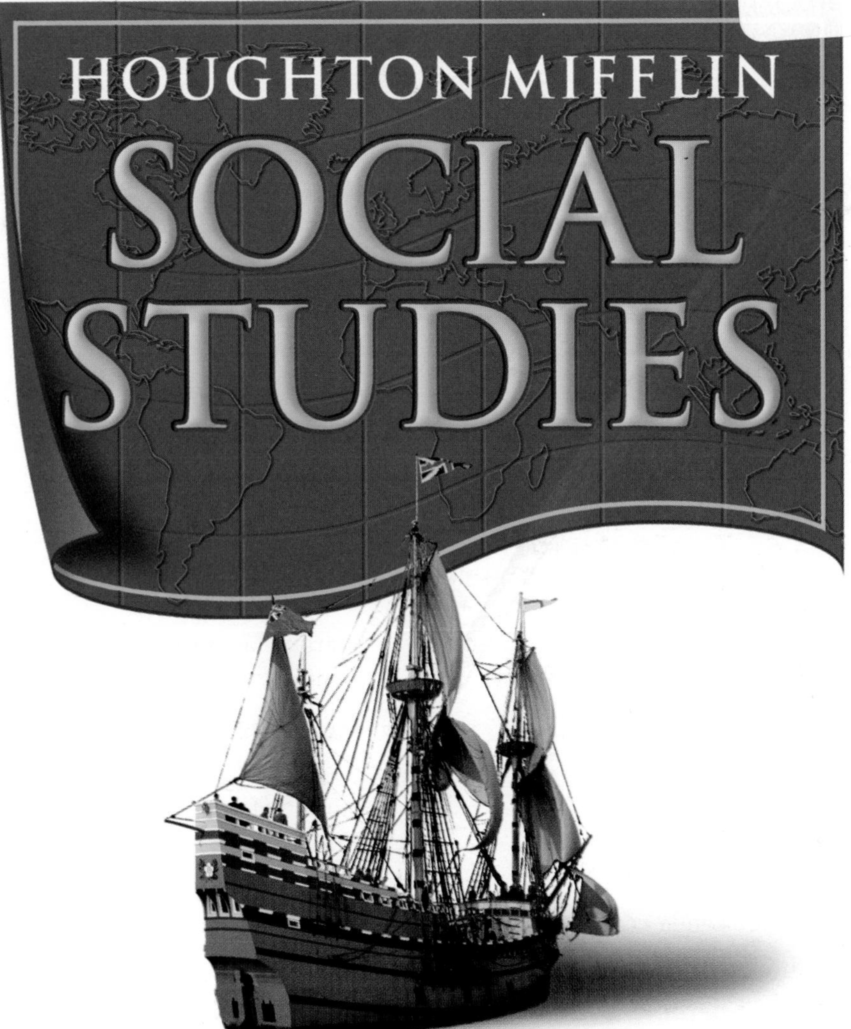

UNITED STATES HISTORY

EARLY YEARS

TEACHER'S EDITION

VOLUME 2

Visit Education Place®
www.eduplace.com/kids

BOSTON

Authors and Reviewers

Lead Author
Dr. Herman J. Viola
Smithsonian Institution

Authors
Dr. Sarah Witham Bednarz
Texas A&M University

Dr. Carlos E. Cortés
University of California, Riverside

Dr. Cheryl Jennings
Institute of Education
University of North Florida

Dr. Mark C. Schug
University of Wisconsin, Milwaukee

Dr. Charles S. White
Boston University

Consulting Authors
Dr. Dolores Beltran
California State University — Los Angeles
(Support for English Language Learners)

Dr. MaryEllen Vogt
California State University Center for the Advancement of Reading
(Reading in the Content Area)

Teacher Reviewers

Grade 3

Stacy Acker
Columbia Station, OH

Kerrie Bandyk
Grand Rapids, MI

Julie Bauer
East St. Louis, IL

Rosie Becerra-Davies
Montebello, CA

Cris Ferguson
Chula Vista, CA

Nancy Hassard
Ringwood, NJ

Lynda Lemon-Rush
Covina, CA

Karen Pratt
North Miami Beach, FL

Stephanie Raker
Rochester, NY

Lorrie Soria
Oakland, CA

Sandra Stroud-Pennington
Decatur, GA

Peggy Yelverton
Palm Bay, FL

Grade 4

Kristy Bouck
Port Orchard, WA

Martha Eckhoff
St. Louis, MO

Melanie Gates
Long Beach, CA

Jo Ann Gillespie
Saratoga, CA

Sharon Hawthrone
Medford, NJ

Martha Lewis
Oviedo, FL

Tammy Morici
Piñon Hills, CA

Andrea Orndorff
Ellicott City, MD

Kay Renshaw
Clearwater, FL

Kristin Roemhildt
Moundsview, MN

Cathy Stubbs
Ft. Lauderdale, FL

Tonya Torres
North Miami Beach, FL

Kristen Werk
Pittsburg, CA

Grade 5

Skip Bayliss
Satellite Beach, FL

Annette Bomba
Schenevus, NY

Amy Clark
Travelers Rest, SC

Melissa Cook
Lake Elsinore, CA

Kelli Dunn
Broadview, IL

Peggy Greene
Thomaston, GA

Elyce Kaplan
San Diego, CA

Julia McNeal
Dayton, OH

Theresa Powell
Charleston, SC

Lesa Roberts
Huntsville, AL

Lynn Schew
Clearwater, FL

Linda Whitford
Alpharetta, GA

Lisa Yingling
Williamsport, PA

Credits
Illustration: Timothy Johnson

Photography:
Library of Congress ID # LC-USZ62-77160, p. 534

Printed in the U.S.A.

ISBN: 0-618-50267-X

123456789 — WC — 13 12 11 10 09 08 07 06 05 04

Contents

United States History: Early Years

Volume 2

Authors

Senior Author
Dr. Herman J. Viola
Curator Emeritus
Smithsonian Institution

Dr. Cheryl Jennings
Project Director
Florida Institute of Education
University of North Florida

Dr. Sarah Witham Bednarz
Associate Professor, Geography
Texas A&M University

Dr. Mark C. Schug
Professor and Director
Center for Economic Education
University of Wisconsin, Milwaukee

Dr. Carlos E. Cortés
Professor Emeritus, History
University of California, Riverside

Dr. Charles S. White
Associate Professor
School of Education
Boston University

Consulting Authors
Dr. Dolores Beltran
Assistant Professor
Curriculum Instruction
California State University, Los Angeles
(Support for English Language Learners)

Dr. MaryEllen Vogt
Co-Director
California State University Center for the Advancement of Reading
(Reading in the Content Area)

The United States Mint honors the Louisiana Purchase and the Lewis and Clark expedition in a new nickel series. The first nickel of the series features a rendition of the Jefferson Peace Medal. Thomas Jefferson commissioned this medal for Lewis and Clark's historic trip, which began in 1804.

Louisiana Purchase/Peace Medal nickel circulating coin images courtesy United States Mint. Used with Permission.

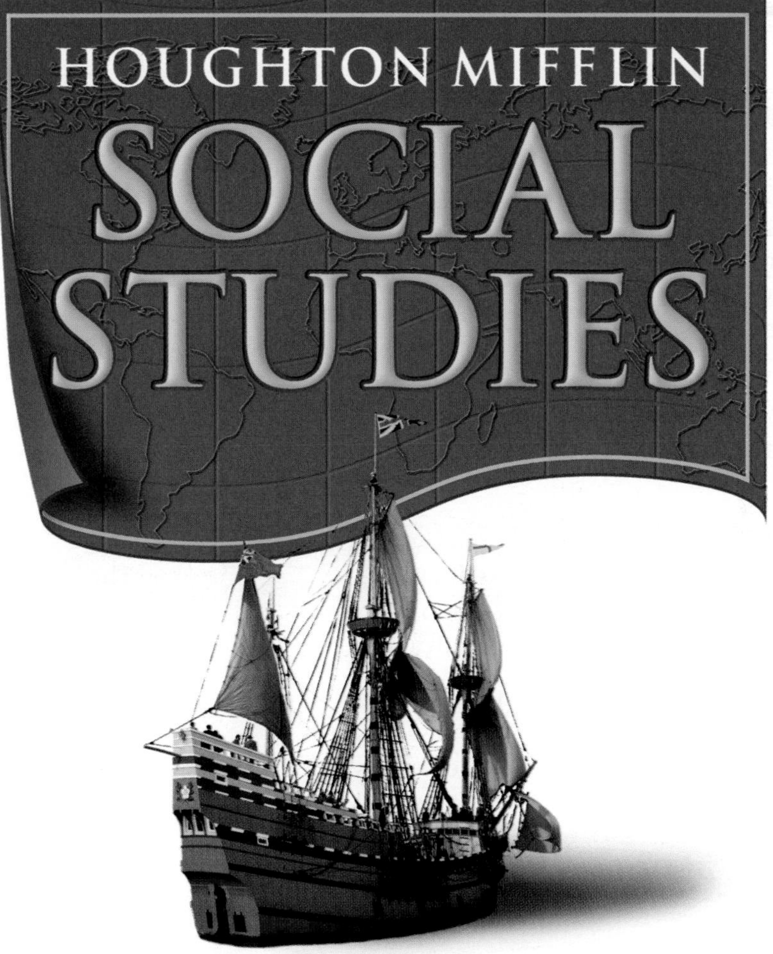

UNITED STATES HISTORY

EARLY YEARS

Visit Education Place®
www.eduplace.com/kids

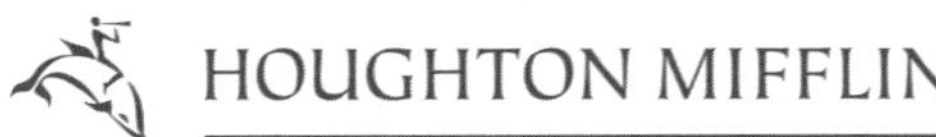

BOSTON

Consultants

Philip J. Deloria
Associate Professor
Department of History and Program in American Studies
University of Michigan

Lucien Ellington
UC Professor of Education and Asia Program Co-Director
University of Tennessee, Chattanooga

Thelma Wills Foote
Associate Professor
University of California

Stephen J. Fugita
Distinguished Professor
Psychology and Ethnic Studies
Santa Clara University

Charles C. Haynes
Senior Scholar
First Amendment Center

Ted Hemmingway
Professor of History
The Florida Agricultural & Mechanical University

Douglas Monroy
Professor of History
The Colorado College

Lynette K. Oshima
Assistant Professor
Department of Language, Literacy and Sociocultural Studies and Social Studies Program Coordinator
University of New Mexico

Jeffrey Strickland
Assistant Professor, History
University of Texas Pan American

Clifford E. Trafzer
Professor of History and American Indian Studies
University of California

Teacher Reviewers

Skip Bayliss
Surfside Elementary
Satellite Beach, FL

Annette Bomba
Schenevus Central School
Schenevus, NY

Amy Clark
Gateway Elementary
Travelers Rest, SC

Melissa Cook
Machado Elementary
Lake Elsinore, CA

Kelli Dunn
Lindop School
Broadview, IL

Peggy Greene
Upson-Lee North Elementary
Thomaston, GA

Elyce Kaplan
Kumeyaay Elementary
San Diego, CA

Julia McNeal
Webster Elementary
Dayton, OH

Theresa Powell
Harbor View School
Charleston, SC

Lesa Roberts
Hampton Cove Middle School
Huntsville, AL

Lynn Schew
Leila G. Davis Elementary
Clearwater, FL

Linda Whitford
Manning Oaks Elementary
Alpharetta, GA

Lisa Yingling
Round Hills Elementary
Williamsport, PA

Printed in the U.S.A.

ISBN: 0-618-42885-2

123456789-DW-13 12 11 10 09 08 07 06 05 04

Contents

Contents .... vi–xxi

UNIT 1 Our Land and First People

CHAPTER 2 The First Americans 36

UNIT 2 Exploration and Settlement 78

CHAPTER 3 Age of Exploration 82

CHAPTER 4 European Settlements 120

viii

UNIT 3 The English Colonies 154

ix

UNIT 4 The American Revolution 222

xi

CHAPTER 10 The Early Republic 342

CHAPTER 11 A Growing Country 376

xii

UNIT 6 The Civil War 410

CHAPTER 12 Causes of the Civil War 414

CHAPTER 13 Civil War and Reconstruction 450

xiii

xiv

References

Extend Lessons

Connect the core lesson to an important concept and dig into it. Extend your social studies knowledge!

Readers' Theater

Geography

Citizenship

Technology

Biography

xvi

Economics

Primary Sources

History

Literature

Skill Lessons

Take a step-by-step approach to learning and practicing key social studies skills.

Map and Globe Skills

Chart and Graph Skills

Study Skills

Citizenship Skills

Reading and Thinking Skills

Reading Skills/Graphic Organizer

xviii

Visual Learning

Become skilled at reading visuals. Graphs, maps, and fine art help you put all the information together.

Maps

xix

Charts and Graphs

Interpreting Fine Art

Diagrams and Infographics

Timelines

About Your Textbook

❶ How It's Organized

Units The major sections of your book are units. Each starts with a big idea.

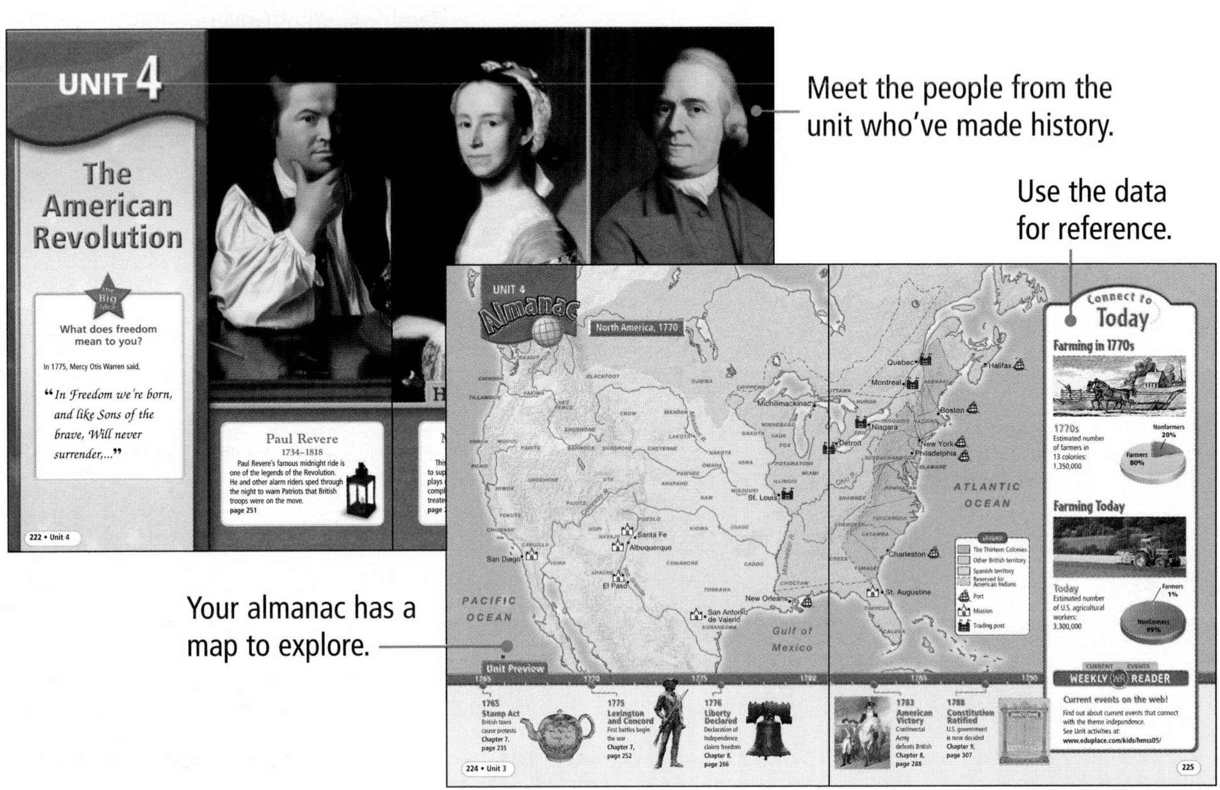

Get ready for reading.

Chapters Units are divided into chapters, and each opens with a vocabulary preview.

Four important concepts get you started.

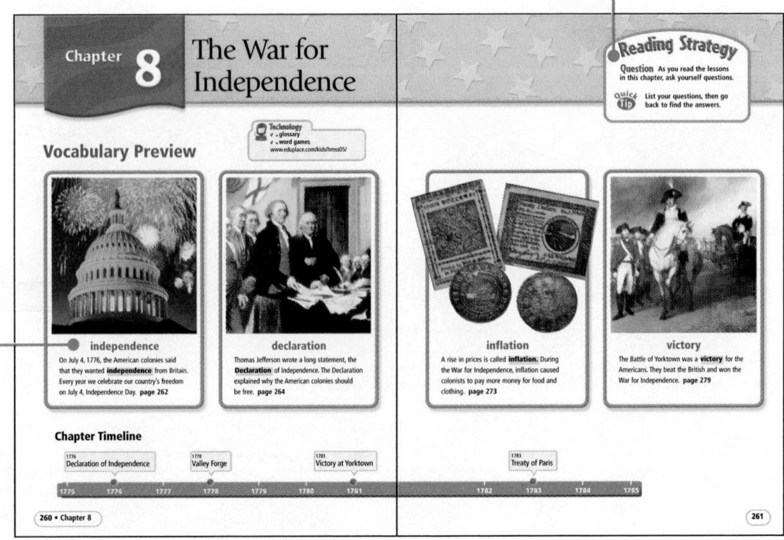

2 Core and Extend

Lessons The lessons in your book have two parts: core and extend.

Core Lessons
Lessons bring the events of history to life and help you meet your state's standards.

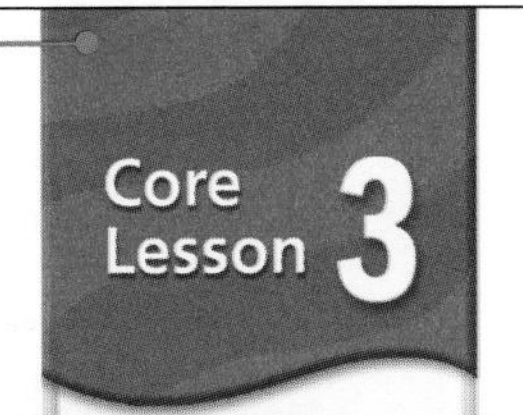

Extend Lessons
Go deeper into an important topic.

Core Lesson

Vocabulary strategies help with word meanings.

Before you read, use your prior knowledge.

Reading skills support your understanding of the text.

The timeline tells you when the lesson takes place.

Main ideas for sections state what is important.

Practice summarizing the lesson.

Studying social studies means asking why ideas are important to remember.

After you read, pull it together!

Core Lesson 3

The War in the North

1774 1776 1778 1780 1782 1784
1776–1778

VOCABULARY
retreat
mercenary
victory

Vocabulary Strategy
retreat
The word **retreat** comes from a word that means to draw back. In battle, retreat means to move back when an enemy attacks.

READING SKILL
Cause and Effect As you read, take notes to show what caused the outcome of each battle of the war.

CAUSE EFFECT

Build on What You Know Think about what it is like to play a game or a sport against a stronger team. How can you win? In the War for Independence, George Washington and his soldiers had to fight Britain's powerful army. To win, they needed careful planning, courage, and help from other countries.

Washington's First Battles

Main Idea Washington's leadership helped the Continental Army continue to fight.

While many Americans were deciding which side to support in the war, battles had already begun. The two armies fighting each other were very different.

At the start of the war, the Continental Army was not as large or as strong as the British army. British soldiers had better training and better weapons. The Continental Army, however, did have some strengths. American soldiers were fighting on home ground, and they could use their knowledge of the land to plan attacks. They had a cause that they believed in and the support of other Patriots. They also had a great leader in **George Washington**.

In the spring of 1776, the soldiers of Washington's army forced the British out of Boston. The British did not give up, though. In August, they defeated the Continental Army in the Battle of Long Island, near New York City.

Signals Drum beats were used as signals for soldiers marching into battle.

278 • Chapter 8

Valley Forge to train the soldiers.

Von Steuben taught the Americans to march together and use their weapons properly. The men of the Continental Army became good soldiers because of their training at Valley Forge. In their next battle, the Americans fought well against the British army.

With the help of France, and men such as Steuben and Lafayette, it looked as though the United States could win the war.

REVIEW What happened at Valley Forge to make the Continental Army better soldiers?
Baron von Steuben taught them to march together and use their weapons properly.

Lesson Summary

Summer 1776	Washington retreats
December 1776	Victory at Trenton
October 1777	Victory at Saratoga
1777–1778	Winter at Valley Forge

Why It Matters ...
The Continental soldiers fought hard during the difficult early years of the war. They kept alive the Patriots' hope of independence.

Lesson Review

1776 Battle of Trenton · 1777 Battle of Saratoga
1776 1777 1778 1779

1. **VOCABULARY** What happened to the Continental Army in 1776? Write a paragraph, using **retreat** and **victory**.
2. **READING SKILL** What was one **cause** of Washington's success at Trenton?
3. **MAIN IDEA: Citizenship** Give two examples of Washington's leadership during the war.
4. **MAIN IDEA: History** Why was the Battle of Saratoga a turning point in the war?
5. **PEOPLE TO KNOW** Who was **Lafayette**, and how did he help during the war?
6. **TIMELINE SKILL** Which battle came first, the one at Trenton or at Saratoga?
7. **CRITICAL THINKING: Analyze** Why was the help of allies such as the French important to the Americans during the war?

WRITING ACTIVITY Write a newspaper account of Washington crossing the Delaware River. Use the questions *Who?, What?, When?, Where?,* and *Why?* as a guide.

281

xxiii

Extend Lesson

Learn more about an important topic from each core lesson.

Dig in and extend your knowledge.

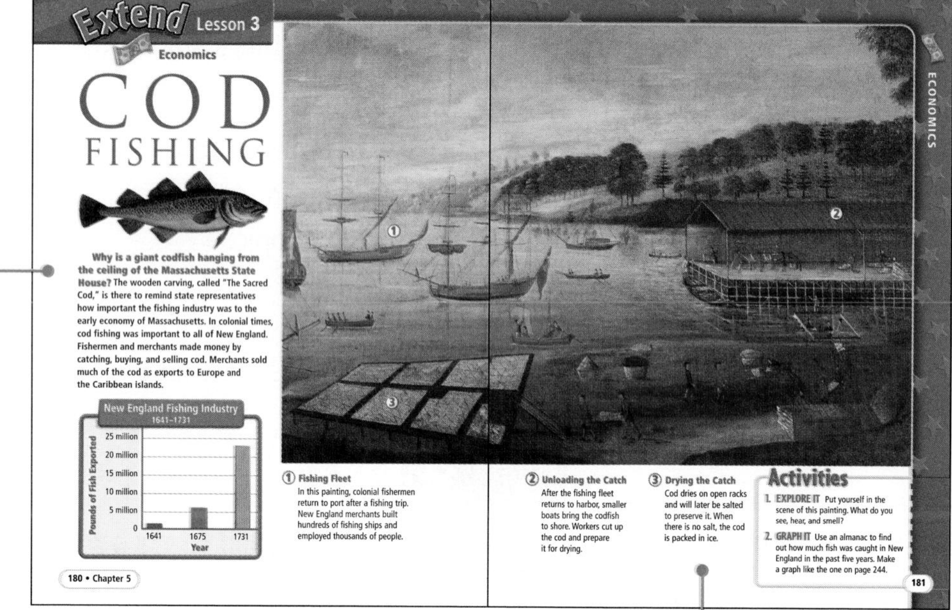

Extend Lesson 3

Economics

COD FISHING

Why is a giant codfish hanging from the ceiling of the Massachusetts State House? The wooden carving, called "The Sacred Cod," is there to remind state representatives how important the fishing industry was to the early economy of Massachusetts. In colonial times, cod fishing was important to all of New England. Fishermen and merchants made money by catching, buying, and selling cod. Merchants sold much of the cod as exports to Europe and the Caribbean islands.

① **Fishing Fleet**
In this painting, colonial fishermen return to port after a fishing trip. New England merchants built hundreds of fishing ships and employed thousands of people.

② **Unloading the Catch**
After the fishing fleet returns to harbor, smaller boats bring the codfish to shore. Workers cut up the cod and prepare it for drying.

③ **Drying the Catch**
Cod dries on open racks and will later be salted to preserve it. When there is no salt, the cod is packed in ice.

Activities

1. **EXPLORE IT** Put yourself in the scene of this painting. What do you see, hear, and smell?
2. **GRAPH IT** Use an almanac to find out how much fish was caught in New England in the past five years. Make a graph like the one on page 244.

180 • Chapter 5

181

ECONOMICS

Look closely. Connect the past to the present.

Look for literature, readers' theater, geography, economics—and more.

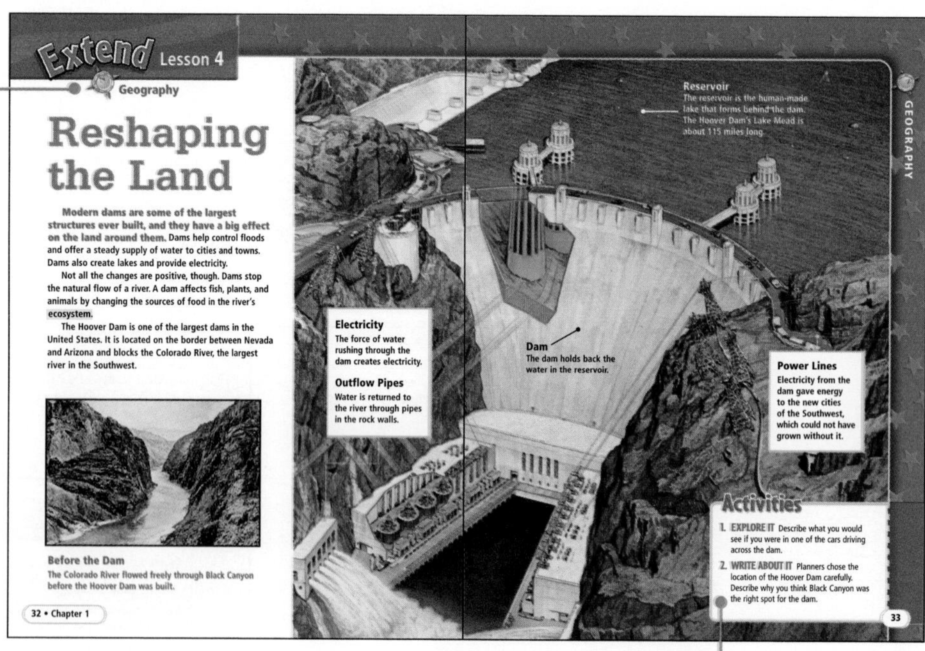

Extend Lesson 4

Geography

Reshaping the Land

Modern dams are some of the largest structures ever built, and they have a big effect on the land around them. Dams help control floods and offer a steady supply of water to cities and towns. Dams also create lakes and provide electricity.

Not all the changes are positive, though. Dams stop the natural flow of a river. A dam affects fish, plants, and animals by changing the sources of food in the river's ecosystem.

The Hoover Dam is one of the largest dams in the United States. It is located on the border between Nevada and Arizona and blocks the Colorado River, the largest river in the Southwest.

Before the Dam
The Colorado River flowed freely through Black Canyon before the Hoover Dam was built.

Activities

1. **EXPLORE IT** Describe what you would see if you were in one of the cars driving across the dam.
2. **WRITE ABOUT IT** Planners chose the location of the Hoover Dam carefully. Describe why you think Black Canyon was the right spot for the dam.

32 • Chapter 1

33

GEOGRAPHY

Write, talk, draw, and debate!

xxiv

3 Skills

Skill Building Learn map, graph, and study skills, as well as citizenship skills for life.

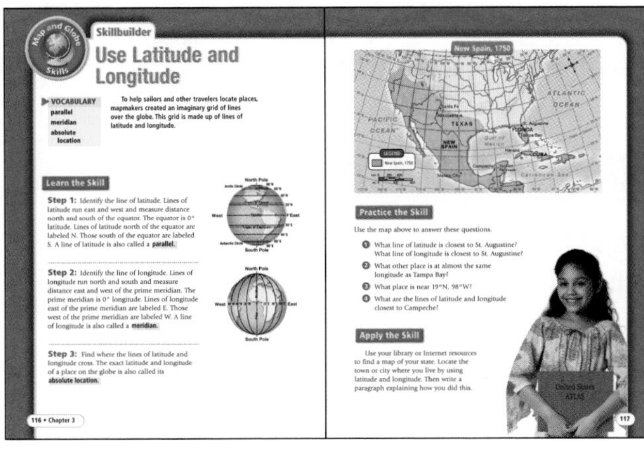

Each Skill lesson steps it out.

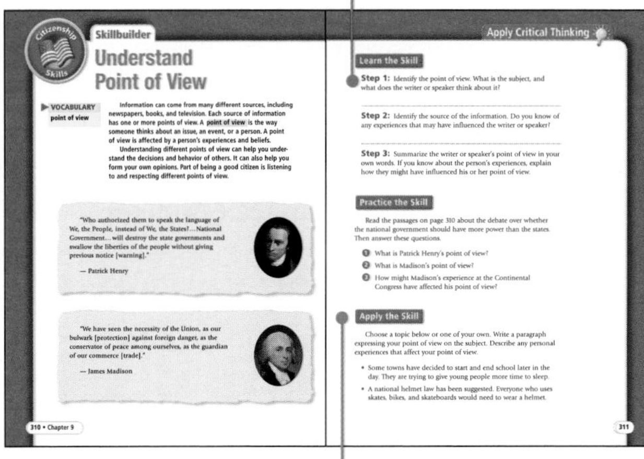

Practice and apply social studies skills.

4 References

Citizenship Handbook

The back of your book includes sections you'll refer to again and again.

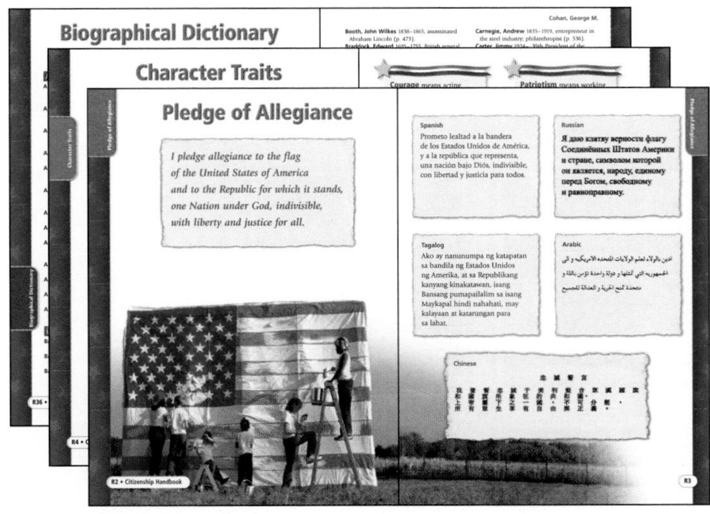

Resources

Look for atlas maps, a glossary of social studies terms, and an index.

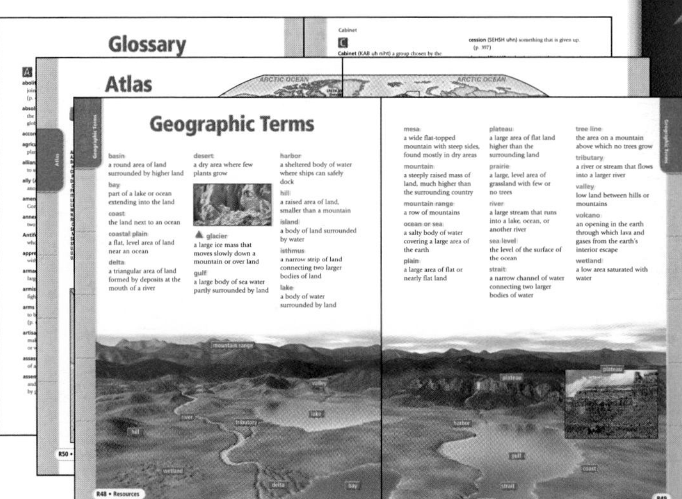

Reading Social Studies

Your book includes many features to help you be a successful reader. Here's what you will find:

VOCABULARY SUPPORT

Every chapter and lesson helps you with social studies terms. You'll build your vocabulary through strategies you're learning in language arts.

Preview
Get a jump start on four important words from the chapter.

Vocabulary Strategies
Focus on word roots, prefixes, suffixes, or compound words, for example.

Vocabulary Practice
Reuse words in the reviews, skills, and extends. Show that you know your vocabulary.

READING STRATEGIES

Look for the reading strategy and quick tip at the beginning of each chapter.

Predict and Infer
Before you read, think about what you'll learn.

Monitor and Clarify
Check your understanding. Could you explain what you just read to someone else?

Question
Stop and ask yourself a question. Did you understand what you read?

Summarize
After you read, think about the most important ideas of the lesson.

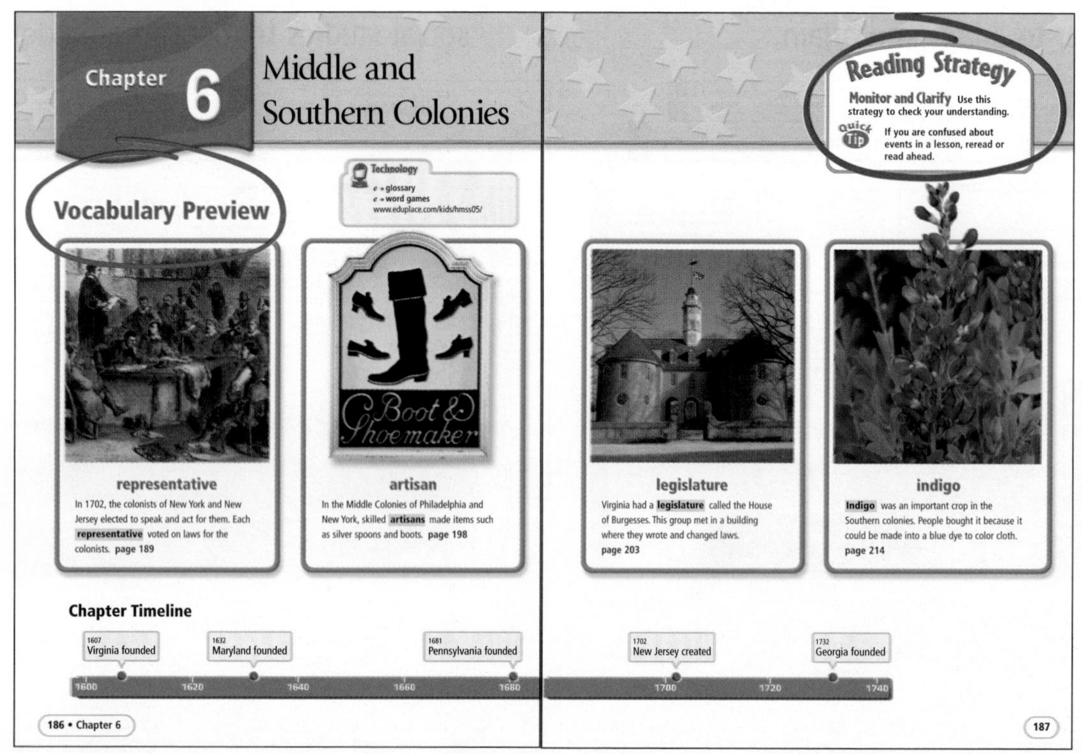

Chapter 6

Middle and Southern Colonies

Vocabulary Preview

Technology
e • glossary
e • word games
www.eduplace.com/kids/hmss05/

representative
In 1702, the colonists of New York and New Jersey elected to speak and act for them. Each **representative** voted on laws for the colonists. **page 189**

artisan
In the Middle Colonies of Philadelphia and New York, skilled **artisans** made items such as silver spoons and boots. **page 198**

Reading Strategy
Monitor and Clarify Use this strategy to check your understanding.
Quick Tip: If you are confused about events in a lesson, reread or read ahead.

legislature
Virginia had a **legislature** called the House of Burgesses. This group met in a building where they wrote and changed laws.
page 203

indigo
Indigo was an important crop in the Southern colonies. People bought it because it could be made into a blue dye to color cloth.
page 214

Chapter Timeline

1607 Virginia founded
1632 Maryland founded
1681 Pennsylvania founded
1702 New Jersey created
1732 Georgia founded

1600 | 1620 | 1640 | 1660 | 1680 | 1700 | 1720 | 1740

186 • Chapter 6

187

xxvi

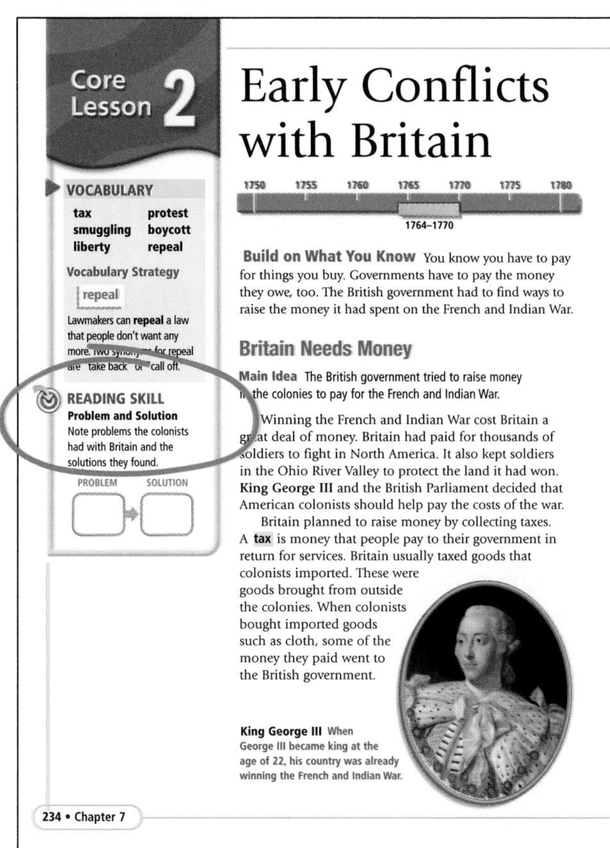

Core Lesson 2

Early Conflicts with Britain

1750 1755 1760 1765 1770 1775 1780
1764–1770

VOCABULARY
tax
smuggling
liberty
protest
boycott
repeal

Vocabulary Strategy
repeal
Lawmakers can **repeal** a law that people don't want any more. Two synonyms for repeal are "take back" or "call off."

READING SKILL
Problem and Solution
Note problems the colonists had with Britain and the solutions they found.
PROBLEM SOLUTION

Build on What You Know You know you have to pay for things you buy. Governments have to pay the money they owe, too. The British government had to find ways to raise the money it had spent on the French and Indian War.

Britain Needs Money

Main Idea The British government tried to raise money in the colonies to pay for the French and Indian War.

Winning the French and Indian War cost Britain a great deal of money. Britain had paid for thousands of soldiers to fight in North America. It also kept soldiers in the Ohio River Valley to protect the land it had won. **King George III** and the British Parliament decided that American colonists should help pay the costs of the war.

Britain planned to raise money by collecting taxes. A **tax** is money that people pay to their government in return for services. Britain usually taxed goods that colonists imported. These were goods brought from outside the colonies. When colonists bought imported goods such as cloth, some of the money they paid went to the British government.

King George III When George III became king at the age of 22, his country was already winning the French and Indian War.

234 • Chapter 7

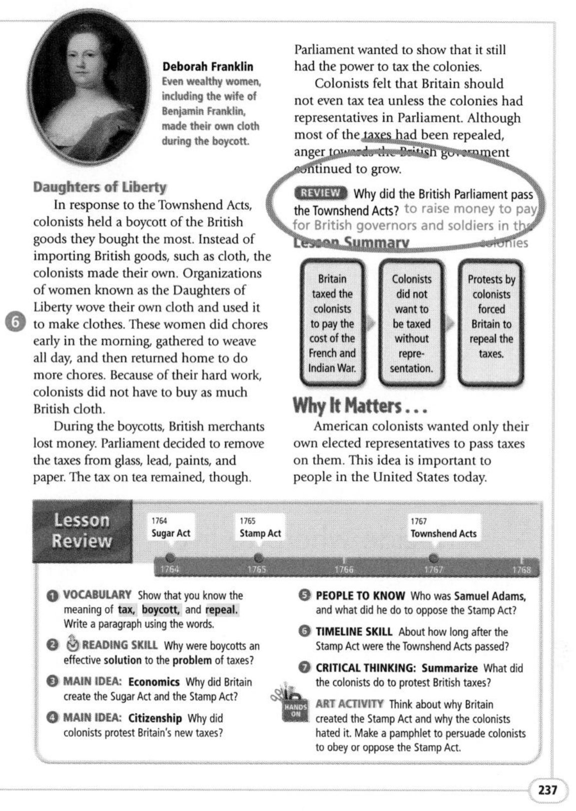

Deborah Franklin Even wealthy women, including the wife of Benjamin Franklin, made their own cloth during the boycott.

Daughters of Liberty

In response to the Townshend Acts, colonists held a boycott of the British goods they bought the most. Instead of importing British goods, such as cloth, the colonists made their own. Organizations of women known as the Daughters of Liberty wove their own cloth and used it to make clothes. These women did chores early in the morning, gathered to weave all day, and then returned home to do more chores. Because of their hard work, colonists did not have to buy as much British cloth.

During the boycotts, British merchants lost money. Parliament decided to remove the taxes from glass, lead, paints, and paper. The tax on tea remained, though. Parliament wanted to show that it still had the power to tax the colonies.

Colonists felt that Britain should not even tax tea unless the colonies had representatives in Parliament. Although most of the taxes had been repealed, anger towards the British government continued to grow.

REVIEW Why did the British Parliament pass the Townshend Acts? to raise money to pay for British governors and soldiers in the colonies

Lesson Summary

Britain taxed the colonists to pay the cost of the French and Indian War.	Colonists did not want to be taxed without representation.	Protests by colonists forced Britain to repeal the taxes.

Why It Matters . . .

American colonists wanted only their own elected representatives to pass taxes on them. This idea is important to people in the United States today.

Lesson Review

1764 Sugar Act · 1765 Stamp Act · 1767 Townshend Acts

1. VOCABULARY Show that you know the meaning of **tax**, **boycott**, and **repeal**. Write a paragraph using the words.
2. READING SKILL Why were boycotts an effective **solution** to the **problem** of taxes?
3. MAIN IDEA: Economics Why did Britain create the Sugar Act and the Stamp Act?
4. MAIN IDEA: Citizenship Why did colonists protest Britain's new taxes?
5. PEOPLE TO KNOW Who was Samuel Adams, and what did he do to oppose the Stamp Act?
6. TIMELINE SKILL About how long after the Stamp Act were the Townshend Acts passed?
7. CRITICAL THINKING: Summarize What did the colonists do to protest British taxes?

ART ACTIVITY Think about why Britain created the Stamp Act and why the colonists hated it. Make a pamphlet to persuade colonists to obey or oppose the Stamp Act.

237

READING SKILLS

As you read, organize the information. These reading skills will help you:

Sequence

Cause and Effect

Compare and Contrast

Problem and Solution

Draw Conclusions

Predict Outcomes

Categorize (or) Classify

Main Idea and Details

COMPREHENSION SUPPORT

Build on What You Know
Check your prior knowledge. You may already know a lot!

Review Questions
Connect with the text. Did you understand what you just read?

Summaries
Look for three ways to summarize–a list, an organizer, or a paragraph.

Social Studies: Why It Matters

Learning social studies will help you know how to get along better in your everyday life, and it will give you confidence when you make important choices in your future.

WHEN I
- decide where to live
- travel
- look for places on a map—

I'll use the geography information I've learned in social studies.

WHEN I
- choose a job
- make a budget
- decide which product to buy—

I'll use economic information.

xxviii

WHEN I
hear the story of a person from the past
read books and visit museums
look closely at the world around me—
I'll use what I've learned about history.
WHEN I
go to a neighborhood meeting
decide who to vote for
get a driver's license—
I can use what I've learned about citizenship.
MUSEUM
HALL
Town Meeting Tonight
Meeting Tonight
xxix

Unit 5

Unit Planner

Begin with Core. Extend for more.

The New Nation

Chapter 10 Pages 342–375

Chapter 11 Pages 376–407

LEVELED BOOKS

The following Social Studies Independent Books are available for extending and supporting students' social studies experience as they read the unit.

Differentiated Instruction

Extra Support

A Tall Tale to Tell

By Becky Cheston

Summary: The tall tale is one of America's most famous additions to the world of storytelling, the legacy of a new nation where the sky was the limit.

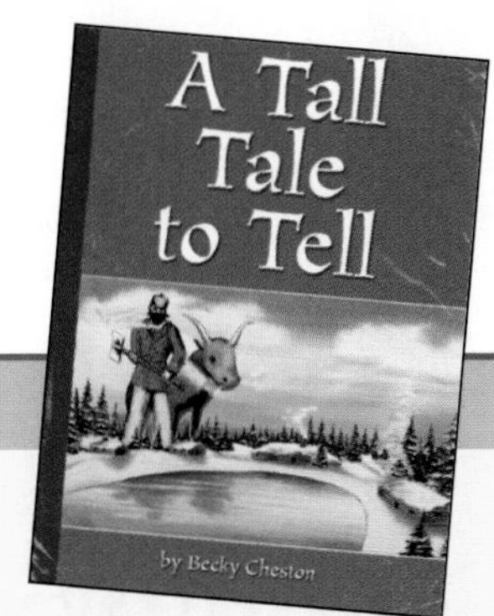

Vocabulary

frontier
pioneer

Extending Understanding

Oral Language: Drama Ask students to work in groups to act out a scene or scenes from one of the tall tales mentioned in the book.

Independent Writing: Narrative Writing Have students write their own tall tale, or a further adventure for one of the tall tales described in the book.

Graphic Organizer: Students can use a Venn diagram to organize the characteristics of a typical tall-tale hero.

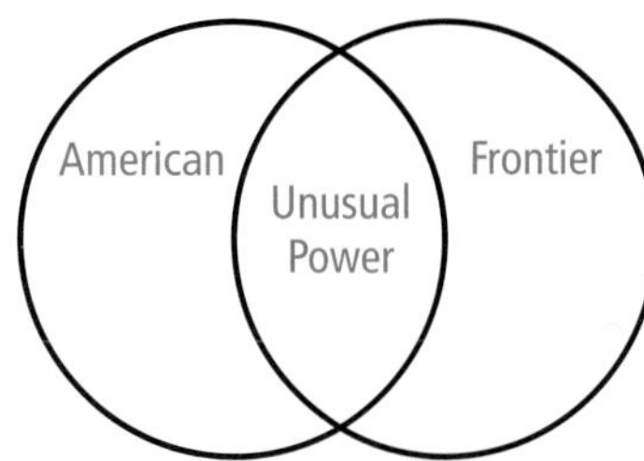

On Level

Flatboat Mondays

By Kathleen E. Jones

Summary: Before the Civil War, flatboats took settlers and traders down the Mississippi and its tributaries, a perilous and exciting journey.

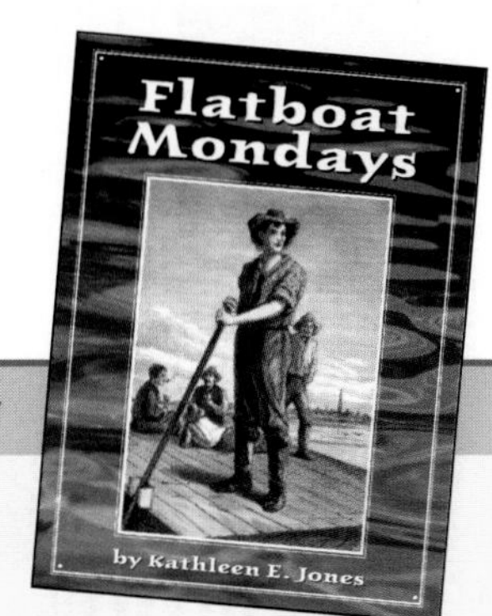

Vocabulary

flatboat
canal
source

Extending Understanding

Oral Language: Monologue Have students act as though riding on a flatboat and describe what they see as the boat floats down the Mississippi.

Independent Writing: Song Using the music of a song that already exists, have students work in small groups to write a folk song about traveling on a flatboat.

Graphic Organizer: Students can use a word web to record words related to flatboats.

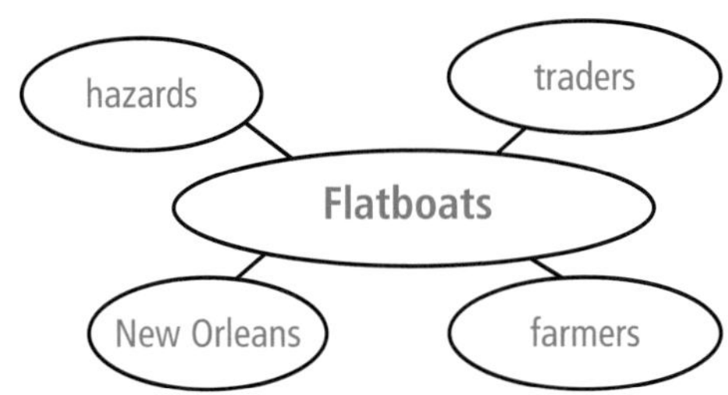

Challenge

Going West—Trials and Trade-Offs

By Starlyn Williams

Summary: A portrait of people who made the long journey across the American West to settle in lands that to them were the Great Unknown.

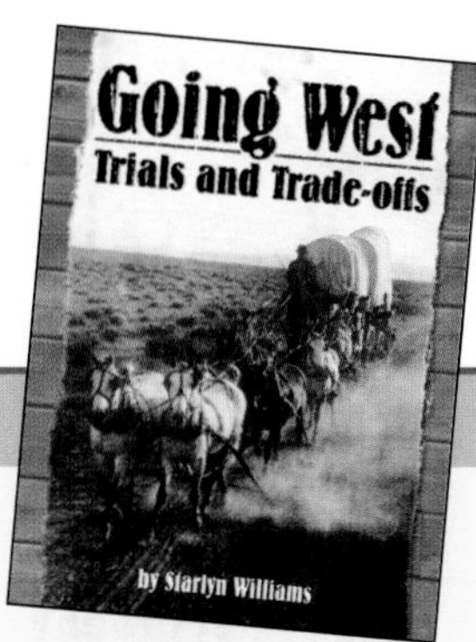

Vocabulary

wagon train
prosperity
injustice

Extending Understanding

Oral Language: Dialogue Have students work in pairs, representing settlers or American Indians who talk with each other about the similarities and differences between their experiences of the westward migration.

Independent Writing: Interview Have students write interview questions they would ask a settler if they had the chance to interview them about life in the West.

Graphic Organizer: Students can use a cause-and-effect diagram as they read.

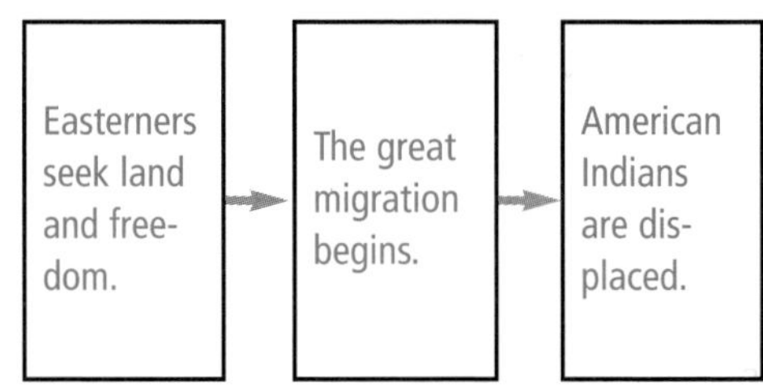

Choices for Reading

- **Extra Support/ELL** Read the selection aloud as students follow along in their books. Pause frequently and help students monitor understanding.
- **On Level** Have partners take turns reading aloud. Students can pause at the end of each page to ask each other questions and check understanding.
- **Challenge** Students can read the selection and write down any questions they have. Then they can work in small groups to answer their questions.

Go to www.eduplace.com/ss/hmss05/ for answers to Responding questions found at the back of the books.

Bibliography

Books for Independent Reading

Social Studies Key

 **Biography**

 **Citizenship**

 **Cultures**

 **Economics**

 **Geography**

 **History**

Social Studies Leveled Readers with lesson plans by Irene Fountas support the content of this unit.

Extra Support

 **The Flag Maker**
by Susan C. Bartoletti
Houghton, 2004

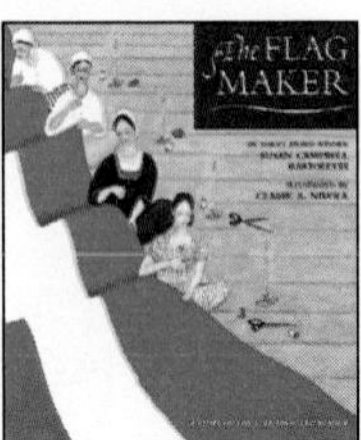

This is the story of the Baltimore girl who helped make the flag that inspired Francis Scott Key's "The Star-Spangled Banner."

Mill
by David Macaulay
Houghton, 1989

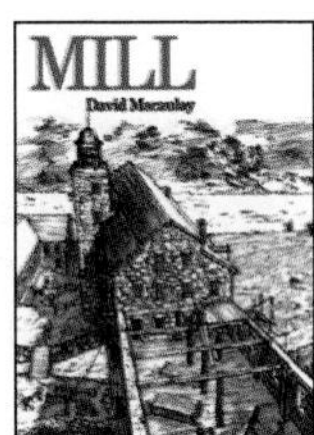

Detailed illustrations and engaging text demonstrate the workings of an eighteenth-century textile mill.

 **The Great Expedition of Lewis and Clark**
by Judith Edwards
Farrar, 2003

The story of the Great Expedition is told from the point of view of Reubin Field, a lesser-known member of the Lewis and Clark team.

 **Benjamin Banneker: Pioneering Scientist**
by Ginger Wadsworth
Carolrhoda, 2003

An accomplished African American astronomer and mathematician, Banneker was one of the foremost thinkers of his time.

 **Elizabeth Cady Stanton**
by Heidi Moore
Heinemann, 2004

Readers learn how Stanton became a leading activist for women's suffrage.

On Level

 **Bold Journey**
by Charles Bohner
Houghton, 2004

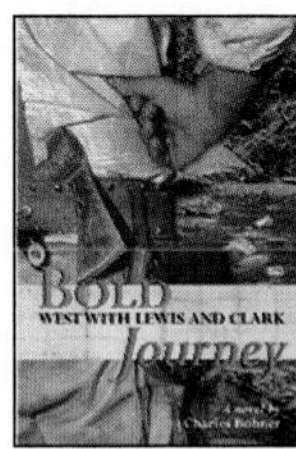

This fast-paced novel follows the Lewis and Clark expedition from the point of view of its youngest member.

 **Andrew Jackson**
by Kieran Doherty
Children's Press, 2003

Jackson's life, and the legacy he left America, are aptly discussed in this *Encyclopedia of Presidents* biography.

 **The Ballad of Lucy Whipple**
by Karen Cushman
Clarion, 1996

Lucy slowly learns to love the wild land of California after her widowed mother moves the family there in 1849.

 **The Coast Mappers**
by Taylor Morrison
Houghton, 2004

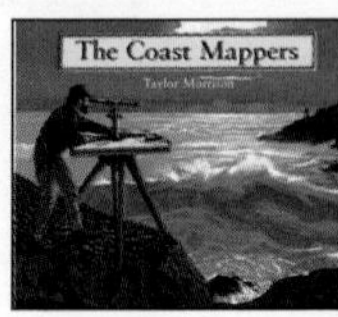

In 1850 George Davidson began the monumental task of surveying and mapping America's entire Pacific coast.

 **Eli Whitney: The Cotton Gin and American Manufacturing**
by Regan A. Huff
Powerkids, 2004

Whitney's invention changed the face of American manufacturing forever.

Challenge

 **Thomas Jefferson: Architect of Democracy**
by John B. Severance
Houghton, 1998

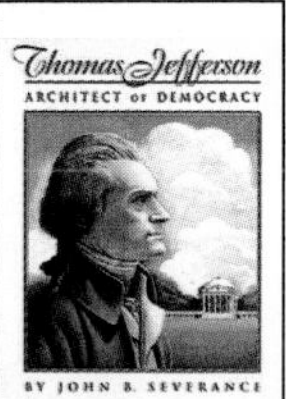

This portrait of America's third president chronicles his life from his school days through his rise in politics.

 **Animals on the Trail with Lewis and Clark**
by Dorothy Henshaw Patent
Clarion, 2002

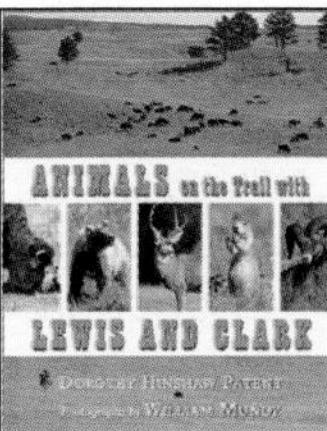

Lewis and Clark documented scores of animals on their 1804–1806 expedition.

 **Inside the Alamo**
by Jim Murphy
Delacorte, 2003

This strong narrative covers the Texas War of Independence, the Alamo battle, and all the key players.

 **Robert Fulton and the Development of the Steamboat**
by Morris A. Pierce
Powerkids, 2003

A complete look at the ambitious inventor and businessman whose ideas changed our nation and the world.

Read Aloud and Reference

Read Aloud Books

Carry On, Mr. Bowditch
by Jean Lee Latham
Houghton, 1955

This is the Newbery Medal-winning true story of the boy who authored *The American Practical Navigator,* "the sailor's bible."

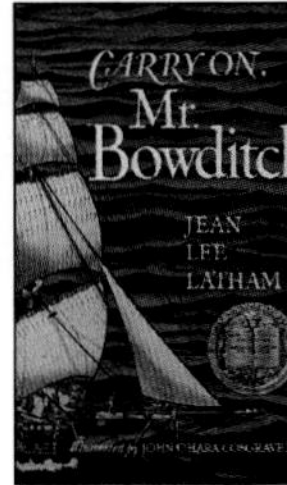

Words West: Voices of Young Pioneers
by Ginger Wadsworth
Clarion, 2003

Nineteenth-century children tell in their own words what it was like to be part of the great western expansion.

Black Potatoes
by Susan C. Bartoletti
Houghton, 2001

This acclaimed book tells of the tragic potato famine that led many Irish people to seek a better life in the United States.

The Sun, the Rain, and the Apple Seed
by Lynda Durrant
Clarion, 2003

This historical novel of John Chapman's life includes an informative afterword.

Reference Books

Battles of the War of 1812
by Diane and Henry Smolinski
Heinemann, 2003

Readers learn about the battles and their effect on people and society. See others in series.

The Louisiana Purchase
by Michael Burgan
Compass Point, 2002

Engaging chapters tell about the political and economic history of the Louisiana Purchase.

Black Frontiers
by Lillian Schlissel
Simon, 2000

The author chronicles the life and times of African Americans in the Old West.

The Industrial Revolution
by S. Connolly, B. January
Heinemann, 2003

The causes and consequences of the Industrial Revolution are explored using primary source materials.

Free and Inexpensive Materials

The Library of Congress
101 Independence Ave. SE
Washington, DC 20540
Phone: (202) 707-5000

The library's website, www.loc.gov, includes historical collections from the National Digital Library.

MULTIMEDIA RESOURCES

PROGRAM RESOURCES

Unit Video
Audio Student's Book with Primary Sources and Songs MP3/CD
Lesson Planner and Teacher Resource CD-ROM
Test Generator CD-ROM
eBook
eBook, Teacher's Edition
Transparencies: Big Idea & Skillbuilder, Interactive
Almanac Map & Graph Practice
Primary Sources Plus: Document-Based Questions
Research and Writing Projects
Bringing Social Studies Alive
Family Newsletter
GeoNet

CD-ROM

The Oregon Trail 3rd Edition. Schlessinger

The Lewis and Clark Picture Show. National Geographic

The Westward Movement Picture Show. National Geographic

VIDEOCASSETTES

Biographies of the Presidents of the United States: Vol. 1. Schlessinger

Lone Star Legacy: The Texas Republic and the Mexican War. Rainbow Educational

American History for Children: United States Expansion. Schlessinger

Let the Women Vote. Schlessinger

AUDIOCASSETTES

The Star-Spangled Banner, *Peter Spier.* Weston Woods

Johnny Appleseed, *Reeve Lindbergh.* Weston Woods

Dear Mr. President: Thomas Jefferson, *Jennifer Armstrong.* Live Oak Media

Assessment Options

You are the best evaluator of your students' progress and attainments. To help you in this task, Houghton Mifflin Social Studies provides you with a variety of assessment tools.

Classroom-Based Assessment

Written and Oral Assessment

In the student book:

Lesson Reviews appear at the end of each lesson.
Chapter Reviews appear on pp. 374–375, 406–407.
Unit Reviews appear on pp. 408–409.

In the *Assessment Options* ancillary:

Lesson Tests appear for all lessons.
Chapter Tests appear for all chapters.
Unit Tests appear for all units.

Technology:

Test Generator provides even more assessment options.

Informal, Continuous Assessment

Comprehension

In the student book:

Review questions appear at the end of each section.

In the teacher's edition:

"Talk About It" questions monitor student comprehension.
Tested Objectives appear at the beginning and end of each lesson.

In the student practice book:

Study Guide pages aid student comprehension.

Reading

In the teacher's edition:

Reading Strategy is featured in every chapter.

Thinking

In the student book:

Critical Thinking questions teach higher-order thinking skills.

In the teacher's edition:

"Think Alouds" let you model thinking critically for your students.

In the *Assessment Options* ancillary:

Observation Checklists give you another option for assessment.

HANDS ON Rubric for Unit 5 Performance Assessment

Score	Description
4	Book describes two inventions for agriculture/industry and two for transportation; thoroughly explains their impact; few, if any, errors.
3	Book describes two inventions for agriculture/industry and two for transportation; explains impact of three inventions; some errors.
2	Book describes one invention for agriculture/industry and one for transportation; explains how they changed daily life; several errors.
1	Book describes several inventions not related to time period; does not explain how they changed daily life; many errors.

In *Assessment Options*, p. 119

Standardized Test Practice

In the student book:

Lesson Review/Test Prep appears at the end of each lesson.
Chapter Review/Test Prep appears at the end of each chapter.
Unit Review/Test Prep appears at the end of each unit.

In the *Assessment Options* ancillary:

Lesson Tests for all lessons.
Chapter Tests for all chapters.
Unit Test for all units.

Technology:

Test Generator provides even more assessment options.

Student Self-Assessment

In the student book:

Hands-On Activities appear in each chapter.
Writing Activities appear in each chapter.

In the Unit Resources:

Reading Skill/Strategy pages give students the chance to practice the skills and strategies of each lesson and chapter.
Vocabulary Review/Study Guide pages provide an opportunity for self-challenge or review.

In the *Assessment Options* ancillary:

Self-Assessment Checklists

Unit 5 Test

Standard Test

TEST PREP

Unit 5 Test

Test Your Knowledge

Circle the letter of the best answer.

1. In what way did Cyrus McCormick's reaper help farmers? Obj. U5–10
   - (A.) It allowed them to harvest their crops faster.
   - B. It made it easier for them to plow thick soil on prairies.
   - C. It helped them transport their crops more easily.
   - D. It eliminated the need to use animals on the farm.
2. Which of the following happened when Thomas Jefferson was President? Obj. U5–4
   - F. The Indian Removal Act
   - G. The Monroe Doctrine
   - H. The War of 1812
   - (J.) The Louisiana Purchase
3. Why did Andrew Jackson sign the Indian Removal Act? Obj. U5–9
   - A. He believed that the law would help American Indians.
   - B. He felt it would help to close the national bank.
   - C. The Supreme Court forced him to sign the law.
   - (D.) He believed that American Indians slowed down the nation's growth by living on land settlers wanted.
4. Which describes the way many Americans felt about their country after the War of 1812? Obj. U5–7
   - F. disappointed
   - G. confused
   - (H.) proud
   - J. angry
5. What is one reason that the United States fought the War of 1812? Obj. U5–6
   - A. It wanted to control the Louisiana Territory.
   - (B.) It wanted to keep the British from helping American Indians who fought the settlers.
   - C. It wanted to move all American Indians west of the Mississippi River.
   - D. It wanted to weaken the British Navy.
6. Why did Americans and Mexicans in Texas fight against Mexico? Obj. U5–15
   - F. They wanted more farmland.
   - G. They thought Mexicans should not support slavery.
   - (H.) They wanted independence from Mexico.
   - J. They wanted to make the Alamo a mission again.

Standard Test

TEST PREP

Test the Skills: Make an Outline; Find and Evaluate Sources

I. The Louisiana Purchase added land to the United States in 1803.
  A. that was west of Mississippi River
  B. that was 530 million acres
  C. that was purchased from France
II. President Jefferson sent Lewis and Clark to explore.
  A. the geography of the land
  B. American Indian cultures
  C. a water route to the Pacific Ocean

Use the passage and the outline to answer the questions below.

7. What title would you give the outline? Obj. U5–3
   Sample answer: The Louisiana Purchase
8. What is the first main idea in the outline? What is one detail that supports the second main idea? Obj. U5–3
   First main idea: The United States bought land in 1803; Detail for second main idea: studied American Indian cultures
9. List three types of sources you might use to find the information in the outline. Obj. U5–12
   Sample answer: encyclopedia, Internet article, book
10. List three questions you might ask to evaluate how reliable your sources are. Obj. U5–12
   Sample answer: Who wrote the source? What is the purpose of this source? Are the facts in the source correct?

Standard Test

TEST PREP

Apply Your Knowledge and Skills

Exploring the Frontier
1. Daniel Boone explored.
  A. He was a hunter pioneer.
  B. He cleared a new road through the Cumberland Gap of the Appalachian Mountains.
II. More people traveled west.
  A. People used wagons and flatboats on the Ohio River.
  B. People crossed the Appalachians looking for inexpensive farmland.

Pioneers explored land west of the Appalachian Mountains in the late 1700s. Daniel Boone, a hunter and pioneer, helped to clear a new road over the mountains through the Cumberland Gap. He called this road, which stretched 200 miles west, the Wilderness Road. Boone guided families across the Appalachians. By the late 1700s, thousands of people had crossed these mountains, looking for inexpensive farmland. They traveled in wagons and in flatboats on the Ohio River.

11. What should be done to correct the outline? Obj. U5–3
   - (A.) Change the number *1* to a Roman numeral.
   - B. Change *A* and *B* to 1 and 2.
   - C. Delete the title.
   - D. Add a conclusion or ending.
12. Where does the following detail belong? Settlers also traveled on canals, such as the Erie Canal.
   Sample answer: as C under II
13. Write a brief essay that describes the trip west for settlers. Write your essay on a separate sheet of paper. Obj. U5–17
   Essays may refer to the difficulties of traveling, the reasons people moved west, and the routes they took.

Standard Test

TEST PREP

Apply the Reading Skills and Strategies

In the 1800s, women did not have the same rights as men. For example, women could not vote, and they were not allowed to speak to an audience with men in it. Only a small number of low-paying jobs were available to women. In most states, a woman could not own property or keep the money she earned. Courageous women spoke out against these injustices, but few people listened. Then, in 1848, a group of women held a convention in Seneca Falls, New York. Over 200 women attended this meeting. It was the start of the women's rights movement.

Reading Skills

Use the passage above to answer each question.

14. **Draw Conclusions** What conclusion can you draw about the character of the women who attended the Seneca Falls Convention? Obj. U5–14
   Sample answer: The women were likely strong-minded, brave, and in favor of women's rights.
15. **Main Idea and Details** What are four details that support the main idea that women in the 1800s did not have the same rights as men? Obj. U5–14
   Sample answer: Women could not vote; they could not own property; they often could not keep the money they earned; there were only a small number of low-paying jobs available to them.

Reading Strategy: Monitor and Clarify

16. Which sentences in the passage would help you clearly understand how some women responded to injustice? List the sentences below. Obj. U5–14
   Sample answer: Courageous women spoke out against these injustices, but few people listened. Then, in 1848, a group of women held a convention in Seneca Falls, New York. It was the start of the women's rights movement.

Reaching All Learners

Extra Support

Indentifying Historical Figures

Class	25 minutes
Objective	To identify historical figures
Materials	pencils, index cards or paper

- Students work in pairs, each pair choosing a significant figure from Unit 5 without revealing the choice to classmates. Students prepare three clues to the figure's identity.
- Each pair of students stands before the class in turn, giving one clue and calling on the class to identify the historical figure. If no one answers correctly, the pair provides the next clue, and so on. If no one guesses correctly after three clues, the pair identifies the figure for the class.

Sacagawea
- Native American (Shoshone)
- interpreter
- helped Lewis and Clark on their expedition

Challenge

Recognize Technological Advances

Singles	25 minutes
Objective	To recognize the merits of technological advances
Materials	heavy paper, markers or pencils

- The Franklin Institute was founded in Pennsylvania in 1824 to honor Benjamin Franklin and promote science and technology. From its beginning, the Institute has granted awards for substantial achievements.
- Have each student select an achievement worthy of such an award, such as a canal, railroads, cotton gin, Conestoga wagon, and so forth, and create a certificate. It might read, *The Franklin Institute Awards The Franklin Medal to,* followed by a name or other identifier and a paragraph explaining the achievement and its benefits.

ELL

Understanding the National Anthem

Singles	30 minutes
Objective	To illustrate the national anthem
Materials	paper, crayons or colored pencils

Beginning
Use photographs and drawings to demonstrate the meaning of *star, spangled, banner, dawn,* and *light.* Point out the 15 stars of the 1814 flag. Have students make a sketch titled "Star-Spangled Banner in the Dawn's Early Light."

Intermediate
Introduce *rockets* and *red glare* as well as *star, spangled, banner, dawn, light.* Differentiate between what rocket means today and what it meant in 1814. Have students make two sketches: The flag seen at night by the red glare of rockets and the flag seen in the morning by the dawn's early light. Have students title the sketches and date them September 13, 1814 and September 14, 1814.

Advanced
Introduce *ramparts.* Have students expand on sketches similar to those described above to include other aspects of the event, such as the British attack or Francis Scott Key's observing from a nearby ship. Students create appropriate titles for their drawings.

Language Arts

Write a Newspaper Article

Pairs	20 minutes
Objective	To write a newspaper article about international conflict
Materials	paper, pencils

- Students imagine themselves to be newspaper reporters. Each pair chooses to report on an aspect of the War of 1812, Texas independence or annexation, or the Mexican-American War.
- Explain that reporters try to follow these guidelines:
  1. Articles are fact, not opinion.
  2. Start with an attention-grabbing sentence or question.
  3. The first paragraph includes who, what, when, where, and why, if possible.
  4. The second paragraph provides more detailed information.
  5. The article ends with a conclusion.
  6. Try for a catchy headline.

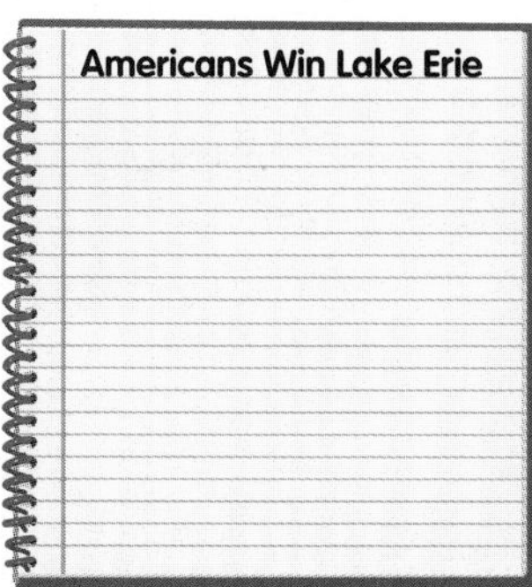

Math

Calculate Travel Times

Singles	15 minutes
Objective	To calculate Oregon Trail travel times then and now
Materials	paper, pencil

- Students can assume each party of travelers arises at 6:00 a.m., is on the road by 7:00 a.m., stops an hour for lunch, then makes camp at 5:00 p.m. in the evening. How long will it take them to make a trip on the Oregon Trail or its modern equivalent—a journey of about 2,000 miles?

By horse and canoe:
10 miles daily

On foot with ox-drawn wagons:
16 miles daily

By bicycle: 62 miles daily

By car: 540 miles daily

Drama

Role-play a Historical Event

Groups	30 minutes
Objective	To use historical imagination
Materials	paper, pencil

- Students draw cards assigning them roles as travelers on the Wilderness Trail, Trail of Tears, immigrant ships, Oregon Trail, or Mormon Trail, at least two or three students to a group.
- The cards also contain a question: *Where did you come from, Why did you leave,* or *Where are you going.* In addition, all cards ask, *What do you hope for.* All students assigned to a group meet around an imaginary campfire or hearth and improvise a conversation based on the questions.

Wilderness Trail
Where did you come from?
What do you hope for?

Trail of Tears
Why did you leave?
What do you hope for?

Begin the Unit

Quick Look

Chapter 10 describes settlement beyond the Appalachians, the purchase and exploration of Louisiana, the War of 1812, and Andrew Jackson.

Chapter 11 discusses the Industrial Revolution, German and Irish immigrants, reform efforts, and migration to the West.

Introduce the Big Idea

Citizenship Although people of the United States have many different ethnic, cultural, and racial identities, they also share an identity as Americans. As students discuss what it means to have an identity as an American, ask them how being an American affects the way they think about themselves.

Explain that this unit will tell them more about events and people that established the new nation as a place that was different from other countries.

Primary Sources

Ask a student to read the quotation on page 338. This phrase is said to have come from several people, including Benjamin Franklin and patriot James Otis. Ask students what they think the saying means. List student responses on the board.

Ask students why they think this might have been a popular saying among people who wanted independence from Britain. Would this saying have the same meaning today? Who might use it today?

UNIT 5

The New Nation

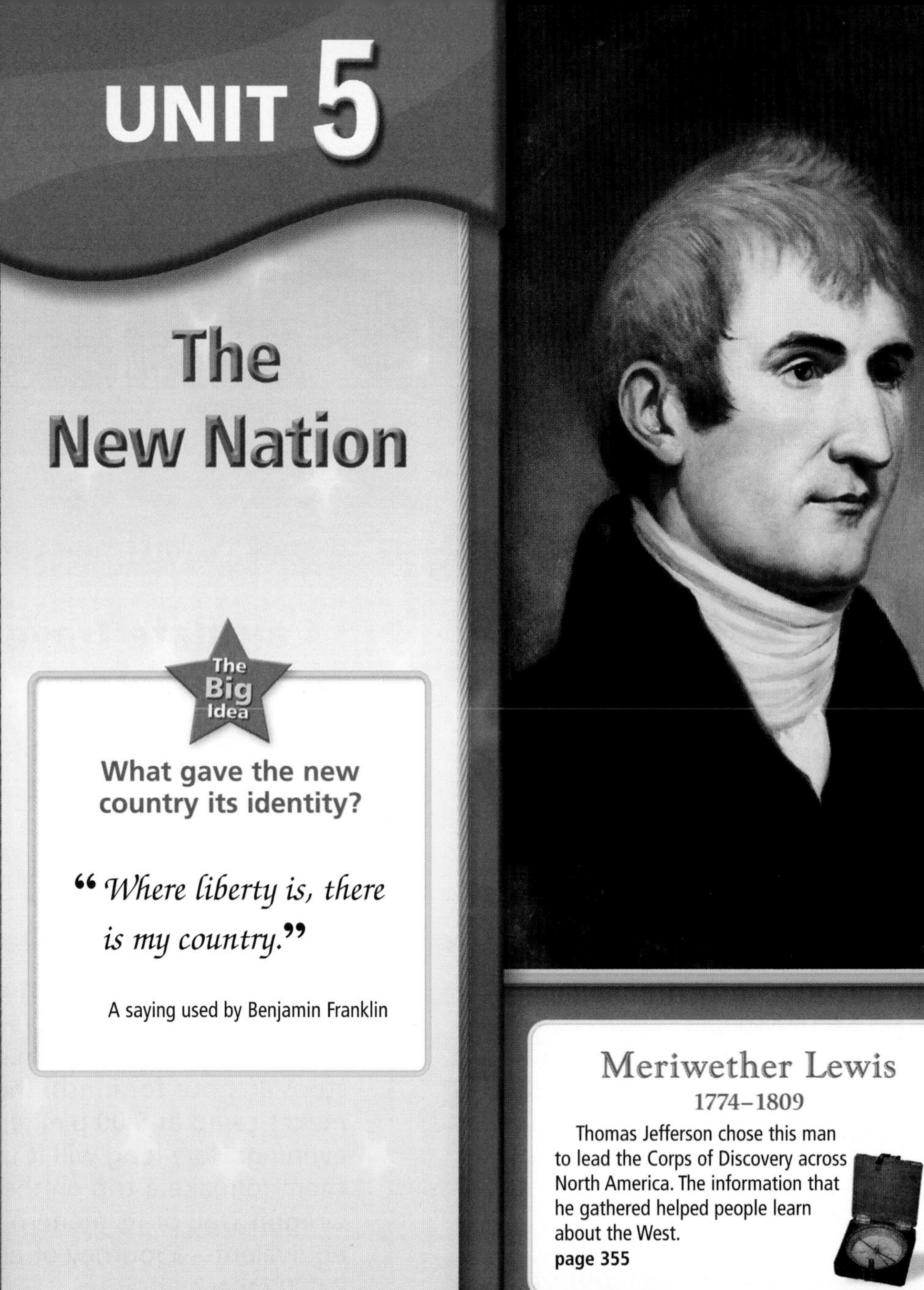

The Big Idea

What gave the new country its identity?

"*Where liberty is, there is my country.*"

A saying used by Benjamin Franklin

Meriwether Lewis
1774–1809

Thomas Jefferson chose this man to lead the Corps of Discovery across North America. The information that he gathered helped people learn about the West.
page 355

Technology

Motivate and Build Background

You may wish to show the Unit Video after students have discussed the Big Idea question on this page.

After viewing, ask students to **summarize** what they already know about the unit content. Ask volunteers to **predict** what else they think they will learn.

You can find more video teaching suggestions on pages R1 and R2 in the Resources Section in the back of the Teacher's Edition.

History Makers

Eli Whitney
1765–1825

Can one person change the way goods are made? An American inventer did. Whitney developed ways to produce many goods quickly and at a low cost.

page 379

Susan B. Anthony
1820–1906

Why was this woman arrested for voting? Because in 1782, it was illegal for women to vote in national elections. Anthony spent most of her life fighting for women's rights.

page 391

339

Web Link

E-Biographies

To learn more about the History Makers on these pages and in this unit, visit www.eduplace.com/kids/hmss05/

Designed to be accessed by your students, these biographies can be used for

- research projects
- Character Education
- developing students' technology skills

Correcting Misconceptions

Ask students what they know about the United States in the early 1800s. Write their responses as a list on the board.

As students read the unit, return to the list periodically to see if any of their responses have been shown to be misconceptions.

Discuss why students may have thought as they did, and what they have learned.

History Makers

Meriwether Lewis Jefferson chose Lewis to lead an expedition to the West because Lewis had lived on the frontier near American Indians while serving in the army. Lewis used a compass like the one shown to lead his group of explorers to the Pacific.

Eli Whitney Whitney invented a cotton gin (shown) that cleaned seeds from cotton fibers. Raw cotton and cotton cloth became important products in the United States. Later, Whitney's gun factory was one of the first to use mass production.

Susan B. Anthony In her fight for equal rights for women, Anthony traveled constantly, giving lectures and handing out petitions and pamphlets. Today a one-dollar coin honors her efforts.

Map and Graph Skills

Interpreting Maps

Talk About It

1. **Q Geography** What can you learn about the history of the United States from this map?
   A what territories were added to the United States, when they were added, and how they were added
2. **Q Geography** After 1783, which territory added the most area to the United States?
   A the Louisiana Purchase
3. **Q History** Was your state a part of the U.S. in 1783, or was it added later on? If it was added later, when was it added?
   A answers will vary
4. **Q History** Of the territories shown here, which was the last one added to the United States? When was it added?
   A the Gadsden Purchase, added in 1853

Interpreting Timelines

Ask students if they can identify any of the images shown on the timeline. cotton gin; bust of Thomas Jefferson; early U.S. flag; gold nugget

UNIT 5 Almanac

Westward Expansion

RED RIVER CESSION–1818
Treaty of 1818
with Great Britain

OREGON TERRITORY–1846
Ceded (given up) by Great Britain

LOUISIANA PURCHASE–1803
Bought from France

MEXICAN CESSION–1848
Treaty of Guadalupe Hildago

TEXAS ANNEXATION–1845

GADSDEN PURCHASE–1853
Bought from Mexico

WEST FLORIDA ANNEXATION 1810, 1813

Portland, San Francisco, Salt Lake City, Kansas City, Milwaukee, Chicago, Indianapolis, St. Louis, Nashville, Memphis, Mobile, San Antonio

Columbia R., Missouri R., Colorado R., Rio Grande, Mississippi R., L. Superior, L. Michigan

PACIFIC OCEAN

Gulf of Mexico

Unit Preview

1790 — 1800 — 1810 — 1820

1793 Cotton Gin
Invention changes agriculture
Chapter 11, page 379

1803 Louisiana Purchase
Jefferson buys French territory
Chapter 10, page 355

1812 War of 1812
"Star-Spangled Banner" is written
Chapter 10, page 363

340 • Unit 5

Technology

GeoNet

To support student geography skills, you may wish to have them go to www.eduplace.com/kids/hmss05/ to play GeoNet.

Math

Growing Strong

Ask students which increased more, the population of Ohio between 1810 and 1830 or the population of California between 1980 and 2000?

Although they need to estimate, students should be able to tell that Ohio grew by about 500,000 people and California grew by between 5 and 10 million people, so the population of California increased more during the time span shown.

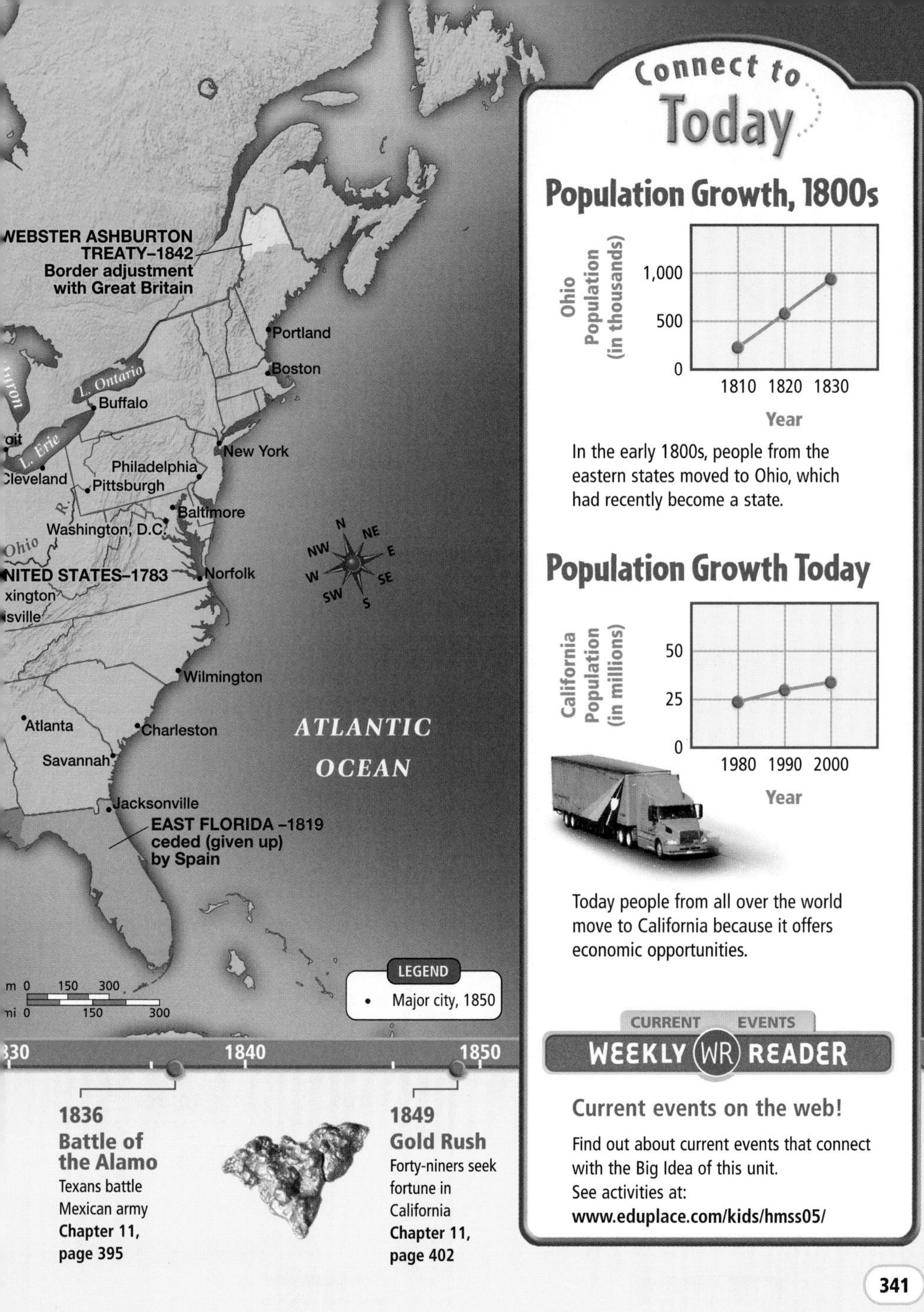

Interpreting Graphs

Talk About It

5 **Q Culture** Do you think someone living in Ohio in 1820 would be happy or unhappy about the state's population growth? Why or why not?

A Answers will vary.

6 **Q Economics** How might a state's economy change after its population increases greatly?

A Possible answers include: land would become more valuable; industries would grow due to greater work force.

Find Out More

Why Here? Ask students to consider what factors may have influenced the growth of their state. Write their answers on the board and have students do library research to determine which ideas were correct.

On the Rise Ask students to construct line graphs showing the population of their town or city since 1950. Then ask students if they expect the town to grow, shrink, or stay the same in the next 50 years.

Current Events

For information about current events related to this unit, visit www.eduplace.com/ss/hmss05/.

Web links to Weekly Reader will help students work on the Current Events Unit Project. The Unit 5 Project will involve creating a poster about people trying to improve the United States today.

As you go through the unit, encourage students to use the web to find people to include on their posters.

Chapter 10 Planning Guide

The Early Republic

Chapter Opener

Pages 342–343

30 minutes

Reading/Vocabulary

Chapter Reading Strategy:
Monitor and Clarify, p. 341F

Resources

Grade Level Resources
- Vocabulary Cards, pp. 43–50

Reaching All Learners
- Challenge Activities, p. 88

Primary Sources Plus, p. 18
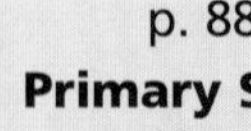

Big Idea Transparency 5

Interactive Transparency 5

Text & Music Audio CD

Lesson Planner & TR CD-ROM

eBook

eTE

Core Lesson 1

People on the Move

Pages 344–347

 40 minutes

Tested Objectives

U5-1 Explain how and why Americans moved west of the Appalachians.

U5-2 Describe life on the trans-Appalachian frontier.

Reading/Vocabulary

Reading Skill: Main Idea & Details

pioneer, flatboat, frontier, canal

Cross-Curricular

Math, p. 346

Science, p. 346

Resources

Unit Resources:
- **Reading Skill/Strategy,** p. 95
- **Vocabulary/Study Guide,** p. 96

Reaching All Learners:
- **Lesson Summary,** p. 38
- **Support for Lang. Dev./ELL,** p. 135

Assessment Options:
- **Lesson Test,** p. 98

Extend Lesson 1

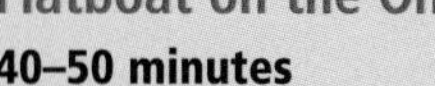

Readers' Theater

Flatboat on the Ohio

40–50 minutes

Pages 348–351

Focus: Students share in a family's river journey past Cincinnati.

Skillbuilder

Study Skill

Make an Outline

Pages 352–353

20 minutes

Tested Objective

U5-3 Organize important information and supporting details in an outline.

Reading/Vocabulary

outline

Resources

Unit Resources:
- **Skill Practice,** p. 97

Skill Transparency 10

Core Lesson 2

The Nation Grows

Pages 354–357

 40 minutes

Tested Objectives

U5-4 Identify important events during Jefferson's presidency.

U5-5 Explain the purchase and exploration of the Louisiana Territory.

Reading/Vocabulary

Reading Skill: Problem and Solution

manufacturer, interpreter, corps, source

Cross-Curricular

Art, p. 356

Resources

Unit Resources:
- **Reading Skill/Strategy,** p. 98
- **Vocabulary/Study Guide,** p. 99

Reaching All Learners:
- **Lesson Summary,** p. 39
- **Support for Lang. Dev./ELL,** p. 136

Assessment Options:
- **Lesson Test,** p. 99

Extend Lesson 2

Geography

Journey of Discovery

20–30 minutes

Pages 358–359

Focus: A look at the difficult route that Lewis and Clark followed to the Pacific Ocean.

National Standards

I a Similarities and differences in addressing human needs and concerns
I d Ways people deal with their physical environment
III a Use mental maps
III h Interaction of human beings and their physical environment
VI c How government does/does not provide for needs and wants, establish order and security, and manage conflict
VI f Factors that contribute to cooperation and cause disputes
IX b Conflict, cooperation, and interdependence
X g Influence of public opinion
X h Public policies and citizen behaviors

Core Lesson 3

The War of 1812

Pages 360–365

 50 minutes

Tested Objectives

U5-6 Describe the causes and events of the War of 1812.

U5-7 Analyze the rise of nationalism in the United States after the War of 1812.

Reading/Vocabulary

Reading Skill: Cause and Effect

prosperity **foreign policy**
nationalism

Cross-Curricular

Art, p. 362 **Math,** p. 364
Music, p. 365

Resources

Unit Resources:
- **Reading Skill/Strategy,** p. 100
- **Vocabulary/Study Guide,** p. 101

Reaching All Learners:
- **Lesson Summary,** p. 40
- **Support for Lang. Dev./ELL,** p. 137

Assessment Options:
- **Lesson Test,** p. 100

Extend Lesson 3

Literature

The National Anthem

40–50 minutes

Pages 366–367

Focus: The words to our national anthem and the story behind it.

Core Lesson 4

Age of Jackson

Pages 368–371

 40 minutes

Tested Objectives

U5-8 Explain Jackson's popularity with ordinary Americans.

U5-9 Summarize important policies of President Jackson, including Indian Removal.

Reading/Vocabulary

Reading Skill: Draw Conclusions

suffrage **ruling**
campaign

Cross-Curricular

Music, p. 370

Resources

Unit Resources:
- **Reading Skill/Strategy,** p. 102
- **Vocabulary/Study Guide,** p. 103

Reaching All Learners:
- **Lesson Summary,** p. 41
- **Support for Lang. Dev./ELL,** p. 138

Assessment Options:
- **Lesson Test,** p. 101

Extend Lesson 4

History

Trail of Tears

20–30 minutes

Pages 372–373

Focus: Where did the Cherokee go when they were forced to move? Students find out.

Chapter Review

Pages 374–375

 30 minutes

Resources

Assessment Options:
- Chapter 10 Test
- Test Generator

Chapter 10 Practice Options

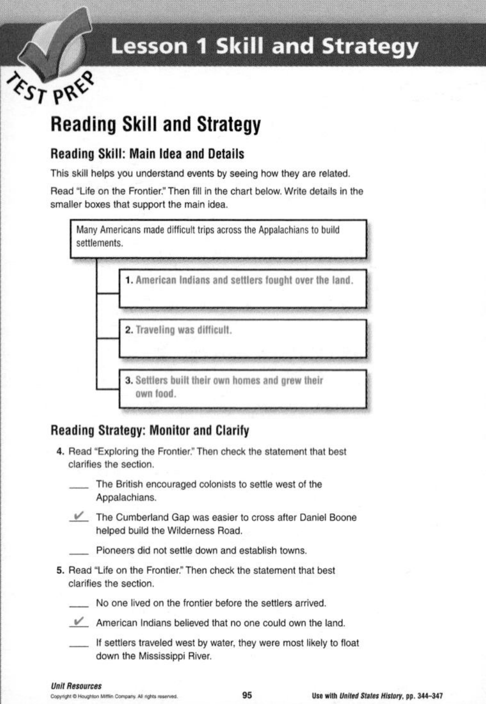

Lesson 1 Skill and Strategy

TEST PREP

Reading Skill and Strategy

Reading Skill: Main Idea and Details

This skill helps you understand events by seeing how they are related.

Read "Life on the Frontier." Then fill in the chart below. Write details in the smaller boxes that support the main idea.

Many Americans made difficult trips across the Appalachians to build settlements.

1. American Indians and settlers fought over the land.
2. Traveling was difficult.
3. Settlers built their own homes and grew their own food.

Reading Strategy: Monitor and Clarify

4. Read "Exploring the Frontier." Then check the statement that best clarifies the section.

___ The British encouraged colonists to settle west of the Appalachians.

✓ The Cumberland Gap was easier to cross after Daniel Boone helped build the Wilderness Road.

___ Pioneers did not settle down and establish towns.

5. Read "Life on the Frontier." Then check the statement that best clarifies the section.

___ No one lived on the frontier before the settlers arrived.

✓ American Indians believed that no one could own the land.

___ If settlers traveled west by water, they were most likely to float down the Mississippi River.

Unit Resources 95 Use with *United States History*, pp. 344–347

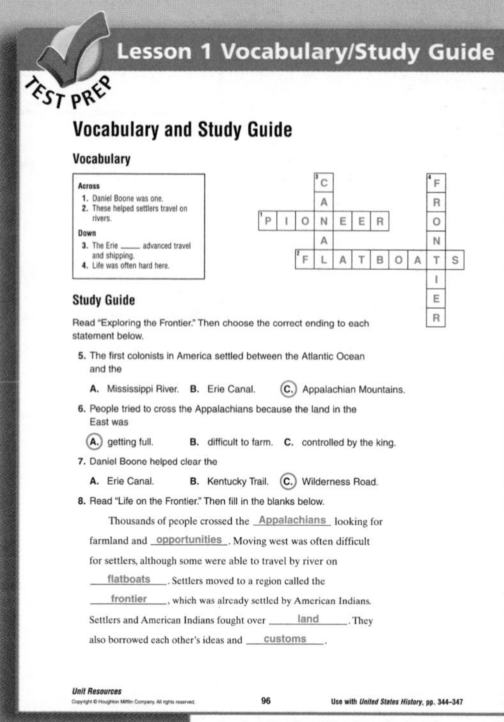

Lesson 1 Vocabulary/Study Guide

TEST PREP

Vocabulary and Study Guide

Vocabulary

Across
1. Daniel Boone was one.
2. These helped settlers travel on rivers.

Down
3. The Erie ___ advanced travel and shipping.
4. Life was often hard here.

Study Guide

Read "Exploring the Frontier." Then choose the correct ending to each statement below.

5. The first colonists in America settled between the Atlantic Ocean and the
   A. Mississippi River. B. Erie Canal. (C.) Appalachian Mountains.
6. People tried to cross the Appalachians because the land in the East was
   (A.) getting full. B. difficult to farm. C. controlled by the king.
7. Daniel Boone helped clear the
   A. Erie Canal. B. Kentucky Trail. (C.) Wilderness Road.
8. Read "Life on the Frontier." Then fill in the blanks below.

Thousands of people crossed the Appalachians looking for farmland and opportunities. Moving west was often difficult for settlers, although some were able to travel by river on flatboats. Settlers moved to a region called the frontier, which was already settled by American Indians. Settlers and American Indians fought over land. They also borrowed each other's ideas and customs.

Unit Resources 96 Use with *United States History*, pp. 344–347

also in *Practice Book*, p. 57

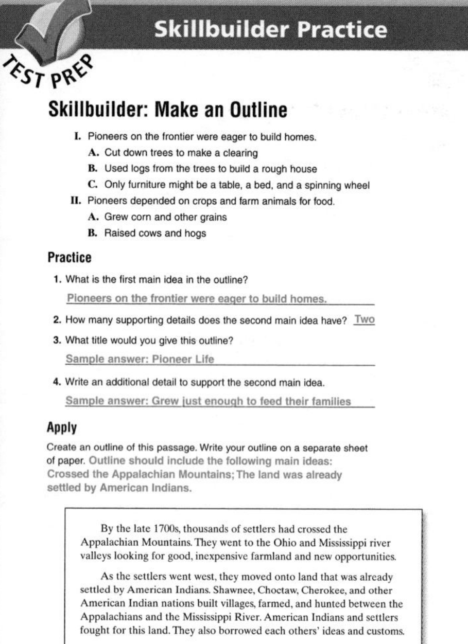

Skillbuilder Practice

TEST PREP

Skillbuilder: Make an Outline

I. Pioneers on the frontier were eager to build homes.
   A. Cut down trees to make a clearing
   B. Used logs from the trees to build a rough house
   C. Only furniture might be a table, a bed, and a spinning wheel
II. Pioneers depended on crops and farm animals for food.
   A. Grew corn and other grains
   B. Raised cows and hogs

Practice

1. What is the first main idea in the outline?
   Pioneers on the frontier were eager to build homes.
2. How many supporting details does the second main idea have? Two
3. What title would you give this outline?
   Sample answer: Pioneer Life
4. Write an additional detail to support the second main idea.
   Sample answer: Grew just enough to feed their families

Apply

Create an outline of this passage. Write your outline on a separate sheet of paper. Outline should include the following main ideas: Crossed the Appalachian Mountains; The land was already settled by American Indians.

By the late 1700s, thousands of settlers had crossed the Appalachian Mountains. They went to the Ohio and Mississippi river valleys looking for good, inexpensive farmland and new opportunities.

As the settlers went west, they moved onto land that was already settled by American Indians. Shawnee, Choctaw, Cherokee, and other American Indian nations built villages, farmed, and hunted between the Appalachians and the Mississippi River. American Indians and settlers fought for this land. They also borrowed each others' ideas and customs.

Unit Resources 97 Use with *United States History*, pp. 352–353

also in *Practice Book*, p. 58

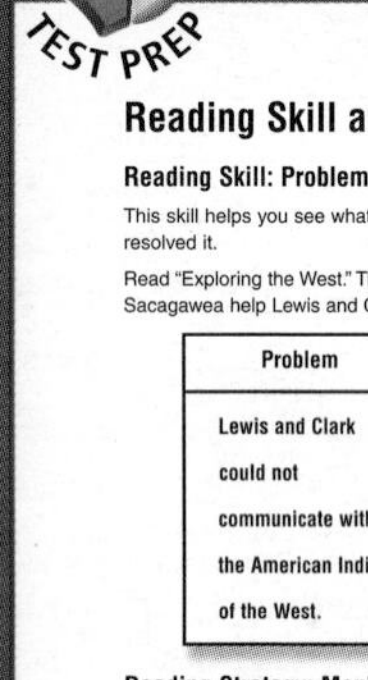

Lesson 2 Skill and Strategy

TEST PREP

Reading Skill and Strategy

Reading Skill: Problem and Solution

This skill helps you see what problem some people faced and how they resolved it.

Read "Exploring the West." Then fill in the problem chart below. How did Sacagawea help Lewis and Clark on their journey?

Problem	Solution
Lewis and Clark could not communicate with the American Indians of the West.	1. Sacagawea was an interpreter and helped trade with the American Indians.

Reading Strategy: Monitor and Clarify

2. Read "President Jefferson." Then check the statement that best clarifies the section.

✓ Thomas Jefferson believed that the government should be smaller.

___ John Adams and the Federalist Party agreed with Jefferson about states' rights.

___ Jefferson sent delegates to France to buy Texas.

3. Read "Exploring the West." Then complete the statement below. Jefferson wanted Lewis and Clark to do three things: learn about the western American Indians, find a water route to the Pacific Ocean, and gather information about the land, plants, and animals of the West.

Unit Resources 98 Use with *United States History*, pp. 354–357

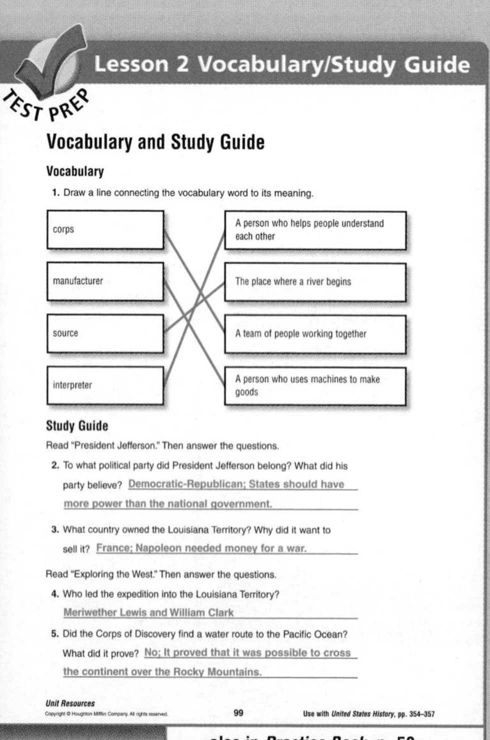

Lesson 2 Vocabulary/Study Guide

TEST PREP

Vocabulary and Study Guide

Vocabulary

1. Draw a line connecting the vocabulary word to its meaning.

Study Guide

Read "President Jefferson." Then answer the questions.

2. To what political party did President Jefferson belong? What did his party believe? Democratic-Republican; States should have more power than the national government.
3. What country owned the Louisiana Territory? Why did it want to sell it? France; Napoleon needed money for a war.

Read "Exploring the West." Then answer the questions.

4. Who led the expedition into the Louisiana Territory?
   Meriwether Lewis and William Clark
5. Did the Corps of Discovery find a water route to the Pacific Ocean? What did it prove? No; It proved that it was possible to cross the continent over the Rocky Mountains.

Unit Resources 99 Use with *United States History*, pp. 354–357

also in *Practice Book*, p. 59

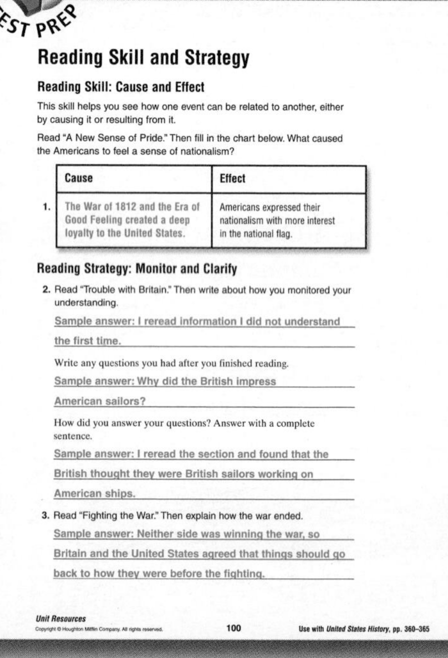

Lesson 3 Skill and Strategy

TEST PREP

Reading Skill and Strategy

Reading Skill: Cause and Effect

This skill helps you see how one event can be related to another, either by causing it or resulting from it.

Read "A New Sense of Pride." Then fill in the chart below. What caused the Americans to feel a sense of nationalism?

	Cause	Effect
1.	The War of 1812 and the Era of Good Feeling created a deep loyalty to the United States.	Americans expressed their nationalism with more interest in the national flag.

Reading Strategy: Monitor and Clarify

2. Read "Trouble with Britain." Then write about how you monitored your understanding.
   Sample answer: I reread information I did not understand the first time.
   Write any questions you had after you finished reading.
   Sample answer: Why did the British impress American sailors?
   How did you answer your questions? Answer with a complete sentence.
   Sample answer: I reread the section and found that the British thought they were British sailors working on American ships.
3. Read "Fighting the War." Then explain how the war ended.
   Sample answer: Neither side was winning the war, so Britain and the United States agreed that things should go back to how they were before the fighting.

Unit Resources 100 Use with *United States History*, pp. 360–365

Lesson 3 Vocabulary/Study Guide

TEST PREP

Vocabulary and Study Guide

Vocabulary

Write the word for each definition below.

1. nationalism A deep loyalty to one's country
2. prosperity Having enough food, clothing, and shelter to be comfortable
3. foreign policy A government's actions towards other nations
4. Use two of the words in a sentence.

Sample answer: After the War of 1812, peace and prosperity created a sense of nationalism in the United States.

Study Guide

Read "The War of 1812." Then fill in the classification chart below.

Question	Dolley Madison	Francis Scott Key	James Monroe	Noah Webster
Who am I?	5. First lady	7. Lawyer who saw a battle	9. U.S. President	11. Writer
What did I do?	6. Saved a painting of George Washington	8. Wrote the words to "The Star-Spangled Banner"	10. Created foreign policy to protect the Western Hemisphere	12. Published the first dictionary of American English

Unit Resources

101 Use with *United States History*, pp. 360–365

also in *Practice Book*, p. 60

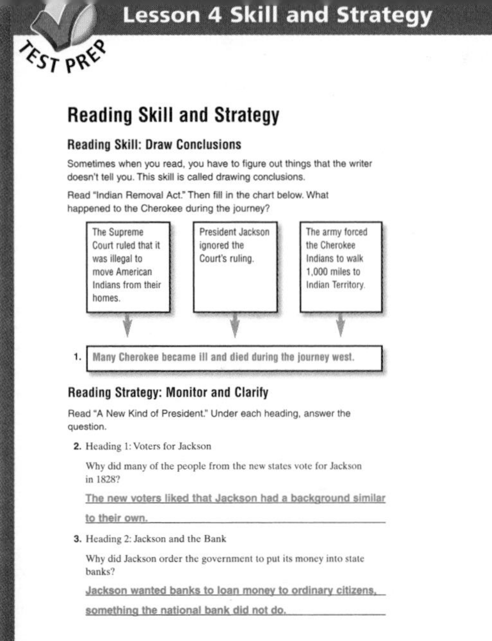

Lesson 4 Skill and Strategy

TEST PREP

Reading Skill and Strategy

Reading Skill: Draw Conclusions

Sometimes when you read, you have to figure out things that the writer doesn't tell you. This skill is called drawing conclusions.

Read "Indian Removal Act." Then fill in the chart below. What happened to the Cherokee during the journey?

The Supreme Court ruled that it was illegal to move American Indians from their homes. | President Jackson ignored the Court's ruling. | The army forced the Cherokee Indians to walk 1,000 miles to Indian Territory.

1. Many Cherokee became ill and died during the journey west.

Reading Strategy: Monitor and Clarify

Read "A New Kind of President." Under each heading, answer the question.

2. Heading 1: Voters for Jackson

Why did many of the people from the new states vote for Jackson in 1828?

The new voters liked that Jackson had a background similar to their own.

3. Heading 2: Jackson and the Bank

Why did Jackson order the government to put its money into state banks?

Jackson wanted banks to loan money to ordinary citizens, something the national bank did not do.

Unit Resources

102 Use with *United States History*, pp. 368–371

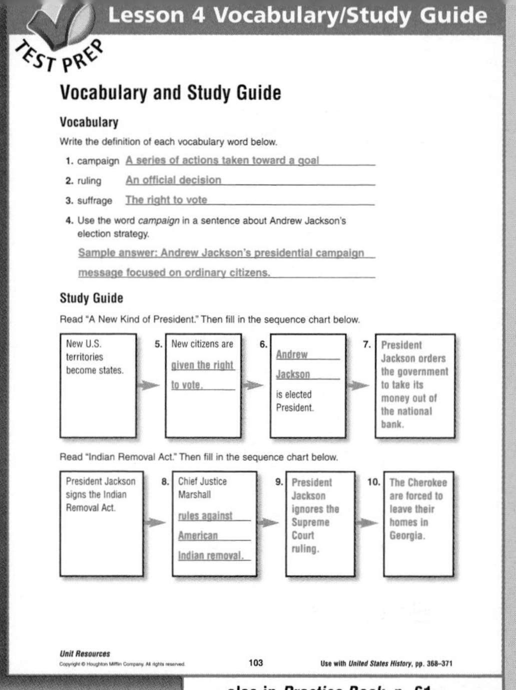

Lesson 4 Vocabulary/Study Guide

TEST PREP

Vocabulary and Study Guide

Vocabulary

Write the definition of each vocabulary word below.

1. campaign A series of actions taken toward a goal
2. ruling An official decision
3. suffrage The right to vote
4. Use the word *campaign* in a sentence about Andrew Jackson's election strategy.

Sample answer: Andrew Jackson's presidential campaign message focused on ordinary citizens.

Study Guide

Read "A New Kind of President." Then fill in the sequence chart below.

New U.S. territories become states. → 5. New citizens are given the right to vote. → 6. Andrew Jackson is elected President. → 7. President Jackson orders the government to take its money out of the national bank.

Read "Indian Removal Act." Then fill in the sequence chart below.

President Jackson signs the Indian Removal Act. → 8. Chief Justice Marshall rules against American Indian removal. → 9. President Jackson ignores the Supreme Court ruling. → 10. The Cherokee are forced to leave their homes in Georgia.

Unit Resources

103 Use with *United States History*, pp. 368–371

also in *Practice Book*, p. 61

Test Your Knowledge

frontier	flatboat	source	campaign

Write *T* if the statement is true or *F* if it is false.

1. T Settlers fought American Indians for land on the frontier. Obj. U5–2
2. T Settlers often hired a flatboat to travel west on the Ohio River. Obj. U5–1
3. F Sacagawea helped Lewis and Clark find the source of important rivers. Obj. U5–5
4. T Jackson's campaign was a message of support for ordinary Americans. Obj. U5–8

Circle the letter of the best answer.

5. Why was life on the frontier often dangerous? Obj. U5–2
   - A. Settlers had to travel on crowded rivers.
   - (B.) Pioneers fought with American Indians over land.
   - C. Settlers did not know how to hunt safely.
   - D. There were no guides to take families west.

6. Which of the following was an example of the rise in nationalism after the war of 1812? Obj. U5–7
   - (F.) The British and the Americans signed the Treaty of Ghent.
   - G. President Madison wanted the United States to stay neutral.
   - H. The British attacked Washington, D.C.
   - J. The first dictionary of American English was published.

7. Why was the Louisiana Purchase an important event for the United States? Obj. U5–4
   - A. The United States paid too much money for it.
   - B. It allowed the French to continue trading through New Orleans.
   - (C.) It doubled the size of the country.
   - D. Jefferson's representatives were able to travel to France.

8. What did President Jefferson ask Lewis and Clark to do? Obj. U5–5
   - (F.) to explore western land and study American Indian cultures
   - G. to make a map of the Arkansas and Red rivers
   - H. to find the source of the Mississippi River
   - J. to meet with the French ruler, Napoleon Bonaparte

Use the map to answer the following questions.

9. Which river marks a border of the Louisiana Territory? Obj. U5–5
   - A. Arkansas River
   - B. Columbia River
   - (C.) Mississippi River
   - D. Ohio River

10. Which of the following did Lewis and Clark explore? Obj. U5–4
    - (F.) the Missouri and Columbia rivers
    - G. the Ohio River
    - H. the Pacific Ocean
    - J. the Appalachian Mountains

Apply the Reading Skill: Cause and Effect

Read the passage below. Then answer the question. Obj. U5–6

> During the war with France, British officers raided American ships to look for British sailors. Sometimes they captured American sailors. The British also helped American Indians fight the settlers. Both of these actions angered Americans, causing Congress to declare war against Britain.

11. What two actions caused Congress to declare war against Britain?
    British officers raided American ships and captured American sailors. The British helped American Indians fight the settlers.

Chapter 10 Test

TEST PREP

Test the Skill: Make an Outline

I. First European colonists settled between the Atlantic Ocean and the Appalachian Mountains.
   - A. Appalachians were difficult to cross.
   - B. British government forbade colonists from settling west of the Appalachians.

II. People began to explore and settle land west of the Appalachians.
   - A. Pioneers followed an American Indian trail through the mountains.
   - B. Pioneers cleared the Wilderness Road.
   - C. Settlers started new towns on the frontier.

12. What are the two main ideas in the outline?
    First European colonists settled between the Atlantic Ocean and the Appalachian Mountains, and people began to explore the land west of the Appalachians. Obj. U5–3
13. How many supporting details does the second main idea have?
    Three Obj. U5–3
14. What title would you give this outline? Obj. U5–3
    Sample answer: Where European Colonists Settled and Why

Apply the Skill

15. Read the passage below. Then fill in the two main ideas in the outline. Obj. U5–3

> Thomas Jefferson made important changes while he was President. He wanted the states to have more power. He also shrank the size of the army. These changes made the national government smaller. President Jefferson also made the country much bigger. He purchased the Louisiana Territory from France in 1803, which added about 530 million acres to the United States.

I. Main Idea
   Jefferson made the national government smaller.

Chapter 10 Test

TEST PREP

Think and Write

16. **Short Response:** Describe two important decisions Andrew Jackson made during his presidency. Obj. U5–9
    President Jackson ordered the government to take money out of the national bank and put it into state banks. He signed the Indian Removal Act, ordering all of the American Indian nations east of the Mississippi River to move to present-day Oklahoma.
17. **Critical Thinking: Draw Conclusions** Why do you think that Americans developed a sense of nationalism after the War of 1812? Obj. U5–7
    Sample answer: Americans developed a sense of nationalism because they enjoyed peace and prosperity after the war and were proud of their country.
18. **Extended Response:** Write a journal entry that a young pioneer living on the frontier west of the Appalachians might have written. Describe how the pioneer traveled west and what life was like. Include information about the land, the pioneer's house, and how he or she got food. Write your journal entry on a separate sheet of paper.
    Obj. U5–2 **Entries may include information about traveling with a full wagon on rough roads or traveling by river on flatboats; about clearing trees and building homes with logs; having only a table, a bed, and dishes; and about planting corn and grains and raising farm animals.**

Self-Assessment

Which person in this chapter do I think had the greatest influence on the United States? Why do I think so?

You can share the following fiction selection with students before beginning the chapter. Ask them to look at the picture on page 346 of their books as you read.

Activate Prior Knowledge

Ask students to discuss what they know about the lives of pioneers traveling west. Tell them that the Read-Aloud selection describes the experience of a young person traveling on the Erie Canal toward a new home further west.

Preview the Chapter

Ask students to find similarities and differences between the picture on page 346 and the details mentioned in the Read Aloud.

Read-Aloud Vocabulary

Explain that a **flatboat** was a large boat with a roof that carried people, animals, and goods. A **canal** is a human-made waterway that allows people to transport goods by boat.

Preview the Reading Strategy

Monitor/Clarify Explain to students that the reading strategy they will use in this chapter is monitor/clarify. When they use this strategy, students pause during their reading and check their understanding. You may wish to use the Read Aloud to model monitor/clarify for your students.

Think Aloud *I've read the first three sentences, and I want to make sure I understand what's going on. Laura is on a flatboat in the Erie Canal, helping her mother make a quilt. I don't understand why she is on the boat, though. I'll keep reading to find out.*

Going West

My name is Laura Kirkpatrick. As I write this, I am floating with my family on a **flatboat** down a long **canal** called the Erie Canal. It is a warm autumn afternoon, and I have just been helping my mother with the quilt she is making. It is hard to imagine wanting one, but by winter, we should be settled in our new home west of here, where it will be extremely cold and windy, I am sure.

Our boat is laden down with as many possessions as we could fit on board, including a milk cow, an ox, and a mule. With all our furniture and trunks, there's barely room left for Ma, Pa, my two brothers, and me.

Pa and Ma tell us that this trip west is the best thing that has ever happened to us. My brothers are excited; Jacob especially loves the new mule. I am excited too, although I must say that I miss my friends already.

And, I admit, I am afraid of the difficulties that lie ahead. But I cannot deny my excitement at the new opportunities that surely await us, too.

Begin the Chapter

Quick Look

Core Lesson 1 focuses on settlers who crossed the Appalachians and their relations with American Indians.

Core Lesson 2 describes the purchase of Louisiana and exploration of the West.

Core Lesson 3 discusses the War of 1812 and the Monroe Doctrine.

Core Lesson 4 presents Andrew Jackson's presidency.

Vocabulary Preview

Use the vocabulary cards to preview the key vocabulary words before starting the lessons and to prepare students to understand the content of the chapter.

Vocabulary Strategy

Vocabulary strategies for this chapter:

- Word roots, pp. 354, 360
- Word origins, pp. 344, 368

Vocabulary Help

Vocabulary card for corps Tell students that the word *corps* is commonly used to refer to divisions of the armed forces, such as the Marine Corps.

Vocabulary card for campaign Explain to students that the word *campaign* comes from a word that means "battlefield." Armed forces use the word *campaign* to refer to military operations. A person who campaigns for the presidency fights for victory in an election.

Chapter 10 The Early Republic

Technology
e • glossary
e • word games
www.eduplace.com/kids/hmss05/

Vocabulary Preview

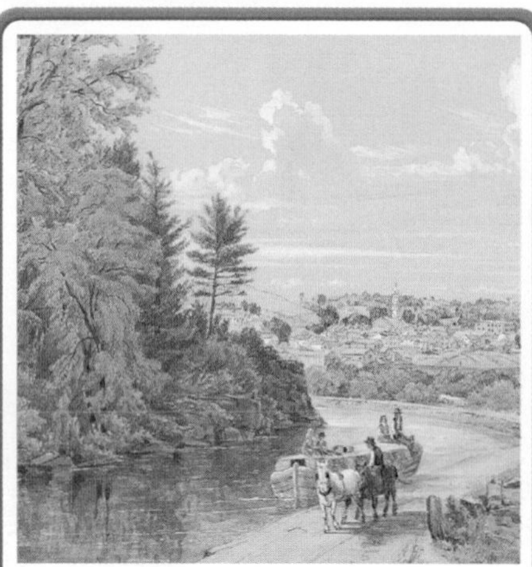

canal

A **canal** was a waterway built to make shipping goods easier. The Erie Canal connected the Great Lakes to the Hudson River.
page 346

corps

More than 30 people explored the West with Lewis and Clark. This **corps** was a team of people who worked together.
page 356

Chapter Timeline

1760	1780	1800
1769 Daniel Boone crosses Appalachians		1803 Louisiana Purchase

Background

Canals

Tell students that people have been building canals for thousands of years. The earliest ones were constructed in China, Egypt, and the Middle East. Canals provided valuable shortcuts on important trade routes.

Vocabulary

Students can use a frame game graphic organizer to further their understanding of the word *prosperity.*

Monitor and Clarify Use this strategy to check understanding.

Stop and ask if the lesson makes sense to you. Reread if you need to.

prosperity

After the War of 1812, the Era of Good Feelings began. It was a time of **prosperity.** Many families had enough money for food, clothing, and shelter. **page 364**

campaign

Andrew Jackson was elected President in 1828. His election **campaign** was successful. Voters liked his promise to support ordinary citizens. **page 369**

343

Leveled Practice

Extra Support

Have students look at the pictures on the vocabulary cards and explain how each picture helps define the word. Visual-spatial

Challenge

Challenge students to name as many words that start with *pro* as they can. Write their words on the board. Ask students to choose two words and find out how "in front" contributes to the meaning of the word. Verbal-linguistic

ELL

All Proficiency Levels

- Have students create an illustration of the Corps of Discovery.
- Ask students to include a caption with the word *corps* in it.
- Hang the illustrations in the classroom for others to enjoy.

Visual-spatial

Using the Timeline

- Direct students to look at the timeline on pages 342 and 343. Point out the segments of the timeline. Ask them how many years this chapter will cover.
- Ask students what they think might have happened during the 1838 event called the Trail of Tears.

Reading Strategy: Monitor and Clarify

To monitor and clarify, the reader reviews the material after reading and draws out important information. The reader also asks questions about the material, to determine what he or she understands or needs clarification on.

Explain to students that to monitor and clarify successfully, they should follow these steps:

- Read the passage.
- Think about what the passage says.
- Ask yourself: What is important about this passage?
- Review the passage.
- Ask yourself: Does this passage make sense? Am I learning what I think I should be learning?
- If you don't understand something, reread, read ahead, or use the headings, graphic organizers, illustrations, and captions.

Students can practice these reading strategies throughout this chapter, including on the Skill and Strategy pages from the unit resources.

Tested Objectives

U5-1 Geography Explain how and why Americans moved west of the Appalachians.

U5-2 Culture Describe life on the trans-Appalachian frontier.

Lesson Quick Look

This lesson describes ways in which settlers from the East and Europe explored the Appalachian frontier, and the resulting interactions they had with American Indians.

Teaching Option **Extend Lesson 1,** a Readers' Theater selection, tells about a flatboat on the Ohio River.

1 Get Set to Read

Preview Have students read the heads on pages 344 and 345. Ask them what they think this lesson is about.

Reading Skill: Main Idea and Details Details can include *who* and *how*.

Build on What You Know Ask students what they think a family of four might need for life on the frontier and how they would pack it all up in one vehicle for a journey that could take a month or more.

Vocabulary

pioneer *noun,* a settler who travels into unknown or unclaimed territory

frontier *noun,* an area just beyond or at the edge of a settled area

flatboat *noun,* a large, rectangular boat with a flat bottom, used for travel over shallow rivers

canal *noun,* a waterway made by people for travel and shipping goods

Core Lesson 1

People on the Move

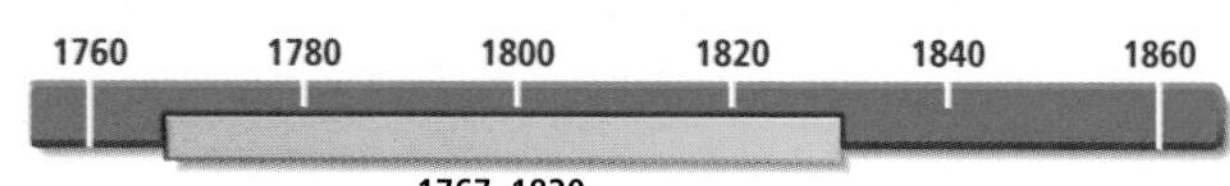

VOCABULARY

pioneer
frontier
flatboat
canal

Vocabulary Strategy

canal

Canal comes from a word meaning passageway. Canals allow boats to pass from one body of water to another.

READING SKILL

Main Idea and Details

As you read, record details that support the second main idea.

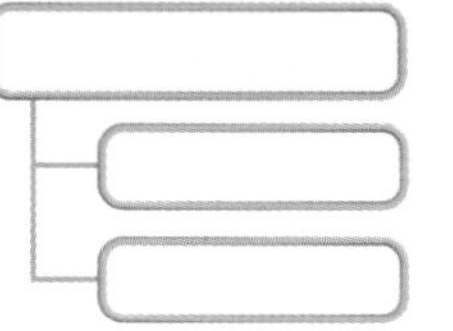

Build on What You Know Have you ever taken a ride in a wagon or on a horse? In the late 1700s and early 1800s, people walked, rode horses, or traveled in wagons over bumpy roads. What is different about travel today?

Exploring the Frontier

Main Idea Pioneers explored land west of the Appalachian Mountains in the late 1700s.

The first colonists who came to the British colonies from Europe settled between the Atlantic Ocean and the Appalachian Mountains. This 2,000-mile-long chain of mountains was difficult to cross. Under the Proclamation of 1763, it was against the law for colonists to settle American Indian lands west of the Appalachians. Yet people did not stop trying to cross these mountains. As land in the East filled with farms and towns, settlers looked for new ways to cross the Appalachians.

Daniel Boone He became a hero for his western explorations. This painting shows him leading settlers west.

Skill and Strategy

Reading Skill and Strategy

Reading Skill: Main Idea and Details

This skill helps you understand events by seeing how they are related.

Read "Life on the Frontier." Then fill in the chart below. Write details in the smaller boxes that support the main idea.

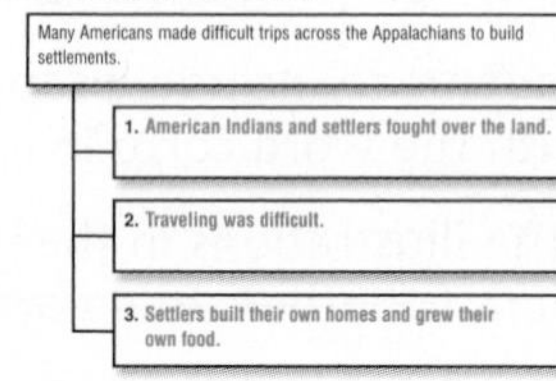

Many Americans made difficult trips across the Appalachians to build settlements.

1. American Indians and settlers fought over the land.
2. Traveling was difficult.
3. Settlers built their own homes and grew their own food.

Reading Strategy: Monitor and Clarify

4. Read "Exploring the Frontier." Then check the statement that best clarifies the section.
   - ___ The British encouraged colonists to settle west of the Appalachians.
   - ✓ The Cumberland Gap was easier to cross after Daniel Boone helped build the Wilderness Road.
   - ___ Pioneers did not settle down and establish towns.
5. Read "Life on the Frontier." Then check the statement that best clarifies the section.
   - ___ No one lived on the frontier before the settlers arrived.
   - ✓ American Indians believed that no one could own the land.
   - ___ If settlers traveled west by water, they were most likely to float down the Mississippi River.

Unit Resources

95 Use with *United States History*, pp. 344–347

Unit Resources, p. 95

Background

Appalachian Wilderness

- The Cumberland Gap is located in the Appalachian Mountains near the place where Tennessee, Kentucky, and Virginia meet.
- In geography, a gap is a pass or a break through the mountains.

Daniel Boone

Daniel Boone, a hunter and pioneer, had heard stories about the land west of the Appalachian Mountains. A **pioneer** is one of the first of a group of people to enter or settle a region. In 1769, Boone and several other men followed an American Indian trail through a narrow
1 passage in the Appalachians in Virginia. On the other side of the Cumberland Gap, as this passage was called, they found a land where American Indians farmed and hunted. Boone wanted to live on this land, too.

Boone helped clear a new road
2 through the Cumberland Gap. The route through the mountains was called the Wilderness Road. It stretched 200 miles west. Boone guided families, including his own wife and children, across the Appalachians. Settlers started towns, such as Harrodsburg and Boonesborough, in present-day Kentucky.

Life on the Frontier

Main Idea American settlers made difficult trips across the Appalachians.

By the late 1700s, thousands of people had crossed the Appalachians. 3
They looked for good, inexpensive farmland and new opportunities in the Ohio and Mississippi river valleys.

As settlers went west, they moved into a region known as the frontier. A **frontier** is the edge of a country or settled region. The frontier, and the land beyond it, was already settled by American Indians. Shawnee, Choctaw, Cherokee, and other American Indian nations built villages, farmed, and hunted between the Appalachians and the Mississippi River. Indians and settlers fought over this land on the frontier, but they also borrowed ideas and customs from one another.

REVIEW In which river valleys did people look for farmland on the frontier?
Ohio and Mississippi

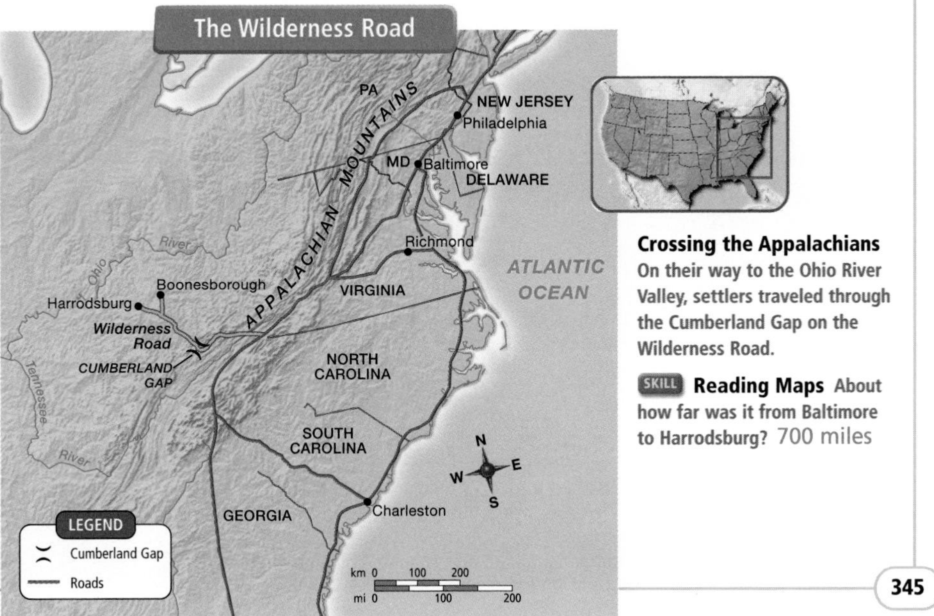

Crossing the Appalachians On their way to the Ohio River Valley, settlers traveled through the Cumberland Gap on the Wilderness Road.

SKILL Reading Maps About how far was it from Baltimore to Harrodsburg? 700 miles

2 Teach

Exploring the Frontier

Talk About It

1 **Q Geography** Where is the Cumberland Gap?

A It is in the Appalachian Mountains in Virginia.

2 **Q History** What did Daniel Boone do?

A He helped clear a new road, the Wilderness Road, through the Cumberland Gap. Then he led settlers along the road west into Kentucky.

Life on the Frontier

Talk About It

3 **Q Economics** Why did the frontier keep moving west?

A People moved west in search of cheap farmland and new opportunities.

Vocabulary Strategy

pioneer Tell students that *pioneer* can be used for someone who accomplishes new and important things: "Amelia Earhart was a pioneer in aviation."

frontier Explain that the word *front* in *frontier* can be used as an aid to recalling its meaning: the *frontier* was always in front of pioneers as they headed west.

Reading Strategy: Monitor/Clarify
Explain to students that monitoring their reading helps them make sure that they understand the information before they move on to other material.

Leveled Practice

Extra Support

Have pairs of students **role-play** early pioneers and tell each other where they went, what they saw, and the problems they faced.
Verbal-linguistic; bodily-kinesthetic

Challenge

Have students **research and create visuals** that show part of the Wilderness Road. Visuals should include some geographic facts.
Visual-spatial

ELL

Beginning/Intermediate

Have students **create a word web** for *pioneer*. Students may gather and record words from the lesson, from other students, and from prior knowledge.

Verbal-linguistic

Life on the Frontier continued

Talk About It

4 **Q History** What did pioneers have in their homes?

A They might have had a table, a bed, a spinning wheel, and a few dishes.

5 **Q History** Why was frontier life hard?

A Settlers worked hard to hunt and farm, and lived far from family and friends.

6 **Q History** Who was Chief Logan?

A He was an American Indian who was friendly to pioneers until settlers killed his family. After that, Chief Logan led attacks against settlers.

Vocabulary Strategy

flatboat Explain that the word *flatboat* is a compound word, a word made up of other words. A *flatboat* is a *boat* that is *flat* on the bottom.

canal Teach this palindrome to help students remember canal: "A man, a plan, a canal, Panama."

Critical Thinking

Decision Making What should a pioneer family take with them to the frontier?

Think Aloud *I know that the pioneers will have to build their own shelter, grow their own food, and make their own clothing. They should probably take enough food to last them until they can grow their own. They should take clothing and tools.*

Traveling West

Many families who traveled west packed large wagons so full of food and supplies that there was little room for people to ride in them. Early roads were rocky dirt paths, and there were no bridges across rivers. Wagons rolling over the rough roads often broke apart and had to be repaired.

Floating on rivers was faster and more comfortable than traveling over bumpy roads. The Ohio River was the most heavily traveled river. Families, furniture, animals, and equipment floated down the Ohio in flatboats. A **flatboat** was a large rectangular boat partly covered by a roof. Settlers also traveled on canals, such as the Erie Canal, that connected bodies of water. A **canal** is a waterway built for boat travel and shipping.

Flatboats on the Ohio In the early 1820s, about 3,000 flatboats a year floated down the Ohio River.

Making a Home

When pioneers arrived on the frontier, they cut down trees to create a clearing in the woods. They used the logs from these trees to build a house. Inside the house they might have only a table, a bed, a spinning wheel, and a few dishes. 4

Settlers grew corn and other grains and raised farm animals. Most early settlers grew just enough to feed their families, with no surplus to trade or sell.

Frontier life was hard, especially for women. They lived far from family and friends. Frontier men and women did the same kinds of work as the American Indian men and women who lived nearby. While men went hunting, women took care of their children and farms. 5

Life was difficult, but many settlers lived better than they had in Europe or in the East. One pioneer wrote: "We were worth nothing when we landed at this place and now we have 1 yoke of oxen, 1 cow, 9 hogs."

346 • Chapter 10

Science

Forces Affecting Travel

Ask students to skim a block of wood over dirt, sticks, and rocks. Then ask them to skim the wood over water. Based on their observations, what can they infer about travel over land and water?

Bodily-kinesthetic

Math

Travel Calendar

How many weeks would it take to walk the Wilderness Road if the pioneer walked eight miles per day, six days per week? $6 \times 8 = 48$ miles/week; 200 miles $\div$ 48 miles/week $\cong$ 4 weeks 1 day

Logical-mathematical

Chief Logan

American Indians did not believe that land could be bought or sold. They agreed to sign treaties letting settlers hunt on the land, but not to own it or live on it.

The Iroquois signed one such treaty in 1768. Settlers quickly moved onto the land where Iroquois, Shawnee, Mingo, and other American Indians were living. **Chief Logan** was a Mingo who had always 6 been friendly to the pioneers. In 1774, however, settlers murdered his family.

Chief Logan
This Mingo leader lived in present-day Ohio.

Chief Logan led many attacks against settlers after his family was killed. Like Logan, American Indians would fight with settlers over land for years to come.

REVIEW What kinds of transportation did settlers use to move west? wagons, flatboats

Lesson Summary

- As the East filled with farms and towns, settlers crossed the Appalachians and built settlements.
- Families traveled west in wagons and on flatboats.
- When settlers moved into areas where American Indians lived, there were conflicts.

Why It Matters ...

Pioneers who crossed the Appalachian Mountains moved the boundaries of American settlement west of the original thirteen colonies.

Lesson Review

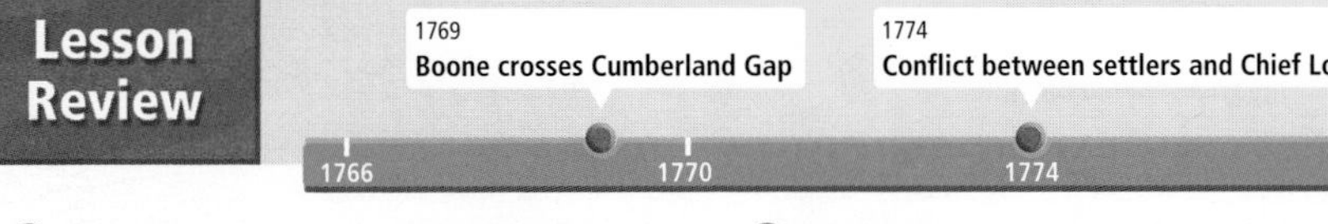

1. **VOCABULARY** Write an announcement for a company that provided transportation for settlers in 1821. Use the words **frontier**, **flatboat**, and **canal**.
2. **READING SKILL** Why did settlers make the difficult trip across the Appalachian Mountains? Use **details** in your answer.
3. **MAIN IDEA: History** What were two reasons that some settlers traveled into the Ohio River Valley by flatboat instead of by wagon?
4. **MAIN IDEA: History** What did women do on the frontier?
5. **TIMELINE SKILL** When did Daniel Boone travel through the Cumberland Gap?
6. **CRITICAL THINKING: Decision Making** An opportunity cost is the thing you give up when you decide to do or have something else. What might have been the opportunity cost for a family who decided to move west across the Appalachians?

HANDS ON **ART ACTIVITY** Reread the section called "Making a Home." Create a model of a house that a pioneer might have built. Use clay or other materials.

3 Review/Assess

Review Tested Objectives

U5-1 Americans were seeking new lands and opportunities. They traveled by wagon and flatboat.

U5-2 Life on the frontier was often harsh. Settlers met and clashed with American Indians.

Lesson Review Answers

1. Possible answers: students might write that the company will take settlers to the *frontier* aboard *flatboats* traveling on a *canal*, which may be their safest, easiest, and fastest way to travel west.
2. They wanted to settle on good, inexpensive farmland and find new opportunities.
3. Traveling by flatboat was faster and more comfortable than traveling by wagon.
4. They took care of their children and farms.
5. 1769
6. Possible answers: safety, comfort, living near friends and family, living in a familiar place, producing surplus farm goods to trade or sell

HANDS ON Performance Task Rubric

4	Details shown are significant; model is accurate; home details are present.
3	Details shown are significant; model is generally accurate; most home details are present.
2	Details shown are significant; model contains some errors; few home details are present.
1	Details shown are not significant; model is inaccurate; home details are absent.

Study Guide/Homework

Vocabulary and Study Guide

Vocabulary

Across
1. Daniel Boone was one.
2. These helped settlers travel on rivers.

Down
3. The Erie ____ advanced travel and shipping.
4. Life was often hard here.

1 PIONEER, 2 FLATBOATS, 3 CANAL, 4 FRONTIER

Study Guide

Read "Exploring the Frontier." Then choose the correct ending to each statement below.

5. The first colonists in America settled between the Atlantic Ocean and the
   A. Mississippi River. B. Erie Canal. (C.) Appalachian Mountains.
6. People tried to cross the Appalachians because the land in the East was
   (A.) getting full. B. difficult to farm. C. controlled by the king.
7. Daniel Boone helped clear the
   A. Erie Canal. B. Kentucky Trail. (C.) Wilderness Road.
8. Read "Life on the Frontier." Then fill in the blanks below.

Thousands of people crossed the Appalachians looking for farmland and opportunities. Moving west was often difficult for settlers, although some were able to travel by river on flatboats. Settlers moved to a region called the frontier, which was already settled by American Indians. Settlers and American Indians fought over land. They also borrowed each other's ideas and customs.

Unit Resources

96 Use with *United States History*, pp. 344–347

Unit Resources, p. 96

Reteach Minilesson

Use a graphic organizer to compare pioneers' lives, traveling west and living on the frontier.

Traveling	Living
large wagons dirt paths floating on rivers	log homes men: hunted women: took care of farms and children

Graphic Organizer 1

Quick Look

Connect to Core Lesson In Lesson 1, students learned about the movement westward and life on the frontier. In Extend Lesson 1, they will share the experiences of an extended family traveling along the Ohio River by flatboat.

1 Preview the Extend Lesson

Connect to the Big Idea

Individuals and the Economy People respond to incentives, such as the promise of good, cheap land, in predictable ways. Their choices affect their future income as well as the nation's economy.

Connect to Prior Knowledge

Explain that the family in this selection has come from Pennsylvania and is traveling westward on the Ohio River. In this selection the family sees Cincinnati, a place they have never seen before. Ask students to predict what the family might do or say when they see it.

Extend Lesson 1

Readers' Theater

Flatboat on the Ohio

What was it like to travel on a flatboat? Imagine that it is spring in the year 1816. A pioneer family is traveling down the Ohio River on a **flatboat** along with their animals, furniture, food, and supplies. On the twelfth day of the journey, the children raise an excited shout—Cincinnati is up ahead!

Characters

Jonah Rees: farmer

Margaret Rees: farmer

Anne: their 15-year-old daughter

Abby: their 12-year-old daughter

Martin: their 10-year-old son

Susie: their 6-year-old daughter

William Rees: Jonah Rees's brother

Tom: William's 16-year-old son

Granny Rees: mother of Jonah and William Rees

Keelboat pilot

348 • Chapter 10

Reaching All Learners

Background

Traveling by Boat

- Flatboats, which were like rafts or barges, were made for one-way travel only. At the end of the journey, passengers often used them for lumber or firewood.
- Keelboats were made for travel in the opposite direction on the Ohio River. They were moved upstream by poling, rowing, sailing, and sometimes towing.

Extra Support

Draw a Family Tree

- Help students keep the characters straight by drawing a family tree with them before the story starts.
- On a handout or on the board, provide a structure showing the two families and their relationship, and have students fill in the names of the characters.

Visual-spatial

On Level

Introduce a Character

- Have students skim the Readers' Theater and choose one of the characters. Ask students to introduce that character.
- Introductions should include the character's age or approximate age and relationship to three other characters. Students should also sum up what their character says, does, and feels on the flatboat journey.

Verbal-linguistic

Tom: Look, cousins! A big town!

Anne: It must be Cincinnati! Mother, please may I go see? I hear it has five thousand people!

Margaret Rees: Be quick about it, Anne. I want to have a look, too. And check if the hens have laid any eggs while you're at it. Granny! It's Cincinnati!

Granny Rees: Yes—I hear all the noise. I'll take a look from one of those crates. Help me up, Martin.

Martin: There you go, Granny. Just look at all those houses!

Abby: What are those buildings near the river?

Tom: Father says there are lots of cotton mills in Cincinnati. I wonder if we'll go ashore. I'd like to see the town.

349

2 Teach the Extend Lesson

Learning Through Drama

Assign each of the roles in this scene to students, and have them read the play aloud to the class. Discuss with students how the scene brings the flatboat journey to life. Ask students whether they would have enjoyed such a journey and have them explain their positions.

Challenge

Make a Model Boat

Invite students to make a model of a flatboat or keelboat using paper, cardboard, clay, or other materials.

- Models should reflect where passengers sat and slept, where goods were stored, and how the boat was steered.
- Students may need to do additional research.

Bodily-kinesthetic

ELL

Intermediate

Have students make a list of details, derived from both the words and illustrations in the Readers' Theater, about travel by flatboat. Students might address the following:

- How many people might be on one boat?
- What animals and goods might be on board?
- What would be a big event during a flatboat journey?
- What did the boat look like?

Visual-spatial

Literature

Mystery

What the Dickens! by Jane Louise Curry. Place this work in your Reading Center for students who want to read a mystery set on a canal boat in 1842.

Critical Thinking

Draw Conclusions Have students draw a conclusion about the direction in which the Ohio River flows.

Generalize Ask students to make a general statement about travel by flatboat. Students might also name some details that led them to their generalization.

Anne: I wish we could live here. It looks so cozy and settled.

Abby: Crowded, you mean! I hate to have people breathing down my neck. I can't wait to get to Indiana.

Granny Rees: You sound like your Pa.

Martin: I just hope we're near a settlement with a school and children my age.

Susie: Where are we going to live in Indiana?

Tom: Don't worry. We're buying land from the government.

Anne: Why do we have to move, anyway? Our farm in Pennsylvania was so close to town, so snug, wasn't it?

Abby: That's exactly why.

Granny Rees: She means it was getting too crowded for your Pa. Land is cheap in Indiana, and he got a good price for the farm.

Tom: And my father says he needs a change, too. He says he likes a new challenge. Oh, here's your father.

Jonah Rees: Martin! Have you milked Sally yet? She doesn't sound too happy!

Martin: I'll do it right now!

Margaret Rees: And what about the chickens, Anne?

Anne: I got six eggs. Look.

Margaret Rees: Good. I'll go have a look at Cincinnati. Don't let the fire get too big, and watch for sparks. Are we stopping here, Jonah?

Jonah Rees: No reason to. We don't need anything. The children won't want to leave if we do.

Reaching All Learners

Language Arts

Write a Friendly Letter

- Ask students to imagine themselves as one of the characters.
- Then have them write a friendly letter home to one of their friends or relatives that describes, from the character's point of view, the events recounted in this scene.
- Students may also wish to convey feelings and hopes about the journey and move as a whole.

Verbal-linguistic

Math

Cramped Quarters

Flatboats ranged in size from 8 to 20 feet wide and 20 to 100 feet long.

- Have students find the area of a flatboat 12 feet wide and 24 feet long.
- Ask students to assume that $\frac{3}{4}$ of the area of the boat is devoted to hauling freight and livestock. What is the remaining space per person on a 9-person boat? Then have students draw that space, which includes sleeping, eating, and all other quarters, and reflect on traveling in it, night and day.

24 ft. × 12 ft. = 288 sq. ft.
288 sq.ft. × $\frac{1}{4}$ = 72 sq. ft.
72 sq. ft. ÷ 9 people = 8 sq. ft. per person

Space Per Person

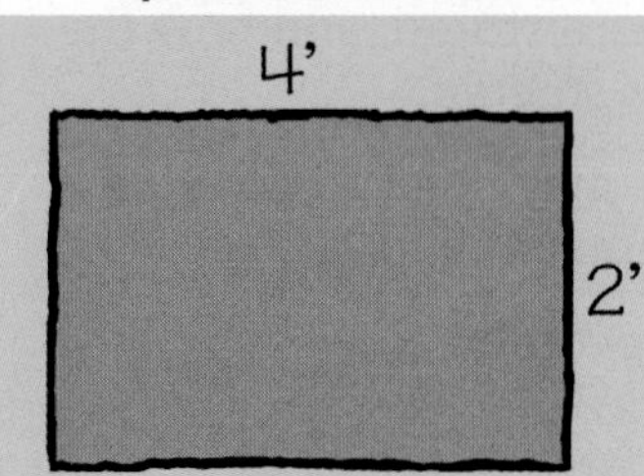

Logical-mathematical

Margaret Rees: The children are a touch homesick. Wouldn't you like to see Cincinnati?

Jonah Rees: I can see it from here. I'd rather get to the land office in Jeffersonville so we can make a claim.

Martin: Look! A keelboat is coming up the river. They're signaling.

Keelboat pilot (shouting): Where are you bound?

William Rees: To Jeffersonville, from Pittsburgh!

Keelboat pilot: Watch for a sandbar below Cincinnati, just past Mill Creek.

William Rees: Much obliged, thank you!

Margaret Rees: Anne, oh no! Check that fire! Get some water! Good—that was close. It was sparking, wasn't it?

Anne: I'm sorry, Mother. We were watching the keelboat and the city, and—

Margaret Rees: Don't fret. We're all getting distracted. Be more careful next time.

William Rees: Jonah, if we're going ashore, we need to bring the boat around now.

Jonah Rees: All right. It seems I'm out-voted. Tom, Anne! Help out, now. Take an oar. We're heading in.

Tom: Cousins, did you hear? We're landing in Cincinnati!

Anne, Abby, Martin, Susie: Hooray!

William Rees: Don't get too worked up, now. We're not staying long.

Jonah Rees: That's right. There's land waiting for us in Indiana!

READERS' THEATER

Activities

1. **TALK ABOUT IT** What were three challenges that flatboat pioneers faced on their journey?
2. **WRITE ABOUT IT** Use a map to locate the route the family is taking. Write another scene about something that could happen before they arrive at their destination.

351

3 Leveled Activities

1 Talk About It *For Extra Support*

Sample answer: Challenges included fires on the boat; getting stuck on sandbars; feeling homesick; traveling with nine people, farm animals, hay bales, barrels, and many other items, all on one boat.

2 Write About It *For Challenge*

Writing Rubric

4	The location of the scene is logical; the scene is built from many interesting and realistic details; grammar, usage, and mechanics are correct.
3	The location of the scene is logical; the scene contains interesting and realistic details; grammar, usage, and mechanics are generally correct.
2	The location of the scene is not completely logical; the scene attempts to use interesting and realistic details; there are several errors in grammar, usage, and mechanics.
1	The location of the scene is not logical; the scene is confused or unrealistic; there are many errors in grammar, usage, and mechanics.

Science

Water Travel

Between 1811 and the 1840s, the Ohio River was crowded with flatboats, keelboats, and steamboats.

- Have students name some of the characteristics of this motion over the water.
- Have students identify forces that would have affected these modes of travel.

Logical-mathematical

Graphic Organizer

A Pioneer Family on the Move

leaves farm in Pennsylvania: "too crowded"

↓

travels on the Ohio River by flatboat

↓

going to Indiana, where land is cheap

Graphic Organizer 5

Tested Objective

U5-3 Organize important information and supporting details in an outline.

1 Teach the Skill

- Read aloud the introductory paragraph on page 352. Then go through the four steps under "Learn the Skill."
- You may want to have students suggest a title, topics, and supporting details for a brief sample outline on the board.
- Remind students that making an outline can help them remember the most important facts of a lesson. An outline can also help them study for a test or plan a report.
- Ask students to brainstorm other uses for outlines.

Skillbuilder

Make an Outline

VOCABULARY
outline

In the last lesson, you read about people moving west across the Appalachian Mountains. You can better understand what you read by creating an outline. An outline identifies the main ideas and supporting details of a piece of writing. Making an outline can also help you organize your ideas before writing a report.

Learn the Skill

Step 1: Identify the topic of the piece of writing in a title at the top of your outline.

Step 2: List each main idea with a Roman numeral. Use your own words to express the ideas.

Step 3: List supporting details under each main idea. Indent each detail and place a capital letter in front of it. Use your own words.

Step 4: Repeat Steps 2 and 3 for the other main ideas in the piece of writing.

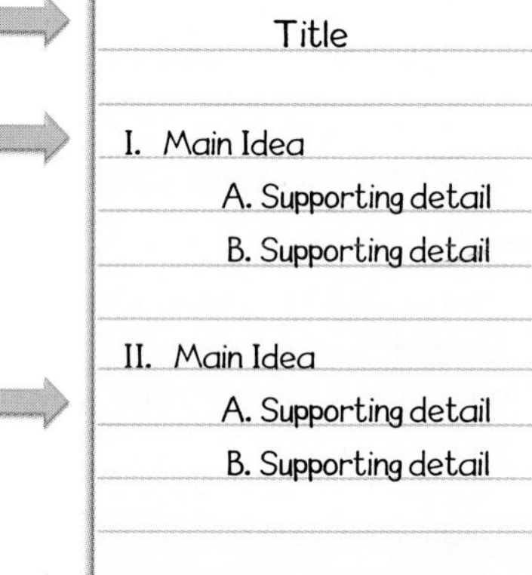

Leveled Practice

Extra Support

Point out that a lesson's title and the headings of different sections provide a kind of outline of the lesson content. Have partners look at a lesson they have already read and make a list of the title and headings. Have them use these to start an outline of the lesson.
Verbal-linguistic

ELL

Beginning/Intermediate

- Explain that the word *outline* can refer to a sketch by an artist. You may wish to show examples of outline drawings.
- Explain that sketches like these do not show every detail of a subject, only the most important features. Similarly, a text outline shows only the most important information.

Visual-spatial

Practice the Skill

Here is an outline of two paragraphs from Lesson 1. Answer the following questions about the outline.

1. What are the two main ideas in the outline?
2. How many supporting details does the first main idea have?
3. What title would you give this outline?

I. Land travel was difficult
   A. Wagons packed full, little room for people
   B. Poor roads, few bridges
   C. Wagons often needed repairs

II. Water travel was easier
   A. Families, furniture, livestock, equipment floated downriver in flatboats
   B. Canals made travel easier

Apply the Skill

Make an outline of this passage about Daniel Boone.

Daniel Boone was a famous pioneer. He was an expert hunter, trapper, and explorer. Boone guided many families, including his own, through the Cumberland Gap and into Kentucky. There he helped settlers survive in the wilderness. Later, Boone moved his family further west to Missouri, where he lived for the rest of his life.

Boone's adventures were published in a book in 1784. He was soon known around the world for his strength and courage. People began writing biographies and poems about him. Although some of the stories about Boone were not true, he became a legend.

353

2 Practice the Skill

1. Travel by land was difficult. Travel by water was easier.
2. three
3. Sample answer: Traveling West

3 Apply the Skill

Ask students to make an outline from the passage about Daniel Boone. When evaluating students' outlines, consider:

- Did the student correctly use the outline format?
- Did the student correctly identify the main ideas and supporting details of the passage?
- Did the student provide an appropriate title for the outline?

Skill Practice

Skillbuilder: Make an Outline

I. Pioneers on the frontier were eager to build homes.
   A. Cut down trees to make a clearing
   B. Used logs from the trees to build a rough house
   C. Only furniture might be a table, a bed, and a spinning wheel

II. Pioneers depended on crops and farm animals for food.
   A. Grew corn and other grains
   B. Raised cows and hogs

Practice

1. What is the first main idea in the outline?
   Pioneers on the frontier were eager to build homes.
2. How many supporting details does the second main idea have? Two
3. What title would you give this outline?
   Sample answer: Pioneer Life
4. Write an additional detail to support the second main idea.
   Sample answer: Grew just enough to feed their families

Apply

Create an outline of this passage. Write your outline on a separate sheet of paper. Outline should include the following main ideas: Crossed the Appalachian Mountains; The land was already settled by American Indians.

By the late 1700s, thousands of settlers had crossed the Appalachian Mountains. They went to the Ohio and Mississippi river valleys looking for good, inexpensive farmland and new opportunities.

As the settlers went west, they moved onto land that was already settled by American Indians. Shawnee, Choctaw, Cherokee, and other American Indian nations built villages, farmed, and hunted between the Appalachians and the Mississippi River. American Indians and settlers fought for this land. They also borrowed each others' ideas and customs.

Unit Resources

97

Use with *United States History*, pp. 352–353

Unit Resources, p. 97

Skill Transparency

Skillbuilder Transparency 10

Make an Outline

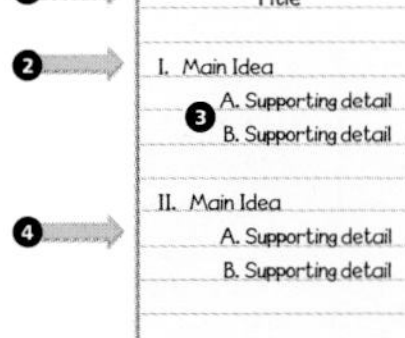

Step 1 Identify the topic of the piece of writing in a title at the top of your outline.

Step 2 List each main idea with a Roman numeral. Use your own words to express the ideas.

Step 3 List supporting details under each main idea. Indent each detail and place a capital letter in front of it. Use your own words.

Step 4 Repeat Steps 2 and 3 for the other main ideas in the piece of writing.

Skillbuilder Transparency

Use with *United States History*, pp. 352–353

Transparency 10

Tested Objectives

U5-4 History Identify important events during Thomas Jefferson's presidency.

U5-5 Geography Explain the purchase and exploration of the Louisiana Territory.

Quick Look

This lesson tells about Thomas Jefferson, who purchased the Louisiana Territory, and about the explorers Meriwether Lewis, William Clark, and Zebulon Pike.

Teaching Option **Extend Lesson 2** features a map showing the geography of the Lewis and Clark expedition.

1 Get Set to Read

Preview Have students look at the map on page 355 and predict what they will learn about in this lesson.

Reading Skill: Problem and Solution Problems included keeping the port of New Orleans open to American farmers.

Build on What You Know You may wish to list students' questions on the board, and relate them to Lewis and Clark's expedition.

Vocabulary

manufacturer *noun,* a person, an enterprise, or an entity that makes goods, especially by large-scale industrial production or using machines.

corps *noun,* an organized group of people who do something together

interpreter *noun,* someone who helps people who speak different languages understand each other

source *noun,* the beginning of a stream or river

Core Lesson 2

The Nation Grows

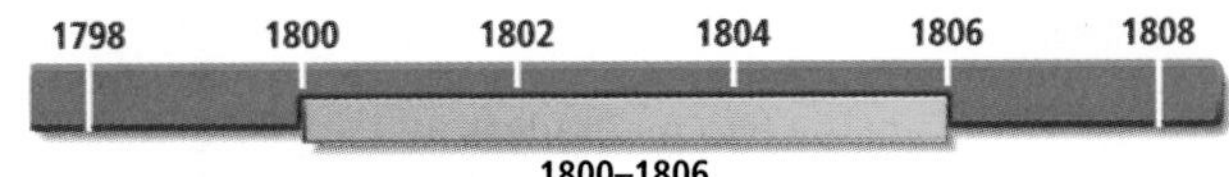

VOCABULARY

manufacturer
corps
interpreter
source

Vocabulary Strategy

interpreter

Interpreter includes the word **interpret**. To interpret is to explain. An interpreter explains a language to people who do not speak it.

READING SKILL

Problem and Solution
Chart problems Jefferson faced as President, and how he solved them.

PROBLEM	SOLUTION

Build on What You Know Think of a place that you've never visited. What would you ask someone who had been there? In the early 1800s, President Jefferson sent explorers to parts of the North American continent that he had never seen.

President Jefferson

Main Idea President Thomas Jefferson made the government smaller and the country bigger.

In 1800, **Thomas Jefferson** was elected the nation's third President. He was a member of a different political party than **John Adams,** who had been President before him. When Jefferson took office, the Federalist party gave up its power to the Democratic-Republican party. This change from one party to another was peaceful and democratic. It showed that the plan in the Constitution for electing leaders worked.

Jefferson and the Democratic-Republican party 1
believed states should be stronger than the national government. Jefferson also wanted to help farmers. Federalists disagreed. They wanted a strong national government and laws that would help merchants and manufacturers. A **manufacturer** is someone who uses machines to make goods.

Thomas Jefferson The third President made the national government smaller by lowering taxes and decreasing the size of the army.

Skill and Strategy

Reading Skill and Strategy

Reading Skill: Problem and Solution

This skill helps you see what problem some people faced and how they resolved it.

Read "Exploring the West." Then fill in the problem chart below. How did Sacagawea help Lewis and Clark on their journey?

Problem	Solution
Lewis and Clark could not communicate with the American Indians of the West.	1. Sacagawea was an interpreter and helped trade with the American Indians.

Reading Strategy: Monitor and Clarify

2. Read "President Jefferson." Then check the statement that best clarifies the section.

✓ Thomas Jefferson believed that the government should be smaller.

___ John Adams and the Federalist Party agreed with Jefferson about states' rights.

___ Jefferson sent delegates to France to buy Texas.

3. Read "Exploring the West." Then complete the statement below. Jefferson wanted Lewis and Clark to do three things: learn about the western American Indians, find a water route to the Pacific Ocean, and gather information about the land, plants, and animals of the West.

Unit Resources 98 Use with *United States History*, pp. 354–357

Unit Resources, p. 98

Background

Sacagawea

- Sacagawea brought her infant son with her on the expedition west. This helped show people they met that the expedition was peaceful.
- Sacagawea may have been a member of the Agaiduka, a Shoshone group whose name means Salmon Eater.

The Louisiana Purchase

A Growing Nation Napoleon sold the Louisiana Territory to the United States in 1803 for $15 million, or less than four cents an acre.

SKILL **Reading Maps** Name the countries that claimed land on the North American continent after the Louisiana Purchase.

United States, Spain, Britain

Louisiana Purchase

The year Jefferson was elected, a large area of land west of the Mississippi River came under French control. This land, known as Louisiana, had been claimed by the French but was given to Spain in 1763, after the French and Indian War. In 1800, France took control of it again.

The biggest port in Louisiana was the city of New Orleans. American farmers worried that the French would close this port to them.

Jefferson sent representatives to France in 1803. They wanted French ruler **Napoleon Bonaparte** to agree that U.S. farmers could trade through New Orleans.

To the surprise of the Americans, the French offered to sell all of Louisiana because they needed money for a war against Great Britain. Jefferson was eager to add this huge area of land to the United States, so he bought it. The Louisiana Purchase doubled the size of
2 the country, adding about 828,000 square miles, or 530 million acres.

Lewis and Clark

Jefferson had always been interested in science and nature. He was curious about the people, land, plants, and animals in this new territory and beyond. He sent an expedition to explore it.

Jefferson chose **Meriwether Lewis** to lead the expedition. Lewis invited his friend **William Clark** to help. Jefferson
asked Lewis and Clark to do three things. 3
First, they were to gather information about the landforms, plants, animals, and climates of the West. Second, he asked them to study the cultures of the western Indians. Finally, he wanted them to explore the Missouri and Columbia rivers. He hoped they would find a water route to the Pacific Ocean.

Lewis and Clark set out from St. Louis in May 1804. More than 30 people, almost all of them soldiers, joined Lewis and Clark on their dangerous journey.

REVIEW Why did Jefferson send representatives to France?

He wanted Napoleon to agree that U.S. farmers could trade through New Orleans.

355

2 Teach

President Jefferson

Talk About It

1 **Q History** In what ways did Jefferson's views differ from those of the first two Presidents?

A He thought state governments should be stronger than the national government. He wanted to help farmers more than business owners and manufacturers.

2 **Q Economics** Why was the Louisiana Purchase a good business deal for the United States?

A The United States doubled its size. It also now had control of the port of New Orleans.

3 **Q History** What did Jefferson ask Lewis and Clark to do?

A gather information about the plants, animals, and climate of the West; study the cultures of the western Indians; look for a water route to the Pacific Ocean

Vocabulary Strategy

manufacturer Tell students that the words *manufacturer* and *factory* both refer to making things. Point out the *-er* ending to *manufacturer,* and ask students for the related verb (*manufacture*).

Reading Strategy: Monitor/Clarify After students read the first page of the lesson, ask them if anything they read did not make sense to them. Help them look back in the text and find answers.

Leveled Practice

Extra Support

Have students **draw a cartoon** showing Jefferson holding a sign that says "Up with ..." or "Down with...". On the sign, students should write three things that Jefferson was for or against. Visual-spatial; verbal-linguistic

Challenge

Ask students to **draw an alternate map** of the United States as it might have looked if Napoleon had refused to sell Louisiana to the Americans. Visual-spatial

ELL

Intermediate/Advanced

Have students name three steps in the Louisiana Purchase land deal and write them in a **sequence chain.** Students can then explain their chain to a partner.

Visual-spatial; verbal-linguistic

Exploring the West

Talk About It

4 **Q History** Why was Sacagawea an important member of the Corps of Discovery?

A She helped the Corps by collecting plants for food and medicine, by talking with the American Indians they met to show they were peaceful, and by helping trade for horses and supplies.

5 **Q Geography** What rivers did Zebulon Pike explore?

A the Mississippi River; the Arkansas River; the Red River

Vocabulary Strategy

corps Explain that the word *corps* comes from the Latin word for *body*. In this case, a corps is a body of people acting together.

interpreter Tell students that the suffix *-er* in *interpreter* means *one who.* Explain that an interpreter is one who interprets.

source Explain that *source* is a word with many meanings, most of them related to the start or beginning of something. In this case, a source is the beginning of a river.

Critical Thinking

Draw Conclusions Why might some people say that the Louisiana Purchase was the most important land deal in U.S. history?

More About It

This nickel is one of a series of nickels issued by the United States Mint to commemorate the bicentennial of the Louisiana Purchase and the Lewis and Clark expedition.

Exploring the West

Main Idea In the early 1800s, explorers traveled into new territory.

The people who traveled with Lewis and Clark called themselves the Corps of Discovery. A **corps** is a team of people who work together. The group included Americans and French-Canadians. An enslaved African American man named **York** and a Shoshone woman named **Sacagawea** (sah KAH guh WEE uh) also made the journey.

4 Sacagawea collected plants for food and medicine. She was an **interpreter,** or someone who helps speakers of different languages understand each other. Sacagawea could talk with some of the American Indians the Corps met and show that it was a peaceful group.

Perhaps most important, Sacagawea helped Lewis and Clark trade for the horses and supplies they needed to cross the western mountains. Without these horses, the expedition probably would have failed.

The Corps of Discovery traveled up the Missouri River, over the Rocky Mountains, and down the Columbia River to the Pacific Ocean. After traveling about 8,000 miles, the expedition returned to St. Louis in September 1806.

Lewis and Clark completed the tasks Jefferson had given them. They kept detailed journals about the land they saw and the people they met. Even though a direct water route to the Pacific Ocean did not exist, the Corps of Discovery proved it was possible to cross the continent through passes in the Rocky Mountains.

Corps of Discovery Lewis and Clark lead the expedition on its return to St. Louis. Sacagawea, carrying her child, and York follow behind. The United States Mint honored the 200th anniversary of the Lewis and Clark expedition with a new nickel (right).

356 • Chapter 10

Language Arts

Journal Entry

Have students write a journal entry about the first time they encountered a specific animal, plant, or landscape. What was it like or unlike? Ask students to describe what they saw, heard, smelled, and touched.

Verbal-linguistic

Art

Drawing Discoveries

Lewis and Clark kept journals in which they drew the things they saw. Have students draw and label three things that Lewis and Clark might have seen and drawn on their trip westward.

Visual-spatial

Zebulon Pike

While Lewis and Clark traveled, another expedition set off into the West. In 1805, **Zebulon Pike** led 20 men up the Mississippi River to look for its source. A
5 **source** is the place where a river begins. Pike and his men explored from St. Louis to northern Minnesota. They never found the Mississippi's source, but Pike learned a lot about this land.

One year later, Pike explored the Arkansas and Red rivers. These rivers run through the southern part of what was the Louisiana Territory. On that journey, Pike tried to climb a high mountain. He failed, but this peak became known as Pikes Peak, now a famous landmark in Colorado. The journeys of Pike, Lewis, and Clark led the way for pioneers and traders to explore the West.

REVIEW What tasks did Lewis and Clark complete on their expedition?
brought back information about the West; crossed the continent

Lesson Summary

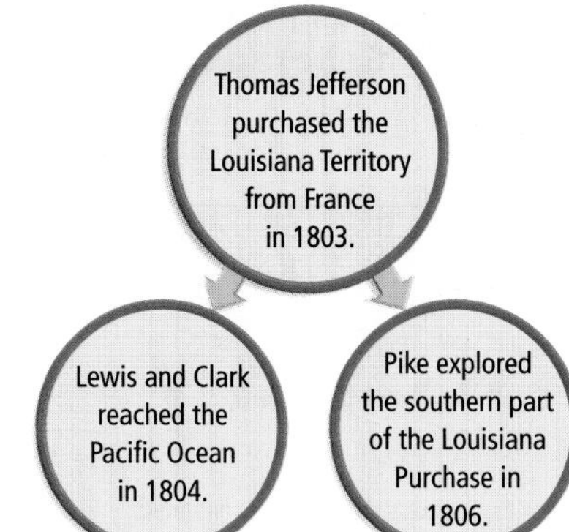

Why It Matters ...

President Thomas Jefferson doubled the size of the United States and sent explorers to learn about the western part of the continent.

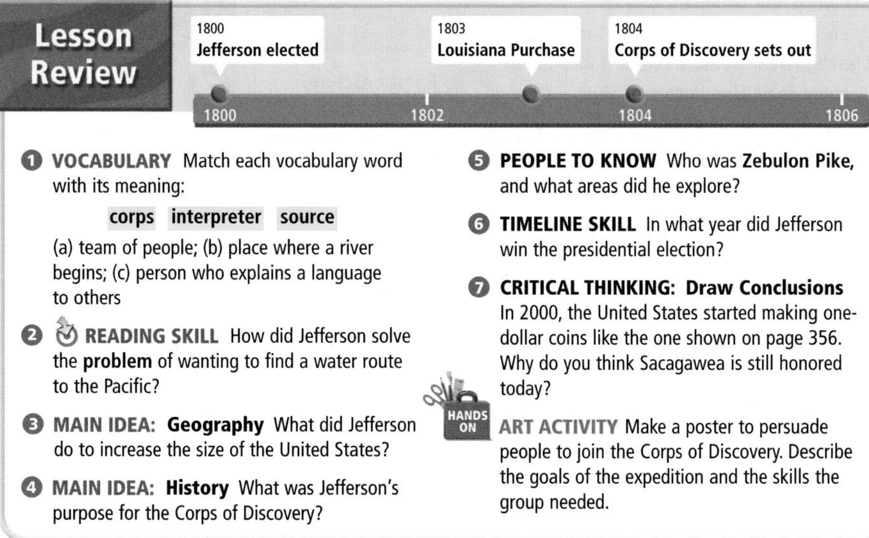

Lesson Review

1. **VOCABULARY** Match each vocabulary word with its meaning:
   corps **interpreter** **source**
   (a) team of people; (b) place where a river begins; (c) person who explains a language to others
2. **READING SKILL** How did Jefferson solve the **problem** of wanting to find a water route to the Pacific?
3. **MAIN IDEA: Geography** What did Jefferson do to increase the size of the United States?
4. **MAIN IDEA: History** What was Jefferson's purpose for the Corps of Discovery?
5. **PEOPLE TO KNOW** Who was **Zebulon Pike,** and what areas did he explore?
6. **TIMELINE SKILL** In what year did Jefferson win the presidential election?
7. **CRITICAL THINKING: Draw Conclusions** In 2000, the United States started making one-dollar coins like the one shown on page 356. Why do you think Sacagawea is still honored today?

HANDS ON **ART ACTIVITY** Make a poster to persuade people to join the Corps of Discovery. Describe the goals of the expedition and the skills the group needed.

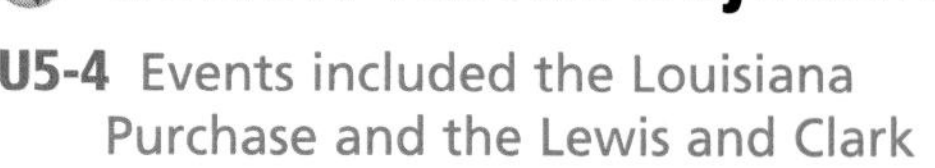

3 Review/Assess

Review Tested Objectives

U5-4 Events included the Louisiana Purchase and the Lewis and Clark expedition.

U5-5 Jefferson bought the Louisiana Territory from France; he sent Lewis and Clark to explore it.

Lesson Review Answers

1. (a) corps; (b) source; (c) interpreter
2. He sent Lewis and Clark to look for one.
3. He purchased the Louisiana Territory.
4. to explore the new territory in the West
5. He was an explorer who led an expedition up the Mississippi River to look for its source; he explored the Arkansas and Red rivers.
6. 1800
7. Sacagawea helped guide one of the most important explorations in our nation's history; she also helps represent the people who lived in the Americas for thousands of years before the Europeans arrived.

HANDS ON Performance Task Rubric

4	The purpose of the poster is clear; the goals and skills are accurate; the writing is persuasive; grammar, usage, and mechanics are correct.
3	The purpose of the poster is generally clear; the goals and skills are mainly accurate; the writing is adequately persuasive; grammar, usage, and mechanics are generally correct.
2	The purpose of the poster is somewhat clear; some goals and skills are accurate; the writing is persuasive in places; some errors in grammar, usage, and mechanics.
1	The purpose of the poster is not clear; the goals and skills are not stated or are not accurate; the writing is not persuasive; many errors in grammar, usage, and mechanics.

Study Guide/Homework

Vocabulary and Study Guide

Vocabulary

1. Draw a line connecting the vocabulary word to its meaning.

corps	A person who helps people understand each other
manufacturer	The place where a river begins
source	A team of people working together
interpreter	A person who uses machines to make goods

Study Guide

Read "President Jefferson." Then answer the questions.

2. To what political party did President Jefferson belong? What did his party believe? Democratic-Republican; States should have more power than the national government.
3. What country owned the Louisiana Territory? Why did it want to sell it? France; Napoleon needed money for a war.

Read "Exploring the West." Then answer the questions.

4. Who led the expedition into the Louisiana Territory? Meriwether Lewis and William Clark
5. Did the Corps of Discovery find a water route to the Pacific Ocean? What did it prove? No; It proved that it was possible to cross the continent over the Rocky Mountains.

Unit Resources 99 Use with United States History, pp. 354–357

Unit Resources, p. 99

Reteach Minilesson

Use a cause-effect chart to reteach the lesson.

Cause
Jefferson purchases the Louisiana Territory from France.

Effect
Lewis and Clark explore the West, opening the way for pioneers and traders.

www.eduplace.com/ss/hmss05/

Quick Look

Connect to Core Lesson In Lesson 2, students were introduced to the work of the Corps of Discovery. In Extend Lesson 2, they can learn more about where the Corps traveled, what they experienced, and what they accomplished.

1 Teach the Extend Lesson

Connect to the Big Ideas

Settlement and Exploration/Expansion of the Nation The explorations of the Corps of Discovery helped open the West to settlers and aided the expansion of the nation.

Geography

Journey of Discovery

They had paddled unmapped rivers and scrambled over mountain passes for more than a year. Finally, the explorers in the Corps of Discovery caught sight of the Pacific Ocean. President Jefferson had asked Lewis and Clark to find a route across the continent to the Pacific. Along the way, they filled their journals with drawings of plants and animals. They described the time that Lewis's dog, Seaman, scared away an attacking bear and the time that Sacagawea saved precious tools and papers from the waters of the Missouri after a boat tipped over.

Lewis and Clark covered thousands of miles. How did the Corps of Discovery travel over this rugged land? Look at the map to find out. Their journey begins on the right side of the map.

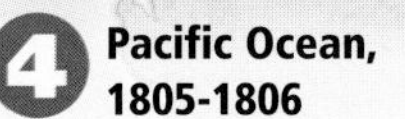

4 Pacific Ocean, 1805-1806
The Corps traveled down the Columbia River and reached the Pacific Ocean in early November 1805. They spent a rainy winter there. In his journal, Clark described his joy at seeing the "immense ocean."

3 Bitterroot Range, 1805
At Camp Fortunate, Sacagawea helped Lewis and Clark trade for horses with the Shoshone. The explorers needed these horses to cross the steep Bitterroot Range of the Rocky Mountains.

Reaching All Learners

Extra Support

Make a List

- Have students make a list of some of the actions and accomplishments of this journey, such as "filled journals" and "paddled boats."
- Ask students to use their lists to tell generally what Lewis and Clark and the Corps of Discovery did on their journey.

Verbal-linguistic

On Level

Make a Timeline

- Have students make a timeline of the Lewis and Clark Expedition by using details in this lesson as well as details on pages 355–356.
- Display the timelines and invite students to discuss what they show.

Visual-spatial

Challenge

Perform a Mock Interview

- Have pairs of students suppose that they can interview Sacagawea.
- Ask them to develop questions and answers for her based on their reading.
- Have them perform a mock interview. Interviews should focus on the role Sacagawea played with the Corps of Discovery.

Bodily-kinesthetic

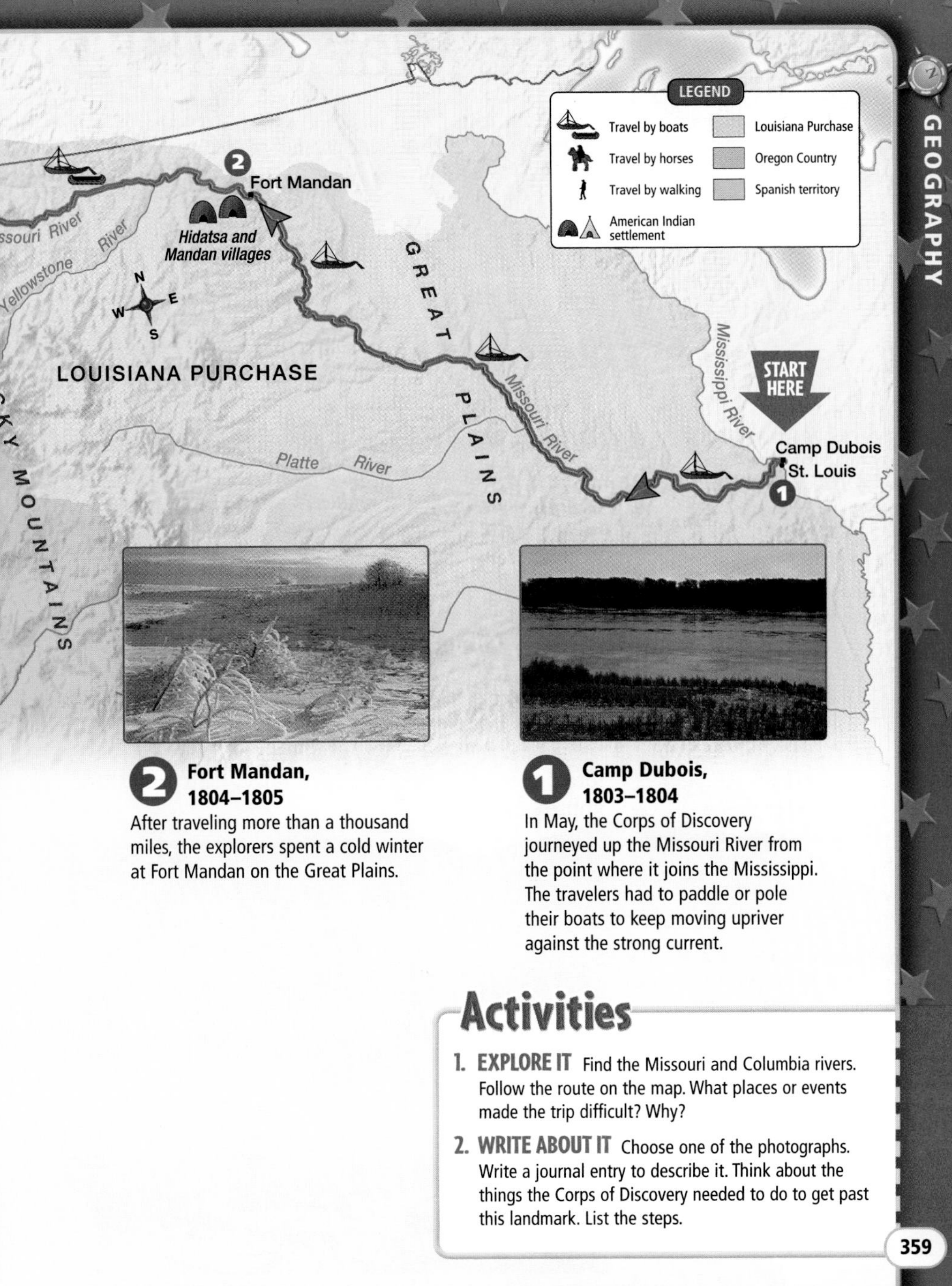

2 Fort Mandan, 1804–1805
After traveling more than a thousand miles, the explorers spent a cold winter at Fort Mandan on the Great Plains.

1 Camp Dubois, 1803–1804
In May, the Corps of Discovery journeyed up the Missouri River from the point where it joins the Mississippi. The travelers had to paddle or pole their boats to keep moving upriver against the strong current.

Activities

1. **EXPLORE IT** Find the Missouri and Columbia rivers. Follow the route on the map. What places or events made the trip difficult? Why?
2. **WRITE ABOUT IT** Choose one of the photographs. Write a journal entry to describe it. Think about the things the Corps of Discovery needed to do to get past this landmark. List the steps.

359

2 Leveled Activities

1 Explore It *For Extra Support*
Answers will vary but might mention crossing the Rocky Mountains, boats tipping over, and encounters with bears.

2 Write About It *For Challenge*

Writing Rubric

4	The description focuses on a geographic landmark; details are interesting and accurate; spelling, usage, and mechanics are correct.
3	The description focuses on a geographic landmark; details are generally accurate; there are a few errors in spelling, usage, and mechanics.
2	The description generally focuses on a geographic landmark; some details are accurate; there are some errors in spelling, usage, and mechanics.
1	The description does not focus on a geographic landmark; details are inaccurate; there are many errors in spelling, usage, and mechanics.

ELL

Beginning

Invite students to **illustrate** the following events:

- glimpsing the Pacific Ocean
- drawing plants and animals in journals
- Lewis's dog scaring away a bear
- Sacagawea saving tools and papers from the river

Have students label their drawings. They might also create an overview heading or statement that identifies the illustrations as a group.

Verbal-linguistic

Physical Education

Paddling Against the Current

- Have small groups of students discuss the job of paddling a boat against a current. What kinds of physical skills do they think this required? Was it more a matter of strength, coordination, or endurance?

Bodily-kinesthetic; verbal-linguistic

Graphic Organizer

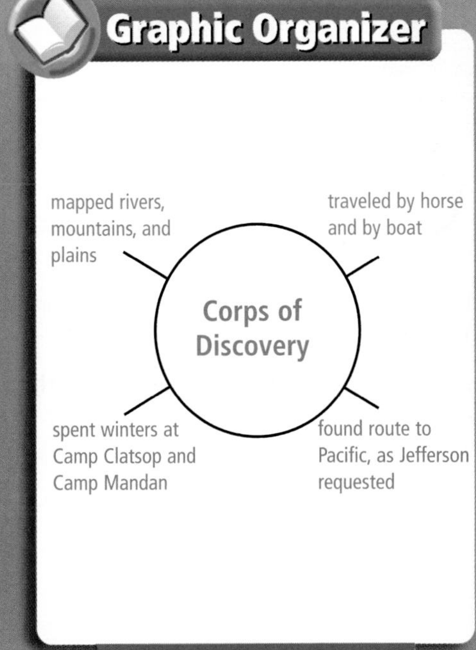

Graphic Organizer 7

Tested Objectives

U5-6 History Describe the causes and events of the War of 1812.

U5-7 History Analyze the rise of nationalism in the United States after the War of 1812.

Quick Look

This lesson gives an overview of the War of 1812 and events that followed it, including the Era of Good Feelings and the Monroe Doctrine.

Teaching Option Extend Lesson 3 explains the story of "The Star-Spangled Banner."

1 Get Set to Read

Preview Have students use the lesson title to predict that they will be reading about a war. Ask them to look for its causes.

Reading Skill: Cause and Effect Students may include impressment of American sailors as a cause.

Build on What You Know Tell students that the title of the national anthem is "The Star-Spangled Banner," and that they will read about it in this lesson. Ask them what *star-spangled banner* means. What do the stars on the flag represent?

Vocabulary

prosperity *noun,* a condition of success; a feeling of having a great deal more than what is necessary to survive

nationalism *noun,* strong loyalty to one's own nation

foreign policy *noun,* decisions and principles that guide a government's actions toward other countries

Core Lesson 3

The War of 1812

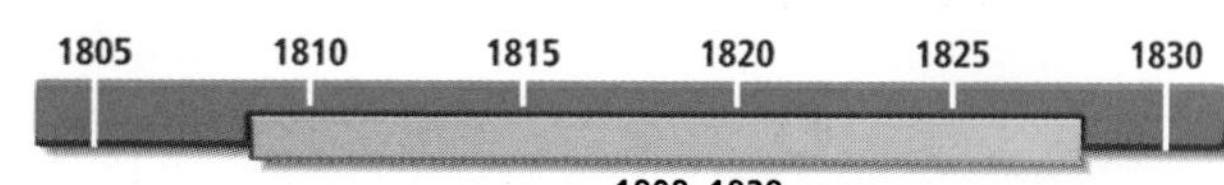

VOCABULARY

prosperity
nationalism
foreign policy

Vocabulary Strategy

nationalism

Look for the word **nation** in **nationalism.** Nationalism means devotion to one's nation, or country.

READING SKILL

Cause and Effect As you read, take notes to show the causes and effects of the War of 1812.

CAUSES	EFFECTS

Build on What You Know What do you feel when you hear the national anthem of the United States? In this lesson, you'll find out when and why this song was written.

Trouble with Britain

Main Idea Conflicts with Britain increased in the early 1800s.

When **James Madison** was elected President in 1808, Britain and France were at war. **Thomas Jefferson** had tried to keep the United States neutral during this war. President Madison also wanted the United States to stay
neutral. He hoped that Americans could keep trading 1
with both Britain and France. But conflicts between the United States and Britain made them enemies.

At this time, Britain had a powerful navy. Yet British sailors often worked on American ships because the Americans paid them more money. British officers raided American ships at sea to look for these British sailors.
Sometimes they captured American sailors instead and 2
forced them to serve in the British navy. This was called impressment.

Impressment About 5,000 American sailors were forced to serve on British ships between 1803 and 1810.

Skill and Strategy

Reading Skill and Strategy

Reading Skill: Cause and Effect

This skill helps you see how one event can be related to another, either by causing it or resulting from it.

Read "A New Sense of Pride." Then fill in the chart below. What caused the Americans to feel a sense of nationalism?

	Cause	Effect
1.	The War of 1812 and the Era of Good Feeling created a deep loyalty to the United States.	Americans expressed their nationalism with more interest in the national flag.

Reading Strategy: Monitor and Clarify

2. Read "Trouble with Britain." Then write about how you monitored your understanding.

Sample answer: I reread information I did not understand the first time.

Write any questions you had after you finished reading.

Sample answer: Why did the British impress American sailors?

How did you answer your questions? Answer with a complete sentence.

Sample answer: I reread the section and found that the British thought they were British sailors working on American ships.

3. Read "Fighting the War." Then explain how the war ended.

Sample answer: Neither side was winning the war, so Britain and the United States agreed that things should go back to how they were before the fighting.

Unit Resources

100
Use with *United States History*, pp. 360–365

Unit Resources, p. 100

Background

American Writers

- Washington Irving's story "The Legend of Sleepy Hollow," about Ichabod Crane and the Headless Horseman, is still popular today.
- James Fenimore Cooper's book "The Last of the Mohicans" was published in 1826. It is set in the 1750s during the French and Indian War.

War Hawks

In 1810, a group in Congress began calling for war against Britain. The group named themselves War Hawks because hawks are seen as aggressive birds. The War Hawks were angry about impressment and even angrier about fighting between American Indians and settlers on the frontier. They believed that people in the British colony of Canada were supplying weapons to American Indians.

The United States government had made treaties that promised it would keep settlers off lands where different groups of American Indians lived. These promises were broken again and again.

Tecumseh (tih CUHM suh), a Shawnee chief, took action. He wanted to unite all the American Indian nations west of the Appalachian Mountains.

Tecumseh and his brother, known as the Prophet, believed that if Indian nations acted together, they could keep settlers away. By 1811, American Indians of many nations had joined Tecumseh.

Tecumseh and nearly 1,000 followers lived near the Tippecanoe River in Indiana Territory. The governor of this territory, **William Henry Harrison**, thought Tecumseh and his followers were a threat. Harrison's army and Tecumseh's followers fought at Tippecanoe. After the Battle of Tippecanoe, Tecumseh went to Canada to join his British allies. 3

REVIEW Why did Tecumseh want American Indian nations to unite? He believed that by acting together, they could keep settlers away.

Battle of Tippecanoe Tecumseh (right) brought American Indians to Tippecanoe. This painting shows the Battle of Tippecanoe.

2 Teach

Trouble with Britain

Talk About It

1 **Q History** Why did President Madison want the United States to stay neutral?

A He wanted Americans to be able to trade with both the British and the French.

2 **Q History** What did Britain do at sea that helped lead to the war?

A British officers raided American ships. They forced some American sailors to work on their ships.

3 **Q History** What happened at the Battle of Tippecanoe?

A William Henry Harrison's army and Tecumseh's followers fought at the Tippecanoe settlement.

Reading Strategy: Monitor/Clarify Have students read the first page, stopping at the end of each paragraph. Ask them to tell what the paragraph was about. If they do not understand something, review the paragraph; if the question is not answered, show them how to read on to find the answer.

Leveled Practice

Extra Support

Have students make **who-what-when-where-why organizers** that help explain why the U.S. went to war. One organizer can be called *Impressment.* The other can be called *Fighting on the Frontier.* Verbal-linguistic

Challenge

Have students **role-play a conversation** between President Madison and the War Hawks. Students should discuss the pros and cons of going to war. Verbal-linguistic; bodily-kinesthetic

ELL

Beginning

Have students **illustrate** one of the events that led to the war, such as British impressments. Pair students with proficient speakers who can help them identify events and describe their drawings.

Visual-spatial

Fighting the War

Talk About It

4 **Q Visual Learning** What power do these boats probably use to move?

A wind power

5 **Q Visual Learning** Why might these boats be vulnerable to cannon fire?

A They are in an exposed position out on the water.

Critical Thinking

Analyze What roles did American Indians play in the War of 1812? You may wish to model for students the process of thinking through the question.

Think Aloud *When I reread the text that mentions American Indians, I can see that some, such as Tecumseh, played important roles in the war. I can also see that some Indian nations were allies with the British, while others were allies of the Americans. They were fighters on both sides of the war.*

Saranac River

Plattsburgh

Cumberland Bay

Battle of Lake Champlain

September 11, 1814

The Battle of Lake Champlain was an important victory for the United States in the War of 1812. It forced British commanders to return to Canada and give up their plans to invade New York.

1. Early in the morning, British ships sail into Cumberland Bay to attack U.S. ships.
2. At the same time, soldiers fight near the village of Plattsburgh. British and U.S. troops fire cannons at each other across the Saranac River.

Art

Make a Collage Timeline

What are the images of the War of 1812? Have students find pictures using library sources or the Internet, print them out, and use them to form a collage timeline that shows some of the people, places, and events of the war.

Visual-spatial; logical-mathematical

Music

The Song Few Can Sing

Have students sing the national anthem. Afterwards, ask students why some singers might find the song hard to sing. Ask students to name other patriotic songs that are easier to sing. Have students explain which one they would choose, if the anthem was replaced.

Musical-auditory

Fighting the War

Main Idea In 1812, the United States went to war against Britain.

On June 18, 1812, Congress declared war against Britain. The United States hoped to stop impressment of soldiers and keep the British from helping American Indians who fought with settlers. The United States also wanted to drive the British out of Canada.

Most of the early battles of the war took place near Canada. The U.S. Army tried to invade Canada several times in

6 1812, but it was badly beaten. The British and their American Indian allies captured Detroit, an important city near the Canadian border.

As the war continued, the United States Army began to win more battles. Captain **Oliver Hazard Perry** forced British ships on Lake Erie to surrender. The Americans recaptured Detroit and chased the British into Canada. There they won a battle on the Thames (tehmz) River. Later, Americans won another important victory at the Battle of Lake Champlain.

Tecumseh was killed in the Battle of the Thames, but many American Indian nations continued his fight. In the South, however, several groups of American Indians fought on the side of the Americans against the British and their allies. In battles in Georgia, the Cherokee, Choctaw, Chickasaw, and some Creek Indians all helped the United States during the War of 1812.

Dolley Madison This First Lady, the wife of President Madison, saved George Washington's portrait.

British Invasions

In August 1814, the British attacked Washington, D.C. As the British Army headed toward the White House, First Lady **Dolley Madison** quickly collected important papers to be taken to safety. She didn't have time to pack most of her family's belongings, but she refused to leave one important item behind—a famous painting of **George Washington** that hung in the White House. After she fled, British forces burned the

White House and other buildings in Washington, D.C. 7

Next, the British moved on to Baltimore. British ships fired cannons at Fort McHenry in Baltimore Harbor, but the U.S. Army did not surrender.

Francis Scott Key, a lawyer, watched the battle. The sight of the American flag flying over the fort in the early morning inspired him to write a poem. This poem was later set to music and became "The Star-Spangled Banner," the country's national anthem.

REVIEW What inspired Francis Scott Key to write the poem that became "The Star-Spangled Banner"?

seeing the American flag flying over Fort McHenry

363

Fighting the War *continued*

Talk About It

6 **History** What happened when the United States Army fought near Canada early in the war?

A The U. S. Army was badly beaten each time it tried to invade Canada.

7 **Q History** What happened to the White House during the invasion of Washington?

A The British burned it.

Reading Strategy: Monitor/Clarify As students read, suggest they pause after each paragraph and reflect on what they have read. After that, they should consider if anything is unclear.

Extra Support

Conduct an Interview

Have students prepare an interview with one of the people in the lesson. Questions should be about what the person thought, felt, and experienced. Have pairs of students give responses that the person might have given.

Verbal-linguistic; bodily-kinesthetic

Challenge

Anthem Lyrics

Have students write lyrics for an anthem about Oliver Hazard Perry, Dolley Madison, Francis Scott Key, or another person mentioned in this lesson.

Verbal-linguistic; musical-auditory

Fighting the War *continued*

Talk About It

8 **Q History** When and where was the Treaty of Ghent signed?

A 1814 in Ghent, Belgium

A New Sense of Pride

Talk About It

9 **Q History** What was the Monroe Doctrine?

A It was an official foreign policy statement issued by President James Monroe. It said that the United States might act to keep other countries out of North and South America.

Vocabulary Strategy

prosperity Tell students that an antonym for *prosperity* is *poverty.*

nationalism Explain that the suffix *-ism* usually suggests a way of thinking or a philosophy. Tell students that *nationalism* is a philosophy in which one's own nation is deeply important and worth fighting for.

foreign policy Point out that *foreign policy* is a compound word. It means a nation's *policy* toward what is *foreign,* or outside its borders.

Critical Thinking

Analyze In what ways has the American flag symbolized our nation over the years?

The End of the War

After two years of fighting, neither Britain nor the United States was winning the war. They agreed to end it.

8 A peace treaty was signed in 1814 in Ghent, Belgium. The Treaty of Ghent did not give either side any new land. The agreement simply returned things to the way they were before the war started. Canada still belonged to Britain.

News of peace took a long time to reach the United States from Europe. Two weeks after the treaty was signed, a large British force attacked New Orleans. **Andrew Jackson** led an army that forced the British to retreat. Although the war was over, Jackson's brave defense of New Orleans made him a national hero.

Changes to the U.S. Flag

1777 Flag This was the first official U.S. flag. The 13 stars and stripes stood for each of the original 13 states.

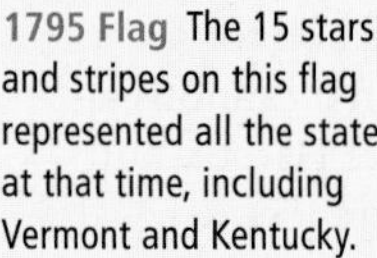

1795 Flag The 15 stars and stripes on this flag represented all the states at that time, including Vermont and Kentucky.

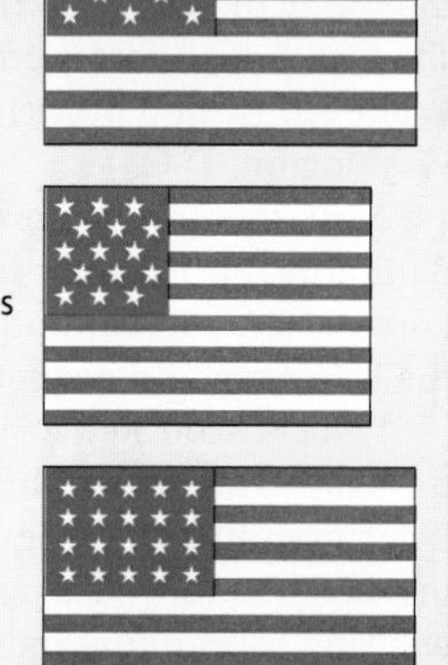

1818 Flag The Flag Act of 1818 gave the flag 13 stripes and 20 stars, one for each of the 20 states.

1960 Flag This is the current American flag. It has 13 stripes and 50 stars.

A New Sense of Pride

Main Idea After the War of 1812, people were proud of their country.

The time after the War of 1812 was one of peace and prosperity. **Prosperity** is economic success and security. This period was called the Era of Good Feelings. During these ten years, people had a new sense of **nationalism,** which is a devotion to one's country.

Pride in the United States created more interest in the national flag. In 1818, Congress passed a law about how many stripes and stars would be on the flag. After this law passed, flags had 13 stripes representing the 13 original colonies. The law also said that as each new state joined the nation, a star would be added. Today, the flag has 50 stars.

The Monroe Doctrine

After the War of 1812, the United States wanted to keep European countries out of the Western Hemisphere. President **James Monroe**, who was elected in 1816, worried that European countries would invade the Americas. He was especially worried that Spain might try to take over former colonies in the Americas.

In a speech to Congress in 1823, Monroe warned European countries to stay out of North and South America. He said that in return, the United States would not get involved in fights between European countries. This was a new foreign policy. **Foreign policy** is a government's actions toward other nations. This policy became known as the Monroe Doctrine. A doctrine 9
is an official statement of policy. The Monroe Doctrine warned other countries that the United States might act to protect the Western Hemisphere.

364 • Chapter 10

Language Arts

Monroe Doctrine Speech

Have students prepare a brief part of the speech they think Monroe might have given to Congress to present the Monroe Doctrine. Encourage students to rehearse and give their speeches to a small group.

Verbal-linguistic; bodily-kinesthetic

Math

- The Treaty of Ghent was signed in December 1814, and the Monroe Doctrine was passed in December 1823.
- Have students calculate how many years and months separated these events. 9 years = 108 months
- Encourage students to calculate how many months they have been in school since first grade and how many months it will be until their 20th birthday.

Logical-mathematical

New American Authors

Another sign of growing pride was a new interest in writers from the United States. In 1828, **Noah Webster** published the first dictionary of English that was uniquely American. Until then, people used dictionaries with British English spellings and meanings. Webster's dictionary showed how people in the United States spoke and included words found only in American English. Many words came from American Indian languages.

Two authors, **Washington Irving** and **James Fenimore Cooper,** set their stories in the United States instead of in Europe. Irving wrote "The Legend of Sleepy Hollow," "Rip Van Winkle," and other stories. Cooper wrote many novels. One of the most famous was *The Last of the Mohicans.*

REVIEW How did the law passed in 1818 change the appearance of the national flag?
The law said that all American flags would have 13 stripes and one star per state.

Noah Webster
After about 22 years of research, Webster published this dictionary. It had 70,000 words.

Lesson Summary

- Congress declared war against Britain in June, 1812.
- After the War of 1812, Americans developed a sense of nationalism.
- In the Monroe Doctrine, Monroe warned that the United States might act to protect the Western Hemisphere.

Why It Matters ...

The United States showed it could stand up to Britain and act as a major power after the War of 1812.

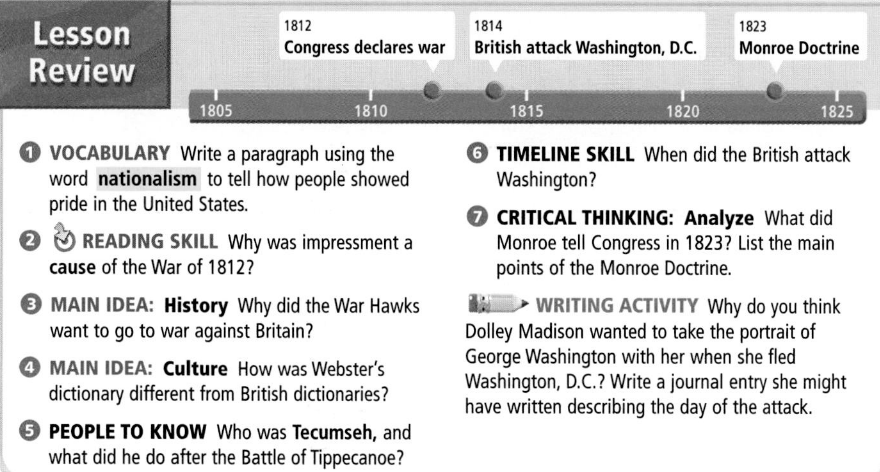

1. **VOCABULARY** Write a paragraph using the word **nationalism** to tell how people showed pride in the United States.
2. **READING SKILL** Why was impressment a **cause** of the War of 1812?
3. **MAIN IDEA: History** Why did the War Hawks want to go to war against Britain?
4. **MAIN IDEA: Culture** How was Webster's dictionary different from British dictionaries?
5. **PEOPLE TO KNOW** Who was **Tecumseh,** and what did he do after the Battle of Tippecanoe?
6. **TIMELINE SKILL** When did the British attack Washington?
7. **CRITICAL THINKING: Analyze** What did Monroe tell Congress in 1823? List the main points of the Monroe Doctrine.

WRITING ACTIVITY Why do you think Dolley Madison wanted to take the portrait of George Washington with her when she fled Washington, D.C.? Write a journal entry she might have written describing the day of the attack.

Study Guide/Homework

Vocabulary and Study Guide

Vocabulary

Write the word for each definition below.

1. nationalism A deep loyalty to one's country
2. prosperity Having enough food, clothing, and shelter to be comfortable
3. foreign policy A government's actions towards other nations
4. Use two of the words in a sentence.
Sample answer: After the War of 1812, peace and prosperity created a sense of nationalism in the United States.

Study Guide

Read "The War of 1812." Then fill in the classification chart below.

Question	Dolley Madison	Francis Scott Key	James Monroe	Noah Webster
Who am I?	5. First lady	7. Lawyer who saw a battle	9. U.S. President	11. Writer
What did I do?	6. Saved a painting of George Washington	8. Wrote the words to "The Star-Spangled Banner"	10. Created foreign policy to protect the Western Hemisphere	12. Published the first dictionary of American English

Unit Resources 101 Use with *United States History*, pp. 360–365

Unit Resources, p. 101

Reteach Minilesson

Use this web to reteach the Era of Good Feelings.

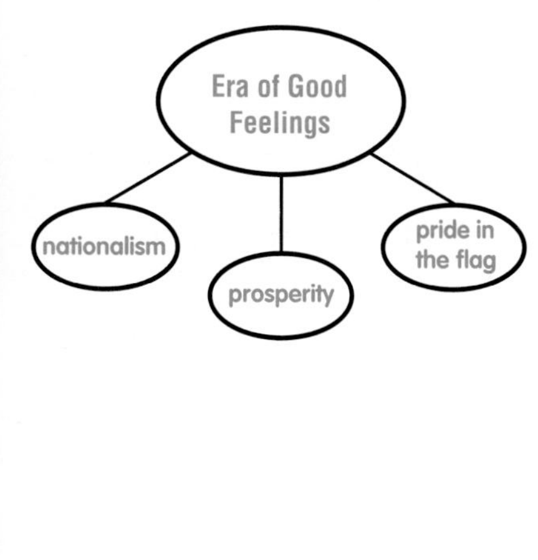

www.eduplace.com/ss/hmss05/

3 Review/Assess

Review Tested Objectives

U5-6 Causes included impressment and frontier fighting; events included the British invasion of Washington, D.C.

U5-7 Nationalism rose because of newfound prosperity following the American victory in the War of 1812.

Lesson Review Answers

1. Paragraphs might explain that Americans showed their nationalism by displaying the national flag.
2. British officers sometimes captured American sailors and forced them to serve in the British navy. This led to increased anger at Britain among Americans.
3. War Hawks were angry about British impressments and fighting between Native Americans and settlers on the frontier.
4. Webster's dictionary showed how Americans spoke and included words found only in American English, including words that came from American Indian languages.
5. Tecumseh was a Shawnee chief. After the battle, he went to Canada to join the British.
6. 1814
7. America was to keep out of Europe's affairs; European countries were to stay out of North and South America.

Writing Rubric

4	The entry uses the first person and a fitting voice; feelings are stated and supported by accurate details; mechanics are correct.
3	The entry generally uses the first person and a fitting voice; feelings are stated and partly supported by details; few errors in mechanics are present.
2	The entry attempts to use the first person and a fitting voice; a few feelings are stated and somewhat supported by details; some errors in mechanics are present.
1	The entry is not in the first person or in a fitting voice; feelings are unstated or illogical; there are many errors in mechanics.

Quick Look

Connect to Core Lesson In Lesson 3, students learned about the British attack on Baltimore and the American victory that inspired Francis Scott Key to write his poem. In this Extend Lesson, students are invited to take a closer look at the words of our national anthem and the circumstances that inspired its creation.

1 Teach the Extend Lesson

Connect to the Big Idea

Democratic Values The flag, the national anthem, and other symbols of our nation represent the democratic principles on which the country was founded. They are central and enduring expressions of patriotism.

Extend Lesson 3

Literature

The National Anthem

Francis Scott Key watches as cannon fire booms in the night sky over Fort McHenry. He is watching from a ship several miles away as the British attack the fort, which is near Baltimore. Key waits for hours to see how the battle will end.

In the early morning, there is a sudden silence. Key looks through his telescope and sees that the American flag still waves over Fort McHenry. He is filled with relief. The United States has not surrendered, and the British have retreated.

Key writes a few lines on the back of a letter to express his feelings of pride. Later he finishes his poem, which he calls "The Defense of Fort McHenry." The poem is printed on September 20, 1814, and people begin singing the first stanza to the tune of an old British song. Both this new song and the American flag itself become known as "The Star-Spangled Banner." In 1931, Key's poem is made the official national anthem of the United States.

The flag that inspired Francis Scott Key to write his poem was constructed by Mary Young Pickersgill. She made the flag large, to be seen from a distance. It measured 30 feet by 42 feet.

The Star-Spangled Banner

Oh, say can you see, by the dawn's early light,
What so proudly we hailed at the twilight's last gleaming?
Whose broad stripes and bright stars, through the perilous fight,
O'er the ramparts we watched, were so gallantly streaming?
And the rockets' red glare, the bombs bursting in air,
Gave proof through the night that our flag was still there.
O say, does that star-spangled banner yet wave
O'er the land of the free and the home of the brave?

(first stanza of "The Defense of Fort McHenry")
—Francis Scott Key

Reaching All Learners

Extra Support

Paraphrase Lyrics

- Help students with the vocabulary of the anthem by explaining, for example, that a banner is a flag, *gleaming* means "shining," and *perilous* means "dangerous." Explain that something that is spangled is decorated or ornamented.
- Ask students to create a paraphrase of the anthem using the terms you have provided.

Verbal-linguistic

On Level

Make a Sequence Chart

- Have students make a flow chart showing the sequence of events that inspired the writing of the poem, its re-creation as a song, and its designation as our national anthem.
- Ask students to illustrate each step of the chart.

Visual-spatial

Challenge

Create a Poster

- Have students research the British attack on Baltimore and find out more about the circumstances under which the anthem was written.
- Have students create a poster to show what they learn.

Visual-spatial

Francis Scott Key gestures toward the American flag. This picture was painted about a hundred years after Key wrote his poem. What feelings do you think the painter was trying to express?

LITERATURE

Activities

1. **SPEAK ABOUT IT** Retell the first four lines of the anthem in your own words.
2. **WRITE ABOUT IT** Key's first stanza includes three questions. Write a poem in the form of questions. Describe being relieved, proud, or curious about something.

367

2 Leveled Activities

1 Speak About It *For Extra Support*
Sample Answer: In the early light of dawn, can you see the flag we saluted at twilight? Whose broad stripes and bright stars flew over the fort walls all through the dangerous fight?

2 Write About It *For Challenge*

Writing Rubric	
4	The poem is comprised of questions; it thoughtfully and creatively evokes feelings of relief, pride, or curiosity; spelling, usage, and mechanics are correct.
3	The poem contains questions; it evokes feelings of relief, pride, or curiosity; spelling, usage, and mechanics are generally correct.
2	The poem attempts to ask questions and evoke feelings of relief, pride, or curiosity; spelling, usage, and mechanics are somewhat correct.
1	The poem does not ask questions or evoke feelings of relief, pride, or curiosity; spelling, usage, and mechanics are generally incorrect.

ELL

Beginning

Have students use the illustrations on pages 366–367 to point out the following:

- the banner
- broad stripes
- bright stars
- the first stanza of the national anthem
- Francis Scott Key

Verbal-linguistic

Music

Respond to the Anthem

Play the anthem, or lead the class in singing it. Have students respond to the music by naming:

- feelings the sound creates
- feelings the words create
- the emotions some people must have felt when the song was first sung

Musical-auditory

Graphic Organizer

The National Anthem

- Francis Scott Key, author
- inspired by victory at Fort McHenry
- written as a poem, became a song

Graphic Organizer 8

Tested Objectives

U5-8 History Explain Andrew Jackson's popularity with ordinary Americans.

U5-9 History Summarize important policies of President Jackson, including Indian Removal.

Lesson Quick Look

This lesson describes changes that took place during the presidency of Andrew Jackson, including Indian removal.

Teaching Option **Extend Lesson 4** teaches students about the history of the Trail of Tears.

1 Get Set to Read

Preview Have students use the headings to predict what happened during Jackson's presidency.

Reading Skill: Draw Conclusions Students should be sure to have at least two details that lead to a valid conclusion.

Build on What You Know Discuss with students the pros and cons of electing a military hero to be President. What qualities does such a hero bring to office? What experience and knowledge may be lacking?

Vocabulary

suffrage *noun,* the right to vote

campaign *noun,* energetic actions or operations taken to accomplish a purpose

ruling *noun,* a decision made by a court

Core Lesson 4

Age of Jackson

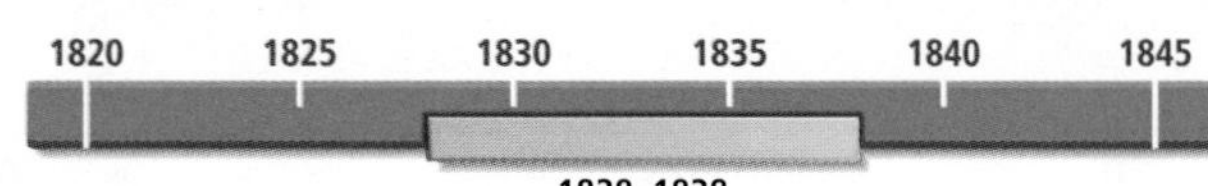

VOCABULARY

suffrage
campaign
ruling

Vocabulary Strategy

suffrage

Suffrage comes from a word that means to show support. In a democracy, people show support by voting.

READING SKILL

Draw Conclusions Note facts and details about Jackson's actions to help you draw a conclusion about him.

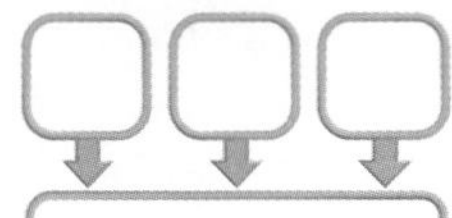

Build on What You Know Do you have a hero, or someone you admire? Many Americans admired **Andrew Jackson** because he was a successful politician who grew up on the frontier.

A New Kind of President

Main Idea Jackson was the first President from the frontier.

The first six people elected President of the United States came from Virginia and Massachusetts. They were all from wealthy families. Andrew Jackson, however, was different.

Jackson grew up on the Carolina frontier. He was poor, but tough and determined. As a young man, Jackson took the Wilderness Trail to Tennessee. In Tennessee, he was a successful lawyer, politician, and business owner. When he became President in 1829, he was the first President to come from a state west of the original thirteen colonies.

After the War of 1812, many people moved to the territories south and west of the original states. When these territories became states, citizens in the new states were guaranteed the right to vote. This right to vote is called **suffrage.**

Jackson's Inauguration When Jackson was sworn into office, people who admired him traveled to Washington for the ceremony.

Skill and Strategy

Reading Skill and Strategy

Reading Skill: Draw Conclusions

Sometimes when you read, you have to figure out things that the writer doesn't tell you. This skill is called drawing conclusions.

Read "Indian Removal Act." Then fill in the chart below. What happened to the Cherokee during the journey?

The Supreme Court ruled that it was illegal to move American Indians from their homes.	President Jackson ignored the Court's ruling.	The army forced the Cherokee Indians to walk 1,000 miles to Indian Territory.

1. Many Cherokee became ill and died during the journey west.

Reading Strategy: Monitor and Clarify

Read "A New Kind of President." Under each heading, answer the question.

2. Heading 1: Voters for Jackson

   Why did many of the people from the new states vote for Jackson in 1828?

   The new voters liked that Jackson had a background similar to their own.

3. Heading 2: Jackson and the Bank

   Why did Jackson order the government to put its money into state banks?

   Jackson wanted banks to loan money to ordinary citizens, something the national bank did not do.

Unit Resources

102
Use with *United States History*, pp. 368–371

Unit Resources, p. 102

Background

Understanding Jackson

- Andrew Jackson was an excellent military leader. One of his most famous victories was at the Battle of New Orleans at the end of the War of 1812.
- In this battle, about 2,000 British soldiers were killed, wounded, captured, or declared missing. By contrast, Jackson only lost about a dozen soldiers.

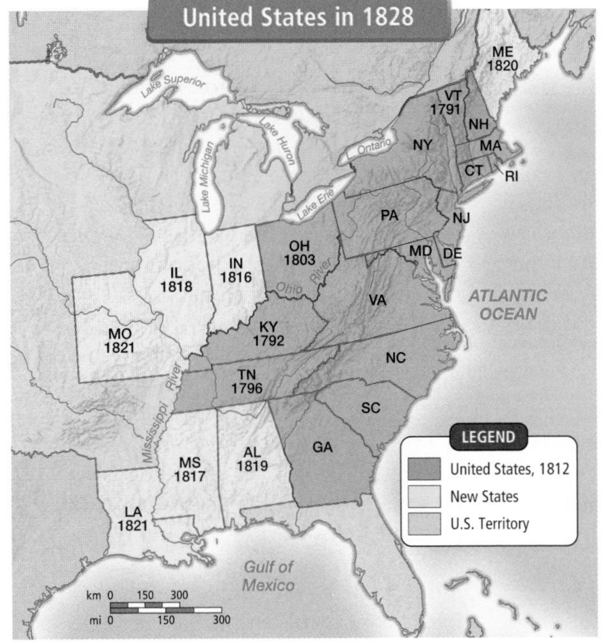

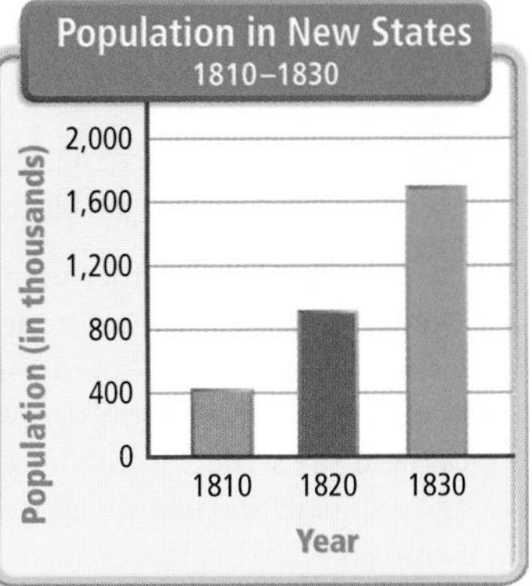

Frontier States Territories became states as more settlers moved west.

SKILL Reading Graphs How many people lived in the new states in 1830?

Jackson's Election

1 Many of these new voters had little money or education. Before this time only white men who owned land or had a certain amount of money could vote. The United States in the 1800s was the only country in the world that gave
2 suffrage to white men who did not own land. Women and most African Americans, however, still could not vote.

In 1828, new voters helped elect Andrew Jackson as President. They liked his campaign message of support for ordinary citizens. A **campaign** is a series of actions taken toward a goal, such as winning a presidential election. Jackson won a huge victory, especially in the new states. People on the frontier were excited to have someone with a background like theirs in the White House.

Jackson and the Bank

President Andrew Jackson took the side of farmers, working people, and frontier settlers. One example of this was his fight against the national bank. The bank had been created while **George Washington** was President. All the government's money was put into the national bank.

Jackson did not like the national bank because poor people could not borrow money from it. He believed that it only helped wealthy people and that it was unfair to those he called "the humble members of society—the farmers, mechanics, and laborers."

In 1833, Jackson ordered the government to take its money out of the national bank and put it in state banks.
Three years later the national bank closed. 3

REVIEW What types of people did Jackson want to help? farmers, working people, frontier settlers

2 Teach

A New Kind of President

Talk About It

1 **Q History** In what ways were voters in the United States different after the War of 1812?

A Many were new voters from the new states and the western frontier. Many also had little money or education.

2 **Q History** Who could not vote during the election of 1828?

A women and most African Americans

3 **Q Economics** What happened to the national bank when Jackson was President?

A The government took its money out of the national bank. Three years later, the bank closed.

Vocabulary Strategy

suffrage Tell students that people who campaigned for women's right to vote were called *suffragists.*

campaign Synonyms for *campaign* include *crusade* and *drive.*

Reading Strategy: Monitor/Clarify As students read, suggest they pause after each paragraph and reflect on what they have read. After that, they should consider whether anything is unclear.

Leveled Practice

Extra Support

Ask students to **role-play a discussion** between two or three Jackson supporters and someone who voted against Jackson. Verbal-linguistic

Challenge

Have students **draw a political cartoon** showing a new voter or Jackson's inauguration. Display completed cartoons in the classroom. Visual-spatial

ELL

Intermediate

- Have students **design a campaign button or poster** for Jackson.
- It should consist of images that tell what Andrew Jackson will do, fight against, or change as President.
- Share completed work as a group.

Visual-spatial

Indian Removal Act

Talk About It

4 **Q History** What was the Indian Removal Act?

A The Indian Removal Act was a law that ordered all Indians east of the Mississippi River to move west of that river.

5 **Q Citizenship** What peaceful methods did John Ross use to fight injustice?

A He went to the Supreme Court to get a decision on Indian removal.

6 **Q History** Who was Chief Osceola?

A Osceola was a Seminole chief who lived in what is now Florida. He fought against Indian removal.

Vocabulary Strategy

ruling Explain that *ruling* has multiple meanings. When the courts *rule,* or have the final say about the laws, their official decisions are called *rulings.*

Critical Thinking

Compare and Contrast How were the new voters of Jackson's day different from the voters before them?

Indian Removal Act

Main Idea Jackson forced American Indian nations to move west of the Mississippi.

Settlers moved farther west every year. They often fought with American Indians. Jackson thought that American Indians slowed down the nation's growth by living on land the settlers wanted. Congress
4 agreed. In 1830, Jackson signed the Indian Removal Act. This law ordered all the Indian nations east of the Mississippi River to move west of that river. Families had to leave their homes and businesses behind.

In the Southeast, the United States Army forced Choctaw, Creek, and Chickasaw people to move to present-day Oklahoma. Congress called this area Indian Territory.

Sequoya's Alphabet Sequoya created 85 symbols, one for each syllable in the Cherokee language. Sequoya's alphabet was used for the *Cherokee Phoenix.* This newspaper, first printed in 1828, is still published today.

The Trail of Tears

In Georgia, the Cherokee had added parts of the settlers' culture to their own traditions. Many became farmers. They built roads, schools, and churches. **Sequoya** (sih KWOY uh) invented a writing system for the Cherokee language. The Cherokee published books and a newspaper using this alphabet.

John Ross, a Cherokee chief, led the
fight against Indian removal. He went to 5
the Supreme Court, the highest court in the country. The head of the Supreme Court, Chief Justice **John Marshall,** made a ruling. A **ruling** is an official decision. He said that it was against the law to force the Cherokee to move.

President Jackson ignored Marshall's ruling. In 1838, the United States Army forced the Cherokee to make the 1,000-mile trip to Indian Territory. The Cherokee had little to eat. The winter was cold and disease spread quickly. About one-fifth of the Cherokee died along the way. This heartbreaking journey came to be known as the Trail of Tears.

Art

Have students work in pairs or small groups to design a memorial to those who perished on the Trail of Tears. Students should write the text of the memorial's inscription, if any, to accompany their designs.

Visual-spatial

Language Arts

Write a News Article

Have students write a brief article that might have been filed by a reporter who witnessed the Trail of Tears. Remind students that their articles should tell who, what, where, when, and why.

Verbal-linguistic

Osceola Fights Back

The United States Army also tried to remove the Seminole from their land in
6 Florida. **Chief Osceola** (AHS ee OH luh) refused to give up his land and convinced many Seminole to join his fight. He and others fought back with surprise attacks. After Chief Osceola was tricked into coming out of hiding to discuss peace, soldiers put him in jail.

Chief Osceola He was a leader in the Seminole Wars in Florida.

Osceola died in prison several months later, but other Seminoles carried on his fight. The struggle of American Indians to keep their homes continued for decades.

REVIEW What did the Cherokee do to fight against removal?
They went to the Supreme Court.

Lesson Summary

By 1828, many small farmers, frontier settlers, and working men had gained suffrage. Their votes helped elect Andrew Jackson. To provide land to frontier settlers, Jackson ordered thousands of American Indians off their land. Their difficult journey west was known as the Trail of Tears.

Why It Matters ...

American Indians were forced to move west, and live in a new environment. Their removal changed the history of people both east and west of the Appalachians.

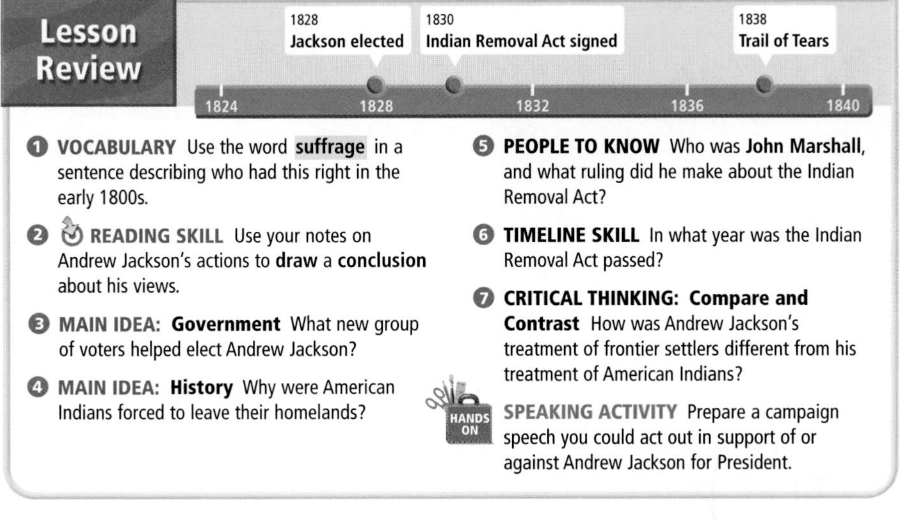

1. **VOCABULARY** Use the word **suffrage** in a sentence describing who had this right in the early 1800s.
2. **READING SKILL** Use your notes on Andrew Jackson's actions to **draw a conclusion** about his views.
3. **MAIN IDEA: Government** What new group of voters helped elect Andrew Jackson?
4. **MAIN IDEA: History** Why were American Indians forced to leave their homelands?
5. **PEOPLE TO KNOW** Who was **John Marshall**, and what ruling did he make about the Indian Removal Act?
6. **TIMELINE SKILL** In what year was the Indian Removal Act passed?
7. **CRITICAL THINKING: Compare and Contrast** How was Andrew Jackson's treatment of frontier settlers different from his treatment of American Indians?

HANDS ON **SPEAKING ACTIVITY** Prepare a campaign speech you could act out in support of or against Andrew Jackson for President.

3 Review/Assess

Review Tested Objectives

U5-8 Americans saw Jackson as an ordinary citizen much like themselves.

U5-9 Policies included removal of money from the national bank to state banks, and the policy of removing Indians from their homelands.

Lesson Review Answers

1. Possible answer: Citizens in new states were granted suffrage and were able to vote in the 1828 election.
2. Sample answer: He believed the national bank was unfair to farmers, mechanics, and laborers.
3. Workers from the new frontier states elected Jackson.
4. Jackson and Congress wanted the frontier settlers to have the American Indians' land.
5. He was Chief Justice of the Supreme Court. He made a ruling that the Cherokee could not be forced to move.
6. 1830
7. Jackson helped settlers by fighting the national bank and hurt American Indians by forcing them off their land.

HANDS ON Performance Task Rubric

4	Speech states position clearly; conveys ideas effectively; facts are accurate.
3	Speech states position well; conveys ideas adequately; most facts cited are accurate.
2	Speech states position in a somewhat disorganized way; conveys ideas adequately; some errors are present.
1	Speech states no position or one that is off topic; conveys ideas in a very general or incomprehensible way; many errors are present.

Study Guide/Homework

Vocabulary and Study Guide

Vocabulary

Write the definition of each vocabulary word below.

1. campaign A series of actions taken toward a goal
2. ruling An official decision
3. suffrage The right to vote
4. Use the word *campaign* in a sentence about Andrew Jackson's election strategy.
   Sample answer: Andrew Jackson's presidential campaign message focused on ordinary citizens.

Study Guide

Read "A New Kind of President." Then fill in the sequence chart below.

New U.S. territories become states. → 5. New citizens are given the right to vote. → 6. Andrew Jackson is elected President. → 7. President Jackson orders the government to take its money out of the national bank.

Read "Indian Removal Act." Then fill in the sequence chart below.

President Jackson signs the Indian Removal Act. → 8. Chief Justice Marshall rules against American Indian removal. → 9. President Jackson ignores the Supreme Court ruling. → 10. The Cherokee are forced to leave their homes in Georgia.

Unit Resources

103
Use with *United States History*, pp. 368–371

Unit Resources, p. 103

Reteach Minilesson

Use this chart to reteach ways in which Jackson was a new kind of President.

A New Kind of President	
1.	first President from West
2.	on side of farmers, working people, settlers
3.	elected by ordinary people

www.eduplace.com/ss/hmss05/

Quick Look

Connect to Core Lesson Students have just read about the Indian Removal Act. In this Extend Lesson, details about the Trail of Tears provide students with a deeper understanding of what Indian removal actually meant.

1 Teach the Extend Lesson

Connect to the Big Idea

Influences on History/Responsibilities of Citizenship Citizens must learn to recognize how laws such as the Indian Removal Act and actions of individuals such as Andrew Jackson have influenced our history and created lasting pain for some cultures.

Pronunciation Help

Tahlequah (TA luh kwaw)

Extend Lesson 4

History

Trail of Tears

The Cherokee had traveled several months when they reached the Mississippi River. Many were sick. Many had died. All were hungry. How their hearts must have ached as they gazed at the ice-clogged waters. No wonder people called the journey "Nunna daul Tsuny," which means "the trail where they cried."

Between 1838 and 1839, about 15,000 Cherokee were forced to leave their homes in the southeastern United States. They traveled more than 800 miles west to what is now the state of Oklahoma, then known as Indian Territory.

The Cherokee were organized into 16 groups. Three groups traveled by steamboat. The rest traveled by foot, horse, and wagon. Their routes are shown on this map.

It took years for the Cherokee to rebuild their lives, but in time, they held elections, built new courthouses and schools, and set up farms. The village of Tahlequah became the new capital of the Cherokee Nation.

3 Arrival

The last group of Cherokee arrived in the newly created Indian Territory in March 1839. They joined Choctaw, Creek, Chickasaw, and Seminole people who had made similar journeys. They waited under the watchful eyes of U.S. soldiers to find out where they would be allowed to settle.

372 • Chapter 10

Reaching All Learners

Extra Support

Create an Organizer

- Guide students in creating a *who, what, when, where, why* organizer that will help them understand the Trail of Tears.
- Emphasize that the Trail of Tears is not one actual trail but an experience of the Cherokee people during one of the most painful episodes of their history.

Verbal-linguistic

On Level

Compare and Contrast

Have students make a compare-and-contrast chart to help them note how the land the Cherokee were forced to settle in differed from the land they had always lived in.

Visual-spatial

Challenge

Write a Letter

- Challenge students to write a letter to the editor that might have been written by a concerned citizen who witnessed any part of the removal of the Cherokee people.
- Encourage students to draw information from these pages to specify a point along the journey and tell what happened there.

Verbal-linguistic

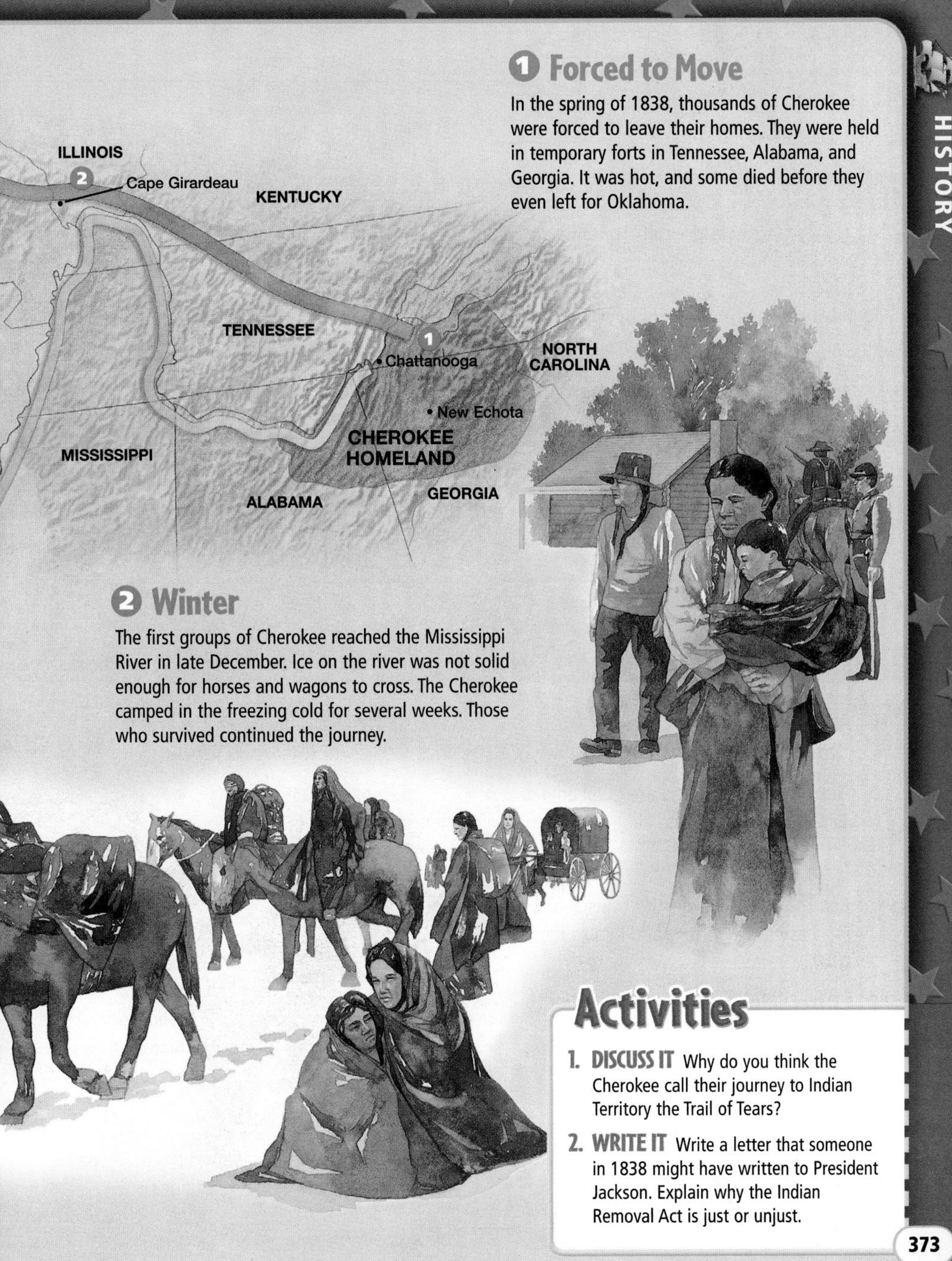

1 Forced to Move

In the spring of 1838, thousands of Cherokee were forced to leave their homes. They were held in temporary forts in Tennessee, Alabama, and Georgia. It was hot, and some died before they even left for Oklahoma.

2 Winter

The first groups of Cherokee reached the Mississippi River in late December. Ice on the river was not solid enough for horses and wagons to cross. The Cherokee camped in the freezing cold for several weeks. Those who survived continued the journey.

Activities

1. **DISCUSS IT** Why do you think the Cherokee call their journey to Indian Territory the Trail of Tears?
2. **WRITE IT** Write a letter that someone in 1838 might have written to President Jackson. Explain why the Indian Removal Act is just or unjust.

373

2 Leveled Activities

1 Discuss It *For Extra Support*

Sample Answer: Many Cherokee might have cried as they were marched away from their homes into an unknown land. They also might have cried because of the terrible conditions of their journey and because so many people died during it.

2 Write It *For Challenge*

Writing Rubric

4	Letter format is used correctly; position and main ideas are supported by accurate details; mechanics are correct.
3	Letter format is used; position and most main ideas are supported by accurate details; most mechanics are generally correct.
2	Letter format is attempted; main ideas and details contain some errors or omissions; some errors in mechanics are present.
1	Letter format is not used; main ideas/details contain many errors or omissions; many errors in mechanics are present.

ELL

Beginning

- Have students **create a word map** with the words "Trail of Tears" in the center. Ask them to write related terms and ideas in secondary circles.
- Invite students to share their work with a partner and explain what it shows.

Verbal-linguistic

Language Arts

Write a Report

- The text in item 3 mentions that the Choctaw, Creek, Chickasaw, and Seminole made similar journeys to Indian Territory.
- Have students do research to find out where each group came from, when the journey took place, and what the conditions of the journey were. Students should present their findings in short reports.

Verbal-linguistic

Graphic Organizer

Trail of Tears

1	Indian Removal Act
2	Cherokee held in forts
3	long, difficult journey westward
4	begin rebuilding lives in Indian Territory

Graphic Organizer 15

Chapter Review

Visual Summary

1. Daniel Boone helped clear this road through the Cumberland Gap. *(Obj. U5-1)*
2. President Jefferson bought this land from France. The land doubled the size of the country. *(Obj. U5-5)*
3. President Madison declared war on Britain to stop impressments and aid to American Indians fighting settlers. *(Obj. U5-6)*
4. In 1838, the U.S. Army forced the Cherokee to walk 1,000 miles to Indian Territory. *(Obj. U5-9)*

Facts and Main Ideas

5. It allowed a passage through the Appalachians. *(Obj. U5-1)*
6. He was a Mingo Indian who lived in Ohio. After settlers killed his family, he fought against them. *(Obj. U5-2)*
7. It doubled the size of the U.S., and gave the country control of New Orleans, an important port city on the Mississippi River. *(Obj. U5-5)*
8. Francis Scott Key wrote it as after watching the battle at Fort McHenry during the War of 1812. *(Obj. U5-7)*
9. American Indians had to give up their land. *(Obj. U5-9)*

Vocabulary

10. **foreign policy** *(Obj. U5-9)*
11. **pioneer** *(Obj. U5-1)*
12. **suffrage** *(Obj. U5-9)*
13. **interpreter** *(Obj. U5-5)*

Visual Summary

1–4. Write a description of each item named below.

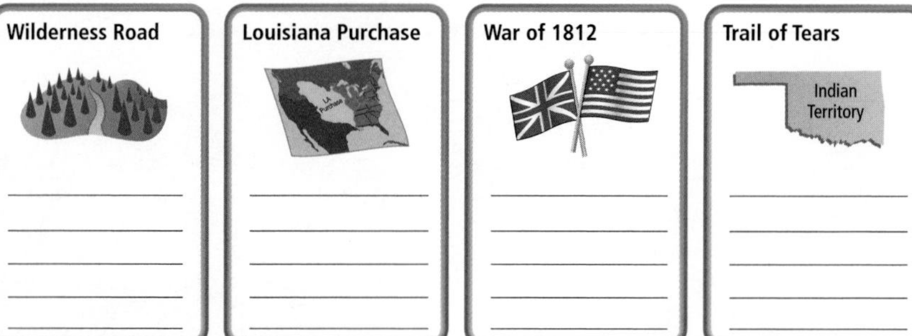

Facts and Main Ideas

TEST PREP Answer each question with information from the chapter.

5. **Geography** Why was the Cumberland Gap a help to pioneers?
6. **History** Who was Chief Logan?
7. **Economics** Why was the Louisiana Purchase an important addition to the United States?
8. **Citizenship** Who wrote "The Star-Spangled Banner" and why?
9. **History** Name one effect of the Indian Removal Act?

Vocabulary

TEST PREP Choose the correct word to complete each sentence.

pioneer, p. 345
interpreter, p. 356
foreign policy, p. 364
suffrage, p. 368

10. The Monroe Doctrine said that the _____ of the United States was to stay out of Europe's problems.
11. Daniel Boone was a _____ who led settlers west of the Appalachians.
12. As new states were added to the United States, the settlers were given _____.
13. Sacagawea was sometimes an _____ on the Lewis and Clark expedition.

Reading/Language Arts Wrap-Up

Reading Strategy: Monitor/Clarify

Review with students the process of monitoring their understanding and clarifying anything they do not understand.

Have students work in pairs, taking turns to model the process as they read.

Partners can help each other clarify important points.

Writing Strategy

As students write, they can apply what they have learned about monitoring and clarifying text.

After writing a draft, students can go back and read their own writing, applying the strategy as they do. By monitoring their reading, students can find points that need clarification.

CHAPTER SUMMARY TIMELINE

1769	1803	1812	1838
Boone crosses Appalachians	Louisiana Purchase	War of 1812	Trail of Tears

1760 1770 1780 1790 1800 1810 1820 1830 1840

Apply Skills

TEST PREP **Study Skill** Read the outline below. Use what you have learned about Andrew Jackson and making an outline to answer each question.

Andrew Jackson
I. Who he was
A. Grew up poor on the Carolina frontier
B. Successful lawyer, politician, and business owner
C.
What he did
A. Fought against the national bank
B. Signed the Indian Removal Act

14. Which supporting detail fits best for "C" under the first main idea?
- **A.** Took the Wilderness Trail to Tennessee
- **B.** Women and most African Americans were not allowed to vote.
- **C.** Hero who fought in the War of 1812
- **D.** Hero who fought in the Revolutionary War

15. What should be placed in front of the second main idea?
- **A.** A.
- **B.** B.
- **C.** I.
- **D.** II.

Critical Thinking

TEST PREP Write a short paragraph to answer each question.

16. Cause and Effect What effect did the movement of pioneers have on American Indians already living on the frontier?

17. Fact and Opinion In your opinion, was the War of 1812 worth fighting? Use facts from the chapter to support your opinion.

Timeline

Use the Chapter Summary Timeline above to answer the question.

18. How many years before the Louisiana Purchase did Daniel Boone cross the Appalachian Mountains?

Activities

Map Activity Make a map showing the route of the Trail of Tears. Label three major landforms or bodies of water on the map.

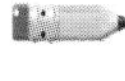
Writing Activity Write a description of what pioneers crossing the Appalachian Mountains might have experienced. Describe the weather, the geography, and any challenges they might have faced.

Technology
Writing Process Tips
Get help with your description at **www.eduplace.com/kids/hmss05/**

Apply Skills

14. C *(Obj. U5-3)*
15. D *(Obj. U5-3)*

Critical Thinking

16. Treaties cheated them out of land; battles resulted in many injuries and deaths; they were forced to leave their homes and relocate. *(Obj. U5-2, U5-9)*

17. Yes, because a time of peace and prosperity came after the war. No, because there was no good reason for the war, many people died in battles, and no land was gained on either side. *(Obj. U5-6, U5-7)*

Timeline

18. 4 years *(Obj. U5-1, U5-5)*

Leveled Activities

HANDS ON Performance Task Rubric

4	Trail is accurate; map and landform details are all present.
3	Trail is generally accurate; most map and landform details are present.
2	Trail contains some errors; few map and landform details are present.
1	Trail is inaccurate; map and landform details are absent.

Writing Rubric

4	Description is well organized and shows considerable creative effort; mechanics are correct; details are accurate.
3	Description is adequately organized and shows creative effort; few errors; details are mostly accurate.
2	Description is somewhat organized and shows some creative effort; some errors; details are somewhat inaccurate.
1	Description is disorganized and shows little effort; many errors in mechanics; details are inaccurate.

Technology

Test Generator

You can generate your own version of the chapter review by using the **Test Generator CD-ROM.**

Web Link

For more ideas, visit **www.eduplace.com/ss/hmss05/**

Standards

National Standards

I a Similarities and differences in addressing human needs and concerns **I d** Ways people deal with their physical environment **III a** Use mental maps **III h** Interaction of human beings and their physical environment **VI c** How government does/does not provide for needs and wants, establish order and security, and manage conflict **VI f** Factors that contribute to cooperation and cause disputes **IX b** Conflict, cooperation, and interdependence **X g** Influence of public opinion **X h** Public policies and citizen behaviors

Chapter 11 Planning Guide

A Growing Country

Chapter Opener

pp. 376–377

30 minutes

Reading/Vocabulary

Chapter Reading Strategy:
Question, p. 375F

Resources

Grade Level Resources
- **Vocabulary Cards,** pp. 43–50

Reaching All Learners
- **Challenge Activities,** p. 89

Primary Sources Plus, p. 19

Big Idea Transparency 5

Interactive Transparency 5

Text & Music Audio CD

Lesson Planner & TR CD-ROM

eBook

eTE

Core Lesson 1

The Industrial Revolution

Pages 378–383

50 minutes

Tested Objectives

U5-10 Explain the effects of new machines on industry and agriculture in the early 1800s.

U5-11 Describe new forms of transportation and explain their impact.

Reading/Vocabulary

Reading Skill: Problem and Solution

textile, interchangeable parts, mass production, productivity, entrepreneur

Cross-Curricular

Science, p. 380 **Drama,** p. 382

Resources

Unit Resources:
- **Reading Skill/Strategy,** p. 104
- **Vocabulary/Study Guide,** p. 105

Reaching All Learners:
- **Lesson Summary,** p. 42
- **Support for Lang. Dev./ELL,** p. 139

Assessment Options:
- **Lesson Test,** p. 106

Extend Lesson 1

Technology

Inside a Cotton Mill

20–30 minutes

Pages 384–385

Focus: A cutaway view of a New England Mill shows how cotton became cloth.

Skillbuilder

Study Skill

Find and Evaluate Sources

Pages 386–387

20 minutes

Tested Objective

U5-12 Conduct research and determine the quality of sources.

Reading/Vocabulary

research

Resources

Unit Resources:
- **Skill Practice,** p. 106

Skill Transparency 11

Core Lesson 2

Immigrants and Reformers

Pages 388–391

40 minutes

Tested Objectives

U5-13 Describe the causes and effects of European immigration during the mid-1800s.

U5-14 Summarize the goals and accomplishments of reform movements of the mid-1800s.

Reading/Vocabulary

Reading Skill: Compare and Contrast

famine, reform, temperance, injustice

Cross-Curricular

Drama, p. 390

Resources

Unit Resources:
- **Reading Skill/Strategy,** p. 107
- **Vocabulary/Study Guide,** p. 108

Reaching All Learners:
- **Lesson Summary,** p. 43
- **Support for Lang. Dev./ELL,** p. 140

Assessment Options:
- **Lesson Test,** p. 107

Extend Lesson 2

Citizenship

The Reform Movements

20–30 minutes

Pages 392–393

Focus: Students meet some of the important reformers who worked for change.

National Standards
II b Vocabulary associated with time, timelines; examples of change; and cause and effect relationships **II d** Sources for reconstructing the past **III h** Interaction of humans and the environment **V e** Tension between an individual's beliefs and government policies and laws **V g** Meet individual needs and promote the common good **VII a** Scarcity and choice in economic decisions **VII f** Influence of incentives, values, traditions, and habits **VIII b** How science and technology affected the environment **IX b** Conflict, cooperation, and interdependence **X e** How citizens can influence public policy **X f** Formal and informal actors that shape public policy **X h** Public policies and citizen behaviors **X j** How the "common good" can be strengthened

Core Lesson 3

Texas and the Mexican War

Pages 394–397

 40 minutes

 **Tested Objectives**

U5-15 List the events that led to Texas's independence and annexation.

U5-16 Explain the causes and effects of the Mexican-American War.

Reading/Vocabulary

Reading Skill: Main Idea and Details

annexation, front, manifest destiny, cession

Cross-Curricular

Music, p. 396

Resources

Unit Resources:
- **Reading Skill/Strategy,** p. 109
- **Vocabulary/Study Guide,** p. 110

Reaching All Learners:
- **Lesson Summary,** p. 44
- **Support for Lang. Dev./ELL,** p. 141

Assessment Options:
- **Lesson Test,** p. 108

www.eduplace.com/ss/hmss05/

Extend Lesson 3

Biographies

At the Alamo

20–30 minutes

Pages 398–399

Focus: Profiles of three people who were at the Alamo.

Core Lesson 4

Moving West

Pages 400–403

 40 minutes

Tested Objectives

U5-17 Identify how and why different groups of people migrated to the West.

U5-18 Describe the events and effects of the California Gold Rush.

Reading/Vocabulary

Reading Skill: Cause and Effect

wagon train, gold rush, forty-niner, boomtown

Cross-Curricular

Math, p. 402

Resources

Unit Resources:
- **Reading Skill/Strategy,** p. 111
- **Vocabulary/Study Guide,** p. 112

Reaching All Learners:
- **Lesson Summary,** p. 45
- **Support for Lang. Dev./ELL,** p. 142

Assessment Options:
- **Lesson Test,** p. 109

Extend Lesson 4

History

Wagons West!

20–30 minutes

Pages 404–405

Focus: Look inside a covered wagon to find out what settlers took with them.

Chapter Review

Pages 406–407

30 minutes

Resources

Assessment Options:
- Chapter 11 Test
- Test Generator

Chapter 11 Practice Options

Lesson 1 Skill and Strategy

TEST PREP

Reading Skill and Strategy

Reading Skill: Problem and Solution

This skill helps you see what problem some people faced and how they resolved it.

Read "The Industrial Revolution." Then fill in the problem and solution chart below. How did transportation become more efficient?

Problem	Solution
Roads were narrow and unusable in bad weather.	1. The federal government built the National Road to connect Ohio with the East.
Boats needed oars, wind, or water currents to move.	2. Robert Fulton invented the steamboat.
Rivers and canals were the fastest way to ship goods.	3. Canals were built to connect the Great Lakes.

Reading Strategy: Question

4. Read "The Industrial Revolution Begins." Then check the question that you might ask while reading this section.
   - ✔ How did Eli Whitney's cotton gin help make yarn production easier?
   - ___ What materials did Eli Whitney use to build the cotton gin?
   - ___ How much yarn can be made from 10 pounds of cotton?
5. Read "Changes in Transportation." Then check the question that you might ask while reading this section.
   - ✔ What made it easier for factories and farms to ship their goods?
   - ___ In what year was the automobile invented?
   - ___ What was the fastest speed railroad locomotives could reach in 1850?

Unit Resources

104
Use with *United States History*, pp. 378–383

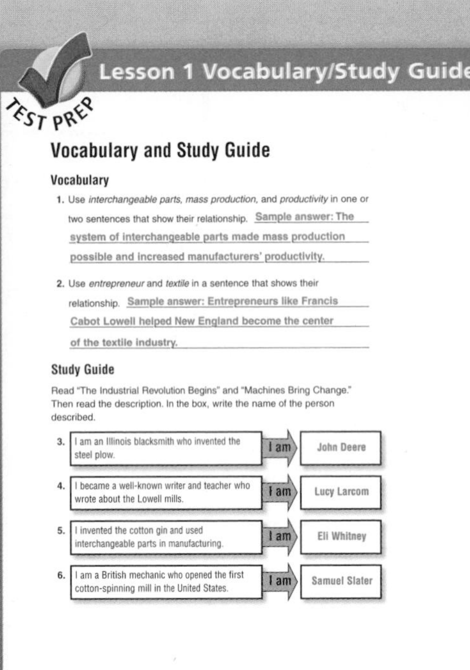

Lesson 1 Vocabulary/Study Guide

TEST PREP

Vocabulary and Study Guide

Vocabulary

1. Use *interchangeable parts, mass production,* and *productivity* in one or two sentences that show their relationship. Sample answer: The system of interchangeable parts made mass production possible and increased manufacturers' productivity.
2. Use *entrepreneur* and *textile* in a sentence that shows their relationship. Sample answer: Entrepreneurs like Francis Cabot Lowell helped New England become the center of the textile industry.

Study Guide

Read "The Industrial Revolution Begins" and "Machines Bring Change." Then read the description. In the box, write the name of the person described.

3. I am an Illinois blacksmith who invented the steel plow. → I am → John Deere
4. I became a well-known writer and teacher who wrote about the Lowell mills. → I am → Lucy Larcom
5. I invented the cotton gin and used interchangeable parts in manufacturing. → I am → Eli Whitney
6. I am a British mechanic who opened the first cotton-spinning mill in the United States. → I am → Samuel Slater

Unit Resources

105
Use with *United States History*, pp. 378–383

also in *Practice Book*, p. 62

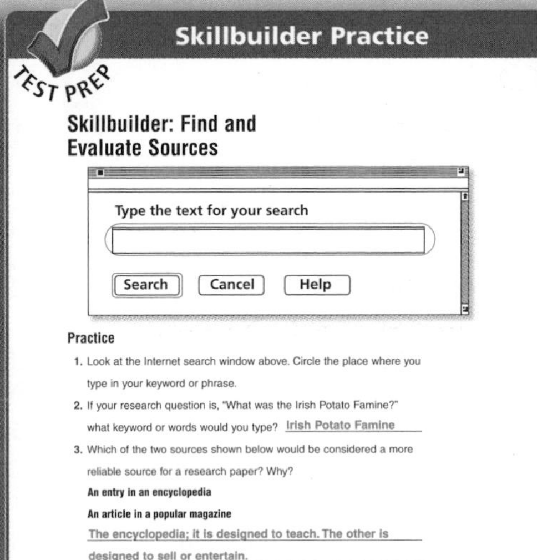

Skillbuilder Practice

TEST PREP

Skillbuilder: Find and Evaluate Sources

Practice

1. Look at the Internet search window above. Circle the place where you type in your keyword or phrase.
2. If your research question is, "What was the Irish Potato Famine?" what keyword or words would you type? Irish Potato Famine
3. Which of the two sources shown below would be considered a more reliable source for a research paper? Why?

   An entry in an encyclopedia

   An article in a popular magazine

   The encyclopedia; it is designed to teach. The other is designed to sell or entertain.

Apply

Start a plan for a research paper about the Irish Potato Famine. Write a question about what you want to research. Then use the Internet and/or the library to find two reliable sources to answer your question. Explain why each resource is a reliable resource.

Unit Resources

106
Use with *United States History*, pp. 386–387

also in *Practice Book*, p. 63

Lesson 2 Skill and Strategy

TEST PREP

Reading Skill and Strategy

Reading Skill: Compare and Contrast

This skill helps you understand how historical events or people are similar and different.

Read "Making a Better Society." Then fill in the Venn diagram below to compare and contrast the rights of men and women.

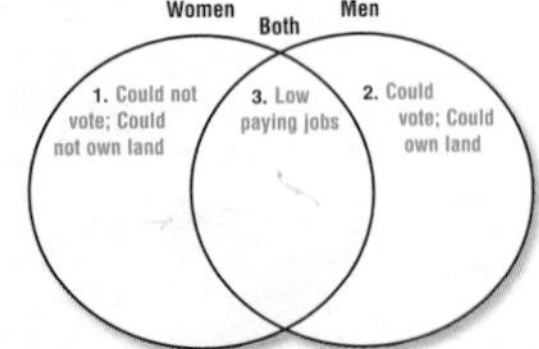

Reading Strategy: Question

4. Read "German and Irish Immigrants." Then check the question that you might ask while reading this section.
   - ___ From which country do most visitors to the United States come?
   - ✔ Why did German and Irish immigrants come to the United States in the mid-1800s?
   - ___ How did people from Germany and Ireland pay for their trips to the United States?
5. Read "Making a Better Society." Read the answer. Then complete the question for the answer.

   Answer: Elizabeth Cady Stanton

   Question: Who was the leader of the Seneca Falls Convention ?

Unit Resources

107
Use with *United States History*, pp. 388–391

Lesson 2 Vocabulary/Study Guide

TEST PREP

Vocabulary and Study Guide

Vocabulary

Across

1. When people work to improve society
2. The movement to control the drinking of alcohol
3. Denying a person's right to speak in a public meeting is an example.

Down

4. Caused many Irish people to leave their country
5. Elizabeth Cady Stanton said, "All _____ and women are created equal."

1 Across: REFORM
2 Across: TEMPERANCE
3 Across: INJUSTICE
4 Down: FAMINE
5 Down: MEN

Study Guide

6. Read "German and Irish Immigrants." Then fill in the blanks below.

   Irish and German people came to the United States for job opportunities and to own land. Thousands of Germans left Europe because of war and crop failure. Many settled in the Midwest. Some bought land, and some found work in cities. Many Irish people immigrated because of the Irish Potato Famine. Most Irish immigrants settled in the Northeast.

7. Read "Making a Better Society." Then fill in the blanks below.

   During the Second Great Awakening, people worked to improve society through reform. Many women who worked in the antislavery movement realized that they also faced injustices as women. Women were not allowed to vote or own property. In 1848, a group of women led by Elizabeth Cady Stanton held a convention to talk about these rights. Stanton and Susan B. Anthony worked to change laws.

Unit Resources

108
Use with *United States History*, pp. 388–391

also in *Practice Book*, p. 64

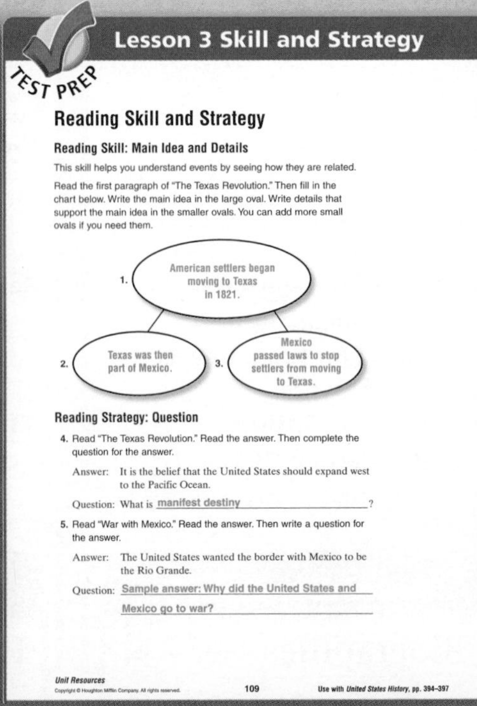

Lesson 3 Skill and Strategy

TEST PREP

Reading Skill and Strategy

Reading Skill: Main Idea and Details

This skill helps you understand events by seeing how they are related.

Read the first paragraph of "The Texas Revolution." Then fill in the chart below. Write the main idea in the large oval. Write details that support the main idea in the smaller ovals. You can add more small ovals if you need them.

Reading Strategy: Question

4. Read "The Texas Revolution." Read the answer. Then complete the question for the answer.

   Answer: It is the belief that the United States should expand west to the Pacific Ocean.

   Question: What is manifest destiny?
5. Read "War with Mexico." Read the answer. Then write a question for the answer.

   Answer: The United States wanted the border with Mexico to be the Rio Grande.

   Question: Sample answer: Why did the United States and Mexico go to war?

Unit Resources

109
Use with *United States History*, pp. 394–397

Lesson 3 Vocabulary/Study Guide

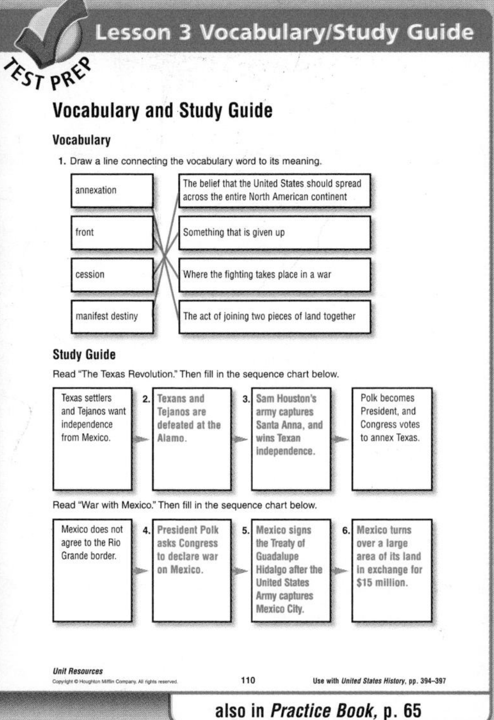

TEST PREP

Vocabulary and Study Guide

Vocabulary

1. Draw a line connecting the vocabulary word to its meaning.

annexation	The belief that the United States should spread across the entire North American continent
front	Something that is given up
cession	Where the fighting takes place in a war
manifest destiny	The act of joining two pieces of land together

Study Guide

Read "The Texas Revolution." Then fill in the sequence chart below.

Texas settlers and Tejanos want independence from Mexico. → 2. Texans and Tejanos are defeated at the Alamo. → 3. Sam Houston's army captures Santa Anna, and wins Texan independence. → Polk becomes President, and Congress votes to annex Texas.

Read "War with Mexico." Then fill in the sequence chart below.

Mexico does not agree to the Rio Grande border. → 4. President Polk asks Congress to declare war on Mexico. → 5. Mexico signs the Treaty of Guadalupe Hidalgo after the United States Army captures Mexico City. → 6. Mexico turns over a large area of its land in exchange for $15 million.

Unit Resources

110

Use with *United States History*, pp. 394–397

also in *Practice Book*, p. 65

Lesson 4 Skill and Strategy

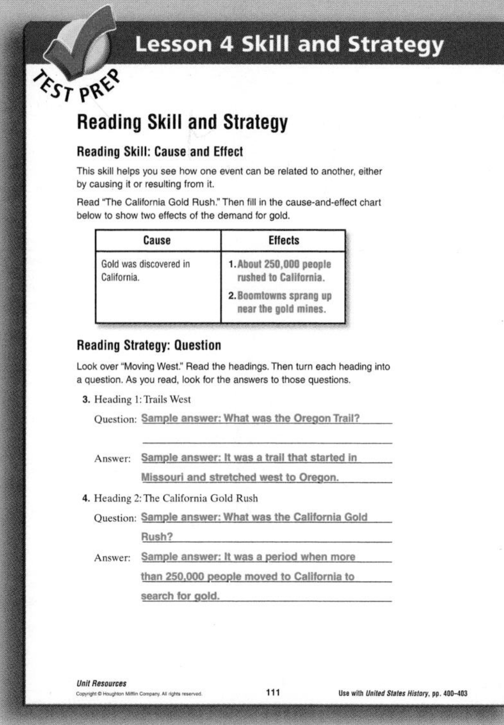

TEST PREP

Reading Skill and Strategy

Reading Skill: Cause and Effect

This skill helps you see how one event can be related to another, either by causing it or resulting from it.

Read "The California Gold Rush." Then fill in the cause-and-effect chart below to show two effects of the demand for gold.

Cause	Effects
Gold was discovered in California.	1. About 250,000 people rushed to California. 2. Boomtowns sprang up near the gold mines.

Reading Strategy: Question

Look over "Moving West." Read the headings. Then turn each heading into a question. As you read, look for the answers to those questions.

3. Heading 1: Trails West

   Question: Sample answer: What was the Oregon Trail?

   Answer: Sample answer: It was a trail that started in Missouri and stretched west to Oregon.

4. Heading 2: The California Gold Rush

   Question: Sample answer: What was the California Gold Rush?

   Answer: Sample answer: It was a period when more than 250,000 people moved to California to search for gold.

Unit Resources

111

Use with *United States History*, pp. 400–403

Lesson 4 Vocabulary/Study Guide

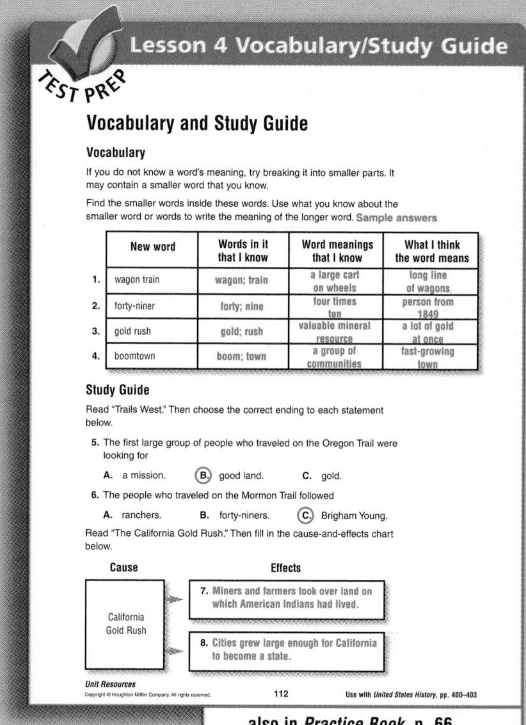

TEST PREP

Vocabulary and Study Guide

Vocabulary

If you do not know a word's meaning, try breaking it into smaller parts. It may contain a smaller word that you know.

Find the smaller words inside these words. Use what you know about the smaller word or words to write the meaning of the longer word. Sample answers

	New word	Words in it that I know	Word meanings that I know	What I think the word means
1.	wagon train	wagon; train	a large cart on wheels	long line of wagons
2.	forty-niner	forty; nine	four times ten	person from 1849
3.	gold rush	gold; rush	valuable mineral resource	a lot of gold at once
4.	boomtown	boom; town	a group of communities	fast-growing town

Study Guide

Read "Trails West." Then choose the correct ending to each statement below.

5. The first large group of people who traveled on the Oregon Trail were looking for

   A. a mission. (**B.**) good land. **C.** gold.

6. The people who traveled on the Mormon Trail followed

   A. ranchers. **B.** forty-niners. (**C.**) Brigham Young.

Read "The California Gold Rush." Then fill in the cause-and-effects chart below.

Cause	Effects
California Gold Rush	7. Miners and farmers took over land on which American Indians had lived.
	8. Cities grew large enough for California to become a state.

Unit Resources

112

Use with *United States History*, pp. 400–403

also in *Practice Book*, p. 66

Chapter 11 Assessment Options

Chapter 11 Test

Chapter 11 Test

Test Your Knowledge

interchangeable parts	famine	Cession	boomtown

Fill in the blank with the correct word from the box.

1. Over a million Irish people died after 1846 due to a shortage of food called a famine. Obj. U5–13
2. Merchants and traders helped the miners in a boomtown get supplies. Obj. U5–18
3. Manufacturers used interchangeable parts to make many new types of tools. Obj. U5–10
4. In the Mexican Cession, Mexico gave up a large area of land. Obj. U5–16

Circle the letter of the best answer.

5. How was the National Road an improvement over older roads? Obj. U5–11
   - A. It connected Lake Erie to the Hudson River.
   - (B.) It was wide and paved for smooth travel.
   - C. It allowed boats to travel against water currents.
   - D. It was narrow and covered in dirt.
6. How did the California Gold Rush change the lives of many Californios? Obj. U5–18
   - F. Californios were given more land.
   - G. Californios were forced to work for the forty-niners.
   - H. Californios lost their American citizenship.
   - (J.) Californio property owners were forced off their land.
7. Which right did some women fight for in the 1800s? Obj. U5–14
   - (A.) the right to vote
   - B. the right to own enslaved people
   - C. the right to marry
   - D. the right to travel
8. With what Mexican law did the Texas settlers disagree? Obj. U5–15
   - (F.) the law that did not allow settlers to own enslaved people
   - G. the law that did not allow settlers to move west
   - H. the law that did not allow settlers to form an army
   - J. the law that did not allow settlers to travel the Oregon Trail

Chapter 11 Test

Apply Your Knowledge

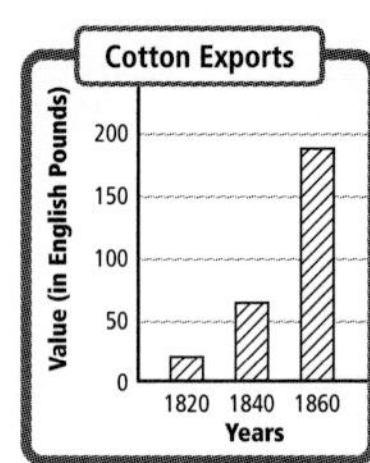

Use the graph to answer the following questions.

9. Which year were cotton exports the largest? Obj. U5–10
   - A. 1800
   - B. 1820
   - C. 1840
   - (D.) 1860
10. Why did U.S. cotton exports increase between 1820 and 1860? Obj. U5–10
    - (F.) The cotton gin helped production.
    - G. No one wanted to sell cotton.
    - H. No more cotton was needed.
    - J. England began to produce cotton.

Apply the Reading Skill: Compare and Contrast

Read the passage below. Then answer the question. Obj. U5–17

> The Whitmans traveled west on the Oregon Trail and settled in present-day Oregon in 1836. They moved west to teach American Indians about Christianity. The Mormons moved west to practice religion freely. They traveled on the Mormon Trail and settled in present-day Utah.

11. How were the Whitmans and the Mormons similar? How were they different?
    Both settled in the West. The Whitmans traveled on the Oregon Trail, settled in Oregon, and taught Christianity. The Mormons traveled on the Mormon Trail, settled in Utah, and moved to practice their religion freely.

Chapter 11 Test

Test the Skill: Find and Evaluate Sources

12. What is the subject of this poster? Cotton mills Obj. U5–12
13. What towns with cotton mills are listed on the poster? Lowell and Chicopee Obj. U5–12
14. Using this source, what research question could you write?
    Sample answers: Where were the cotton mills in Massachusetts? How old were the young women in the mills? How did young women learn about work in the mills? Obj. U5–12

Apply the Skill

15. Using your research question, write the key words you would use to do more research. What sources would you use to do your research?
    Sample answers: Cotton mills; Lowell, Massachusetts; Chicopee, Massachusetts; Massachusetts mills. Students may write that they could use encyclopedias or the Internet. Obj. U5–12

Chapter 11 Test

TEST PREP

Think and Write

16. **Short Response:** Describe the goals of the women's movement of the mid-1800s. Obj. U5–14
    Sample answers: To gain the right to vote, to own property, and to speak in public
17. **Critical Thinking: Infer** Why was the annexation of Texas important to many people in the United States? Obj. U5–15
    Sample answer: Many supporters of annexation believed that it was the nation's destiny to expand west and stretch from the Atlantic to the Pacific Ocean.
18. **Extended Response:** Write a letter that a German or Irish immigrant to the United States might have written to a family member. Include answers to these questions. Why did this person leave home and immigrate to the United States? Where did this person settle? What did this person do for work? How was he or she treated by other Americans? Write your letter on a separate sheet of paper. Obj. U5–13 Letters may include descriptions about working on a farm or in a factory, hoping to buy land, and finding opportunities in the United States. Letters might also tell about how people in cities were upset that immigrants might take jobs away from them.

Self-Assessment

What do I think was an important change of the early and mid-1800s? Why do I think it was important?

You can share the following fiction selection with students before beginning the chapter.

Activate Prior Knowledge

Ask students if they can name any inventions that were used during the Industrial Revolution of the 1800s. Explain that the Read-Aloud selection describes one such device. In this chapter, students will read about the Industrial Revolution and the changes it brought.

Preview the Chapter

Have students skim the section Changes on the Farm on page 381 of their books. Ask them why farmers might have been excited about the inventions described in this section and in the Read Aloud.

Read-Aloud Vocabulary

Explain that an **entrepreneur** is a person who takes a risk in starting a new business. **Productivity** is the amount of work done in a certain amount of time.

Preview the Reading Strategy

Question Explain to students that the reading strategy they will use in this chapter is questioning, or asking about what is happening. You may wish to use the Read Aloud to model this strategy.

Think Aloud *The brothers in the first two paragraphs are staring at a strange contraption in front of the general store. The store's owner, Mr. Zwicker, is talking loudly about it to a crowd. I wonder what the contraption is, and why the brothers are so interested.*

Something New

"What's all the noise?" Papa asked. My brother, Ezra, and I poked our heads over the side of the wagon to stare at the crowd outside Mr. Zwicker's general store.

Papa halted our mules, and Ezra and I jumped out of the wagon almost before it stopped rolling. We wormed our way through the crowd to where Mr. Zwicker stood, talking loudly, in front of a strange contraption. Mr. Zwicker fancied himself an **entrepreneur,** but he really just tried to sell other people's inventions at his store.

Ezra interrupted Mr. Zwicker's speech. "What's that?" he asked. It looked like a plow, but where Papa's plow had a blade of worn wood, this plow had a shiny metal blade. Papa came up behind Ezra and me and looked at the strange plow, too.

"As I was saying, folks," Mr. Zwicker continued with a stern glance at my brother. "With this new plow, you'll be able to break sod like you've never broken sod before. Your **productivity** will soar! Why, farming will never be the same!"

"Ebenezer Zwicker, you've been saying that about every new contraption you've ever shown us," called one of the farmers from the crowd. "Why should we believe you now?"

"Because of me, friend," said another man, who had been standing so quietly that I hadn't even noticed him before. Or, maybe I hadn't noticed him because Mr. Zwicker was so noisy.

"And who are you?" asked the farmer who had spoken.

"I invented this plow," said the man. "And it does what he says. The steel plow is going to make a big difference."

"A steel plow?" my father said, "Well, I've seen everything now!"

Begin the Chapter

Quick Look

Core Lesson 1 explains how the Industrial Revolution changed factories and transportation.

Core Lesson 2 describes German and Irish immigration in the mid-1800s and efforts of reformers.

Core Lesson 3 discusses how Texas became part of the United States.

Core Lesson 4 focuses on American migration to the West.

Vocabulary Preview

Use the vocabulary cards to preview the key vocabulary words before starting the lessons and to prepare students to understand the content of the chapter.

Vocabulary Strategy

Vocabulary strategies for this chapter:

- Structural analysis, p. 378
- Root words, p. 394
- Prefixes and suffixes, p. 388
- Word origins, p. 400

Vocabulary Help

Vocabulary card for textile Ask students to study the picture on this card. Ask them to identify the *textiles* in the picture. Ask what else is shown in the picture. Ask students to describe the relationship between the people, the machines, and the textiles in the picture. (The people are using the machines to make textiles.)

Vocabulary card for reform Ask students to describe what they see in this picture. Invite them to think about the relationship between the woman giving the speech and the definition of *reform*. (Students may guess that the woman is giving a speech that urges people to work for change.)

Chapter 11 A Growing Country

Vocabulary Preview

productivity

New machines increased **productivity.** Workers produced more goods in a shorter time.
page 379

reform

Both women and men worked for **reform.** They gave speeches and held meetings to tell people about ways to improve society.
page 390

Chapter Timeline

- 1825 Erie Canal opens
- 1833 National Road completed
- 1836 Texas wins independence

1825 — 1830 — 1835

376 • Chapter 11

Background

Economics terms

Tell students that as they read this chapter, they will find economics terms:

- *manufacturing, Industrial Revolution, factory,* p. 378
- *export, interchangeable parts, mass production, productivity,* p. 379
- *entrepreneur, industry,* p. 380
- *gold rush, boomtown,* p. 402

Vocabulary

Use the following graphic organizer to discuss the word *productivity* and how it is related to other words.

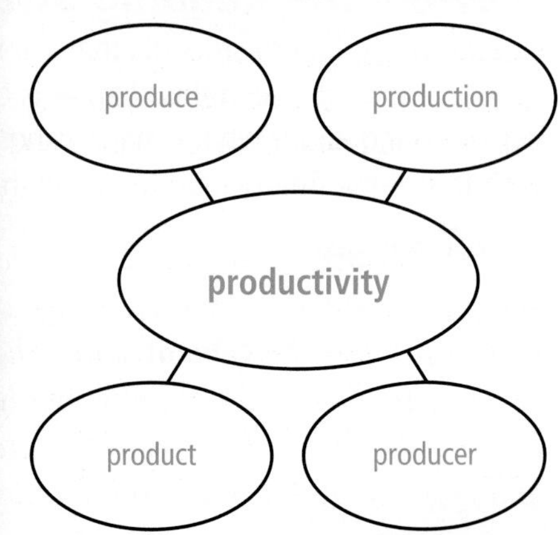

Question Use this strategy as you read the lessons in this chapter.

Stop and ask yourself questions. Do you need to go back and reread?

annexation

People in the independent Republic of Texas voted for **annexation.** Congress also voted to make Texas part of the United States.

page 395

boomtown

During the Gold Rush, people quickly built towns near each new gold mine. These **boomtowns** seemed to spring up overnight.

page 402

1848
Seneca Falls Convention

1840 1845 1850

377

Leveled Practice

Extra Support

Have students find the vocabulary word in the captions under each picture. Pronounce the word aloud, and give students the chance to pronounce it as well. Ask them to restate each definition in their own words. Verbal-linguistic

Challenge

Have students use a dictionary to identify related words and terms for *reform,* for example, *reformer* and *Reformation*. Ask them to make vocabulary cards for three of these words. Verbal/linguistic

ELL

All Proficiency Levels

- Have students work in pairs to create an illustrated report about a factory.
- One student may write the text, and the other draw the pictures.
- Place the illustrated stories in the class reading center for others to enjoy.

Visual-spatial

Using the Timeline

- Direct students to look at the timeline on pages 376 and 377. Point out the segments of the timeline. Ask them how many years this chapter will cover.
- You may wish to use a KWL chart to access students' prior knowledge of the events on the timeline. This is also an excellent opportunity to determine what, if any, misconceptions students may hold about the material.

Reading Strategy: Question

To question, the reader asks questions to himself or herself about the material, in order to better understand it. The reader then attempts to answer these questions as he or she reads on or finishes a section.

Explain to students that to question successfully, they should follow these steps:

- Read the passage.
- Think about what the passage says.
- Ask yourself: Is there anything I don't understand or find confusing?
- Write a question about what you don't understand on a self-stick note. Place the note in the margin near the passage.
- Read on.
- If you find the answer to your question, go back to the note and either orally or in writing answer your question.
- If you can't find the answer to your question by reading on, then reread the passage. Then try answering the question.

Students can practice this reading strategy throughout the chapter, including on their Skill and Strategy pages.

Tested Objectives

U5-10 History Explain how new machines affected industry and agriculture in the early 1800s.

U5-11 History Describe new forms of transportation and explain their effect.

Lesson Quick Look

This lesson provides an overview of the Industrial Revolution.

Teaching Option: Technology Extend Lesson 1 teaches about the technology of a cotton mill.

1 Get Set to Read

Preview Before they read, ask students to look at the headings and tell what kinds of changes, or revolutions, in American life they will be learning about.

Reading Skill: Problem and Solution Students should consider increased productivity and lower costs of goods.

Build on What You Know Discuss with students some of the machines and electronics that make their lives easier.

Vocabulary

textile *noun,* cloth or fabric

interchangeable parts *noun,* identical parts that can replace each other

mass production *noun,* the making of goods in large quantities, using interchangeable parts and an assembly line

productivity *noun,* how fast goods and services are produced by a person, machine, or group

entrepreneur *noun,* a person who starts his or her own business rather than working for someone else

Core Lesson 1

The Industrial Revolution

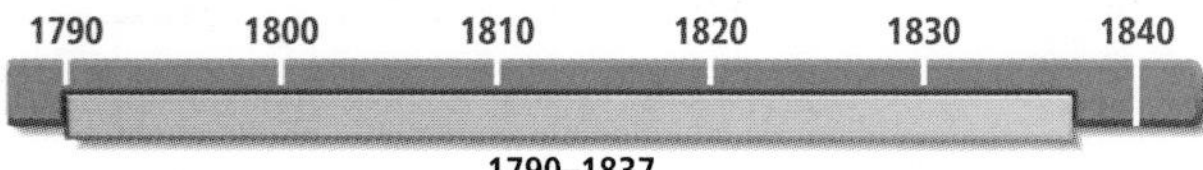

VOCABULARY

textile
interchangeable parts
mass production
productivity
entrepreneur

Vocabulary Strategy

productivity

Look for the word **product** in **productivity.** Productivity is the number of products made in a given time.

READING SKILL
Problem and Solution
Chart the problems that people tried to solve during the Industrial Revolution and the solutions they offered.

PROBLEMS	SOLUTIONS

Build on What You Know Do you have a chore at home, such as taking out the trash? What if a machine took out the trash twice as fast as you do? During the Industrial Revolution, new machines helped people do things faster.

The Industrial Revolution Begins

Main Idea New inventions brought changes to manufacturing.

In the 1700s, most people were farmers. Cloth, tools, and furniture were made by hand in homes or small shops. By the early 1800s, people began making cloth and other goods in factories. New forms of transportation moved people and goods faster than ever before. These changes in manufacturing and transportation are called the Industrial Revolution.

The Industrial Revolution started in Britain. Inventors created machines for the British textile industry. **Textile** means cloth or fabric. These machines spun cotton into yarn much faster than the old hand-powered spinning wheel, or spinning ginny. 1

In 1790, a British mechanic named **Samuel Slater** opened the first cotton-spinning mill in the United States. He built machines like the ones he used in Britain. His mill was set on a river in Rhode Island. Water power drove the machines in the mill.

Cotton Before cotton could be spun, the seeds deep inside the cotton (right) had to be removed.

Skill and Strategy

Reading Skill and Strategy

Reading Skill: Problem and Solution

This skill helps you see what problem some people faced and how they resolved it.

Read "The Industrial Revolution." Then fill in the problem and solution chart below. How did transportation become more efficient?

Problem	Solution
Roads were narrow and unusable in bad weather.	1. The federal government built the National Road to connect Ohio with the East.
Boats needed oars, wind, or water currents to move.	2. Robert Fulton invented the steamboat.
Rivers and canals were the fastest way to ship goods.	3. Canals were built to connect the Great Lakes.

Reading Strategy: Question

4. Read "The Industrial Revolution Begins." Then check the question that you might ask while reading this section.
   - ✓ How did Eli Whitney's cotton gin help make yarn production easier?
   - ___ What materials did Eli Whitney use to build the cotton gin?
   - ___ How much yarn can be made from 10 pounds of cotton?
5. Read "Changes in Transportation." Then check the question that you might ask while reading this section.
   - ✓ What made it easier for factories and farms to ship their goods?
   - ___ In what year was the automobile invented?
   - ___ What was the fastest speed railroad locomotives could reach in 1850?

Unit Resources
 104 Use with *United States History,* pp. 378–383

Unit Resources, p. 104

Background

Industry and the Economy

- During the Industrial Revolution, northern mills used more and more southern cotton.
- As the North industrialized, the South became more agricultural. Cotton growers used more enslaved people to produce greater amounts of cotton.

Eli Whitney

New machines turned cotton into yarn very quickly, but getting cotton ready for the mills took a long time. A lot of work went into cleaning the seeds from cotton so it could be spun. In 1793, **Eli Whitney** invented a cotton engine, or cotton gin. Its wire teeth cleaned cotton very quickly.

Cotton was soon the nation's largest export. Cotton production rose from less than 2 million pounds per year in 1790 to 60 million pounds per year in 1805.

A few years after inventing the cotton gin, Whitney was hired to make 10,000 guns for the U.S. government. At that time, guns were made by hand. A part made for one gun would not fit in another gun. To make guns quickly and at less cost, Whitney used interchangeable parts.
2 **Interchangeable parts** are parts made by a machine to be exactly the same in size and shape. Any part could then fit into any gun of the same design. If one part of a gun broke, a new part could replace it.

Cotton Gin With the help of Whitney's invention (below), cotton production increased during the period from 1790–1830.

SKILL **Reading Graphs** How many pounds of cotton were produced in 1830?

Mass Production

Whitney used a system of mass production to make the guns. Mass is another word for "many." **Mass production** means making many products at once. Instead of one person making a complete gun, each worker put together the same section of many guns. Fitting together the same parts over and over was faster than making a single gun from start to finish.

Manufacturers used interchangeable parts and mass production to make many types of tools and machines. The new ways of making goods increased the productivity of the whole United States. **Productivity** is the amount of goods and services produced by workers in a certain amount of time.

REVIEW What did Whitney do to manufacture guns more quickly and cheaply?
He used interchangeable parts and mass production to make his guns.

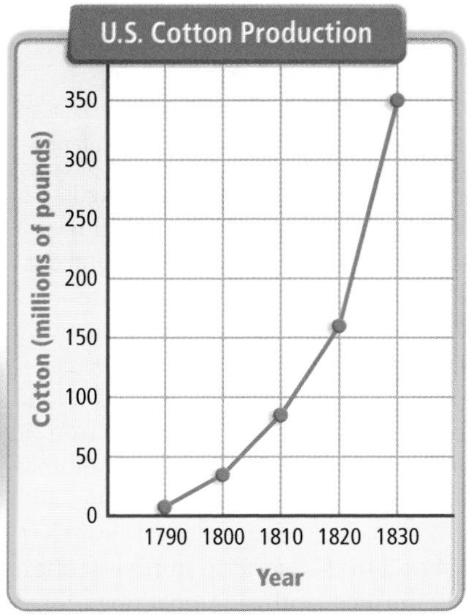

2 Teach

The Industrial Revolution Begins

Talk About It

1 **Q History** In what way did the new textile machines in Britain change the textile industry?

A They spun cotton much faster than the old machines.

2 **Q History** What effect did interchangeable parts have on production?

A They made it possible to produce many more tools and machines.

Vocabulary Strategy

textile Tell students that a synonym for *textile* is *fabric.*

interchangeable parts Explain to students that the prefix *inter-* often means "between." The suffix *-able* means "able to be."

mass production The opposite of *mass production* is making items one by one.

productivity Have students find the word *product* in *productivity.* Explain that productivity is how fast products are made.

Reading Strategy: Question Explain to students that asking questions helps them focus on what they want to find out while reading a lesson. You may wish to model the strategy for students.

Think Aloud *These first two pages talk about the beginning of the Industrial Revolution. It sounds like work could go much faster with these new inventions. I wonder if people liked their lives better before or after this change.*

Leveled Practice

Extra Support

Have partners **draw a diagram** that shows the meaning of interchangeable parts. Suggest that students choose something familiar to diagram; for example, the parts of a skateboard. Visual-spatial

Challenge

Ask students to **write a contract** that one of the entrepreneurs in this lesson might have given to people hired to work in a factory. Verbal-linguistic

ELL

Beginning

Have students **use sound and movement** to contrast an environment in which mass production is taking place with an environment in which goods are being produced one by one.

Musical-auditory; bodily-kinesthetic

Machines Bring Change

Talk About It

3 **Q Visual Learning** What do you notice about the mill in this picture?

A large room; many machines

4 **Q History** What made Lowell's mill different from other mills before it?

A Lowell's mill was the first to turn raw cotton into finished cloth all under one roof. It produced more cloth than other mills before it.

Vocabulary Strategy

entrepreneur Tell students that a synonym for *entrepreneur* is *businessman* or *businesswoman.*

Critical Thinking

Generalize What are some ways that workers' lives changed during the Industrial Revolution? You may wish to model for students the process of thinking through the question. For example:

Think Aloud *I read that during the Industrial Revolution many people stopped working on farms or in workshops and got jobs at the new large mills and factories. On a farm or in a small shop, a worker would probably do many different things during one day. In a factory, a worker would only do one thing over and over all day long. This would be a big change for people to get used to.*

3

Lowell Factories These workers use machines that prepare cotton for spinning. Labels like the one on the right showed that the cloth was made in the Lowell Mills.

CASSIMERES EXTRA HEAVY LOWELL MILLS FOR MEN'S WEAR.

Machines Bring Change

Main Idea The Industrial Revolution changed the way people worked in mills and on farms.

In 1814, an entrepreneur named **Francis Cabot Lowell** built a mill near Boston, Massachusetts. An **entrepreneur** takes risks to start a business. Entrepreneurs can lose money and time by starting and running a business. They take risks because they are excited about an idea and hope to earn money from it.

4 Lowell's idea was to build a mill that had both cotton-spinning machines and power looms to weave cloth. It was the first mill in the world to turn raw cotton into finished cloth, all under one roof.

Lowell's factory was a great success. Within five years, the mill was spinning 30 miles of cloth a day. Other cotton and wool factories soon opened. New England became the center of a growing textile industry.

Many people went to work in these factories. Their lives and workdays changed as they found jobs in the mill towns. Before the Industrial Revolution, Americans did different kinds of work on their own farms or in small workshops. In factories built during the Industrial Revolution, people did the same task, over and over, all day long.

380 • Chapter 11

Science

Make a Water Wheel

Have students create a water wheel, using a paper plate. Help them make six to eight equally spaced cuts going from the edge of the plate to about two inches from the middle. Fold each section away from the plate to make angled blades. Insert a pencil through the middle of the plate to act as an axle; make sure the pencil is not in too tightly or the plate will not turn. Hold the plate under a faucet or a pitcher and gently pour water over the blades. Have students compare the movements of wheels with fewer or more blades, and experiment with how the wheel's movement is affected if you make shorter or longer cuts.

Bodily-kinesthetic

The workers in the first textile mills were girls and young women from the New England countryside. They left home to earn money for themselves and their families. Some were as young as 10 years old.

5 Mill workers lived in boardinghouses. Their workday began at 5:00 A.M. and ended at 7:00 P.M., with only one hour of free time. They still found time to take classes, learn new languages, and write poems, stories, and essays. They published these in a magazine called *The Lowell Offering*.

One mill worker, **Lucy Larcom**, became a well-known writer and teacher. Later in her life, she wrote about what it was like to work in the Lowell mills. She described:

> "The buzzing and hissing and whizzing of pulleys and rollers and spindles and flyers...."

6 The Industrial Revolution changed life for people who stayed on farms, too. In 1831, **Cyrus McCormick** built a horse-drawn reaper. A reaper has sharp blades that cut grain. Harvesting an acre of wheat by hand took about 20 hours. McCormick's reaper did the same job in less than an hour.

In 1837, **John Deere**, a blacksmith from Illinois, invented the steel plow. This plow could cut through tough soil that would break a wooden plow. Deere's invention made it easier for farmers to plow thick soil on prairies and plains.

REVIEW In what ways did the workday change for many people during the Industrial Revolution? They began working in factories where they did the same task all day long.

Cyrus McCormick
He planned, built, and tested his first reaper in just six weeks.

McCormick's Reaper
This advertisement, showing a reaper from 1875, illustrates how the machine helped farmers quickly cut wheat.

SKILL Reading Visuals What does the advertisement say to persuade the reader to buy a McCormick reaper? light, superior, clean, and rapid

381

Machines Bring Change *continued*

Talk About It

5 **Q History** What was life like for young women working at the Lowell mills?

A They worked long days and lived in boardinghouses, away from their families. They also made time to read, write, study, and publish a magazine.

6 **Q Economics** In what ways did McCormick's reaper and John Deere's steel plow change farming?

A The reaper allowed farmers to harvest grain much faster. The steel plow could cut through tough soil, helping farmers on the prairies and plains.

Reading Strategy: Question Model for students the process of formulating questions based on the middle two pages of the lesson.

Extra Support

Explore Meaning

- Create a chart with these headings: What an Entrepreneur Needs to Have, What an Entrepreneur Needs to Do.
- Have small groups work together to come up with as many ideas as possible to write in the chart.
- Have groups share their ideas.

Verbal-linguistic

Challenge

Research

Have students find out about the effect of the steel plow on farming.

- Did farmers have more leisure time, or did farmers farm more land so they could grow more crops and make more money?

Verbal-linguistic

Changes in Transportation

Talk About It

7 Q History Why did the federal government build the National Road?

A to connect Ohio to the East; earlier roads were muddy, unpaved, and difficult to travel.

8 Q History What did Robert Fulton do to improve travel by water?

A He invented the steamboat, which made water travel much faster and easier.

9 Q Economics How did the railroads help American business?

A They let farmers and factories ship their goods all over the country quickly.

Critical Thinking

Generalize Ask students how the life of a businessperson, such as a merchant or a banker, was different before and after the Industrial Revolution.

Transportation Routes In the 1850s, canals helped farmers and manufacturers near the Great Lakes ship their goods to the East Coast.

Changes in Transportation

Main Idea People and goods traveled faster in the 1800s.

In the early 1800s, settlers headed west in search of land. At the same time, factories and farms produced more goods to be shipped to distant cities to be sold.

Overland travel was slow, difficult, and expensive. Early roads were narrow dirt paths barely wide enough for a horse and carriage. Rain turned roads to mud. Snow and ice blocked roads in winter.

In 1811, the federal government began building the National Road to connect Ohio with the East. By 1833, the new road stretched from Cumberland, Maryland, to Columbus, Ohio. It was wide and paved with flat stones. The National Road, which later went as far as Vandalia, Illinois, became the most heavily traveled road in the United States. Towns and businesses, such as blacksmith shops and inns, were built along the roadsides.

Steamboats and Canals

On August 9, 1807, Americans watched a strange-looking boat travel up the Hudson River. **Robert Fulton's** new steam-powered boat was making its first trip from New York City to Albany, New York, in a record 32 hours. The boat's paddlewheel powered it against the flow of water. Until then, boats needed oars, wind, or water currents to move. No one had ever seen a steamboat. Within a few years, however, steamboats were widely used on rivers.

Because roads were so poor at this time, rivers and canals were the fastest and cheapest ways to ship goods. Canals are waterways built for travel and shipping. In 1825, the Erie Canal opened. This canal connected the Hudson River to Lake Erie. More canals were built throughout the East. By 1840, more than 3,000 miles of canals crossed the eastern part of the nation.

Drama

Act Out a Scene

- Ask students to think about people watching Fulton's steamboat for the first time. What do they see? What do they say?
- Have students work in small groups to plan and rehearse a scene about watching the steamboat.
- Have groups perform their scenes for the class.

Bodily-kinesthetic

Language Arts

Write a Letter

- Have students write a letter a young person might have written on the day when the first train came to the new railroad station in his or her town.
- Remind them to include historical details in their letter.
- Have students read their letters aloud to the class or in small groups.

Verbal-linguistic

Railroads

Wagons on new roads, steamboats on rivers, and barges on canals all changed transportation. But the steam locomotive created even greater changes. Trains pulled by steam locomotives were fast. They could go up and down hills effortlessly. A trip from New York City to Albany, New York, took 32 hours by steamboat. It took only 10 hours by train.

By 1850, the nation had 9,000 miles of railroad track. New tracks were added every day. Soon factories and farmers
9 could ship their goods to almost any city or town in the country by train.

REVIEW Why were steam locomotives better than other forms of transportation?
faster; could travel up and down hills easily

Lesson Summary

- The Industrial Revolution came to the United States in the late 1700s.
- New inventions increased productivity and changed the way people worked in factories and on farms.
- New roads, canals, steamboats, and steam locomotives made travel and shipping cheaper and faster.

Why It Matters ...

The Industrial Revolution changed the way people worked and the goods that were produced in the United States.

Fulton's Steamboat

Lesson Review

1793	1814	1825
Whitney invents cotton gin	Lowell builds mill	Erie Canal opened

1790 — 1800 — 1810 — 1820 — 1830

1. **VOCABULARY** Which vocabulary word is a synonym, or has the same meaning, as *cloth*?
   productivity **textile** **entrepreneur**
2. **READING SKILL** Using your chart, write a paragraph about how one **problem** in the early 1800s was solved by new machines.
3. **MAIN IDEA: Economics** How did mass production increase productivity?
4. **MAIN IDEA: History** In what way was Fulton's steamboat different from other boats?
5. **PEOPLE TO KNOW** Who was **Eli Whitney**, and how did his invention increase cotton production?
6. **TIMELINE SKILL** How many years after the invention of the cotton gin did Lowell build his mill?
7. **CRITICAL THINKING: Evaluate** Why is the Industrial Revolution a good name for the period of 1790 to 1840?

HANDS ON **DRAMA ACTIVITY** With a partner, act out a scene between two cotton mill workers discussing mass production.

3 Review/Assess

Review Tested Objectives

U5-10 Machines like the reaper and the cotton gin made harvesting and textile production much faster and easier.

U5-11 Steamboats, canals, and railroads let people travel longer distances more easily.

Lesson Review Answers

1. textile
2. Paragraph should include information from lesson.
3. Mass production allowed many more items to be made faster.
4. It had a paddlewheel that allowed it to move against the current.
5. Eli Whitney invented the cotton gin, which cleaned cotton quickly amd made processing faster.
6. 21 years
7. Answers should discuss the great impact of the new technology on American life.

HANDS ON Performance Task Rubric

4	Scene is well organized and shows considerable creative effort; uses cotton mill setting clearly.
3	Scene is fairly well organized and shows creative effort; uses cotton mill setting.
2	Scene is somewhat organized and shows minimal creative effort; is not clear in cotton mill setting.
1	Scene is not organized and shows no creative effort; does not use cotton mill setting.

Study Guide/Homework

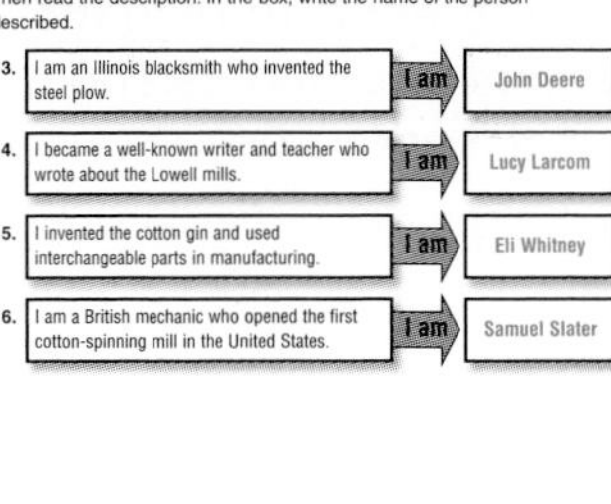

Vocabulary and Study Guide

Vocabulary

1. Use *interchangeable parts, mass production,* and *productivity* in one or two sentences that show their relationship. Sample answer: The system of interchangeable parts made mass production possible and increased manufacturers' productivity.
2. Use *entrepreneur* and *textile* in a sentence that shows their relationship. Sample answer: Entrepreneurs like Francis Cabot Lowell helped New England become the center of the textile industry.

Study Guide

Read "The Industrial Revolution Begins" and "Machines Bring Change." Then read the description. In the box, write the name of the person described.

3. I am an Illinois blacksmith who invented the steel plow. I am John Deere
4. I became a well-known writer and teacher who wrote about the Lowell mills. I am Lucy Larcom
5. I invented the cotton gin and used interchangeable parts in manufacturing. I am Eli Whitney
6. I am a British mechanic who opened the first cotton-spinning mill in the United States. I am Samuel Slater

Unit Resources 105 Use with United States History, pp. 378–383

Unit Resources, p. 105

Reteach Minilesson

Use a three-column chart to reteach the Industrial Revolution.

New Inventions	New Transportation	New Ways of Life
machines for the textiles cotton gin interchangeable parts McCormick's reaper steel plow	National Road steamboats canals railroads	movement from farm to city doing same job over and over all day long women work outside the home

Graphic Organizer 2

Quick Look

Connect to the Core Lesson Students read how new inventions brought changes to manufacturing and ways of life. In Extend Lesson 1, they can learn about the specific activities that took place inside a cotton mill.

1 Teach the Extend Lesson

Connect to the Big Idea

Market Economies Freedom of enterprise and a strong profit motive enabled Francis Cabot Lowell to create the factory system that helped change the United States forever. Without a market economy, Lowell might not have had the capital or the freedom to dare on such a large and complex scale.

Extend Lesson 1

Technology

Inside a Cotton Mill

How does cotton become cloth? The process involves many steps, including cleaning, spinning, and weaving the cotton. The first cotton mills only spun cotton into yarn. Weavers wove yarn into cloth in homes or small shops. When Francis Cabot Lowell put power looms in his Massachusetts textile factory, he made it possible to do all of the steps of making cloth in one building.

The cloth-making process began on the bottom floor of the mill. After the raw cotton was cleaned, cotton fibers were carded, or combed into loose ropes. These ropes were spun into thread on the second floor of the mill. Next, the thread was prepared for weaving. This process, called warping, took place on the third floor. Finally, the thread was woven into finished cloth. Each of these steps required a different machine.

The mill's machines used water power. Lowell's company built canals along the Merrimack River. The canals carried rushing water to the mills where it turned waterwheels. The waterwheels were attached to belts that powered the machines in the factory.

Bales of Cotton
Workers rip open huge bales of cotton weighing about 500 pounds. The raw cotton is run through machines that clean and sort the cotton fibers.

384 • Chapter 11

Reaching All Learners

Extra Support

Perform Charades

- Have students perform charades of various activities that took place in a cotton mill.
- Have classmates guess at the activities and describe them in their own words.

Bodily-kinesthetic; verbal-linguistic

On Level

Create a Journal Entry

- Ask students to create an illustrated journal entry that might have been written by a cotton mill worker.
- Have students read and look at each other's entries and check them for accuracy.

Visual-spatial; verbal-linguistic

Challenge

Categorize Challenges

- Have students brainstorm a list of challenges mill workers might have faced.
- They can categorize the challenges as mental or physical.
- Encourage students to read more about the mills to understand the lives of mill workers better.

Verbal-linguistic

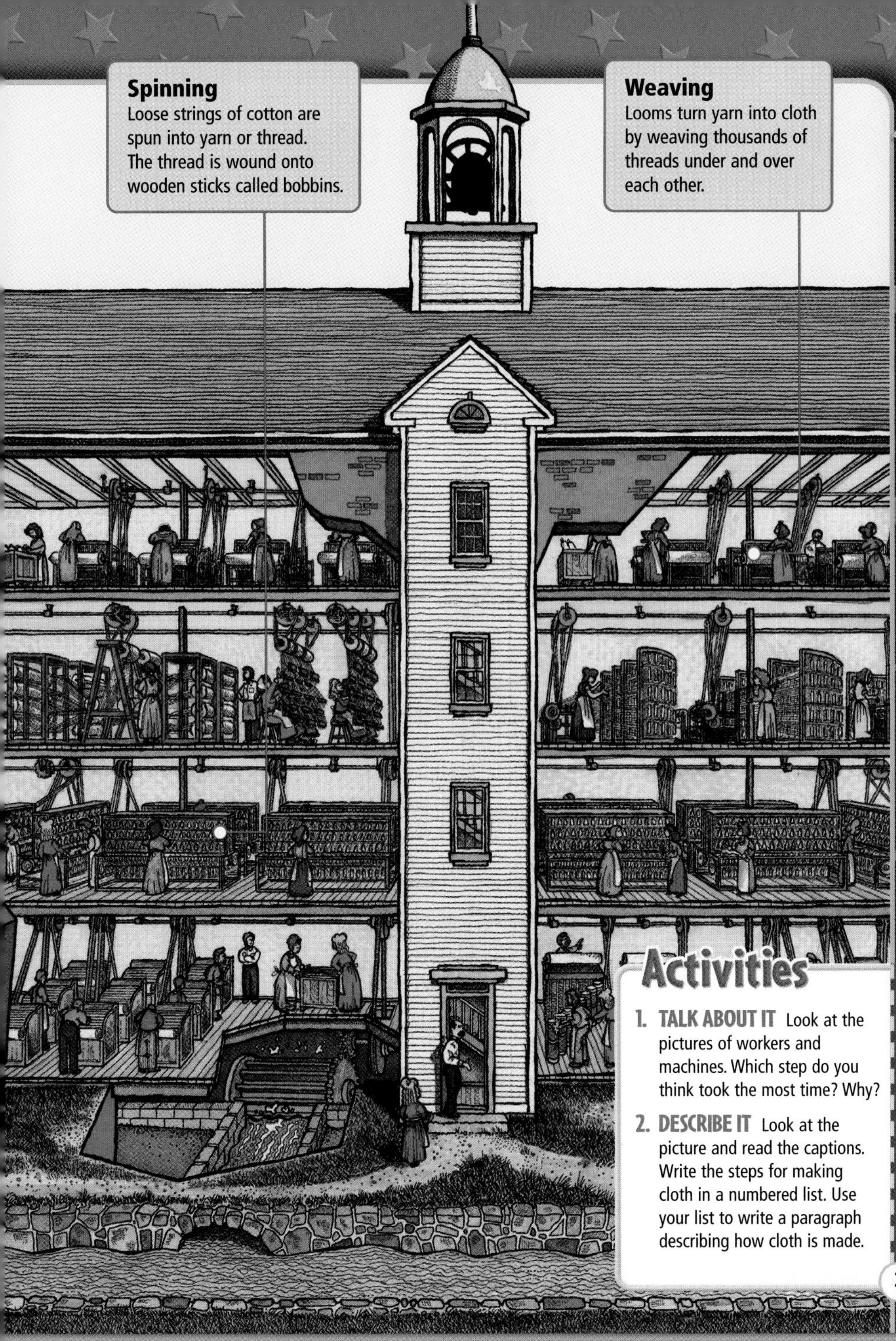

Spinning
Loose strings of cotton are spun into yarn or thread. The thread is wound onto wooden sticks called bobbins.

Weaving
Looms turn yarn into cloth by weaving thousands of threads under and over each other.

Activities

1. **TALK ABOUT IT** Look at the pictures of workers and machines. Which step do you think took the most time? Why?
2. **DESCRIBE IT** Look at the picture and read the captions. Write the steps for making cloth in a numbered list. Use your list to write a paragraph describing how cloth is made.

2 Leveled Activities

1 Talk About It *For Extra Support*
Sample answer: weaving, because it is the most complex

2 Describe It *For Challenge*

Writing Rubric

4	The paragraph clearly describes how cloth is made; the steps are in order and linked by transition words such as *first* and *second;* mechanics are correct.
3	The paragraph describes how cloth is made; the steps are in order; mechanics are generally correct.
2	The paragraph attempts to describe how cloth is made; some steps are in order; mechanics are somewhat correct.
1	The paragraph does not describe how cloth is made; steps are missing or out of order; many errors in mechanics are present.

ELL

Beginning

- Have partners discuss terms from the lesson that are unfamiliar, such as *warping, bale,* and *bobbin.*
- Have them work together to illustrate or act out the meanings of these terms.

Bodily-kinesthetic; visual-spatial

Math

Calculate Weights and Work Times

- If one bale of cotton weighed 500 pounds, how much would four bales weigh altogether? 2,000 pounds
- If a mill worker worked ten hours every workday and got one day off a week, how many hours would he or she work per week? 60 hours

Logical-mathematical

Graphic Organizer

1	Clean the cotton.
2	Card cotton fiber into loose ropes.
3	Spin ropes into threads.
4	Warp thread and weave it into cloth.

Graphic Organizer 15

Tested Objective

U5-12 Conduct research and determine the quality of sources.

1 Teach the Skill

- Remind students of past assignments they have completed that required research.
- Discuss with students what sources they used in their research. Ask how they knew that these sources were reliable.
- Go through the four steps under "Learn the Skill" on page 386. Discuss any questions students have.
- Ask students to explain why having a very specific question on a topic makes doing research easier.

Skillbuilder

Find and Evaluate Sources

VOCABULARY
research

In Lesson 1, you read about the Industrial Revolution. To learn more about that time period, you can do research. Research is the search for facts. These steps will help you to use encyclopedias and websites to research a topic.

Learn the Skill

Step 1: Form a question about what you want to research.

Step 2: Identify a key word or phrase in your question. Key words are the most important words.

- **Encyclopedias** — Look in the volume that includes the first letter of your key word. If there is no information on that topic, look for a list of related topics or try another key word.
- **The Internet** — Use a search engine. When you type your key word into a search engine, it will show you a list of websites related to the word. If those websites aren't helpful, try another key word or phrase.

Step 3: Evaluate your sources to see if they are reliable and accurate. Use these questions to evaluate them:

- What is the purpose of the source? Is it designed to teach, to entertain, or to sell?
- Is the source written by an expert or an average person?
- Is the information correct? Check it in another source.

Step 4: Make sure the sources answer your original question. If they do not, look for new sources. If they do, take notes.

386 • Chapter 11

Leveled Practice

Extra Support

Have students brainstorm questions about the Industrial Revolution that they might want to research. Work together to create a large word web on the board to give students ideas of specific questions they would like to answer. Verbal-linguistic

Challenge

Have students write a paragraph about one hazard workers faced during the Industrial Revolution. Students should list their sources and explain how they chose them. Verbal-linguistic

ELL

Intermediate/Advanced

- Demonstrate or discuss with students how different Internet search engines work.
- Have students do online searches for terms such as "textile industry" and names from the lesson.
- Discuss how many websites they found and whether they think any are reliable.

Verbal-linguistic

Practice the Skill

Think of a question about the Industrial Revolution that you would like to research. Find an encyclopedia article and a website that provide the information you want. Then answer the questions.

1. What related articles listed after the encyclopedia entry might also be helpful?
2. What information about the author and the website lead you to believe that they are reliable?
3. How are the two articles similar? How are they different?

Apply the Skill

Using the two sources you found, write a paragraph that answers your research question about the Industrial Revolution.

2 Practice the Skill

1. Answers will vary. Students should explain why they think the articles might be helpful.
2. Answers will vary. Students might mention government websites or those from universities as reliable sources.
3. Answers will vary. Students should explain how the two articles are similar and different.

3 Apply the Skill

Ask students to write a paragraph answering their research question. When evaluating students' paragraphs, consider:

- Did the student form a question about the Industrial Revolution?
- Did the student use reliable articles (at least one encyclopedia article and one website) to answer the question?
- Did the student's sources answer the research question?

Skill Practice

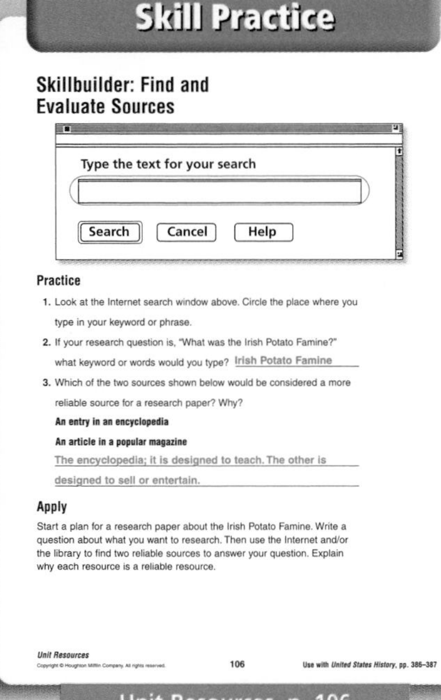

Skillbuilder: Find and Evaluate Sources

Type the text for your search

Search | Cancel | Help

Practice

1. Look at the Internet search window above. Circle the place where you type in your keyword or phrase.
2. If your research question is, "What was the Irish Potato Famine?" what keyword or words would you type? Irish Potato Famine
3. Which of the two sources shown below would be considered a more reliable source for a research paper? Why?

   An entry in an encyclopedia

   An article in a popular magazine

   The encyclopedia; it is designed to teach. The other is designed to sell or entertain.

Apply

Start a plan for a research paper about the Irish Potato Famine. Write a question about what you want to research. Then use the Internet and/or the library to find two reliable sources to answer your question. Explain why each resource is a reliable resource.

Unit Resources

106 Use with *United States History*, pp. 386–387

Unit Resources, p. 106

Skill Transparency

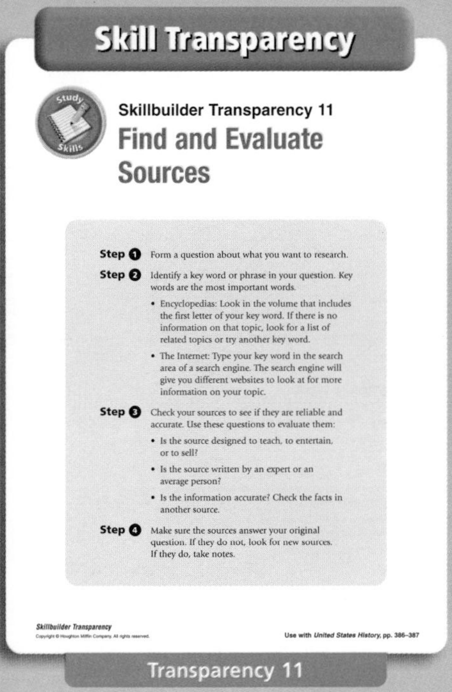

Skillbuilder Transparency 11

Find and Evaluate Sources

Step 1 Form a question about what you want to research.

Step 2 Identify a key word or phrase in your question. Key words are the most important words.

- Encyclopedias: Look in the volume that includes the first letter of your key word. If there is no information on that topic, look for a list of related topics or try another key word.
- The Internet: Type your key word in the search area of a search engine. The search engine will give you different websites to look at for more information on your topic.

Step 3 Check your sources to see if they are reliable and accurate. Use these questions to evaluate them:

- Is the source designed to teach, to entertain, or to sell?
- Is the source written by an expert or an average person?
- Is the information accurate? Check the facts in another source.

Step 4 Make sure the sources answer your original question. If they do not, look for new sources. If they do, take notes.

Skillbuilder Transparency

Use with *United States History*, pp. 386–387

Transparency 11

Tested Objectives

U5-13 History Describe the causes and effects of European immigration to the United States during the mid-1800s.

U5-14 History Summarize the goals and accomplishments of reform movements of the mid-1800s.

Quick Look

This lesson tells about immigration, its effects on cities, and reform movements.

Teaching Option: Extend Lesson 2 shows students some of the reforms achieved during this time.

1 Get Set to Read

Preview Ask students to use the circle graph to determine what percentages of all immigrants came from Ireland and Germany.

Reading Skill: Compare and Contrast Students should consider why immigrants left their home countries and where they settled.

Build on What You Know Have students discuss ways in which they have celebrated St. Patrick's Day. Ask them to think of other holidays brought to the U.S. from other countries.

Vocabulary

famine *noun,* a widespread shortage of food

reform *noun,* change for the better

temperance *noun,* the decision to drink little alcohol or none at all

injustice *noun,* something one person does to another that is wrong

Core Lesson 2

Immigrants and Reformers

VOCABULARY

famine
reform
temperance
injustice

Vocabulary Strategy

reform

The prefix **re-** in **reform** means again. Reform forms something again, or changes it. People who worked for reform wanted to change society.

READING SKILL

Compare and Contrast

Chart the similarities and differences between German and Irish immigrants.

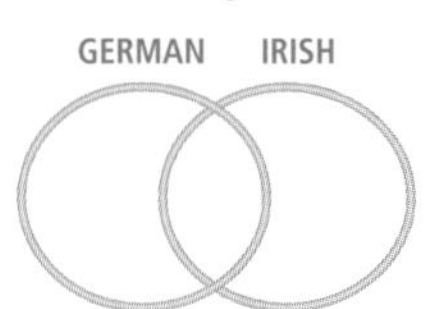

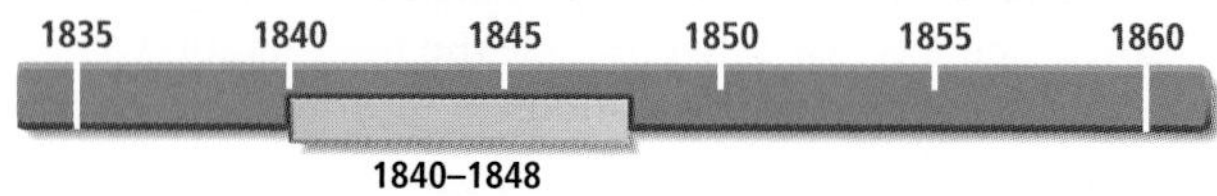

Build on What You Know You may have celebrated St. Patrick's Day by wearing green. Irish immigrants brought this holiday to the United States.

German and Irish Immigrants

Main Idea Millions of German and Irish immigrants came to the United States in the mid-1800s.

People had been moving to North America from European countries since the 1500s. They were immigrants, that is, people who move to another country to live. Between 1840 and 1860, the numbers of immigrants rose sharply. About four million Europeans came to the United States during this time. Almost half of these immigrants were Irish. About one-third were German. The rest came from other parts of Europe.

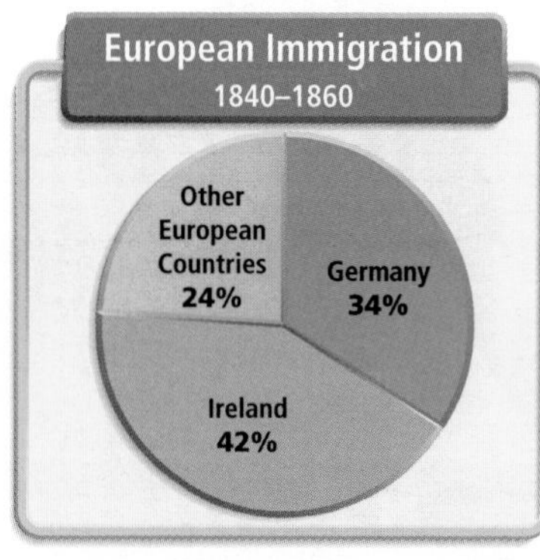

SKILL **Reading Graphs** What percentage of immigrants coming to the United States between 1840 and 1860 were German? 34%

Skill and Strategy

Reading Skill and Strategy

Reading Skill: Compare and Contrast

This skill helps you understand how historical events or people are similar and different.

Read "Making a Better Society." Then fill in the Venn diagram below to compare and contrast the rights of men and women.

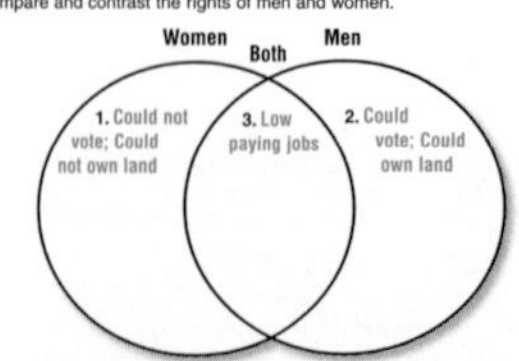

Reading Strategy: Question

4. Read "German and Irish Immigrants." Then check the question that you might ask while reading this section.

___ From which country do most visitors to the United States come?

✓ Why did German and Irish immigrants come to the United States in the mid-1800s?

___ How did people from Germany and Ireland pay for their trips to the United States?

5. Read "Making a Better Society." Read the answer. Then complete the question for the answer.

Answer: Elizabeth Cady Stanton

Question: Who was the leader of the Seneca Falls Convention ?

Unit Resources 107 Use with United States History, pp. 388–391

Unit Resources, p. 107

Math

Using Fractions

Have students express the information in the circle graph in fractions. Then ask them to use one of the fractions to write a sentence about the information in the graph. For example, they might write: "About 2/5 of European immigrants between 1840 and 1860 came from Ireland."

Why They Came

Irish and German people learned about what to expect in the United States from relatives who lived there. They were told of the land and job opportunities that could be found across the Atlantic Ocean.

Thousands of Germans left Europe because of war and crop failures. When they arrived in the United States, many
1 Germans settled in the Midwest where land was plentiful. Those who had the money, education, and skills bought land and started farms. Some found work in midwestern cities such as Chicago, St. Louis, and Milwaukee.

The Irish Potato Famine caused many Irish people to leave their country. **Famine** is a widespread shortage of food. Potatoes were the main source of food for the poor in Ireland. When a disease destroyed Ireland's potato crop in 1846, more than a million Irish people died.

Irish Immigration Immigrants wait to board ships to the United States. The city names on the signs show where these immigrants are going.

Finding Work

Over the next 10 years, about 1.5 million people left Ireland and came to the United States. When they arrived, most didn't have enough money to buy land or even to leave the port cities in which they landed. Irish men and women settled in the cities of the Northeast to work in factories, as household servants, or as builders of canals and railroads.

Some people disliked immigrants because their customs seemed unusual. Many immigrants worked for very little money because they needed jobs. People in cities often thought immigrants were taking jobs away from them.

Immigrants were not the only people who wanted jobs. Blacksmiths, weavers, and other craftspeople were losing work. Goods they had made by hand, such as tools and cloth, were now produced at lower cost in factories. Rural people left farms and workshops to find jobs in cities. 2

REVIEW Why did Irish immigrants usually stay in northeastern cities, while most Germans moved to the Midwest? Most Irish immigrants lacked money to leave cities where they landed. Many German immigrants had enough money to buy land in the Midwest.

2 Teach

German and Irish Immigrants

Talk About It

1 **Q History** In what region of the United States did German immigrants tend to settle?

A Many Germans settled in the Midwest.

2 **Q Economics** Other than immigration, what caused U.S. cities to grow so fast?

A People were leaving farms to move to the cities in search of jobs.

Vocabulary Strategy

famine Tell students that *famine* comes from the Latin word *fames,* which means "hunger." Have they ever heard someone say "I'm famished"? *Famished* means "very hungry."

Reading Strategy: Question Have students read the first two pages of the lesson. As they read, they should ask themselves, "What was life like for new immigrants to the United States at this time?"

Leveled Practice

Extra Support

Have students work in pairs to **list problems** immigrants faced. Verbal-linguistic

Challenge

Ask students to use the library or the Internet to **find pictures** and descriptions of immigrants in the mid-1800s. Invite students to share and discuss their pictures with the class. Visual-spatial

ELL

Intermediate/Advanced

- Have students **write a script for a conversation** between an Irish immigrant and a German immigrant who have just arrived in America around 1850.
- Conversations might include why each came and what each hopes to do.

Verbal-linguistic

Making a Better Society

Talk About It

3 **Q Citizenship** What reform movements were people working for in the mid-1800s?

A antislavery, temperance, women's rights

4 **Q Citizenship** What was the Seneca Falls Convention?

A It was a meeting held in Seneca Falls, New York, to discuss women's rights.

Vocabulary Strategy

reform Note that the prefix *re-* means "again." When society is reformed, it is built again or made over.

temperance Explain that *temper* can mean to lessen or make more moderate. Temperance reformers wanted to lessen the drinking of alcohol.

injustice Explain to students that the prefix *in-* in *injustice* means "not."

Critical Thinking

Compare and Contrast How was the temperance movement different from other reform movements? You may wish to model for students the process of thinking through the question.

Think Aloud *Let me make sure I understand temperance first. Temperance focused on getting people to drink less alcohol. The other reform movements focused on ending injustices. I guess temperance was different because it encouraged people to behave a certain way, while the other movements tried to change the system to protect people's rights.*

Making a Better Society

Main Idea In the 1800s, people tried to improve society by joining reform movements.

Beginning in the 1820s, a rise in religious feeling spread throughout the United States. Thousands of people joined Christian churches. This widespread religious movement was called the Second Great Awakening.

During the Second Great Awakening, many people were inspired to change society. Society is all the people living in the same country.

People worked to improve society through reform. **Reform** is an action that makes something better. Several impor-
3 tant reform movements came about at
this time, including the antislavery and temperance movements. **Temperance** means controlling or cutting back on the drinking of alcohol.

Seneca Falls In the 1800s, reformers held conventions to gather support. Here, Elizabeth Cady Stanton addresses the crowd at the Seneca Falls Convention and calls for rights for women.

Seneca Falls Convention

Religion wasn't the only cause of reform movements. Many women who worked for reform, especially in the antislavery movement, realized they also faced injustice. **Injustice** means unfair treatment that abuses a person's rights. For example, women were not allowed to speak to an audience that included men. They had to be silent in public meetings.

Women could not vote either. Only a small number of low-paying jobs were available to women. In most states, a married woman could not own property or keep the money she earned. Everything she had belonged to her husband.

Courageous women spoke out against this injustice, but few people listened. Then, in 1848, a group of women held a convention in Seneca Falls, New York, to
discuss their rights. Nearly 300 people 4
attended this meeting. The convention marked the beginning of the women's rights movement.

Elizabeth Cady Stanton was the leader of the Seneca Falls Convention. Drawing on the words of the Declaration of Independence, which says that "all men are created equal," Stanton said,

> **"all men and women are created equal."**

Many excited discussions followed her bold speech.

Drama

Stage a Street Scene

- Have small groups stage a street scene in which several people get into an argument about women's rights.
- Have groups begin with a brief planning session to determine the different points of view they will represent.

Verbal-linguistic; bodily-kinesthetic

Language Arts

Give a Speech

- Have students work in pairs to write a short speech on temperance, the end of slavery, or women's rights.
- They should try to express the values and beliefs of a reformer of the mid-1800s.

Verbal-linguistic

Susan B. Anthony joined Stanton as a movement leader. Anthony traveled across the country, giving powerful speeches and working to change laws.

Many felt that a woman's role should not change. Newspapers published attacks against Stanton, Anthony, and others in the women's rights movement. The attacks did not stop women from joining the movement.

REVIEW Why did women reformers decide to start a movement to protect their own rights?
They realized that they faced injustice as women.

Susan B. Anthony
She and Elizabeth Cady Stanton founded several organizations that fought for women's rights.

Lesson Summary

Millions of German and Irish immigrants came to America in the mid-1800s. Cities and jobs changed as people moved to cities from farms and other countries in search of work. During the Second Great Awakening, people worked for important reform movements, including temperance, antislavery, and women's rights. Women demanded recognition of their rights at the Seneca Falls Convention of 1848.

Why It Matters...

In the 1800s, women and other reformers began working for change in growing numbers. They led the way for others to work to improve society.

Lesson Review

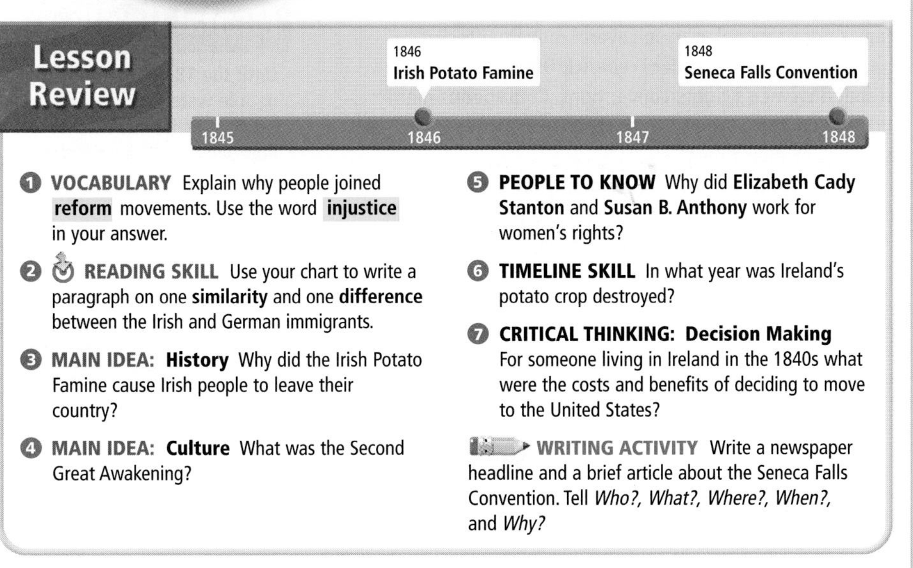

1. **VOCABULARY** Explain why people joined **reform** movements. Use the word **injustice** in your answer.
2. **READING SKILL** Use your chart to write a paragraph on one **similarity** and one **difference** between the Irish and German immigrants.
3. **MAIN IDEA: History** Why did the Irish Potato Famine cause Irish people to leave their country?
4. **MAIN IDEA: Culture** What was the Second Great Awakening?
5. **PEOPLE TO KNOW** Why did **Elizabeth Cady Stanton** and **Susan B. Anthony** work for women's rights?
6. **TIMELINE SKILL** In what year was Ireland's potato crop destroyed?
7. **CRITICAL THINKING: Decision Making** For someone living in Ireland in the 1840s what were the costs and benefits of deciding to move to the United States?

WRITING ACTIVITY Write a newspaper headline and a brief article about the Seneca Falls Convention. Tell *Who?, What?, Where?, When?,* and *Why?*

391

3 Review/Assess

Review Tested Objectives

U5-13 Causes included war and crop failures in Germany and the Irish Potato Famine; effects included growth of cities and job competition.

U5-14 Goals included temperance and women's rights; accomplishments included the Seneca Falls Convention.

Lesson Review Answers

1. Answers should explain that people joined reform movements to fight against the injustice that many people faced.
2. Similarities might include challenges upon arrival; differences might include reasons for departure and where they settled in the U.S.
3. The potato crop was destroyed, leaving many Irish people without food.
4. a rise in religious feeling that inspired people to change society
5. They believed that women deserved equal treatment in society, and should have the right to vote and to own property.
6. 1846
7. Benefits included escaping the famine; costs included working for low pay and poor treatment by other Americans.

Writing Rubric

4	News article format used correctly; all questions answered; mechanics correct.
3	News article format used; one question not answered; few errors in mechanics.
2	News article format attempted; two or three questions unanswered; some errors in mechanics.
1	News article format not used; four or five questions unanswered; many errors in mechanics.

Study Guide/Homework

Vocabulary and Study Guide

Vocabulary

Across
1. When people work to improve society
2. The movement to control the drinking of alcohol
3. Denying a person's right to speak in a public meeting is an example.

Down
4. Caused many Irish people to leave their country
5. Elizabeth Cady Stanton said, "All ___ and women are created equal."

REFORM, TEMPERANCE, INJUSTICE, FAMINE, MEN

Study Guide

6. Read "German and Irish Immigrants." Then fill in the blanks below.
Irish and German people came to the United States for job opportunities and to own land. Thousands of Germans left Europe because of war and crop failure. Many settled in the Midwest. Some bought land, and some found work in cities. Many Irish people immigrated because of the Irish Potato Famine. Most Irish immigrants settled in the Northeast.

7. Read "Making a Better Society." Then fill in the blanks below.
During the Second Great Awakening, people worked to improve society through reform. Many women who worked in the antislavery movement realized that they also faced injustices as women. Women were not allowed to vote or own property. In 1848, a group of women led by Elizabeth Cady Stanton held a convention to talk about these rights. Stanton and Susan B. Anthony worked to change laws.

Unit Resources 108 Use with United States History, pp. 388–391

Unit Resources, p. 108

Reteach Minilesson

Use a flow chart to reteach the relationship between the Second Great Awakening and reform movements.

Cause	Effect
Second Great Awakening makes people want to change society for the better.	Reformers work to • end slavery • end problems caused by drinking alcohol • give equal rights to women

Graphic Organizer 3

Quick Look

Connect to the Core Lesson Students have just learned about reform movements. In Extend Lesson 2, they can learn more about the people who helped lead these movements.

1 Teach the Extend Lesson

Connect to the Big Idea

Rights and Responsibilities In addition to their rights, American citizens have responsibilities and duties to preserve the principles and values of democracy and an obligation to understand and appreciate their patriotic identity. Each reformer spotlighted in this lesson took seriously his or her responsibility to protect the rights of others.

Citizenship

The Reform Movements

"We'll have our rights ... and you can't stop us from them." Sojourner Truth spoke those forceful words at a women's rights convention in 1853. Some people disagreed with Truth, an African American woman. Others nodded their heads in agreement as she spoke.

Sojourner Truth was a reformer in the mid-1800s. Reformers held conventions all over the United States so that they could meet others who shared their views and work together to meet their goals.

The antislavery movement was one of the first important reform movements. It led to many others. Many reformers took part in several movements. For example, antislavery leader Frederick Douglass also attended women's rights conventions. Courageous men and women encouraged one another to fight the injustices of their times.

Change came slowly. People fought for these causes for decades, and women did not win the right to vote in national elections until 1920, more than 70 years after Elizabeth Cady Stanton and others demanded suffrage.

Education

Old buildings, short school years, and a lack of teacher training caused problems in public schools in the early 1800s.

Women's Rights

Women worked for recognition of their right to vote, own property, and earn money.

Mental Health

Until the 1840s, mentally ill people were locked up in jails. Reform leaders worked to improve conditions for the mentally ill.

Temperance

People who drank too much alcohol caused problems in their families and workplaces. Temperance workers wanted to make selling alcohol illegal.

Reaching All Learners

Extra Support

Summarize Passages

- Have partners reread one of the four short passages on page 393 and discuss the reformer or reformers in it.
- Have pairs summarize the achievements of one reformer for the class or larger group.

Verbal-linguistic

On Level

Make a Chart

- Have students make a who, what, and why chart of reform movements.
- In the *who* category, they should list the names of all reformers mentioned on pages 390–393.
- In the *what* category, students should list the type of reform.
- In the *why* category, they should explain the problem or issue reformers addressed.

Visual-spatial

Challenge

Biographies

- Have each student choose a reformer.
- Have students describe the reform work, beliefs and goals of the reformer.

Verbal-linguistic

Horace Mann
He led efforts to provide textbooks, increase pay and training for teachers, and build schoolhouses. Mann also worked in the temperance and mental health movements.

Elizabeth Cady Stanton and Susan B. Anthony
After they met in 1851, they worked together to improve women's rights for the rest of their lives. While Anthony traveled and gave speeches, Stanton stayed at home with her family and organized their campaigns.

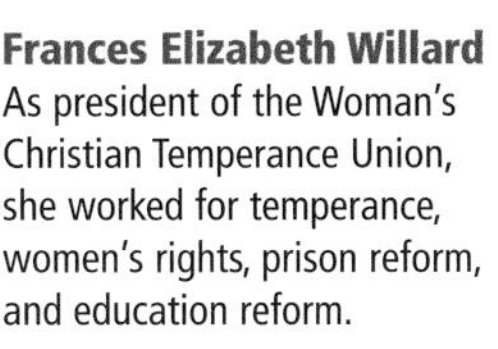

Dorothea Dix
She led a movement to help mentally ill people. Dix wrote state leaders to say mentally ill people should not be punished and put in jail, and she founded hospitals for their care.

Frances Elizabeth Willard
As president of the Woman's Christian Temperance Union, she worked for temperance, women's rights, prison reform, and education reform.

Activities

1. **THINK ABOUT IT** How did reform leaders show good citizenship?
2. **CHART IT** Research one of the people described. Make a chart or timeline of major events or accomplishments in the life of that person.

2 Leveled Activities

1 Think About It *For Extra Support*
Reformers showed good citizenship by identifying problems in society and working to address them.

2 Chart It *For Challenge*

HANDS ON Performance Task Rubric

Score	Description
4	The chart or timeline shows many important events; events are clearly labeled and accurate; mechanics are correct.
3	The chart or timeline shows important events; most events are clearly labeled and accurate; mechanics are mostly correct.
2	The chart or timeline shows a few important events; some events are not clearly labeled or are inaccurate; some errors in mechanics are present.
1	The chart or timeline does not show important events; events are illegible or very inaccurate; many errors in mechanics are present.

ELL

Intermediate

- Divide students into small groups. Give each student a nametag with the name of one of the reformers described in the lesson.
- Have students introduce themselves to each other in character as the reformer whose name they are wearing.
- They should ask and answer each other's questions about their reform work, beliefs, and goals.

Bodily-kinesthetic; verbal-linguistic

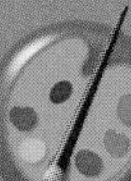

Art

Create a Floor Plan

- Have small groups of students work together to create a floor plan for a museum called the Reformers' Hall of Fame.
- What rooms will it have? What will each room contain? Which rooms might lead to others or contain similar items?
- Invite students to share their floor plans with the class.

Visual-spatial

Graphic Organizer

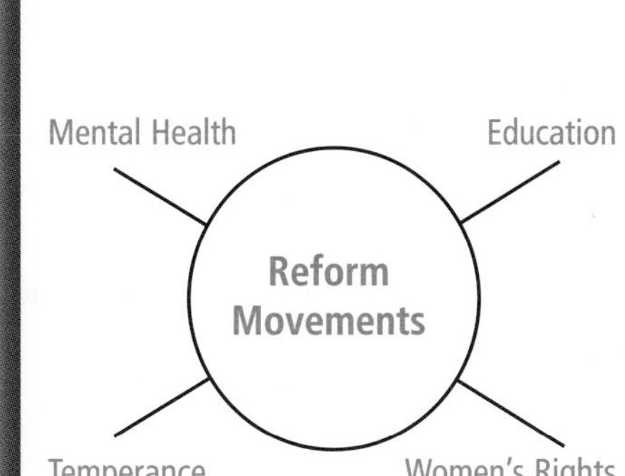

Graphic Organizer 7

Tested Objectives

U5-15 History List the events that led to Texas' independence and annexation.

U5-16 History Explain the causes and effects, including territorial changes, of the Mexican War.

Lesson Quick Look

This lesson explains how Texas was established and how its statehood led to war with Mexico and new territory for the United States.

Teaching Option: **Extend Lesson 3** provides students with biographies of some soldiers and survivors of the Alamo.

1 Get Set to Read

Preview Ask students to use the headings to predict what the lesson will be about.

Reading Skill: Main Idea and Details A sample detail is that settlers often disobeyed Mexican laws.

Build on What You Know Have students discuss why the American Revolution occurred, and look for reasons for Texas to want independence.

Vocabulary

annexation *noun,* the act of adding more territory to a country

manifest destiny *noun,* the belief that the United States could and should expand across the continent

front *noun,* place where fighting occurs in a war

cession *noun,* something that is given up or surrendered, such as land

Core Lesson 3

Texas and the Mexican War

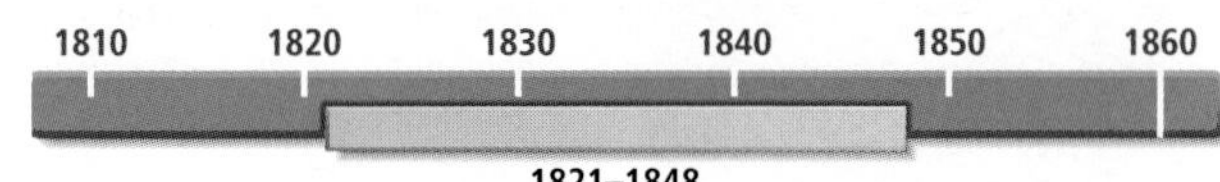

VOCABULARY

annexation
manifest destiny
front
cession

Vocabulary Strategy

front

In a war, the **front** is where battles take place. The soldiers at the front of an army do the fighting.

READING SKILL
Main Idea and Details
Chart the details that support the main idea of Texas independence.

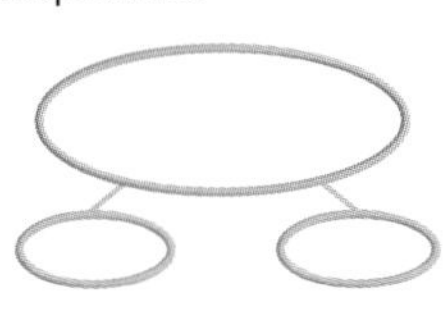

Build on What You Know You know that American colonists fought for independence from Britain during the American Revolution. When Texas was part of Mexico, Texans also fought a war for independence.

The Texas Revolution

Main Idea Americans and Mexicans in Texas fought for independence from the Mexican government.

In 1821, the first settlers from the United States arrived in Texas in search of inexpensive land. Texas was then a part of Mexico. The leader of these settlers was **Stephen Austin.** Within ten years, there were more Americans than Mexicans in Texas. Mexico passed laws to stop settlers from moving to Texas, but they continued to come. 1

These new settlers did not always obey Mexican laws. For example, Texas settlers brought slaves with them from the United States even though slavery was illegal in Mexico. Because of differences over slavery and other issues, the settlers wanted to break away from Mexico.

Stephen Austin Called the "Father of Texas," Austin set up the first American colony in Texas.

394 • Chapter 11

Skill and Strategy

Reading Skill and Strategy

Reading Skill: Main Idea and Details

This skill helps you understand events by seeing how they are related.

Read the first paragraph of "The Texas Revolution." Then fill in the chart below. Write the main idea in the large oval. Write details that support the main idea in the smaller ovals. You can add more small ovals if you need them.

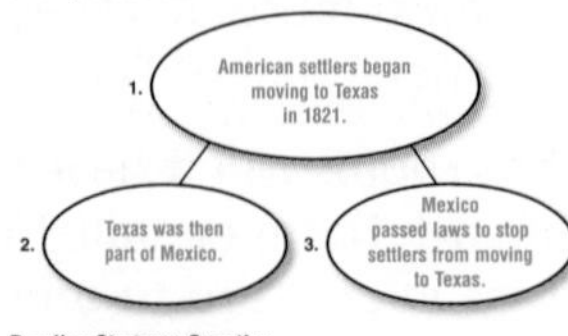

Reading Strategy: Question

4. Read "The Texas Revolution." Read the answer. Then complete the question for the answer.

   Answer: It is the belief that the United States should expand west to the Pacific Ocean.

   Question: What is manifest destiny?

5. Read "War with Mexico." Read the answer. Then write a question for the answer.

   Answer: The United States wanted the border with Mexico to be the Rio Grande.

   Question: Sample answer: Why did the United States and Mexico go to war?

Unit Resources

109
Use with *United States History*, pp. 394–397

Unit Resources, p. 109

Background

The Mexican Cession

- The Treaty of Guadalupe Hidalgo added more than 1.2 million square miles to the United States.
- The addition of this land brought the western borders of the United States to the Pacific Ocean.

The Fighting Begins

Many Tejanos (teh HAHN ohs), as the Mexicans who lived in Texas were called, also wanted to break away from Mexico. They did not like laws made by **Antonio López de Santa Anna,** Mexico's President. Tejanos and Texans rebelled against Mexico to win independence.

In early 1836, Santa Anna led a large army to San Antonio to stop this rebellion. His goal was to capture the Alamo, an old mission that was used as a military fort.
2 Fewer than 200 American Texans and Tejanos defended the fort. During the Battle of the Alamo, most of them were killed.

Meanwhile, Texan leaders voted to officially declare independence from Mexico and form the Republic of Texas. They chose **Sam Houston** to lead their army. He was an experienced soldier who had fought alongside **Andrew Jackson** in the War of 1812.

Houston led a surprise attack on
3 Santa Anna's army at San Jacinto (sahn hah SEEN toh). At that battle, Texans shouted

> **"Remember the Alamo!"**

as they defeated Mexican troops and captured Santa Anna. To gain his freedom, Santa Anna agreed to give Texas its independence.

The Republic Becomes a State

The Republic of Texas held its first election in September 1836. Texans elected Sam Houston as their president. They made slavery legal, and they voted to join the United States. Texans had not wanted to be part of Mexico, but they were in favor of annexation by the United States. **Annexation** is the act of joining two countries or pieces of land together.

Martin Van Buren, the U.S. President, was against annexation. He feared it would lead to war with Mexico because Mexico wanted Texas back. He also did
not want to add a new state that allowed 4
slavery. Many Americans were against slavery.

Supporters of annexation argued that it was the nation's destiny to expand west. They believed the United States should spread across the entire North American continent, from the Atlantic Ocean to the Pacific Ocean. This belief is called **manifest destiny.** Manifest means obvious, and destiny is what will happen in the future. People who supported manifest destiny thought that Texas should become part of the United States. In 1845, when **James Polk** became President, Congress voted to annex Texas.

REVIEW Why didn't President Van Buren want to annex Texas? didn't want war with Mexico or to annex a new slave state

The Alamo This former mission is where the Battle of the Alamo took place. It still stands in San Antonio, Texas.

2 Teach

The Texas Revolution

Talk About It

1 **Q History** Why did Mexico pass laws to stop Americans from settling in Texas?

A There were more Americans than Mexicans in Texas; some of their actions, such as owning slaves, went against Mexican law.

2 **Q History** Who fought and what happened at the Battle of the Alamo?

A A small group of American Texans and Tejanos tried to defend the Alamo against an attack by Santa Anna's army. Most who tried to defend the fort died.

3 **Q History** What was the result of the fighting at San Jacinto?

A Santa Anna was captured and agreed to give Texas independence.

4 **Q History** Why were some Americans against annexing Texas? Why did some people support it?

A Some opposed it because they feared war with Mexico and didn't want to admit another slave state. Others supported annexation as part of manifest destiny.

Vocabulary Strategy

annexation Tell students that the suffix *-tion* in *annexation* means "action of" or "process of."

manifest destiny Tell students that the letters *m* and *d* in *manifest destiny* can help them remember its meaning. For many Americans, manifest destiny was a *must do:* it was the nation's right and duty.

Reading Strategy: Question As students read, suggest that they keep in mind the question, "What was the result of the Texas Revolution?"

Leveled Practice

Extra Support

Have students **create a sequence chain** called "Steps to Statehood." It should show major events that occurred between 1821 and 1836. Visual-spatial

Challenge

Have students **make a list of words** that describe the people who settled and fought for Texas, such as *brave, determined,* or *rebellious.* For each word they select, ask for a fact that supports that choice. Verbal-linguistic

ELL

Intermediate/Advanced

- Have students **make a glossary** of names and terms related to the Texas Revolution.
- They might include Stephen Austin, Tejanos, Santa Anna, Sam Houston, San Jacinto, and the Alamo.

Verbal-linguistic

War with Mexico

Talk About It

5 Q History What disagreement did Mexico and the United States have about the border between them?

A Mexico wanted the border to be at the Nueces River; the U.S. wanted it at the Rio Grande, which would give the U.S. more land.

6 Q History What were the three fronts where the war was fought?

A The war was fought in northern Mexico, in New Mexico, and in southern Mexico.

7 Q History What was the Mexican Cession?

A It was the land Mexico gave up after the war in the Treaty of Guadalupe Hidalgo.

Vocabulary Strategy

front Explain that *front* is a multiple-meaning word. Students can remember it as a place to confront, or meet, the enemy.

cession Point out the homophone *session* and discuss its meeting. Use this sentence to illustrate: "In this session of Congress, we discussed the Mexican Cession."

Critical Thinking

Draw Conclusions Why do you think people believed in manifest destiny, even at the cost of war?

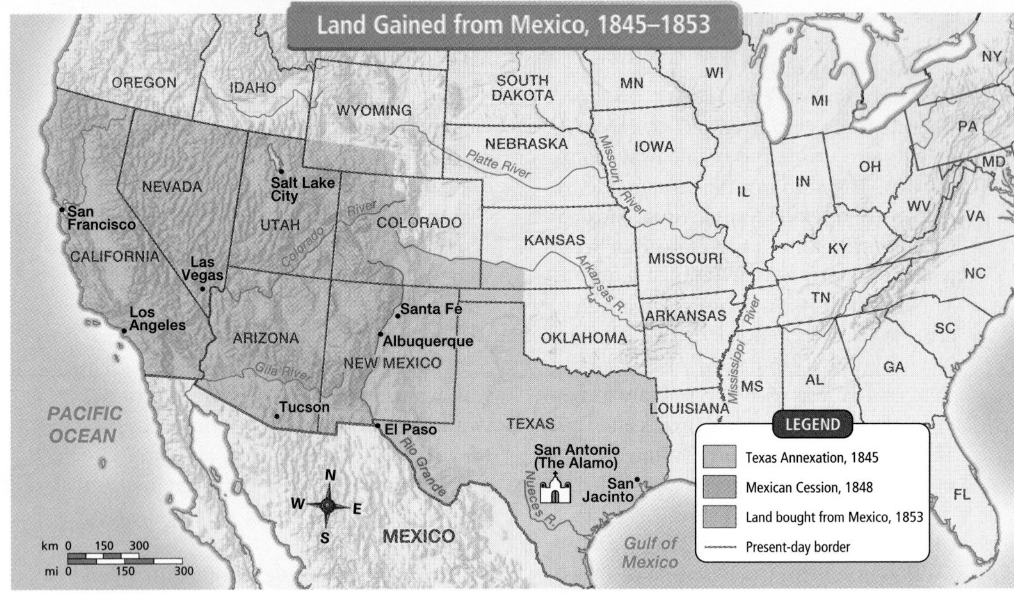

A Growing Nation The United States gained present-day California, Nevada, Utah, and parts of Colorado, Arizona, New Mexico, and Wyoming after the Mexican War.

SKILL **Reading Maps** Which river forms the border between Mexico and Texas? Rio Grande

War with Mexico

Main Idea After Texas became a state, the United States went to war with Mexico.

When Texas joined the United States, Mexico wanted the border between Texas and Mexico to be at the Nueces (NWEH sehs) River. President Polk wanted the boundary to be the Rio Grande (REE oh
5 GRAHN deh), a river that lay 150 miles south of the Nueces. The Rio Grande boundary would give the United States more land. The Mexican government would not agree to this border. Polk sent soldiers led by General **Zachary Taylor** into Texas and asked Congress to declare war with Mexico. Congress declared war on May 13, 1846.

The Mexican War was fought on three fronts. A **front** is where fighting takes place in a war. The first front was in 6
northern Mexico. The second was in New Mexico where American soldiers captured Santa Fe and then headed west to help the U.S. Navy take control of California. The third front was in southern Mexico. U.S. soldiers invaded Mexico by sea and marched inland to capture Mexico City in September 1847.

Lone Star State The Republic of Texas chose this flag in 1839.

Music

Texas Independence: The Musical

- Ask partners to write a plan for one scene from a musical about Texas independence.
- Have them describe the type of music, costumes, and scenery that would help bring it to life.
- Students might list the kinds of instruments or voices, the tempo of the music, and its overall message.

Musical-auditory

Language Arts

Write a Poem

- Have students write a poem about the Battle of the Alamo or Houston's attack on San Jacinto.
- Tell them to write about the event as a Tejano, an American Texan, or a member of Santa Anna's army might have seen it.
- Have students share their poems with the class.

Verbal-linguistic

The Treaty of Guadalupe Hidalgo

After the U.S. Army captured Mexico City, Mexico's leaders agreed to discuss a peace treaty. In 1848, the United States and Mexico signed the Treaty of Guadalupe Hidalgo (gwah dah LOO peh ee DAHL goh). Mexico agreed to accept the annexation of Texas and the Rio Grande as the border between Texas and Mexico. Mexico was also forced to turn over a large
7 area of land called the Mexican Cession. A **cession** is something that is given up.

The United States paid Mexico $15 million for the cession. Mexicans living on this land were allowed to become citizens of the United States. Laws protected them from losing their property, but these laws were often ignored. Many new American citizens lost their land.

REVIEW What did Mexico agree to under the Treaty of Guadalupe Hidalgo? Mexico agreed to let the United States annex Texas and to make the Rio Grande the border between Texas and Mexico.

Lesson Summary

- **1820s** United States settlers come to Texas
- **1836** Texas war for independence
- **1845** Texas annexed by United States
- **1846** United States goes to war with Mexico

Why It Matters ...

Texas, California, and nearly all of the present-day American Southwest became part of the United States after the Mexican War.

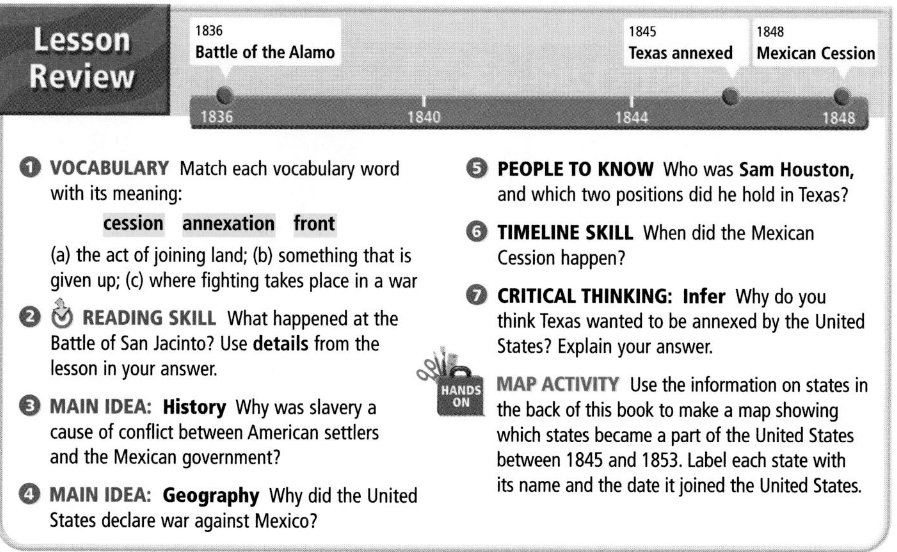

Lesson Review

1. **VOCABULARY** Match each vocabulary word with its meaning:
   cession **annexation** **front**
   (a) the act of joining land; (b) something that is given up; (c) where fighting takes place in a war
2. **READING SKILL** What happened at the Battle of San Jacinto? Use **details** from the lesson in your answer.
3. **MAIN IDEA: History** Why was slavery a cause of conflict between American settlers and the Mexican government?
4. **MAIN IDEA: Geography** Why did the United States declare war against Mexico?
5. **PEOPLE TO KNOW** Who was **Sam Houston,** and which two positions did he hold in Texas?
6. **TIMELINE SKILL** When did the Mexican Cession happen?
7. **CRITICAL THINKING: Infer** Why do you think Texas wanted to be annexed by the United States? Explain your answer.

HANDS ON **MAP ACTIVITY** Use the information on states in the back of this book to make a map showing which states became a part of the United States between 1845 and 1853. Label each state with its name and the date it joined the United States.

397

Study Guide/Homework

Vocabulary and Study Guide

Vocabulary

1. Draw a line connecting the vocabulary word to its meaning.

annexation	The belief that the United States should spread across the entire North American continent
front	Something that is given up
cession	Where the fighting takes place in a war
manifest destiny	The act of joining two pieces of land together

Study Guide

Read "The Texas Revolution." Then fill in the sequence chart below.

Texas settlers and Tejanos want independence from Mexico. → 2. Texans and Tejanos are defeated at the Alamo. → 3. Sam Houston's army captures Santa Anna, and wins Texan independence. → Polk becomes President, and Congress votes to annex Texas.

Read "War with Mexico." Then fill in the sequence chart below.

Mexico does not agree to the Rio Grande border. → 4. President Polk asks Congress to declare war on Mexico. → 5. Mexico signs the Treaty of Guadalupe Hidalgo after the United States Army captures Mexico City. → 6. Mexico turns over a large area of its land in exchange for $15 million.

Unit Resources 110 Use with *United States History*, pp. 394–397

Unit Resources, p. 110

Reteach Minilesson

Use a flow chart to review the effects of Texas statehood on the nation.

Texas annexation → War with Mexico → Mexican cession

www.eduplace.com/ss/hmss05/

3 Review/Assess

Review Tested Objectives

U5-15 Events included the Battle of the Alamo and Santa Anna's surrender at San Jacinto.

U5-16 Events included border disputes, fighting on several fronts, and resolution of conflict through the Treaty of Guadalupe Hidalgo.

Lesson Review Answers

1. (a) annexation; (b) cession; (c) front
2. Answers should include that Texans defeated Mexican troops and captured Santa Anna; Santa Anna agreed to give Texas its independence.
3. Slavery was illegal in Mexico, yet Americans living there owned slaves.
4. The United States wanted the border between Texas and Mexico to be the Rio Grande, while Mexico wanted to set it at the Nueces River.
5. Sam Houston was a soldier. He was the leader of the Texan army and the first president of the Republic of Texas.
6. 1848
7. Answers may include the desire to be linked to a larger country and the fact that many Texans had lived in the United States before moving to Texas.

HANDS ON Performance Task Rubric

4	Map is drawn accurately; states and dates are labeled correctly; mechanics are correct.
3	Map is mostly drawn accurately; most states and dates are labeled correctly; mechanics are mostly correct.
2	Map is drawn with some inaccuracies; some states and dates are labeled incorrectly; some errors in mechanics are present.
1	Map is not accurate; many states and dates are absent or labeled incorrectly; many errors in mechanics are present.

Quick Look

Connect to the Core Lesson In Core Lesson 3, students learned about the Texas Revolution, including the Battle of the Alamo. In this Extend Lesson, they can learn about some of the individuals who were there.

1 Teach the Extend Lesson

Connect to the Big Idea

Individuals in American History Our history is made up of the stories of people who have struggled and, in some cases, given their lives for what they believed in. Davy Crockett and the other people profiled in this lesson are examples..

Extend Lesson 3

Biographies

AT THE ALAMO

Who took part in the fierce 13-day attack on the Alamo? The painting shows the Mexican leader, Santa Anna, and his troops attacking the mission in 1836. Nearly all those who defended the Alamo lost their lives, including Davy Crockett, a famous pioneer. Two survivors who saw the fight were Susanna Wilkerson Dickinson and Juan Seguin.

Davy Crockett 1786–1836

A well-known hunter and trapper, Davy Crockett was the subject of many tall tales. One writer said Crockett could "run faster, jump higher, squat lower, dive deeper, stay under longer, and come out drier, than any man in the whole country." He was elected to Congress, where he voted against President Andrew Jackson's Indian Removal Act.

Crockett went to Texas to help his friend Sam Houston fight for independence from Mexico. Crockett hoped to become a political leader in the independent Texas. He lost his life at the Battle of the Alamo, but his courage in the face of death inspired others.

398 • Chapter 11

Reaching All Learners

Extra Support

Write a Summary

- Have pairs of students write a summary of each biography by following these steps.
- Photocopy the biographies.
- Have students underline the most important words or phrases.
- Have students write a summary that tells the most important things each person did.

Verbal-linguistic

On Level

Write Clues

- Have students write "who's who" clues for each person, such as "I lived at the Alamo" or "I carried Santa Anna's letter to Sam Houston."
- Invite pairs of students to exchange clues and identify each person.

Verbal-linguistic

Challenge

Write a Tall Tale

- Invite students to write their own tall tale about Davy Crockett, Susanna Dickinson, or Juan Seguin.
- Students may want to read more about other tall tale heroes to get a feel for the genre.
- Ask students to share their tall tales with the class.

Verbal-linguistic

BIOGRAPHIES

Susanna Wilkerson Dickinson 1814–1883

Susanna Dickinson lived at the Alamo. Her husband, a soldier, was killed in the battle, but she and her baby survived. Mexican soldiers found them, and Santa Anna gave her money and a blanket for her journey home. He also ordered her to deliver a letter to Sam Houston. Santa Anna wanted Dickinson to tell about the defeat of the Texans at the Alamo. He hoped the story would terrify those who were fighting for Texas independence. It didn't. Six weeks later, the Texans defeated Santa Anna.

Juan Seguin 1806–1890

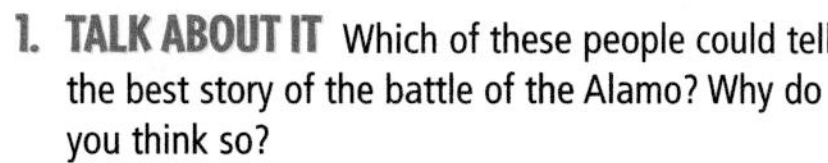

Juan Seguin was a Mexican Texan, or Tejano, from a wealthy family in San Antonio. As an army captain in the Texas revolution, Seguin helped force Santa Anna's troops out of San Antonio in 1835. The next year he joined the troops defending the Alamo. When Santa Anna attacked, Seguin was told to run from the fort and get help. That order probably saved his life. He fought against Santa Anna again at the battle of San Jacinto.

Later, when Texas became independent, Seguin served in the state senate. As a senator, he worked to have the laws of the new republic printed in Spanish. From 1841 to 1842, Seguin was the mayor of San Antonio.

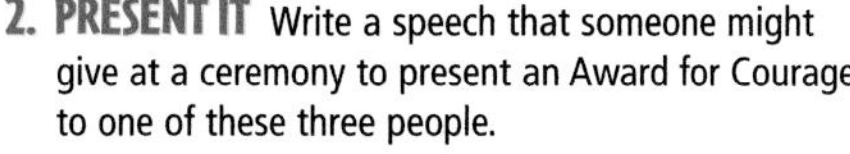

Activities

1. **TALK ABOUT IT** Which of these people could tell the best story of the battle of the Alamo? Why do you think so?
2. **PRESENT IT** Write a speech that someone might give at a ceremony to present an Award for Courage to one of these three people.

Technology Visit Education Place for more biographies of people in this unit. www.eduplace.com/kids/hmss05/

399

2 Leveled Activities

1 Talk About It *For Extra Support*

Sample Answer: Susanna Wilkerson Dickinson, because she survived the fighting and met Santa Anna

2 Present It *For Challenge*

Writing Rubric

4	Speech states achievements clearly; conveys ideas effectively; facts cited are accurate.
3	Speech states achievements; conveys ideas adequately; most facts cited are accurate.
2	Speech states achievements in a somewhat disorganized way; conveys ideas adequately; some factual errors are present.
1	Speech states no achievements or is off topic; conveys ideas in a very general or incomprehensible way; many factual errors are present.

Pronunciation Help

Seguin (seh GEEN)

ELL

Intermediate

- Have students practice the correct pronunciation of the names of the people and places mentioned in this lesson.
- Then have them make up sentences using these names, for example, "Juan Seguin fought at the Alamo and at the Battle of San Jacinto."
- You may wish to have students repeat each other's sentences.

Verbal-linguistic

Math

Create a Timeline

- Have students create a timeline that includes events mentioned in the lesson.
- Remind them to divide their timelines into equal segments and to label dates clearly.
- Compare completed timelines as a group.

Visual-spatial; logical-mathematical

Graphic Organizer

Texan Independence: People Who Made a Difference

- Davy Crockett
- Susanna Wilkerson Dickinson
- Juan Seguin

Graphic Organizer 8

Tested Objectives

U5-17 History Identify why different groups of people migrated to the West and the trails they took to get there.

U5-18 History Describe the events and effects of the California Gold Rush.

Quick Look

This lesson describes movement westward on the Oregon, Mormon, and other trails, as well as the California Gold Rush.

Teaching Option: **Extend Lesson 4** teaches students about travel in a covered wagon.

1 Get Set to Read

Preview Have students skim the headings in this lesson and predict what they will be reading about.

Reading Skill: Cause and Effect Students should include *religion* and *making money* in the first column, and tell about the growth of towns in the second.

Build on What You Know Ask students to evaluate the book recommendation—was it as good as their friend said? How might stories the settlers heard be similar?

Vocabulary

wagon train *noun,* a line of covered wagons moving together cross-country

forty-niner *noun,* a person who went to look for gold in California in 1849

gold rush *noun,* the quick movement of people to California and other places following the discovery of gold

boomtown *noun,* a town offering many chances to make money and filled with people just arriving

Core Lesson 4

Moving West

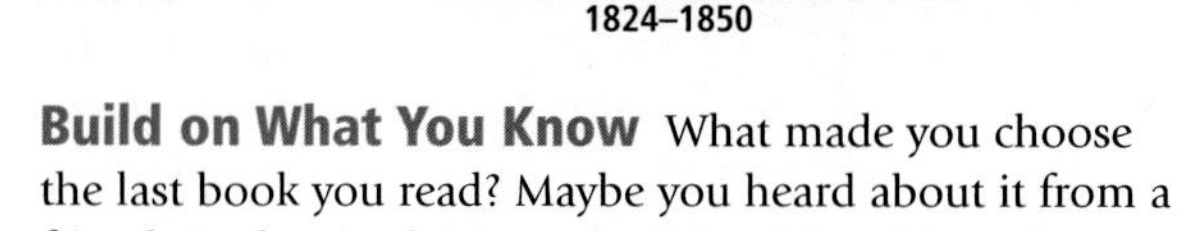

VOCABULARY

wagon train
forty-niner
gold rush
boomtown

Vocabulary Strategy

forty-niner

Many people went to California in 1849. They were called **forty-niners.**

READING SKILL

Cause and Effect Note reasons pioneers moved west and what happened as a result.

CAUSES	EFFECTS

Build on What You Know What made you choose the last book you read? Maybe you heard about it from a friend. Settlers in the 1840s heard exciting things about the West and decided to move there.

Trails West

Main Idea Pioneers made difficult journeys to settle in the West.

In 1824, Crow Indians showed a trapper a way through the Rocky Mountains that was wide enough for wagons. The route was called the South Pass. By the end of the 1850s, thousands of people had traveled through the South Pass on a route known as the Oregon Trail.

The Oregon Trail was about 2,000 miles long. It started in Missouri and stretched west across the Rocky
Mountains to present-day Oregon. In some places, the 1
trail was wide and open. When it crossed rivers and mountains, the path became very narrow.

Marcus and **Narcissa Whitman** were two of the first pioneers to travel the Oregon Trail. They were missionaries who settled in eastern Oregon in 1836. They wanted to teach American Indians about Christianity. The Whitman mission became a place where travelers could rest.

John Frémont explored parts of the West and helped make maps of the Oregon Trail. He wrote reports describing the beauty of the land. People on the Oregon Trail used Frémont's maps and reports as guides.

Narcissa Whitman She was the first American woman to travel through the South Pass.

Skill and Strategy

Reading Skill and Strategy

Reading Skill: Cause and Effect

This skill helps you see how one event can be related to another, either by causing it or resulting from it.

Read "The California Gold Rush." Then fill in the cause-and-effect chart below to show two effects of the demand for gold.

Cause	Effects
Gold was discovered in California.	1. About 250,000 people rushed to California. 2. Boomtowns sprang up near the gold mines.

Reading Strategy: Question

Look over "Moving West." Read the headings. Then turn each heading into a question. As you read, look for the answers to those questions.

3. Heading 1: Trails West
   Question: Sample answer: What was the Oregon Trail?
   Answer: Sample answer: It was a trail that started in Missouri and stretched west to Oregon.
4. Heading 2: The California Gold Rush
   Question: Sample answer: What was the California Gold Rush?
   Answer: Sample answer: It was a period when more than 250,000 people moved to California to search for gold.

Unit Resources

111
Use with *United States History*, pp. 400–403

Unit Resources, p. 111

Background

The Canada/Oregon Border

- In the 1840s, the border between Canada and the Oregon Territory was disputed. At that time, Canada belonged to Britain.
- President James K. Polk's campaign slogan "54–40 or Fight," promised to set the border at 54 degrees, 40 minutes, or to fight Britain over it.
- The border was set at the forty-ninth parallel in 1846. This gave the United States less land than Polk's slogan promised, but war was avoided.

Traveling West Settlers traveled in wagon trains for safety and to keep each other company on the long trip.

Wagon Trains

The first large group of about 1,000 people set out on the Oregon Trail in 1843. They came from Ohio, Indiana, Illinois, Kentucky, and Tennessee. They were looking for good, inexpensive land.

Pioneers on the Oregon Trail traveled by wagon train. A **wagon train** was a line of covered wagons that moved together. Oxen, mules, or horses pulled each wagon.

Travelers on the Oregon Trail faced
2 injuries, diseases, and bad weather. Lack
of food and water were problems, too. One woman described the trail in her journal:

> **“Not a drop of water, nor a spear of grass to be seen, nothing but barren hills, bare and broken rock, sand and dust.”**

Despite the hardships, many people settled in Oregon.

President **James Polk** believed in manifest destiny. He wanted Oregon to belong to the United States. At the time, Oregon was claimed by both the United States and Britain. In 1846, Polk signed a treaty with Britain to set the border between the western United States and Canada. The land south of this border became the Oregon Territory in 1848.

Pioneers also took other trails to the
West. People who traveled on the Mormon 3
Trail were members of the Church of Jesus Christ of Latter-Day Saints. Members of this church, which was founded in 1830 in New York, were called Mormons.

Some people opposed the Mormons' teachings and would not allow them to practice their religion. In 1847, Mormon leader **Brigham Young** took his people west. They settled in present-day Utah.

REVIEW Why did the first large group of people set out on the Oregon Trail? They wanted to find good, inexpensive land.

401

2 Teach

Trails West

Talk About It

1 **Q Geography** What did the Oregon Trail allow settlers to do?

A cross the Rocky Mountains; travel from Missouri to present-day Oregon by wagon

2 **Q History** Why was travel on the Oregon Trail difficult?

A Settlers faced injuries, diseases, and bad weather on the trail, and there was not enough food and water.

3 **Q History** Who were the Mormons?

A The Mormons were members of the Church of Jesus Christ of Latter-Day Saints who searched for a place to practice their religion freely. They eventually settled in present-day Utah.

Vocabulary Strategy

wagon train Tell students that the word *train* has many meanings. A *wagon train* means a long line of moving wagons.

Reading Strategy: Question As students read, suggest they formulate their own questions and seek the answers. You may wish to use any unanswered questions as a jumping-off point for class discussion.

Leveled Practice

Extra Support

Ask students to list points that might be raised in **a discussion** between two people from the East who want to travel across the Oregon Trail in 1845 and two who do not. Verbal-linguistic

Challenge

Have students **design a home page** for a website about the California Gold Rush. (This may be done on paper or computer.) The home page should name at least five categories of information, with illustrations or icons that visitors can click on to learn more. Visual-spatial

ELL

Intermediate

- Have students **categorize information** by making a chart that lists the trails, the explorers, and the settlers mentioned in this chapter.
- Students may share their charts with a partner.

Visual-spatial; verbal-linguistic

The California Gold Rush

Talk About It

4 Q History Who lived in California before the gold rush?

A American Indians and Californios (Mexicans who lived in California)

5 Q Geography Why did boomtowns spring up during the gold rush?

A because many miners, merchants, and traders moved to town, near the gold mines

6 Q History How long after becoming a territory did California have enough people to be a state?

A just two years

Vocabulary Strategy

forty-niner Teach students this verse from "Oh My Darling Clementine":

In a cavern, in a canyon,
Excavating for a mine,
Dwelt a miner, forty-niner,
And his daughter Clementine.

gold rush Explain to students that *rush* is a multiple-meaning word; here, it means a race to obtain something.

boomtown Tell students that an antonym for *boomtown* is *ghost town.* Some boomtowns eventually turned into ghost towns.

Critical Thinking

Cause and Effect Why did many boomtowns disappear after the gold rush ended?

Think Aloud *Boomtowns grew up around the gold mines. When the gold rush ended, people left these mining towns and moved elsewhere. That's why the boomtowns often didn't survive.*

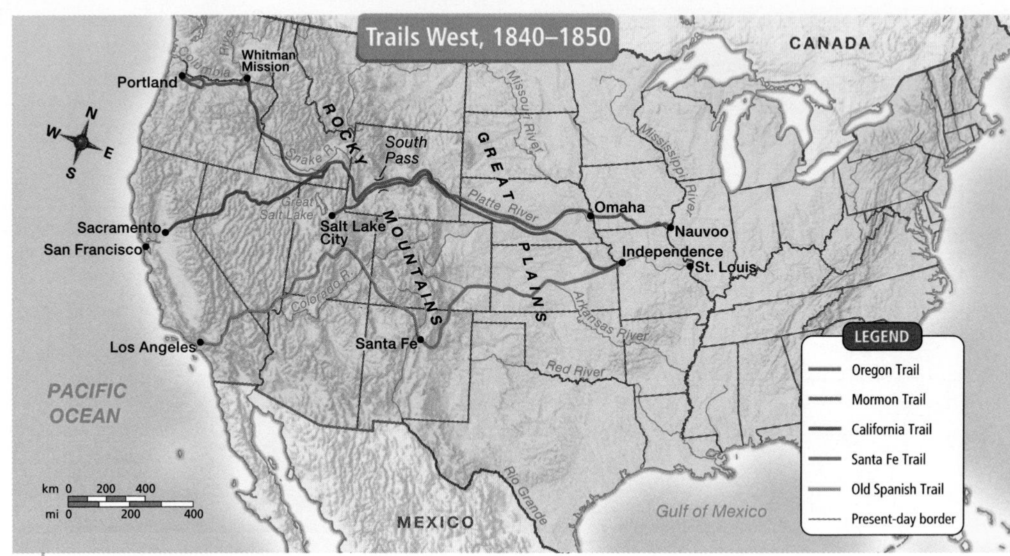

Overland Trails This map shows the trails most settlers traveled to get to the West. The trails led pioneers along rivers and through mountain passes.

SKILL **Reading Maps** Which trail ends in Sacramento? California Trail

The California Gold Rush

Main Idea Thousands rushed to California to dig for gold in the mid-1800s.

4 Before the 1700s, California Indians lived in villages where they hunted, gathered plants, and fished. When California became part of New Spain, many American Indians were forced to live and work on Spanish missions.

When Mexico gained independence in 1821, California became part of it. Californios, as Mexican citizens in California were called, built large ranches on old mission lands. American Indians were forced to work on the ranches. In 1848, when California joined the United States, Californios could become U.S. citizens. Very little changed for the American Indians living there.

That same year, gold was discovered in California. Thousands of people from the United States, Mexico, China, Europe, and South America rushed to California to dig for gold. These people became known as forty-niners. A **forty-niner** was a miner who went to California around 1849.

During the California Gold Rush, more than 250,000 people poured into California. A **gold rush** takes place when many people hurry to the same area to
look for gold. Boomtowns sprang up 5
near the gold mines. A **boomtown** is a town whose population booms, or grows very quickly. Merchants and traders in boomtowns sold food and clothing to the miners. People in boomtowns published newspapers and opened banks and inns. Lawyers found work settling arguments.

Math

Use Data

- Ask students how population in a boomtown might have changed between 1849 and 1854.
- Have students create a hypothetical data table. It should show the population for each of those years in a boomtown that peaked at 15,000 people.
- Have students use their data table to make a line graph or bar graph.

Logical-mathematical

Language Arts

Write Historical Fiction

- Have students write the beginning of a short story about a young person living at the time of the gold rush.
- Have them trade their story beginnings with a partner, identify historical facts in each other's stories, and suggest what might happen next.

Verbal-linguistic

Forty-Niners Miners dug for gold with picks and shovels.

After the Gold Rush

The California Gold Rush lasted only about five years. Though a few miners found gold, most did not. Some forty-niners went back home, but thousands stayed and settled in California.

The gold rush changed California. Miners and farmers killed California Indians and took over their land. Newcomers also forced many Californio property owners off their land.

Cities such as San Francisco grew. By 1850, only two years after becoming a U.S. territory, California had enough people to become a state. The new state included American Indians and people from Mexico, China, South America, Europe, and other parts of the United States. 6

REVIEW Who lived in the boomtowns around the gold mines? miners, merchants, bankers, innkeepers, and lawyers

Lesson Summary

- Missionaries, farmers, and other settlers traveled west in wagon trains.
- The discovery of gold in 1848 brought thousands of people to California.
- Growth in California led to conflicts with American Indians and Californios.

Why It Matters ...

In their search for land, religious freedom, and gold, pioneers started new towns in many present-day western states.

Lesson Review

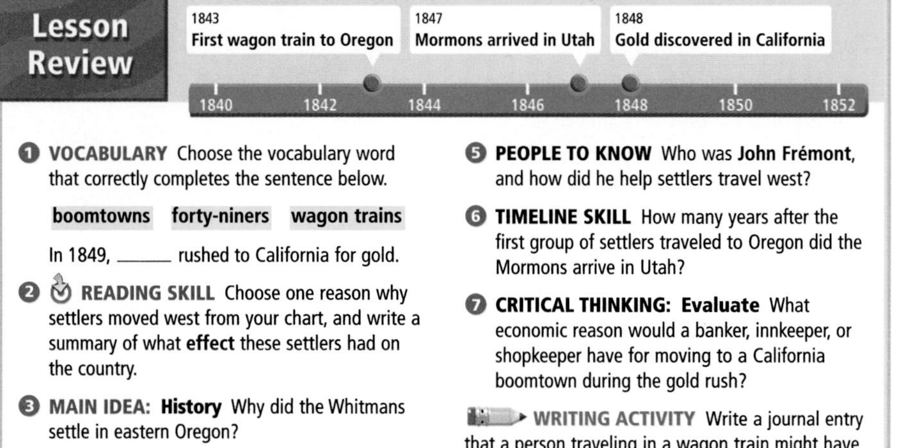

1. **VOCABULARY** Choose the vocabulary word that correctly completes the sentence below.

   boomtowns **forty-niners** **wagon trains**

   In 1849, ______ rushed to California for gold.

2. **READING SKILL** Choose one reason why settlers moved west from your chart, and write a summary of what **effect** these settlers had on the country.

3. **MAIN IDEA: History** Why did the Whitmans settle in eastern Oregon?

4. **MAIN IDEA: History** List two changes that took place in California after the gold rush ended.

5. **PEOPLE TO KNOW** Who was **John Frémont**, and how did he help settlers travel west?

6. **TIMELINE SKILL** How many years after the first group of settlers traveled to Oregon did the Mormons arrive in Utah?

7. **CRITICAL THINKING: Evaluate** What economic reason would a banker, innkeeper, or shopkeeper have for moving to a California boomtown during the gold rush?

WRITING ACTIVITY Write a journal entry that a person traveling in a wagon train might have written. Describe the hardships he or she might have faced.

403

3 Review/Assess

Review Tested Objectives

U5-17 Reasons for moving included missionary work and religious freedom; trails included the Oregon Trail and the Mormon Trail.

U5-18 During the gold rush, thousands of people headed to California to mine for gold. Results included the spread of farms and ranches and increased population.

Lesson Review Answers

1. forty-niners
2. Answers will vary; should include information from the lesson.
3. to do missionary work among American Indians
4. Changes included the killing of California Indians; the taking over by settlers of Indian and Californio lands; the growth of cities; and statehood.
5. Frémont helped make maps of the Oregon Trail and wrote reports; these were useful to people moving west.
6. four
7. Answers might describe the opportunities to be found in boomtowns, including new business opportunities and little regulation.

Writing Rubric

4	The entry is clearly stated and shows considerable creative effort; the information is based accurately on facts; the writing is mechanically correct.
3	The entry is generally clear and shows creative effort; the information is mainly based on facts; most of the writing is mechanically correct.
2	The entry is somewhat clear; some information is based accurately on fact; the writing is mechanically correct in places.
1	The entry is not clear; the facts are missing or inaccurate; the writing has many errors in mechanics.

Study Guide/Homework

Vocabulary and Study Guide

Vocabulary

If you do not know a word's meaning, try breaking it into smaller parts. It may contain a smaller word that you know.

Find the smaller words inside these words. Use what you know about the smaller word or words to write the meaning of the longer word. Sample answers

	New word	Words in it that I know	Word meanings that I know	What I think the word means
1.	wagon train	wagon; train	a large cart on wheels	long line of wagons
2.	forty-niner	forty; nine	four times ten	person from 1849
3.	gold rush	gold; rush	valuable mineral resource	a lot of gold at once
4.	boomtown	boom; town	a group of communities	fast-growing town

Study Guide

Read "Trails West." Then choose the correct ending to each statement below.

5. The first large group of people who traveled on the Oregon Trail were looking for
   A. a mission. (B.) good land. C. gold.
6. The people who traveled on the Mormon Trail followed
   A. ranchers. B. forty-niners. (C.) Brigham Young.

Read "The California Gold Rush." Then fill in the cause-and-effects chart below.

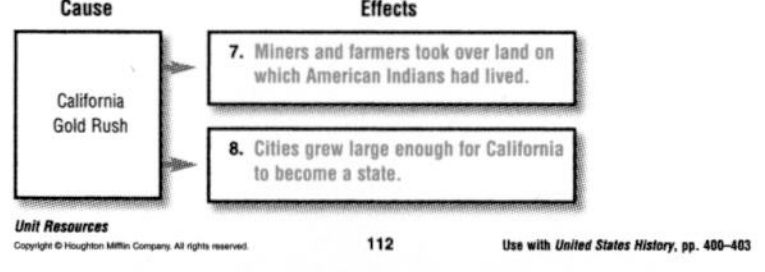

Cause: California Gold Rush

Effects:

7. Miners and farmers took over land on which American Indians had lived.
8. Cities grew large enough for California to become a state.

Unit Resources 112 Use with *United States History*, pp. 400–403

Unit Resources, p. 112

Reteach Minilesson

Use a flow chart to review some effects of the gold rush.

Gold is discovered in California.
↓
Boomtowns appear.
↓
Boomtowns disappear.
↓
California grows and changes.

www.eduplace.com/ss/hmss05/

Quick Look

Connect to the Core Lesson In Core Lesson 4, students read about some of the early travelers to the West and the trails they followed. In this Extend Lesson, students can learn some details about traveling in a covered wagon.

History

Wagons West!

There wasn't much room in a covered wagon for passengers. People packed as many belongings as they could for their new homes. They brought quilts and bedding, tools, lanterns, and staple foods—flour, sugar, salt, dried beef, rice, and coffee, for example. Water was stored in large wooden barrels, which were refilled along the way.

Wagons were so crammed with supplies that pioneers and their children might have to walk alongside or behind their wagons. In the photograph, the people are walking the Mormon Trail the way their pioneer ancestors did. They might be singing a pioneer song popular in the 1850s:

"For some must push, and some must pull
As we go marching up the hill!
So merrily on our way we go,
Until we reach the Valley, O!"

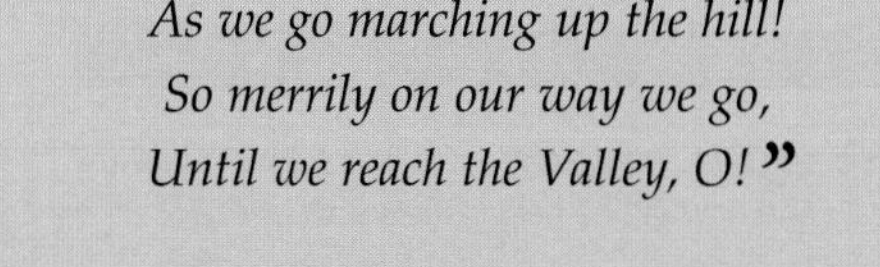

① Household Goods

② Treasures

① Household Goods
Everyday items such as candles, scissors, and medicines were brought along for emergencies.

② Treasures
Dishes, books, games, and toys were reminders of home. If they made the wagon too heavy, they had to be left behind.

③ Pioneer Kitchens
When the wagons stopped for meals, pioneers built a cooking fire and unpacked the kettle, skillet, and other wares for making food.

④ Tools
Wagon repairs were often needed, and pioneers also needed tools for building their new homes and barns.

1 Teach the Extend Lesson

Connect to the Big Idea

Expansion of the Nation Over time, the United States has grown and developed in its physical space, democratic institutions, and economic opportunities for its citizens. The history of westward expansion and settlement includes the stories of daily challenges met by ordinary settlers.

Reaching All Learners

Extra Support

Find Details

Have students find details in the lesson that support each of the following main ideas:

- There wasn't much room in a covered wagon for passengers.
- It was expensive to get ready for the journey in a covered wagon.
- Everyday life in a covered wagon was challenging.

Verbal-linguistic

On Level

Make a List

- Have students make a things-to-do list of tasks for pioneers to complete before the day they leave on their journey west by covered wagon.
- Lists can include things to pack, things to give away, and good-byes.

Visual-spatial

Challenge

Rank Items by Importance

- Ask students to make a list of items mentioned in this lesson that pioneers carried in their wagons.
- Then have students rank them in order of importance.
- Invite students to share their lists and their reasoning with the class.

Logical-mathematical

HISTORY

③ Pioneer Kitchens

④ Tools

Activities

1. **EXPLORE IT** Look at the items in the painting. What else would people need on a long journey across the country?
2. **WRITE A SCHEDULE** Think about a 24-hour period on a wagon train. What would people do? How many times would they pack and unpack? Write a schedule for a typical day on the trail.

405

2 Leveled Activities

1 Explore It *For Extra Support*
Sample answer: People would need clothing for different types of weather and sturdy shoes or boots. They might need their farm animals for food.

2 Write a Schedule *For Challenge*

Writing Rubric

4	The schedule shows many logical daily activities; includes packing, unpacking, and other reasonable tasks; mechanics are correct.
3	The schedule shows daily activities; includes reasonable tasks; mechanics are generally correct.
2	The schedule attempts to show daily activities; includes some fairly reasonable tasks; some errors in mechanics are present.
1	The schedule does not show daily activities or is confused or illegible; few or no reasonable tasks are included; many errors in mechanics are present.

ELL

Beginning

- Have pairs of students match some of the nouns on these pages with the pictures that illustrate them.
- Students might also work together to create and enlarge idea maps for categories such as household goods and tools.

Verbal-linguistic

Math

Calculate: What Did It Weigh?

- Ask pairs of students to create weight estimates for each of the items listed in the lesson.
- Have students add their estimates to arrive at an estimate of the total weight of these items.
- Pairs can then compare their estimates and talk about how this weight might have affected speed of movement.

Logical-mathematical

Graphic Organizer

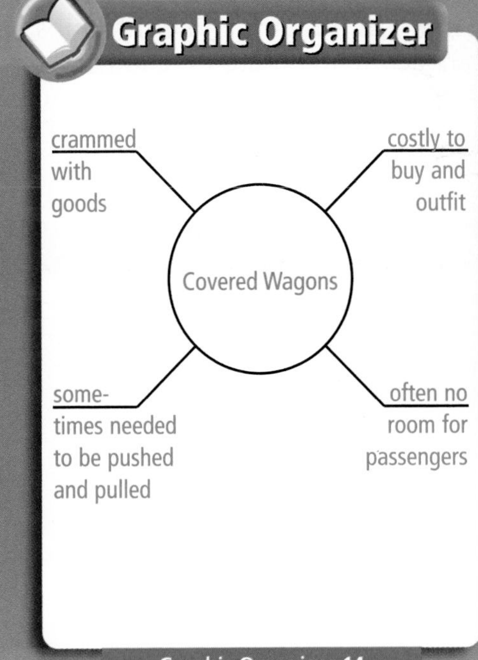

Graphic Organizer 14

Chapter Review

Tested Objectives

The lesson objective assessed by each question is shown in parentheses after the answer.

Visual Summary

1. connected the Hudson River to Lake Erie, making travel and trade easier *(Obj. U5-11)*
2. A meeting to discuss women's rights *(Obj. U5-14)*
3. The peace treaty signed in February 1848, after the Mexican War. *(Obj. U5-16)*
4. People rushed to California in 1849 to dig for gold. *(Obj. U5-18)*

Facts and Main Ideas

5. Interchangeable parts allowed more products to be made quickly and easily and at a lower cost. *(Obj. U5-13)*
6. Most immigrants worked for less money. *(Obj. U5-13)*
7. They did not like many of Mexico's laws, such as the law against slavery. *(Obj. U5-15)*
8. It started in Missouri and ended in Portland, Oregon. *(Obj. U5-17)*
9. American Indians and Californios already living there were joined by people from other places who came during the Gold Rush. *(Obj. U5-18)*

Vocabulary

10. **reform** *(Obj. U5-14)*
11. **boomtown** *(Obj. U5-18)*
12. **entrepreneur** *(Obj. U5-10)*
13. **annexation** *(Obj. U5-15)*

Chapter 11 Review and Test Prep

Visual Summary

1.–4. Write a description of each event named below.

Erie Canal, 1825

Seneca Falls, 1848

Treaty of Guadalupe, 1848

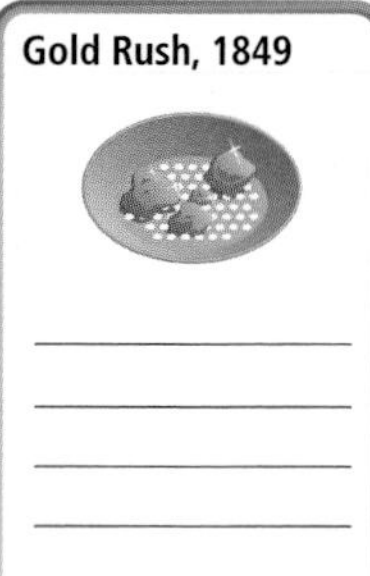

Gold Rush, 1849

Facts and Main Ideas

TEST PREP Answer each question with information from the chapter.

5. **Economics** What was the effect of interchangeable parts on the production of guns and other products?
6. **History** Why did some U. S. citizens feel that immigrants might take away their jobs?
7. **History** Why did settlers in Texas want independence from Mexico?
8. **Geography** Where did the Oregon Trail start and where did it end?
9. **Citizenship** Why did California have such a diverse population when it became a state?

Vocabulary

TEST PREP Choose the correct word from the list below to complete each sentence.

entrepreneur, p. 380
reform, p. 390
annexation, p. 395
boomtown, p. 402

10. The temperance movement was a _____ movement that tried to make life better for people.
11. San Francisco was a _____ that grew during the California Gold Rush.
12. Francis Cabot Lowell was an _____ who took the risk of starting a cotton mill.
13. People in favor of _____ wanted Texas to become part of the United States.

Reading/Language Arts Wrap-Up

Reading Strategy: Question

Review with students the steps involved when they develop questions about a passage of text.

In pairs, have students take turns modeling the process of questioning as they read.

Ask students to do a self-check: "How well did I practice questioning as I read?"

Writing Strategy

Explain to students that the process they use in questioning as they read can be used when they have to write questions.

You may wish to review questions that students wrote for the chapter. Guide students who want to revise their questions based on the discussion.

CHAPTER SUMMARY TIMELINE

1825 Erie Canal opens	1833 National Road completed	1836 Texas wins independence	1848 Seneca Falls Convention

1825 — 1830 — 1835 — 1840 — 1845 — 1850

Apply Skills

TEST PREP Reading and Thinking Skill Read the paragraph below. Then evaluate the source to answer each question.

> No one needs Robert Fulton's steamboat. The boats are ugly and dangerous. I don't think travelers care whether they can get from New York City to Albany in five or ten days. I've made the trip many times, and if a boat cannot make the trip one day, it can just wait for the winds to pick up the next day. In my opinion, we don't need steamboats at all.

14. What key word might have been used to find this source?
- **A.** Albany
- **B.** New York City
- **C.** Steamboats
- **D.** Erie Canal

15. Which of the following suggests that the article is not reliable?
- **A.** It supports facts you read in a textbook.
- **B.** It presents more opinions than facts.
- **C.** It presents many sides of an argument.
- **D.** It supports its arguments with facts.

Critical Thinking

TEST PREP Write a short paragraph to answer each question.

16. Synthesize How were the experiences of Tejanos and Californios similar?

17. Fact and Opinion Which invention discussed in this chapter was the most important? Support your opinion with facts from the chapter.

Timeline

Use the Chapter Summary Timeline above to answer the question.

18. How many years after the opening of the Erie Canal was the National Road completed?

Activities

Science Activity Think about an invention from the last 100 years. Find out more about it. Make a drawing or model to show how it works.

Writing Activity Write a persuasive essay that Susan B. Anthony or Elizabeth Cady Stanton might have written to explain her views on women's rights.

Technology
Writing Process Tips
Get help with your essay at
www.eduplace.com/kids/hmss05/

Technology

Test Generator

You can generate your own version of the chapter review by using the **Test Generator CD-ROM**.

Web Link

For more ideas, visit
www.eduplace.com/ss/hmss05/

Standards

National Standards

II b Vocabulary associated with time and timelines **II d** Sources **III h** Interaction of humans and the environment **V e** Individual beliefs and government policies **V g** Meet individual needs and promote the common good **VII a** Scarcity and choice in economic decisions **VII f** Incentives, values, traditions, and habits **VIII a** How technology has changed lives **VIII b** How science and technology have affected the environment **IX b** Conflict, cooperation, and interdependence **X e** Citizens and public policy **X f** Public policy **X h** Public policies and citizen behaviors **X j** Strengthening the "common good"

Apply Skills

14. C *(Obj. U5-12)*
15. B *(Obj. U5-12)*

Critical Thinking

16. Both Tejanos and Californios were Mexican citizens who became American citizens when the territories in which they lived became part of the U.S. *(Obj. U5-15)*

17. Sample answer: The steam locomotive was the most important because it allowed people to travel faster, and it is still used today. *(Obj. U5-10)*

Timeline

18. 8 years *(Obj. U5-11)*

Leveled Activities

HANDS ON Performance Task Rubric

4	Invention clearly depicted; drawing or model very creative; mechanics correct.
3	Invention adequately depicted; drawing or model is creative; few errors in mechanics.
2	Invention is depicted; drawing or model is fairly creative; some errors in mechanics.
1	Invention not depicted; creativity lacking; many errors in mechanics.

Writing Rubric

4	Position clearly stated and persuasive; reasons supported by information from the text; mechanics are correct.
3	Position adequately stated and mostly persuasive; most reasons supported by information from the text; few errors in mechanics.
2	Position is stated and somewhat persuasive; reasons confused or poorly supported by text information; some errors in mechanics.
1	Position not stated and not persuasive; reasons not supported; many errors in mechanics.

Unit Review

Vocabulary and Main Ideas

1. Wagons traveled on bumpy roads and could break apart, while flatboats were more comfortable. *(Obj. U5-11)*
2. She could communicate with other Indians. She could show that the Corps was peaceful. *(Obj. U5-5)*
3. He told other countries that the United States would protect the Western Hemisphere. *(Obj. U5-7)*
4. He built mills that turned raw cotton into finished cloth. *(Obj. U5-10)*
5. They couldn't speak to an audience of men, vote, work in many jobs, or own property. *(Obj. U5-13)*
6. Wagon trains kept settlers company on long trips, and they were safer than traveling alone. *(Obj. U5-1)*

Critical Thinking

7. **Sample answer:** The settler meant that because so many people were moving away from "Old America" to the West, the original thirteen colonies were changing. *(Obj. U5-1)*
8. **Sample answer:** Before the Industrial Revolution, people traveled by horse and carriages over poor dirt roads. It took a long time to get anywhere. Beginning in the 1800s, the government built new roads and canals. Steam-powered transportation, such as the steamboat and steam locomotive, also improved travel. After 1800, travel was much easier, quicker, and less expensive. *(Obj. U5-11)*

Apply Skills

9. C *(Obj. U5-3)*
10. A *(Obj. U5-3)*

UNIT 5

Review and Test Prep

Vocabulary and Main Ideas

TEST PREP Write a sentence to answer each question.

1. Why was traveling on a **flatboat** easier than traveling in a wagon in the early 1800s?
2. How did Sacagawea's skill as an **interpreter** help Lewis and Clark?
3. In what way did President Monroe change U.S. **foreign policy** in 1823?
4. What did Francis Cabot Lowell do to help New England become a center of the **textile** industry?
5. List three kinds of **injustice** women faced in the 1800s.
6. Why did settlers often travel by **wagon train** when moving west?

Critical Thinking

TEST PREP Write a short paragraph to answer each question.

7. **Infer** In the early 1800s, a British settler said, "Old America seems to be breaking up and moving westward." What did the settler mean by that?
8. **Evaluate** Explain the ways in which transportation improved during the Industrial Revolution. Describe methods of transportation used before and after 1800.

Apply Skills

TEST PREP Study Skill Use the outline below to answer each question.

I. Changes in Manufacturing
  A. Slater's Cotton-spinning mill
  B. Whitney's cotton gin
  C. Interchangable parts
  D. Mass Production
II. Changes in Transportation
  A. The National Road
  B. The Erie Canal
  C. Steam locomotives

9. Which of the following topics is the title of the outline?
   - **A.** Changes in Manufacturing
   - **B.** The National Road
   - **C.** The Industrial Revolution
   - **D.** Changes in Transportation
10. Which supporting detail could be added under the main idea "Changes in Transportation"?
    - **A.** Fulton's steamboat
    - **B.** Lowell's mill
    - **C.** Deere's steel plow
    - **D.** McCormick's reaper

Technology

Test Generator

- Use the **Test Generator CD-ROM** to create tests customized to your class.
- Access hundreds of test questions and make lesson, chapter, and unit quizzes and tests.

Web Updates

Curious about new trade book titles that you can use with the program? Visit www.eduplace.com/ss/hmss05/ to update your Unit Bibliography.

Extra Support

Act It Out

Students may benefit from choosing an event described in the unit and acting it out. They may wish to write and perform a Readers' Theater or go a step further and use props and costumes.

Unit Activity

Write a Poem about Being an American

- Brainstorm a list of details about what it means to be an American.
- Use your ideas in a poem. The first line might ask, "What does it mean to be an American?" The following lines might answer the question.
- Illustrate your poem and read it aloud.

At the Library

You may find these books at your school or public library.

The Flag Maker by Susan C. Bartoletti

A Baltimore girl helped make the flag that inspired "The Star-Spangled Banner."

Animals on the Trail with Lewis and Clark by Dorothy Henshaw Patent

Lewis and Clark identified dozens of animals on their 1804–1806 expedition.

CURRENT EVENTS

WEEKLY WR READER

Connect to Today

Create a poster about people who are trying to improve the United States today.

- Find articles about current reformers, or people who are trying to improve the United States.
- Write a summary of each article. Draw a picture to illustrate each summary.
- Arrange your summaries on a poster, and display it in your classroom.

Technology

Get information for the poster from the Weekly Reader at **www.eduplace.com/kids/hmss05/**

Read About It

Look for these Social Studies Independent Books in your classroom.

409

Unit Activity

HANDS ON Performance Task Rubric

4	Poem is well organized and shows considerable creative effort; mechanics are correct.
3	Poem is adequately organized and shows creative effort; few errors.
2	Poem is somewhat organized and shows some creative effort; some errors.
1	Poem is disorganized and shows little effort; many errors in mechanics.

WEEKLY WR READER

Unit Project

- Have students present their posters to the class. Have them discuss what each of the reformers has in common.

At the Library

- You may wish to wrap up the unit by reading aloud from one of these suggested titles or from one of the Read-Aloud selections included in the Unit Bibliography.

Read About It

- You may wish to provide students with the appropriate Leveled Social Studies Books for this unit. Turn to page 337B for teaching options.
- If students have written summaries or reviews of the Leveled Books or the books in the Unit Bibliography, you may wish to display them in the classroom.

Language Arts

Test Taking Tip

Remind students that when they encounter a passage in a text, they should read all of it before answering questions about it.

Standards

National Standards

III h Interaction of human beings and their physical environment; **V e** Tension between an individual's beliefs and government policy and laws; **VI c** How government does/does not provide for needs and wants, establish order and security, and manage conflict; **VII f** Influence of incentives, values, traditions, and habits; **VIII a** How transportation and technology have changed lives; **X e** How citizens can influence public policy; **X f** Formal and informal actors that shape public policy

Unit 6 Unit Planner

Begin with Core.
Extend for more.

The Civil War

Chapter 12 Pages 414–449

Causes of the Civil War

Core Lesson 1 pp. 416–419
Worlds Apart

Extend Lesson 1 pp. 420–421
Economics King Cotton

Skillbuilder
Compare Bar, Line, and Circle Graphs pp. 422–423

Core Lesson 2 pp. 424–427
The Struggle for Freedom

Extend Lesson 2 pp. 428–431
Literature *Stealing Freedom* by Elisa Carbone

Core Lesson 3 pp. 432–435
Compromise and Conflict

Extend Lesson 3 pp. 436–439
Readers' Theater A Troubling Law

Core Lesson 4 pp. 440–445
Civil War Begins

Extend Lesson 4 pp. 446–447
Primary Sources Blue and Gray

Chapter Review pp. 448–449

Chapter 13 Pages 450–489

The Civil War and Reconstruction

Core Lesson 1 pp. 452–457
A Nation at War

Extend Lesson 1 pp. 458–459
Primary Source The Gettysburg Address

Core Lesson 2 pp. 460–463
The Human Face of War

Extend Lesson 2 pp. 464–465
Biographies Courageous Women

Core Lesson 3 pp. 466–469
The War Ends

Extend Lesson 3 pp. 470–471
Geography A Global View, 1865

Core Lesson 4 pp. 472–477
Reconstruction

Extend Lesson 4 pp. 478–479
Economics The South After the War

Skillbuilder
Compare Primary and Secondary Sources pp. 480–481

Core Lesson 5 pp. 482–485
The Challenge of Freedom

Extend Lesson 5 pp. 486–487
History African American Education

Chapter Review pp. 488–489

Unit Review
pp. 490–491

LEVELED BOOKS

The following Social Studies Independent Books are available for extending and supporting students' social studies experience as they read the unit.

Differentiated Instruction

Extra Support

Wake Up, Young Soldier

By Michelle Laliberte

Summary: Boys who served as soldiers on both sides of the Civil War brought the conflict directly into their homes and their families.

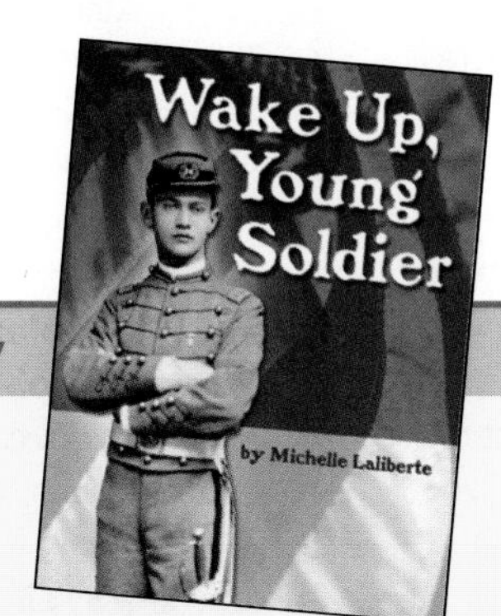

Vocabulary

Confederacy
Union
draft
casualties

Extending Understanding

Oral Language: Debate Ask students to work in pairs, with one taking the role of a boy who wants to enlist and the other taking the role of his parent who doesn't want the boy to join the army.

Independent Writing: Descriptive Letter Have students imagine they are young soldiers writing a letter home to their families describing life in the army and in battle.

Graphic Organizer: Students can use a sequence chart to keep track of the sequence of events.

1	A young man decides to enlist.
2	He suffers hardships in camp and battle.
3	His family must cope with his absence and their fears.

On Level

Mighty Ironclads and Other Amazements

By Alison Wells

Summary: The Civil War was a crisis that fueled remarkable technical innovation whose impact eventually reached well beyond the battlefield.

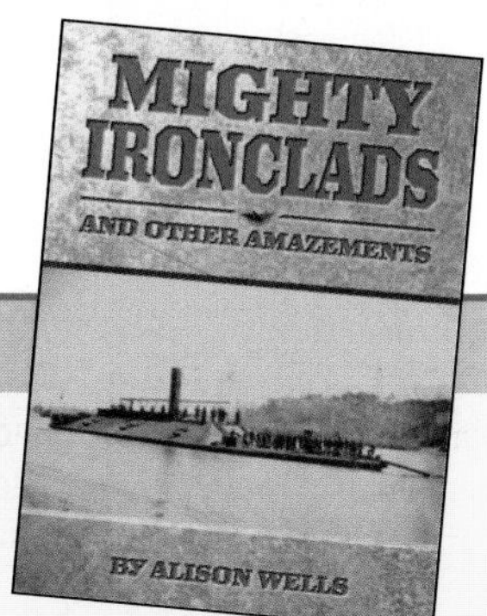

Vocabulary

telegraph
home front
civilian

Extending Understanding

Oral Language: Descriptive Speech Ask students to present one of the new technologies or devices mentioned in the book to a government war committee that might purchase it.

Independent Writing: Poster Have students create posters that advertise one of the new inventions described in the book, detailing its uses and how it works.

Graphic Organizer: Students can use a cause-and-effect diagram as they read.

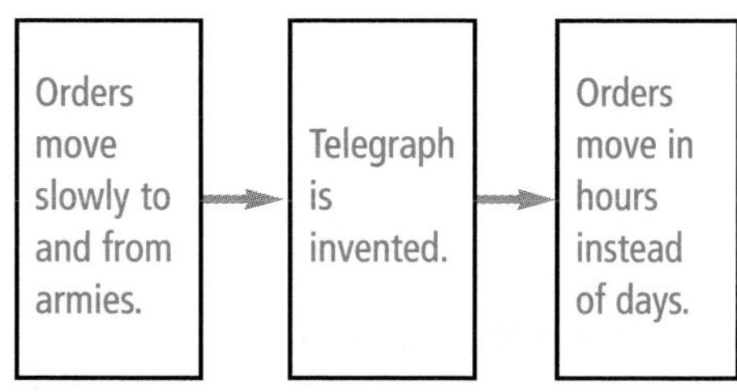

Challenge

Woman Writers: Voices from the 1800s

By Jonathan Wing

Summary: The lives and works of this group of women who lived ordinary lives but had an extraordinary impact on American literature and society.

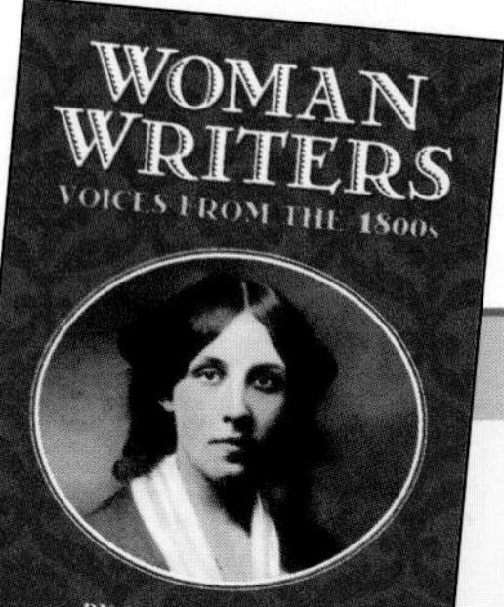

Vocabulary

abolitionist
Underground Railroad
fugitive

Extending Understanding

Oral Language: Drama Have students work in groups to act out a conversation about slavery between the three writers.

Independent Writing: Persuasive Essay Have students write about the one author whose life and work most appeals to them, describing why they think this writer is particularly important or interesting.

Graphic Organizer: Students can use a Venn diagram to organize information about the three authors.

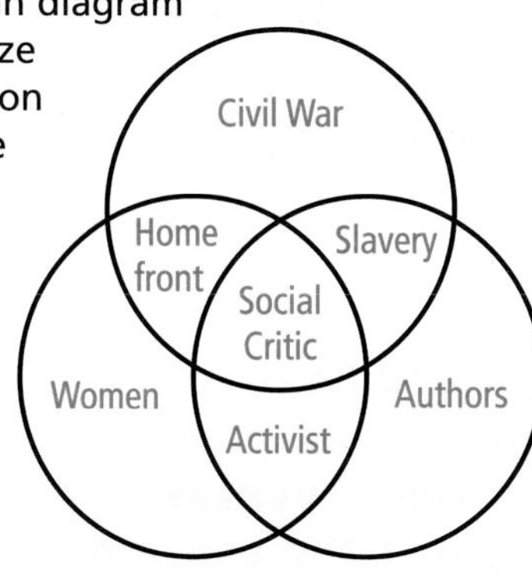

Choices for Reading

- **Extra Support/ELL** Read the selection aloud as students follow along in their books. Pause frequently and help students monitor understanding.
- **On Level** Have partners take turns reading aloud. Students can pause at the end of each page to ask each other questions and check understanding.
- **Challenge** Students can read the selection and write down any questions they have. Then they can work in small groups to answer their questions.

 Go to www.eduplace.com/ss/hmss05/ for answers to Responding questions found at the back of the books.

Bibliography

Books for Independent Reading

Social Studies Key

 Biography

 Citizenship

 Cultures

 Economics

 Geography

 History

Extra Support

The Daring Escape of Ellen Craft
by Cathy Moore
Carolrhoda, 2002
This is the true story of Ellen and William Craft's escape from slavery.

Harriet Tubman
by George Sullivan
Scholastic, 2002
Primary sources enhance this biography of Tubman. See others in the *In Their Own Words* series.

Clara Barton: Founder of the American Red Cross
by Dorothy Francis
Millbrook, 2003
Readers learn how Barton founded the American Red Cross.

Duel of the Ironclads: The Monitor vs. the Virginia
by Patrick O'Brien
Walker, 2003
On March 9, 1862, two unusual-looking warships faced each other in battle and changed naval warfare forever.

Only Passing Through: The Story of Sojourner Truth
by Anne Rockwell
Knopf, 2000
This is the story of one of the most powerful African American voices in the abolitionist movement.

On Level

Seaward Born
by Lea Wait
Simon, 2003
Michael escapes from slavery to Boston, but even in the North there is danger for an escaped slave.

Women in the Civil War
by Douglas Savage
Chelsea House, 2000
Short chapters focus on different roles filled by women in the Civil War. See others in series.

Dear Ellen Bee: A Civil War Scrapbook of Two Union Spies
by Mary E. Lyons and Muriel M. Branch
Atheneum, 2002
Based on real persons and events, this Civil War story is told through letters, newspaper clippings, documents, and photographs.

How I Found the Strong
by Margaret McMullan
Houghton, 2004
Shanks is too young to enlist, but not too young to consider the important issues of the war, including his own family's divided sympathies.

Shades of Gray
by Carolyn Reeder
Simon, 1999
Ben must rethink his definition of honor and courage when he goes to Virginia to live with an uncle who refused to fight in the war.

Challenge

Frederick Douglass: For the Great Family of Man
by Peter Burchard
Atheneum, 2003
This is an extensive biography of one of the most influential African Americans of the nineteenth century.

Lincoln: A Photobiography
by Russell Freedman
Clarion, 1987
This Newbery Medal-winning biography of Lincoln includes numerous photos and excerpts from Lincoln's own writing.

The War Within
by Carol Matas
Simon, 2001
Hannah reconsiders her view on slavery and what it is to be a Jewish Southerner.

Hear the Wind Blow
by Mary Downing Hahn
Clarion, 2003
Young Haswell Magruder uses compassion to triumph over violence during the last days of the war.

Girl in Blue
by Ann Rinaldi
Scholastic, 2001
Sarah disguises herself as a boy to join the Union army and ends up as a spy.

Social Studies Leveled Readers with lesson plans by Irene Fountas support the content of this unit.

Read Aloud and Reference

Read Aloud Books

Bound for the North Star: True Stories of Fugitive Slaves
by Dennis Brindell Fradin
Houghton, 2000

Readers learn about 12 true daring escapes from slavery.

No More! Stories and Songs of Slave Resistance
by Doreen Rappaport
Candlewick, 2002

This unique collection of stories, songs, and poetry reflects the dignity and determination of enslaved Africans.

The Boy's War
by Jim Murphy
Clarion, 1993

The author shares first-hand accounts of boys under 16 who served in both the Confederate and Union armies.

Moon Over Tennessee
by Craig Crist-Evans
Houghton, 1999

A free-verse diary format is used to relay the experiences of a 13-year-old boy who follows his Confederate father into battle.

Songs and Stories of the Civil War
by Jerry Silverman
21st Century, 2002

This illustrated songbook includes music and lyrics, as well as information about the importance of songs to soldiers and civilians.

Reference Books

The Civil War A to Z
by Norman Bolotin
Dutton, 2002

This comprehensive history has more than 130 entries of the most important people, places, and events of the Civil War.

A Three Minute Speech: Lincoln's Remarks at Gettysburg
by Jennifer Armstrong
Simon, 2003

Armstrong explains why the Gettysburg Address became one of America's most important speeches.

Outrageous Women of Civil War Times
by Mary Furbee
Wiley, 2003

Confederate spy Belle Boyd, Mary Todd Lincoln, and Sojourner Truth are some of the women discussed here.

Free and Inexpensive Materials

National Park Service Headquarters
1849 C Street NW
Washington, DC 20240
Phone: (202) 208-6843

Through the National Park Service's website, www.nps.gov, you can find information about Civil War locations that have been preserved as national parks and historic sites. Also, many state official websites contain pages concerning state and local history of the Civil War.

MULTIMEDIA RESOURCES

PROGRAM RESOURCES

Unit Video
Audio Student's Book with Primary Sources and Songs MP3/CD
Lesson Planner and Teacher Resource CD-ROM
Test Generator CD-ROM
eBook
eBook, Teacher's Edition
Transparencies: Big Idea & Skillbuilder, Interactive
Almanac Map & Graph Practice
Primary Sources Plus: Document-Based Questions
Research and Writing Projects
Bringing Social Studies Alive
Family Newsletter
GeoNet

CD-ROM

The Civil War. National Geographic

United and Divided. Creative Teaching Press

VIDEOCASSETTES

A Picture of Freedom, *Kathryn Lasky.* Weston Woods

Just a Few Words, Mr. Lincoln, *Jean Fritz.* Weston Woods

The Civil War: Why, Who, What & When? Library Video

Underground Railroad. History Channel

A History of Slavery in America, Schlessinger

AUDIOCASSETTES

Across Five Aprils, *Irene Hunt.* Audio Bookshelf

Soldier's Heart, *Gary Paulsen.* Listening Library

Bull Run, *Paul Fleischman.* Audio Bookshelf

Assessment Options

You are the best evaluator of your students' progress and attainments. To help you in this task, Houghton Mifflin Social Studies provides you with a variety of assessment tools.

Classroom-Based Assessment

Written and Oral Assessment

In the student book:

Lesson Reviews appear at the end of each lesson.
Chapter Reviews appear on pp. 448–449, 488–489.
Unit Reviews appear on pp. 490–491.

In the *Assessment Options* ancillary:

Lesson Tests appear for all lessons.
Chapter Tests appear for all chapters.
Unit Tests appear for all units.

Technology:

Test Generator provides even more assessment options.

Informal, Continuous Assessment

Comprehension

In the student book:

Review questions appear at the end of each section.

In the teacher's edition:

"Talk About It" questions monitor student comprehension.
Tested Objectives appear at the beginning and end of each lesson.

In the student practice book:

Study Guide pages aid student comprehension.

Reading

In the teacher's edition:

Reading Strategy is featured in every chapter.

Thinking

In the student book:

Critical Thinking questions teach higher-order thinking skills.

In the teacher's edition:

"Think Alouds" let you model thinking critically for your students.

In the *Assessment Options* ancillary:

Observation Checklists give you another option for assessment.

HANDS ON Rubric for Unit 6 Performance Assessment

Score	Description
4	Debate shows clear understanding of conflict and relative strengths; refers to numerous events; structure is excellent.
3	Debate shows satisfactory understanding of conflict and relative strengths; refers to several events; structure is good.
2	Debate shows partial understanding of conflict and relative strengths; refers to one or two events; structure lacks clear beginning, middle, or conclusion.
1	Debate shows little or no understanding of conflict and relative strengths; refers to no events; structure is poor and/or confusing.

In *Assessment Options*, p. 141

Standardized Test Practice

In the student book:

Lesson Review/Test Prep appears at the end of each lesson.
Chapter Review/Test Prep appears at the end of each chapter.
Unit Review/Test Prep appears at the end of each unit.

In the *Assessment Options* ancillary:

Lesson Tests for all lessons.
Chapter Tests for all chapters.
Unit Test for all units.

Technology:

 **Test Generator** provides even more assessment options.

Student Self-Assessment

In the student book:

Hands-On Activities appear in each chapter.
Writing Activities appear in each chapter.

In the Unit Resources:

Reading Skill/Strategy pages give students the chance to practice the skills and strategies of each lesson and chapter.
Vocabulary Review/Study Guide pages provide an opportunity for self-challenge or review.

In the *Assessment Options* ancillary:

Self-Assessment Checklists

Unit 6 Test

Standard Test

TEST PREP

Unit 6 Test

Test Your Knowledge

Circle the letter of the best answer.

1. Who was elected President of the Confederate States of America in 1861? Obj. U6–9
   - A. Thomas Jefferson
   - **(B.)** Jefferson Davis
   - C. Andrew Jackson
   - D. Abraham Lincoln

2. What important event took place at Appomattox Court House in 1865? Obj. U6–16
   - F. General Sherman began his March to the Sea.
   - G. Abraham Lincoln was assassinated.
   - H. Southern states voted to secede.
   - **(J.)** General Lee surrendered to General Grant.

3. What did it mean if a state had *popular sovereignty?* Obj. U6–6
   - A. The state must allow slavery for its citizens.
   - B. The federal government would make decisions about whether or not slavery should be allowed in the state.
   - **(C.)** The state would make its own decisions about whether or not to allow slavery.
   - D. The state would not allow slavery for any of its citizens.

4. Why did Jim Crow laws harm African Americans? Obj. U6–21
   - **(F.)** They enforced the segregation of African Americans from other Americans.
   - G. They forced African Americans to become successful sharecroppers.
   - H. They began the period known as Reconstruction.
   - J. They required federal troops to leave the South.

5. What was the purpose of the Underground Railroad? Obj. U6–5
   - A. It helped capture runaway slaves.
   - B. It helped abolish slavery.
   - **(C.)** It helped enslaved people escape.
   - D. It helped return fugitives to their owners.

6. What is one advantage the North had during the Civil War? Obj. U5–11
   - F. Most of the fighting took place in the North.
   - **(G.)** The North had more factories for making weapons and supplies.
   - H. The North had an excellent military leader in Robert E. Lee.
   - J. The North had help from Britain.

Standard Test

TEST PREP

Test the Skills: Compare Bar, Line, and Circle Graphs; Compare Primary and Secondary Sources

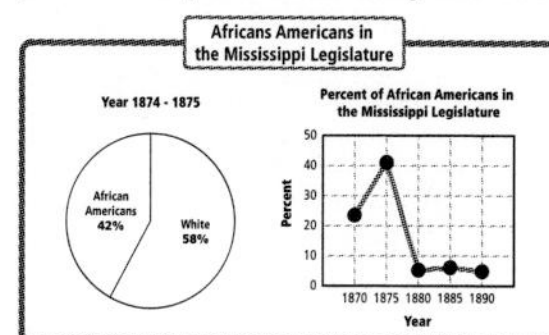

Use the graphs to answer the questions below.

7. How is the information in the two graphs similar? How is it different? Obj. U6–3
   Both graphs show data about the percent of African Americans in the Mississippi legislature; circle graph shows only 1874–1875; bar graph shows 1870–1890.

8. What does the bar graph show about African Americans in the Mississippi legislature from 1875 to 1890? Obj. U6–3
   The number decreased significantly after 1875.

Read the passage. Then answer the questions below.

> "I wish to speak. . . not as a Massachusetts man, nor as a Northern man, but as an American. . . . I speak today for the preservation of the Union."
>
> —Senator Daniel Webster of Massachusetts speaking to Congress in 1850

9. Is the text shown above a primary or a secondary source? Obj. U6–19
   primary source

10. Name one characteristic of a primary source and one characteristic of a secondary source. Obj. U6–19
    Sample answer: A primary source is written by someone who was at the event. A secondary source is written by someone who did not witness the event.

Standard Test

TEST PREP

Apply Your Knowledge and Skills

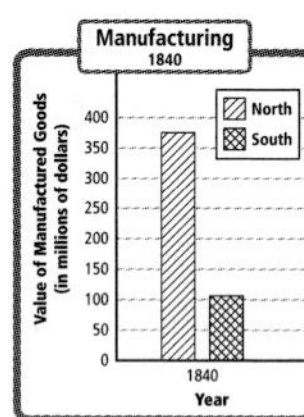

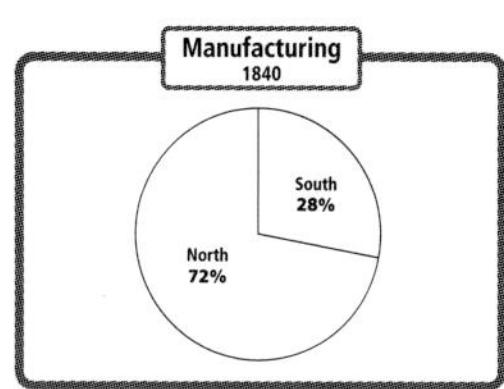

> In the early 1800s, the economies of the North and the South became increasingly different. By 1940, the North was relying more and more on factories to produce goods. Meanwhile, the South remained a farming society, mainly growing crops and raising animals.

11. What tells you that the passage above is a secondary source? Obj. U6–19
    - **(A.)** It provides an overview or summary.
    - B. It contains information that is inaccurate or outdated.
    - C. It includes the words *I* or *my*.
    - D. It gives firsthand information.

12. Based on the graphs and passage, which of the following statements is true? Obj. U6–3
    - F. The South earned more money from manufactured goods than the North.
    - **(G.)** The North earned more money from manufactured goods than the South.
    - H. The North and South manufactured the same amount of goods.
    - J. More manufacturing was done in the South.

13. Write a brief essay about how manufacturing may have been an advantage to the North during the Civil War. Write your essay on a separate sheet of paper. Obj. U6–10
    Essays may refer to factories making weapons, the economy not depending on crops, and how the North could withhold products from the South during the war.

Standard Test

TEST PREP

Apply the Reading Skills and Strategies

> On July 1, 1863, General Lee decided to attack the Union army near Gettysburg, Pennsylvania. For two days, the armies battled back and forth. On the third day, Lee ordered a final attack. Fourteen thousand Confederate soldiers charged across open fields towards the Union army. The Union soldiers stopped the attack with rifle and cannon fire. About half of the Confederate soldiers were killed or wounded. Lee's weakened army had to retreat. The Union army had won an important victory! It was the turning point of the war.

Reading Skills

Use the passage above to answer each question.

14. **Cause and Effect** What caused the war to turn in favor of the Union in July 1863? Obj. U6–16
    the Union army's victory at Gettysburg

15. **Draw Conclusions** Draw a conclusion about how the surviving Confederate soldiers might have felt after the Battle of Gettysburg. Give details from the passage that support your conclusion. Obj. U6–16
    Sample answer: The soldiers may have felt discouraged because they had to retreat and give the Union army an important victory or angry because so many of their fellow soldiers were killed or wounded.

Reading Strategy: Summarize

16. Write a short summary of the passage. Obj. U6–16
    Sample answer: General Lee and the Confederate army attacked the Union army at Gettysburg on July 1, 1863. Half of the Confederate soldiers were wounded or lost their lives. The Confederate army had to retreat. The Union's victory was a turning point in the war.

Reaching All Learners

Extra Support

Make a Cause-and-Effect Flow Chart

Pairs	20 minutes
Objective	To identify causes and effects
Materials	Paper, markers

- Have each partner select a major event from Unit 6 and construct a three-part flow chart with the event at the center. Students then may add to the chart one or more causes and one or more effects. Have partners display their flow charts and explain to the class how the items in their cause-and-effect chains are linked.

Verbal-linguistic

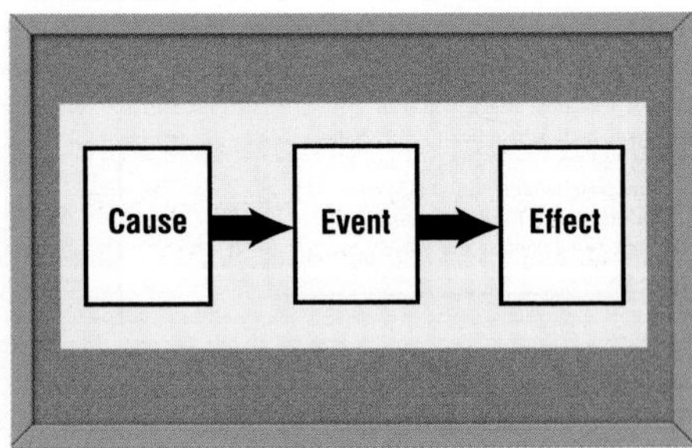

Challenge

Display a Range of Opinion

Groups	25 minutes
Objective	To summarize views on Civil War and Reconstruction
Materials	Poster paper, markers, crayons

- Have small groups create a bulletin board displaying a range of opinions on slavery, states' rights, the Civil War, and Reconstruction. Each group should select one to three historical figures and post simple statements expressing their views. Remind students to write legibly and in large letters. Groups may include an illustration or other visual symbol with the printed statement.

Visual-spatial; verbal-linguistic

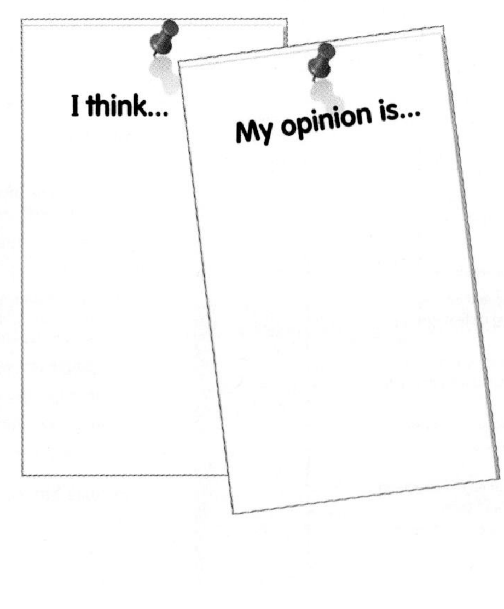

ELL

Sort and Match Key Terms

Groups	25 minutes
Objective	To sort and match key Civil War terms
Materials	Outline maps, index cards with key phrases, cloze sentences and lists of key terms

Beginning
Give students two outline maps, one for Union states and another for Confederate states. Then give students index cards with printed phrases such as North, South, factories, plantations, slavery, no slavery, won, lost. Have students sort the cards into two stacks and place each stack with the correct map.

Intermediate/Advanced
Give students a list of terms from which to choose, then read aloud a summary similar to the one below, calling on them to fill in blanks. The North had many *industries* and the South had many large farms called *plantations*. Plantation owners used *enslaved people* to work their land. The North and South argued. The South tried to *secede* from the Union and become its own country—the *Confederacy*. The Union and the Confederacy fought a war called the *Civil War*. The Union won. After the war, the United States ended *slavery*.

Verbal-linguistic; visual-spatial

Language Arts

Write a Summary

Singles	20 minutes
Objective	To describe the South before and after the Civil War
Materials	Paper, pencils

- Ask students to write two paragraphs. One paragraph should summarize what life was like in the South before the Civil War. The other paragraph should summarize what life was like after the war.
- Paragraphs should include main ideas and supporting details from the unit about Southern industry, resources, and population.

Verbal-linguistic

Math

Make a Circle Graph

Pairs	25 minutes
Objective	To make a circle graph of Civil War states
Materials	Paper or graph paper, rulers, pencils, colored pencils

- Remind students that during the Civil War, there were free Union states, Confederate slave states, and border states, which were Union slave states.
- Write the following data from the unit on the board:
  Union states: 20
  Confederate states: 11
  Border states: 4
- Ask students to use the data to calculate the total number of Civil War states. 35
- What fraction of Civil War states were slave states? $\frac{3}{7}$
- What fraction of Civil War states were free states? $\frac{4}{7}$
- Ask students to show their answers in a circle graph.

Logical-mathematical

Art

Memorialize Civil War Heroes

Singles	25 minutes
Objective	To plan a memorial for a Civil War hero
Materials	Paper or poster paper, pencils, markers or crayons

- Explain that a memorial honoring a person or event can take many forms, for example, a building, garden, statue, stone slab, or fountain.
- Have students design a memorial to someone who lived during the Civil War. They can pick a famous person or unknowns, such as travelers on the Underground Railroad or women who ran farms while the men were away. Students should create a model, diagram, or sketch for a memorial that includes wording telling whom they are honoring and why.

Visual-spatial

Travelers on the Underground Railroad

- Memorial fountain?
- Gardens along travel route?

Begin the Unit

Unit Quick Look

Chapter 12 describes the conflict within the United States over slavery, the election of Abraham Lincoln, and the secession of southern states.

Chapter 13 discusses the causes of the Civil War, its major battles, the end of the war, and the period of Reconstruction.

Introduce the Big Idea

Citizenship The United States has had many leaders who have guided citizens through difficult times. Courage, perseverance, compassion, and wisdom are some of the traits of an effective leader. Ask students how they think Harriet Tubman, Abraham Lincoln, and Booker T. Washington embodied the traits of good leaders.

Explain that this unit will tell about the leaders who guided the nation through the challenge of ending slavery.

Primary Sources

Ask a student to read the quote by Abraham Lincoln on page 410. Ask students what they think Lincoln's words mean. Make a list of their responses on the board.

Ask students what Lincoln's speech might have meant to a person in the 1800s. Would people have the same response to a President who said these words today?

UNIT 6

The Civil War

The Big Idea

What makes a good leader?

In 1865, Abraham Lincoln said that the country should act,

"With malice toward none, with charity for all . . ."

Harriet Tubman
1820?–1913

Why would someone risk her life over and over again? Tubman knew what slavery was like, and she wanted to help others to reach freedom, as she had.
page 427

Technology

Motivate and Build Background

You may wish to show the Unit Video after students have discussed the Big Idea question on this page.

After viewing, ask students to **summarize** what they already know about the unit content. Ask volunteers to **predict** what else they think they will learn.

You can find more video teaching suggestions on pages R1 and R2 in the Resources Section in the back of the Teacher's Edition.

History Makers

Abraham Lincoln
1809–1865

Lincoln's election angered southern states so much that they broke away from the Union. Yet no President had ever worked as hard to keep the nation together.
page 440

Booker T. Washington
1856–1915

This teacher helped former slaves gain new skills. At his Tuskegee Institute in Alabama, students of all ages learned to make and grow the things they needed.
page 484

411

Web Link

E-Biographies

To learn more about the History Makers on these pages and in this unit, visit www.eduplace.com/kids/hmss05/

Designed to be accessed by your students, these biographies can be used for

- research projects
- Character Education
- developing students' technology skills

Correcting Misconceptions

Ask students what they know about slavery and the Civil War. Write their responses as a list on the board.

As students read the unit, return to the list periodically to see if any of their responses have been shown to be misconceptions.

Discuss why students may have thought as they did, and what they have learned.

History Makers

Harriet Tubman Harriet Tubman escaped from slavery but returned to the South 19 times to lead hundreds of enslaved people to freedom. She inspired others to make the same journey. Today, her heroism is commemorated on a U.S. postage stamp.

Abraham Lincoln President Lincoln was reelected in 1864, shortly before the end of the Civil War. The quotation on page 410 comes from his Second Inaugural Address, as he looked forward to a time of peace. The hat pictured here is similar to one he often wore.

Booker T. Washington Booker T. Washington was a former slave who fought for his own educational opportunities. When he was sixteen, he traveled 500 miles by himself to enroll in a new school for African Americans. With his own school, he wanted to provide African Americans with skills they could use to improve their lives.

Map and Graph Skills

Interpreting Maps

Talk About It

1. **Q Geography** What can you learn about the United States in 1863 from this map?
   A how the country was divided during the Civil War, the economic strengths for the North and the South, and the location of western forts, textile mills, and cotton growing areas
2. **Q Economics** What differences does the map show between the northern and southern economies?
   A The North was more industrial, while the South's economy was based more on agriculture
3. **Q Geography** What conclusions can you draw about Texas from the map?
   A While the eastern part of the state was involved in cotton production, the western part was still considered frontier at the time.

Critical Thinking

Infer Point out the states that had slavery but did not secede from the Union. Ask students why those states might have chosen to remain in the Union. Those states were closest to the Union and may have had more ties to the Union than other slave states. They might also have feared attack from the Union army.

Interpreting Timelines

Ask students if they can identify any of the images shown on the timeline. William Lloyd Garrison; Dred Scott; attack on Fort Sumter; Abraham Lincoln

UNIT 6 Almanac

The United States, 1860s

Seattle, WASHINGTON TERRITORY, Portland, Columbia R., Snake R., Fort Walla Walla, OREGON, Fort Boise, Fort Hall, Fort Benton, Fort Union, DAKOTA TERRITORY, Missouri R., Fort Pierre, Fort Randall, MINNESOTA, L. Superior, MICHIGAN, L. Michigan, WISCONSIN, IOWA, Chicago, INDIANA, ILLINOIS, St. Louis, Fort Bridger, Fort Laramie, NEBRASKA TERRITORY, Platte R., Fort Kearny, NEVADA TERRITORY, UTAH TERRITORY, COLORADO TERRITORY, Colorado R., San Francisco, CALIFORNIA, Fort Riley, KANSAS, Fort Leavenworth, MISSOURI, Bent's New Fort, Arkansas R., Fort Defiance, Santa Fe, Fort Union, NEW MEXICO TERRITORY, INDIAN TERRITORY, Fort Smith, ARKANSAS, MISSISSIPPI, Los Angeles, San Diego, Fort Yuma, Pecos R., Fort Belknap, Brazos R., LOUISIANA, TEXAS, Fort Davis, Rio Grande, New Orleans, PACIFIC OCEAN, Gulf of Mexico

Unit Preview

1830 — 1840 — 1850 — 1860

1831 Abolitionism Grows
William Lloyd Garrison publishes *The Liberator*
Chapter 12, page 425

1857 Dred Scott Decision
Slavery is legal in territories
Chapter 12, page 434

1861 Fort Sumter
Civil War begins
Chapter 12, page 445

Technology

GeoNet

To support student geography skills, you may wish to have them go to www.eduplace.com/kids/hmss05/ to play GeoNet.

Math

All Together Now

Have students use the first bar graph to estimate how much more valuable the farms in Virginia were than the farms in Massachusetts in 1860. Students should estimate that Virginia farms were worth over $200 million more than Massachusetts farms. Actual numbers are $371,761,661 (VA) – $123,255,948 (MA) = $248,505,713 (difference).

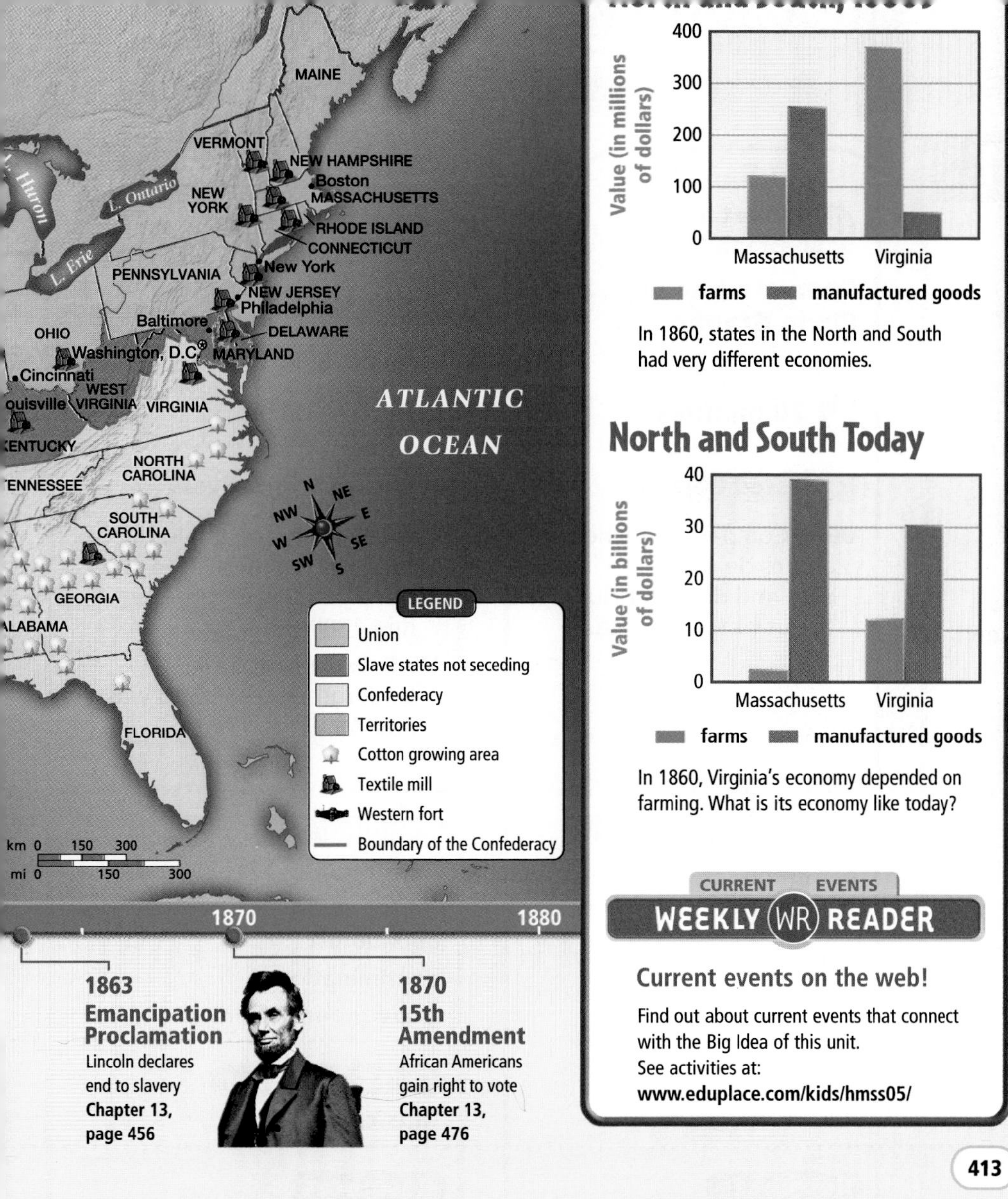

Talk About It

4 Q Economics How has the economy of Massachusetts changed since the Civil War?

A It has become even more focused on industry rather than farming.

5 Q Geography What natural advantages would farming in Virginia have over farming in Massachusetts?

A Possible answers include: Virginia has shorter and milder winters; Virginia is larger geographically, so it has more land available for farming.

Find Out More

For What it's Worth Ask students to perform library or Internet research on the economy of either Massachusetts or Virginia today. Then have students use their findings to create a bar graph showing the top three products for that state.

Home and Away Ask students to research the top manufactured product for their state. Do other states manufacture this product as well? Have students consider why different states might produce different goods.

Current Events

For information about current events related to this unit, visit www.eduplace.com/ss/hmss05/.

Web links to Weekly Reader will help students work on the Current Events Unit Project. The Unit 6 Project will involve creating a biographical poster about a modern-day leader.

As you go through the unit, have students use the web to find information for their posters.

Chapter Opener

pp. 414–415

30 minutes

Reading/Vocabulary

Chapter Reading Strategy:
Predict and Infer, p. 413F

Resources

Grade Level Resources
- Vocabulary Cards, pp. 51–58

Reaching All Learners
- Challenge Activities, p. 90

Primary Sources Plus, p. 22

Big Idea Transparency 6

Interactive Transparency 6

Text & Music Audio CD

Lesson Planner & TR CD-ROM

eBook

eTE

Core Lesson 1

Worlds Apart

Pages 416–419

40 minutes

Tested Objectives

U6-1 Analyze the effects of slavery in the South.

U6-2 Identify economic and political differences between the North and South.

Reading/Vocabulary

Reading Skill: Compare and Contrast

tariff
sectionalism
states' rights

Cross-Curricular

Math, p. 418

Resources

Unit Resources:
- Reading Skill/Strategy, p. 115
- Vocabulary/Study Guide, p. 116

Reaching All Learners:
- Lesson Summary, p. 46
- Support for Lang. Dev/.ELL, p. 143

Assessment Options:
- Lesson Test, p. 120

Extend Lesson 1

Economics

King Cotton

20–30 minutes

Pages 420–421

Focus: From the field to the factory, here's the path that cotton followed.

Skillbuilder

Chart and Graph Skill

Compare Bar, Line, and Circle Graphs

Pages 422–423

20 minutes

Tested Objective

U6-3 Compare bar, line, and circle graphs to interpret and draw conclusions about historical data.

Reading/Vocabulary

bar graph
circle graph

Resources

Unit Resources:
- Skill Practice, p. 117

Skill Transparency 12

Core Lesson 2

The Struggle for Freedom

Pages 424–427

40 minutes

Tested Objectives

U6-4 Identify the goals, methods, and leaders of the antislavery movement of the mid-1800s.

U6-5 Explain what the Underground Railroad was and how it worked.

Reading/Vocabulary

Reading Skill: Problem and Solution

abolitionist
discrimination
Underground Railroad

Cross-Curricular

Music, p. 426

Resources

Unit Resources:
- Reading Skill/Strategy, p. 118
- Vocabulary/Study Guide, p. 119

Reaching All Learners:
- Lesson Summary, p. 47
- Support for Lang. Dev./ELL, p. 144

Assessment Options:
- Lesson Test, p. 121

Extend Lesson 2

Literature

Stealing Freedom

40–50 minutes

Pages 428–431

Focus: This exciting story is based on a real girl's escape to freedom.

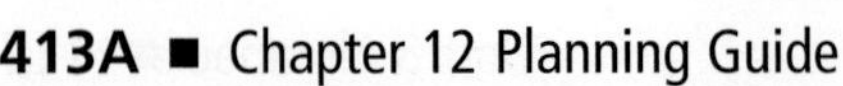

National Standards
I a Addressing human needs and concerns **II c** Stories or accounts about the past **III c** Resources, data sources, and geographic tools **III h** Interaction of human beings and the environment **V d** Internal conflicts **V e** Tension between individual beliefs and government policies and laws **V g** Meet individual needs and promote the common good **VI f** Factors that contribute to cooperation and cause disputes **VI h** Tensions between the wants and needs and fairness, equity, and justice **VII d** Economic systems **VII i** Supply, demand, and price **IX b** Conflict, cooperation, and interdependence **X e** How citizens can influence public policy **X h** Public policies and citizen behaviors **X j** How the "common good" can be strengthened

Core Lesson 3

Compromise and Conflict

Pages 432–435

 40 minutes

 **Tested Objectives**

U6-6 Describe the conflict between North and South over the spread of slavery.

U6-7 Identify events that increased tension between the North and the South in the mid-1800s.

Reading/Vocabulary

Reading Skill: Cause and Effect

slave state, free state, Union, popular sovereignty, fugitive

Cross-Curricular

Drama, p. 434

Resources

Unit Resources:
- **Reading Skill/Strategy,** p. 120
- **Vocabulary/Study Guide,** p. 121

Reaching All Learners:
- **Lesson Summary,** p. 48
- **Support for Lang. Dev./ELL,** p. 145

Assessment Options:
- **Lesson Test,** p. 122

Extend Lesson 3

Readers' Theater

A Troubling Law

40–50 minutes

Pages 436–439

Focus: Townspeople predict many problems in enforcing the Fugitive Slave Act.

Core Lesson 4

Civil War Begins

Pages 440–445

 50 minutes

Tested Objectives

U6-8 Describe Lincoln's early life, views on slavery, and role in the Republican Party.

U6-9 Explain the events that led to the secession of the Confederate states.

Reading/Vocabulary

Reading Skill: Sequence

secession, Confederacy, civil war

Cross-Curricular

Art, p. 442 **Math,** p. 444

Resources

Unit Resources:
- **Reading Skill/Strategy,** p. 122
- **Vocabulary/Study Guide,** p. 123

Reaching All Learners:
- **Lesson Summary,** p. 49
- **Support for Lang. Dev./ELL,** p. 146

Assessment Options:
- **Lesson Test,** p. 123

www.eduplace.com/ss/hmss05/

Extend Lesson 4

Primary Sources

Blue and Gray

20–30 minutes

Pages 446–447

Focus: Students compare and contrast two young Civil War soldiers.

Chapter Review

Pages 448–449

30 minutes

Resources

Assessment Options:
- Chapter 12 Test
-  Test Generator

Chapter 12 Practice Options

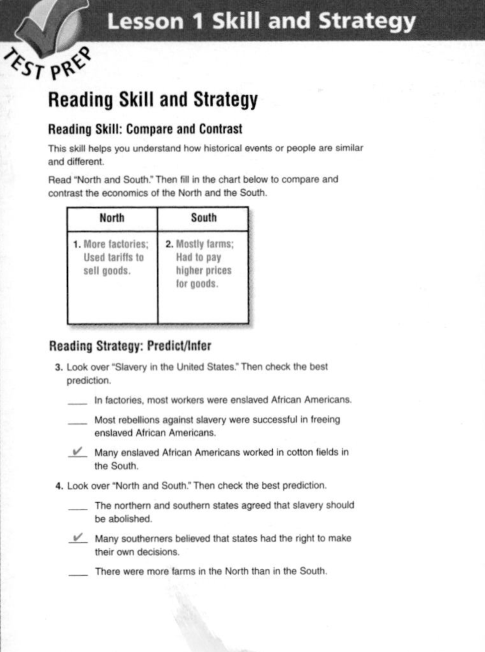

Lesson 1 Skill and Strategy

TEST PREP

Reading Skill and Strategy

Reading Skill: Compare and Contrast

This skill helps you understand how historical events or people are similar and different.

Read "North and South." Then fill in the chart below to compare and contrast the economics of the North and the South.

North	South
1. More factories; Used tariffs to sell goods.	2. Mostly farms; Had to pay higher prices for goods.

Reading Strategy: Predict/Infer

3. Look over "Slavery in the United States." Then check the best prediction.

___ In factories, most workers were enslaved African Americans.

___ Most rebellions against slavery were successful in freeing enslaved African Americans.

✓ Many enslaved African Americans worked in cotton fields in the South.

4. Look over "North and South." Then check the best prediction.

___ The northern and southern states agreed that slavery should be abolished.

✓ Many southerners believed that states had the right to make their own decisions.

___ There were more farms in the North than in the South.

Unit Resources 115 Use with *United States History*, pp. 416–419

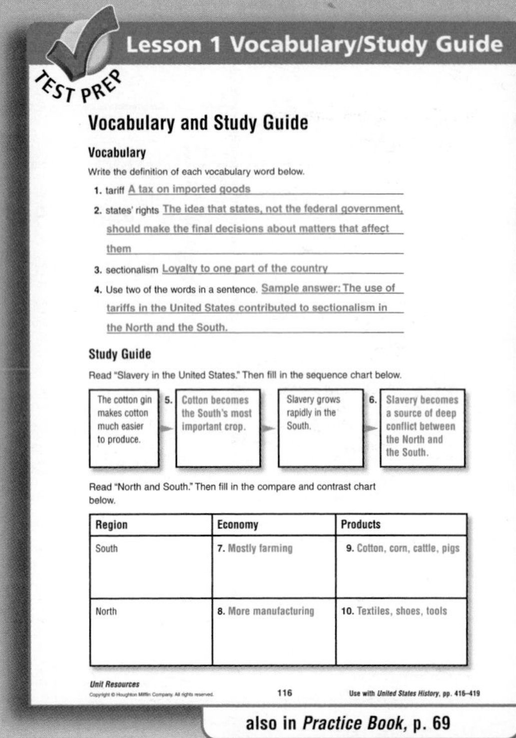

Lesson 1 Vocabulary/Study Guide

TEST PREP

Vocabulary and Study Guide

Vocabulary

Write the definition of each vocabulary word below.

1. tariff A tax on imported goods
2. states' rights The idea that states, not the federal government, should make the final decisions about matters that affect them
3. sectionalism Loyalty to one part of the country
4. Use two of the words in a sentence. Sample answer: The use of tariffs in the United States contributed to sectionalism in the North and the South.

Study Guide

Read "Slavery in the United States." Then fill in the sequence chart below.

The cotton gin makes cotton much easier to produce. → 5. Cotton becomes the South's most important crop. → Slavery grows rapidly in the South. → 6. Slavery becomes a source of deep conflict between the North and the South.

Read "North and South." Then fill in the compare and contrast chart below.

Region	Economy	Products
South	7. Mostly farming	9. Cotton, corn, cattle, pigs
North	8. More manufacturing	10. Textiles, shoes, tools

Unit Resources 116 Use with *United States History*, pp. 416–419

also in *Practice Book*, p. 69

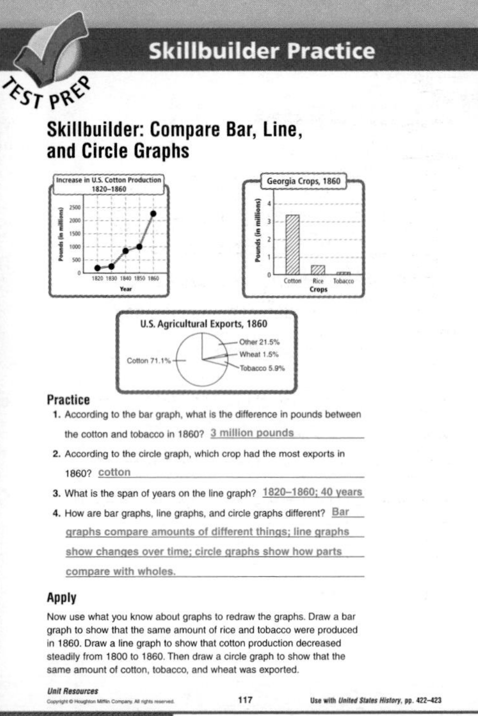

Skillbuilder Practice

TEST PREP

Skillbuilder: Compare Bar, Line, and Circle Graphs

Practice

1. According to the bar graph, what is the difference in pounds between the cotton and tobacco in 1860? 3 million pounds
2. According to the circle graph, which crop had the most exports in 1860? cotton
3. What is the span of years on the line graph? 1820–1860; 40 years
4. How are bar graphs, line graphs, and circle graphs different? Bar graphs compare amounts of different things; line graphs show changes over time; circle graphs show how parts compare with wholes.

Apply

Now use what you know about graphs to redraw the graphs. Draw a bar graph to show that the same amount of rice and tobacco were produced in 1860. Draw a line graph to show that cotton production decreased steadily from 1800 to 1860. Then draw a circle graph to show that the same amount of cotton, tobacco, and wheat was exported.

Unit Resources 117 Use with *United States History*, pp. 422–423

also in *Practice Book*, p. 70

Lesson 2 Skill and Strategy

TEST PREP

Reading Skill and Strategy

Reading Skill: Problem and Solution

This skill helps you see what problem some people faced and how they resolved it.

Read "The Struggle for Freedom." Then fill in the chart below with solutions for the problem. How did some Americans show their opposition to slavery?

Problem	Solutions
Some Americans opposed slavery.	1. Abolitionists spoke out against slavery. 2. The Underground Railroad helped enslaved people escape. 3. Free African Americans worked in the abolitionist movement.

Reading Strategy: Predict/Infer

4. Look over "The Antislavery Movement." Then check the best prediction.

✓ Many former enslaved African Americans were leading abolitionists.

___ Most Americans agreed that slavery was good for the nation's economy.

___ African Americans in the North were treated as equals.

5. Read "The Underground Railroad." Then complete the statement that you can infer.

Many abolitionists believed that Harriet Tubman Sample answer: was a heroic woman.

Unit Resources 118 Use with *United States History*, pp. 424–427

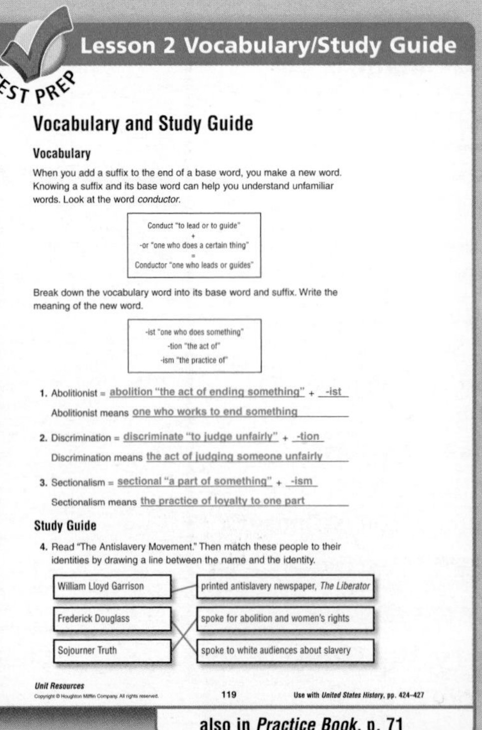

Lesson 2 Vocabulary/Study Guide

TEST PREP

Vocabulary and Study Guide

Vocabulary

When you add a suffix to the end of a base word, you make a new word. Knowing a suffix and its base word can help you understand unfamiliar words. Look at the word *conductor*.

Conduct "to lead or to guide" + -or "one who does a certain thing" = Conductor "one who leads or guides"

Break down the vocabulary word into its base word and suffix. Write the meaning of the new word.

-ist "one who does something"
-tion "the act of"
-ism "the practice of"

1. Abolitionist = abolition "the act of ending something" + -ist
   Abolitionist means one who works to end something
2. Discrimination = discriminate "to judge unfairly" + -tion
   Discrimination means the act of judging someone unfairly
3. Sectionalism = sectional "a part of something" + -ism
   Sectionalism means the practice of loyalty to one part

Study Guide

4. Read "The Antislavery Movement." Then match these people to their identities by drawing a line between the name and the identity.

William Lloyd Garrison	printed antislavery newspaper, *The Liberator*
Frederick Douglass	spoke for abolition and women's rights
Sojourner Truth	spoke to white audiences about slavery

Unit Resources 119 Use with *United States History*, pp. 424–427

also in *Practice Book*, p. 71

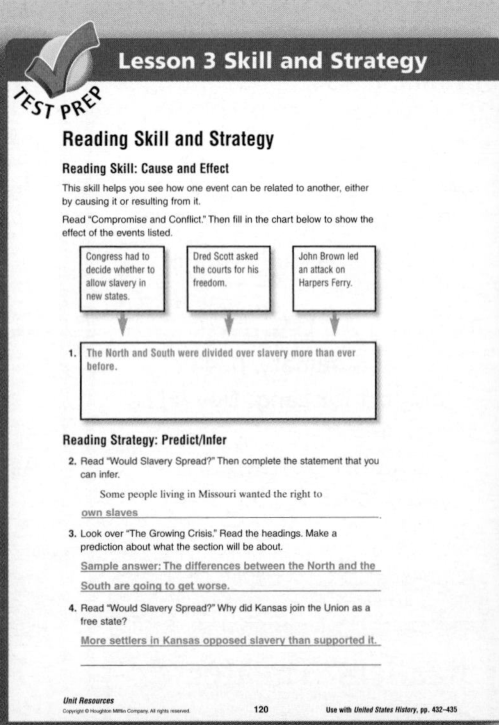

Lesson 3 Skill and Strategy

TEST PREP

Reading Skill and Strategy

Reading Skill: Cause and Effect

This skill helps you see how one event can be related to another, either by causing it or resulting from it.

Read "Compromise and Conflict." Then fill in the chart below to show the effect of the events listed.

Congress had to decide whether to allow slavery in new states. | Dred Scott asked the courts for his freedom. | John Brown led an attack on Harpers Ferry.

1. The North and South were divided over slavery more than ever before.

Reading Strategy: Predict/Infer

2. Read "Would Slavery Spread?" Then complete the statement that you can infer.

Some people living in Missouri wanted the right to own slaves

3. Look over "The Growing Crisis." Read the headings. Make a prediction about what the section will be about.

Sample answer: The differences between the North and the South are going to get worse.

4. Read "Would Slavery Spread?" Why did Kansas join the Union as a free state?

More settlers in Kansas opposed slavery than supported it.

Unit Resources 120 Use with *United States History*, pp. 432–435

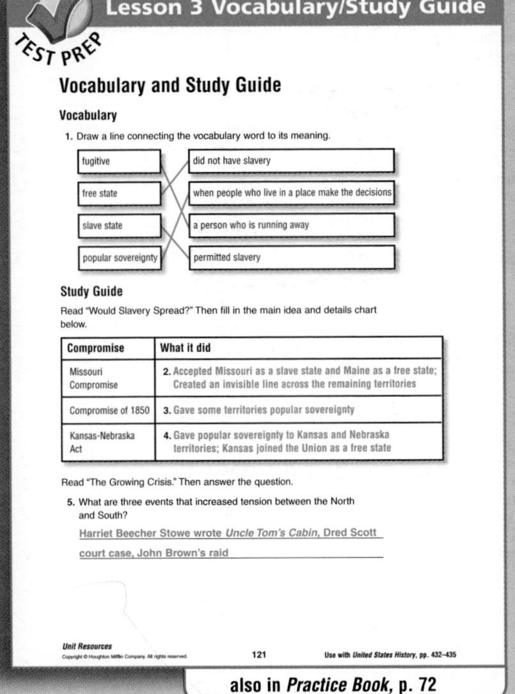
Lesson 3 Vocabulary/Study Guide

TEST PREP

Vocabulary and Study Guide

Vocabulary

1. Draw a line connecting the vocabulary word to its meaning.

fugitive	did not have slavery
free state	when people who live in a place make the decisions
slave state	a person who is running away
popular sovereignty	permitted slavery

Study Guide

Read "Would Slavery Spread?" Then fill in the main idea and details chart below.

Compromise	What it did
Missouri Compromise	2. Accepted Missouri as a slave state and Maine as a free state; Created an invisible line across the remaining territories
Compromise of 1850	3. Gave some territories popular sovereignty
Kansas-Nebraska Act	4. Gave popular sovereignty to Kansas and Nebraska territories; Kansas joined the Union as a free state

Read "The Growing Crisis." Then answer the question.

5. What are three events that increased tension between the North and South?
Harriet Beecher Stowe wrote *Uncle Tom's Cabin*, Dred Scott court case, John Brown's raid

Unit Resources
Copyright © Houghton Mifflin Company. All rights reserved. 121 Use with United States History, pp. 432–435

also in *Practice Book*, p. 72

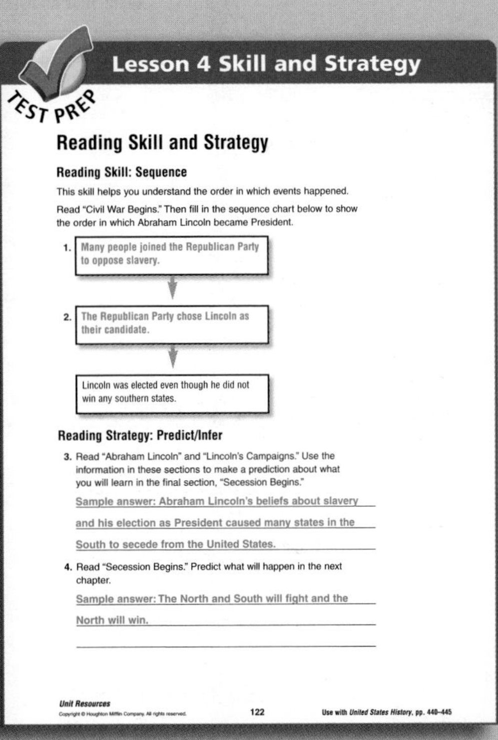
Lesson 4 Skill and Strategy

TEST PREP

Reading Skill and Strategy

Reading Skill: Sequence

This skill helps you understand the order in which events happened.

Read "Civil War Begins." Then fill in the sequence chart below to show the order in which Abraham Lincoln became President.

1. Many people joined the Republican Party to oppose slavery.
2. The Republican Party chose Lincoln as their candidate.

Lincoln was elected even though he did not win any southern states.

Reading Strategy: Predict/Infer

3. Read "Abraham Lincoln" and "Lincoln's Campaigns." Use the information in these sections to make a prediction about what you will learn in the final section, "Secession Begins."
Sample answer: Abraham Lincoln's beliefs about slavery and his election as President caused many states in the South to secede from the United States.
4. Read "Secession Begins." Predict what will happen in the next chapter.
Sample answer: The North and South will fight and the North will win.

Unit Resources
Copyright © Houghton Mifflin Company. All rights reserved. 122 Use with United States History, pp. 440–445

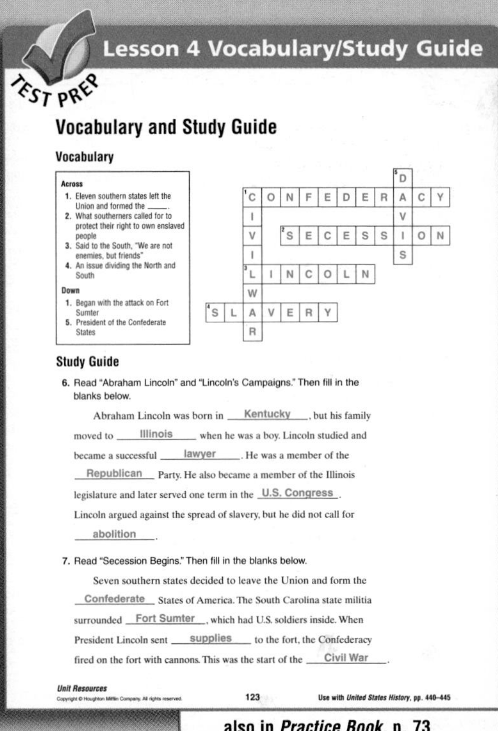
Lesson 4 Vocabulary/Study Guide

TEST PREP

Vocabulary and Study Guide

Vocabulary

Across
1. Eleven southern states left the Union and formed the ____.
2. What southerners called for to protect their right to own enslaved people
3. Said to the South, "We are not enemies, but friends"
4. An issue dividing the North and South

Down
1. Began with the attack on Fort Sumter
5. President of the Confederate States

Study Guide

6. Read "Abraham Lincoln" and "Lincoln's Campaigns." Then fill in the blanks below.

Abraham Lincoln was born in Kentucky, but his family moved to Illinois when he was a boy. Lincoln studied and became a successful lawyer. He was a member of the Republican Party. He also became a member of the Illinois legislature and later served one term in the U.S. Congress. Lincoln argued against the spread of slavery, but he did not call for abolition.

7. Read "Secession Begins." Then fill in the blanks below.

Seven southern states decided to leave the Union and form the Confederate States of America. The South Carolina state militia surrounded Fort Sumter, which had U.S. soldiers inside. When President Lincoln sent supplies to the fort, the Confederacy fired on the fort with cannons. This was the start of the Civil War.

Unit Resources
Copyright © Houghton Mifflin Company. All rights reserved. 123 Use with United States History, pp. 440–445

also in *Practice Book*, p. 73

Chapter 12 Assessment Options

Chapter 12 Test

TEST PREP

Chapter 12 Test

Test Your Knowledge

Match each word to its definition.

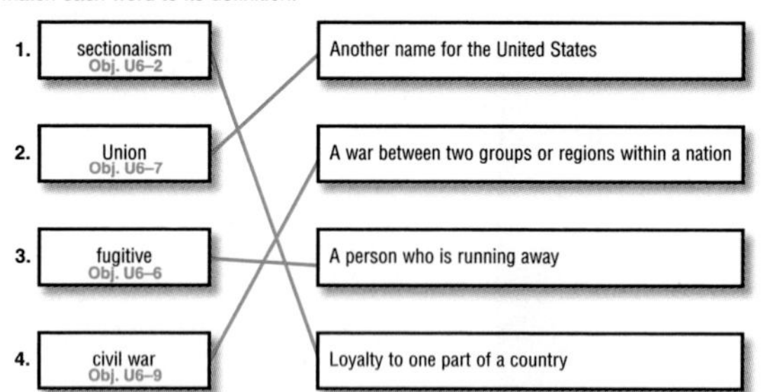

Circle the letter of the best answer.

5. Why was slavery so important to many people in the South? Obj. U6–1
   - A. Businesses wanted enslaved people to build factories.
   - B. Factory owners wanted enslaved people to build machines.
   - C. The government wanted enslaved people to pay tariffs.
   - (D.) Southern farmers wanted more enslaved people to produce cotton.
6. What did some abolitionists do to try to end slavery? Obj. U6–4
   - (F.) They printed antislavery newspapers and spoke against slavery.
   - G. They formed their own towns.
   - H. They used the Underground Railroad.
   - J. They sent enslaved people food.
7. Why were tariffs good for the North? Obj. U6–2
   - A. Tariffs made local goods more expensive than imported goods.
   - (B.) Tariffs made imported goods more expensive than local goods.
   - C. Tariffs were lower in the North than in the South.
   - D. Tariffs made imported goods easier to buy in the North.
8. What did Abraham Lincoln believe about slavery? Obj. U6–8
   - F. Slavery should spread to new territories.
   - G. All states should have slavery.
   - H. Only the North should have slavery.
   - (J.) Slavery was morally and socially wrong.

Assessment Options

Chapter 12 Test

TEST PREP

Apply Your Knowledge

> The Underground Railroad was a secret network of men and women called "conductors," who led enslaved workers to freedom. Some fled to the North and Canada, and others went south to Florida, Mexico, or the Caribbean. Harriet Tubman was the most famous conductor. After escaping, Tubman traveled between Maryland and the North 19 times to help about 300 enslaved Africans escape to freedom.

Use the passage to answer the following questions.

9. Where did enslaved people traveling south on the Underground Railroad go? Obj. U6–5
   - (A.) Florida, Mexico, and the Caribbean
   - B. Florida, Mexico, and Canada
   - C. The North and Canada
   - D. The North and the Caribbean
10. Who gave most of the money to support the Underground Railroad? Obj. U6–5
   - F. enslaved African Americans
   - (G.) free African Americans
   - H. white abolitionists in the North
   - J. white Southern abolitionists

Apply the Reading Skill: Problem and Solution

Read the passage below. Then answer the question. Obj. U6–6

> Politicians from the North and the South argued over which territories would have slavery. Congress tried to keep a balance between demands of the slave and free states. To do this, Congress passed the Missouri Compromise and the Compromise of 1850. In 1854, Congress passed the Kansas-Nebraska Act, which allowed the settlers in these territories to decide what they wanted to do about slavery.

11. Name the problem the United States had and tell how Congress tried to solve it.

    The country was divided over the issue of slavery. Congress created compromises to keep both the slave states and free states satisfied.

Assessment Options

Chapter 12 Test

TEST PREP

Test the Skill: Compare Bar, Line, and Circle Graphs

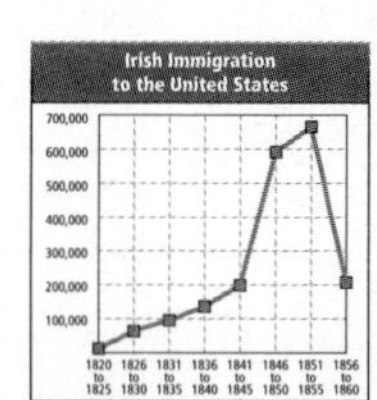

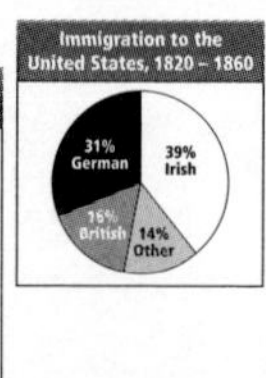

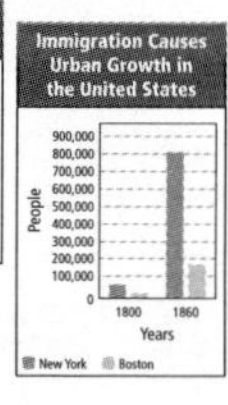

12. How is the information on the three graphs related?

    All three graphs have to do with immigration to the United States. Obj. U6–3
13. How does the information on the line graph differ from the information on the circle graph?

    Sample answer: The line graph shows only Irish immigration in exact numbers, and the circle graph shows Irish immigration as well as immigration of other groups expressed as a percentage. Obj. U6–3
14. According to the line graph, in which years did the highest number of Irish immigrants come to the United States? 1851 to 1855 Obj. U6–3

Apply the Skill

15. Write a paragraph describing immigration to the United States between1800 and 1860. In your paragraph, include data from each of the three graphs.

    Sample answer: Irish immigration steadily increased until 1855. About 39 percent of the people coming to the United States were Irish, 31 percent were German, 16 percent were British, and 14 percent were from other countries. The city of New York grew from about 50,000 people in 1800 to 800,000 in 1860 because immigrants settled there.

Assessment Options

Chapter 12 Test

TEST PREP

Think and Write

16. **Short Response:** Describe how southerners felt about the results of the election of 1860. Obj. U6–9

    Sample answer: Southerners thought Lincoln's election was a disaster; they thought that the federal government was too powerful and feared it would grow stronger.
17. **Critical Thinking: Generalize** What point of view did Congress have about slavery? Obj. U6–7

    Sample answer: Congress as a whole was not for or against slavery. Congress tried to settle the disagreement between the North and the South.
18. **Extended Response:** Write a journal entry from someone who witnessed the Lincoln-Douglas debates. What did each think about the spread of slavery? Write what each might say. Write your journal entry on a separate sheet of paper. Obj. U6–8 Entries may refer to Douglas speaking in favor of popular sovereignty and not thinking that slavery was wrong, Douglas asking why the country could not go on being split into free and slave states, Lincoln saying that slavery was a "moral, social, and political evil," and Lincoln saying that the country could not go on divided but not calling for abolition.

Self-Assessment

What important thing did I learn about slavery in the United States? Why is it important to me?

Assessment Options

You can read the following fiction selection to students before beginning the chapter.

Activate Prior Knowledge

Ask students to share what they know about the history of slavery in the United States. Explain that the Read-Aloud selection helps them imagine the experience of someone who helped enslaved people escape from the South to freedom in the North. Note that many of the people who did this work were former slaves themselves.

Preview the Chapter

Ask students to look at the map on page 426 of their books and trace the various routes that slaves could take to freedom.

Read-Aloud Vocabulary

Explain that an **abolitionist** was a person who was part of the movement to end slavery. Some abolitionists started the **Underground Railroad,** which was a series of escape routes used to help slaves reach freedom.

Preview the Reading Strategy

Predict/Infer Explain to students that the reading strategy they will use in this chapter is predicting, or guessing what will happen next based on information they already have. You may wish to use the Read Aloud to model the strategy.

Think Aloud *The character in the first paragraph helps slaves escape to freedom. It's midnight, but this person is awake, expecting something. The title is "Escape Route," so I think I'm going to hear about how this person helps a slave escape along the route in the middle of the night.*

Escape Route

It's midnight, and you're lying safe and warm in your bed. But an endless stream of late-night taps at your door and windows has taught you to sleep lightly. After all, you're an **abolitionist** and a member of the **Underground Railroad,** whose mission is to help slaves escape to freedom. You don't expect to get a good night's rest until slavery is ended.

"What's that?" you whisper, sitting up in bed. A knock on the door, or just a tree branch brushing against a window? You leap out of bed, light a candle, and creep down the stairs.

All is dark outside—perhaps you imagined the sound. You peer out the front door to be sure. And it's a good thing, too, for there you find a family of four runaway slaves from a cotton farm in the South. They're exhausted and shivering in the nighttime chill. A former runaway yourself, you know just how they feel.

"Come in, come in," you whisper. "You'll be safe here."

They enter the house quietly, making no more noise than wind across the grass. "Thank you," says the man.

You smile. "We do what we can. Come into the kitchen. I'll fix you something warm to eat. And I just might have a peppermint drop or two," you say, looking at the children.

The little boys smile up at you, their eyes bright at the thought of a treat.

"After that, you can sleep safe and sound," you add, ushering them into the kitchen.

Tomorrow you will help them continue on their journey north, to a new life.

Begin the Chapter

Quick Look

Core Lesson 1 focuses on slavery in the United States.

Core Lesson 2 describes the antislavery movement.

Core Lesson 3 discusses compromise and conflict over slavery.

Core Lesson 4 describes the beginning of the Civil War.

Vocabulary Preview

Use the vocabulary cards to preview the key vocabulary words before starting the lessons and to prepare students to understand the content of the chapter.

Vocabulary Strategy

Vocabulary strategies for this chapter:

- Word roots, pp. 416, 424
- Related words, pp. 432, 440

Vocabulary Help

Vocabulary card for secession The words *succeed* and *secede* sound similar, but have very different meanings. To secede means to leave an organization or country. Secession is the act of seceding, or leaving a country.

Vocabulary card for fugitive Fugitive slaves were slaves who ran away from their masters. The cover of *Uncle Tom's Cabin* shows a woman running away with her son. This novel portrayed the hardships of slavery through the life of Uncle Tom, a fictional character. It was the best-selling novel in the United States in the 1800s.

Chapter 12 Causes of the Civil War

Technology
e • glossary
e • word games
www.eduplace.com/kids/hmss05/

Vocabulary Preview

states' rights

John C. Calhoun favored **states' rights.** He wanted states to have more power than the federal government. **page 419**

abolitionist

An **abolitionist** was someone who fought to end slavery. Sojourner Truth gave powerful speeches about the cruelty of slavery. **page 424**

Chapter Timeline

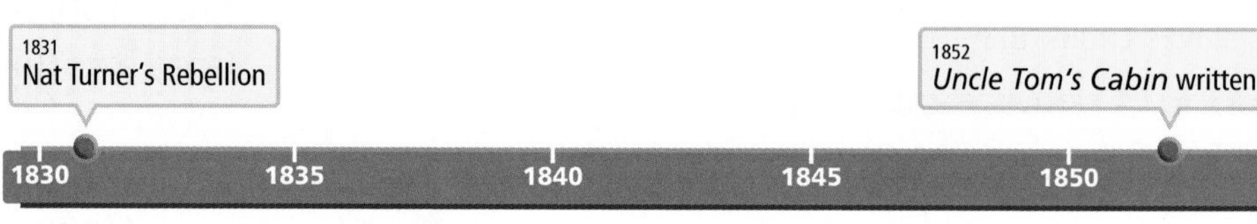

Background

Fugitive Slave Law

This law affected communities across the United States. African Americans who had lived in the same place for years were dragged away from their homes and into slavery. People who were accused of being fugitives were not allowed to have a trial by jury or to testify at their trial, and officials received more money when they ruled that a person was a fugitive rather than a free person.

Vocabulary

Use a graphic organizer to help students list two-word phrases in the chapter.

Lesson 1: states' rights, p. 416, etc.
Lesson 2: Underground Railroad, p. 424, etc.
Lesson 3: popular sovereignty, p. 433, etc.
Lesson 4: civil war, p. 445, etc.

Reading Strategy

Predict and Infer Before you read each lesson, use this strategy.

Quick Tip Look at each lesson title and the pictures. What do you think you will learn about?

fugitive

Many people believed it was wrong to return an escaped **fugitive** to slavery. Harriet Beecher Stowe wrote *Uncle Tom's Cabin* in protest over the Fugitive Slave Law. **page 434**

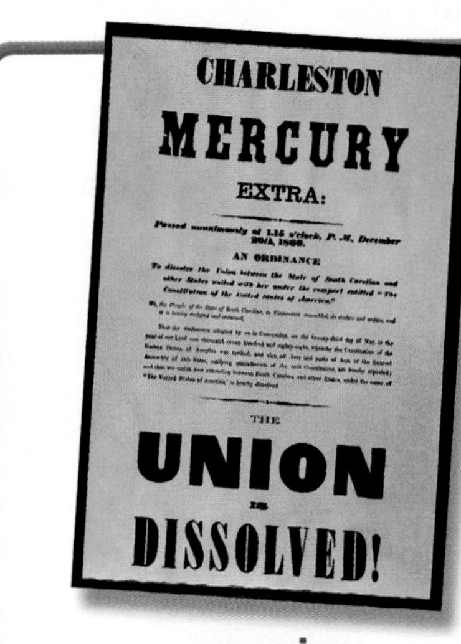

secession

After the **secession** of 11 southern states, war broke out between the North and the South. States that left the Union formed the Confederacy. **page 440**

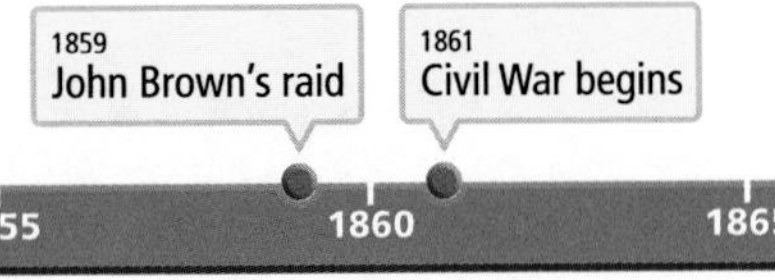

415

Leveled Practice

Extra Support

Ask students to write newspaper headlines using each vocabulary word. Verbal-linguistic

Challenge

Have students identify four words related to the vocabulary words in this opener. Ask them to work with a partner to make a cross-word puzzle using all eight words. Challenge them to write clues that define each word. Verbal-linguistic

ELL

All Proficiency Levels

- Have students work together to create an illustrated story about the abolitionists and the Underground Railroad.
- One student may write the text, and the other draw the pictures.
- Place the stories in the class reading center for other students to enjoy.

Visual-spatial

Using the Timeline

- Direct students to look at the timeline on pages 414 and 415. Point out how far Nat Turner's Rebellion is from the start of the Civil War. Ask them how many years this chapter will cover.
- Ask students if they see any words that they know on the timeline. Make a list of the words and ask students what each word means. This is also an excellent opportunity to determine what, if any, misconceptions students may hold about the material.

Reading Strategy: Predict and Infer

To predict or infer, the reader uses information that he or she has. When predicting, the reader uses that information to make an informed guess about what will happen next. When inferring, the reader uses information to "read between the lines," and draw out information that the author has not explicitly stated.

Explain to students that *predict* and *infer* are different, but related. Both are based on using knowledge at hand to determine what is not known.

To predict, a reader should ask the question, "What will happen next?"

To infer, a reader should ask the question, "Based on what I know, what can I figure out about this?"

Students can practice this reading strategy throughout this chapter, including on their Skill and Strategy pages.

Tested Objectives

U6-1 History Analyze the effects of slavery in the South.

U6-2 Economics Identify economic and political differences between the North and South.

Lesson Quick Look

This lesson describes the differences between the northern and southern states in the early 1800s.

Teaching Option: Extend Lesson 1 tells students more about the economic differences between North and South.

1 Get Set to Read

Preview Direct students to the graph on page 418. Ask them if the two economies may have affected the way the North and South viewed slavery.

Reading Skill: Compare and Contrast
North: no slavery, industrial, strong federal government; South: slavery, agricultural, strong state's rights

Build on What You Know Ask students why people who have different ideas from one another might seem as if they live in separate worlds. The North and South had very different economies. This fact and the issue of slavery became a major disagreement between the two sides.

Vocabulary

tariff *noun,* a tax charged by a government on imported goods

states' rights *noun,* the political belief in limiting the powers of federal government and preserving those of the state governments

sectionalism *noun,* loyalty to local and regional interests and customs

Core Lesson 1

Worlds Apart

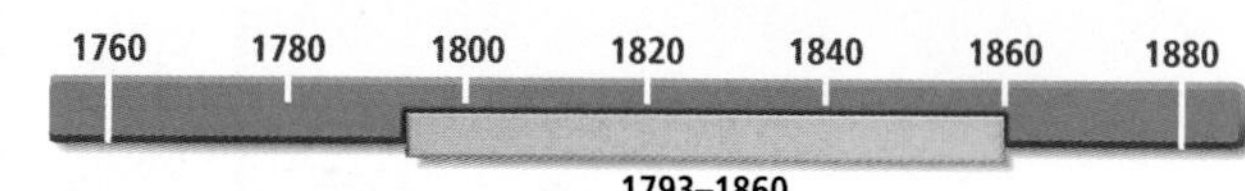

VOCABULARY

tariff
states' rights
sectionalism

Vocabulary Strategy

sectionalism

Find the word **section** in **sectionalism.** Sectionalism is loyalty to one section, or part, of a country.

READING SKILL

Compare and Contrast
What differences were there between the North and South in the early 1800s? Write them down as you read.

NORTH	SOUTH

Build on What You Know When people have very different ideas from one another, it can seem as if they live in separate worlds. In the early 1800s, the South and the North were worlds apart from each other in many ways.

Slavery in the United States

Main Idea Slavery grew in the South after the invention of the cotton gin.

Slavery had a long history in the United States. The thirteen colonies had all allowed slavery, though slaves were less common in the North than in the South. After the War for Independence, several northern states passed laws to abolish, or end, slavery. Southern states chose not to.

At the Constitutional Convention, some delegates tried to stop slavery in all states. As one delegate said, slavery did not fit with "the principles of the Revolution."

Skill and Strategy

Reading Skill and Strategy

Reading Skill: Compare and Contrast

This skill helps you understand how historical events or people are similar and different.

Read "North and South." Then fill in the chart below to compare and contrast the economics of the North and the South.

North	South
1. More factories; Used tariffs to sell goods.	2. Mostly farms; Had to pay higher prices for goods.

Reading Strategy: Predict/Infer

3. Look over "Slavery in the United States." Then check the best prediction.
   ___ In factories, most workers were enslaved African Americans.
   ___ Most rebellions against slavery were successful in freeing enslaved African Americans.
   ✓ Many enslaved African Americans worked in cotton fields in the South.
4. Look over "North and South." Then check the best prediction.
   ___ The northern and southern states agreed that slavery should be abolished.
   ✓ Many southerners believed that states had the right to make their own decisions.
   ___ There were more farms in the North than in the South.

Unit Resources

115
Use with *United States History*, pp. 416–419

Unit Resources, p. 115

Background

Leaders to Know

- Eli Whitney invented the cotton gin, a machine that separated cottonseed from fiber. Whitney's gin cleaned raw cotton faster than workers could by hand.
- Nat Turner was a preacher who led over 40 slaves in his uprising. He was captured and tried. After Turner was hanged, white mobs killed many African Americans.

The Growth of Slavery

George Mason, a slaveowner from Virginia, called slavery a "national sin." Delegates at the Continental Congress could not agree to end slavery. Many hoped that it would soon die out. However, changes in southern farming caused slavery to grow in coming years.

After the invention of the cotton gin in 1793, southern farmers wanted more enslaved people to work in their cotton fields. The cotton gin made cotton much easier to produce. At the same time, the value of cotton was rising. New textile
1 mills in Britain and New England needed more cotton, and the South could grow it.

Cotton became the South's most important crop. By 1840, the South was growing most of the world's cotton. Plantation owners used their profits to buy more land and more slaves. Slavery grew rapidly. In 1790, there were about 800,000 enslaved people in the South. By 1860, there were nearly four million.

Resistance to Slavery

Sometimes enslaved people fought against slaveowners. In Virginia in 1831, an enslaved African American named **Nat Turner** led a rebellion against slave owners. He and his followers killed 59 people before being stopped by the local militia. After Nat Turner's Rebellion, southern states passed laws to control both enslaved and free blacks. For example, black ministers were no longer allowed to preach without a white person present. By the 1850s, slaves and free blacks had fewer rights than ever. 2

Slavery became a source of deep conflict between the North and South. Many southerners argued that slavery was too important to their economy to give up. Some people in the North argued that slavery kept the country's economy from growing faster. They also believed that slavery was unfair and wrong.

REVIEW What led to the growth of slavery in the early 1800s? As cotton became the South's most important crop, plantation owners used more and more slaves to grow it.

Cotton Plantations

1 Enslaved people worked in the fields, picking cotton.

2 Cotton was packed into bales before being shipped.

3 Many plantations were near the Mississippi River, where steamboats carried the cotton south to New Orleans.

2 Teach

Slavery in the United States

Talk About It

1 **Q Economics** Why did the value of cotton grow?

A Mills in Britain and New England needed it.

2 **Q History** What did the southern states do after Nat Turner's rebellion?

A They passed laws to control both enslaved and free blacks.

Reading Strategy: Predict/Infer Ask students to think about what they have just read. Explain that they can use this information to predict what might happen next.

Think Aloud *I read that slavery became a source of conflict between the North and South. When two groups are in conflict, they sometimes talk to see if they can end the conflict peacefully. Sometimes they fight. I predict that northerners and southerners will fight if they cannot work out their differences.*

Leveled Practice

Extra Support

Ask students to **create a chart** listing the differences between the North and South. Have them chart the different ways of life, the economies, and views of government and slavery in each region. Visual-spatial

Challenge

Have students use library or Internet resources to **research** the cotton gin and how it worked. Verbal-linguistic

ELL

Beginning

Have students work in pairs to **create a word web** with *cotton* in the central circle. Then have them fill in the outer circles.

Verbal-linguistic

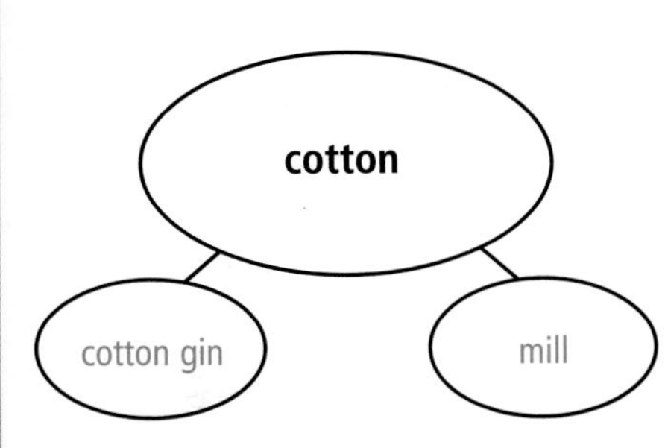

North and South

Talk About It

3 **Q Economics** What were the differences between the economies of the North and South?

A The South's economy was agricultural. The North's economy was industrial.

4 **Q Economics** Why were there fewer farmers in the North by 1860?

A Manufacturing jobs drew more people to cities where the factories were.

Vocabulary Strategy

tariff Some synonyms of *tariff* are *tax, duty,* and *levy.* All of them are fees that support a government.

states' rights Remind students that the apostrophe after *states* means "belonging to more than one." *States' rights* are rights that belong to more than one state.

sectionalism Have students find the word *section* in *sectionalism.* Explain that *sectionalism* is loyalty to one section of a country.

Critical Thinking

Cause and Effect What effect did tariffs have on the North?

Think Aloud *I know that tariffs are taxes on imported goods, and that when imported goods are more expensive, people tend to buy local goods. I think tariffs were economic incentives. They encouraged people in the North to buy more goods from their local factories and strengthened the Northern economy.*

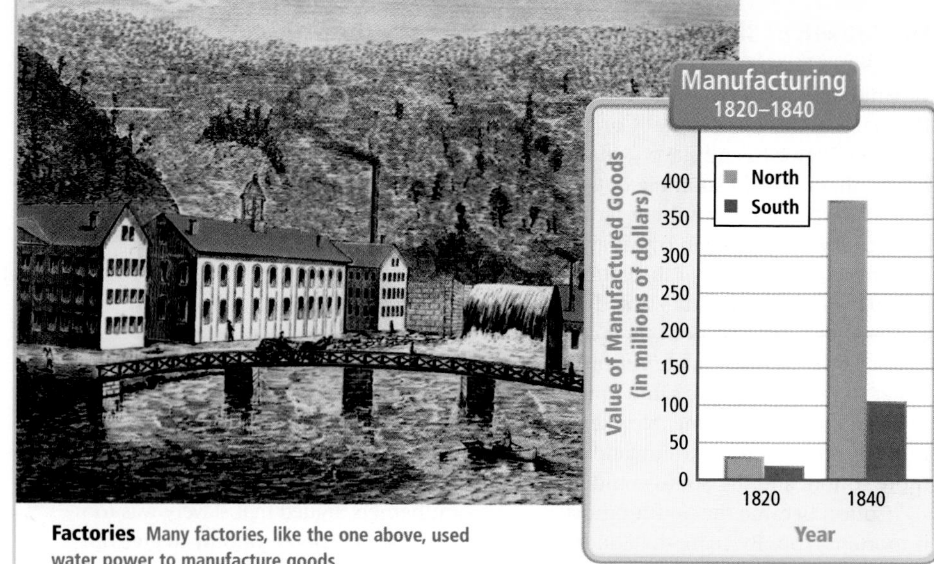

Factories Many factories, like the one above, used water power to manufacture goods.

SKILL **Reading Graphs** What was the value of goods made in the North in 1840? about $375 million

North and South

Main Idea The many differences between the North and South divided the two regions.

The North and the South had
3 different economies. The South's economy was agricultural, or mostly based on farming. Some southerners worked on large cotton plantations. Many more had small farms and grew food crops such as corn, or raised cattle and pigs. These farmers usually had only a few enslaved people or none at all.

Northern states had many farmers as
4 well, but the economy of the North was changing. Cities in the North were growing quickly and factories were being built throughout the region. In factories, people made textiles, shoes, tools, and other goods. By 1860, fewer than half of people in the North were farmers.

The Tariff

The different economies in the North and South led to disagreements between the regions about tariffs. A **tariff** is a tax on imported goods.

Between 1816 and 1832, Congress passed high tariffs on goods made outside the country. British textiles, for example, became very expensive. The only cloth most people could afford came from the mills of New England.

Congress used tariffs to help American manufacturing. Tariffs were good for northern industry, but they did not help the South, where there was less industry. Southerners, like all consumers, had to pay higher prices for manufactured goods they wanted, such as steel and cloth. When prices of these goods went up, southerners blamed it on tariffs and the North.

Math

Calculation: Multiplication

- In 1790, there were almost 800,000 enslaved people in the United States. By 1860, there were about four million. About how many more enslaved people were there in 1860? about 3,200,000 more people
- By what percent did the population increase? about 400%

Logical-mathematical

Language Arts

Write an Editorial

Have students think about what it would be like for a southern farmer after Congress has just passed another high tariff on imported goods. Ask students to write an editorial on the tariffs.

Verbal-linguistic

States' Rights

One southerner who argued against tariffs was **John C. Calhoun** of South Carolina. Calhoun was Vice President in 1828. He believed the Constitution did not allow the federal government to create tariffs. He argued for states' rights.
5 **States' rights** is the idea that states, not the federal government, should make the final decisions about matters that affect them. Calhoun believed that states had the right to veto tariffs. States' rights became a popular idea in the South.

John C. Calhoun
He became a U.S. senator after serving as Vice President. Calhoun argued for slavery and states' rights.

Disagreements over slavery, tariffs, and other economic issues increased sectionalism in the North and South. Loyalty to one part of the country is called **sectionalism.** As conflicts grew, it seemed that many people cared more about their own section of the country than for the country as a whole.

Tariffs made prices on certain goods higher.

REVIEW Why did southerners dislike tariffs?

Some thought tariffs were unconstitutional.

Lesson Summary

- Slavery grew with the demand for cotton.
- Tariffs helped the growing number of northern factories.
- The North and South argued over slavery, tariffs, and states' rights.

Why It Matters ...

The North and South were headed toward war. It began with arguments about slavery and the power of the national and state governments.

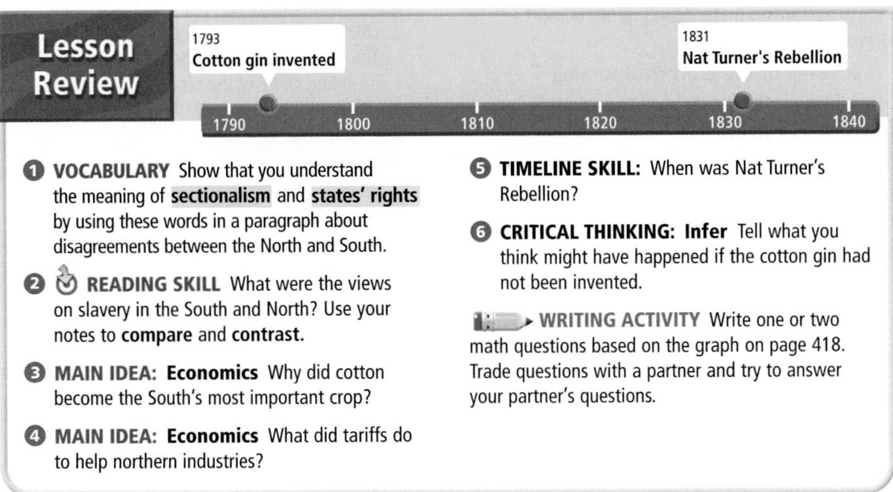

Lesson Review

1. **VOCABULARY** Show that you understand the meaning of **sectionalism** and **states' rights** by using these words in a paragraph about disagreements between the North and South.
2. **READING SKILL** What were the views on slavery in the South and North? Use your notes to **compare** and **contrast.**
3. **MAIN IDEA: Economics** Why did cotton become the South's most important crop?
4. **MAIN IDEA: Economics** What did tariffs do to help northern industries?
5. **TIMELINE SKILL:** When was Nat Turner's Rebellion?
6. **CRITICAL THINKING: Infer** Tell what you think might have happened if the cotton gin had not been invented.

WRITING ACTIVITY Write one or two math questions based on the graph on page 418. Trade questions with a partner and try to answer your partner's questions.

Study Guide/Homework

Vocabulary and Study Guide

Vocabulary

Write the definition of each vocabulary word below.

1. tariff A tax on imported goods
2. states' rights The idea that states, not the federal government, should make the final decisions about matters that affect them
3. sectionalism Loyalty to one part of the country
4. Use two of the words in a sentence. Sample answer: The use of tariffs in the United States contributed to sectionalism in the North and the South.

Study Guide

Read "Slavery in the United States." Then fill in the sequence chart below.

The cotton gin makes cotton much easier to produce. → 5. Cotton becomes the South's most important crop. → Slavery grows rapidly in the South. → 6. Slavery becomes a source of deep conflict between the North and the South.

Read "North and South." Then fill in the compare and contrast chart below.

Region	Economy	Products
South	7. Mostly farming	9. Cotton, corn, cattle, pigs
North	8. More manufacturing	10. Textiles, shoes, tools

Unit Resources 116 Use with *United States History*, pp. 416–419

Unit Resources, p. 116

Reteach Minilesson

Use a two-column chart to list the differences between the North and South.

North	South
Abolished slavery	Allowed slavery
Industrial economy	Agricultural economy
Believed in strong federal government	Believed in states' rights

Graphic Organizer 1

3 Review/Assess

Review Tested Objectives

U6-1 Slavery fueled the growth of the South's agricultural economy. Slavery became a source of conflict between different groups in the South.

U6-2 The North abolished slavery, had an industrial economy, and believed in a strong federal government. The South allowed slavery, had an agricultural economy, and believed in states' rights.

Lesson Review Answers

1. Answers should describe the differences, including each side's views of sectionalism and states' rights.
2. Answers should show how North and South differed on slavery.
3. Mills in Britain and New England needed cotton, and the South grew most of the world's cotton.
4. Tariffs made imported goods more expensive than ones produced in the North.
5. 1831
6. If the cotton gin had not been invented, cotton might not have become so important to the southern economy and slavery might not have grown in the South.

Writing Rubric

4	Two questions written and answered; shows keen understanding of graph data and lesson; mechanics are correct.
3	Two questions written and answered; shows adequate understanding of graph data and lesson; few errors in mechanics.
2	One question written and answered; shows partial understanding of graph data and lesson; some errors in mechanics.
1	No questions written or answered; does not seem to understand graph data and lesson; many errors in mechanics.

Quick Look

Connect to Core Lesson Students have just learned about the different issues that divided the North and South. In Extend Lesson 1, students will trace the journey of cotton from the South, to mills in the North, and to ports of other countries.

1 Teach the Extend Lesson

Connect to the Big Idea

Production As demand for cotton from mills in the North and Britain grew, cotton became the South's most important crop. The invention of the cotton gin made cotton easier to produce, and each improvement made in the production of cotton expanded the economies of those involved in the process.

Connect to Prior Knowledge

Ask students to look at the flow chart. Even if the captions were not visible, what predictions might students make about the steps involved in the production of cotton?

Extend Lesson 1

Economics

King Cotton

In the 1840s and 1850s, cotton was called "king." It was the most valuable crop raised in the South and an important part of the North's growing industrial economy. In some years, more than two million bales of cotton were harvested. Bales weighed about 500 pounds. All that cotton was turned into shirts, pants, jackets, and other useful products.

Each step of the process of turning cotton into clothing was done separately by workers who did only that step. This specialization made each part of the process faster. As the cotton industry became more productive, people could buy more and more cotton goods.

1 **Working in the Fields** Cotton grows in the South's fertile soil and mild climate. It is often grown on large plantations and picked by enslaved workers.

3 **Unloading at the Docks** Bales of cotton arrive in northern ports such as Boston. The North has most of the nation's mills, including some of the biggest in the world.

5 **Train Delivery** The finished cloth is loaded onto trains and shipped to buyers throughout the United States and other countries.

420 • Chapter 12

Reaching All Learners

Extra Support

Trace the Journey

- Have students use visuals by looking at the flow chart and tracing the journey cotton takes on a United States map.
- Ask students to number and describe each step in the process.

Visual-spatial

On Level

Draw a Cartoon

- Ask students to create a cartoon strip showing the production of a garment from woven cloth.
- Working in pairs, students can illustrate the panels and write captions or speech balloons.

Visual-spatial

Challenge

Make the Longest List

- Have students work in small groups. Ask each group to list as many cotton products as they can. See which group can come up with the longest list.
- Invite groups to share their lists with the class. How many different cotton products did the class list?

Verbal-linguistic

2 **Shipping North** Bundled into bales, the cotton is sent by wagon and steamboat to port cities such as New Orleans and Charleston. Then it is loaded onto ships and sent to the North and to other countries.

4 **Weaving the Thread** The cotton arrives at the mills. There, it is spun into thread and woven into cloth by women and girls working at huge spinning and weaving machines.

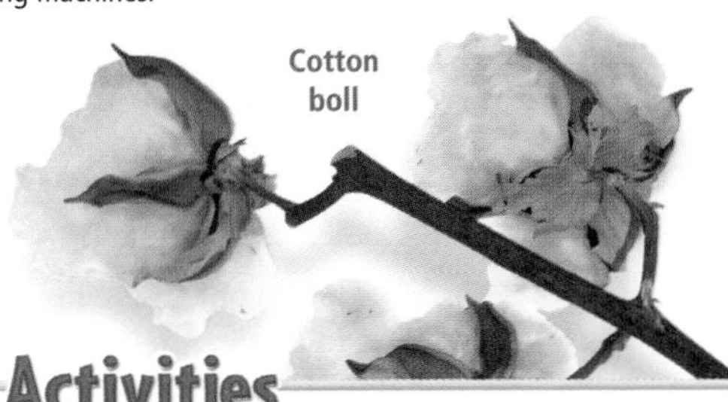

ECONOMICS

Activities

1. **DISCUSS IT** Use the pictures to compare all of the different places cotton traveled, from when it was picked to the finished cloth.
2. **REPORT IT** Where does cotton come from today? Using library resources, research cotton and write a summary of what you find out.

2 Leveled Activities

1 Discuss It *For Extra Support*
Answers should reflect each student's understanding of the lesson.

2 Report It *For Challenge*

Writing Rubric

4	Topic is clearly described; summary is well organized; mechanics are correct.
3	Topic is adequately described; summary is adequately organized; few errors in mechanics.
2	Topic is described in a confused or disorganized way; summary is somewhat organized; some errors in mechanics.
1	No topic given; summary is disorganized; many errors in mechanics.

ELL

Beginning

Ask students to create a list of five products that are made of cotton. Then have them illustrate the products on their lists.

Visual-spatial

Math

Calculate: Conversions

Have students answer the following questions.

- If each bale of cotton weighed about 500 pounds, how much did 2 million bales weigh? about 1 billion pounds
- If a ton is equal to 2,000 pounds, about how much did a cotton bale weigh in tons? About 1/4 ton
- How much did 2 million bales weigh in tons? about 500,000 tons

Logical-mathematical

Graphic Organizer

1	Cotton grows in the South.
2	Cotton is shipped to the North.
3	Cotton is unloaded at northern ports.
4	Cotton is woven into cloth at northern mills.
5	Cloth is delivered to buyers in the United States and around the world.

Graphic Organizer 15

Tested Objective

U6-3 Compare bar, line, and circle graphs to interpret and draw conclusions about historical data.

1 Teach the Skill

- Discuss with students the types of graphs they have seen. Explain that they can use different graphs to present different types of information.
- Have students sketch samples of each kind of graph on the board. Discuss what information each graph shows.
- Ask students why it might be helpful to look at more than one kind of graph about a subject they are studying.

Skillbuilder

Compare Bar, Line, and Circle Graphs

VOCABULARY
bar graph
line graph
circle graph

Graphs can give you a better understanding of historical information, such as the importance of cotton to the United States economy. Different kinds of graphs present different kinds of information.

- **Bar graphs** compare amounts of things.
- **Line graphs** show changes over time.
- **Circle graphs** illustrate how a part compares with the whole.

Together, these graphs can show overall patterns. The steps below will help you to read and describe information from these three kinds of graphs.

Learn the Skill

Step 1: Read the title and identify the kind of graph. The title tells you about the subject and purpose of each graph.

Step 2: Examine the labels. They explain the units of measurement and the type of information presented.

Step 3: Look at the information on each of the graphs. Look for increases, decreases, or sudden changes on line graphs. Compare amounts on bar graphs and the parts of the whole on circle graphs. How is the information on the three graphs related?

422 • Chapter 12

Leveled Practice

Extra Support

Have students use modeling clay or math manipulatives to present the information shown in the bar graph. Display completed models in the classroom. Visual-spatial

Challenge

Have students create bar, line, and circle graphs that convey population information about the United States. Have volunteers explain how the graphs are related. Visual-spatial

ELL

Beginning

Ask volunteers to locate different graphs in their textbook and identify them by type. Then have students discuss in small groups the subject of each graph and the information each graph presents about its topic.

Visual-spatial; verbal-linguistic

Practice the Skill

Compare the information on the bar, line, and circle graphs by answering the following questions.

1. How is the information on the three graphs related?
2. How does the information on the bar graph differ from the facts in the other two graphs?
3. On the line graph, what 10-year period had the greatest change in cotton production?
4. Based on your reading of Lesson 1 and the circle graph, what crop was exported more than any other crop in 1860? Why?

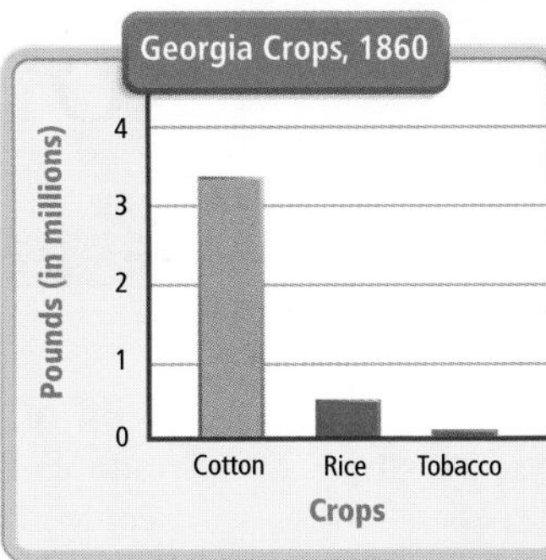

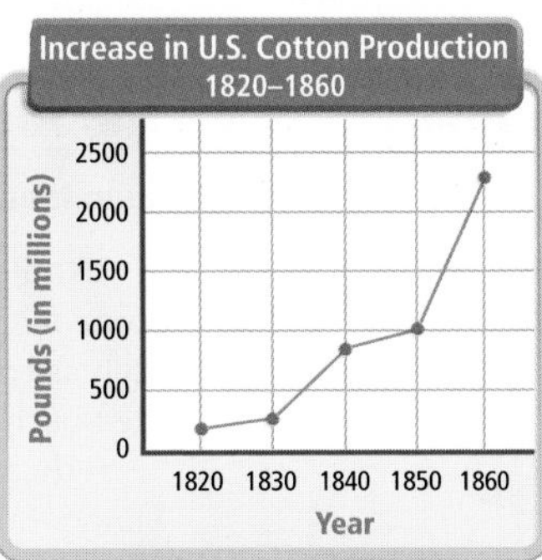

Apply the Skill

Write a paragraph describing cotton production in the United States and Georgia in 1860. In your paragraph, include data from each of the three graphs.

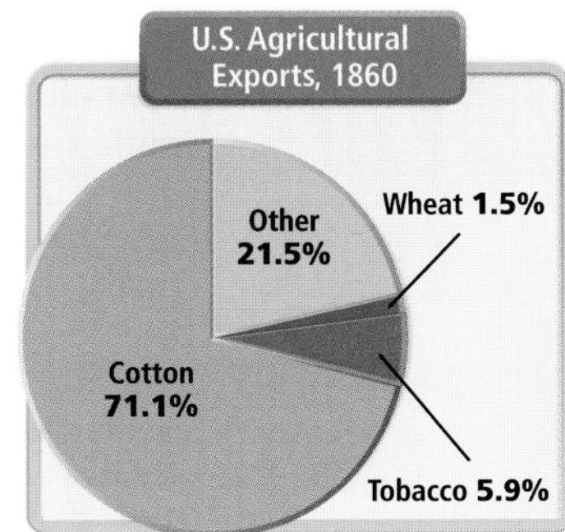

423

Skill Practice

Skillbuilder: Compare Bar, Line, and Circle Graphs

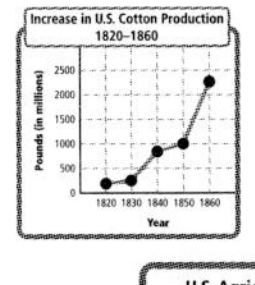

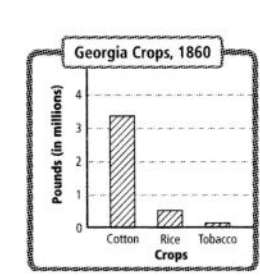

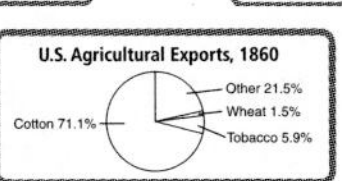

Practice

1. According to the bar graph, what is the difference in pounds between the cotton and tobacco in 1860? 3 million pounds
2. According to the circle graph, which crop had the most exports in 1860? cotton
3. What is the span of years on the line graph? 1820–1860; 40 years
4. How are bar graphs, line graphs, and circle graphs different? Bar graphs compare amounts of different things; line graphs show changes over time; circle graphs show how parts compare with wholes.

Apply

Now use what you know about graphs to redraw the graphs. Draw a bar graph to show that the same amount of rice and tobacco were produced in 1860. Draw a line graph to show that cotton production decreased steadily from 1800 to 1860. Then draw a circle graph to show that the same amount of cotton, tobacco, and wheat was exported.

Unit Resources

117 Use with *United States History*, pp. 422–423

Unit Resources, p. 117

Skill Transparency

Skillbuilder Transparency 52

Compare Bar, Line, and Circle Graphs

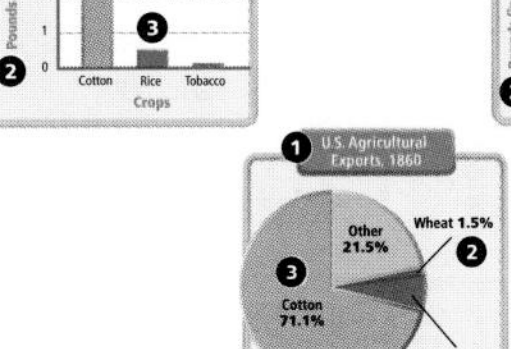

Step 1 Read the title and identify the kind of graph. The title tells you about the subject and purpose of each graph.

Step 2 Examine the labels. They explain the units of measurement and the type of information presented.

Step 3 Look at the information on each of the graphs. Look for increases, decreases, or sudden changes on line graphs. Compare amounts on bar graphs and the parts of the whole on circle graphs. How is the information on the three graphs related?

Skillbuilder Transparency

Use with *United States History*, pp. 422–423

Transparency 12

2 Practice the Skill

1. All three include information about cotton and the year 1860.
2. It focuses on one state rather than the whole United States.
3. 1850–1860
4. Cotton. The demand for cotton was greatest because it was not grown in Britain, where mills used it for producing textiles.

3 Apply the Skill

Ask students to write a paragraph describing cotton production in the United States and Georgia in 1860. When you evaluate students' paragraphs, consider:

- Did the student include information from all three graphs?
- Did the student understand the graphs correctly?
- Did the student use correct mechanics in the paragraph?

Tested Objectives

U6-4 History Identify the goals, methods, and leaders of the antislavery movement of the mid-1800s.

U6-5 History Explain what the Underground Railroad was and how it worked.

Quick Look

This lesson describes the people who worked to end slavery and the different methods they used.

Teaching Option: Extend Lesson 2 features a story about the Underground Railroad.

1 Get Set to Read

Preview Ask students to find *abolitionist* on page 424. Ask them what they think it means.

Reading Skill: Problem and Solution Solutions include writing or speaking out publicly against slavery and helping people escape slavery.

Build on What You Know Ask students to recall another conflict they have learned about in this book. What resulted from the conflict?

Vocabulary

abolitionist *noun,* an antislavery activist

discrimination *noun,* treatment of people based on a class or category rather than on individual merit

Underground Railroad *noun,* a secret system that helped runaway slaves escape to the free states or Canada

Core Lesson 2

The Struggle for Freedom

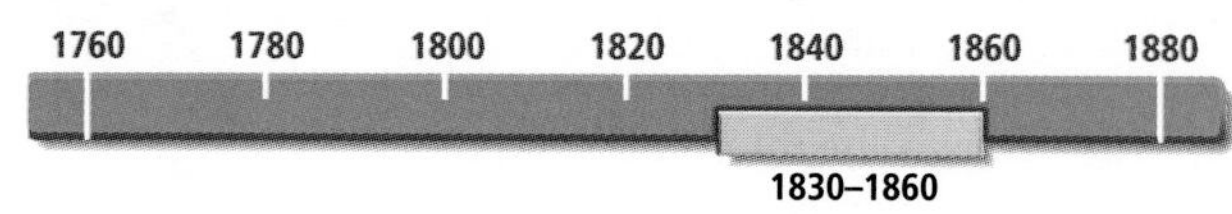

VOCABULARY

abolitionist
discrimination
Underground Railroad

Vocabulary Strategy

abolitionist

Abolitionist comes from the word **abolish**. Abolitionists were people who wanted to abolish, or end, slavery.

READING SKILL
Problem and Solution
Look for solutions abolitionists found to fight slavery.

PROBLEM	SOLUTIONS
Slavery	

Build on What You Know Think about how important freedom is to you. In the early 1800s, not all people in the United States were free. Many lived in slavery. They struggled to win freedom, with help from the antislavery movement.

The Antislavery Movement

Main Idea Groups against slavery formed in the mid-1800s.

People could not agree about the issue of slavery. Some felt that slavery was needed to grow cash crops such as cotton and tobacco. As cotton farming spread in the South, they wanted slavery to spread as well.

Other people felt it was wrong to enslave people. Many of them became abolitionists. An **abolitionist** is someone who joined the movement to abolish, or end, slavery. Most abolitionists felt that slavery went against the ideas of Christianity.

Abolitionists included people in the North and South, whites and free blacks, men and women. They 1
wrote pamphlets and traveled across the country, speaking against slavery. The abolitionist movement grew quickly in the 1830s and 1840s.

Slavery Some enslaved people had to wear tags that told where they lived and what they did.

SKILL Primary Sources What city is stamped on this tag? Charleston

Skill and Strategy

Reading Skill and Strategy

Reading Skill: Problem and Solution

This skill helps you see what problem some people faced and how they resolved it.

Read "The Struggle for Freedom." Then fill in the chart below with solutions for the problem. How did some Americans show their opposition to slavery?

Problem	Solutions
Some Americans opposed slavery.	1. Abolitionists spoke out against slavery. 2. The Underground Railroad helped enslaved people escape. 3. Free African Americans worked in the abolitionist movement.

Reading Strategy: Predict/Infer

4. Look over "The Antislavery Movement." Then check the best prediction.
   - ✓ Many former enslaved African Americans were leading abolitionists.
   - ___ Most Americans agreed that slavery was good for the nation's economy.
   - ___ African Americans in the North were treated as equals.
5. Read "The Underground Railroad." Then complete the statement that you can infer.

   Many abolitionists believed that Harriet Tubman Sample answer: was a heroic woman.

Unit Resources

118
Use with *United States History*, pp. 424–427

Unit Resources, p. 118

Background

Abolitionists

- Many abolitionists felt that slavery violated fundamental human rights.
- William Lloyd Garrison believed that if all enslaved people were freed immediately, they could adjust to society. His views made him unpopular among those who favored gradual abolition.

William Lloyd Garrison
"I will not retreat a single inch — AND I WILL BE HEARD," Garrison wrote in *The Liberator.*

Frederick Douglass
After escaping to the North, Douglass raised enough money to buy his freedom.

Sojourner Truth
When she preached against slavery, she attracted large crowds.

Leading Abolitionists

2 In 1831, **William Lloyd Garrison** began printing an antislavery newspaper called *The Liberator*. In it, he demanded that all enslaved people be freed.

Frederick Douglass was a well-known black abolitionist. Douglass had escaped from slavery. He was a writer and often spoke to white audiences about slavery. He told one audience,

3 > **"I can tell you what I have seen with my own eyes, felt on my own person, and know to have occurred in my own neighborhood."**

Sojourner Truth, another important abolitionist, had also been born into slavery. Truth spoke in favor of abolition and women's rights.

Sarah Grimké (GRIM kee) and **Angelina Grimké** of South Carolina saw the cruelty of slavery from another point of view. They were daughters of a slave-owner. As adults, the sisters moved north and spoke out against slavery.

Free Blacks

By 1860, about 500,000 free blacks lived in the United States. About half lived in the North, half in the South.

Free blacks in the South often faced discrimination. **Discrimination** is the unfair treatment of particular groups. State laws limited the rights of free blacks. For example, they could not travel without permission or meet in groups without a white person present.

African Americans in the North also faced discrimination. However, they could travel freely, organize groups, and publish newspapers. These rights made it possible for free blacks in the North to work openly against slavery. Free black leaders joined whites in creating the American Anti-Slavery Society in 1833. 4 This group called for the immediate end of slavery. Many free blacks gave money to the group. *The Liberator* also received most of its money from free blacks.

REVIEW What did free blacks in the North do to convince people that slavery was wrong? gave speeches; wrote pamphlets and newspapers; organized anti-slavery groups

425

2 Teach

The Antislavery Movement

Talk About It

1 **Q History** When did the abolitionist movement grow quickly?
A in the 1830s and 1840s

2 **Q History** What did William Lloyd Garrison do in 1831?
A began printing *The Liberator*

3 **Q Primary Source** What effect do you think Frederick Douglass had on his audience?
A His words made the horrors of slavery real to his audience because they knew he was an escaped slave.

4 **Q History** When was the American Anti-Slavery Society created?
A 1833

Vocabulary Strategy

abolitionist Explain to students that the *-ist* suffix added to a word means "a supporter of a specific belief." An *abolitionist* supports the *abolition* of slavery.

discrimination Explain to students that to *discriminate* is to distinguish or make a distinction.

Reading Strategy: Predict/Infer Ask students to read the first two pages of the lesson. Work with them to apply the infer strategy to abolitionists and the antislavery movement. What challenges might abolitionists have faced?

Leveled Practice

Extra Support

Encourage students to **create trading cards** depicting various members of the antislavery movement. Have them illustrate the person's picture on the front and list at least two details about the person on the back. Visual-spatial

Challenge

Ask students to **read a biography** of one the abolitionists they have learned about. Then have them describe why that person was important to the abolitionist movement. Verbal-linguistic

ELL

Advanced

Suggest that students work in small groups to **write headlines** that might have appeared in *The Liberator* or another antislavery newspaper.

Verbal-linguistic

The Underground Railroad

Talk About It

5 **Q History** What was the Underground Railroad?

A a series of escape routes and hiding places to bring slaves out of the South.

6 **Q History** What features of the Underground Railroad made it seem like a real railroad?

A Hiding places were known as "stations" and "conductors" guided runaways from station to station.

7 **Q History** Who was Harriet Tubman?

A She was the most famous conductor on the Underground Railroad.

Vocabulary Strategy

Underground Railroad Tell students that when something is *underground,* it can mean that it is done in secret or hidden—like the *Underground Railroad.*

Critical Thinking

Compare and Contrast What were some of the similarities and differences between Harriet Tubman and Sojourner Truth?

Think Aloud *Both were free African American women who had been born into slavery. Both fought against slavery. They fought against slavery in different ways. Tubman was the most famous conductor on the Underground Railroad. Truth was an abolitionist speaker.*

The Underground Railroad

Main Idea The Underground Railroad helped people escape from slavery.

Some abolitionists worked in secret
to help slaves escape to freedom. They set
up a system known as the Underground
5 Railroad. The **Underground Railroad** was a
series of escape routes and hiding places
to bring slaves out of the South.

Runaways, the people who fled slavery, could head for the North and Canada, or go south to Florida, Mexico, or the Caribbean.

Runaways often walked at night. Sometimes they hid in carts driven by members of the Underground Railroad. Escaping took great courage. Runaways who were caught would be punished and returned to slavery.

Escape to Freedom The Underground Railroad was not really underground, and not really a railroad. It was the routes that led slaves to freedom.

Music

Play a Recording

- Play a recording of "Follow the Drinking Gourd." Have students discuss the lyrics. What is the song about? Who might have sung it, and why?
- Explain to students that the song contained coded directions for escaping slaves. The "drinking gourd" refers to the Big Dipper, which points to the North Star. Gourds were used as dippers to scoop drinking water out of buckets.

Musical-auditory

Language Arts

Write a Poem

Have students write a poem about a conductor such as Harriet Tubman, a Railroad member, or a traveler on the Underground Railroad.

Verbal-linguistic

Harriet Tubman This photograph shows Harriet Tubman (left) with a group of enslaved people she helped to escape.

Stations and Conductors

Free blacks gave most of the money and did most of the work to support the Underground Railroad. Members of the Railroad gave food, clothing, and medical aid to runaways. They hid them until it was safe to move on. Hiding places were
6 known as stations. "Conductors" guided runaways on to the next station.

The most famous conductor was 7
Harriet Tubman, who escaped from slavery in Maryland. She then returned 19 times to lead others to freedom. Each time, she risked being caught and enslaved again. Tubman helped about 300 people escape to the North. She became a symbol of the abolitionist movement.

REVIEW What was the purpose of the Underground Railroad? to help people escape slavery and get to places where they could be free

Lesson Summary

Abolitionists worked to end slavery. Free blacks and women played important roles in the abolitionist movement. Many people worked against slavery by helping enslaved people escape to freedom on the Underground Railroad.

Why It Matters ...

As abolitionists struggled to free enslaved people, they convinced others that slavery was wrong.

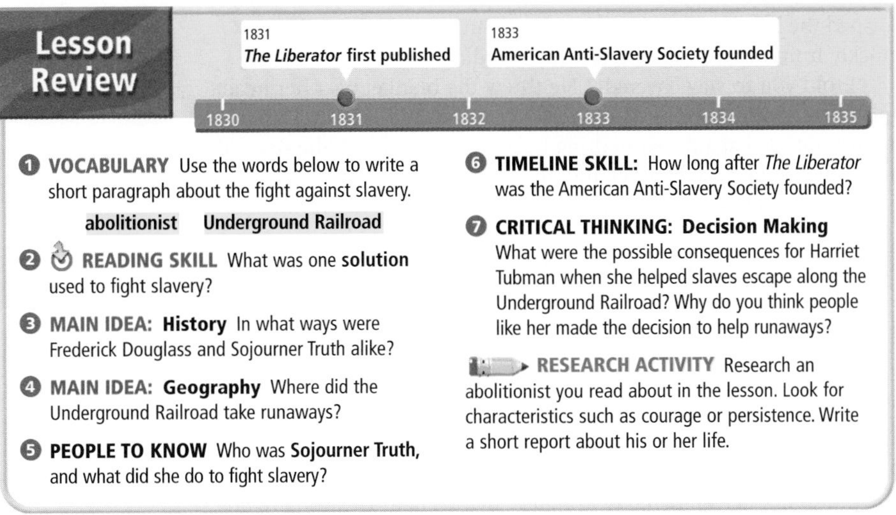

1. **VOCABULARY** Use the words below to write a short paragraph about the fight against slavery.
   abolitionist **Underground Railroad**
2. **READING SKILL** What was one **solution** used to fight slavery?
3. **MAIN IDEA: History** In what ways were Frederick Douglass and Sojourner Truth alike?
4. **MAIN IDEA: Geography** Where did the Underground Railroad take runaways?
5. **PEOPLE TO KNOW** Who was **Sojourner Truth**, and what did she do to fight slavery?
6. **TIMELINE SKILL:** How long after *The Liberator* was the American Anti-Slavery Society founded?
7. **CRITICAL THINKING: Decision Making** What were the possible consequences for Harriet Tubman when she helped slaves escape along the Underground Railroad? Why do you think people like her made the decision to help runaways?

RESEARCH ACTIVITY Research an abolitionist you read about in the lesson. Look for characteristics such as courage or persistence. Write a short report about his or her life.

Study Guide/Homework

Vocabulary and Study Guide

Vocabulary

When you add a suffix to the end of a base word, you make a new word. Knowing a suffix and its base word can help you understand unfamiliar words. Look at the word *conductor*.

Conduct "to lead or to guide"
+
-or "one who does a certain thing"
=
Conductor "one who leads or guides"

Break down the vocabulary word into its base word and suffix. Write the meaning of the new word.

-ist "one who does something"
-tion "the act of"
-ism "the practice of"

1. Abolitionist = abolition "the act of ending something" + -ist
   Abolitionist means one who works to end something
2. Discrimination = discriminate "to judge unfairly" + -tion
   Discrimination means the act of judging someone unfairly
3. Sectionalism = sectional "a part of something" + -ism
   Sectionalism means the practice of loyalty to one part

Study Guide

4. Read "The Antislavery Movement." Then match these people to their identities by drawing a line between the name and the identity.

William Lloyd Garrison	printed antislavery newspaper, *The Liberator*
Frederick Douglass	spoke for abolition and women's rights
Sojourner Truth	spoke to white audiences about slavery

Unit Resources 119 Use with *United States History*, pp. 424–427

Unit Resources, p. 119

Reteach Minilesson

Use a main idea/details chart to reteach the lesson.

Antislavery Movement
- Leading abolitionists
- Free blacks
- Underground Railroad

Graphic Organizer 8

3 Review/Assess

Review Tested Objectives

U6-4 The movement worked to abolish slavery. Abolitionists wrote pamphlets and spoke out against slavery across the country. Leaders included Sojourner Truth, William Lloyd Garrison, Frederick Douglass, Sarah Grimké, and Angelina Grimké.

U6-5 The Underground Railroad was a series of secret routes and hiding places that helped people escape slavery.

Lesson Review Answers

1. Answers should make clear that students understand the meaning of *abolitionist* and *Underground Railroad.*
2. Solutions include writing or speaking out publicly against slavery and helping people escape slavery.
3. Both were important abolitionists and had escaped slavery. They were also well-known speakers.
4. north toward Canada or south toward Mexico or the Caribbean
5. She spoke out against slavery and for abolition.
6. two years
7. One consequence is that she would have been returned to slavery if she had been caught. She helped runaways because she believed in freedom.

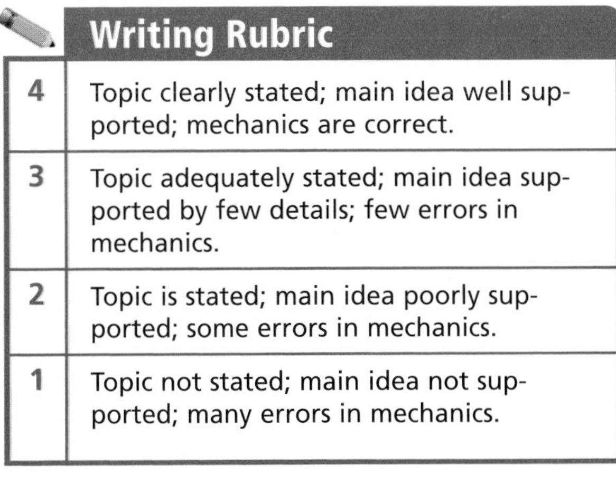

Writing Rubric	
4	Topic clearly stated; main idea well supported; mechanics are correct.
3	Topic adequately stated; main idea supported by few details; few errors in mechanics.
2	Topic is stated; main idea poorly supported; some errors in mechanics.
1	Topic not stated; main idea not supported; many errors in mechanics.

Quick Look

Connect to Core Lesson Students have learned about the antislavery movement and the people who were actively involved in it. In Extend Lesson 2, students will read about characters who worked for the Underground Railroad.

1 Preview the Extend Lesson

Connect to the Big Idea

Influences on History Some abolitionists, instead of making speeches or printing pamphlets, actively helped slaves escape to freedom. Members of the Underground Railroad performed their secret tasks well aware of the risks and danger involved. Harriet Tubman was so successful as a conductor she became a symbol of the abolitionist movement.

Connect to Prior Knowledge

Ask students to read the introduction note. Then ask them to make predictions about what might happen to Ann.

Literature

Stealing Freedom

by Elisa Carbone

This story is based on the life of a real person, Ann Weems, an enslaved servant who lived in the Maryland home of Charles Price in the 1850s. Ann, age thirteen, hopes to be freed. A lawyer, Jacob Bigelow, promised to help her escape on the Underground Railroad. But tonight a man whom Ann saw at the county fair has kidnapped her from the Prices and bundled her into the back of a carriage. She has been riding in the carriage a long time. Where is he taking her?

The horse stopped. In an instant, Ann threw off the blanket and grasped the handle of the carriage door. But the man leaped so quickly from his seat, he was already standing over her.

"I told you to stay covered!" He threw the blanket over her head and lifted her in it, his arms tight as a vise around her chest. Ann's mouth bumped against something bony—his shoulder? She opened her mouth wide and, blanket and all, bit him as hard as she could.

The man yelped and dropped her. She landed on her rump and struggled to get untangled from the blanket. He grabbed her again and, this time with no blanket to cushion him, she bit down on his arm.

A door opened and a slice of yellow light brightened the dark street.

"Help!" Ann cried.

But the blanket came down over her head again.

"Are you mad?" It was another man's hushed voice. "The constable patrols this street every hour all night!"

"The wench bit me!"

Ann found herself being held tightly by two pairs of strong hands.

Reaching All Learners

Background

Underground Railroad

- No one knows exactly when the Underground Railroad started, but there have been reports of help given to runaways as early as the 1700s.
- One of Harriet Tubman's routes using modern roads would be 560 miles long. The journey, depending on the runaway's health and the weather, may have taken two months to a year.

Extra Support

Write a Review

- Have students write a review of the excerpt from *Stealing Freedom.* Remind them that a good review evaluates whether the author did a good job.
- Explain that the review should not give away the ending, but should help possible readers to understand the basic plot. Make sure students understand that they should share their opinions in a review.

Verbal-linguistic

On Level

Write a Book Jacket

- Explain to students that often a book will have information on the back cover telling what it is about.
- Have students write a short passage that creatively summarizes the excerpt they have read.
- Remind them that their passages should not give away the ending and should make people want to read more to find out what happens.

Verbal-linguistic

"Just get her inside."

She heard a door shut and as it did, her heart sank. She was trapped.

"You've scared her half to death, is what you've done."

"I got her here, ain't I?" came the voice of her captor.

The blanket was lifted off her head. A hand grasped hers and helped her to her feet. She blinked, uncomprehending. She was standing in the foyer of a narrow row house. One candle flickered on a table nearby. In the dancing light she saw the stubbly face of the tobacco-chewing man from the fair. He was calmly picking his teeth. When she turned to see the other man who'd helped him drag her inside, she let out a yelp and stepped back, her hands covering her mouth. It was Jacob Bigelow.

"Welcome to my home," said Mr. Bigelow.

Ann took in a sharp breath. "You're . . . I mean . . ." She pointed to the other man. "He's . . ."

Mr. Bigelow smoothed the sweaty hair away from her forehead. "There will be time for explanation," he said. "Are you in one piece?"

She nodded.

Mr. Bigelow handed the man a fat wad of paper money. "You got her here safely. Now be off before the constable comes by to find out why there's a brawl going on in my foyer at three A.M."

The man tipped his hat to Ann and slipped out the door.

"I apologize for his conduct," said Mr. Bigelow, "but often it's only the roughest sort who are willing to do such risky work. And I'm sure you understand why we had to do it this way."

Ann screwed up her face. "I don't think I understand anything," she said, bewildered.

LITERATURE

2 Teach the Extend Lesson

Learning Through Historical Fiction

After students read the selection, discuss with them how the selection explains why members of the Underground Railroad had to perform their tasks in secret. Ask students if they agree or disagree with Jacob Bigelow's methods of helping Ann escape to freedom.

Challenge

Support the Railroad

Jacob Bigelow is a lawyer by day and a kidnapper by night. Have students write an anonymous editorial that Bigelow might have written defending his actions and those of other members of the Underground Railroad.

Verbal-linguistic

ELL

Intermediate

Have students reread the selection and fill out the appropriate spaces in a story map for the selection.

Verbal-linguistic

Literature

Historical Fiction

Obtain copies of *Bright Freedom's Song* by Gloria Houston, and *F is for Freedom* by Roni Schotter. Place these works of historical fiction in your Reading Center for students who want to find out what it was like for young people to be in the Underground Railroad.

Critical Thinking

Predict Have students predict what might have happened if the constable had heard Ann's cry for help. What might have happened to Ann and Mr. Bigelow? What might the characters have said?

Evaluate The Powder Boy was paid by Jacob Bigelow to kidnap Ann. He also smuggles gunpowder. Ask students if they agree with how the Powder Boy makes his living. They should support their statements with details from the selection.

Mr. Bigelow helped her to a chair in the parlor, carrying the candle with them. She sat stiff and uncomfortably. It was the first time she'd ever sat in a parlor.

"We had to steal you from your master this way," he said.

Ann felt a quiver go from her throat to her belly as it dawned on her what had actually happened this night.

"You see—" Mr. Bigelow adjusted his spectacles. "If you'd known that you were escaping, you would not have played the part so convincingly. But as it was, if you'd been taken up by the sheriff, what would you have told him?"

"That I'd been kidnapped!"

"Exactly," said Mr. Bigelow. "And you would have been returned to your master without harm or suspicion."

Ann's eyes widened as the plan began to make sense.

"And if anyone has seen you, the rumor mill will serve us well. You were not seen running away. You were being carried away against your will."

Ann rubbed the bump on her head—what a small price to pay for a clean escape! "Thank you," she said. She held her hands together toward him in a gesture like prayer. "Thank you so much."

Mr. Bigelow pressed his fingertips together. "Ah, yes," he said. "A lawyer by day, a lawless kidnapper by night. It's a wonder I get any sleep at all."

There was the sound of footsteps in the street. They stopped briefly outside the door, then moved on.

"That's Sergeant Orme on his parol," Mr. Bigelow said quietly. "I'd better show you to the guest quarters now."

He led Ann into the hallway and, with one wiry eyebrow raised, pointed to the ceiling. "There you are," he said. "The most comfortable lodging in town for kidnapping victims."

The candlelight flickered and Ann squinted at the place where he'd pointed. All she could see was wide ceiling boards that fit tightly together. Was he playing a joke on her?

Mr. Bigelow hummed as he opened a nearby closet and pulled out a ladder.

Then he climbed up and pushed carefully on the ceiling. Ann's mouth dropped open as a piece of the ceiling lifted up and he slid it aside.

"Up you go," he said, stepping down off the ladder. He gave her the candle.

430 • Chapter 12

Reaching All Learners

Language Arts

Write the Next Chapter

- What is the next stop for Ann on the Underground Railroad? What other dangers might Ann face on her journey to freedom?
- Suggest that students envision what might happen next in the selection and write the next chapter. Chapter should be about two pages.

Verbal-linguistic

Physical Education

Role-Play the Story

Ask volunteers to pantomime the actions of the characters in the selection (such as Ann throwing off the blanket or climbing the ladder to Jacob Bigelow's attic) while others take turns reading the selection aloud.

Bodily-kinesthetic

Drama

Rewrite Scenes

Ask students to rewrite the selection as scenes from a play.

- Have students list the characters involved and create dialogue for each character.
- Ann's thoughts in the beginning may become a monologue and additional lines may be written for the scenes.

Verbal-linguistic

Ann climbed up until her head entered a stuffy, attic-like room. She lifted the candle and saw a pitcher of water, a dish of corn bread, a straw mat and quilt, and a chamber pot over in the corner. She looked down at Mr. Bigelow. "No one will know I'm here!" she exclaimed.

"My thoughts exactly," he replied.

Ann scrambled up, then lay on her stomach to peer down before closing up the opening. "May I know his name?" she asked. "The man who brought me here?" He had given her several hours of terror and a rather large bump on her head, but he had, in fact, been her savior. She wanted to remember him.

Mr. Bigelow rested one foot on the bottom rung of the ladder. "The Powder Boy," he answered. "He takes both gunpowder and fugitives on his sailing vessel. Of course, that's not his real name, but that is how he's known on the road—and since you are now a passenger on the road, that is how you should know him."

The Powder Boy. She would never forget. She looked quizzically at Mr. Bigelow. "The road?" she asked, shaking her head slightly.

"The Underground Railroad. You have just begun to ride it, my dear. I am one of the conductors, and this is your first stop. It runs all the way to Canada."

Canada. She felt the quiver run through her again. She could not turn back now. And Canada was so far away.

They said good night, and Ann slid the ceiling boards back into place. They fit perfectly. The hiding place must have been built, she thought, like a hidden closet behind one of the upstairs bedrooms.

When she blew out the candle the room went quite dark. Her stomach had been through too much this night for her to eat the corn bread, but she drank thirstily from the pitcher. The air was hot and close. Sweat dripped down her neck as she lay on the mat. Her heart pounded in her ears with a new rhythm—one she'd never heard before. It said, "I'm free, I'm free, I'm free . . . ."

Activities

1. **TALK ABOUT IT** Why was Ann kidnapped? What do you think of Joseph Bigelow's plan?
2. **MAP IT** Where will Ann go next? Plan a route that Ann might follow from Baltimore, Maryland to Canada. Show the route on a map. Mark places on the map where she might stop along the Underground Railroad.

3 Leveled Activities

❶ **Talk About It** *For Extra Support*
Ann was kidnapped so it looked like she was being taken against her will instead of running away. Students may agree or disagree that Jacob Bigelow's plan was a good one.

❷ **Map It** *For Challenge*

HANDS ON Performance Task Rubric

4	Routes and stops are thoughtfully planned and clearly marked; map is complete and accurate; mechanics are correct.
3	Most routes and stops are planned and clearly marked; map is complete and contains few inaccuracies; most mechanics are correct.
2	Some routes and stops are planned and marked; map is complete but contains some inaccuracies; some mechanical errors.
1	Routes and stops are not planned or marked; map is incomplete or inaccurate; many mechanical errors.

Art

Illustrate a Book Cover

- Ask students to think about how the cover of a book can affect what they think that book will be about.
- Have students design a book cover for *Stealing Freedom*. Encourage them to think carefully about which scene is the most dramatic.

Visual-spatial

Graphic Organizer

1	Ann finds herself wrapped in a blanket and thrown into a carriage.
2	Ann tries to escape her kidnapper but is brought into a house.
3	Ann meets Jacob Bigelow.
4	Jacob Bigelow explains why he had Ann kidnapped and shows Ann her hiding place.

Graphic Organizer 15

Tested Objectives

U6-6 History Describe the conflict between the North and the South over the spread of slavery into the new territories.

U6-7 History Identify events that increased tension between the North and the South in the mid-1800s.

Quick Look

This lesson covers the legal debate over slavery, which resulted in compromises and increased tension between free and slave states.

Teaching Option: Extend Lesson 3 dramatizes the decisions people had to make after the Fugitive Slave Law was passed.

1 Get Set to Read

Preview Look at the maps on the next page. What will you find out about in this lesson?

Reading Skill: Cause and Effect Causes may include the Kansas-Nebraska Act, Fugitive Slave Law, Dred Scott decision, and John Brown's raid on Harpers Ferry.

Build on What You Know Ask students if they have ever made a compromise. To settle their differences over the issue of slavery, both the North and South made compromises.

Vocabulary

slave state *noun,* a state in which slavery is allowed

free state *noun,* a state in which slavery is not allowed

Union *noun,* the United States of America; the northern states during the Civil War

popular sovereignty *noun,* authority carried out by the people at large

fugitive *noun,* one who runs away from the law

Core Lesson 3

Compromise and Conflict

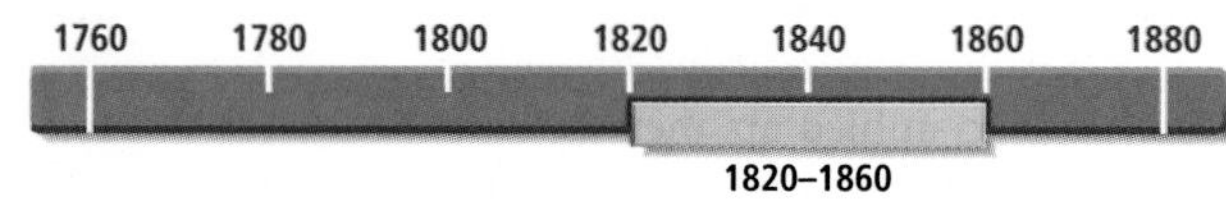

VOCABULARY

slave state
free state
Union
popular sovereignty
fugitive

Vocabulary Strategy

fugitive

Fugitive and refuge come from a word meaning to flee. A fugitive flees to find refuge, or safety.

READING SKILL

Cause and Effect Note the causes that made the conflict over slavery grow worse.

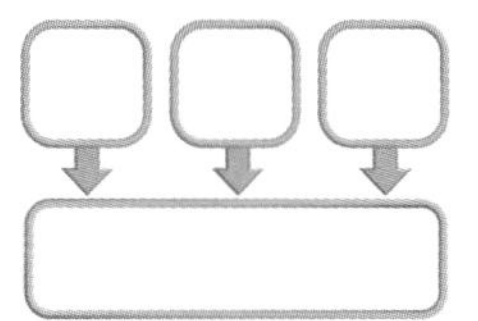

Build on What You Know To solve a disagreement, you give a little to get something back. That is a compromise. During the 1800s, Congress made several compromises over slavery to keep the country together.

Would Slavery Spread?

Main Idea Congress had to decide whether to allow slavery in new territories and states.

The United States grew in the 1800s. The Louisiana
Purchase and the Mexican War had opened new lands to 1
settlers. Congress set up governments for these lands, and some of the regions became territories. When a territory's population was large enough, it could become a state.

Congress had to decide whether to allow slavery in each territory. Territories that allowed slavery became slave states. A **slave state** permitted slavery. Territories where slavery was illegal became free states. A **free state** did not permit slavery. For a time, Congress tried to keep an equal number of free and slave states.

Henry Clay Known as the Great Compromiser, Kentucky senator Henry Clay tried to keep arguments over slavery from dividing the nation.

Skill and Strategy

Reading Skill and Strategy

Reading Skill: Cause and Effect

This skill helps you see how one event can be related to another, either by causing it or resulting from it.

Read "Compromise and Conflict." Then fill in the chart below to show the effect of the events listed.

Congress had to decide whether to allow slavery in new states.	Dred Scott asked the courts for his freedom.	John Brown led an attack on Harpers Ferry.

1. The North and South were divided over slavery more than ever before.

Reading Strategy: Predict/Infer

2. Read "Would Slavery Spread?" Then complete the statement that you can infer.

   Some people living in Missouri wanted the right to own slaves.

3. Look over "The Growing Crisis." Read the headings. Make a prediction about what the section will be about.

   Sample answer: The differences between the North and the South are going to get worse.

4. Read "Would Slavery Spread?" Why did Kansas join the Union as a free state?

   More settlers in Kansas opposed slavery than supported it.

Unit Resources

120
Use with *United States History*, pp. 432–435

Unit Resources, p. 120

Background

Compromise and Conflict

- When Missouri applied for statehood, northerners wanted to stop slavery from spreading in that territory. As a compromise, Maine was admitted as a free state.
- *Uncle Tom's Cabin* was published in 1851. The novel describes how a man maintains his dignity even after being separated from his friends and family.

Compromises in Congress

Through the first half of the 1800s, Congress argued over which territories would have slavery. Northerners wanted free states to have a majority of representatives in Congress, so they could pass laws against slavery. Southerners wanted more slave states.

Missouri wanted to join the Union as a slave state in 1820. The **Union** is another name for the United States. To satisfy both sides, Congress created the
2 Missouri Compromise. It accepted Missouri as a slave state and Maine as a free state. Congress then created an invisible line across the rest of the territories. Only territories south of that line would allow slavery.

3 Congress continued to debate the spread of slavery into new territories. In the Compromise of 1850, Congress allowed settlers in some territories to make the decision for themselves. The right of people to make political decisions for themselves is called **popular sovereignty.**

In 1854, Congress passed the Kansas-Nebraska Act. This law gave popular sovereignty to the Kansas and Nebraska territories. Abolitionists opposed the act because it allowed slavery north of the line created in the Missouri Compromise. Settlers supporting and opposing slavery rushed into Kansas. Both sides wanted to win the vote on whether to allow slavery. Soon the two sides fought for control of the territory. In 1861, Kansas joined the Union as a free state.

REVIEW What compromises did Congress make as the nation grew?
the Missouri Compromise, the Compromise of 1850, and the Kansas-Nebraska Act

Growth and Compromise Compromises in Congress affected where slavery was allowed.

SKILL Reading Maps Which state joined the Union as a free state in 1850? California

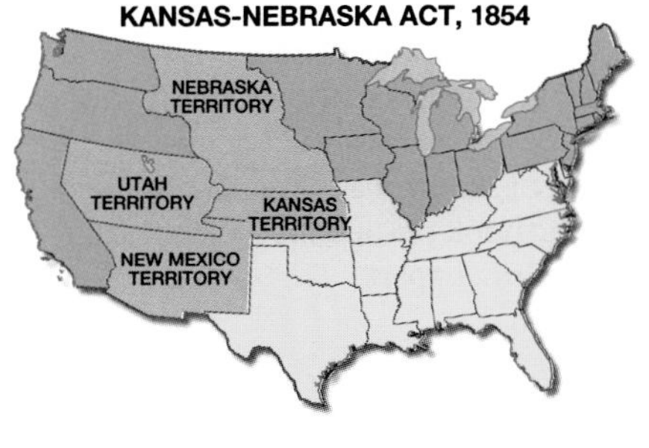

2 Teach

Would Slavery Spread?

Talk About It

1 **Q Geography** Why did the territory of the United States expand in the 1800s?
A The Louisiana Purchase and the Mexican War opened up new lands for settlers.

2 **Q Geography** What free state joined the Union as part of the Missouri Compromise?
A Maine

3 **Q Citizenship** What did the Compromise of 1850 do?
A It allowed popular sovereignty in some territories so that they could choose whether to allow slavery.

Vocabulary Strategy

slave state A *slave state* is one where *slavery* is permitted or practiced.

free state A *free state* is one that is *free* of slavery.

Union Explain to students that the prefix *uni-* in *Union* means *one.*

popular sovereignty Have students look at the meanings of *popular* (enjoyed by many people) and *sovereign* (one who governs a state) to put together the meaning of *popular sovereignty.*

Reading Strategy: Predict/Infer Have students read the first heading, "Would Slavery Spread?" What do you think the answer is? Share your inferences, and ask students to share theirs.

Leveled Practice

Extra Support

Have students **use visuals** by looking at the maps and their titles on page 433. Ask them to list the changes in the territories as each compromise took place.
Visual-spatial

Challenge

Have students research the conflict over slavery in Kansas known as "Bleeding Kansas." Have them write a one-page report on the topic. Verbal-linguistic

ELL

Intermediate

Ask students to **locate the eight states** mentioned in this lesson on a wall map. Have them look up which ones entered the Union as slave or free states. Using red pins for slave states and blue ones for free states, students can mark them on the map. What other states were in the Union by 1860?

Visual-spatial

The Growing Crisis

Talk About It

4 Q History Who was Harriet Beecher Stowe?

A She wrote *Uncle Tom's Cabin,* a book that pushed the North and South further apart.

5 Q History Why did John Brown attack a U.S. Army post in Harpers Ferry, Virginia?

A He wanted to start a rebellion against slavery.

Vocabulary Strategy

fugitive *Fugitive* comes from the Latin verb meaning "to flee." A *fugitive* is someone who flees or runs away.

Critical Thinking

Cause and Effect What effect did the Dred Scott decision have on the conflict over slavery?

Think Aloud *In the Dred Scott decision, the Supreme Court said that enslaved people were property and that the government could not ban slavery in any territory. Slave owners felt that they had won the right to keep enslaved people as property. Abolitionists were afraid that slavery would spread across the country. The Dred Scott decision increased the conflict between slave owners and abolitionists.*

Harriet Beecher Stowe
Her book, *Uncle Tom's Cabin,* described the suffering of slaves. Many people in the North began to feel new sympathy for enslaved people after reading the book.

The Growing Crisis

Main Idea Events in the 1850s made the split between the North and South worse.

As part of the Compromise of 1850, Congress passed the Fugitive Slave Law, which upset northerners. A **fugitive** is a person who is running away. The law said that slaves who had escaped to the North had to be returned to slavery. The Fugitive Slave Law also ordered citizens to help catch fugitives. Many northerners refused to obey the law.

4 **Harriet Beecher Stowe,** a writer from New England, was against the Fugitive Slave Law. She decided to write a story describing the cruelty of slavery. Her book, *Uncle Tom's Cabin,* sold 300,000 copies in one year. Stowe pointed out in the book that slavery was not just the South's problem. It was the nation's problem. *Uncle Tom's Cabin* convinced many northerners that slavery was wrong. Some southerners insisted that Stowe's picture of slavery was false. The arguments over the book pushed the North and South further apart.

Dred Scott

A legal case about slavery came to the Supreme Court in 1857. **Dred Scott,** an enslaved man from Missouri, asked the court for his freedom. Scott argued that he should be free because he had once lived in Illinois, a free state, and Wisconsin, a free territory. The Supreme Court disagreed. It said that enslaved people were property, and that living in a free state did not make them citizens. The Supreme Court also said that the government could not keep slavery out of any territory, because that would prevent slaveowners from moving their property to new territories.

The Dred Scott decision was a victory for slaveowners. It meant that slavery had to be legal in all territories, even if most settlers did not want it. Abolitionists feared that slavery would spread over the whole country.

Dred Scott

Drama

Role-Play a Scene

Have students work in small groups to write dialogue for a dramatic scene depicting a group of people discussing the Dred Scott decision.

- Have them use details from the lesson to make the dialogue seem real.

Bodily-kinesthetic; verbal-linguistic

Language Arts

Write a Persuasive Essay

- The Fugitive Slave Law ordered northern citizens to help catch runaway slaves.
- Ask students to write a persuasive essay arguing why northerners should not have to obey this law.

Verbal-linguistic

Attack at Harpers Ferry

John Brown's Raid

An abolitionist named **John Brown** decided to fight slavery on his own. In
5 1859, he tried to start a rebellion against slavery by attacking a U.S. Army post at Harpers Ferry, Virginia. Soldiers quickly surrounded his group and captured Brown. The government accused Brown of treason. At his trial, he insisted that he had done "no wrong but right." Brown was found guilty and hanged. Many northerners saw Brown as a hero. Southerners saw him as a violent man out to destroy their way of life.

By 1860, the North and South were deeply divided. As antislavery feeling grew stronger in the North, some southerners argued that they should leave the Union to protect their way of life.

REVIEW Why did John Brown attack Harpers Ferry? He wanted to start a rebellion against slavery.

Lesson Summary

Americans disagreed about whether slavery should be allowed to spread.

Congress tried to settle the slavery issue with a series of compromises.

The Fugitive Slave Law and John Brown's raid drove the North and South further apart.

Why It Matters ...

Over time, it became much harder for Americans to compromise over slavery. This conflict started to split the nation.

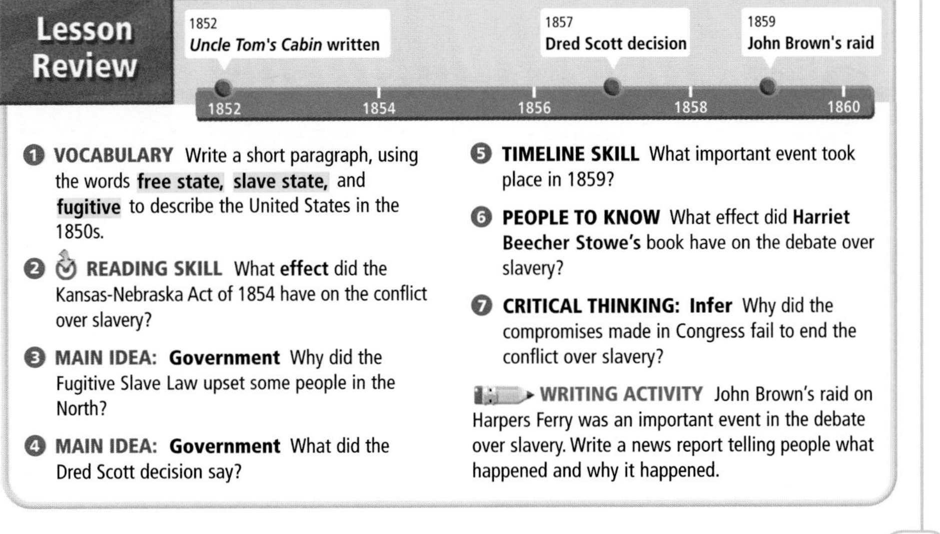

1. **VOCABULARY** Write a short paragraph, using the words **free state, slave state,** and **fugitive** to describe the United States in the 1850s.
2. **READING SKILL** What **effect** did the Kansas-Nebraska Act of 1854 have on the conflict over slavery?
3. **MAIN IDEA: Government** Why did the Fugitive Slave Law upset some people in the North?
4. **MAIN IDEA: Government** What did the Dred Scott decision say?
5. **TIMELINE SKILL** What important event took place in 1859?
6. **PEOPLE TO KNOW** What effect did **Harriet Beecher Stowe's** book have on the debate over slavery?
7. **CRITICAL THINKING: Infer** Why did the compromises made in Congress fail to end the conflict over slavery?

WRITING ACTIVITY John Brown's raid on Harpers Ferry was an important event in the debate over slavery. Write a news report telling people what happened and why it happened.

435

3 Review/Assess

Review Tested Objectives

U6-6 The North wanted new territories to ban slavery and become free states, while the South wanted new territories to allow slavery and become slave states. Congress tried to settle the slavery issue with several compromises.

U6–7 The Kansas-Nebraska Act, Fugitive Slave Law, Dred Scott decision, and John Brown's raid all increased conflict between the North and South.

Lesson Review Answers

1. Paragraphs should discuss popular sovereignty and the Fugitive Slave Law.
2. It did not prevent deepening conflicts over the spread of slavery.
3. Many northerners did not want to be forced to help slave owners recover runaway slaves.
4. It said that enslaved people were property and had no rights to citizenship even if they had lived in free states.
5. John Brown's raid
6. It made more northerners oppose slavery and angered many southerners.
7. because the North and South were too different in their beliefs about slavery

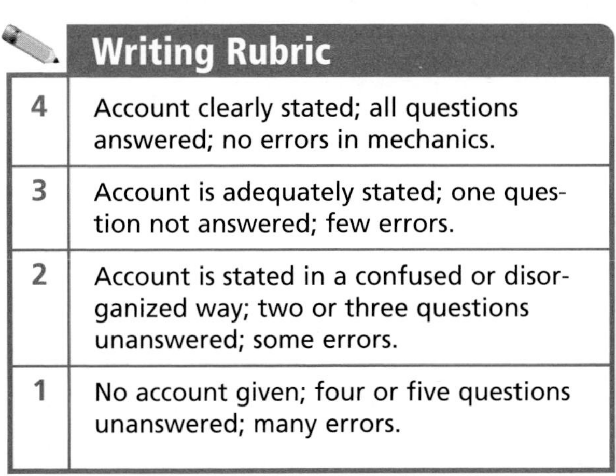

Writing Rubric

4	Account clearly stated; all questions answered; no errors in mechanics.
3	Account is adequately stated; one question not answered; few errors.
2	Account is stated in a confused or disorganized way; two or three questions unanswered; some errors.
1	No account given; four or five questions unanswered; many errors.

Study Guide/Homework

Vocabulary and Study Guide

Vocabulary

1. Draw a line connecting the vocabulary word to its meaning.

fugitive	did not have slavery
free state	when people who live in a place make the decisions
slave state	a person who is running away
popular sovereignty	permitted slavery

Study Guide

Read "Would Slavery Spread?" Then fill in the main idea and details chart below.

Compromise	What it did
Missouri Compromise	2. Accepted Missouri as a slave state and Maine as a free state; Created an invisible line across the remaining territories
Compromise of 1850	3. Gave some territories popular sovereignty
Kansas-Nebraska Act	4. Gave popular sovereignty to Kansas and Nebraska territories; Kansas joined the Union as a free state

Read "The Growing Crisis." Then answer the question.

5. What are three events that increased tension between the North and South?
Harriet Beecher Stowe wrote *Uncle Tom's Cabin*, Dred Scott court case, John Brown's raid

Unit Resources

121
Use with *United States History*, pp. 432–435

Unit Resources, p. 121

Reteach Minilesson

Use a flow chart to review compromises made by Congress.

Causes	Effects
Missouri Compromise	Missouri becomes a slave state; Maine becomes a free state
Compromise of 1850	Popular sovereignty in some states; Fugitive Slave Act
Kansas-Nebraska Act	Popular sovereignty in Kansas and Nebraska

www.eduplace.com/ss/hmss05/

Quick Look

Connect to Core Lesson Students have just read about the compromises the North and South made over the issue of slavery. In Extend Lesson 3, students will hear from characters who were affected by the Fugitive Slave Law.

1 Preview the Extend Lesson

Connect to the Big Idea

Conflict and Compromise Because the Fugitive Slave Law ordered citizens to help catch fugitive slaves, many northerners were angered by it. The Fugitive Slave Law not only made northerners choose sides in the slavery debate, it made the issue personal. One major effect of the Fugitive Slave Law is that it strengthened the abolitionist movement in the North.

Connect to Prior Knowledge

Ask students to look at the list of characters. Then ask them to make predictions about each character's feelings about the Fugitive Slave Law.

Readers' Theater

A Troubling Law

Was the Fugitive Slave Law a bad law? The setting is dusk in a northern town in 1850. Citizens have gathered to decide how to respond to the new Fugititve Slave Law, meant to help slave owners. Should people in free states follow it or resist it?

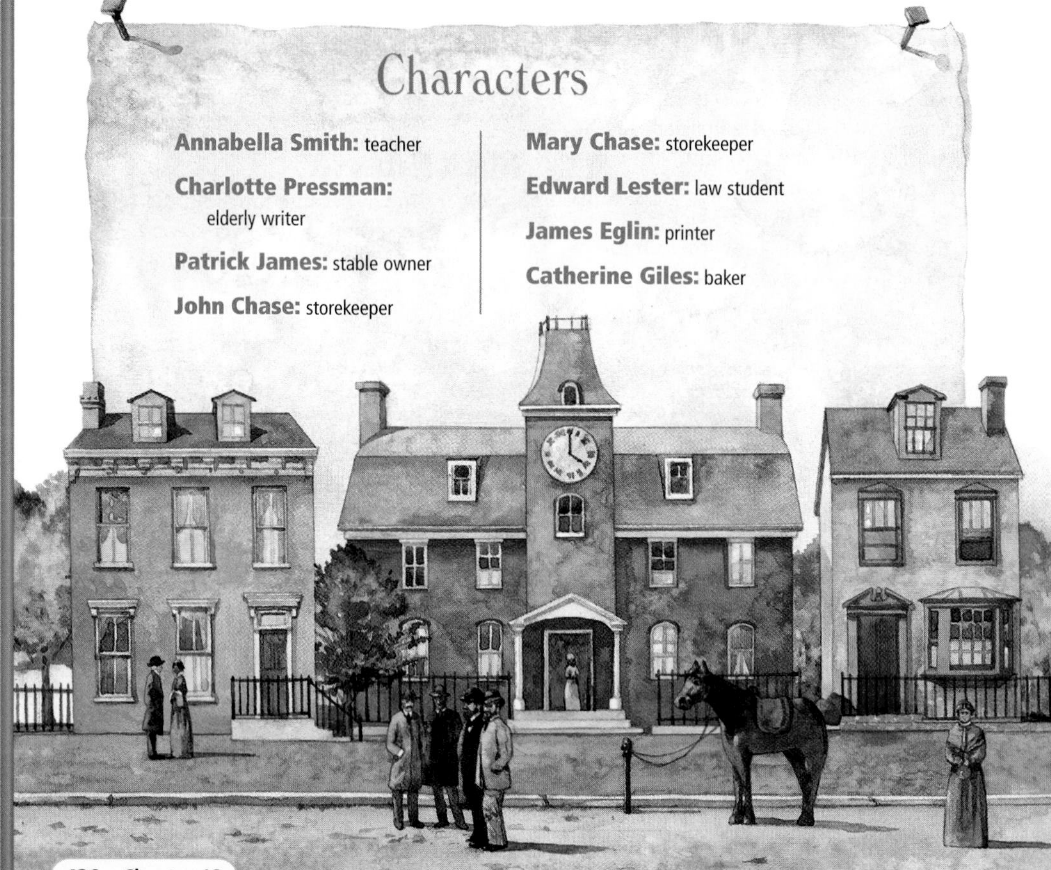

Reaching All Learners

Background

Fugitive Slave Law

- Under the Fugitive Slave Law, federal marshals were authorized to issue warrants, gather posses, and force citizens to help catch runaways under penalty of fines or imprisonment.
- Mobs in several northern cities forced federal officials to rule in favor of accused runaways or stopped slave owners from returning to the South with captured slaves.

Extra Support

Take a Poll

- Have students prepare a poll of questions to ask each character. They could ask about the character's occupation, and initial feelings about Robert Simms's plight.
- Have designated students answer the questions in character.
- After the poll, encourage students to share what they have learned with the class.

Verbal-linguistic; bodily-kinesthetic

On Level

Hold a Debate

- Tell students that in some northern cities, mobs stopped slave owners and their agents from returning to the South with their captives.
- Have students form two groups, for and against, and debate whether this was the best way to resist the Fugitive Slave Law.

Verbal-linguistic

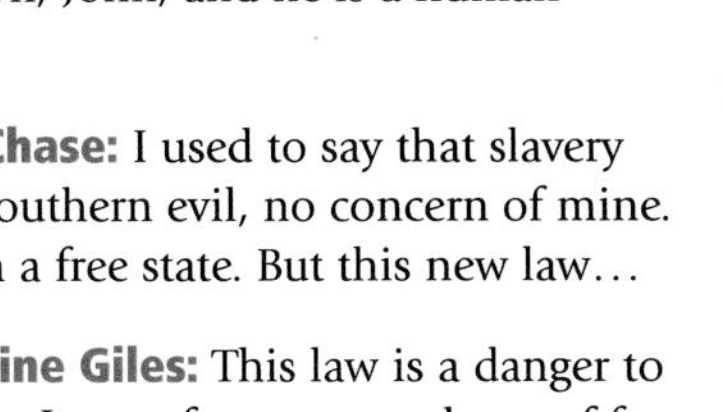

Annabella Smith: I have bad news. Robert Simms has been arrested — taken from his house last night!

John Chase: What happened? What was his offense?

Charlotte Pressman: I'm sure he did nothing wrong. We all know Robert. He has lived in this town for five years since he came here from Virginia.

Patrick James: It's that new slave law! He will be dragged back to slavery unless we do something.

Edward Lester: It is a very troubling law. It strikes a blow to the heart of our efforts to free people.

John Chase: That's easy for you to say, Edward. Mary and I are storekeepers, and radical talk about abolition isn't good for business.

Patrick James: But Simms worked in our town, John, and he is a human being.

Mary Chase: I used to say that slavery was a southern evil, no concern of mine. I live in a free state. But this new law…

Catherine Giles: This law is a danger to all of us. I am a free woman, born of free parents. But because I am black, I could be kidnapped and sold into slavery, and there would be no help for me.

James Eglin: It's true! I ran away from slavery. I earn an honest living as a printer. Now the law says my old master can come after me, and you have to help him.

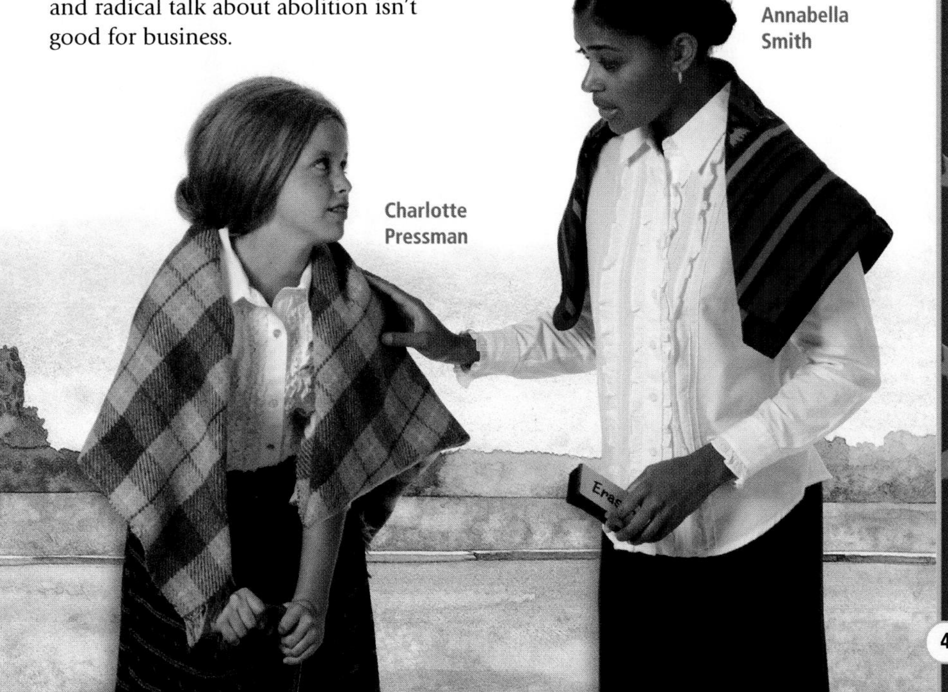

READERS' THEATER

2 Teach the Extend Lesson

Learning Through Drama

Assign each of the roles in the play to students and have them read the play aloud to the class. Then discuss with students how the play helps explain why northerners were upset about the Fugitive Slave Law. Ask students if they agree with their character's point of view and have them explain why or why not.

Character Trait: Courage

Ask students to predict the ways in which the townspeople might show courage as they decide what to do when Robert Simms is arrested.

For more on character traits, turn to pages R4–R5.

Challenge

Plan a Meeting

Have students work in a group to brainstorm ideas to organize and run a local abolitionist meeting.

- Students should create such materials as posters and pamphlets, or newspaper editorials to promote the meeting.
- If time allows, have students hold the meeting. They should prepare persuasive speeches to inspire people to become abolitionists, as well as discuss new ways to fight slavery.

Bodily-kinesthetic; visual-spatial

ELL

Intermediate/Advanced

- Instruct students to work in pairs to create a chart of all the characters from the play.
- Next, they should write a few sentences describing each character's views about the Fugitive Slave Law and what they think should be done about it.

Visual-spatial; verbal-kinesthetic

Literature

Historical Fiction

Trouble Don't Last by Shelley Pearsall, and *The Second Escape of Arthur Cooper* by Cynthia M. Stowe. Place these works of historical fiction in your Reading Center for students who want to read about what it was like for fugitive slaves to escape to the North.

Critical Thinking

Infer Have students reread the position stated by Edward Lester. Ask them why isn't he, a law student, in favor of obeying the Fugitive Slave Law. Students should support their answer with information from his statements.

Fact and Opinion Ask students to review Charlotte Pressman's statement that "there is a higher law than the Fugitive Slave Law." Have students explain why Charlotte Pressman's statement is fact or opinion.

Annabella Smith: Help him?

James Eglin: And if my old master catches me, I don't get a trial. I can't speak in my own defense. Just his word alone can send me back in chains.

Edward Lester: Did you know that the judge who hears the case is paid $5 when he frees a fugitive and $10 when he sends him back to slavery?

Annabella Smith: We must disobey this law. We must help Mr. Simms.

John Chase: I hear the punishment for helping a fugitive is a $1,000 fine or six months in jail.

James Eglin: That's nothing compared to a person's freedom.

John Chase: A thousand dollars is still a lot of money. If I spent six months in jail, my business would collapse.

Patrick James: I am willing to risk it.

Reaching All Learners

Language Arts

Write a Flyer

Ask students to suppose that Edward Lester or Catherine Giles wanted to write a flyer to encourage other townspeople to oppose the Fugitive Slave Law.

- Have students write the flyer from a character's point of view. Flyers should state the character's position and support it with details from the Readers' Theater.

Verbal-linguistic

Drama

Write the Next Act

What will happen next if the characters succeed in rescuing Mr. Simms? Suggest that students imagine what happens next and write the next act of the Readers' Theater.

Verbal-linguistic

Charlotte Pressman: The question is, what can we do? It's too late to hide him. He has already been caught.

Patrick James: Then we must rescue him by force. Don't look so shocked! It has already happened in Boston. A group broke into the courthouse and rescued a fugitive.

John Chase

James Eglin: It wouldn't be easy. My uncle says a slaveowner and his hunters tried to capture some fugitives in Pennsylvania. People were badly wounded. A man died.

Annabella Smith: This could be dangerous.

Catherine Giles: It could lead to terrible violence.

Edward Lester: Then we will set out to rescue Mr. Simms without violence. We will gather a group large enough to overpower the guards and try to persuade them to let Robert go. We will carry no firearms.

James Eglin: I will do it.

Patrick James: You know I will.

Mary Chase: So will I.

John Chase: What if you get hurt? What if you are thrown in jail? I just don't know what to do.

Mary Chase: This is a free state, John. We cannot let the slaveholders take away our freedom.

Charlotte Pressman: I will defy this law, no matter what may come of it!

Activities

1. **THINK ABOUT IT** In what ways do you think the townspeople showed **courage**?
2. **WRITE ABOUT IT** Write a letter to the editor of a newspaper in 1850 telling your beliefs about the Fugitive Slave Law.

3 Leveled Activities

1 Think About It *For Extra Support*
Sample answer: some of the townspeople decided to risk jail time, injury, or even their lives to rescue Mr. Simms. They were brave because they decided to attempt the rescue without carrying firearms to defend themselves.

2 Write About It *For Challenge*

Writing Rubric

4	Editorial is clearly written; position is well stated and supported with several details; no errors in mechanics.
3	Editorial is adequately written; position is adequately stated and supported with details; few errors in mechanics.
2	Editorial is somewhat unclear or confusing; position is not well stated or well supported; some errors in mechanics.
1	Editorial is unclear, confusing, or unwritten; position is not stated or supported; many errors in mechanics.

Art

Design a Playbill

Suggest that students create and design a playbill for "A Troubling Law." Have students illustrate the cover and list the characters on the back.

Visual-spatial

Graphic Organizer

Should characters obey the Fugitive Slave Law, or should they rescue Mr. Simms?

Obey the law	Rescue Simms
Punishment for helping a fugitive is $1,000 fine or six months in jail. A rescue could be violent.	The law is unjust. We cannot let slaveholders take away our freedom. We will try to rescue him without violence.

Graphic Organizer 1

Tested Objectives

U6-8 History Describe Abraham Lincoln's early life, views on slavery, and role in the Republican Party.

U6-9 History Explain the events that led to the secession of the Confederate states.

Lesson Quick Look

This lesson discusses the political career of Abraham Lincoln, whose election as President led to the secession of the South and the start of the Civil War.

Teaching Option: Extend Lesson 4 shows students what real people were feeling at the time of secession.

1 Get Set to Read

Preview Ask students to look at the lesson title. Ask them what they think it is about.

Reading Skill: Sequence The sequence of events includes Lincoln's election, the secession of the South, and the Confederate attack on Fort Sumter.

Build on What You Know Have students describe people whose strong beliefs led them to make their community a better place. Discuss what the people believed and the effect of their beliefs on their actions.

Vocabulary

secession *noun,* the act of withdrawing membership from an organization or union

Confederacy *noun,* the eleven Southern states that seceded from the United States in 1860 and 1861

civil war *noun,* a war between opposing groups of the same country

Core Lesson 4

Civil War Begins

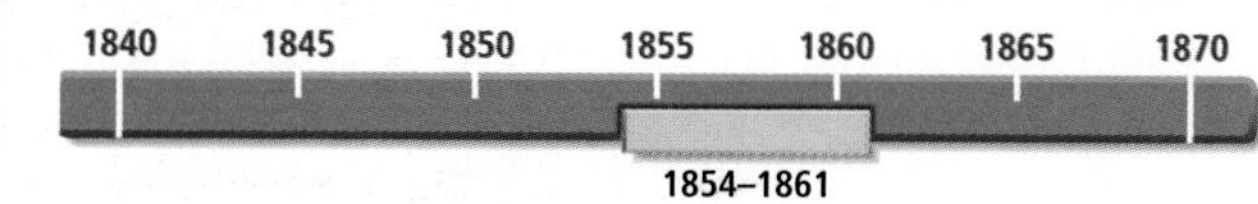

VOCABULARY

secession
Confederacy
civil war

Vocabulary Strategy

Confederacy

A confederation is a group that unites for a purpose. The **Confederacy** was a confederation formed by 11 southern states.

READING SKILL

Sequence As you read, note in order the events that began the Civil War.

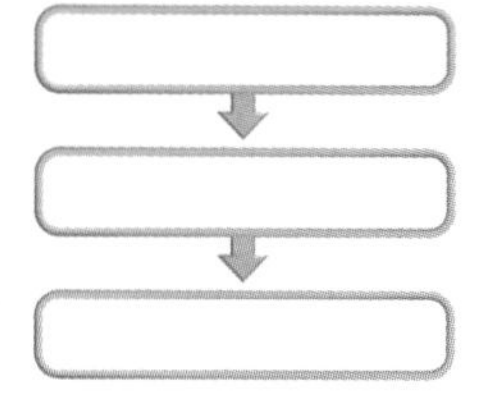

Build on What You Know You know that strong beliefs can make a difference in people's lives. President Abraham Lincoln strongly believed that the Union should not be allowed to split apart. When southern states tried to leave the Union, Lincoln went to war to stop them.

Abraham Lincoln

Main Idea Many people joined a new political party that opposed the spread of slavery.

By 1860, the conflict over slavery was becoming worse. **John Brown's** raid on Harpers Ferry in 1859 had worried people in the South. They thought abolitionists
wanted to start a slave rebellion. Some southerners 1
believed secession was the only way to protect their states' rights and continue as a slave-owning region. When part of a country leaves or breaks off from the rest it is called **secession.**

Northerners were upset as well. Many disliked the Kansas-Nebraska Act and the **Dred Scott** decision. They feared that slavery would spread across the country.
Some formed a new political party, the Republican Party. 2
Republicans wanted to keep slavery out of the territories. **Abraham Lincoln** was a famous Republican. In these difficult years, he became one of the most important leaders the United States has ever had.

Abraham Lincoln He earned a reputation for hard work and honesty.

Skill and Strategy

Reading Skill and Strategy

Reading Skill: Sequence

This skill helps you understand the order in which events happened.

Read "Civil War Begins." Then fill in the sequence chart below to show the order in which Abraham Lincoln became President.

1. Many people joined the Republican Party to oppose slavery.
2. The Republican Party chose Lincoln as their candidate.

Lincoln was elected even though he did not win any southern states.

Reading Strategy: Predict/Infer

3. Read "Abraham Lincoln" and "Lincoln's Campaigns." Use the information in these sections to make a prediction about what you will learn in the final section, "Secession Begins."
Sample answer: Abraham Lincoln's beliefs about slavery and his election as President caused many states in the South to secede from the United States.
4. Read "Secession Begins." Predict what will happen in the next chapter.
Sample answer: The North and South will fight and the North will win.

Unit Resources

122
Use with *United States History*, pp. 440–445

Unit Resources, p. 122

Background

The Confederacy

- The constitution created by the Confederate States of America was based on the U.S. Constitution, but it gave more power to the states, and it protected slavery.
- From February to May of 1861, Montgomery, Alabama, was the Confederate capital. After Virginia joined the Confederacy, the Confederate government moved to Richmond, Virginia.

Log cabin This is a copy of the cabin where Lincoln was born. As a boy, he studied math, grammar, spelling, and history. A page of his math homework is on the right.

Lincoln's Early Years

Abraham Lincoln was born in a small
3 cabin in Kentucky, a slave state. His father was a farmer there. The family later moved to Indiana and then to Illinois, both free states. As a boy, Lincoln worked hard on his father's farm. He did not have much time to go to school. He loved reading, though, and read all the books he could.

Lincoln did not want to be a farmer. He studied law and became a lawyer. Lincoln also wanted to be a member of the Illinois legislature. He first won an election at age 25 and served four terms. Each term was for two years.

Later, Lincoln served one term as a representative in the United States Congress. He argued against allowing slavery to expand into new territories. After his time in Congress, Lincoln returned to his job as a lawyer.

REVIEW Why did some southerners want their states to leave the Union?
They believed it was the only way to continue as a slave-owning region and protect their states' rights.

2 Teach

Abraham Lincoln

Talk About It

1 **Q History** Why did some southerners want their states to withdraw from the Union?

A They believed secession was the only way to protect slavery.

2 **Q Citizenship** What did Republicans think about slavery in the territories?

A Republicans wanted to keep slavery out of the territories.

3 **Q Geography** In what states did Abraham Lincoln's family live while he grew up?

A He was born in Kentucky. The family moved from there to Indiana and then to Illinois.

Vocabulary Strategy

secession Explain to students that *secede* comes from the Latin word meaning "to withdraw." A *secession* is a withdrawal.

Reading Strategy: Predict/Infer Ask students to infer why Lincoln became one of America's most important leaders. After reading the lesson, ask students to share their inferences and whether their view of Lincoln's leadership has changed.

Leveled Practice

Extra Support

Ask students to consider what questions they would like to ask Abraham Lincoln or Stephen Douglas if they had the chance. Have them **prepare questions** for each candidate. Invite them to share with the class responses they think the candidates might have made. Verbal-linguistic

Challenge

Have students **debate** whether President Lincoln should have tried to keep the Union together or let the Confederacy continue as a separate nation. Verbal-linguistic

ELL

Beginning

Ask students to **create a collage** using the quotes of Abraham Lincoln. They can illustrate the quotes with their own drawings or pictures from old magazines.

Visual-spatial; verbal-linguistic

Lincoln's Campaigns

Talk About It

4 **Q Primary Source** What did Abraham Lincoln mean when he said, "A house divided against itself cannot stand"?

A He meant that the country could not go on forever divided by slavery.

5 **Q History** What were Stephen Douglas's views on slavery?

A He didn't feel slavery was wrong and thought it should be legal if people wanted it.

Critical Thinking

Infer If Abraham Lincoln hated slavery so much, why wasn't he an abolitionist?

Think Aloud *Lincoln believed that the national government had no legal right to interfere with the rights of the slave states. Instead, he wanted to prohibit slavery in all the territories. This way, slavery would stop spreading and end on its own. So even though Lincoln hated slavery, he didn't think he could abolish it in the slave states.*

Lincoln's Campaigns

Main Idea Abraham Lincoln opposed slavery when he ran for the Senate and for President.

After Congress passed the Kansas-Nebraska Act, Lincoln decided to run for office again. In 1858, he ran for the Senate in Illinois as a Republican against **Stephen Douglas.** The two men held seven debates. In the debates, they argued about slavery.

Lincoln saw slavery as a "moral, social, and political evil." He argued that the United States could not go on forever divided by slavery. He said,

4
> "A house divided against itself cannot stand. I believe this government cannot endure [last] permanently half slave and half free. . . . It will become all one thing, or all the other."

Douglas wanted popular sovereignty in the territories. He did not believe slavery was wrong and thought it should be legal if people wanted it. Douglas also thought the country could remain split over slavery. He asked, "Why can it not exist divided into free and slave states?" 5

Lincoln hated slavery, but he did not think that the national government had the power to end slavery in slave states. The Constitution did not mention slavery. He said, "I have no purpose . . . to interfere with the institution of slavery in the states where it exists. I believe I have no lawful right to do so."

Although Lincoln did not argue for abolition, he wanted to keep slavery from spreading into the territories. Like many Republicans, Lincoln believed that slavery would end on its own if it were not allowed to spread across the country.

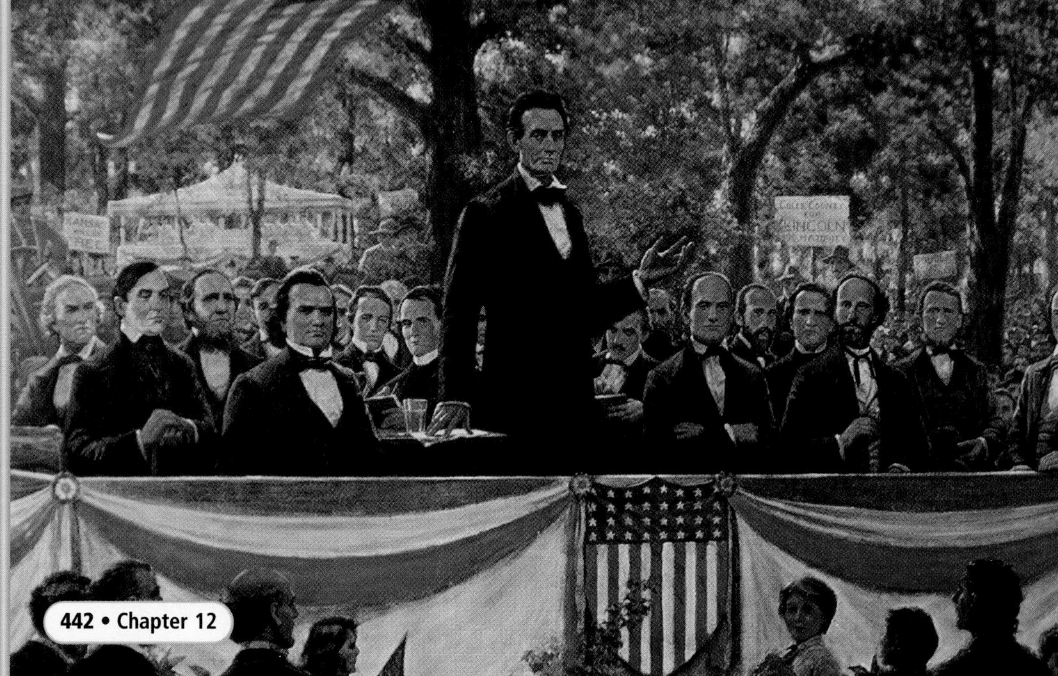

Art

Design a Campaign Poster

- Tell students that campaign posters were used to inform people about a candidate for public office.
- Ask students to pick either Abraham Lincoln or Stephen Douglas and create an informational campaign poster for their candidate.

Visual-spatial

Language Arts

Write a Magazine Profile

- Students can research Abraham Lincoln's childhood and early years to write a magazine profile of the young Lincoln as a rising political star.
- Encourage them to illustrate their articles and post their profiles on a classroom project board.

Verbal-linguistic; visual-spatial

A Divided Nation

Lincoln lost the election to Douglas, but the debates made Lincoln famous. Reporters printed what the two men said. Across the country, people read Lincoln's words. Many northerners agreed with his views on slavery. In the South, people saw him as an enemy.

In 1860, the country held an election for President. The Democratic Party was
6 split and could not agree on only one candidate. Northern Democrats chose Stephen Douglas. Southern Democrats chose **John Breckinridge** of Kentucky. Breckinridge owned slaves. He wanted slavery allowed in all the territories.

The Republican Party chose Abraham Lincoln as its candidate. Lincoln was the only candidate against slavery. He had support in the North, but very little in the South. In 10 southern states, voters were
7 not given Lincoln's name as a choice.

Lincoln won the election, but the result showed how divided Americans were. He did not win in a single southern state. To southerners, Lincoln's election was a disaster. One southern newspaper called it "the greatest evil that has ever befallen [happened to] this country."

Many southerners felt that the federal government had become too powerful. When the government passed tariffs or tried to limit slavery, southerners argued that their states' rights were under attack. With Lincoln as President, they feared that the government would grow stronger and that Lincoln would try to end slavery. They believed that secession was the only way to protect their rights.

REVIEW Why did southerners see Lincoln as an enemy?
They thought he would make the federal government too strong and that he would try to end slavery.

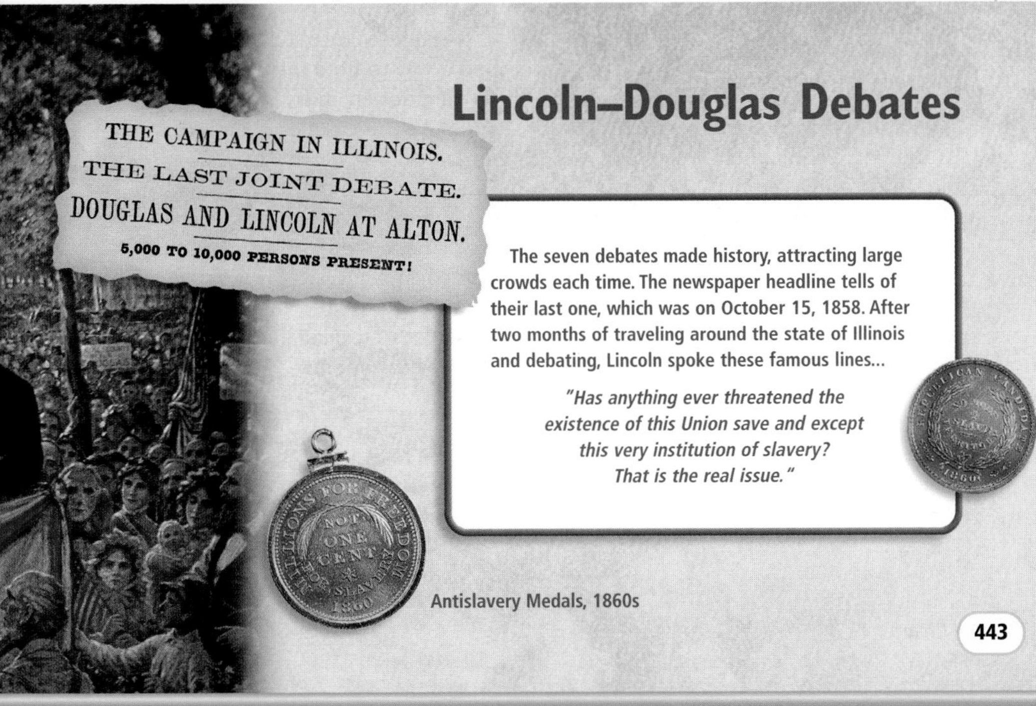

The seven debates made history, attracting large crowds each time. The newspaper headline tells of their last one, which was on October 15, 1858. After two months of traveling around the state of Illinois and debating, Lincoln spoke these famous lines...

"Has anything ever threatened the existence of this Union save and except this very institution of slavery? That is the real issue."

Antislavery Medals, 1860s

Lincoln's Campaigns

continued

Talk About It

6 **Q Citizenship** Who were the Democratic candidates for President in 1860?

A Northern Democrats voted for Stephen Douglas. Southern Democrats voted for John Breckenridge.

7 **Q Citizenship** Why would it have been difficult to vote for Lincoln in the South?

A Voters in 10 southern states were not given Lincoln's name as a choice.

Reading Strategy: Predict/Infer Ask students to predict what they think will happen when the South secedes from the North. After they read the lesson, ask students to share their predictions and whether they were the same as or different from what actually happened.

Extra Support

Report a News Story

- Have students divide up into reporters, anchor people, and eyewitnesses to create a newscast about the firing on Fort Sumter.
- Reporters should describe the causes of this event and opinions about it from both the Confederates and federal troops.

Visual-spatial; bodily-kinesthetic

Challenge

Research an Election

- Abraham Lincoln won the election for President in 1860 but did not win a single southern state.
- Have students research this election to find how many votes each candidate received and in what states they won majorities.
- Students can trace the map on page 444 to illustrate their findings, or they may create their own.

Verbal-linguistic

Secession Begins

Talk About It

8 Q History Which state was the first to leave the Union?

A South Carolina

Vocabulary Strategy

Confederacy Tell students that a *confederacy* is a political union of peoples, such as the Haudenosaunee, or states. The *Confederacy* was a political union of eleven southern states.

civil war *Civil* comes from the Latin word *civis,* citizen. A *civil war* is a war between a country's citizens.

Critical Thinking

Infer If Jefferson Davis had been elected President instead of Lincoln, what do you think would have happened?

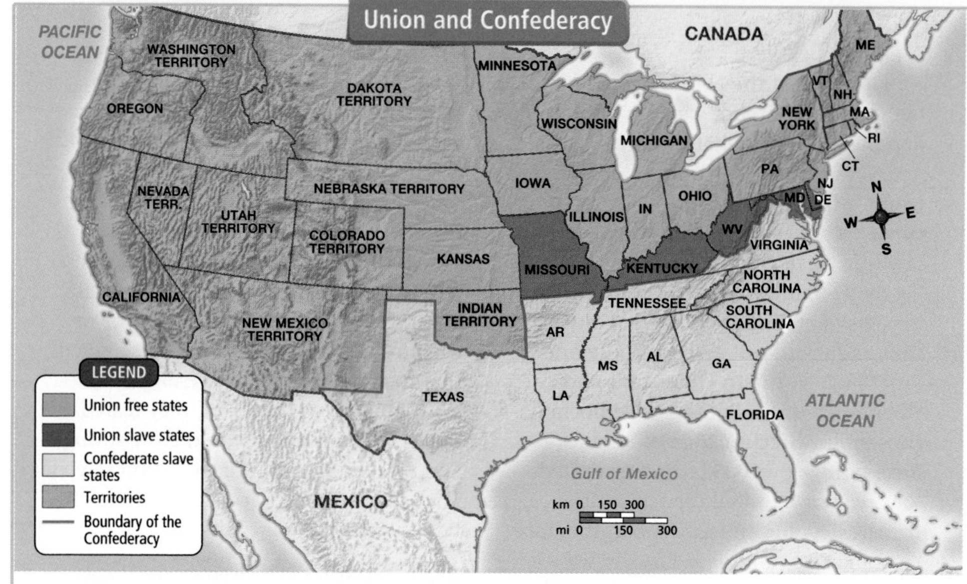

Secession Eleven slave states decided to secede from the Union. Four slave states chose to stay in the Union. SKILL **Reading Maps** How many states were part of the Union? 24

Secession Begins

Main Idea Eleven southern states left the Union and formed their own government.

8 South Carolina withdrew from the Union first. People there voted to leave the Union on December 20, 1860. Mississippi, Florida, Alabama, Georgia, Louisiana, and Texas soon did the same.

On February 4, 1861, delegates from the seven states met in Montgomery, Alabama. They voted to form their own confederation. In this confederation, the states would have more power than the central government. These states called themselves the Confederate States of America, or the **Confederacy.** The delegates elected **Jefferson Davis** as President.

Attack on Fort Sumter

President Lincoln was determined to find a way to hold the country together. "We are not enemies, but friends," he said. "We must not be enemies."

It was too late. In Charleston, South Carolina, the state militia had surrounded Fort Sumter, a federal fort with United States soldiers inside. The Confederate government wanted control of the fort, but Lincoln refused to surrender it. Instead, he sent a ship with supplies to the fort.

Jefferson Davis After serving as an officer in the Mexican War, he became a senator from Mississippi and argued for states' rights.

Math

Make a Circle Graph

Ask students to make a circle graph showing the results of the 1860 Presidential electoral vote:

- Lincoln: 180 votes
- Breckenridge: 72 votes
- Bell: 39 votes
- Douglas: 12 votes

Logical-mathematical; visual-spatial

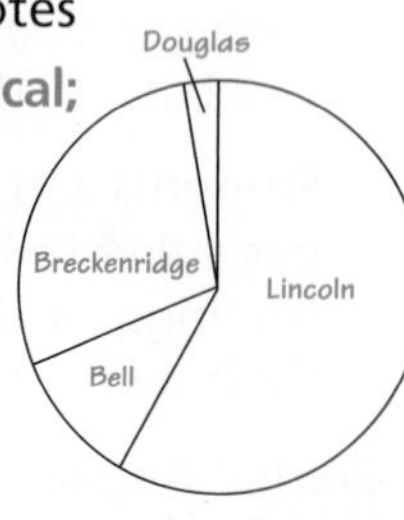

Language Arts

Write a Speech

- President Lincoln told the South "We must not be enemies."
- Ask students to write a speech that Lincoln might have given before Congress expressing why it was important to keep the country together.
- Have them begin with a strong introduction and end with a conclusion.

Verbal-linguistic

Lincoln wanted to show that he would not give in to the Confederacy. However, he also did not want to start a war. He hoped that the southern states would return to the Union peacefully.

Confederate leaders saw the refusal to surrender of Fort Sumter as an act of war. They ordered cannons to fire on the fort. The first shot was fired on April 12, 1861.

The cannons fired on Fort Sumter for 34 hours. At last, the soldiers in the fort had to surrender. The attack on Fort Sumter marked the beginning of the Civil War. A **civil war** is a war between two groups or regions within a nation.

Fort Sumter

President Lincoln called for 75,000 soldiers to fight the rebellion. Some states refused to send men to help Lincoln. Arkansas, North Carolina, Tennessee, and Virginia joined the Confederacy instead. Citizens in the North and the South prepared to fight.

REVIEW What event began the Civil War? the Confederate attack on Fort Sumter

Lesson Summary

- Americans who opposed slavery formed the Republican Party.
- Abraham Lincoln became famous for his speeches against slavery.
- After Lincoln's election, southern states began to leave the Union.

Why It Matters ...

For the first time in United States history, states tried to leave the Union. This began a terrible war.

Lesson Review

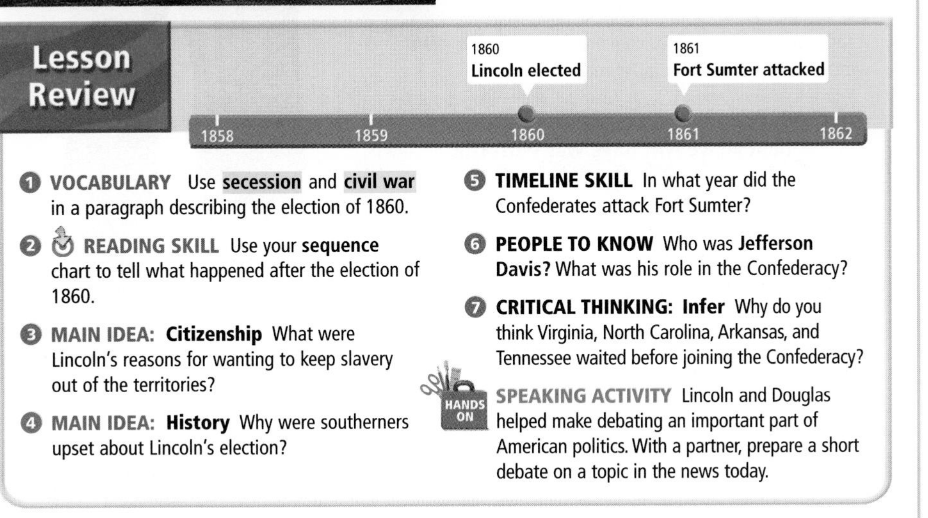

1. **VOCABULARY** Use **secession** and **civil war** in a paragraph describing the election of 1860.
2. **READING SKILL** Use your **sequence** chart to tell what happened after the election of 1860.
3. **MAIN IDEA: Citizenship** What were Lincoln's reasons for wanting to keep slavery out of the territories?
4. **MAIN IDEA: History** Why were southerners upset about Lincoln's election?
5. **TIMELINE SKILL** In what year did the Confederates attack Fort Sumter?
6. **PEOPLE TO KNOW** Who was **Jefferson Davis?** What was his role in the Confederacy?
7. **CRITICAL THINKING: Infer** Why do you think Virginia, North Carolina, Arkansas, and Tennessee waited before joining the Confederacy?

HANDS ON **SPEAKING ACTIVITY** Lincoln and Douglas helped make debating an important part of American politics. With a partner, prepare a short debate on a topic in the news today.

3 Review/Assess

Review Tested Objectives

U6-8 Lincoln was born to a Kentucky farmer and lived in both free and slave states. He opposed slavery and believed it would end on its own if it did not spread. He won the Presidency in 1860 for the Republicans.

U6-9 After Lincoln was elected, southern states decided that the only way to protect their states' rights was to secede. South Carolina voted to secede on December 20, 1860, and other states soon followed.

Lesson Review Answers

1. Answers should discuss why the election led to the secession, and the start of the Civil War.
2. South Carolina withdrew from the Union, then other southern states followed; South Carolina tried to force Union soldiers out of Fort Sumter; they fired cannon at the fort, starting the war.
3. He wanted to keep slavery from spreading.
4. They worried that Lincoln would pass laws that would abolish slavery.
5. 1861
6. Jefferson Davis was elected President of the Confederacy after southern states seceded.
7. They waited until they had to choose sides.

HANDS ON Performance Task Rubric

Score	Description
4	Debates position clearly; conveys ideas effectively; facts are correct.
3	Debates position well; conveys ideas adequately; most facts cited are accurate.
2	Debates position in a somewhat disorganized way; conveys ideas adequately; some errors.
1	Debates no position or one that is off topic; conveys ideas in a very general or incomprehensible way; many errors.

Study Guide/Homework

Vocabulary and Study Guide

Vocabulary

Across
1. Eleven southern states left the Union and formed the _____.
2. What southerners called for to protect their right to own enslaved people
3. Said to the South, "We are not enemies, but friends"
4. An issue dividing the North and South

Down
1. Began with the attack on Fort Sumter
5. President of the Confederate States

CONFEDERACY
SECESSION
LINCOLN
SLAVERY
CIVIL WAR
DAVIS

Study Guide

6. Read "Abraham Lincoln" and "Lincoln's Campaigns." Then fill in the blanks below.

Abraham Lincoln was born in Kentucky, but his family moved to Illinois when he was a boy. Lincoln studied and became a successful lawyer. He was a member of the Republican Party. He also became a member of the Illinois legislature and later served one term in the U.S. Congress. Lincoln argued against the spread of slavery, but he did not call for abolition.

7. Read "Secession Begins." Then fill in the blanks below.

Seven southern states decided to leave the Union and form the Confederate States of America. The South Carolina state militia surrounded Fort Sumter, which had U.S. soldiers inside. When President Lincoln sent supplies to the fort, the Confederacy fired on the fort with cannons. This was the start of the Civil War.

Unit Resources 123 Use with *United States History*, pp. 440–445

Unit Resources, p. 123

Reteach Minilesson

Use a cause-and-effect chart to show the various causes of the Civil War.

Causes

The election of Abraham Lincoln as President angers many southerners.	Seven southern states secede from the Union to form the Confederacy.	Confederates fire on Fort Sumter.

Effect

The Civil War begins.

www.eduplace.com/ss/hmss05/

Quick Look

Connect to Core Lesson Students have just read about the issues and events that led to the beginning of the Civil War. In Extend Lesson 4, students will read from primary sources written by people on both sides of the war.

1 Teach the Extend Lesson

Connect to the Big Idea

Conflict and Compromise People in the North and South had already feared that war was approaching before the attack on Fort Sumter took place. The issues that divided the nation also divided communities and families, often pitting neighbor against neighbor and forcing relatives to join opposing armies.

Connect to Prior Knowledge

Ask students to note the authors of the letters. Now that they know who wrote the letters, ask students to predict what the letters have in common.

Primary Sources

Blue and Gray

"I fear our happy days are gone," wrote Sarah Rousseau Espey of Alabama in her diary in March, 1861. The threat of war was tearing the United States apart. States, towns, and even families were divided over which side to support. Only a few people guessed how terrible the war would be.

Americans in the North and South wrote many letters and diary entries expressing their feelings about the causes of the war and what had to be done. Many of these letters have been saved. Today, we can read the words and think about how the writers felt.

Confederate Soldier

After South Carolina and six other southern states seceded, Americans wondered whether war was coming. One young Virginian wrote home to his mother in February 1861:

"I believe we will have war with the North in less than sixty days... I am a man who knows my rights... One of those rights is secession... But like that gallant Henry [Patrick Henry] who rose in rebellion against the mightiest empire on earth my words are 'give me liberty or give me death.'"

—John H. Cochran

Gray

Confederate soldiers often wore uniforms that were gray, or a shade of brown called butternut.

Reaching All Learners

Extra Support

Describe Primary Sources

- Have students describe the positions and feelings expressed in the letters featured in this lesson.
- Ask them to support their statements with details from the letters.

Verbal-linguistic

On Level

Add to the Letters

- Ask students to provide the beginnings and endings to the primary source letters in this lesson.
- Beginnings should include a greeting and an introduction to the text of the letters featured.
- Endings should include additions to the text and a closing.

Verbal-linguistic

Challenge

Perform a Scene

- Ask students to create and perform a scene in which the two soldiers shown above talk to one another.
- Have students consider what each character might say to the other about their feelings about the war.

Bodily-kinesthetic

PRIMARY SOURCES

Union Soldier Once the Confederacy fired on Fort Sumter, people all across the North prepared for war. A young man on his way to join the Union army wrote to the people of his home town in Middle Spring, Pennsylvania:

"I think it is my duty as well as those of my neighbors to go and join with those that have gone before; and help to fight the battles of our country... And every young single man that is healthy and will not go when his country needs him is either a coward or a rebel and I don't care which. No good country loving Patriot will stay at home when he hears of his country's flag being trampled in the dust by the Southern confederacy."

—George Traxler

Blue

At the beginning of the war Union soldiers wore many different uniforms, but soon they all wore blue.

Activities

1. **TALK ABOUT IT** How are the Union and Confederate uniforms the same? How are they different? Why are the differences important?
2. **WRITE ABOUT IT** Write a personal narrative from the point of view of one of the letter writers. Describe his feelings about going to war. Include setting, events, and other people.

Technology Learn about other primary sources for this unit at Education Place. www.eduplace.com/kids/hmss05/

447

2 Leveled Activities

1 Talk About It *For Extra Support*

Confederate soldiers wore gray uniforms and Union soldiers wore blue uniforms. Both uniforms had shirts, pants, and hats in common. The differences are important because they helped soldiers on both sides tell whether someone was an ally or enemy on the battlefield.

2 Write About It *For Challenge*

Writing Rubric

4	Narrative is well organized and shows considerable creative effort; mechanics are correct; written in past tense.
3	Narrative is adequately organized and shows creative effort; few errors; written in past tense.
2	Narrative is somewhat organized and shows some creative effort; some errors, including shifts in tense.
1	Narrative is disorganized and shows little creative effort; many errors in mechanics; past tense is absent.

ELL

Intermediate

- Encourage students to draw diagrams that show the differences and similarities between the Confederate and Union uniforms.
- Have students label the hat, shirt, and pants of each uniform, as well as its color.

Visual-spatial

Language Arts

Write a Letter

- Ask students to write a letter in response to one of the letters featured in this lesson.
- Response letters may support or oppose the views of the primary source letters.

Verbal-linguistic

Graphic Organizer

Confederate Soldier	Union Soldier
Believes there will be war in less than 60 days Believes in the right of secession Compares himself to Patrick Henry	Believes it is his duty to fight his country's battles Every healthy young man who doesn't go is a coward or a rebel No patriot will stay at home when the Confederacy dishonors the flag

Graphic Organizer 1

Chapter Review

Visual Summary

1. Nat Turner was an enslaved person who began a rebellion against slavery in Virginia. *(Obj. U6-4)*
2. In 1859, John Brown led an attack on a U.S. army post in Harpers Ferry, Virginia, hoping to begin a rebellion against slavery. *(Obj. U6-4)*
3. The Confederate government fired cannons at the federal fort. This battle began the Civil War. *(Obj. U6-7)*

Facts and Main Ideas

4. plantation owners used more enslaved African Americans. *(Obj. U6-2)*
5. Southerners passed laws to control both enslaved and free blacks. They still believed that slavery was necessary. *(Obj. U6-4)*
6. The act recognized the right to vote on slavery in the Kansas and Nebraska territories. Settlers supporting and opposing slavery fought each other. Kansas joined the Union as a free state. *(Obj. U6-6)*
7. It helped enslaved people escape to the North, Canada, Florida, Mexico, or the Caribbean. *(Obj. U6-5)*
8. Lincoln was the only candidate against slavery. Many feared he would make the federal government stronger and try to end slavery. *(Obj. U6-9)*

Vocabulary

9. **popular sovereignty** *(Obj. U6-6)*
10. **tariff** *(Obj. U6-7)*
11. **fugitive** *(Obj. U6-5)*

Chapter 12 Review and Test Prep

Visual Summary

1–3. Write a description of each event named below.

Conflicts before the Civil War	
Nat Turner's Rebellion	
Attack on Harpers Ferry	
Attack on Fort Sumter	

Facts and Main Ideas

TEST PREP Answer each question with information from the chapter.

4. **Economics** What happened to slavery as states grew more cotton?
5. **History** What effect did Nat Turner's rebellion have on southerners and their opinion of freedom for African Americans?
6. **Geography** What were the results of the Kansas-Nebraska Act?
7. **History** How did the Underground Railroad help people escape slavery?
8. **Government** Why were many southerners unhappy when Abraham Lincoln was elected President?

Vocabulary

TEST PREP Choose the correct word from the list below to complete each sentence.

tariff, p. 418
popular sovereignty, p. 433
fugitive, p. 434

9. In some territories, settlers had _____ and decided for themselves whether to allow slavery.
10. When Congress passed a _____, people had to pay higher prices for imported goods.
11. An escaped slave was called a _____.

Reading/Language Arts Wrap-Up

Reading Strategy: Predict/Infer

Review with students the process of evaluating information in order to make a prediction.

Based on what students have read in the chapter, you may wish to involve the class in making predictions about what they will read next.

Writing Strategy

As students write, they can apply what they know about predicting and inferring to how their readers will react to their text.

Have students review their written work and look for places where the reader has to infer or predict. Have students do a self-check: "Have I given the reader enough information to predict or infer correctly?"

CHAPTER SUMMARY TIMELINE

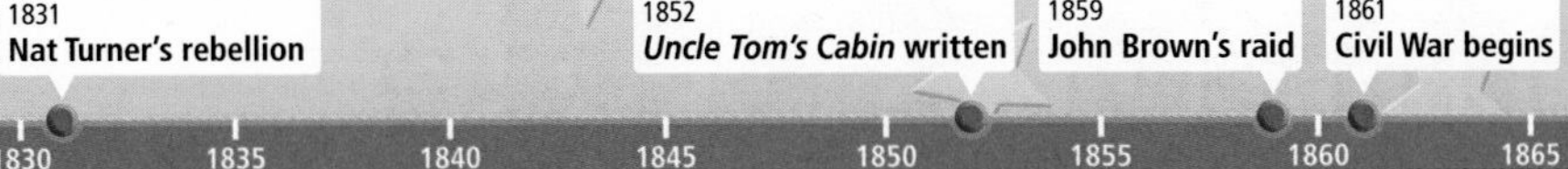

Apply Skills

✓ **TEST PREP Chart and Graph Skill**
Use the graphs about African American population before the Civil War to answer each question.

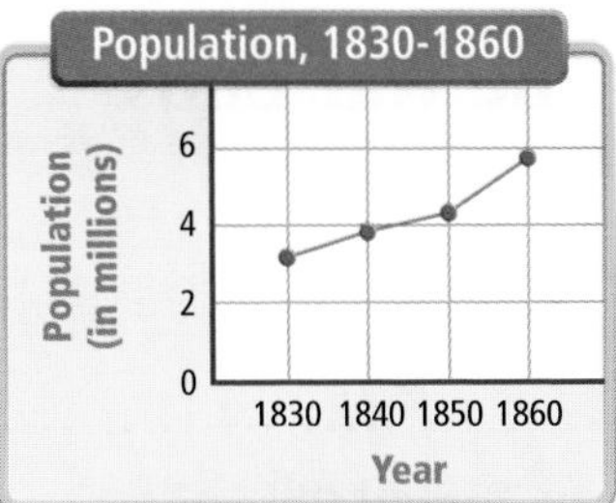

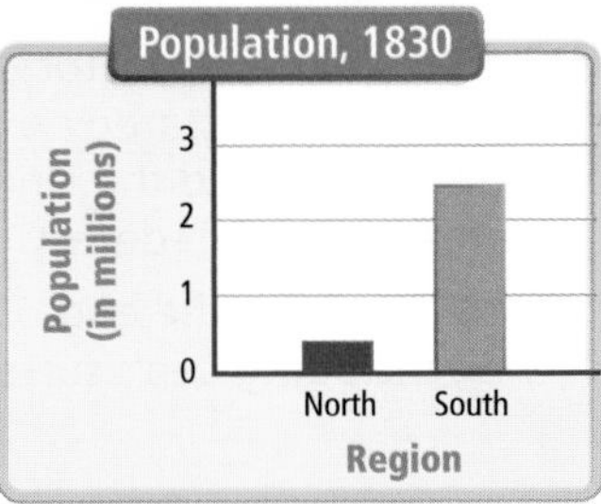

12. Which statement is most accurate?

A. The number of African Americans in the North grew quickly.

B. The number of African Americans in the North and South was equal in 1830.

C. The number of African Americans decreased over time.

D. The number of African Americans in the South was greater than in the North.

13. What do the two graphs have in common?

Critical Thinking

✓ **TEST PREP** Write a short paragraph to answer each question.

14. Cause and Effect What were the causes of sectionalism in the United States?

15. Compare and Contrast In what way was Abraham Lincoln's view of slavery different from that of Stephen Douglas?

Timeline

Use the Chapter Summary Timeline above to answer the question.

16. Which events took place during the 1850s?

Activities

Research Activity With a partner, find out more about an abolitionist in this chapter. Write and illustrate a short biography of that person.

Writing Activity Write a dialogue for a story in which a member of the Underground Railroad asks friends to help rescue enslaved people. Have the characters discuss the dangers and importance of the work.

Technology
Writing Process Tips
Get help with your story at
www.eduplace.com/kids/hmss05/

449

Apply Skills

12. D *(Obj. U6-3)*

13. Both give data about the African American population in 1830. *(Obj. U6-3)*

Critical Thinking

14. different economies of the North and South, disagreements about slavery and tariffs *(Obj. U6-7)*

15. Lincoln believed that the United States could not survive if it were divided by slavery. He thought the country could be divided into slave and free states. *(Obj. U6-8)*

Timeline

16. *Uncle Tom's Cabin* was written and John Brown's raid *(Obj. U6-7)*

Leveled Activities

HANDS ON Performance Task Rubric

4	Biography is thorough, clear, accurate, and well organized; mechanics correct.
3	Biography is fairly clear, accurate, organized; most mechanics correct.
2	Biography is somewhat confusing or inaccurate; some mechanical errors.
1	Biography is incomplete or inaccurate; many mechanical errors.

Writing Rubric

4	Dialogue is creative, vivid, and reflects thorough understanding of lesson; mechanics correct.
3	Dialogue reflects understanding of lesson, most mechanics correct.
2	Dialogue reflects partial understanding of lesson, some mechanical errors.
1	Dialogue is incomplete or does not reflect an understanding of lesson; many mechanical errors.

Technology

Test Generator

You can generate your own version of the chapter review by using the **Test Generator CD-ROM.**

Web Links

For more ideas, visit **www.eduplace.com/ss/hmss05/**

Standards

National Standards

I a Addressing human needs and concerns **II c** Accounts of the past **III c** Resources, data sources, and geographic tools **III h** Humans and the environment **V d** Internal conflicts **V e** Individual beliefs and government policies and laws **V g** Individual needs and the common good **VI f** Cooperation and disputes **VI h** Wants and needs and fairness, equity, and justice **VII d** Economic systems **VII i** Supply, demand, and price **IX b** Conflict, cooperation, and interdependence **X e** Citizens and public policy **X f** Formal and informal actors that shape public policy **X h** Public policies and citizen behaviors **X j** How the "common good" can be strengthened

Chapter 13 Planning Guide

Civil War and Reconstruction

Chapter Opener

pp. 450–451

30 minutes

Reading/Vocabulary

Chapter Reading Strategy: Summarize, p. 449F

Resources

Grade Level Resources
- Vocabulary Cards, pp. 51–58

Reaching All Learners
- Challenge Activities, p. 91

Primary Sources Plus, p. 23

Big Idea Transparency 6

Interactive Transparency 6

Text & Music Audio CD

Lesson Planner & TR CD-ROM

eBook

eTE

Core Lesson 1

A Nation at War

Pages 452–457

 50 minutes

Tested Objectives

U6-10 Compare the Confederacy and the Union.

U6-11 Identify important battles and events in the early years of the Civil War.

U6-12 Describe the significance of the Emancipation Proclamation.

Reading/Vocabulary

Reading Skill: Classify

border states, draft, casualties, emancipation

Cross-Curricular

Math, p. 454 **Art,** p. 454 **Drama,** p. 456

Resources

Unit Resources:
- **Reading Skill/Strategy,** p. 124
- **Vocabulary/Study Guide,** p. 125

Reaching All Learners:
- **Lesson Summary,** p. 50
- **Support for Lang. Dev./ELL,** p. 147

Assessment Options:
- **Lesson Test,** p. 128

www.eduplace.com/ss/hmss05

Extend Lesson 1

Primary Source

Gettysburg Address

20–30 minutes

Pages 458–459

Focus: Students read and understand President Lincoln's short speech.

Core Lesson 2

The Human Face of War

Pages 460–463

 40 minutes

Tested Objectives

U6-13 Describe the conditions that soldiers faced during the Civil War.

U6-14 Explain how the war affected people on the home fronts in both the North and the South.

Reading/Vocabulary

Reading Skill: Main Idea and Details

camp, civilian, home front

Cross-Curricular

Science, p. 462

Resources

Unit Resources:
- **Reading Skill/Strategy,** p. 126
- **Vocabulary/Study Guide,** p. 127

Reaching All Learners:
- **Lesson Summary,** p. 51
- **Support for Lang. Dev./ELL,** p. 148

Assessment Options:
- **Lesson Test,** p. 129

www.eduplace.com/ss/hmss05

Extend Lesson 2

Biographies

Courageous Women

20–30 minutes

Pages 464–465

Focus: Profiles of three women whose courage inspired others.

Core Lesson 3

The War Ends

Pages 466–469

 40 minutes

Tested Objectives

U6-15 Explain the factors, including the strategy of total war, that helped the Union defeat the Confederacy.

U6-16 Describe the end of the war, including Lee's surrender.

Reading/Vocabulary

Reading Skill: Predict Outcomes

telegraph, desert, total war

Cross-Curricular

Math, p. 468

Resources

Unit Resources:
- **Reading Skill/Strategy,** p. 128
- **Vocabulary/Study Guide,** p. 129

Reaching All Learners:
- **Lesson Summary,** p. 52
- **Support for Lang. Dev./ELL,** p. 149

Assessment Options:
- **Lesson Test,** p. 13

Extend Lesson 3

Geography

A Global View, 1865

20–30 minutes

Pages 470–471

Focus: A world map shows important events in other countries.

National Standards

II b Vocabulary associated with time, timelines; examples of change; and cause and effect relationships
II d Sources for reconstructing the past
IV g Analyze a particular event
VI h Tensions between the wants and needs and fairness, equity, and justice
IX b Conflict, cooperation, and interdependence among individuals, groups, and nations
IX f Universal human rights
X a K key ideals
X b Citizen rights and responsibilities
X h Public policies and citizen behaviors

Core Lesson 4

Reconstruction

Pages 472–477

 50 minutes

Tested Objectives

U6-17 Compare the different plans for reuniting the country and rebuilding the South after the Civil War.

U6-18 Describe how the Constitution changed to protect the rights of African Americans after the war.

Reading/Vocabulary

Reading Skill: Draw Conclusions

Reconstruction **impeach**
assassination
Freedmen's Bureau

Cross-Curricular

Math, p. 474
Drama, p. 476

Resources

Unit Resources:
- **Reading Skill/Strategy,** p. 130
- **Vocabulary/Study Guide,** p. 131

Reaching All Learners:
- **Lesson Summary,** p. 53
- **Support for Lang. Dev./ELL,** p. 150

Assessment Options:
- **Lesson Test,** p. 131

Extend Lesson 4

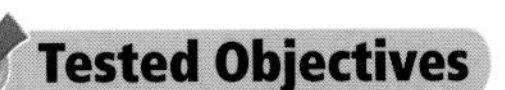

Economics

The South After the War

20–30 minutes

Pages 478–479

Focus: What problem did the South face after the Civil War? Students find out.

Skillbuilder

Study Skill

Compare Primary and Secondary Sources

Pages 480–481

 20 minutes

Tested Objectives

U6-19 Identify and interpret the difference between primary and secondary sources.

Reading/Vocabulary

primary source
secondary source

Resources

Unit Resources:
- **Skill Practice,** p. 132

Skill Transparency 13

Core Lesson 5

The Challenge of Freedom

Pages 482–485

 40 minutes

Tested Objectives

U6-20 Explain the effects of Reconstruction policies on the South after the Civil War.

U6-21 Describe the end of Reconstruction in the South.

Reading/Vocabulary

Reading Skill: Problem and Solution

sharecropping **segregation**
Jim Crow

Cross-Curricular

Science, p. 484

Resources

Unit Resources:
- **Reading Skill/Strategy,** p. 133
- **Vocabulary/Study Guide,** p. 134

Reaching All Learners:
- **Lesson Summary,** p. 54
- **Support for Lang. Dev./ELL,** p. 151

Assessment Options:
- **Lesson Test,** p. 132

Extend Lesson 5

History

African American Education

20–30 minutes

Pages 486–487

Focus: A look inside a classroom at the Tuskegee Institute in the 1870s.

Chapter Review

Pages 488–489

30 minutes

Resources

Assessment Options:
- **Chapter 13 Test**
- **Test Generator**

Chapter 13 Practice Options

Lesson 1 Skill and Strategy

TEST PREP

Reading Skill and Strategy

Reading Skill: Classify

This skill helps you understand and remember what you have read by organizing facts into groups or categories.

Read "North Against South." What were the advantages for the Union and the Confederacy?

Union	Confederacy
1. More factories to make weapons	2. Knew the land where the fighting took place
3. More railroads for supplies	4. Excellent military leaders

Reading Strategy: Summarize

5. Read "North Against South." Then check the best summary.
   - ✓ The North and the South had different advantages in the war.
   - ___ There were more people in the North than in the South.
   - ___ The Confederacy defeated the Union at the First Battle of Bull Run.
6. Read "The War's Leaders." Then check the best summary.
   - ___ The Union had many more generals than the Confederacy.
   - ___ General Lee and General Grant fought each other in many battles.
   - ✓ Political and military leaders were very important during the Civil War.

Unit Resources 124 Use with *United States History*, pp. 452–457

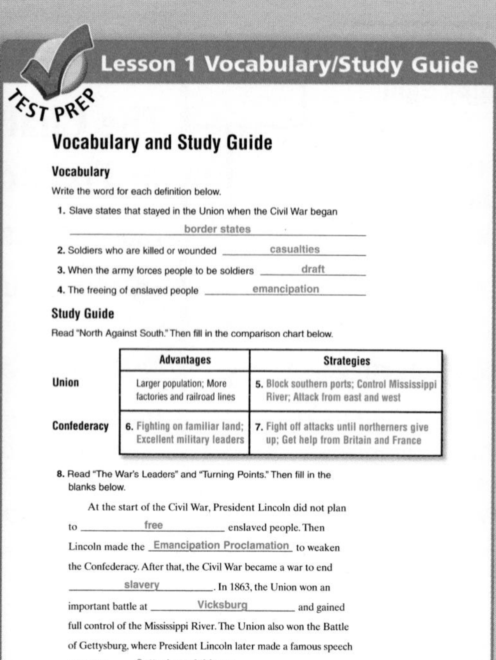

Lesson 1 Vocabulary/Study Guide

TEST PREP

Vocabulary and Study Guide

Vocabulary

Write the word for each definition below.

1. Slave states that stayed in the Union when the Civil War began border states
2. Soldiers who are killed or wounded casualties
3. When the army forces people to be soldiers draft
4. The freeing of enslaved people emancipation

Study Guide

Read "North Against South." Then fill in the comparison chart below.

	Advantages	Strategies
Union	Larger population; More factories and railroad lines	5. Block southern ports; Control Mississippi River; Attack from east and west
Confederacy	6. Fighting on familiar land; Excellent military leaders	7. Fight off attacks until northerners give up; Get help from Britain and France

8. Read "The War's Leaders" and "Turning Points." Then fill in the blanks below.

At the start of the Civil War, President Lincoln did not plan to free enslaved people. Then Lincoln made the Emancipation Proclamation to weaken the Confederacy. After that, the Civil War became a war to end slavery. In 1863, the Union won an important battle at Vicksburg and gained full control of the Mississippi River. The Union also won the Battle of Gettysburg, where President Lincoln later made a famous speech called the Gettysburg Address.

Unit Resources 125 Use with *United States History*, pp. 452–457

also in *Practice Book*, p. 74

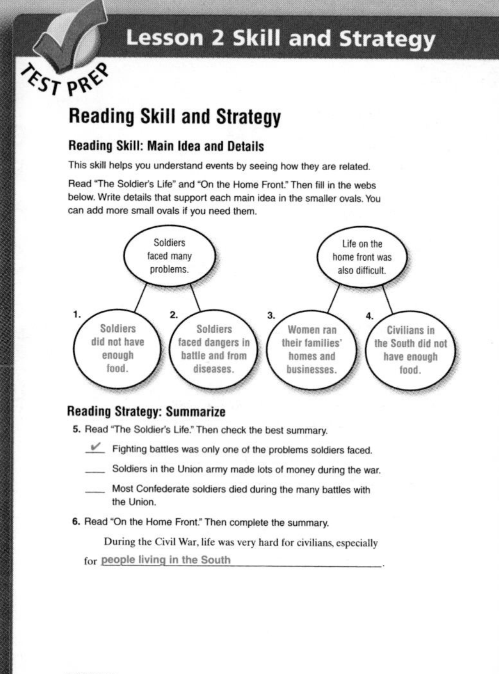

Lesson 2 Skill and Strategy

TEST PREP

Reading Skill and Strategy

Reading Skill: Main Idea and Details

This skill helps you understand events by seeing how they are related.

Read "The Soldier's Life" and "On the Home Front." Then fill in the webs below. Write details that support each main idea in the smaller ovals. You can add more small ovals if you need them.

Reading Strategy: Summarize

5. Read "The Soldier's Life." Then check the best summary.
   - ✓ Fighting battles was only one of the problems soldiers faced.
   - ___ Soldiers in the Union army made lots of money during the war.
   - ___ Most Confederate soldiers died during the many battles with the Union.
6. Read "On the Home Front." Then complete the summary.

During the Civil War, life was very hard for civilians, especially for people living in the South.

Unit Resources 126 Use with *United States History*, pp. 460–463

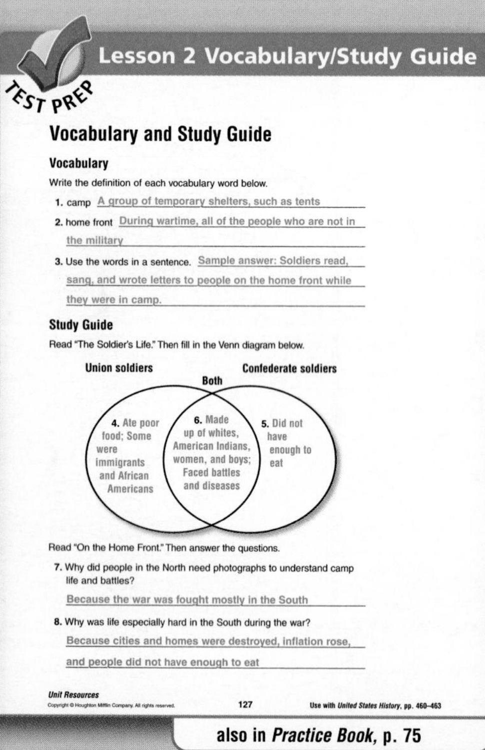

Lesson 2 Vocabulary/Study Guide

TEST PREP

Vocabulary and Study Guide

Vocabulary

Write the definition of each vocabulary word below.

1. camp A group of temporary shelters, such as tents
2. home front During wartime, all of the people who are not in the military
3. Use the words in a sentence. Sample answer: Soldiers read, sang, and wrote letters to people on the home front while they were in camp.

Study Guide

Read "The Soldier's Life." Then fill in the Venn diagram below.

Read "On the Home Front." Then answer the questions.

7. Why did people in the North need photographs to understand camp life and battles?
   Because the war was fought mostly in the South
8. Why was life especially hard in the South during the war?
   Because cities and homes were destroyed, inflation rose, and people did not have enough to eat

Unit Resources 127 Use with *United States History*, pp. 460–463

also in *Practice Book*, p. 75

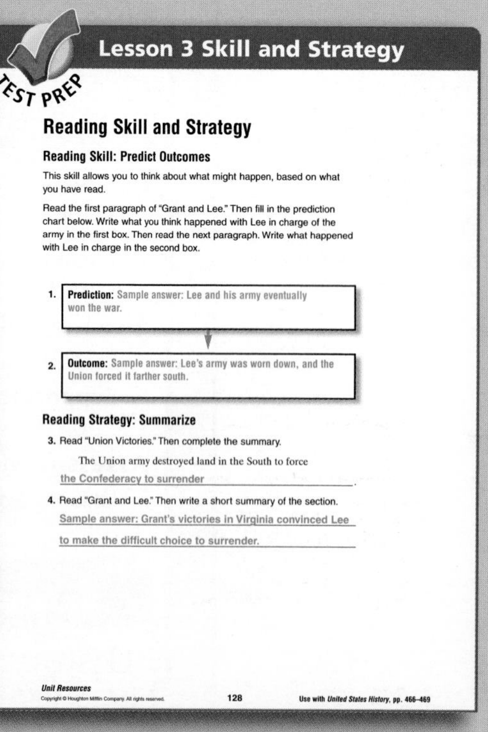

Lesson 3 Skill and Strategy

TEST PREP

Reading Skill and Strategy

Reading Skill: Predict Outcomes

This skill allows you to think about what might happen, based on what you have read.

Read the first paragraph of "Grant and Lee." Then fill in the prediction chart below. Write what you think happened with Lee in charge of the army in the first box. Then read the next paragraph. Write what happened with Lee in charge in the second box.

1. **Prediction:** Sample answer: Lee and his army eventually won the war.
2. **Outcome:** Sample answer: Lee's army was worn down, and the Union forced it farther south.

Reading Strategy: Summarize

3. Read "Union Victories." Then complete the summary.

The Union army destroyed land in the South to force the Confederacy to surrender.

4. Read "Grant and Lee." Then write a short summary of the section.
   Sample answer: Grant's victories in Virginia convinced Lee to make the difficult choice to surrender.

Unit Resources 128 Use with *United States History*, pp. 466–469

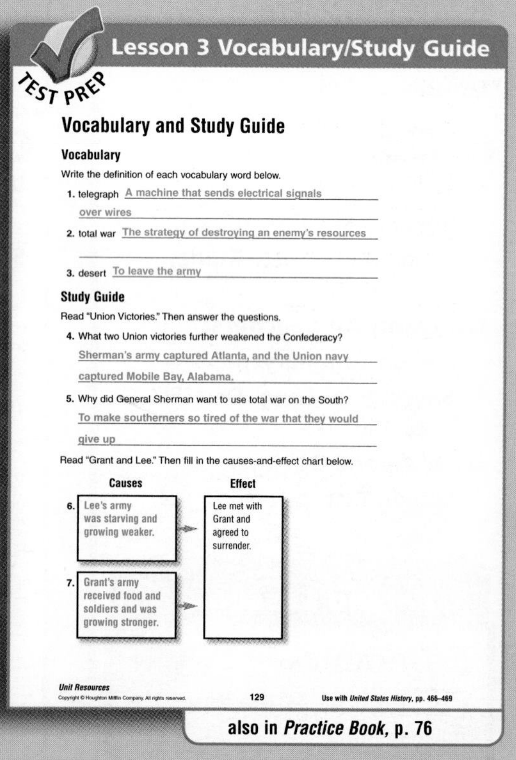

Lesson 3 Vocabulary/Study Guide

TEST PREP

Vocabulary and Study Guide

Vocabulary

Write the definition of each vocabulary word below.

1. telegraph A machine that sends electrical signals over wires
2. total war The strategy of destroying an enemy's resources
3. desert To leave the army

Study Guide

Read "Union Victories." Then answer the questions.

4. What two Union victories further weakened the Confederacy?
   Sherman's army captured Atlanta, and the Union navy captured Mobile Bay, Alabama.
5. Why did General Sherman want to use total war on the South?
   To make southerners so tired of the war that they would give up

Read "Grant and Lee." Then fill in the causes-and-effect chart below.

Causes	Effect
6. Lee's army was starving and growing weaker.	Lee met with Grant and agreed to surrender.
7. Grant's army received food and soldiers and was growing stronger.	

Unit Resources 129 Use with *United States History*, pp. 466–469

also in *Practice Book*, p. 76

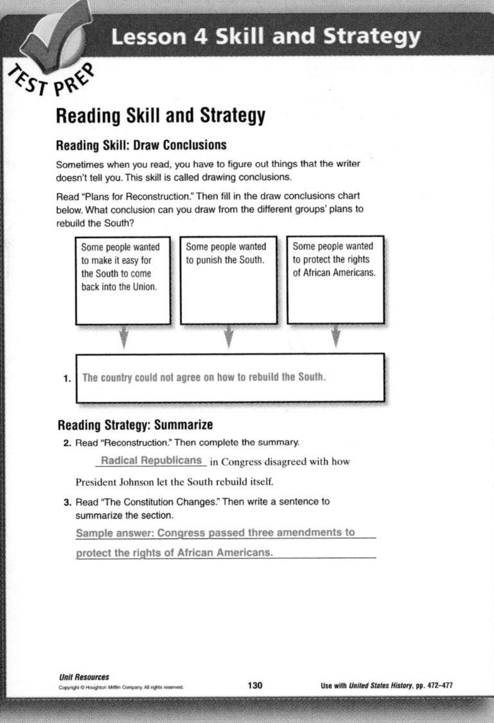

Lesson 4 Skill and Strategy

TEST PREP

Reading Skill and Strategy

Reading Skill: Draw Conclusions

Sometimes when you read, you have to figure out things that the writer doesn't tell you. This skill is called drawing conclusions.

Read "Plans for Reconstruction." Then fill in the draw conclusions chart below. What conclusion can you draw from the different groups' plans to rebuild the South?

Some people wanted to make it easy for the South to come back into the Union.	Some people wanted to punish the South.	Some people wanted to protect the rights of African Americans.

1. The country could not agree on how to rebuild the South.

Reading Strategy: Summarize

2. Read "Reconstruction." Then complete the summary.
   Radical Republicans in Congress disagreed with how President Johnson let the South rebuild itself.
3. Read "The Constitution Changes." Then write a sentence to summarize the section.
   Sample answer: Congress passed three amendments to protect the rights of African Americans.

Unit Resources

130
Use with *United States History*, pp. 472–477

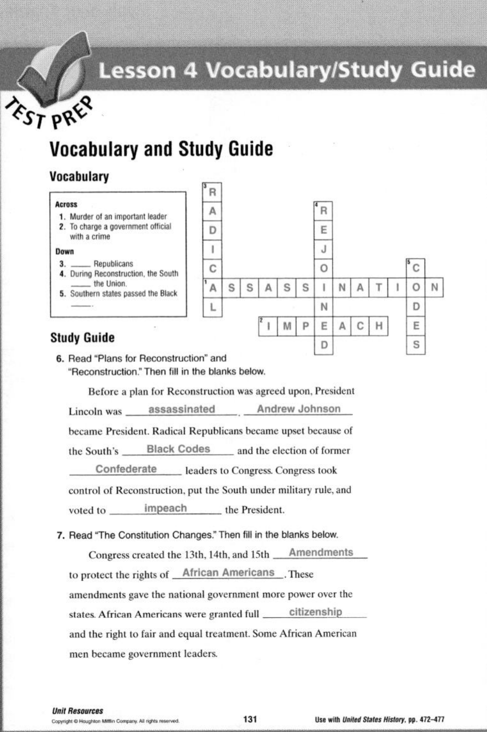

Lesson 4 Vocabulary/Study Guide

TEST PREP

Vocabulary and Study Guide

Vocabulary

Across
1. Murder of an important leader
2. To charge a government official with a crime

Down
3. ____ Republicans
4. During Reconstruction, the South ____ the Union.
5. Southern states passed the Black ____

Crossword answers: 1 ASSASSINATION; 2 IMPEACH; 3 RADICAL; 4 REJOINED; 5 CODES

Study Guide

6. Read "Plans for Reconstruction" and "Reconstruction." Then fill in the blanks below.
   Before a plan for Reconstruction was agreed upon, President Lincoln was assassinated. Andrew Johnson became President. Radical Republicans became upset because of the South's Black Codes and the election of former Confederate leaders to Congress. Congress took control of Reconstruction, put the South under military rule, and voted to impeach the President.
7. Read "The Constitution Changes." Then fill in the blanks below.
   Congress created the 13th, 14th, and 15th Amendments to protect the rights of African Americans. These amendments gave the national government more power over the states. African Americans were granted full citizenship and the right to fair and equal treatment. Some African American men became government leaders.

Unit Resources

131
Use with *United States History*, pp. 472–477

also in *Practice Book*, p. 77

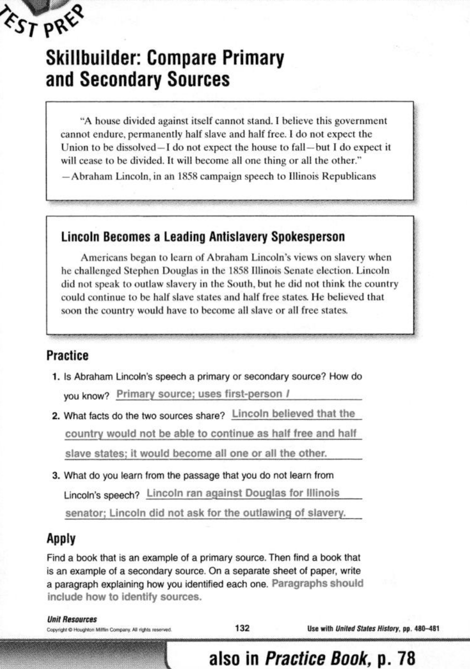

Skillbuilder Practice

TEST PREP

Skillbuilder: Compare Primary and Secondary Sources

"A house divided against itself cannot stand. I believe this government cannot endure, permanently half slave and half free. I do not expect the Union to be dissolved—I do not expect the house to fall—but I do expect it will cease to be divided. It will become all one thing or all the other."
—Abraham Lincoln, in an 1858 campaign speech to Illinois Republicans

Lincoln Becomes a Leading Antislavery Spokesperson

Americans began to learn of Abraham Lincoln's views on slavery when he challenged Stephen Douglas in the 1858 Illinois Senate election. Lincoln did not speak to outlaw slavery in the South, but he did not think the country could continue to be half slave states and half free states. He believed that soon the country would have to become all slave or all free states.

Practice

1. Is Abraham Lincoln's speech a primary or secondary source? How do you know? Primary source; uses first-person *I*
2. What facts do the two sources share? Lincoln believed that the country would not be able to continue as half free and half slave states; it would become all one or all the other.
3. What do you learn from the passage that you do not learn from Lincoln's speech? Lincoln ran against Douglas for Illinois senator; Lincoln did not ask for the outlawing of slavery.

Apply

Find a book that is an example of a primary source. Then find a book that is an example of a secondary source. On a separate sheet of paper, write a paragraph explaining how you identified each one. Paragraphs should include how to identify sources.

Unit Resources

132
Use with *United States History*, pp. 480–481

also in *Practice Book*, p. 78

Lesson 5 Skill and Strategy

TEST PREP

Reading Skill and Strategy

Reading Skill: Problem and Solution

This skill helps you see what problem some people faced and how they resolved it.

Read "The Challenge of Freedom." Then fill in the problem-and-solution chart below. What happened to the freed people during and after Reconstruction?

Problems	Solutions
1. Freed African Americans wanted to farm for themselves.	Many African Americans became sharecroppers.
Government soldiers left the South.	2. Southern states passed Jim Crow laws.

Reading Strategy: Summarize

3. Read "The Challenge of Freedom." Then write a short summary of each section.
   Section 1: Freedom and Hardship
   Summary: Sample answer: African Americans experienced difficult times after being freed.
   Section 2: The End of Reconstruction
   Summary: Sample answer: Many of the rights African Americans gained during Reconstruction were lost afterward.

Unit Resources

133
Use with *United States History*, pp. 482–485

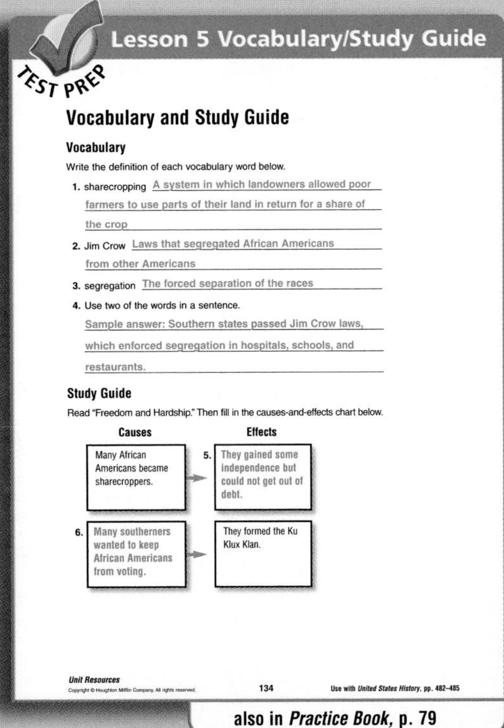

Lesson 5 Vocabulary/Study Guide

TEST PREP

Vocabulary and Study Guide

Vocabulary

Write the definition of each vocabulary word below.

1. sharecropping A system in which landowners allowed poor farmers to use parts of their land in return for a share of the crop
2. Jim Crow Laws that segregated African Americans from other Americans
3. segregation The forced separation of the races
4. Use two of the words in a sentence.
   Sample answer: Southern states passed Jim Crow laws, which enforced segregation in hospitals, schools, and restaurants.

Study Guide

Read "Freedom and Hardship." Then fill in the causes-and-effects chart below.

Causes	Effects
Many African Americans became sharecroppers.	5. They gained some independence but could not get out of debt.
6. Many southerners wanted to keep African Americans from voting.	They formed the Ku Klux Klan.

Unit Resources

134
Use with *United States History*, pp. 482–485

also in *Practice Book*, p. 79

Chapter 13 Assessment Options

Chapter 13 Test

Chapter 13 Test

Test Your Knowledge

casualties	home front	desert	Jim Crow

Fill in the blank with the correct word from the box.

1. At the Battle of Antietam, the Union and Confederate armies suffered 22,000 casualties. Obj. U6–11
2. Toward the end of the war, hungry Confederate soldiers began to desert. Obj. U6–16
3. Many civilians on the southern home front could not afford to buy enough food. Obj. U6–14
4. The Jim Crow laws segregated African Americans from other Americans and made it difficult for them to vote. Obj. U6–21

Circle the letter of the best answer.

5. How did the Emancipation Proclamation change the war? Obj. U6–12
   - (A.) It made the war a war to end slavery in the heart of the South.
   - B. It made the war a war to end the Union.
   - C. It started the draft for the war.
   - D. It forced the Confederate armies to retreat.
6. Where did most of the battles in the Civil War take place? Obj. U6–11
   - F. in the East
   - G. in the West
   - H. in the North
   - (J.) in the South
7. How did General Sherman's strategy of total war help the Union defeat the Confederacy? Obj. U6–15
   - A. It helped the Union draft more soldiers.
   - B. It cleared a path to the sea for transporting Union supplies.
   - (C.) It destroyed the resources southerners needed for the war.
   - D. It helped Union soldiers get good training.
8. Which constitutional amendment gave full citizenship to African Americans? Obj. U6–18
   - F. the Thirteenth Amendment
   - (G.) the Fourteenth Amendment
   - H. the Fifteenth Amendment
   - J. the Sixteenth Amendment

Assessment Options

133
Use with *United States History*

Chapter 13 Test

Apply Your Knowledge

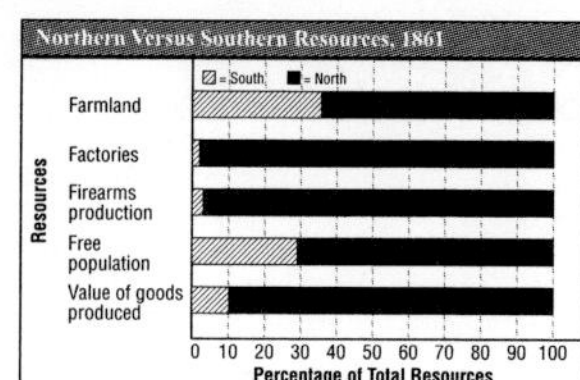

Use the graph to answer the following questions.

9. In 1861, about what percentage of the free population lived in the South? Obj. U6–10
   - A. 10 percent
   - B. 70 percent
   - (C.) 30 percent
   - D. 5 percent
10. What advantage did the Confederate states have in fighting the Civil War? Obj. U6–10
    - F. The Confederate states had help from France and Britain.
    - G. Most of the weapon factories were in the Confederate states.
    - H. The Confederate states had more free states.
    - (J.) Most of the fighting took place in the Confederate states.

Apply the Reading Skill: Classify

Read the passage below. Then answer the questions. Obj. U6–17

> Americans could not agree on how to bring the South back into the Union. President Lincoln asked northerners not to punish the South. He wanted to make it easy for the South to rejoin the Union. The Radical Republicans in Congress wanted to change the South greatly and protect the rights of African Americans.

11. Classify the two opinions about Reconstruction plans. Whose opinion was about reuniting the country? Whose opinion was about rebuilding the South?
    President Lincoln wanted to reunite the country. The Radical Republicans wanted to change the South.

Assessment Options

134
Use with *United States History*

Chapter 13 Test

Test the Skill: Compare Primary and Secondary Sources

> "All persons held as slaves within any State or designated part of a State . . . shall be then, thenceforward, and forever free; and the Executive Government of the United States, including the military and naval authority thereof, will recognize and maintain the freedom of such persons, and will do no act or acts to repress such persons, or any of them, in any efforts they may make for their actual freedom."
>
> —Emancipation Proclamation, 1862

> President Abraham Lincoln issued the Emancipation Proclamation in 1862. The proclamation stated that all enslaved people in the Confederate states would become free. The Confederate states, however, did not obey the proclamation. Most enslaved people in the South did not gain their freedom until after the Union won the war.
>
> —encyclopedia article

12. Is the Emancipation Proclamation a primary or secondary source? How do you know? Primary source; it includes words from an original document. Obj. U6–19
13. What facts are similar in the two sources? Obj. U6–19 Sample answer: Enslaved people were declared free by the Emancipation Proclamation.
14. How is the primary source different from the secondary source? Obj. U6–19
    Sample answer: The primary source includes more details.

Apply the Skill

15. Based on what you have learned about primary and secondary sources, which source would provide a more useful summary? Obj. U6–19
    Secondary source

Assessment Options

135
Use with *United States History*

Chapter 13 Test

Think and Write

16. **Short Response:** Explain sharecropping and how it affected African Americans during Reconstruction. Obj. U6–20
    Most freed African Americans could not afford to buy their own land. Landowners let poor farmers use their land in return for a share of crops. Most sharecroppers could not repay landowners for seeds and tools and went into debt.
17. **Critical Thinking: Analyze** In what way did President Johnson and Congress disagree on Reconstruction? Obj. U6–21
    The President allowed the southern states to elect former Confederate leaders into Congress and pass Black Codes. Congress voted to keep southern representatives out of Congress and passed laws protecting freed people.
18. **Extended Response:** General Lee has just surrendered. Write a letter from a Union soldier to his family. Describe the events of the last few days. Write your letter on a separate sheet of paper. Obj. U6–16 **Sample response: The letter should tell how Grant and the Union army kept attacking despite terrible losses; how both armies fought near Richmond for almost a year; how additional food, supplies, and soldiers helped the Union army; and what brought about the surrender of General Lee.**

Self-Assessment

Who was an important leader or hero of the Civil War? Why do I think so?

Assessment Options

136
Use with *United States History*

You can share the following fiction selection with students before beginning the chapter.

Activate Prior Knowledge

Ask students to discuss what they know about the Civil War. Explain that the Read-Aloud selection describes what it felt like to anticipate being sent to fight in that war. They will read about the real events of the Civil War in this chapter.

Preview the Chapter

Have students skim the section The Governments Respond on page 455 of their books. Ask them to find similarities and differences between the information in this section and the details mentioned in the Read Aloud.

Read-Aloud Vocabulary

Explain that in a **draft,** people are chosen to serve in the military and are required to do so. **Casualties** are those injured or killed in a war.

Preview the Reading Strategy

Summarize Explain to students that the reading strategy they will use in this chapter is summarizing, or putting something in their own words. You may wish to use the Read Aloud to model summarizing for your students.

Think Aloud *A young man is sitting in a room waiting to hear if his name will be called. If it is, he will have to go fight in the Union army against the South. He is frightened. Then he thinks of how much he wants the country to be whole again. He straightens in his chair, ready to hear his name if it is called.*

Waiting for the News

The crowded room is almost silent. All the men there are listening nervously to hear if their name is called. One young man slumps in his chair, his hands shaking.

He knows that if his name is chosen in the **draft,** he will have to join the Union army to fight against the South in the war. He realizes he must go, but he is frightened. He has been listening to people who are angry about the war and say it should not be fought. He has also heard about the large number of **casualties.**

He's been hurt before—kicked by horses, mules, and cows, fallen out of trees. War is different, though. The horses and mules were just trying to tell him they didn't like something. In war, someone is trying to shoot you. To hurt you. That makes him afraid.

The thought of leaving everyone he loves is hard to bear. He thinks about his parents and wonders how his father will be able to manage the farm without his help. His father is getting on in years, and his mother's been ill. His sister is young, but strong. She is brave, too, a real firebrand. He smiles as he thinks about her. Eleven is not so little, he supposes.

After a moment, an image of President Lincoln comes into his mind. He remembers reading the President's speech about keeping the Union together. He thinks of how much he wants the country to be whole again, not divided between North and South. The young man straightens up in his chair and watches as the next name is chosen. If it is his, he will be ready.

Begin the Chapter

Quick Look

Core Lesson 1 discusses the early years of the Civil War.

Core Lesson 2 focuses on the hardships faced by soldiers and civilians during the war.

Core Lesson 3 describes how the North won the war.

Core Lesson 4 focuses on the Reconstruction era.

Core Lesson 5 describes the challenges faced by former slaves after the end of Reconstruction.

Vocabulary Preview

Use the vocabulary cards to preview the key vocabulary words before starting the lessons and to prepare students to understand the content of the chapter.

Vocabulary Strategy

Vocabulary strategies for this chapter:

- Structural analysis, p. 452, 482
- Root words, p. 460, 472
- Prefixes and suffixes, p. 466

Vocabulary Help

Vocabulary card for emancipation Tell students that words that end in *-ion* are usually nouns. Many words that end in *-ion* are the name of an action. Suggest that they remember this by noticing that action ends with *-ion*. *Emancipation* is the action of freeing slaves.

Vocabulary card for telegraph Explain that *telegraph* includes *tele-*, which means "distance", and *-graph*, which means "write." Say that *telephone* and *television* are familiar words that include *tele-* and that *autograph* is a word that includes *-graph*.

Chapter 13 Civil War and Reconstruction

Technology
e • glossary
e • word games
www.eduplace.com/kids/hmss05/

Vocabulary Preview

emancipation

In 1862, President Lincoln ordered the **emancipation** of all the slaves in the Confederacy. He declared that they were free.
page 456

civilian

The war touched the lives of everyone, whether soldier or **civilian.** Family photographs were a comfort to civilians who stayed at home.
page 462

Chapter Timeline

Background

Segregation

- "Jim Crow" was an insulting term for African Americans during the 19th century.
- Today it is used to refer to laws that promoted segregation and unequal treatment during this time.

Vocabulary

Use the following graphic organizer to discuss the word *civilian* and how it is related to other words and phrases that begin with *civil.*

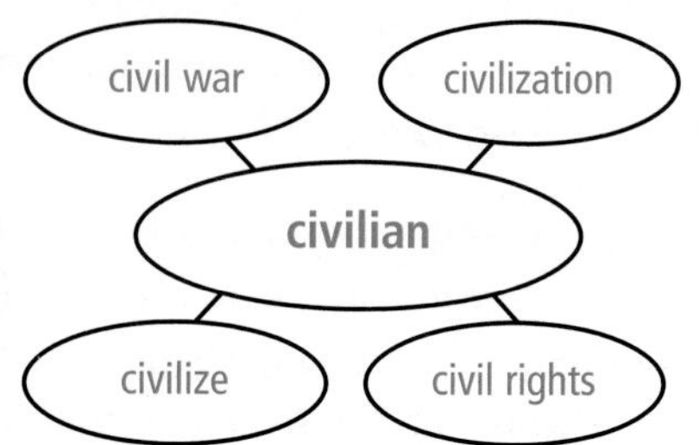

Challenge students to define all the words in the organizer, using dictionaries if necessary, and discuss how they are related.

Summarize Use this strategy to focus on important ideas.

Review the main ideas. Then look for important details that support those ideas.

telegraph

Generals used the **telegraph** to give President Lincoln information about the war. Their messages traveled quickly over wires. **page 467**

sharecropping

After the war, many African Americans began **sharecropping.** They gave the owner of the land they farmed a share of the crops they raised. **page 482**

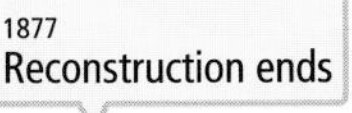

1877 Reconstruction ends

1881 Tuskegee Institute opens

1875 — 1880 — 1885

Using the Timeline

- Direct students to look at the timeline on pages 450 and 451. Point out the segments of the timeline. Ask them in what year the first event on the timeline takes place.

Reading Strategy: Summarize

To summarize, a reader identifies and pulls together the essential information in a longer text passage and restates that information in a condensed fashion.

Explain to students that to summarize successfully, they should follow these steps:

- Read the passage twice.
- Think about what the passage says.
- Ask yourself: What is the main topic this passage is describing?
- Find the main point of the passage. Jot it down (or underline it).
- Use your own words to tell what the passage means.
- Look back at the passage to check if your summary is accurate.

Students can practice this reading strategy throughout the chapter, including on their Skill and Strategy pages.

Leveled Practice

Extra Support

Have students use index cards to make their own word cards for these vocabulary words. Ask them to illustrate the word on the unlined side and write a definition, in their own words, on the side with lines. Verbal-linguistic

Challenge

Have students play vocabulary charades using the four words in the opener. Ask them to work in teams of two or three and act out each word so that other students can guess what is being portrayed. Bodily-kinesthetic

ELL

Intermediate

- Have students make up sentences using each of the four words on the vocabulary cards.
- Ask them to rewrite their sentences on a separate sheet of paper, leaving a blank where the vocabulary word would appear.
- Then ask students to exchange papers with another student and fill in the blanks on each other's papers.

Verbal-linguistic

Tested Objectives

U6-10 History Compare strengths of the Confederacy and the Union.

U6-11 History Identify important early battles and events of the Civil War.

U6-12 Citizenship Describe the significance of the Emancipation Proclamation.

Quick Look

This lesson describes what happened during the first few years of the Civil War.

Teaching Option: Extend Lesson 1 provides the text of the Gettysburg Address.

1 Get Set to Read

Preview Direct students to look at the map on page 453. Ask them what it shows.

Reading Skill: Classify The Union's advantages included a larger population; the Confederacy's, excellent military leaders.

Build on What You Know Explain that at the start of the Civil War, each side thought that it would win the war quickly.

Vocabulary

border states *noun,* slave states that remained part of the Union during the Civil War

casualties *noun,* people who are killed, wounded, captured, or missing during a military action

draft *noun,* forced enrollment in the armed forces

emancipation *noun,* liberation, especially from slavery

Core Lesson 1

A Nation at War

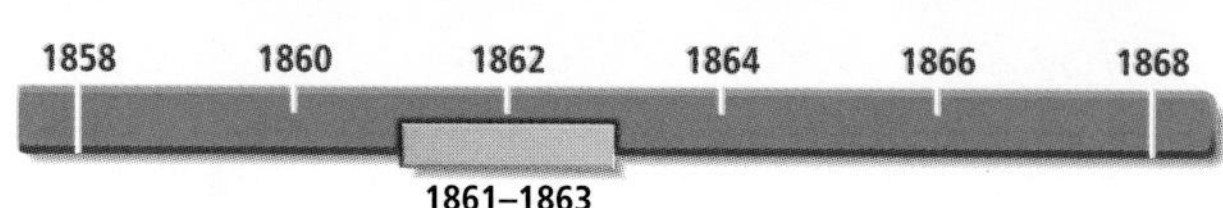

VOCABULARY

border states
casualties
draft
emancipation

Vocabulary Strategy

draft

Draft is a homograph, a word with more than one meaning. In this lesson, it means a system for bringing people into the military.

READING SKILL

Classify List the advantages and disadvantages that the North and the South had at the start of the war.

NORTH	SOUTH

Build on What You Know Have you ever started a task that was harder than it seemed at first? At the start of the Civil War, both sides thought they could win quickly. Soon, they knew that winning would be far from easy.

North Against South

Main Idea The Union and Confederacy had different strengths.

When the Civil War began, 11 southern states seceded 1
and formed the Confederacy. Four other slave states, Missouri, Kentucky, Maryland, and Delaware, stayed in the Union. Slave states that stayed in the Union were known as **border states.**

The North had many advantages in the war. About 22 million people lived in the North. The South only had around nine million people, and about one-third of them were enslaved and could not become soldiers. The North had more factories for making weapons and supplies. It also had more railroad lines than the South. Soldiers and supplies could move quickly by railroad.

The Confederate states had some advantages, too. Most of the fighting took place in the South, and Confederate soldiers were defending land they knew. The South also had excellent military leaders, such as General **Robert E. Lee.**

General Lee He was a skilled and respected Confederate general who had fought in the Mexican War.

Skill and Strategy

Reading Skill and Strategy

Reading Skill: Classify

This skill helps you understand and remember what you have read by organizing facts into groups or categories.

Read "North Against South." What were the advantages for the Union and the Confederacy?

Union	Confederacy
1. More factories to make weapons	2. Knew the land where the fighting took place
3. More railroads for supplies	4. Excellent military leaders

Reading Strategy: Summarize

5. Read "North Against South." Then check the best summary.
   - ✓ The North and the South had different advantages in the war.
   - ___ There were more people in the North than in the South.
   - ___ The Confederacy defeated the Union at the First Battle of Bull Run.
6. Read "The War's Leaders." Then check the best summary.
   - ___ The Union had many more generals than the Confederacy.
   - ___ General Lee and General Grant fought each other in many battles.
   - ✓ Political and military leaders were very important during the Civil War.

Unit Resources

124
Use with *United States History*, pp. 452–457

Unit Resources, p. 124

Background

Bravery and Eloquence

- Confederate General Thomas Jackson held his ground and led his soldiers to victory in chaotic battle conditions. This earned him the nickname by which he is still known today: "Stonewall" Jackson.
- Lincoln read the Gettysburg Address at a ceremony four months after the Battle of Gettysburg. The speaker before him spoke for two hours; Lincoln's speech lasted two minutes.

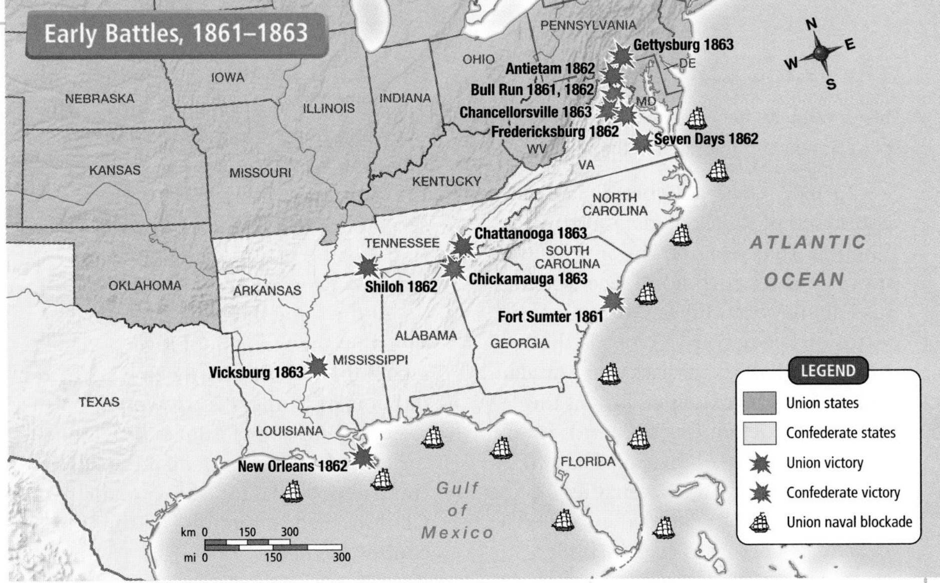

Early Battles The Union plan to block Confederate ports and attack by land was called the Anaconda Plan, after a snake that squeezes its prey.

SKILL **Reading Maps** In which state were most of the Confederate victories? Virginia

Plans for War

Union leaders created a strategy, or

2 plan, to defeat the South. The navy would block southern seaports so that the Confederacy could not trade with other countries. The navy would also take control of the Mississippi River. Then the Union army would attack in the East and West at the same time.

The South's strategy was to fight off northern attacks until the Confederacy could survive as a separate nation. Southerners knew that many people in the North were already against the war. If the Union lost too many battles, northerners might give up. Southerners also hoped for help from Britain and France because those countries needed southern cotton.

The War in the East

At the start of the war, both sides expected a quick, easy victory. Thousands of men from the North and South joined the Union and Confederate armies.

In July 1861, a Union army marched south from Washington. Its goal was to capture the Confederate capital of Richmond, Virginia, about 100 miles away. On July 21, the two armies fought at a stream called Bull Run, near the town of Manassas. Both sides fought hard all day. At the end of the battle, called the First Battle of Bull Run, the Union army retreated in a panic. The battle was worse than expected. People began to realize that the war would not end soon.

REVIEW What was the Confederacy's plan for winning the war? to fight off northern attacks until the Union gave up and to get help from Britain and France

Leveled Practice

Extra Support

Have partners look at the map on page 453 and **list the battles** and when they happened. Then ask students to describe a battle from the list in terms of its importance.
Visual-spatial

Challenge

Have students use library or Internet resources to **find several interesting facts** about the First Battle of Bull Run. Have students share their findings with the class.
Verbal-linguistic

ELL

Advanced

Have partners **write down the advantages** the North and South had at the start of the war. Encourage students to discuss how these advantages might affect the course of the war.

Verbal-linguistic

2 Teach

North Against South

Talk About It

1 **Q Geography** What were the four border states at the start of the Civil War?

A Missouri, Kentucky, Maryland, and Delaware

2 **Q History** What was the Union's plan for achieving victory?

A The Union planned to block seaports, control the Mississippi River, and attack from east and west at once.

Vocabulary Strategy

border states Explain that a border is the place where two regions, states, or countries meet.

Reading Strategy: Summarize Explain to students that a summary is always shorter than the original text. Summarize the first paragraph under "North Against South."

Think Aloud *The main idea in this paragraph is that some states seceded to form the Confederacy, while others remained part of the Union. My summary might sound like this: Out of the slave states, eleven seceded from the Union and formed the Confederacy. Four border states remained part of the Union.*

The War's Leaders

Talk About It

3 **Q History** What happened at the Battle of Antietam?

A The Union army stopped General Lee from invading the North. The armies suffered a combined 22,000 casualties.

4 **Q Geography** Why was Vicksburg the only major Confederate town left to capture on the Mississippi River?

A Vicksburg sat on cliffs above the river where Confederates could shoot at Union ships.

Vocabulary Strategy

casualties Tell students that *casualty* is related to the word *casual,* which can mean "happening by chance." Explain that it is hard to control events during a battle, and that injuries or deaths can happen without warning—seemingly by chance.

Critical Thinking

Infer The Southern strategy was to protect its borders. Why do you think General Lee tried to invade the North?

Think Aloud *General Lee knew that some northerners were against the war. Maybe he tried to invade the North to scare more northerners into being against the war. He also may have hoped to get some more supplies by invading the North.*

The War's Leaders

Main Idea Military and political leaders played important roles during the war.

In 1862, General Robert E. Lee took command of the Confederate army in Virginia. That year, the Union tried twice more to attack Richmond. Lee defeated his enemies both times. After these victories, Lee decided to invade the North. He led his soldiers into Maryland. The Union army stopped him at the
3 Battle of Antietam (an TEE tam). It was the deadliest day of the war. The two armies suffered 22,000 casualties. Soldiers who are killed or wounded are called **casualties.** Lee's army had such high casualties that he returned to Virginia.

The War in the West

In the West, the Union army and navy had more success. General **Ulysses S. Grant** led a Union army south from Illinois into Tennessee. He captured several Confederate forts along the way. In the Battle of Shiloh, he defeated a large Confederate army.

At the same time, the Union navy sailed up the Mississippi River and attacked New Orleans. By early 1863, the only major Confederate town left on the 4
river was Vicksburg, Mississippi. From Vicksburg's cliffs, Confederate soldiers could shoot at Union ships on the river. Grant needed to capture Vicksburg to control the river.

Battle of Antietam Look at the map and the description on the next page to learn more about this fierce battle.

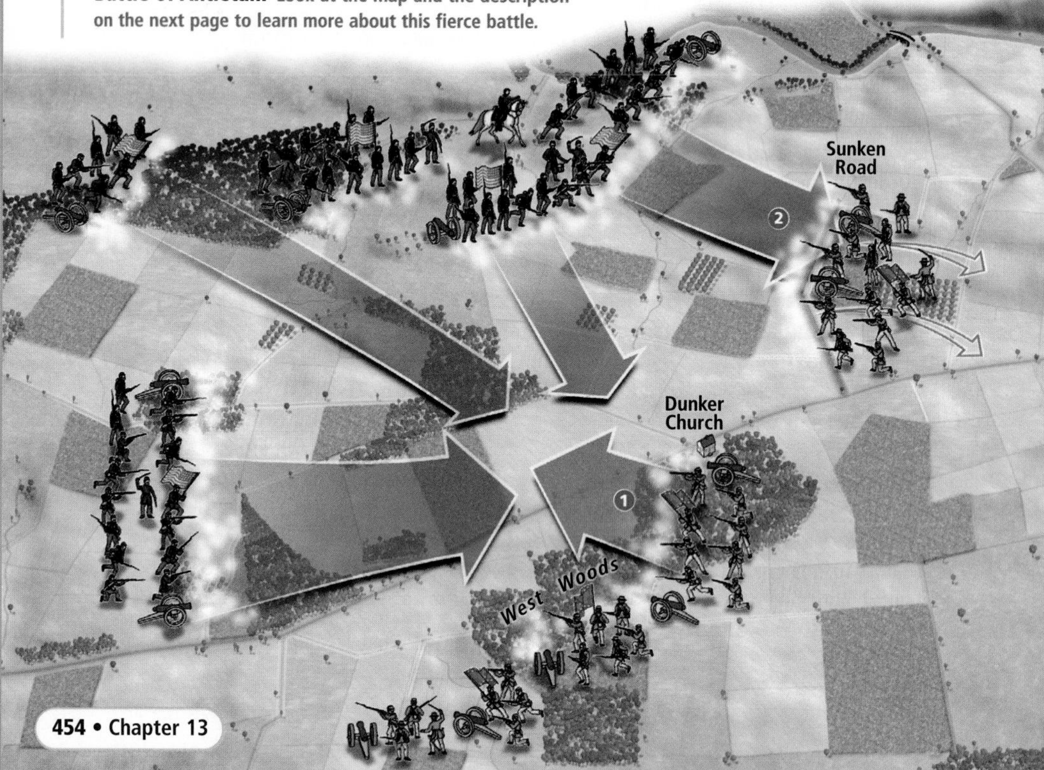

Math

Calculate Fractions

The North had a numerical advantage over the South. The North had about twenty-two million people and the South only had about nine million people.

- If one-third of the people in the South were enslaved, how many southerners were free? about six million
- How many were enslaved? about three million

Logical-mathematical

Art

Create a Diorama

Have students work in pairs or small groups to research and create a diorama of one of the battles mentioned in this lesson. Display completed dioramas in the classroom.

Visual-spatial

The Governments Respond

5 **Jefferson Davis,** the president of the Confederacy, faced many problems. The Union blockade closed most Confederate ports. The South had trouble getting enough food, weapons, or money to fight. Not enough people wanted to join the army. To find more soldiers, Davis had to start a draft. During a **draft,** a government selects people to serve in the military. The Confederate states often ignored Jefferson Davis's orders.

President **Abraham Lincoln** also faced challenges. As the number of casualties rose, he had to work hard to win support for the war.

Like the Confederacy, the Union had to start a draft. Rich people could pay to get out of the draft. This upset people who could not afford the money and those who were against the war. In New York City, people opposed to the draft started a riot that lasted for days. A riot is a violent protest. The government had to send in thousands of soldiers to stop the riots.

REVIEW Why did people in the North oppose the draft? because rich people could pay to avoid it while poor people could not, or because they were opposed to the war

Battle of Antietam
September 17, 1862

1. 6 A.M. – 9 A.M. Confederate soldiers fight off three powerful Union attacks near the Dunker Church.
2. 9 A.M. – 1 P.M. Union attacks on the Sunken Road force Confederate soldiers to retreat toward Sharpsburg. Both sides suffer many casualties.
3. 1 P.M. – 3 P.M. After hours of fighting, Union soldiers cross Antietam Creek and attack Sharpsburg. The bridge is later renamed for their commander, General Burnside.
4. 3:30 P.M. Confederate soldiers take the Union soldiers by surprise, forcing them to retreat back across the river and saving Lee's army from defeat.

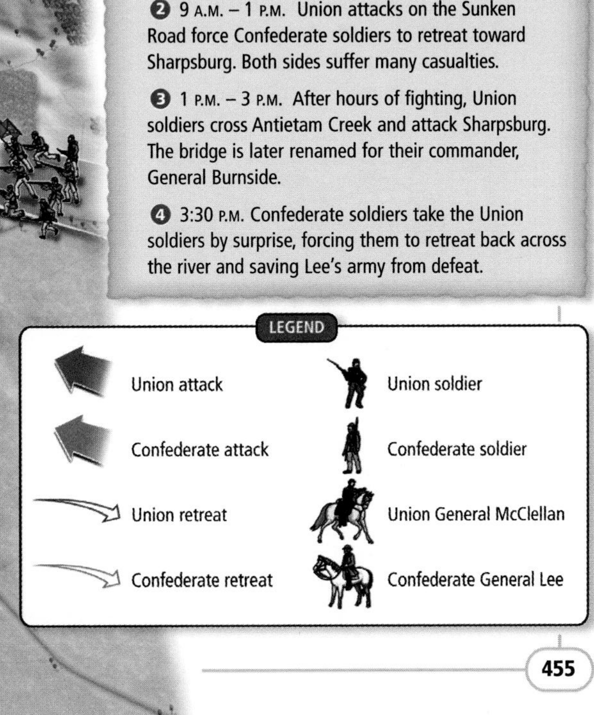

The War's Leaders

continued

Talk About It

5 **Q History** What were some of the problems Jefferson Davis faced?

A The Confederates couldn't get enough food, money, or weapons because the Union blockade closed most southern ports. Davis had to start a draft because not enough people wanted to join the army. The Confederate states ignored his orders because they didn't want to give up their power.

Vocabulary Strategy

draft Tell students that the word *draft* comes from an Old English word meaning "to draw or pull." They can picture drafted soldiers being pulled into service.

Reading Strategy: Summarize

Demonstrate for students how to summarize the first paragraph under "The Governments Respond" on page 455.

Extra Support

Create a Presidential Plan

- Both Jefferson Davis and Abraham Lincoln faced many problems as Presidents. Have partners create an agenda or plan for both Presidents.
- Have them keep in mind the challenges the President must face.
- They can make Venn diagrams using their agendas and compare and contrast the problems Lincoln and Davis faced.

Visual-spatial

Challenge

Write a Response

- Have students write a short story, poem, or scene in which someone responds to being drafted to fight in the Civil War.
- Have them share their work with the class.

Verbal-linguistic

Turning Points

Talk About It

6 Q History Why did President Lincoln issue the Emancipation Proclamation?

A Lincoln knew that freeing enslaved people could hurt the Confederacy. Enslaved people who worked on Southern farms could help the North instead.

7 Q History Why was the Battle of Gettysburg a turning point of the war?

A General Lee lost many of his men at Gettysburg. After the battle, his weakened army had to retreat.

Vocabulary Strategy

emancipation Point out the related verb *emancipate.* Have students help you list other verb/noun pairs with the suffixes *-ate* and *-ation* (*create/creation; anticipate/anticipation*).

Critical Thinking

Predict What might have happened if the North had lost the Battle of Gettysburg?

Turning Points

Main Idea Events in 1863 helped the Union become stronger in the Civil War.

At the start of the war, President Lincoln's only goal was to keep the Union together. He did not plan to free enslaved people. By 1862, however, he changed his mind. Many people in the North wanted him to end slavery, and
6 freeing enslaved people could weaken the Confederacy. He also hoped that freed slaves would work to help the Union.

Lincoln put the Emancipation Proclamation into effect on January 1, 1863. **Emancipation** is the freeing of enslaved people. This proclamation declared that slaves in the Confederacy were free. It did not end slavery in the border states. Confederates ignored the new law. The North would have to defeat the South to free the slaves. The Civil War had started as a war to save the Union. The Emancipation Proclamation made it a war to end slavery in the South.

Emancipation Proclamation
President Lincoln decided to issue the proclamation to free the slaves. This is a copy that was made so that people could put it up in their homes and schools.

Vicksburg and Gettysburg

In 1863, the Union won two important battles. In the West, General Grant's army surrounded Vicksburg and fired cannons into the town for six weeks. On July 4, Vicksburg surrendered. The Union now controlled the Mississippi River. This cut off Texas and Arkansas from the rest of the South.

The Union also won a major battle in the East. After stopping two more attacks on Richmond, General Lee decided to invade the Union again. He marched north into Pennsylvania. The Union army met Lee's soldiers on July 1, near the town of Gettysburg.

For two days the armies battled back and forth. On the third day, Lee ordered a final attack. Nearly 14,000 Confederate soldiers charged across open fields towards the Union army.

The Union soldiers were ready. They stopped the attack with rifle and cannon
fire. The heavy fire killed or wounded 7
about half of the Confederate soldiers. Lee's weakened army had to retreat.

July 1863 was the turning point of the war. The Union victories at Vicksburg and Gettysburg gave the Union a better chance of winning.

Drama

Give a Dramatic Reading

- Ask students to give a dramatic reading of part or all of the Gettysburg Address on pages 458–459.
- Encourage students to perform in front of classmates or at a community gathering.

Bodily-kinesthetic

Language Arts

Write a Report

- Both General Ulysses S. Grant and General Robert E. Lee attended the United States Military Academy at West Point.
- Have students research and write either a short biography of one of the generals or a short history of West Point.
- Remind them to include interesting details.

Verbal-linguistic

Gettysburg This painting shows the Confederate attack on the third day of the battle. The attack is known as Pickett's Charge, after one of the generals who led it.

Later that year, President Lincoln gave a short speech at Gettysburg, known as the Gettysburg Address. He declared that the Union was fighting to make sure that American democracy would survive. The speech is famous as a powerful statement about the purpose of the Civil War.

REVIEW Why was the victory at Vicksburg important to the Union? It gave the Union control of the Mississippi River.

Lesson Summary

At first, the Confederacy won most battles in the East, while the Union won battles in the West. However, victories at Vicksburg and Gettysburg gave the Union the advantage in the war.

Why It Matters ...

With the Emancipation Proclamation, the Civil War became a fight to end slavery in the Confederate States.

Lesson Review

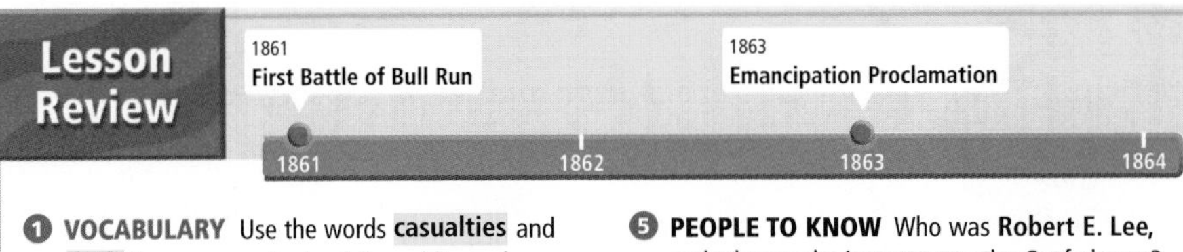

1. **VOCABULARY** Use the words **casualties** and **draft** in a paragraph about the soldiers who fought the Civil War.
2. **READING SKILL** Would you **classify** having control of Vicksburg as an advantage or disadvantage for the Union? Why?
3. **MAIN IDEA: History** What was the Union strategy in the Civil War?
4. **MAIN IDEA: Government** Why did both the Union and the Confederacy need to use the draft?
5. **PEOPLE TO KNOW** Who was **Robert E. Lee**, and why was he important to the Confederacy?
6. **TIMELINE SKILL** When did the First Battle of Bull Run take place?
7. **CRITICAL THINKING: Infer** Why do you think having a larger population was an advantage for the Union?

WRITING ACTIVITY News of the Civil War was very important to Americans. Prepare a news report about an event from the Civil War from the Union or Confederate point of view.

3 Review/Assess

Review Tested Objectives

U6-10 Confederacy strengths included fighting on home turf and talented military commanders. Union advantages were greater population, more factories, and more railroad lines.

U6-11 Important battles and events included the First Battle of Bull Run, General Lee and General Grant assuming control of their armies, and the Battle of Antietam.

U6-12 The Emancipation Proclamation declared enslaved people in the Confederacy free and turned slavery into the key issue of the war.

Lesson Review Answers

1. Paragraphs may focus on anger over the draft and the large number of casualties.
2. advantage; it split the South
3. attack in the east and west at the same time; control Mississippi River; block seaports
4. The fighting required many soldiers on both sides, and many people did not want to fight.
5. Lee was a talented Confederate general.
6. 1861
7. It meant more soldiers and more people to make supplies and weapons.

Writing Rubric

4	Report accurately describes event; uses Union or Confederate perspective; is easy to understand.
3	Report describes event; uses Union or Confederate perspective; is fairly easy to understand.
2	Report describes event with some errors; attempts to use Union or Confederate perspective; is somewhat confusing.
1	Report does not describe event; does not attempt to use Union or Confederate perspective; is confusing or disorganized.

Study Guide/Homework

Vocabulary and Study Guide

Vocabulary

Write the word for each definition below.

1. Slave states that stayed in the Union when the Civil War began: border states
2. Soldiers who are killed or wounded: casualties
3. When the army forces people to be soldiers: draft
4. The freeing of enslaved people: emancipation

Study Guide

Read "North Against South." Then fill in the comparison chart below.

	Advantages	Strategies
Union	Larger population; More factories and railroad lines	5. Block southern ports; Control Mississippi River; Attack from east and west
Confederacy	6. Fighting on familiar land; Excellent military leaders	7. Fight off attacks until northerners give up; Get help from Britain and France

8. Read "The War's Leaders" and "Turning Points." Then fill in the blanks below.

At the start of the Civil War, President Lincoln did not plan to free enslaved people. Then Lincoln made the Emancipation Proclamation to weaken the Confederacy. After that, the Civil War became a war to end slavery. In 1863, the Union won an important battle at Vicksburg and gained full control of the Mississippi River. The Union also won the Battle of Gettysburg, where President Lincoln later made a famous speech called the Gettysburg Address.

Unit Resources, p. 125

Reteach Minilesson

Use a sequence chart to list the events that occurred during the first years of the Civil War.

1	First Battle of Bull Run
2	Battle of Antietam
3	Emancipation
4	Gettysburg Address

Graphic Organizer 15

Quick Look

Connect to the Core Lesson Students have just learned about the events that took place during the first years of the Civil War. In Extend Lesson 1, students will read and learn about the meaning of Abraham Lincoln's Gettysburg Address.

1 Teach the Extend Lesson

Connect to the Big Idea

Democratic Principles When Lincoln said, "Government of the people, by the people, for the people, shall not perish," he meant that the Union must win the war in order to preserve American democracy. The fate of the Union and the ideals of freedom and equality were at stake.

Connect to Prior Knowledge

Ask students to read the first sentence in the Gettysburg Address. Lincoln is making a direct connection to the Declaration of Independence. Four score and seven years is 87 years. Eighty-seven years before 1863 was 1776, the year the Declaration was written. Lincoln is saying that the principles of that document, especially "All men are created equal," still apply.

Extend Lesson 1

Primary Source

The GETTYSBURG ADDRESS

The speech President Lincoln gave on that November day in 1863 was short. It took him barely two minutes to read it. The speech that came before his had lasted for two hours. But Americans still remember the Gettysburg Address more than 140 years later.

Lincoln gave the address just four months after the Battle of Gettysburg. In a ceremony honoring the Union soldiers who had died in the battle, Lincoln spoke about the meaning of the war and its terrible cost. His words captured the feelings of Americans as they struggled to meet a serious danger to their country.

① *Four score and seven years ago our fathers brought forth on this continent, a new nation, conceived in Liberty, and dedicated to the proposition that all men are created equal.*

② *Now we are engaged in a great civil war, testing whether that nation, or any nation so conceived and so dedicated, can long endure.*

③ *We are met on a great battle-field of that war. We have come to dedicate a portion of that field, as a final resting place for those who here gave their lives that that nation might live. It is altogether fitting and proper that we should do this.*

458 • Chapter 13

Reaching All Learners

Extra Support

Write a Short Speech

- Encourage students to write a short speech introducing President Lincoln.
- Introductions should state who the speaker is and what he will speak about.

Verbal-linguistic

On Level

Math Summaries

- Make photocopies of the Gettysburg Address and summaries featured in this lesson.
- Then ask students to cut up the Address into numbered sections and to cut out the numbered summaries.
- Partners can then match sections of the Address with their correct summaries.

Visual-spatial

Challenge

Perform the Gettysburg Address

- Have students memorize sections of the Gettysburg Address and perform them for the class.
- After each student performs, have classmates restate in their own words the main ideas of the section.

Verbal-linguistic

④ But, in a larger sense, we can not dedicate—we can not consecrate—we can not hallow—this ground. The brave men, living and dead, who struggled here, have consecrated it, far above our poor power to add or detract. The world will little note, nor long remember what we say here, but it can never forget what they did here. It is for us the living, rather, to be dedicated here to the unfinished work which they who fought here have thus far so nobly advanced. It
⑤ is rather for us to be here dedicated to the great task remaining before us—that from these honored dead we take increased devotion to that cause for which they gave the last full measure of devotion—that we here highly resolve that these dead shall not have died in vain—that this nation, under God, shall have a new birth of freedom—and that government of the people, by the people, for the people, shall not perish from the earth.

PRIMARY SOURCE

1. Eighty-seven years ago, our nation was founded on the ideals of freedom and equality.
2. Now we are fighting a war to see if our nation and our ideals can survive.
3. We are here to honor soldiers who died fighting in this war.
4. The best way we can honor them is to stay dedicated to our ideals.
5. We promise to uphold freedom so that our democracy will survive.

Activities

1. **TALK ABOUT IT** What do you think Lincoln meant by "unfinished work"?
2. **WRITE ABOUT IT** Explain why you think Lincoln's speech is famous today. Choose two of his ideas and write a one-page paper about why they are still important.

Technology Learn about other primary sources for this unit at Education Place. www.eduplace.com/kids/hmss05/

459

2 Leveled Activities

1 Talk About It *For Extra Support*

Sample answer: a Union victory in the war

2 Write About It *For Challenge*

Writing Rubric

4	Paper discusses two important ideas from speech; explains their importance effectively; mechanics are correct.
3	Paper discusses one or two important ideas from speech; explains their importance; mechanics are mostly correct.
2	Paper discusses one or two important ideas from speech; attempts to explain their importance; several errors in mechanics are present.
1	Paper does not discuss important ideas from speech; does not explain speech's importance effectively; many errors in mechanics are present.

ELL

Intermediate

- Ask students to create a list of vocabulary words from the Gettysburg Address.
- Then, have them use the words in sentences.

Verbal-linguistic

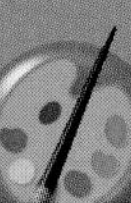

Art

Design a Poster

- Ask students to design and illustrate a poster announcing President Lincoln's speech at the dedication of the Gettysburg cemetery.
- Details should include the place and date.

Visual-spatial

Graphic Organizer

American Ideals
- Freedom
- Equality
- Democracy

Graphic Organizer 8

Tested Objectives

U6-13 History Describe the conditions that soldiers faced during the Civil War.

U6-14 History Explain how the war affected people on the home fronts in both the North and the South.

Lesson Quick Look

This lesson focuses on how soldiers coped with camp life and how civilians on the home front coped with the war.

Teaching Option: Extend Lesson 2 tells students about several women who displayed bravery and ingenuity during the Civil War.

1 Get Set to Read

Preview Have students look at the graph on page 462. Ask what it shows about prices in the South.

Reading Skill: Main Idea and Details Difficulties on the Southern home front included destruction of property, inflation, and hunger.

Build on What You Know Not only did the war take men from their families, but it also divided some families when members supported different sides.

Vocabulary

camp *noun,* a place where tents or other temporary shelters are set up, especially for soldiers or travelers

home front *noun,* the civilian population or the civilian activities of a country at war

civilian *noun,* a person not serving in the armed forces

Core Lesson 2

The Human Face of War

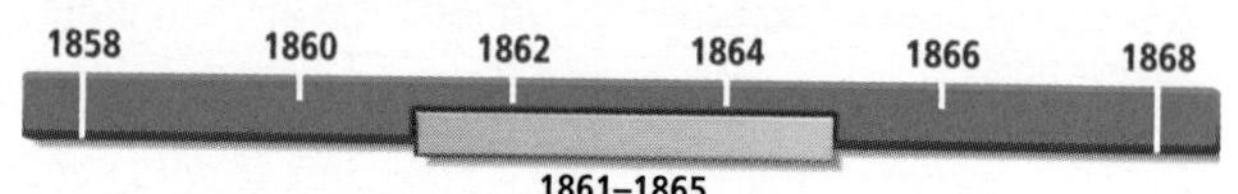

VOCABULARY

camp
home front
civilian

Vocabulary Strategy

civilian

Look at the word **civilian.** Think of other words that end in **-ian** that describe a person, such as musician.

READING SKILL
Main Idea and Details
As you read, note details that support the second main idea.

Build on What You Know Have you ever missed someone or waited for a card from a friend or family member? If you have, then you know part of what it was like to live during the Civil War. During the war, soldiers and their families missed each other's company.

The Soldier's Life

Main Idea Soldiers in the Civil War faced problems other than fighting battles.

Men from all parts of the country fought in the Civil War. Many hoped for excitement and glory. Instead, they found terror in battle and boredom in camp. A **camp** is a group of temporary shelters, such as tents.

Soldiers read, sang, or wrote letters to pass the time 1
in camp. Some put on shows or printed newspapers. They loved to get letters. "It made the boys shout with Joy to heare from home once more," wrote one soldier.

Food in the army was usually poor. Union soldiers grew tired of eating the same food almost every day. However, Confederate soldiers suffered more because they often did not have enough to eat.

Camp Life Soldiers in camp often slept on the ground in tents, with nothing to sit on but the ground or wooden boxes.

Skill and Strategy

Reading Skill and Strategy

Reading Skill: Main Idea and Details

This skill helps you understand events by seeing how they are related.

Read "The Soldier's Life" and "On the Home Front." Then fill in the webs below. Write details that support each main idea in the smaller ovals. You can add more small ovals if you need them.

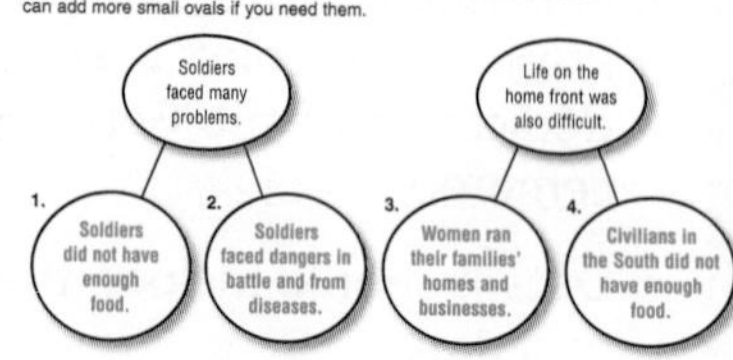

Reading Strategy: Summarize

5. Read "The Soldier's Life." Then check the best summary.

✓ Fighting battles was only one of the problems soldiers faced.

___ Soldiers in the Union army made lots of money during the war.

___ Most Confederate soldiers died during the many battles with the Union.

6. Read "On the Home Front." Then complete the summary.

During the Civil War, life was very hard for civilians, especially for people living in the South.

Unit Resources 126 Use with United States History, pp. 460–463

Unit Resources, p. 126

Background

People Who Made a Difference

- Clara Barton taught school before she nursed the Union wounded. Besides heading the American Red Cross, Barton lobbied the U.S. to join the Geneva Convention.
- Although Mathew Brady is credited with taking many Civil War photographs, most were actually shot by his assistants because he had poor eyesight.

New Soldiers African American soldiers fought for the Union in many battles. Several won the Congressional Medal of Honor, shown at right, for their courage.

Who Were the Soldiers?

Civil War soldiers came from many different backgrounds. At first, almost all were white and born in the United States. As the war went on, the Union allowed African Americans to join the army. About 180,000 African Americans served in the Union army. They fought in many battles, including Vicksburg.

Immigrants also joined the Union army. They included people from
2 Germany, Ireland, and Italy. American Indians fought on both sides.

Thousands of boys went into battle even though they were too young. Some served as drummers who sent signals to soldiers in battle. Hundreds of women on both sides disguised themselves as men and joined the army. Women also worked as spies for one side or the other.

Casualties of War

The Civil War was the deadliest war
in American history. Rifles could shoot 3
farther and more accurately than ever before. Casualties were much higher than people had expected. However, battle was not the only danger of war. Disease killed twice as many soldiers as the fighting did.

Women helped care for the sick and wounded. More than 3,000 northern women served as nurses. One was **Clara Barton,** who later founded the American Red Cross. Southern women also cared for wounded soldiers in hospitals and in their homes.

The Civil War affected the lives of most Americans. Soldiers had to face the dangers of battle and disease, as well as the boredom of camp life. Thousands of families lost loved ones.

 **REVIEW** What did women on both sides of the war do to help their side?
dressed as men and joined the army; spied; cared for sick and wounded

461

2 Teach

The Soldier's Life

Talk About It

1. **Q History** What did soldiers do to fight the boredom of camp life?
   A They read, sang, or wrote letters. Some put on shows or printed newspapers.
2. **Q Geography** What are some countries that immigrants who joined the Union army came from?
   A Germany, Ireland, and Italy
3. **Q History** What made the Civil War so deadly?
   A Rifles could shoot farther and more accurately than ever, and disease killed twice as many soldiers as fighting did.

Vocabulary Strategy

camp Ask students if they have ever been to summer camp. Explain that a camp is not a permanent place to live.

Reading Strategy: Summarize Ask a student to read the topic sentence of the first paragraph under "The Soldier's Life." Write the topic sentence on the board. With student help, edit the sentence to make it shorter but keep its essence. Explain that a summary of text is always shorter than the original text.

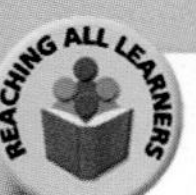

Leveled Practice

Extra Support

Have partners **create a chart** comparing and contrasting camp life and life on the home front. Display charts on the board. Visual-spatial

Challenge

Have students **make a collage** of images about the Civil War. They may photocopy pictures from library books, find photographs online, and draw their own images. Display finished collages in the classroom. Visual-spatial

ELL

Intermediate

Have students **make a list** of supplies they would put into a "CARE package" for soldiers who are bored with camp life. Encourage them to illustrate their lists.

Visual-spatial; verbal-linguistic

On the Home Front

Talk About It

4 **Q Economics** What tasks did women take on during the Civil War?

A They ran farms and businesses. Thousands sewed uniforms, knitted socks, made bandages, and raised money for both armies. Some were nurses.

5 **Q Economics** What effect did inflation have in the South?

A Confederate money became almost worthless, making food and other items very expensive.

6 **Q History** Why is June 19 a day of celebration in Texas and other parts of the South?

A News of the Emancipation Proclamation reached Texas on June 19, 1865. This is celebrated in parts of the South as the day slavery ended.

Vocabulary Strategy

home front Tell students that *front* is used here to mean "a field of activity."

civilian *Civilian* is related to the adjective *civil,* which means "of ordinary citizens or ordinary community life."

Critical Thinking

Draw Conclusions How, do you think, did new technology affect people's feeling toward the war?

On the Home Front

Main Idea The Civil War was difficult for people at home, especially in the South.

Many soldiers left families behind when they went to war. Those families were part of the home front. When a country is at war, the **home front** is all the people who are not in the military. Soldiers and their families did not want to be separated. "My Dear Dear Father," wrote the daughter of one officer, "I do miss you so much. . . ." With men gone,
4 women took on new tasks. They ran farms and businesses. Thousands of women sewed uniforms, knitted socks, made bandages, and raised money for their armies.

Most of the battles in the Civil War took place in the South. Few people in the North could see the war happening. The new technology of photography let civilians see what the war looked like. A **civilian** is a person who is not in the military. **Mathew Brady** took pictures of soldiers, camp life, and battlefields. He showed his photographs in the North. Civilians there saw that war was much worse than they had realized.

Money Each Confederate state printed its own money. Because of inflation, most of the bills became almost worthless.

Confederate Inflation

Dollars per pound (0, 5, 10, 15, 20, 25); Year (1861, 1862, 1863, 1864, 1865); bacon; butter

Inflation Food and other necessary goods became too expensive for many southerners to afford. SKILL **Reading Graphs** How expensive was butter in 1864? 25 dollars per pound

The Southern Home Front

Life on the home front was especially hard in the South. Their farms became battlefields. Their cities, homes, and barns were destroyed.

In the South, soldiers and civilians often did not have enough to eat.
Inflation, or a rise in prices, made food 5
very expensive. The money printed by the Confederate government became almost worthless. A barrel of flour that cost $6 in 1861 might cost $1,000 in 1865. In Richmond and other towns, hungry women attacked shops in search of food.

Enslaved people in the South suffered as well, but most still welcomed the war. The Emancipation Proclamation in 1863 gave them the hope of freedom.

Science

History of the Camera

- Remind students that photography was still new technology around the time of the Civil War. Have them research the history of photography or how early cameras worked.
- They may bring in examples of pictures taken with different kinds of cameras from different periods in history.

Visual-spatial

Language Arts

Write a Fundraising Letter

- Have students write a letter that a Union or Confederate general might have written to either Abraham Lincoln or Jefferson Davis requesting more supplies for his army.
- Letters could include details of camp life and efforts of relatives on the home front.

Verbal-linguistic

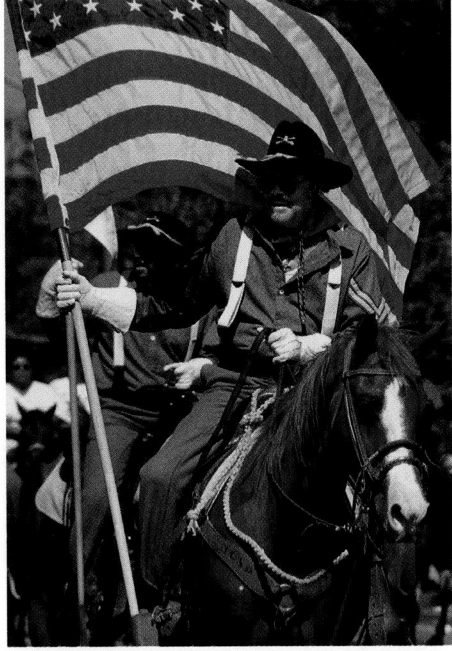

Juneteenth African American communities celebrate Juneteenth. This parade was held in Austin, Texas, where it is a yearly event.

Some enslaved people only learned of the proclamation at the end of the war. News of the Emancipation Proclamation reached Texas on June 19, 1865. This day became a day of celebration. Known as Juneteenth, June 19 is still celebrated in Texas and other parts of the country as the day slavery ended. 6

REVIEW What happened to prices in the South during the Civil War? They increased, making food and other goods expensive.

Lesson Summary

- During the war soldiers faced danger in battle and from disease.
- Soldiers came from many different backgrounds.
- The Civil War affected the lives of all Americans, not just soliders.

Why It Matters ...

During the Civil War, Americans lived through of the hardest years in the nation's history.

Lesson Review

1. **VOCABULARY** Write a pargraph about the lives of ordinary people during the Civil War. Use **home front** and **civilian** in your paragraph.
2. **READING SKILL** Use the details in the chart on page 462 to explain why life was hard during the Civil War.
3. **MAIN IDEA: History** What made camp life hard for Civil War soldiers?
4. **MAIN IDEA: Citizenship** In what ways did women contribute to the war effort?
5. **PEOPLE TO KNOW** Who was **Mathew Brady** and what did he do during the Civil War?
6. **CRITICAL THINKING: Draw Conclusions** Use information you have learned to tell why women and children joined the army on both sides.
7. **CRITICAL THINKING: Analyze** What was the point of view of enslaved people in the South toward the war? How was it different from the view of most other southerners?

MAP ACTIVITY Trace a map of the United States. Identify the states that fought in the Civil War. Use different colors for the Union, the Confederacy, and the border states.

463

3 Review/Assess

Review Tested Objectives

U6-13 Soldiers lived in camps, where they waited for news from home. Powerful rifles and rampant disease led to many casualties.

U6-14 Home front effects included inflation and hunger in the South and personal losses to many families. Many women had to take over traditionally male responsibilities.

Lesson Review Answers

1. Paragraph should show an understanding of vocabulary.
2. Answers should include detail about inflation.
3. Camp life was often boring, and soldiers were far from home and family.
4. Women ran farms and businesses; made socks, uniforms, and bandages; and raised money for the war effort.
5. Mathew Brady was a photographer. His pictures showed people in the North what battlefield and camp conditions were really like.
6. Answers might describe the importance of the war to all people in both the North and South.
7. Many enslaved southerners supported the war because of the promise of emancipation. Some other southerners opposed it because of the difficult living conditions it brought to them.

Study Guide/Homework

Vocabulary and Study Guide

Vocabulary

Write the definition of each vocabulary word below.

1. camp A group of temporary shelters, such as tents
2. home front During wartime, all of the people who are not in the military
3. Use the words in a sentence. Sample answer: Soldiers read, sang, and wrote letters to people on the home front while they were in camp.

Study Guide

Read "The Soldier's Life." Then fill in the Venn diagram below.

Union soldiers: 4. Ate poor food; Some were immigrants and African Americans

Both: 6. Made up of whites, American Indians, women, and boys; Faced battles and diseases

Confederate soldiers: 5. Did not have enough to eat

Read "On the Home Front." Then answer the questions.

7. Why did people in the North need photographs to understand camp life and battles?
Because the war was fought mostly in the South
8. Why was life especially hard in the South during the war?
Because cities and homes were destroyed, inflation rose, and people did not have enough to eat

Unit Resources

127
Use with *United States History*, pp. 460–463

Unit Resources, p. 127

Reteach Minilesson

Use a Venn diagram to chart the effects the Civil War had on soldiers' lives and the home front.

Graphic Organizer 11

Performance Task Rubric

4	Map of the U.S. is accurate; states are accurately designated.
3	Map is mostly accurate; almost all states are accurately designated.
2	Map contains inaccuracies; several states are not accurately designated.
1	Map is extremely inaccurate or does not show the U.S.; most or all states are not accurately designated.

Extend Lesson 2 Pages 464–465

Quick Look

Connect to the Core Lesson Students have just read about what it was like to live during the Civil War. In Extend Lesson 2, students will discover several remarkable women who made a difference during the war.

1 Teach the Extend Lesson

Connect to the Big Idea

Influences on History Women contributed in many ways to help both sides in the Civil War. Women on both sides of the conflict raised money, sewed uniforms, and nursed the wounded. Their efforts and strong beliefs influenced the course of the war.

Connect to Prior Knowledge

Ask students to read the introduction. Remind students that women have made wartime contributions since the American Revolution. Then discuss dangers and risks women took in joining a war effort on the home front or on the battlefield.

Extend Lesson 2

Biographies

Courageous Women

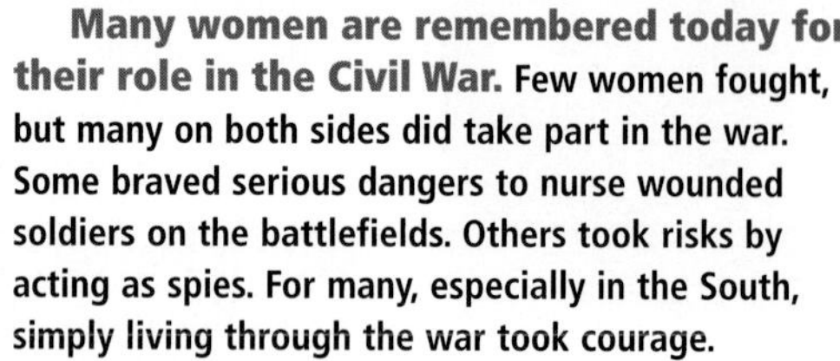

Many women are remembered today for their role in the Civil War. Few women fought, but many on both sides did take part in the war. Some braved serious dangers to nurse wounded soldiers on the battlefields. Others took risks by acting as spies. For many, especially in the South, simply living through the war took courage.

CLARA BARTON

1821–1912

When Clara Barton volunteered as a Union army nurse, she saw that hospitals had no medicines or bandages. She wrote letters to newspapers asking people to make donations. When she arrived at battlefields with loads of supplies, she sometimes risked her life. But the troops cheered. "I went in while the battle raged," she once recalled. After the war, in 1881, she was asked to start the American Red Cross, an organization that still helps people in times of war and peace.

Reaching All Learners

Extra Support

Create a Chart

- Have students create a compare and contrast chart of the women featured in this lesson.
- Ask them to list how the women are alike and how they are different.

Verbal-linguistic

On Level

Create Trading Cards

- Encourage students to create trading cards of the Civil War women.
- Have them illustrate an image of each one for the front of the cards and list at least two facts about each one on the back.

Visual-spatial

Challenge

Write a Report

- Ask students to research and briefly report on two other women who made a difference during the Civil War.
- Ask them to share their reports with the class.

Verbal-linguistic

CHARACTER TRAIT: Courage

ELIZABETH VAN LEW

1818 – 1890

Even before the Civil War began, Elizabeth Van Lew opposed slavery. She lived in Virginia, a southern state, and she convinced her mother to free the family's slaves. During the war, Van Lew became a spy for the Union army. She got important information from Confederate sources. She asked former slaves to carry her secret coded messages in hollow eggshells or in the soles of their shoes. In 1865, when Union troops arrived in Richmond, Van Lew flew the Union flag for all to see.

MARY CHESNUT

1823 – 1886

Mary Chesnut kept a diary during the Civil War. She was a wealthy South Carolinian whose husband was a Confederate general. In her diary, she described the collapse of the Confederate government. She recorded the thoughts and fears of people involved in the war, including her own true beliefs—she was against slavery. Her writing is valued today as a full portrait of the Confederacy, and a rich source of information for historians.

Activities

1. **TALK ABOUT IT** Discuss how each of these women showed **courage** during the Civil War.
2. **DEBATE IT** Do you think it was harder or easier for women to take part in the war than for men? Debate your opinion. Support your opinion with facts.

Technology Visit Education Place for more biographies of people in this unit. www.eduplace.com/kids/hmss05/

BIOGRAPHIES

465

2 Leveled Activities

❶ **Talk About It** *For Extra Support*
Sample answer: Barton showed courage through battlefield nursing; Van Lew by spying; Chesnut through her honest writing.

❷ **Debate It** *For Challenge*

HANDS ON Performance Task Rubric

4	States position clearly; conveys ideas effectively; facts are accurate.
3	States position well; conveys ideas adequately; most facts cited are accurate.
2	States position in a somewhat disorganized way; conveys ideas adequately; some errors.
1	States no position or one that is off topic; conveys ideas in a very general or incomprehensible way; many errors.

Character Trait: Courage

Ask students to describe what inspired each of these women to be courageous.

For more on character traits, turn to pages R4–R5.

ELL

REACHING ALL LEARNERS

Intermediate

- Have students draw a cartoon or comic strip illustrating one of the women making her contribution.
- Then have them write captions for their drawings.

Visual-spatial; verbal-linguistic

Math

Make a Bar Graph

- Have students make a horizontal bar graph of the life spans of the women featured in this lesson.
- Ask students to compare the spans.
- Who lived the longest? Barton
- Whose life spanned the 19th and 20th centuries? Barton
- Who was born first? Van Lew

Logical-mathematical

Graphic Organizer

Clara Barton	Mary Chesnut	Elizabeth Van Lew
Union army nurse	Kept Civil War diary	Helped free her family's slaves
Founder of American Red Cross	Wife of Confederate general	Union army spy

Graphic Organizer 2

Tested Objectives

U6-15 History Explain the factors, including the strategy of total war, which helped the Union to defeat the Confederacy.

U6-16 History Describe the end of the war, including Lee's surrender to Grant.

Quick Look

This lesson describes how Generals Grant and Sherman used their armies to defeat General Lee and end the war.

Teaching Option: Extend Lesson 3 explains events going on around the world in 1865.

1 Get Set to Read

Preview Have students look at the map on page 467. Discuss the meaning of the symbols.

Reading Skill: Predict Outcomes Students' predictions might include continued destruction in the South and Union victory.

Build on What You Know Ask students why having enough supplies is important to completing a task. Note that the Union had more supplies and soldiers than the Confederacy did.

Vocabulary

telegraph *noun,* a communications system that uses electric impulses to send messages by wire

total war *noun,* a method of warfare where anything connected to an enemy's resources is destroyed

desert *verb,* to leave, abandon, or withdraw, especially from an army

Core Lesson 3

The War Ends

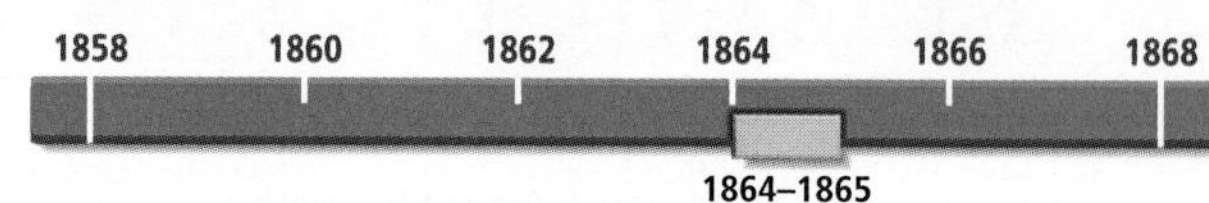

VOCABULARY

telegraph
total war
desert

Vocabulary Strategy

telegraph

The prefix **tele-** in the word **telegraph** means "far away." A telegraph sends messages to distant places.

READING SKILL

Predict Outcomes

As you read, make a prediction about how the Civil War will finally end.

PREDICTION

OUTCOME

Build on What You Know To finish a job, you need to have enough supplies. In the Civil War, the Union had more soldiers, weapons, and food than the Confederacy. These supplies helped the Union win the war.

Union Victories

Main Idea The Union tried to force the South to surrender by destroying southerners' resources.

By the end of 1863, the Union had won several important battles in the Civil War. Victories at Vicksburg and Gettysburg gave northerners hope of winning the war. But the Confederate armies were still fighting hard. To end the war, the North had to destroy the South's ability to fight.

President Lincoln needed a tough army general to defeat the South. He chose **Ulysses S. Grant.** Grant proved in the West that he could fight hard. Lincoln made him the commander of all Union armies.

Grant planned to lead an army into Virginia to defeat 1
General **Robert E. Lee's** army and capture Richmond. Grant also ordered General **William Tecumseh Sherman** to lead the Union army in Tennessee. Sherman planned to attack Atlanta, Georgia, a major Confederate city.

General Grant Little known before the war, he became famous for his determination to win.

Skill and Strategy

Reading Skill and Strategy

Reading Skill: Predict Outcomes

This skill allows you to think about what might happen, based on what you have read.

Read the first paragraph of "Grant and Lee." Then fill in the prediction chart below. Write what you think happened with Lee in charge of the army in the first box. Then read the next paragraph. Write what happened with Lee in charge in the second box.

1. **Prediction:** Sample answer: Lee and his army eventually won the war.
2. **Outcome:** Sample answer: Lee's army was worn down, and the Union forced it farther south.

Reading Strategy: Summarize

3. Read "Union Victories." Then complete the summary.
The Union army destroyed land in the South to force the Confederacy to surrender.
4. Read "Grant and Lee." Then write a short summary of the section.
Sample answer: Grant's victories in Virginia convinced Lee to make the difficult choice to surrender.

Unit Resources
 128 Use with *United States History*, pp. 466–469

Unit Resources, p. 128

Background

General Sherman

- William Tecumseh Sherman went to West Point as a young man. After graduating, he served several military assignments in the South, which helped him learn about southern people and geography.
- In the 1850s, Sherman lived in California and worked as a banker.

Later Battles This map shows the major battles from the last two years of the Civil War. During their march through Georgia, Union soldiers wrecked railroads (above) by bending the rails.

Sherman's March

Sherman began his attack on Atlanta in May 1864. His experienced soldiers quickly marched into Georgia. The Confederates fought all summer, but Sherman's army captured Atlanta in September. Sherman sent a message to President Lincoln by telegraph. A **telegraph** is a machine that sends electric signals over wires. Sherman's message said, "Atlanta is ours, and fairly won." That summer, the Union navy won another important battle by capturing Mobile Bay in Alabama.

Lincoln welcomed these victories. He was running for reelection in 1864 and worried about losing. He needed military victories like Atlanta and Mobile Bay to gain voters' support.

From Atlanta, Sherman's army marched to Savannah, on Georgia's coast. This march became known as the March to the Sea. Along the way, the soldiers destroyed anything southerners needed for the war. They stole food, killed animals, and wrecked factories and railroad tracks. Sherman used total war to make southerners so tired of fighting that they would give up. **Total war** is the strategy of destroying an enemy's resources. 2

After reaching Savannah, Sherman's army turned north once again destroying everything in its path. One woman described how the soldiers "roamed about setting fire to every house . . ."

REVIEW Why did Sherman decide to use total war against the South? He thought total war would make the South stop fighting.

467

2 Teach

Union Victories

Talk About It

1 Q History What was General Grant's plan to end the war?

A He would lead an army to defeat General Lee's soldiers and capture Richmond. At the same time, General Sherman's army would attack Atlanta.

2 Q Geography What happened during Sherman's March to the Sea?

A Sherman's army marched through Georgia from Atlanta to Savannah, destroying nearly everything they passed.

Vocabulary Strategy

telegraph Explain to students that the suffix *-graph* means "something written or drawn."

total war Explain that synonyms for *total* include *complete* and *absolute.*

Reading Strategy: Summarize Have students read the first paragraph under "Union Victories." Work with the students to find the topic sentence. With student suggestions, write a summary of the paragraph on the board.

Leveled Practice

Extra Support

Have students **look at the map** on page 467. Ask them to tell the location and outcome of each battle. Verbal-linguistic

Challenge

Have students **write a trivia quiz** about General Grant and General Lee. Have them use the quiz to test their classmates. Verbal-linguistic

ELL

Intermediate

Encourage students to create newspaper headlines describing the events in this lesson. They may want to use the names or quotes of the leaders included in the lesson. Display the headlines around the classroom.

Visual-spatial

Grant and Lee

Talk About It

3 **Q History** Why was Robert E. Lee a respected general?

A He had defeated larger armies.

4 **Q History** What advantage did Grant's army have over Lee's at Richmond?

A The Union army received food, supplies, and soldiers. The Confederate army was running out of reinforcements.

5 **Q History** What happened at Appomattox Court House on April 9, 1865?

A Lee surrendered to Grant, ending the war.

Vocabulary Strategy

desert Review with students the meanings and pronunciations of *desert* (to leave or abandon), *desert* (a dry and sandy region), and *dessert* (sweet food eaten to finish a meal).

Critical Thinking

Decision Making Why do you think Sherman decided to destroy everything the South needed in his March to the Sea?

Think Aloud *I see that because Sherman's army destroyed much of the South's supplies, Lee's army couldn't fight off Grant's army for very long. If Sherman hadn't done what he did, Lee's army would have had more supplies, and the war might have lasted longer.*

Grant and Lee

Main Idea Grant's attacks in Virginia wore down Lee's army and forced it to surrender.

While Sherman marched into Georgia in 1864, Grant led a huge army toward Richmond, Virginia. He was opposed by
3 Robert E. Lee's army. Lee was a brilliant general who had defeated larger armies. Grant's strength was his determination. He kept attacking, even after a defeat.

Lee used all of his skill to fight off Grant's army. The Union suffered terrible losses, but Grant kept attacking. His attacks wore down the Confederate army in a series of battles. Lee was forced farther and farther south.

In June 1864, the two armies faced each other near Richmond. They stayed there for almost a year. Neither side could defeat the other. However, the Union army was growing stronger.

Lee's Surrender

The Union's resources helped Grant. 4
He received a steady supply of food and equipment. The North sent thousands more soldiers to join his army. President Lincoln said, "We have more men now than we had when the war began."

At the same time, Lee's army was struggling. The Confederate government had no more soldiers or supplies to send Lee. Confederate soldiers went hungry, and some began to desert. To **desert** means to leave the army without permission.

By early April 1865, Lee's army was too weak to defend Richmond any longer. Lee retreated. The Union army captured Richmond and chased Lee's army west. Finally, near a town called Appomattox Court House, Lee made a hard decision. His starving army was nearly surrounded. He had to surrender. He said,

> **"There is nothing left for me to do but go and see General Grant..."**

Surrender Lee surrendered to Grant on April 9, 1865 at Appomattox Court House. "We are all Americans," one of Grant's officers told Lee afterwards.

Lee's Chair

Math

Send a Morse Code Message

- Telegraph messages were sent by Morse code, a system of patterns of dots and dashes created by the inventor Samuel Morse.
- Have students use library or Internet resources to learn about Morse code.
- Then ask pairs of students to create and send messages in Morse code to each other.

Visual-spatial; verbal-linguistic

Language Arts

Write a Speech

- Have students write a speech that a Civil War general might have given to his soldiers at the end of the war.
- Ask them to include ideas about what changes the end of the war may bring to the country.

Verbal-linguistic

5 On April 9, 1865, Grant and Lee met in a home in the village of Appomattox Court House. Grant said that Lee's soldiers could go home. Lee agreed to surrender. Grant then sent 25,000 meals to the hungry Confederate soldiers.

Grant told his soldiers not to celebrate. "The war is over," he said. "The rebels are our countrymen again." A few days later, Lee's soldiers marched past the Union army to surrender. As they passed, the Union soldiers saluted their old enemies.

News of Lee's surrender spread quickly. In Washington, people celebrated in the streets. Confederate soldiers in North Carolina surrendered to Sherman. Fighting continued in a few places, but by late June all was quiet. The war was over at last.

Lesson Summary

- General Sherman used total war to destroy the South's ability to fight.
- General Lee's army could not get enough food or equipment.
- Lee had to surrender to General Grant.

Why It Matters ...

The victory of the Union made certain that the United States would remain one nation.

REVIEW Why did Lee have to surrender? He could not get more supplies, soldiers were deserting, and he almost surrounded.

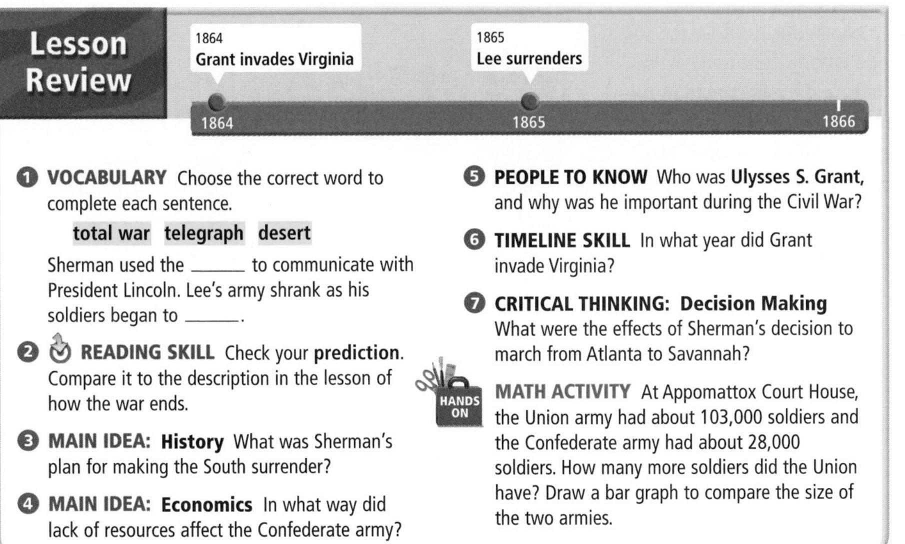

Lesson Review

1864 Grant invades Virginia — 1865 Lee surrenders (timeline: 1864, 1865, 1866)

1. **VOCABULARY** Choose the correct word to complete each sentence.
   total war **telegraph** **desert**
   Sherman used the ______ to communicate with President Lincoln. Lee's army shrank as his soldiers began to ______.
2. **READING SKILL** Check your **prediction.** Compare it to the description in the lesson of how the war ends.
3. **MAIN IDEA: History** What was Sherman's plan for making the South surrender?
4. **MAIN IDEA: Economics** In what way did lack of resources affect the Confederate army?
5. **PEOPLE TO KNOW** Who was **Ulysses S. Grant,** and why was he important during the Civil War?
6. **TIMELINE SKILL** In what year did Grant invade Virginia?
7. **CRITICAL THINKING: Decision Making** What were the effects of Sherman's decision to march from Atlanta to Savannah?

HANDS ON **MATH ACTIVITY** At Appomattox Court House, the Union army had about 103,000 soldiers and the Confederate army had about 28,000 soldiers. How many more soldiers did the Union have? Draw a bar graph to compare the size of the two armies.

3 Review/Assess

Review Tested Objectives

U6-15 Factors included greater availability of soldiers and supplies in the North and Sherman's strategy of total war, which devastated much of the South.

U6-16 The war ended with Lee's surrender to Grant after a long face-off near Richmond and increased desertion by Confederate troops.

Lesson Review Answers

1. telegraph; desert
2. Answers will vary; should cite previous predictions and lesson details.
3. Sherman's plan was to destroy everything the South needed for the war.
4. It weakened the Confederate army and led to desertion.
5. Grant was the commander of the Union armies. His leadership led to victory for the North.
6. 1864
7. Sherman's decision to march to Savannah led to the destruction of southern resources in Georgia.

HANDS ON Performance Task Rubric

4	Labels are correct and clear; both bars are accurate; graph includes a title.
3	Most labels are correct; both bars are accurate; graph includes a title.
2	Some labels are correct; only one bar is accurate; title inaccurate.
1	Labels are inaccurate or missing; neither bar is accurate, or both bars are absent; no title.

Study Guide/Homework

Vocabulary and Study Guide

Vocabulary

Write the definition of each vocabulary word below.

1. telegraph A machine that sends electrical signals over wires
2. total war The strategy of destroying an enemy's resources
3. desert To leave the army

Study Guide

Read "Union Victories." Then answer the questions.

4. What two Union victories further weakened the Confederacy? Sherman's army captured Atlanta, and the Union navy captured Mobile Bay, Alabama.
5. Why did General Sherman want to use total war on the South? To make southerners so tired of the war that they would give up

Read "Grant and Lee." Then fill in the causes-and-effect chart below.

Causes	Effect
6. Lee's army was starving and growing weaker.	Lee met with Grant and agreed to surrender.
7. Grant's army received food and soldiers and was growing stronger.	

Unit Resources 129 Use with *United States History*, pp. 466–469

Unit Resources, p. 129

Reteach Minilesson

Use a sequence chart to list the events that led to the end of the Civil War.

1	Sherman's March
2	Lee and Grant face each other near Richmond
3	Confederate Army runs out of supplies
4	Lee surrenders

Graphic Organizer 15

Quick Look

Connect to the Core Lesson Students have learned about the events and ending of the Civil War. In Extend Lesson 3, students will look at changes that took place in other parts of the world during the same time period.

1 Teach the Extend Lesson

Connect to the Big Idea

Change While the Civil War was taking place in the United States, changes were taking place in other parts of the world. Discoveries and new technologies increased trade between nations. Conflicts erupted into rebellions and wars. It was a time of rapid change and progress.

Connect to Prior Knowledge

Ask students to read the introduction. Then discuss with them what kinds of changes took place during this time in other parts of the world.

Extend Lesson 3

Geography

A Global View, 1865

During the 1860s, the Civil War changed life for most Americans. At the same time, changes were taking place elsewhere. Powerful nations in Europe tried to conquer land in other continents. Some countries grew more wealthy. People in other countries rebelled against their leaders and governments.

New technology made travel and communication easier, so trade among continents grew. Goods and ideas spread more quickly than ever before. Look on the map to see what was happening around the world.

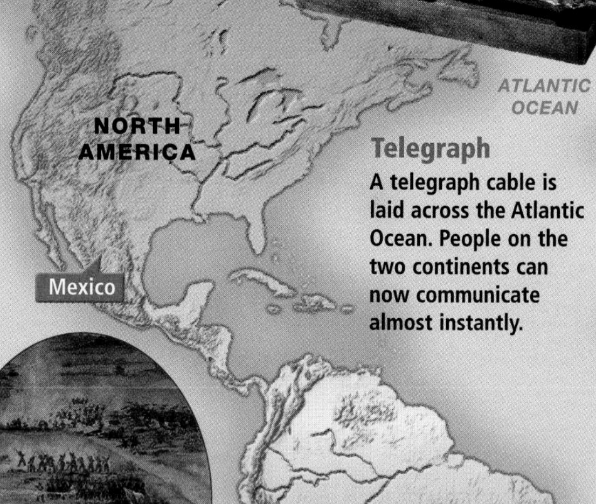

Telegraph
A telegraph cable is laid across the Atlantic Ocean. People on the two continents can now communicate almost instantly.

Mexico
In 1867, Mexican soldiers defeat a French army that had tried to occupy the country.

470 • Chapter 13

Reaching All Learners

Extra Support

Describe Changes

- Have students locate the various places featured in this lesson on a world map or globe.
- Ask them to describe the changes that took place in at least three countries.

Visual-spatial; verbal-linguistic

On Level

Create a Chart

- Ask students to create a three-column classification chart listing the changes taking place in other parts of the world as *Political, Economic,* or *Technological.*
- Have them explain their choices of classification.

Verbal-linguistic

Challenge

Prepare a Report

- Ask students to research and briefly report on another change that took place during this time period.
- Students may also create a poster showing the effects of this change.

Verbal-linguistic; visual-spatial

Italy
Italy, which had been made up of many small states, is united for the first time in almost 1,500 years.

India
The British government takes over large parts of India. India is ruled by Britain until 1947.

EUROPE

Italy

ASIA

Egypt

AFRICA

India

PACIFIC OCEAN

Australia
The discovery of gold in Australia brings thousands of new settlers to the colonies there.

AUSTRALIA

Egypt
The Suez Canal opens in 1869. Ships traveling between Europe and Asia no longer have to sail all the way around Africa.

INDIAN OCEAN

ANTARCTICA

GEOGRAPHY

Activities

1. **TALK ABOUT IT** How do you think the Suez Canal or a telegraph across the Atlantic Ocean changed people's lives?
2. **CREATE IT** Find out the different ways people could travel and communicate in 1865. Make a poster comparing travel and communication in 1865 and today.

471

2 Leveled Activities

❶ **Talk About It** *For Extra Support*
Sample answer: by making travel, trade, and communication faster and easier

❷ **Create It** *For Challenge*

HANDS ON

	Performance Task Rubric
4	Modes of transportation and communication are clearly shown; poster is well researched; mechanics are correct.
3	Modes are shown; poster is well researched; few errors in mechanics are present.
2	Modes are partially shown; poster is fairly well researched; some errors in mechanics are present.
1	Modes are not shown; research lacking; many errors in mechanics are present.

ELL

Intermediate/Advanced

- Have students draw the flags of three of the countries shown in this lesson.
- Ask them to find out about a famous monument or natural feature in one of these countries.

Visual-spatial; verbal-linguistic

Science

Write a Report

- Suggest that students research and report on either the building of the Suez Canal or the laying of the transatlantic cable.
- Have students explain in their reports why these projects are still important today.

Verbal-linguistic

Graphic Organizer

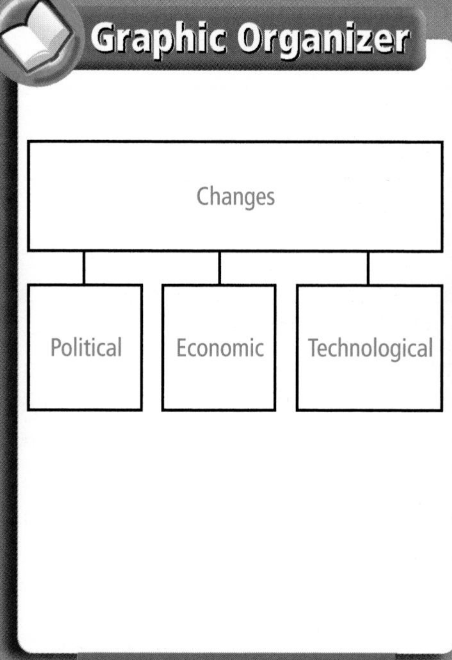

Graphic Organizer 8

 Tested Objectives

U6-17 History Compare different plans for reuniting the country and rebuilding the South after the Civil War.

U6-18 Citizenship Describe how the Constitution changed to protect the rights of African Americans after the war.

Lesson Quick Look

This lesson describes what happened during the period of Reconstruction.

Teaching Option: Extend Lesson 4 uses graphs to show students the economic effects of Reconstruction.

1 Get Set to Read

Preview Have students look at the photograph on page 473. Ask them what it shows.

Reading Skill: Draw Conclusions Students might conclude that African Americans gained some political power during Reconstruction.

Build on What You Know Ask students to think about important turning points in their lives. Explain that Reconstruction was a turning point in U.S. history.

Vocabulary

Reconstruction *noun,* the period following the Civil War during which the Confederate states rejoined the Union

assassination *noun,* the murder of a public figure by surprise attack, usually for political reasons

Freedmen's Bureau *noun,* a federal agency formed to aid and protect former enslaved people in the South after the Civil War

impeach *verb,* to formally charge a public official with misconduct in office

Core Lesson 4

Reconstruction

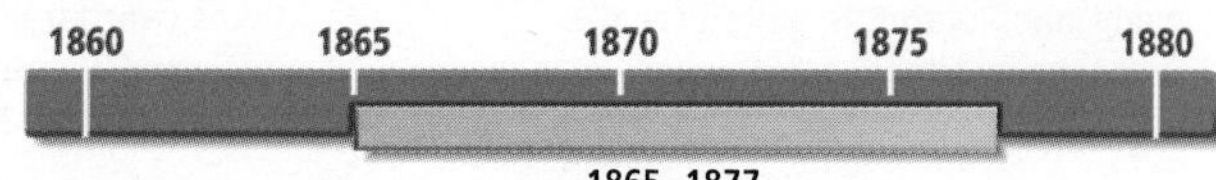

VOCABULARY

Reconstruction
assassination
Freedmen's Bureau
impeach

Vocabulary Strategy

Reconstruction

Find the word **construct** in **Reconstruction.** When you reconstruct something, you construct, or build, it again.

READING SKILL

Draw Conclusions

Use facts and details to come to a conclusion about how Reconstruction affected people's lives.

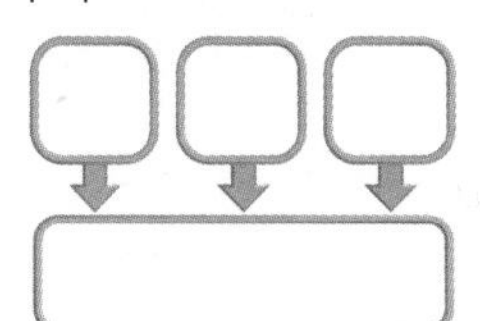

Build on What You Know Have you ever had a moment when you knew that your life has changed forever? That is a turning point. The Civil War was a turning point for the United States. After the war, the nation would never be the same again.

Plans for Reconstruction

Main Idea President Lincoln and Congress disagreed about how to rebuild the South.

As the Civil War ended, Americans faced a great challenge. When the South tried to leave the Union, the nation had nearly split apart. During Reconstruction, the country had to be reunited. The period when the South rejoined the Union is called **Reconstruction.**

Reconstruction was a difficult time. Americans could
not agree on how to bring the South back into the 1
Union. Some wanted to make it easy for southern states to rejoin. They hoped that the nation could be almost the way it had been before the war.

Many northerners felt differently. They were bitter about the war and blamed the South for it. Some of them wanted to use Reconstruction to punish the South.

President Lincoln Saving the Union was Lincoln's greatest concern. He wanted to reunite the nation quickly.

Skill and Strategy

Reading Skill and Strategy

Reading Skill: Draw Conclusions

Sometimes when you read, you have to figure out things that the writer doesn't tell you. This skill is called drawing conclusions.

Read "Plans for Reconstruction." Then fill in the draw conclusions chart below. What conclusion can you draw from the different groups' plans to rebuild the South?

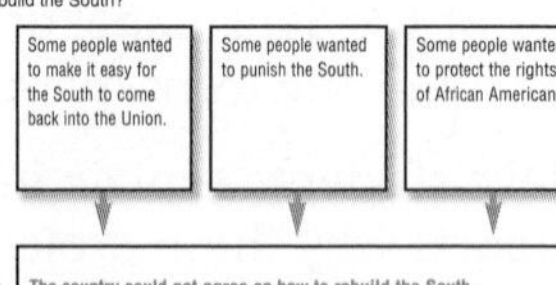

Reading Strategy: Summarize

2. Read "Reconstruction." Then complete the summary.

Radical Republicans in Congress disagreed with how President Johnson let the South rebuild itself.

3. Read "The Constitution Changes." Then write a sentence to summarize the section.

Sample answer: Congress passed three amendments to protect the rights of African Americans.

Unit Resources

130
Use with *United States History*, pp. 472–477

Unit Resources, p. 130

Background

Andrew Johnson

- Andrew Johnson was apprenticed to a tailor as a boy. When Johnson was fifteen, he ran away, causing his employer to post a reward of $10 for his apprehension.
- Johnson served in the Tennessee legislature and in the state senate. He admired Andrew Jackson and Thomas Jefferson and modeled some of his political ideas after theirs.

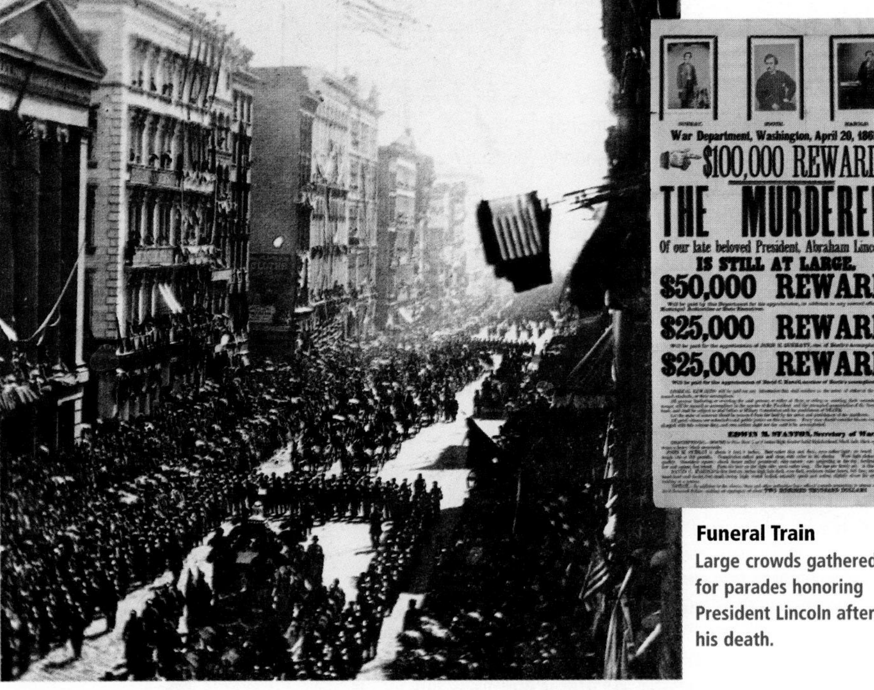

Funeral Train
Large crowds gathered for parades honoring President Lincoln after his death.

President Lincoln did not want to punish the South. He asked northerners to forget their anger. Lincoln said,

> **"With malice [meanness] toward none, with charity for all . . . let us strive on [try] to finish the work we are in, to bind up the nation's wounds . . ."**

2 Lincoln planned to let the defeated states set up new state governments and rejoin the Union quickly.

Many people disagreed with Lincoln, especially the Radical Republicans. These senators and representatives wanted to greatly change the South. For example, they hoped to use Reconstruction to protect the rights of African Americans. Because they disagreed with the President, Republicans in Congress wanted to control Reconstruction.

Lincoln's Death

Before Lincoln and Congress could agree on a plan, disaster struck. On the evening of April 14, 1865, Lincoln went to a play at Ford's Theater in Washington. **John Wilkes Booth,** an actor, crept up behind Lincoln. Booth supported the Confederacy and was angry about the South's defeat. He pulled out a gun and shot the President. Abraham Lincoln died the next day. 3

Lincoln's assassination shocked the nation. **Assassination** is the murder of an important leader. Lincoln had become a hero to many people. His death filled them with sadness. They would miss his leadership during the difficult years of Reconstruction.

REVIEW What was Lincoln's plan for Reconstruction? to let southern states set up new state governments and rejoin the Union quickly

473

2 Teach

Plans for Reconstruction

Talk About It

1 **Q History** What made Reconstruction a huge challenge for Americans?

A The South had to be reunited with the rest of the country, but Americans could not agree on how it should be done.

2 **Q Citizenship** What were President Lincoln's plans for Reconstruction?

A He planned to let the southern states set up new state governments and quickly rejoin the Union.

3 **Q History** Why did John Wilkes Booth assassinate President Lincoln?

A He supported the Confederacy and was angry about the South's defeat.

Vocabulary Strategy

Reconstruction Remind students that *construct* means "to build" and the prefix *re-* means "again."

assassination Point out the related words *assassin* and *assassinate.* Remind students that the ending *-tion* shows that *assassination* is a noun.

Reading Strategy: Summarize As students read the first section, ask them to use what they know about summarizing to produce a summary of the section. Ask students to share their summaries with the class.

Leveled Practice

Extra Support

Have students **discuss with a partner** Lincoln's and the Radical Republicans' plans for Reconstruction. Ask them to list the differences between the two plans. Verbal-linguistic

Challenge

Have students **write an editorial** someone might have written at the end of the Civil War. The editorial should express their opinions about the best plan for Reconstruction. Verbal-linguistic

ELL

Intermediate

Have students **perform a scene** in which several people with conflicting ideas about Reconstruction discuss their ideas. Encourage them to share their scenes with the class.

Bodily-kinesthetic

Reconstruction

Talk About It

4 Q Citizenship What were the Black Codes?

A They were laws passed by southern states to limit the rights of former enslaved people to travel, vote, and work in certain jobs.

5 Q History What was the purpose of the Freedmen's Bureau?

A The Bureau provided food, clothing, medical care, and legal advice to poor blacks and whites. It set up hospitals and schools for newly freed people.

Vocabulary Strategy

Freedmen's Bureau Explain to students that *bureau* can mean "a department of a government."

Critical Thinking

Evaluate Do you think it was a good idea for Congress to put the South under military rule? Why or why not?.

Reconstruction

Main Idea Congress took control of Reconstruction from President Andrew Johnson.

After Lincoln's death, Vice President **Andrew Johnson** of Tennessee became President. Johnson put Lincoln's plan for Reconstruction into action in 1865. The southern states quickly set up new state governments. The federal government forced them to abolish slavery in their state constitutions. At the same time, though, most southern states passed
4 harsh laws called Black Codes. The Black Codes limited the rights of former slaves to travel, vote, and work in certain jobs.

Radical Republicans in Congress were unhappy about the Black Codes. President Johnson upset them more by allowing southern states to elect former Confederate leaders to Congress.

Congress fought back. Members voted not to let the new southern representatives join Congress. They passed a law to protect the rights of freedmen, who were the people freed from slavery. Congress also created the Freedmen's Bureau. The **Freedmen's Bureau** provided food, clothing,
medical care, and legal advice to poor 5
blacks and whites. It set up hospitals and schools and found jobs for many.

Reconstruction The mural below shows several scenes from Reconstruction: 1 Students attend a new school opened by the Freedmen's Bureau. 2 Radical Republicans impeach President Johnson. 3 African Americans vote for the first time. 4 African Americans serve in Congress.

Math

Make a Graph

- Have small groups plan a budget for the Freedmen's Bureau. Have each group make a list of several projects that they would like the Bureau to fund, such as job training for sharecroppers or new health clinics.
- Then have them create a circle graph indicating how much of their budget they will devote to each project. Discuss finished graphs as a class.

Visual-spatial; verbal-linguistic

Language Arts

Write a Short Story

- Have students write a short story about people whose lives are affected by Reconstruction.
- Have students share their stories with the class.

Verbal-linguistic

Congress Takes Control

In 1867, Congress began its own Reconstruction plan. It put the South under military rule. Soldiers from the national army marched into the region. When they arrived, they forced southern states to obey Congress. The states had to allow all men, including blacks, to vote.

After taking over Reconstruction, Congress tried to remove President Johnson. In 1868, the House of
6 Representatives voted to impeach Johnson. To **impeach** means to charge a government official with a crime. They accused him of breaking one of their new laws. Congress almost forced Johnson out of office, but they did not succeed, and he finished his presidency.

Carpetbaggers and Scalawags

Some southerners supported the Republicans during Reconstruction. They were unpopular with southerners. Southerners who helped the government during Reconstruction were known as scalawags. Scalawag was a slang word for an old worthless horse.

Many northerners traveled south during Reconstruction. Some wanted to help rebuild the South, but others just wanted to make money. These people were known as carpetbaggers, because
they often carried suitcases made of carpet 7
material. Southerners disliked carpetbaggers and did not want them there.

REVIEW Why were soldiers sent to the South?
to force southern states to obey Congress

475

Reconstruction *continued*

Talk About It

6 **Q History** What did Congress try to do after taking over Reconstruction?

A They tried to impeach President Johnson, but failed.

7 **Q History** Who were the "carpetbaggers"?

A They were people from the North who went South to make money during Reconstruction.

Vocabulary Strategy

impeach Tell students that *impeach* comes from a Latin word meaning "to catch or ensnare."

Reading Strategy: Summarize As students read the next section, ask them to use what they know about summarizing to produce a summary of the section. Ask students to share their summaries with the class.

Extra Support

Write a Speech

Have partners prepare a speech explaining and supporting one of the amendments mentioned in this lesson. They can deliver or display their speeches.

Verbal-linguistic

Challenge

Create Trading Cards

Have students research and illustrate trading cards of famous people from the Reconstruction Era, including President Lincoln and President Johnson, John Wilkes Booth, and the first African Americans to hold elected office. Ask students to list three facts about each person on the back of each card.

Visual-spatial

The Constitution Changes

Talk About It

8 **Q Citizenship** What was the purpose of the Thirteenth Amendment?

A It abolished slavery in the United States.

9 **Q Citizenship** In what ways did the Fourteenth Amendment and Fifteenth Amendment protect the rights of African Americans?

A Fourteenth Amendment: gave African Americans full citizenship and guaranteed due process of law. Fifteenth Amendment: gave African American men the right to vote.

10 **Q Citizenship** What did many African Americans do after winning the right to vote?

A began taking part in government; ran for office; became government leaders

Critical Thinking

Infer What might have happened if the Thirteenth, Fourteenth, and Fifteenth Amendments to the Constitution had not been ratified?

The Constitution Changes

Main Idea Congress changed the Constitution to protect the rights of African Americans.

During Reconstruction, Congress created three new amendments to the Constitution. The new amendments gave the national government more power over the states. They also protected the rights of African Americans.

The first of the new amendments, the
8 Thirteenth Amendment, ended slavery
throughout the United States. In 1865,
the states ratified the amendment, which
means they approved it.

Black Codes still limited the rights of
African Americans. To protect those
9 rights, Congress passed the Fourteenth
Amendment, which gave citizenship to
African Americans. It said that a citizen's
life, liberty, or property cannot be taken
away without a fair trial. This is called
"due process of law." It also said that all
citizens must be treated equally under
the law.

Almost every southern state refused to ratify the Fourteenth Amendment. They did not want the national government to interfere with their state laws. Congress declared that southern states had to ratify the Fourteenth Amendment to rejoin the Union. The states then agreed to the demands of Congress.

A year later, Congress passed the
Fifteenth Amendment, guaranteeing
African American men the right to vote.
The Fifteenth Amendment had an effect
right away. African Americans began
taking part in government. Religious
leaders, former soldiers, and others ran
for office. Some became leaders in
community and state government. 10

Many African Americans served in state legislatures. They worked to create the first public schools for whites and blacks in the South. Seventeen African Americans joined the United States Congress. **Blanche K. Bruce** and **Hiram Revels** of Mississippi became two of the first black senators.

Three New Amendments

Thirteenth Amendment

The Thirteenth Amendment declared that slavery would not be allowed to exist in the United States. It ended the long argument in the United States over whether slavery should be legal.

Fourteenth Amendment

The Fourteenth Amendment declared that the states could not limit the rights of citizens. States could not take away life, liberty, or property without due process of the law, or deny equal protection of the law.

Fifteenth Amendment

The Fifteenth Amendment gave all men the right to vote, no matter what their skin color was or if they had been enslaved. However, women were still not allowed to vote until the 1920s.

Drama

Debate in Congress

- Have small groups evaluate Congress's actions during Reconstruction.
- Ask them to consider other actions Congress might have taken during this time.
- Then bring the groups together to act out a scene in which Congress holds a debate about this issue.

Verbal-linguistic

Language Arts

Write a Newspaper Article

- Have students write a newspaper article describing the day when Hiram Revels, the first African American senator, joined the U.S. Senate.
- Remind them to tell *who*, *what*, *where*, *when*, and *why* in their article.

Verbal-linguistic

The Struggle for Rights Continues

The amendments passed during Reconstruction helped all Americans. They protected people's rights and made laws fairer. For example, the Fourteenth Amendment requires both the federal and the state governments to treat all citizens equally and fairly.

The amendments, however, did not solve all of the nation's problems. Some people, both in the North and in the South, did not want African Americans to vote or to have equal rights.

Hiram Revels
He served in the Mississippi state senate, and later became the first African American elected to the U.S. Senate.

Sometimes laws protecting rights were ignored. The struggle for equality would continue for African Americans.

REVIEW Why did Congress pass the Fourteenth Amendment? to protect African Americans from the Black Codes and assure equal treatment

Lesson Summary

- Congress and President Lincoln had different plans for Reconstruction.
- President Lincoln was assassinated just after the war ended.
- Congress took control of Reconstruction from President Johnson.
- Three important amendments were ratified during Reconstruction.

Why It Matters ...

During Reconstruction, the nation's laws became fairer, with new constitutional protection for citizens' rights and freedoms.

Lesson Review

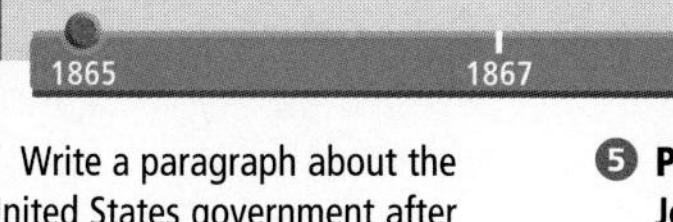

1. **VOCABULARY** Write a paragraph about the actions of the United States government after the Civil War, using the words **Reconstruction, Freedmen's Bureau,** and **impeach.**
2. **READING SKILL** Review your **conclusion.** What effect do you think Reconstruction had on the lives of freedmen?
3. **MAIN IDEA: Government** Why did Congress fight against President Johnson?
4. **MAIN IDEA: Citizenship** What right did the Fifteenth Amendment protect for African American men?
5. **PEOPLE TO KNOW** Why was **Andrew Johnson** important after Lincoln's death?
6. **TIMELINE SKILL** What did Congress do in 1868?
7. **CRITICAL THINKING: Infer** How do you think Reconstruction might have been different if President Lincoln had not been assassinated?

HANDS ON **RESEARCH ACTIVITY** The Fourteenth Amendment guarantees due process of law and equal protection under the law. Use library or Internet resources to find out more about this amendment and create a mural explaining it.

477

3 Review/Assess

Review Tested Objectives

U6-17 Some northerners wanted to punish the South; Lincoln wanted to let the South rejoin the Union easily; Radical Republicans wanted to change the South, especially with regard to African Americans' rights.

U6-18 The Constitution's 13th Amendment ended slavery; the 14th gave full citizenship to African Americans and guaranteed due process of law; and the 15th gave African American men the right to vote.

Lesson Review Answers

1. Paragraph should use all three vocabulary words.
2. Answers will vary; should incorporate details from the lesson.
3. Congress disliked President Johnson because he resisted Congress's Reconstruction plan.
4. The Fifteenth Amendment protected the right of African American men to vote.
5. Johnson was President after Lincoln's death, and tried to put Lincoln's plan for Reconstruction into effect.
6. They impeached President Andrew Johnson.
7. Answers should show awareness of ways in which Lincoln's plans for the South differed from Congress's.

HANDS ON Performance Task Rubric

4	Information is accurate; mural is easily understood; mechanics are correct.
3	Information is mostly accurate; mural is understood; few errors in mechanics are present.
2	Some information is inaccurate; mural is fairly understandable; some errors in mechanics are present.
1	Most or all information is inaccurate; mural is not understandable; many errors in mechanics are present.

Study Guide/Homework

Vocabulary and Study Guide

Vocabulary

Across
1. Murder of an important leader
2. To charge a government official with a crime

Down
3. ___ Republicans
4. During Reconstruction, the South ___ the Union.
5. Southern states passed the Black ___.

ASSASSINATION / IMPEACH / RADICAL / REJOIN / CODES

Study Guide

6. Read "Plans for Reconstruction" and "Reconstruction." Then fill in the blanks below.

Before a plan for Reconstruction was agreed upon, President Lincoln was assassinated. Andrew Johnson became President. Radical Republicans became upset because of the South's Black Codes and the election of former Confederate leaders to Congress. Congress took control of Reconstruction, put the South under military rule, and voted to impeach the President.

7. Read "The Constitution Changes." Then fill in the blanks below.

Congress created the 13th, 14th, and 15th Amendments to protect the rights of African Americans. These amendments gave the national government more power over the states. African Americans were granted full citizenship and the right to fair and equal treatment. Some African American men became government leaders.

 131 Use with United States History, pp. 472–477

Unit Resources, p. 131

Reteach Minilesson

Use a graphic organizer to review Reconstruction.

Reconstruction
- Freedmen's Bureau
- South Under Military Rule
- 13th, 14th, and 15th Amendments Ratified

Graphic Organizer 8

Quick Look

Connect to the Core Lesson Students have just read about Reconstruction and how it affected the South after the Civil War. In Extend Lesson 4, students will learn more about the southern economy after the war.

1 Teach the Extend Lesson

Connect to the Big Idea

Economic Performance The economy of the South suffered greatly after the Civil War. Many lives were lost and much property was destroyed. Such losses made a slow recovery for the South's farm-based economy inevitable. Some Republicans in Congress wanted to punish the South, and its economy would be directly affected by Congress's policies.

Connect to Prior Knowledge

Have students read the introduction. Then ask them what kinds of visual aids they would suggest that would depict the information about the South's economy after the Civil War.

Extend Lesson 4

Economics

The South After the War

After the Civil War, the economy of the United States grew faster than ever before. The South, however, did not see as much growth as other regions. Manufacturing in the South grew more slowly than in the rest of the country. Southern farmers struggled to produce as much as they had before the war.

The economy of the South suffered for many reasons. The region lost two-thirds of its wealth. Many young men who would have been farmers or workers lost their lives in the war. The war ruined homes, farms, machinery, factories, and railroads.

People in the South worked hard to rebuild their homes, cities, and factories. Cities such as Atlanta, Richmond, and Charleston became centers of trade and industry again.

Charleston (above) was left in ruins by the end of the Civil War. However, people rebuilt quickly. By 1893, Charleston (below) had grown into a large and busy city.

Reaching All Learners

Extra Support

Interpret Graphs

- Ask students to look at the graphs and captions in this lesson and write down the regions shown.
- Then have them list which region's production and farm values did the best and which region's did the worst.

Visual-spatial

On Level

Create a Chart

- Have students create a compare and contrast chart of the regions' economies featured in this lesson.
- Ask them to list ways in which the economies are alike and different.

Verbal-linguistic

Challenge

Write a Report

- Have students research and report on what goods the South produced around the time of the Civil War and what it produces today.
- Ask them to share their reports with their classmates.

Verbal-linguistic

In 1870, the value of a southern farm was only one-third of what it had been before the war.

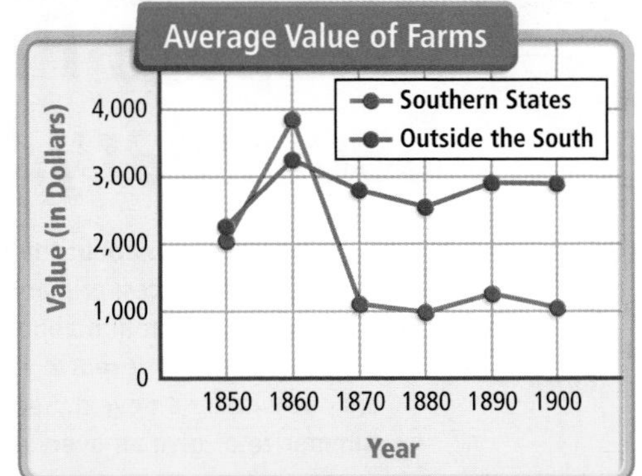

The economy of the South improved after the war. However, the value of goods made in the South remained lower than in the rest of the country.

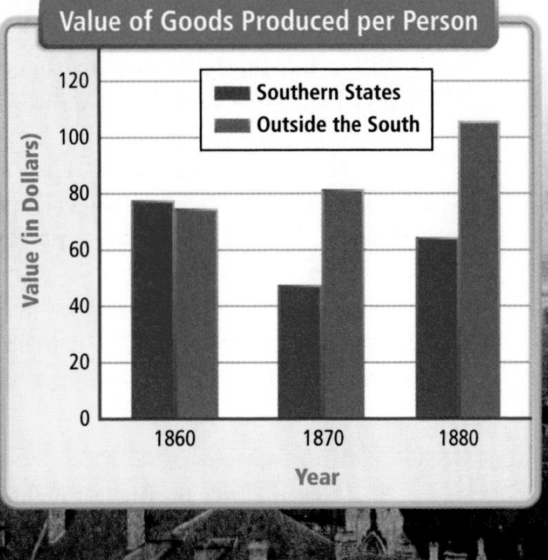

ECONOMICS

Activities

1. **THINK ABOUT IT** Why do you think so much property was destroyed in the South, but not in the North?
2. **MAKE YOUR OWN** Look at the line graph of farm values. Make a bar graph showing farm values.

479

2 Leveled Activities

1 Think About It *For Extra Support*
Answers should discuss how much of the war was fought in the South and that many lives and property were lost.

2 Make Your Own *For Challenge*

HANDS ON Performance Task Rubric

4	Graph is clear, accurate, and complete; mechanics are correct.
3	Graph is mostly clear, accurate, and complete; few errors in mechanics.
2	Graph is somewhat unclear, inaccurate, or incomplete; some errors in mechanics, grammar, and punctuation.
1	Graph is incomplete, unclear, inaccurate; many errors in spelling, grammar, and punctuation.

ELL

Intermediate

- Suggest that students create three-dimensional models of the bar graphs by gluing and stacking sugar cubes or by using modeling clay.
- Have them color the sugar cubes or use different clays to differentiate the bar graphs.

Bodily-kinesthetic; visual-spatial

Art

Design Icons

- Ask students to create icons for the various products in the South's economy before and after the Civil War.
- They can use these icons to symbolize the changes in the South's economy shown in this lesson.

Visual-spatial

Graphic Organizer

Many farmers and workers died. → Southern economy grew more slowly.

War ruined property. → Southern economy grew more slowly.

Graphic Organizer 9

Skillbuilder Pages 480–481

Tested Objective

U6-19 Identify and interpret the difference between primary and secondary sources.

1 Teach the Skill

- Have students talk about an important event in their lifetimes, one that was reported in newspapers and on television. Ask how they learned about the event.
- Read with students the two accounts of President Lincoln's assassination shown on page 480. Discuss how they are similar and how they are different.
- Make sure students understand all the vocabulary in the two accounts.
- Point out that primary sources tend to contain stronger emotions and opinions than secondary sources. Secondary sources may be supported by more facts and may provide a more general overview of events than primary sources.
- Ask students why it is a good idea to use both types of sources when studying events from the past.

Skillbuilder

Compare Primary and Secondary Sources

VOCABULARY
primary source
secondary source

People learned about the death of President Lincoln from two types of sources: primary and secondary. A primary source is firsthand information about an event, a place, or a time period. A secondary source is information from someone who did not witness an event. Secondary sources sometimes summarize or give an overview of what happened.

The New York Herald

J. Wilkes Booth, the Actor, the Alleged Assassin of the President

War Department – Washington, April 15, 1865 – 1:30 a.m. – Major General Dix, New York:

This evening, at about 9:30 p.m., at Ford's Theatre [Washington, D.C.], the President, while sitting in his private box with Mrs. Lincoln,... was shot by an assassin, who suddenly entered the box and approached behind the President.

The assassin then leaped upon the stage, brandishing [waving] a large dagger or knife, and made his escape in the rear of the theatre.

...I was at Ford's theatre last night, seated in the left hand side nearly opposite the President's box. About half past ten I heard a shot. I thought it was in the play. A man appeared in front of the President's box and got upon the stage swinging himself down partly by the curtains and partly jumping. I noticed he had a large dagger in his left hand I think. He appeared to stagger but recovered himself. He held the dagger up just as he got upon the stage and said in a tragical tone very clearly...sic semper tyrannis [thus always to tyrants].

- Will T. Kent, testimony given to Supreme Court on April 15, 1865

Leveled Practice

Extra Support

- Have students work in teams to find several accounts of Lincoln's assassination.
- Have the teams assemble facts from these sources on note cards, labeling each one as a primary or a secondary source. Verbal-linguistic

Challenge

Have students compare several primary and secondary sources on Lincoln's assassination. Discuss students' findings. Verbal-linguistic

ELL

Beginning

- Discuss other meanings of the words *primary* and *secondary.* Give the examples of *primary school, secondary school,* and *primary election.*
- Have students make up sentences using these words in various contexts.

Verbal-linguistic

Apply Critical Thinking

Learn the Skill

Step 1: Read the sources. Look for clue words such as *I* and *my*, which are sometimes used in primary sources.

Step 2: Identify the information as a primary or secondary source. Ask yourself, Who wrote the information? Was the writer at the event?

Step 3: Make a list of the similarities and differences in the sources. Does the primary source give a different account of the event than the secondary source? What information did you learn from each source?

Practice the Skill

Read the two accounts of President Lincoln's assassination on page 480. Then answer these questions.

1. Is the news article a primary or a secondary source? How do you know?
2. Is Will T. Kent's account a primary or a secondary source? How do you know?
3. What facts do the two accounts share?
4. What differences do you see between sources?

Apply the Skill

Find an example of a primary source in a book, newspaper, or magazine article. Then find an article that is an example of a secondary source. In a paragraph, explain how you identified each one.

481

Skill Practice

Skillbuilder: Compare Primary and Secondary Sources

"A house divided against itself cannot stand. I believe this government cannot endure, permanently half slave and half free. I do not expect the Union to be dissolved—I do not expect the house to fall—but I do expect it will cease to be divided. It will become all one thing or all the other."
—Abraham Lincoln, in an 1858 campaign speech to Illinois Republicans

Lincoln Becomes a Leading Antislavery Spokesperson

Americans began to learn of Abraham Lincoln's views on slavery when he challenged Stephen Douglas in the 1858 Illinois Senate election. Lincoln did not speak to outlaw slavery in the South, but he did not think the country could continue to be half slave states and half free states. He believed that soon the country would have to become all slave or all free states.

Practice

1. Is Abraham Lincoln's speech a primary or secondary source? How do you know? Primary source; uses first-person *I*
2. What facts do the two sources share? Lincoln believed that the country would not be able to continue as half free and half slave states; it would become all one or all the other.
3. What do you learn from the passage that you do not learn from Lincoln's speech? Lincoln ran against Douglas for Illinois senator; Lincoln did not ask for the outlawing of slavery.

Apply

Find a book that is an example of a primary source. Then find a book that is an example of a secondary source. On a separate sheet of paper, write a paragraph explaining how you identified each one. Paragraphs should include how to identify sources.

Unit Resources 132 Use with *United States History*, pp. 480–481

Unit Resources, p. 132

Skill Transparency

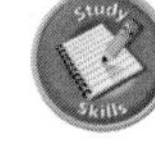

Skillbuilder Transparency 63

Compare Primary and Secondary Sources

The New York Herald

J. Wilkes Booth, the Actor, the Alleged Assassin of the President
War Department – Washington, April 15, 1865 – 1:30 a.m. – Major General Dix, New York:

This evening, at about 9:30 p.m., at Ford's Theatre [Washington, D.C.], the President, while sitting in his private box with Mrs. Lincoln,... was shot by an assassin, who suddenly entered the box and approached behind the President.

The assassin then leaped upon the stage, brandishing [waving] a large dagger or knife, and made his escape in the rear of the theatre.

...I was at Ford's theatre last night, seated in the left hand side nearly opposite the President's box. About half past ten I heard a shot. I thought it was in the play. A man appeared in front of the President's box and got upon the stage swinging himself down partly by the curtains and partly jumping. I noticed he had a large dagger in his left hand I think. He appeared to stagger but recovered himself. He held the dagger up just as he got upon the stage and said in a tragical tone very clearly...sic semper tyrannis [thus always to tyrants].

- Will T. Kent, testimony given to Supreme Court on April 15, 1865

Step 1 Read the sources. Look for clue words such as *I* and *my*, which are sometimes used in primary sources.

Step 2 Identify the information as a primary or a secondary source. Who wrote the information? Was he or she at the event?

Step 3 Make a list of the similarities and differences in the sources. Do the sources have different ways of telling the information? What did you learn from each source?

Skillbuilder Transparency Use with *United States History*, pp. 480–481

Transparency 13

2 Practice the Skill

1. Secondary source; does not use the words *I* or *my*. The writer does not claim to have been at the theater when Lincoln was shot.
2. Primary source; comes from Kent's court testimony. He says he was at the theater and witnessed the shooting. His account uses the word *I*.
3. Both accounts say that the shooting occurred in the President's box at Ford's Theater, that the assassin carried a dagger, and that he jumped from the box to the stage.
4. time of the assassination (10:30 p.m. in the primary source, 9:30 p.m. in the secondary source); Kent uses the word *I* and shares firsthand observations, for example, saying that the assassin spoke in a "tragical tone."

3 Apply the Skill

Ask students to find one primary source article and one secondary source article. Then have them write a paragraph explaining how they identified each type of source. When evaluating students' paragraphs, consider:

- Did the student find and correctly identify a primary source article and a secondary source article?
- Did the student effectively explain how they identified each type of article?
- Did the student use correct mechanics in the paragraph?

Tested Objectives

U6-20 Economics Explain the effects of Reconstruction policies on the South after the Civil War.

U6-21 History Describe the end of Reconstruction in the South.

Lesson Quick Look

This lesson focuses on how freed African Americans coped with opportunities and challenges during and after Reconstruction.

Teaching Option: Extend Lesson 5 uses photographs to teach students about the African American educational movement.

1 Get Set to Read

Preview Have students look at the photograph and chart on page 483. Ask what these visuals show.

Reading Skill: Problem and Solution Problems included debt, Jim Crow laws, and attacks by the Ku Klux Klan. Solutions included new schools such as the Tuskegee Institute.

Build on What You Know Discuss opportunities Americans share. Point out that although freedom opens up opportunities, it may also bring challenges.

Vocabulary

sharecropping *noun,* a system of farming in which a tenant farmer pays a share of the crops as rent to the landowner

Jim Crow *noun,* the practice of discriminating against and segregating African Americans after Reconstruction

segregation *noun,* the practice of separating a group of people from the rest of society

Core Lesson 5

The Challenge of Freedom

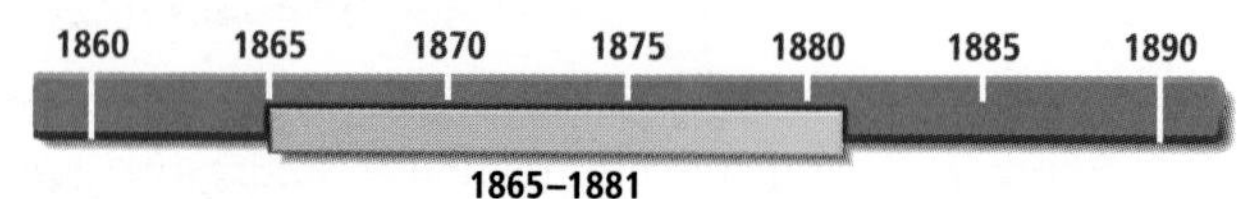

VOCABULARY

sharecropping
Jim Crow
segregation

Vocabulary Strategy

share|cropping

In **sharecropping,** a farmer only gets to keep a part, or **share,** of a crop and gives the rest to the landowner.

READING SKILL

Problem and Solution

Take notes to identify the problems facing African Americans after the Civil War and their solutions.

PROBLEMS	SOLUTIONS

Build on What You Know You know how important freedom is to people in the United States. Millions of African Americans were free after the Civil War. Freedom brought new opportunities, but also new challenges.

Freedom and Hardship

Main Idea Freed African Americans looked for ways to make a living after the end of slavery.

> **"No more iron chain for me, no more, no more!"**

African Americans sang with joy to celebrate their new freedom. Reconstruction was a time of hope for them. Slavery had ended at last. They had the chance to make new lives for themselves.

Freedom was exciting, but it was not easy. Newly freed African Americans had to struggle to make a living. They also had to prepare for their new roles as full citizens. They worked to educate themselves and took part in politics. However, times were hard in the South and some people did not want African Americans to be truly free.

Sharecropping This photograph shows sharecroppers at work in the fields they rent from a landowner.

Skill and Strategy

Reading Skill and Strategy

Reading Skill: Problem and Solution

This skill helps you see what problem some people faced and how they resolved it.

Read "The Challenge of Freedom." Then fill in the problem-and-solution chart below. What happened to the freed people during and after Reconstruction?

Problems	Solutions
1. Freed African Americans wanted to farm for themselves.	Many African Americans became sharecroppers.
Government soldiers left the South.	2. Southern states passed Jim Crow laws.

Reading Strategy: Summarize

3. Read "The Challenge of Freedom." Then write a short summary of each section.

Section 1: Freedom and Hardship

Summary: Sample answer: African Americans experienced difficult times after being freed.

Section 2: The End of Reconstruction

Summary: Sample answer: Many of the rights African Americans gained during Reconstruction were lost afterward.

Unit Resources

133
Use with *United States History*, pp. 48[illegible]

Unit Resources, p. 133

Background

The Tuskegee Institute

- The Tuskegee Institute began with $2000 for teachers' salaries but nothing for land or buildings.
- Booker T. Washington got a $200 loan to purchase land for the school. Students built its first buildings and grew food for the school.

The Rise of Sharecropping

Reconstruction ended the plantation system in the South, leaving many people there very poor. Freed people wanted to farm for themselves. However, few had enough money to buy land.

Landowners set up a system called
1 sharecropping that let poor whites and former slaves become farmers. In **sharecropping,** poor farmers used a landowner's fields. In return, the farmer gave the landowner a share of the crop. Landowners often loaned sharecroppers tools and seeds as well.

Sharecropping gave African Americans some independence. It also kept poor
2 farmers in debt. After selling their crops, many sharecroppers did not have enough money to pay the landowners what they owed. They had to keep borrowing and could not get out of debt. Sharecropping made it hard for poor farmers to save money and provide a good life for their families.

Responses to Reconstruction

Reconstruction angered some people in the South. They opposed the new laws that protected African Americans' rights. They also disliked having federal soldiers in the South to enforce the laws.

Some people wanted to stop African Americans from taking part in government. They formed secret organizations, such as the Ku Klux Klan. The Ku Klux Klan threatened, beat, and even killed African Americans to keep them from voting. The Ku Klux Klan also attacked people who helped African Americans. In 1871, African Americans in Kentucky asked Congress for protection. They described the Klan's "riding nightly over the country . . . robbing, whipping . . . and killing our people." 3

REVIEW Why did many freed African Americans become sharecroppers?
They wanted to be farmers, but could not afford to buy land.

Debts Landowners often charged high prices. This chart shows how much a sharecropper might owe after a year of hard work.

SKILL Reading Charts How much more did this farmer need to earn to make a profit?
$134.81

Sharecropper's Account for the Year 1870

Money Borrowed		Money Earned		Debt
Food	-$83.25	Cotton	+$90.45	
Clothing	-$64.75			
Farm Supplies	-$75.08			
Medicine	-$2.17			
TOTAL:	-$225.25		+$90.45	-$134.80

2 Teach

Freedom and Hardship

Talk About It

1 **Q Economics** What benefits did landowners and poor farmers get from sharecropping?

A Landowners let poor farmers farm small areas of their land in return for a share of the crop.

2 **Q Economics** Why did sharecroppers usually stay poor?

A They owed money to the landowners, making it hard to get out of debt.

3 **Q History** What was the Ku Klux Klan?

A It was a secret organization that planned to keep African Americans from voting by threatening, beating, or killing them.

Vocabulary Strategy

sharecropping Explain that *share* can be a noun or a verb: "She had to share her toys with her sister"; "The landowner demanded his share of the crop."

Reading Strategy: Summarize As students read each section, ask them to use what they know about summarizing to produce a summary of the section. Ask students to share their summaries with the class.

Leveled Practice

Extra Support

Have students **make a list** of opportunities and challenges freed African Americans faced. Then ask students if they faced more opportunities or challenges.
Verbal-linguistic

Challenge

Have students research and **create a report** describing life at the Tuskegee Institute. Ask them to include details that show the benefits of studying there.
Visual-spatial

ELL

Intermediate

Have partners **write a journal entry** from the perspective of a sharecropper. Remind them to include details about daily life and the advantages and disadvantages of sharecropping.

Verbal-linguistic

The End of Reconstruction

Talk About It

4 **Q History** Why did many Americans feel disappointed with Reconstruction?

A Many Americans did not feel that it had successfully reunited the nation.

5 **Q History** What places did the Jim Crow laws segregate?

A schools, hospitals, cemeteries

6 **Q Technology** What plant did George Washington Carver study?

A the peanut

Vocabulary Strategy

Jim Crow Explain to students that *Jim Crow* was a derogatory term used at this time. It is now used to refer to the set of laws and practices that enforced segregation and inequality in the South.

segregation Synonyms include *isolation* and *separation.*

Critical Thinking

Compare and Contrast In what ways was life for African Americans in the South different after President Hayes removed government soldiers?

The End of Reconstruction

Main Idea African Americans worked and studied to overcome new laws that limited their rights.

4 People grew disappointed with Reconstruction over time. They did not feel that it had successfully reunited the nation. In 1877, the new President, **Rutherford B. Hayes**, ended Reconstruction and ordered government soldiers to leave the South. Without protection, many African Americans were unable to vote and they lost their political power.

Southern states began passing Jim Crow laws. **Jim Crow** was a nickname for laws that kept African Americans separate from other Americans. These laws made segregation legal. **Segregation** is the
5 forced separation of the races. Jim Crow laws segregated schools, hospitals, and even cemeteries. States usually spent less money on schools and hospitals for African Americans.

New Schools

African Americans did not want to let Jim Crow laws ruin their hopes for the future. Many believed that education would give them a chance for a better life. Eager students filled the new schools and colleges for African Americans that opened in the South. Churches in the North sent money and teachers to support these new schools. African American churches in the South also took a leading role. These churches became important centers in African American communities.

In 1881, a former slave named **Booker T. Washington** opened the Tuskegee Institute in Alabama. All of Tuskegee's students and teachers were African Americans. Washington believed that African Americans would receive equal treatment in time if they were educated and learned useful skills. Students at the Tuskegee Institute studied writing, math, and science. They also learned trades such as printing, carpentry, and farming.

Tuskegee Schools such as the Tuskegee Institute (right) gave African Americans the education they had not received under slavery. Booker T. Washington, (below) was the president of Tuskegee.

Science

Carver's Inventions

- Have students find out more about George Washington Carver and his inventions.
- Have them choose an invention and make a poster about it.
- Remind them to include details about the product's benefits.
- Display completed posters in the classroom.

Visual-spatial

Language Arts

Write a Fundraising Letter

- Wealthy people such as Andrew Carnegie and John D. Rockefeller contributed to the Tuskegee Institute.
- Ask students to write a letter to one of these men explaining why donating to the Tuskegee Institute is a worthy cause.

Verbal-linguistic

The most famous teacher at Tuskegee was **George Washington Carver**. Carver studied how to improve the lives of poor southern farmers. He taught them to grow crops such as peanuts, pecans, and sweet potatoes instead of cotton.

Carver invented over 300 products
6 made from peanuts. His inventions included peanut butter, peanut cheese, and peanut milk. Carver's discoveries helped farmers across the South.

REVIEW What was the purpose of the Tuskegee Institute? to educate African Americans in the South

Lesson Summary

- Many freed African Americans became sharecroppers.
- The Ku Klux Klan used violence to stop African Americans from voting.
- Reconstruction ended when government soldiers left the South in 1877.
- After Reconstruction, Jim Crow laws required segregation in many public places in the South.

Why It Matters ...

Reconstruction did not solve all of the nation's problems. After Reconstruction, African Americans had to continue their struggle for freedom.

George Washington Carver
He worked at the Tuskegee Institute for more than 40 years. He invented new products that could be made from common crops.

Lesson Review

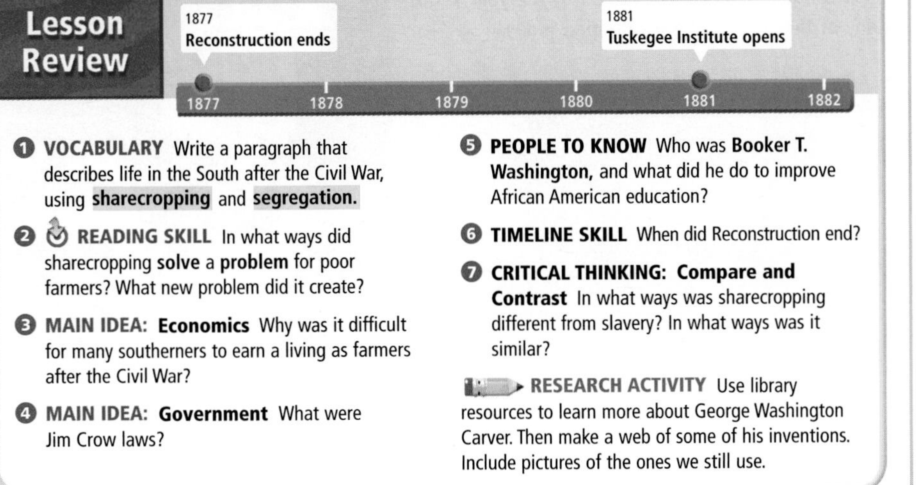

1. **VOCABULARY** Write a paragraph that describes life in the South after the Civil War, using **sharecropping** and **segregation.**
2. **READING SKILL** In what ways did sharecropping **solve** a **problem** for poor farmers? What new problem did it create?
3. **MAIN IDEA: Economics** Why was it difficult for many southerners to earn a living as farmers after the Civil War?
4. **MAIN IDEA: Government** What were Jim Crow laws?
5. **PEOPLE TO KNOW** Who was **Booker T. Washington,** and what did he do to improve African American education?
6. **TIMELINE SKILL** When did Reconstruction end?
7. **CRITICAL THINKING: Compare and Contrast** In what ways was sharecropping different from slavery? In what ways was it similar?

RESEARCH ACTIVITY Use library resources to learn more about George Washington Carver. Then make a web of some of his inventions. Include pictures of the ones we still use.

3 Review/Assess

Review Tested Objectives

U6-20 Effects included the rise of sharecropping and the formation of the Ku Klux Klan.

U6-21 Events included the formation of Jim Crow laws and the formation of new schools for African Americans, such as the Tuskegee Institute.

Lesson Review Answers

1. Answers will vary; paragraphs may address poverty and racism in the South during Reconstruction.
2. Sharecropping solved the problem of making a living, but also kept many farmers in debt.
3. The end of the plantation system meant that many farmers had to seek out new jobs, often as sharecroppers.
4. The Jim Crow laws segregated African Americans and made it difficult for them to vote.
5. Washington founded the Tuskegee Institute, a school where all the teachers and students were African Americans.
6. 1877
7. Different: sharecroppers were not enslaved and could choose where to work. Similar: sharecroppers were often deeply in debt to landowners, making it difficult for them to be financially independent.

Study Guide/Homework

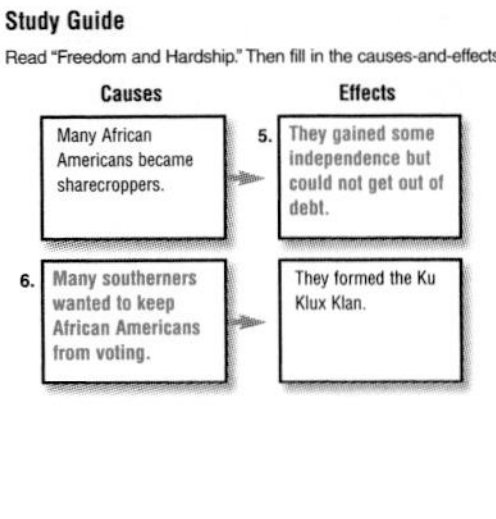

Vocabulary and Study Guide

Vocabulary

Write the definition of each vocabulary word below.

1. sharecropping A system in which landowners allowed poor farmers to use parts of their land in return for a share of the crop
2. Jim Crow Laws that segregated African Americans from other Americans
3. segregation The forced separation of the races
4. Use two of the words in a sentence. Sample answer: Southern states passed Jim Crow laws, which enforced segregation in hospitals, schools, and restaurants.

Study Guide

Read "Freedom and Hardship." Then fill in the causes-and-effects chart below.

Causes	Effects
Many African Americans became sharecroppers.	5. They gained some independence but could not get out of debt.
6. Many southerners wanted to keep African Americans from voting.	They formed the Ku Klux Klan.

Unit Resources 134 Use with United States History, pp. 482–485

Unit Resources, p. 134

Reteach Minilesson

Use a graphic organizer to list the challenges that newly freed African Americans faced.

Graphic Organizer 13

HANDS ON Performance Task Rubric

4	Web is well organized and shows considerable effort; pictures are correct; no errors in mechanics.
3	Web is adequately organized and shows effort; one picture incorrect; few errors in mechanics.
2	Web is somewhat organized and shows some effort; some errors in pictures and/or in mechanics.
1	Web is disorganized and shows little effort; many errors in mechanics and pictures.

Quick Look

Connect to the Core Lesson Students have just learned about the opportunities and challenges African Americans faced during and after Reconstruction. In Extend Lesson 5, students will learn more about the importance of education to African Americans during this period in history.

1 Teach the Extend Lesson

Connect to the Big Idea

Individuals and Communities in American History Even though African Americans faced challenges after the Civil War, many sought a better life through a good education.

Connect to Prior Knowledge

Ask students to read the introduction and look at the photographs and captions. Discuss with students what impact they think these schools made on the students' lives.

History

African American Education

The Freedmen's Bureau closed, but African Americans kept their schools open. After the Civil War, the Freedmen's Bureau gave money to set up schools and colleges for African Americans in the South. The head of the bureau said that they helped start 4,239 schools. More than 240,000 students attended these schools.

When the Freedmen's Bureau closed in 1872, African Americans raised money to keep their schools open. Their efforts increased the number of African American colleges to 34 by the year 1900. Many of these schools are still open today.

A Freedmen's Bureau School

Tuskegee One of the most famous Freedmen's Bureau schools was the Tuskegee Institute, shown above. It specialized in practical education. Students learned skills such as shoemaking, carpentry, and cabinetmaking.

Reaching All Learners

Extra Support

Sketch a Photo Album

- Encourage students to sketch ideas for a photo album of your school.
- What special activities or classes would they highlight for future classes to see?

Visual-spatial

On Level

Calculate and Compare

Have students use information from the lesson to answer the questions:

- If more than 240,000 students attended 4,239 schools for African Americans in the South, how many students might have attended each school? about 56 students
- How many students did the Tuskegee Institute have in 1888? more than 400
- Do you think the Tuskegee Institute had more or fewer students than most schools for African Americans in the South? more

Logical-mathematical

Challenge

List Ideas for Fundraising

- Ask students to imagine that they are in charge of raising funds for a Freedmen's Bureau school.
- Have them list ideas to raise funds for the school and reasons they can give potential donors about why the school is important.

Verbal-linguistic

HISTORY

The Institute Grows
The Institute started in a small building. By 1888, the Institute covered 540 acres and had more than 400 students.

Long Days at School
Students at the Institute studied and worked as many as 16 hours per day.

Activities

1. **MAKE YOUR OWN** Create a poster that might have appeared in the 1870s to raise money for a new African American college.
2. **WRITE ABOUT IT** What courses do you think would have been important for elementary school students to learn in the 1870s? Write a brief description of a typical school day.

487

2 Leveled Activities

❶ **Make Your Own** *For Extra Support*
Posters should show understanding of the importance of education to African Americans during this time period.

❷ **Write About It** *For Challenge*

Writing Rubric

4	Description clearly describes a typical elementary school day in the 1870s; courses and activities mentioned are reasonable; mechanics are correct.
3	Description describes a typical school day in the 1870s; courses and activities mentioned are reasonable; mechanics are mostly correct.
2	Description attempts to describe a typical school day in the 1870s; courses and activities mentioned are somewhat reasonable; several errors in mechanics are present.
1	Description does not attempt to describe a typical school day in the 1870s; courses and activities are not mentioned or not reasonable; many errors in mechanics are present.

ELL

Intermediate/Advanced

- Have students research and illustrate the skills taught at the Tuskegee Institute.
- Then have them write short captions for their illustrations.

Visual-spatial

Art

Make a Collage

- Have students make collages about a typical day at their school.
- Suggest that they organize their pictures and plan layouts.
- Additions to pictures can be word balloons or quotes from magazines; covers can be decorated with paints and stick-on letters.

Visual-spatial

Graphic Organizer

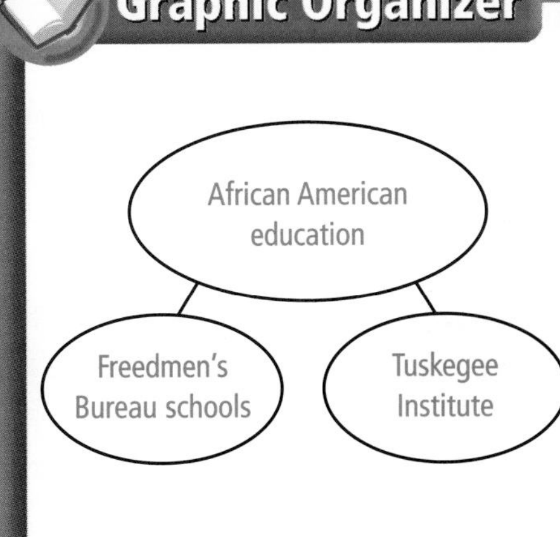

www.eduplace.com/ss/hmss05/

Chapter Review

Visual Summary

1. Lincoln's proclamation declared that slaves in the Confederacy were free. *(Obj. U6-12)*
2. These laws made segregation legal in southern states. *(Obj. U6-21)*
3. 13th Amendment ended slavery in the U.S. 14th gave full citizenship to African Americans and recognized the right of all citizens to equal treatment under the law. 15th gave African American men the right to vote. *(Obj. U6-18)*
4. founded by Booker T. Washington as a school for African Americans *(Obj. U6-21)*

Facts and Main Ideas

5. Cities, homes, farms, and transportation routes were destroyed. Inflation made food expensive. *(Obj. U6-14)*
6. The Union wanted to cut off Texas, Louisiana, and Arkansas from the rest of the South *(Obj. U6-15)*
7. His army was surrounded and did not have enough food or supplies. *(Obj. U6-16)*
8. Advantage: gave freed slaves a chance to become farmers and keep part of their crops; Disadvantage: kept farmers in debt *(Obj. U6-20)*
9. to provide food, clothing, medical care, and legal advice *(Obj. U6-17)*

Vocabulary

10. **home front** *(Obj. U6-14)*
11. **segregation** *(Obj. U6-21)*
12. **total war** *(Obj. U6-15)*
13. **draft** *(Obj. U6-13)*

Chapter 13 Review and Test Prep

Visual Summary

1–4. Write a description of each item named below.

Emancipation Proclamation, 1863

Jim Crow Laws

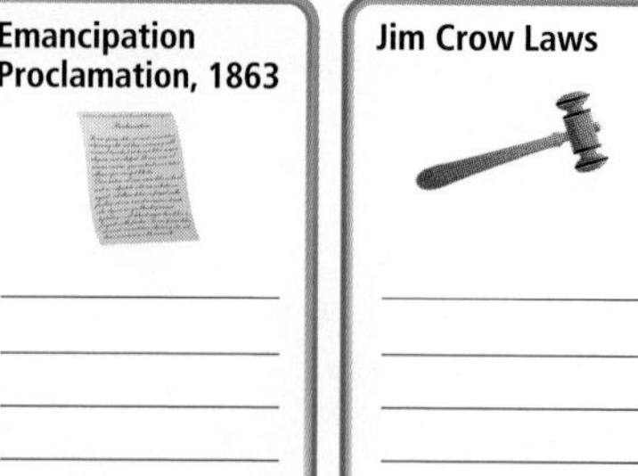

Three New Amendments

Tuskegee Institute

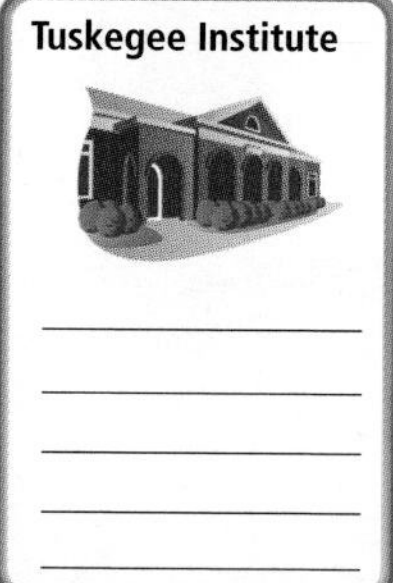

Facts and Main Ideas

TEST PREP Answer each question with information from the chapter.

5. **Citizenship** What were the effects of the Civil War on civilians in the South?
6. **Geography** Why did the Union army want to control the Mississippi River?
7. **History** Why did General Robert E. Lee decide to surrender?
8. **Economics** What were some advantages and disadvantages of sharecropping?
9. **Government** Why did Congress create the Freedmen's Bureau?

Vocabulary

TEST PREP Choose the correct word to complete each sentence.

draft, p. 455
home front, p. 462
total war, p. 467
segregation, p. 484

10. People who are not in the military when a country is at war are part of the _____.
11. After the Civil War, some states passed laws making _____ legal.
12. Sherman used the strategy of destroying an enemy's resources known as _____.
13. Jefferson Davis started a _____ to get enough soldiers for his army.

Reading/Language Arts Wrap-Up

Reading Strategy: Summarize

Review with students the steps involved when they summarize a passage of text.

Have students work in small groups. Each member of the group should take a paragraph and summarize it for the rest of the group.

Ask students to do a self-check: "How well did I do in summarizing?"

Writing Strategy

Explain to students that summarizing will be a valuable tool when they need to write.

For example, if students are taking a test in which they must write short answers to questions, they can use the summarizing strategy as they review what they know and choose the details most pertinent to the answer.

CHAPTER SUMMARY TIMELINE

1863 Battle of Gettysburg — 1865 Civil War ends — 1877 Reconstruction ends — 1881 Tuskegee Institute opens

1860 · 1865 · 1870 · 1875 · 1880 · 1885

Apply Skills

TEST PREP **Study Skill** Read the quotes about the final charge at Gettysburg to answer the question.

> We saw the enemy with colors [flags] flying...until this moment I had not gazed upon so grand a sight as was presented by that beautiful mass of grey.
>
> — Thomas Galwey, Union soldier

> About 13,000 troops advanced across an open field and up Cemetery Ridge in what has become known as "Pickett's Charge."...Only a few of the Southern troops reached the top of the ridge.
>
> — from the *World Book* encyclopedia article for the Battle of Gettysburg

14. What does the first source tell you that the second source does not?
- **A.** who led the charge
- **B.** when the charge took place
- **C.** how many soldiers were in the battle
- **D.** how the charge looked to the soldiers

15. How do you know that the *World Book* article is a secondary source?

Critical Thinking

TEST PREP Write a short paragraph to answer each question.

16. Analyze In what ways was life during the war harder in the South than it was in the North?

17. Categorize What two categories could you use to group the following?

Abraham Lincoln, Robert E. Lee, Jefferson Davis, Ulysses S. Grant, William T. Sherman

Timeline

Use the Chapter Summary Timeline above to answer the question.

18. Did the Civil War end before or after the end of Reconstruction?

Activities

Music Activity During the Civil War, songs were written and sung about victory, about missing home, and other topics. Write the words or music for a song about an event in this chapter.

Writing Activity Write a short story about the first day for students at a Freedmen's School in the South. Include details about what life was like after the Civil War.

Technology
Writing Process Tips
Get help with your story at **www.eduplace.com/kids/hmss05/**

489

Technology

Test Generator

- The questions in this review are part of the bank of questions that can be found on the **Test Generator CD-ROM.**
- You can generate your own version of the chapter review by using the Test Generator.

Web Link

For more ideas, visit
www.eduplace.com/ss/hmss05/

Standards

National Standards

II b Vocabulary associated with time, timelines; examples of change; and cause and effect relationships
II d Sources for reconstructing the past **IV g** Analyze a particular event
VI h Tensions between the wants and needs and fairness, equity, and justice
IX b Conflict, cooperation, and interdependence among individuals, groups, and nations **IX f** Universal human rights **X a** Key ideals
X b Citizen rights and responsibilities
X h Public policies and citizen behaviors

Apply Skills

14. D *(Obj. U6-19)*

15. It is not written by someone who was at the event. *(Obj. U6-19)*

Critical Thinking

16. Most of the battles were fought in the South, so many farms, homes and cities were destroyed by the fighting. People in the South also had difficulty buying enough food because of inflation. *(Obj. U6-14)*

17. Union, Confederacy *(Obj. U6-10)*

Timeline

18. The Civil War ended before the end of Reconstruction. *(Obj. U6-21)*

Leveled Activities

HANDS ON Performance Task Rubric

4	Song is well organized and shows considerable creative effort; mechanics are correct.
3	Song is adequately organized and shows creative effort; few errors.
2	Song is somewhat organized and shows some creative effort; some errors.
1	Song is disorganized and shows little effort; many errors in mechanics.

Writing Rubric

4	Story is organized and shows considerable creative effort; mechanics are correct.
3	Story is adequately organized and shows creative effort; few errors.
2	Story is somewhat organized and shows some creative effort; some errors, including shifts in tense.
1	Story is disorganized and shows little effort; many errors in mechanics.

Unit Review

Vocabulary and Main Ideas

1. disagreements over slavery, tariffs and other economic issues, and states' rights *(Obj. U6-7)*
2. It was used as a way to decide which territories would allow slavery and which would not. *(Obj. U6-6)*
3. They felt it was the only way to protect their states' rights and remain a slave-owning region. *(Obj. U6-9)*
4. It said that enslaved people in the Confederacy were free, but it did not end slavery in the border states. *(Obj. U6-12)*
5. The soldiers stole food, killed animals, and wrecked factories and railroad tracks. They also burned houses. *(Obj. U6-15)*
6. They made life harder by forcing African Americans to use schools and hospitals that were not very good, and it became difficult for them to vote. *(Obj. U6-2)*

Critical Thinking

7. **Sample answer:** After the war, slavery was not allowed any more, and all the former slaves were freed. It also became possible for African Americans to receive an education. The southern states were controlled by Congress until 1877, and U.S. soldiers enforced the law. *(Obj. U6-20)*
8. **Sample answer:** The Thirteenth Amendment ended slavery in the United States. The Fourteenth Amendment gave African Americans full citizenship. The Fifteenth Amendment protected the right of African American men to vote. *(Obj. U6-18)*

Apply Skills

9. B *(Obj. U6-19)*
10. C *(Obj. U6-19)*

UNIT 6

Review and Test Prep

Vocabulary and Main Ideas

TEST PREP Write a sentence to answer each question.

1. What issues increased **sectionalism** in the United States during the early 1800s?
2. Why was **popular sovereignty** an important issue as the United States grew?
3. Why did some people in the South argue for **secession**?
4. What did the **Emancipation Proclamation** say?
5. What did General Sherman's army do when it used **total war** against the South?
6. How did **segregation** and **Jim Crow** laws affect life for African Americans?

Critical Thinking

TEST PREP Write a short paragraph to answer each question.

7. **Contrast** In what ways was life in the South after the Civil War different from life before the Civil War?
8. **Synthesize** Explain how the Thirteenth, Fourteenth, and Fifteenth Amendments changed the U.S. Constitution. Use details from the unit to support your answer.

Apply Skills

TEST PREP Study Skill Use the two sources about John Brown's raid on Harpers Ferry below to answer each question.

> ...before me stood four men, three armed with Sharpe's rifles. ...I was then told that I was a prisoner.
>
> — Colonel Washington, Harpers Ferry, 1859

> The next appearance... was at the house of the Colonel Lewis Washington, a large farmer and slave-owner. ...A party [group] rousing Colonel Washington, told him he was their prisoner...
>
> — R.M. DeWitt, New York, 1859

9. What piece of information tells you that Colonel Washington's account is a primary source?
   - **A.** the description of the type of rifles
   - **B.** the words "I was"
   - **C.** the description of the number of men
   - **D.** the date it was written
10. What does the secondary source tell you that the primary source does not?
    - **A.** what time the event occurred
    - **B.** where the event took place
    - **C.** who Colonel Washington was
    - **D.** why Colonel Washington was taken prisoner

Technology

Test Generator

- Use the **Test Generator CD-ROM** to create tests customized to your class.
- Access hundreds of test questions and make lesson, chapter, and unit quizzes and tests.

Web Updates

Curious about new trade book titles that you can use with the program? Visit www.eduplace.com/ss/hmss05/ to update your Unit Bibliography.

Extra Support

Use a Frame Game

Have students use a frame game graphic organizer (Graphic Organizer 12) to review vocabulary words or concepts.

Unit Activity

Write a News Report

- Choose an event in this unit in which one person led others.
- Do research to find out more about the event.
- Write a news report describing the event, the leader, and how well you think this person led others.
- Illustrate your news report and share it with the class.

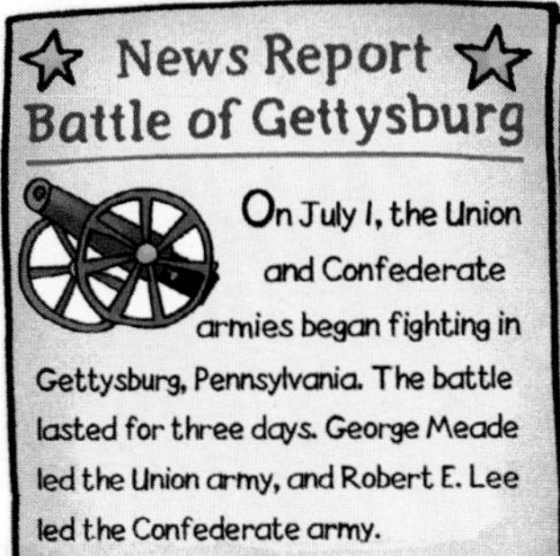

At the Library

Check your school or public library for these books.

Only Passing Through: The Story of Sojourner Truth by Anne Rockwell

Sojourner Truth was one of the most powerful voices in the abolitionist movement.

Lincoln: A Photobiography by Russell Freedman

This biography of Lincoln includes photos and excerpts from Lincoln's own writing.

CURRENT EVENTS WEEKLY WR READER

Connect to Today

Create a poster about the leaders of different countries today.

- Find articles about the leader of another country.
- Write a short biography of this leader. Draw or find a picture of him or her.
- Display your poster in your classroom.

Technology

Get information for the poster from the Weekly Reader at **www.eduplace.com/kids/hmss05/**

Read About It

Look for these Social Studies Independent Books in your classroom.

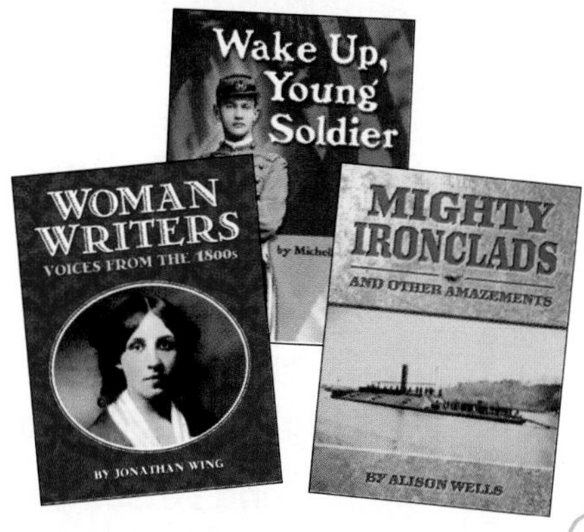

491

Language Arts

Test Taking Tips

Tell students that when they are answering a documents-based question, they should read the document completely. If they read a word they don't understand they should look for main ideas and details to help them.

Standards

National Standards

II d Sources for reconstructing the past
III h Interaction of human beings and their physical environment
V e Tension between an individual's beliefs and government policies and laws
VI h Tensions between wants and needs and fairness, equity, and justice
IX b Conflict, cooperation, and interdependence
IX f Universal human rights
X e How citizens can influence public policy
X f Actors that shape public policy
X h Public policies and citizen behaviors

Unit Activity

HANDS ON Performance Task Rubric

Score	Criteria
4	Questions *who? what? where? why?* and *when?* clearly answered; answers supported by research; shows considerable creative effort; mechanics are correct.
3	Questions adequately answered; most answers supported by research; shows creative effort; few errors in mechanics.
2	Questions are answered; answers confused or poorly supported by research; shows some creative effort; some errors in mechanics.
1	Questions not answered; answers not supported by research; shows no creative effort; many errors in mechanics.

WEEKLY WR READER

Unit Project

- Have volunteers present their world leader posters to the class.

At the Library

- You may wish to wrap up the unit by reading aloud from one of these suggested titles or from one of the Read-Aloud selections included in the Unit Bibliography.

Read About It

- You may wish to provide students with the appropriate Leveled Social Studies Books for this unit. Turn to page 409B for teaching options.
- If students have written summaries or reviews of the Leveled Books or the books in the Unit Bibliography, you may wish to have them give book reports to the class.

Unit 7 Unit Planner

Begin with Core.
Extend for more.

Linking to Today

Chapter 14 Pages 496–521

Immigration

Core Lesson 1 pp. 498–501
Many New Immigrants

Extend Lesson 1 pp. 502–503
Geography Chinatown

Core Lesson 2 pp. 504–507
Twentieth-Century Immigration

Extend Lesson 2 pp. 508–509
Citizenship Changes in Immigration

Skillbuilder
Read Flow Lines on a Map pp. 510–511

Core Lesson 3 pp. 512–515
The American People Today

Extend Lesson 3 pp. 516–519
Literature Poems that Go Places

Chapter Review pp. 520–521

Chapter 15 Pages 522–547

The Promise of America

Core Lesson 1 pp. 524–527
Americans Work for Change

Extend Lesson 1 pp. 528–529
History Women's Rights Movement

Core Lesson 2 pp. 530–535
The Struggle Continues

Extend Lesson 2 pp. 536–537
Biographies Champions for a Cause

Skillbuilder
Resolve Conflicts pp. 538–539

Core Lesson 3 pp. 540–543
Rights and Responsibilities

Extend Lesson 3 pp. 544–545
Citizenship Volunteers

Chapter Review pp. 546–547

Unit Review
pp. 548–549

LEVELED BOOKS

The following **Social Studies Independent Books** are available for extending and supporting students' social studies experience as they read the unit.

Differentiated Instruction

Extra Support

Clean and Clear

By Teresa Domnauer

Summary: The story behind the first Earth Day and the movement to protect the environment.

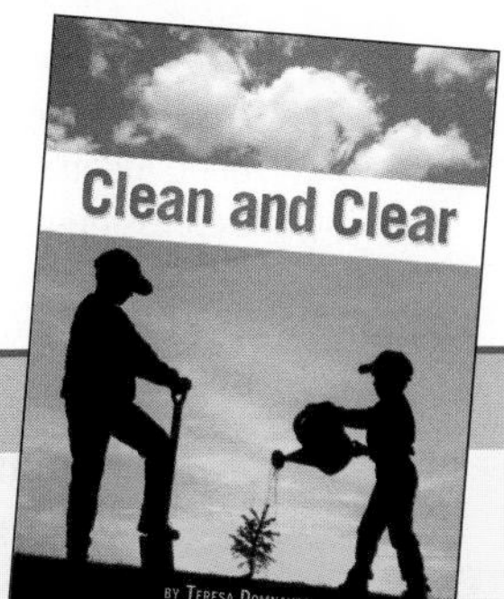

Vocabulary

interdependent

Extending Understanding

Oral Language: Debate Ask students to consider whether they believe the government should do more to protect the environment or whether more should be left to private individuals and businesses and then present their point of view in a short speech.

Independent Writing: Poster Have students create posters advertising the first Earth Day, describing what kinds of celebrations will take place and ways we can help protect the Earth.

Graphic Organizer: Students can use a word web to record words related to Earth Day.

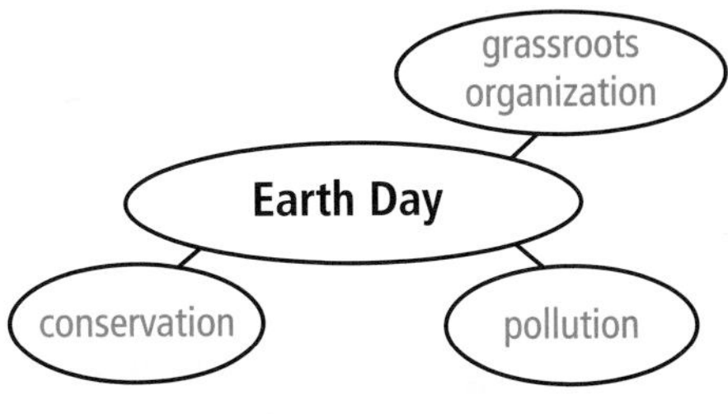

On Level

What Is the Media?

By Julia Jones

Summary: Once newspapers were the ultimate in high-speed mass communication, but new inventions and the quest for faster connections have changed the very nature of the media today.

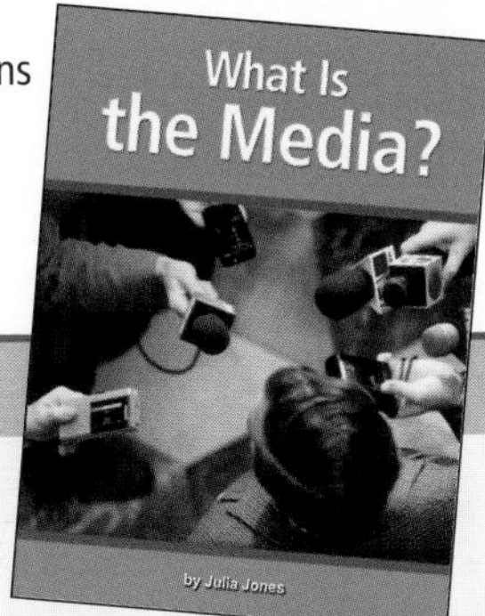

Vocabulary

Internet
high-tech

Extending Understanding

Oral Language: Dialogue Have students work in pairs to discuss the impact of ever-faster modes of communication and predict what innovations the future of mass communication holds.

Independent Writing: News stories Have students pick two media described in the book and write short news bulletins on the same subject for each of the two media. The class can discuss the differences in the bulletins based on which media they were written for.

Graphic Organizer: Students can use a word web to note connections between media.

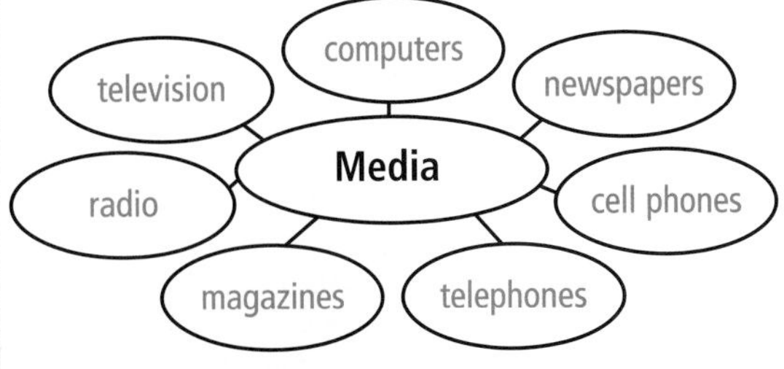

Challenge

Thurgood Marshall and Civil Rights

By Jerome Foster

Summary: Thurgood Marshall rose above the barriers of racism to devote his life to fulfilling the Declaration of Independence's promise that all men are created equal.

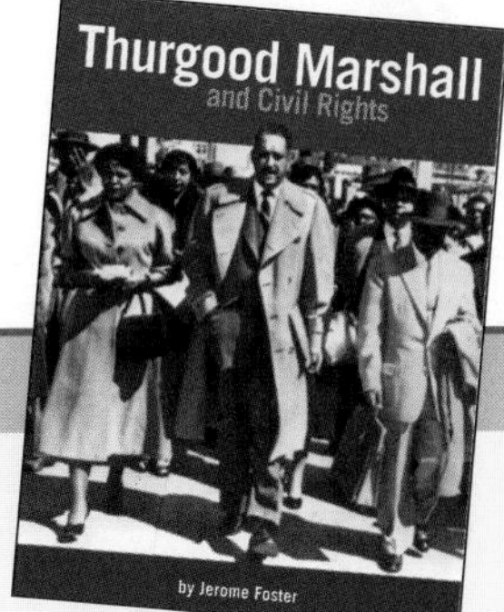

Vocabulary

civil rights
desegregation
nonviolence

Extending Understanding

Oral Language: Trial Have students take the parts of people involved in a case that Thurgood Marshall argued. They can be members of the Supreme Court, other lawyers who worked with Marshall, lawyers who argued against Marshall, etc.

Independent Writing: Journal Have students write a journal entry by Marshall on the eve of his presentation to the Supreme Court for either *Brown v. Board of Education* or *Smith v. Allwright,* describing his worries and his determination to win.

Graphic Organizer: Students can use a sequence chart to keep track of the sequence of events of Marshall's life.

1	Marshall becomes a lawyer.
2	Marshall wins *Brown v. Board of Education.*
3	Marshall become a Supreme Court justice.

Choices for Reading

- **Extra Support/ELL** Read the selection aloud as students follow along in their books. Pause frequently and help students monitor understanding.
- **On Level** Have partners take turns reading aloud. Students can pause at the end of each page to ask each other questions and check understanding.
- **Challenge** Students can read the selection and write down any questions they have. Then they can work in small groups to answer their questions.

Go to **www.eduplace.com/ss/hmss05/** for answers to **Responding** questions found at the back of the books.

Bibliography

Books for Independent Reading

Social Studies Key

 Biography

 Citizenship

 Cultures

 Economics

 Geography

 History

Social Studies Leveled Readers with lesson plans by Irene Fountas support the content of this unit.

Extra Support

Elizabeth Cady Stanton
by Heidi Moor
Heinemann, 2004
Readers learn how Stanton became a leading activist for women's suffrage. See others in series.

Children of the Civil Rights Era
by Catherine A. Welch
Lerner, 2001
Welch recounts the courageous involvement of young people in the civil rights movement. See others in series.

Martin Luther King, Jr.
by Mary Winget
Lerner, 2003
This is a biography of America's most celebrated civil rights leader.

Immigrant Children
by Sylvia Whitman
Lerner, 2000
Readers learn about young immigrants, both on their journeys and in their new country.

The Gold-Threaded Dress
by Carolyn Marsden
Candlewick, 2002
A young girl from Thailand finds what it is to be American in this story about longing to belong.

Coming to America: A Muslim Family's Story
by Bernard Wolf
Lee & Low, 2003
This photo essay chronicles the day-to-day life of a family recently emigrated from Egypt.

On Level

Dolores Huerta
by Rebecca Thatcher Murcia
Mitchell Lane, 2002
Huerta, along with Cesar Chavez, fought for farm workers' rights.

A Real American
by Richard Easton
Clarion, 2002
Eleven-year-old Nathan is surprised at how much he and Arturo, an Italian immigrant, have in common.

Tenement: Immigrant Life on the Lower East Side
by Raymond Bial
Houghton, 2002
Tells what life was like for newly arrived immigrants in New York City.

The Voice That Challenged a Nation
by Russell Freedman
Clarion, 2004
African American opera singer Marian Anderson used her voice to help bring racial equality to our nation.

Remembering Manzanar
by Michael L. Cooper
Clarion, 2002
Cooper examines life in a California relocation camp for Japanese Americans during World War II.

Walking to the Bus-Rider Blues
by Harriette Gillem Robinet
Simon, 2000
This mystery is set against the backdrop of the Alabama bus boycott.

Challenge

Esperanza Rising
by Pam Muñoz Ryan
Scholastic, 2000
Tragedy forces Esperanza to leave the good life in Mexico and join other Depression-era migrant workers in California.

Behind the Mountains
by Edwidge Danticat
Scholastic, 2003
A young Haitian girl narrates this novel about modern day immigrants.

Julian Nava: My Mexican American Journey
by Julian Nava
Arte Publico, 2002
Nava tells how he rose from humble beginnings to become a revered educator and the first Mexican American ambassador to Mexico.

Fight On! Mary Church Terrell's Battle for Integration
by Dennis and Judith Fradin
Clarion, 2003
This is an engrossing biography of an acclaimed civil rights leader.

It's Our World, Too!
by Phillip Hoose
Sunburst, 2002
Fourteen accounts of children who work for human rights are followed by a guide to help readers get involved in social projects of their choice.

Read Aloud and Reference

Read Aloud Books

Remember: A Pictorial Tribute to the Brown v. Board of Education Supreme Court Decision
by Toni Morrison
Houghton, 2004
Morrison pairs archival photographs with storytelling to bring the history of school desegregation to life.

Roll of Thunder, Hear My Cry
by Mildred D. Taylor
Dial, 1976
Taylor's award-winning novel tells of one African American family fighting to stay together in the face of prejudice in the South of the 1930s.

My Chinatown: One Year in Poems
by Kam Mak
Harper, 2001
Everyday life in a Chinatown community is expressed in four seasonal poems.

We Are Americans: Voices of the Immigrant Experience
by Dorothy and Thomas Hoobler
Scholastic, 2003
Immigrants from America's beginnings to the present tell their stories in their own words.

In Defense of Liberty: The Story of America's Bill of Rights
by Russell Freedman
Holiday, 2003
Freedman discusses the Bill of Rights as it applies to contemporary issues.

Reference Books

Failure is Impossible!
by Martha E. Kendall
Lerner, 2001
The history of American women's rights is chronicled from 1607 to 2000.

Black Women Leaders of the Civil Rights Movement
by Zita Allen
Watts, 1996
Readers learn about African American women who fought for civil rights from 1900 to 1964.

Democracy
by David Downing
Heinemann, 2003
Readers gain a deeper understanding of how democracy works in the United States and around the world.

Volunteering to Help in Your Neighborhood
by Claudia Isler
Children's Press, 2000
Readers learn how to volunteer and about the benefits of volunteering.

Free and Inexpensive Materials

International Information Programs of the U.S. State Department

Visit this website (usinfo.state.gov/homepage/htm) to find a valuable collection of links on civil rights and more.

MULTIMEDIA RESOURCES

PROGRAM RESOURCES

Unit Video
Audio Student's Book with Primary Sources and Songs MP3/CD
Lesson Planner and Teacher Resource CD-ROM
Test Generator CD-ROM
eBook
eBook, Teacher's Edition
Transparencies: Big Idea & Skillbuilder, Interactive
Almanac Map & Graph Practice
Primary Sources Plus: Document-Based Questions
Research and Writing Projects
Bringing Social Studies Alive
GeoNet

CD-ROM

American Social Issues. Library Video

Decisions, Decisions® Current Issues series. Tom Snyder

Civil Rights. National Geographic

VIDEOCASSETTES

Black Americans of Achievement series. Schlessinger Media

American Citizenship. Schlessinger

Celebrating Our Differences series. National Geographic

Our North American Neighbors series. Rainbow Educational Media

Martin Luther King's Greatest Speeches. Media Basics

AUDIOCASSETTES

This Land Is Your Land, *Woodie Guthrie.* Weston Woods

What I Had Was Singing, *Jerry Ferris.* Books On Tape

Assessment Options

You are the best evaluator of your students' progress and attainments. To help you in this task, Houghton Mifflin Social Studies provides you with a variety of assessment tools.

Classroom-Based Assessment

Written and Oral Assessment

In the student book:

Lesson Reviews appear at the end of each lesson.
Chapter Reviews appear on pp. 520–521, 546–547.
Unit Reviews appear on pp. 548–549.

In the *Assessment Options* ancillary:

Lesson Tests appear for all lessons.
Chapter Tests appear for all chapters.
Unit Tests appear for all units.

Technology:

Test Generator provides even more assessment options.

Informal, Continuous Assessment

Comprehension

In the student book:

Review questions appear at the end of each section.

In the teacher's edition:

"Talk About It" questions monitor student comprehension.
Tested Objectives appear at the beginning and end of each lesson.

In the student practice book:

Study Guide pages aid student comprehension.

Reading

In the teacher's edition:

Reading Strategy is featured in every chapter.

Thinking

In the student book:

Critical Thinking questions teach higher-order thinking skills.

In the teacher's edition:

"Think Alouds" let you model thinking critically for your students.

In the *Assessment Options* ancillary:

Observation Checklists give you another option for assessment.

HANDS ON Rubric for Unit 7 Performance Assessment

4	Profile accurately explains reasons for immigrating, describes challenges and makes reasonable prediction; includes several quotes that are all punctuated correctly.
3	Profile partially explains reasons for immigrating, describes one challenge and makes prediction; includes several quotations, with one or two errors.
2	Profile does not give reasons for immigrating, states that challenges existed but does not describe; describes future; includes at least one quote, all having errors.
1	Profile does not say the person immigrated; no challenges or prediction present, or prediction is unreasonable; no quotations.

In Assessment Options, p. 162

Standardized Test Practice

In the student book:

Lesson Review/Test Prep appears at the end of each lesson.
Chapter Review/Test Prep appears at the end of each chapter.
Unit Review/Test Prep appears at the end of each unit.

In the *Assessment Options* ancillary:

Lesson Tests for all lessons.
Chapter Tests for all chapters.
Unit Test for all units.

Technology:

Test Generator provides even more assessment options.

Student Self-Assessment

In the student book:

Hands-On Activities appear in each chapter.
Writing Activities appear in each chapter.

In the Unit Resources:

Reading Skill/Strategy pages give students the chance to practice the skills and strategies of each lesson and chapter.
Vocabulary Review/Study Guide pages provide an opportunity for self-challenge or review.

In the *Assessment Options* ancillary:

Self-Assessment Checklists

Unit 7 Test

Standard Test

Unit 7 Test

Test Your Knowledge

Circle the letter of the best answer.

1. What kinds of jobs were immigrants most likely to find in the United States in the early 1900s? Obj. U7–2
   - (A.) jobs in mills, factories, and mines
   - B. jobs in department stores
   - C. jobs in the army and in the navy
   - D. jobs doing laundry and cleaning homes

2. Why were immigration laws passed in the 1920s? Obj. U7–3
   - F. to allow immigrants from more countries into the United States
   - (G.) to limit the total number of immigrants coming from various countries
   - H. to increase the number of immigrants who came from Asia and Africa
   - J. to bring more immigrants from Canada and Latin America

3. What does the Bill of Rights guarantee? Obj. U7–8
   - A. It protects our right to own homes.
   - B. It gives us the right to get a good education.
   - C. It provides us the right to live wherever we want.
   - (D.) It gives us the freedoms of speech, religion, and assembly.

4. What did the NAACP do in the early 1900s? Obj. U7–10
   - (F.) It worked to change laws that did not treat African Americans equally.
   - G. It worked to give women the right to vote.
   - H. It pushed for new laws protecting workers in factories.
   - J. It worked to prevent Congress from passing new immigration laws.

5. How did Martin Luther King Jr. protest the bus policies in Montgomery, Alabama? Obj. U7–11
   - A. He supported violent riots to make people's voices heard.
   - B. He decided to ride in the front of the buses until the policy was changed.
   - (C.) He organized a nonviolent protest to boycott the buses.
   - D. He started a new bus company that served only African Americans.

6. What is one responsibility of young people under age 18 in a democracy? Obj. U7–15
   - F. to vote in elections
   - G. to display a flag in or near their home
   - H. to use their money to support candidates for political office
   - (J.) to go school

Standard Test

Test the Skills: Read Flow Lines on a Map; Resolve Conflicts

Use the map to answer the questions.

7. From which country did people immigrate to San Antonio? Obj. U7–5

   Mexico

8. In which directions did immigrants travel when they left San Antonio?

   They traveled north, east, and west. Obj. U7–5

Read this paragraph about a conflict. Then answer the questions.

> In 1955, an African American woman named Rosa Parks was arrested for breaking a law in Montgomery, Alabama, that stated African Americans must sit at the back of the bus. Some people supported this law. Others, who believed the law should be changed, organized nonviolent protests. They asked African Americans not to ride city buses. In 1956, the Supreme Court agreed that it was illegal to segregate bus riders.

9. What was the conflict? Obj. U7–13

   Sample answer: Whether or not to change a law that segregated bus riders in Montgomery, Alabama

10. How was the conflict resolved? Obj. U7–13

    African Americans protested the law by not riding the buses; the Supreme Court made a decision that the law needed to be changed.

Standard Test

Apply Your Knowledge and Skills

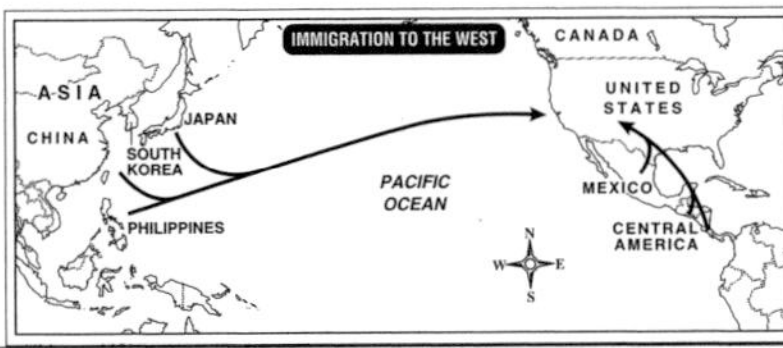

> Like immigrants in the 1800s, immigrants today come to the United States in search of a better life. Some travel east from countries in Asia or north from Central America. Many immigrants want to find better jobs. People who already live in the United States are sometimes afraid that immigrants will take their jobs. Many immigrants work hard to create a new life in the United States.

11. Based on the passage, what is the conflict? Obj. U7–13
    - A. Immigrants cannot find safety and freedom in the United States.
    - B. Other countries will not allow people to immigrate to the United States.
    - (C.) People in the United States may fear that immigrants will take their jobs.
    - D. Traveling to the United States is difficult.

12. Based on the map and the passage, in what direction do immigrants from Japan travel to come to the United States? Obj. U7–5
    - F. north
    - G. south
    - (H.) east
    - J. west

13. Write a brief essay about the immigration laws that were passed in the 1920s. Explain what caused the United States to pass these laws and what the laws said. Give your opinion about these laws and support it with details from the unit. Write your essay on a separate sheet of paper. Obj. U7–3

    Essays may refer to how the large number of immigrants in the 1800s and 1900s led to negative feelings about them; the immigration laws limited immigration and set quotas for each country; should also include student opinion about the laws.

Standard Test

Apply the Reading Skills and Strategies

> Most immigrants in the late 1800s were poor and hoped to find work in the United States. Immigrants from Europe came through the immigration station at Ellis Island near New York City. Most European immigrants were allowed to enter the country. Immigrants from Asia stopped at Angel Island in San Francisco Bay. It was harder for them to enter. One-fourth of Asian immigrants were turned away. Although immigrants had little trouble finding jobs in mills, mines, or factories, these places were often dangerous or unsafe. Immigrants had to work long hours for very little pay. But their hard work helped businesses grow. The United States became one of the richest countries in the world.

Reading Skills

Use the passage above to answer each question.

14. **Compare and Contrast** In what ways were Asian and European immigrants alike? In what ways did they differ? Obj. U7–2

    Alike: were usually poor, came to find work, got jobs in factories; Different: Asians came through Angel Island, and one-fourth were not allowed to enter; Europeans came through Ellis Island, and most were allowed to enter.

15. **Cause and Effect** What is a reason that businesses grew in the United States in the late 1800s? Obj. U7–1

    Sample answer: Immigrants came to the United States and worked hard and for little pay in mills, mines, and factories.

Reading Strategy: Summarize

16. Write a short summary of the passage. Obj. U7–1, U7–2

    Sample answer: In the late 1800s, immigrants came to the United States from Europe and Asia. Many found jobs in factories, mills, and mines. These workplaces were often dangerous and unsafe. But the immigrants worked hard and helped businesses grow. As a result, the United States became rich.

Reaching All Learners

Extra Support

Chart Changes in Immigration

Groups	25 minutes
Objective	To chart changes in immigration
Materials	Chart paper, colored markers

- Select a section of text about one of the periods of immigration, and ask students to read it aloud or silently.
- Have students work together to chart facts that answer these questions:
  - Who immigrated?
  - Why did they immigrate?
  - What problems did they face?
  - How did they solve these problems?
- Assign a different immigration period to each group.
- Have groups share their charts with the class.
- Discuss changes in immigration between 1880 and today.

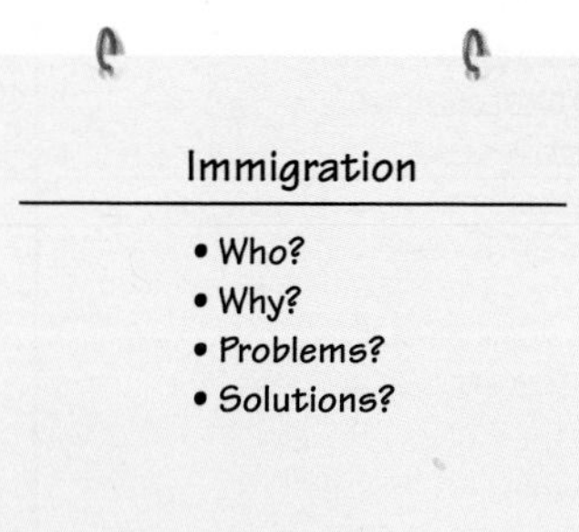

Visual-spatial

Challenge

Sorting Responses to Immigrants

Pairs	25 minutes
Objective	To analyze information and draw conclusions
Materials	Two-column chart, pen or pencil

- Explain that during the three periods of immigration between 1880 and today, Americans responded to immigrants in different ways. Sometimes they were welcoming, and sometimes they were not.
- Have partners reread the text to find ways that Americans responded to immigrants.
- Have students categorize responses in a two-column chart with the headings, "Welcome" and "Unwelcome."

Welcome	Unwelcome
1880–1920	
1920–1965	
1965–2000	

Visual-spatial

ELL

Understanding Protest

Groups	25 minutes
Objective	To understand the struggles for equal rights
Materials	Role-play props, markers, colored pencils, cloze sentences, Venn diagram

Beginning/Intermediate
Ask students to follow in their texts as you read the biography of Martin Luther King, Jr. Have them use role-play to show the meanings of *struggle, overcome, boycott, protest, leader,* and *sit-in.*

Bodily-kinesthetic

Advanced
Discuss the meanings of these related terms: *struggle, equality, overcome, sit-in, nonviolent protest,* and *demonstration.* Then, pair students with more capable language peers to read two of the biographies in Chapter 15. Have students compare the two people and record their observations on a Venn diagram.

Verbal-linguistic

Cross-Curricular Activities

Language Arts

Speechwriting for Change

Singles	25 minutes
Objective	To write a speech that will persuade people to work for change
Materials	writing paper, pens, pencils

- Ask students to write a speech from the point of view an American working for change during the last century—for example, sodbuster, factory worker, woman suffragist, migrant worker, or settlement house resident.
- In their speeches, students should explain what they want to change, why they want to change it, and what their audience can do to help.

Verbal-linguistic

Math

Make a Circle Graph

Singles	20 minutes
Objective	To make a circle graph from raw data
Materials	Unlined paper, ruler, compass, pencils, markers, colored pencils

- Explain that between 1910 and 1920, thousands of African Americans moved from the South to the North. Give students this information:

African Americans Living in the South
1910: 90 percent
1920: 75 percent

- Have students use the data to make two circle graphs showing this change. Remind them to include labels and titles.

Logical-mathematical

Drama

Presenting Rosa Parks

Groups	30 minutes
Objective	To re-enact Rosa Parks' non-violent protest
Materials	Chairs, props, paper and pencils

- Have students work together to write a scene showing Rosa Parks' refusal to give up her seat on the crowded bus.
- Students can divide the parts and act out the scene.
- Use props such as chairs arranged as seats on a bus, a bus driver's hat, police badges, and passenger lunch bags and newspapers.

Verbal-linguistic; bodily-kinesthetic

Begin the Unit

Unit Quick Look

Chapter 14 discusses immigration and immigration policy from 1880 to today, and the diversity of the modern United States.

Chapter 15 describes civil rights movements from the early 20th century through the 1970s, and the rights and responsibilities of citizens.

Introduce the Big Idea

Citizenship Individual citizens do not have to become leaders to help their country. Every individual can participate in government and work for positive change. Ask students what they have seen citizens do to work for positive change. What can students do themselves?

Explain that this unit is about the immigrant heritage of the United States and the movements inspired by the ideal of equality for all.

Primary Sources

Invite a volunteer to read the quote by Senator Barbara Jordan on page 492. Tell students that at the time, Jordan was one of the few African Americans in the U.S. Congress. Ask students how Jordan's words might have affected listeners in 1976. Ask students to think about what Jordan might have meant by the promise of America. List student responses on the board.

Ask students whether they think the promise of America is the same today as in 1976. Why or why not?

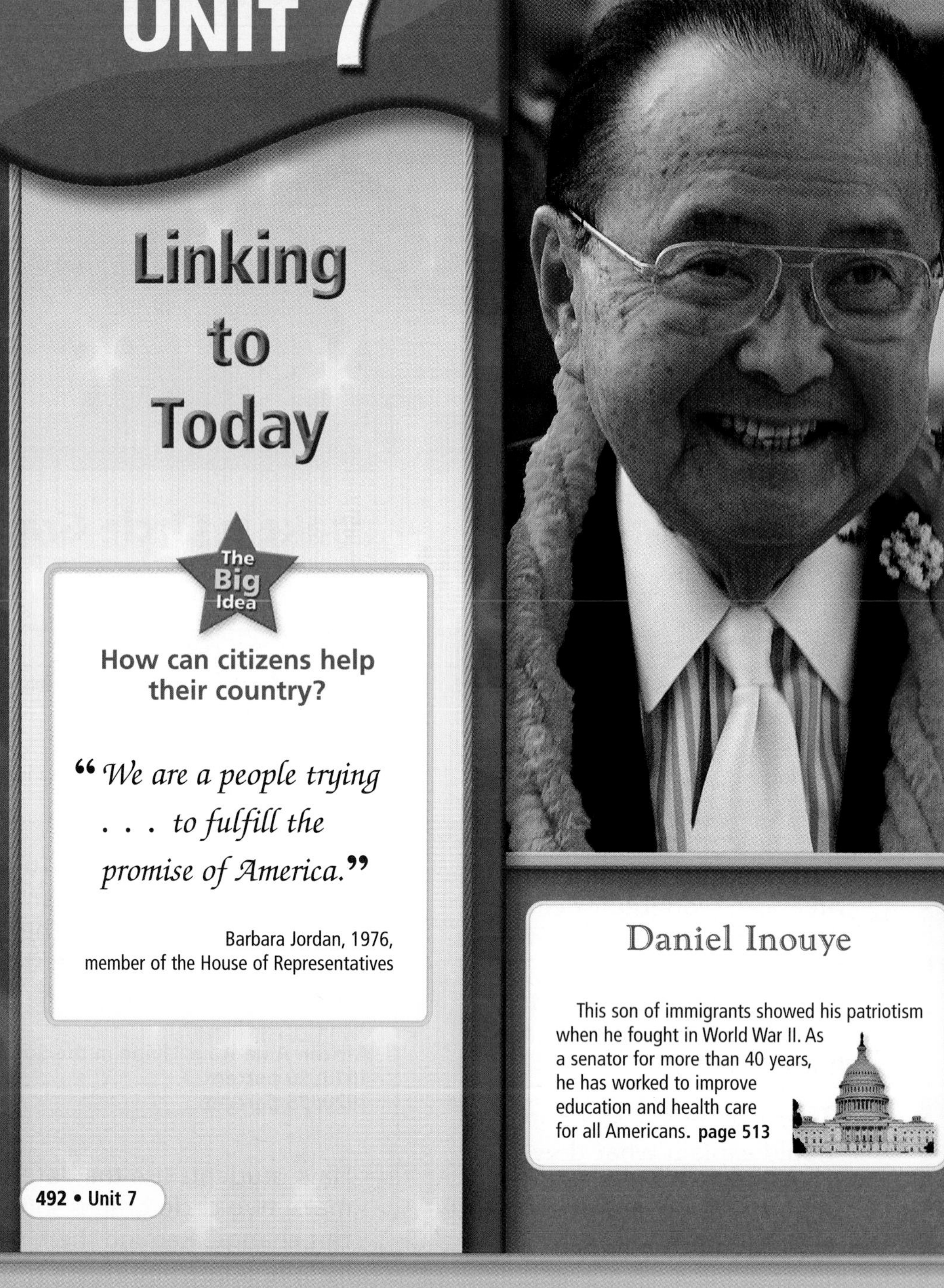

UNIT 7

Linking to Today

The Big Idea

How can citizens help their country?

"We are a people trying . . . to fulfill the promise of America."

Barbara Jordan, 1976, member of the House of Representatives

Daniel Inouye

This son of immigrants showed his patriotism when he fought in World War II. As a senator for more than 40 years, he has worked to improve education and health care for all Americans. **page 513**

Technology

Motivate and Build Background

You may wish to show the Unit Video after students have discussed the Big Idea question on this page.

After viewing, ask students to **summarize** what they already know about the unit content. Ask volunteers to **predict** what else they think they will learn.

You can find more video teaching suggestions on pages R1 and R2 in the Resources Section in the back of the Teacher's Edition.

History Makers

Madeleine Albright

Can a refugee achieve success in the United States? Albright fled Eastern Europe after World War II. She became U.S. Ambassador to the United Nations and then Secretary of State. **page 513**

Cesar Chavez

1927–1993

From years of working on farms, Chavez knew the harsh conditions that migrant farmers faced. To help improve these conditions, he organized marches, sit-ins, and other types of protests. **page 534**

493

Web Link

E-Biographies

To learn more about the History Makers on these pages and in this unit, visit www.eduplace.com/kids/hmss05/

Designed to be accessed by your students, these biographies can be used for

- research projects
- Character Education
- developing students' technology skills

Correcting Misconceptions

Ask students what they know about immigration and diversity. Write their responses as a list on the board.

As students read the unit, return to the list periodically to see if any of their responses have been shown to be misconceptions.

Discuss why students may have thought as they did, and what they have learned.

History Makers

Daniel Inouye Inouye still serves today as a Senator for the state of Hawaii. He was the first American of Japanese descent to serve in Congress. The Capitol building where Congress meets is shown.

Madeleine Albright Albright was the first woman to be appointed Secretary of State. The official seal of the U.S. State Department is shown.

Cesar Chavez Chavez founded an organization for migrant farm workers. Farm workers who joined his movement for better working conditions wore buttons such as the one shown.

Map and Graph Skills

Interpreting Maps

Talk About It

1. **Q Geography** What type of information can you learn about the United States from this map?
   A U.S. state capitals; the range of members of the House of Representatives for each state

2. **Q Geography** Which states have the most members of the House of Representatives?
   A California and Texas

3. **Q Geography** What is the range of representatives for your state?
   A Answers will vary.

Critical Thinking

Evaluate States with more people have more votes in the House of Representatives. How is this balanced by the Senate? Why is this important? All states are represented by two Senators in the Senate. This balance gives the states with more people slightly more power in Congress, but not so much that small states lose their ability to affect lawmaking.

Interpreting Timelines

Ask students if they can identify any of the images shown on the timeline. W.E.B. DuBois; poster supporting women's suffrage; Linda Brown; immigrants to the U.S.; President Bush signing the Americans with Disabilities Act

UNIT 7 Almanac

Members of the U.S. House of Representatives

ARCTIC OCEAN
km 0 300
mi 0 300
ALASKA
Juneau
PACIFIC OCEAN
Olympia
WASHINGTON
Salem
OREGON
MONTANA
Helena
NORTH DAKOTA
Bismarck
MINNESOTA
St. Paul
SOUTH DAKOTA
Pierre
Boise
IDAHO
WYOMING
IOWA
Des Moines
NEBRASKA
Lincoln
Cheyenne
NEVADA
Carson City
Sacramento
Salt Lake City
UTAH
Denver
COLORADO
Topeka
KANSAS
Jefferson City
MISSOURI
CALIFORNIA
PACIFIC OCEAN
OKLAHOMA
Oklahoma City
Little Rock
ARKANSAS
Santa Fe
NEW MEXICO
ARIZONA
Phoenix
TEXAS
Austin
km 0 50 100
mi 0 50 100
Honolulu
HAWAII
PACIFIC OCEAN

Unit Preview

1910 1930 1950

1909
Demand for Equality
W.E.B. Du Bois founds NAACP
Chapter 15, page 526

VOTE
League of Women Voters

1920
19th Amendment Ratified
Women gain right to vote
Chapter 15, page 526

1954
Brown v. *Board of Education*
Segregation ruled unconstitutional
Chapter 15, page 530

494 • Unit 7

Technology

GeoNet

To support student geography skills, you may wish to have them go to www.eduplace.com/kids/hmss05/ to play GeoNet.

Math

Voter Turnout

Tell students that about 105 million women could have voted in the 2000 election, but only about 59 million women actually voted. Ask how many women who could have voted did not do so.
105 million − 59 million = 46 million
46 million women did not vote

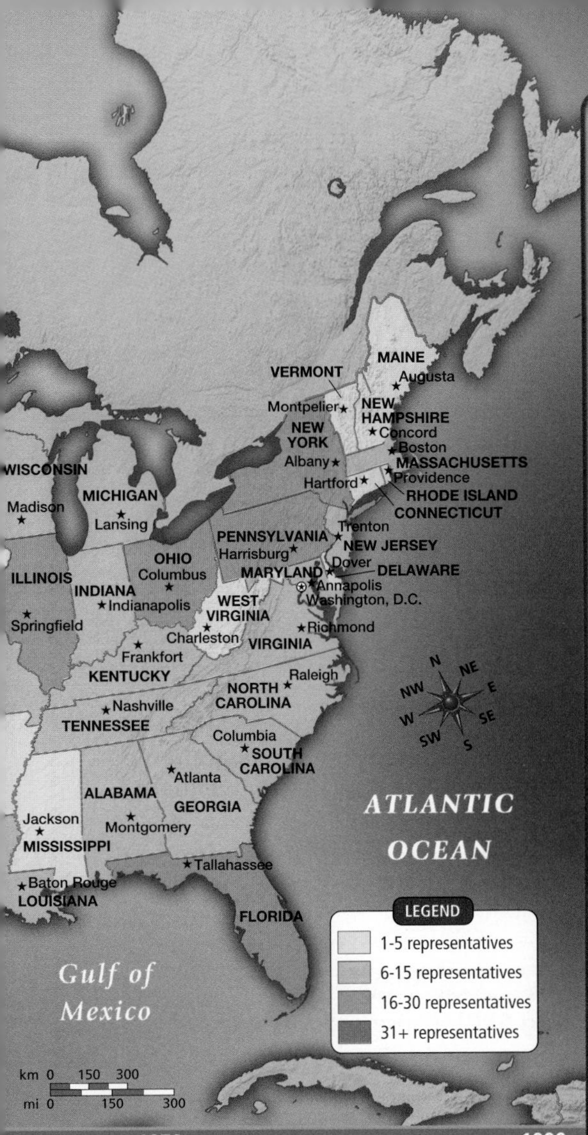

ATLANTIC OCEAN

Gulf of Mexico

LEGEND
1-5 representatives
6-15 representatives
16-30 representatives
31+ representatives

1970 — 1990

1965 Immigration Policy
Immigration and Nationality Act passes
Chapter 14, page 506

1990 Expansion of Rights
Americans with Disabilities Act passes
Chapter 15, page 535

Connect to Today

Election of 1920

1920
Estimated number of women voters in 1920 election: 8 million

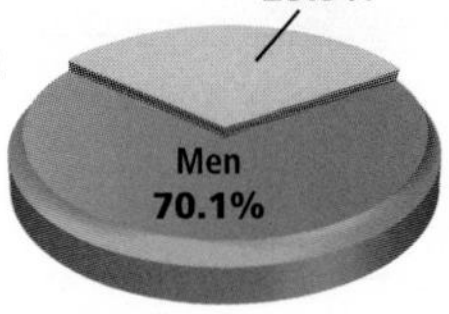

Women 29.9%
Men 70.1%

Election of 2000

Today
Estimated number of women voters in 2000 election: 59 million

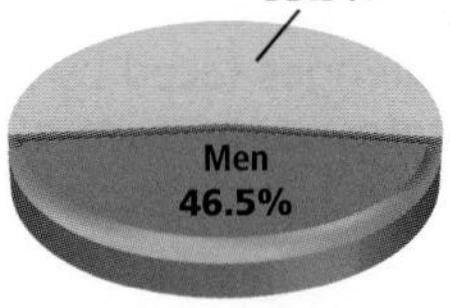

Women 53.5%
Men 46.5%

About how many more women voted in 2000 than in 1920?

CURRENT EVENTS
WEEKLY WR READER

Current events on the web!

Find out about current events that connect with the content of this unit. See Unit activities at: **www.eduplace.com/kids/hmss05/**

495

Current Events

For information about current events related to this unit, visit www.eduplace.com/ss/hmss05/.

Web links to Weekly Reader will help students work on the Current Events Unit Project. The Unit 7 Project will involve designing a volunteer project that the class can do together.

As you go through the unit, ask students to use the web site to find ideas for their project.

Interpreting Graphs

Talk About It

4 **Q Culture** Do you think that the percentage of voters that are women will continue to rise as it has since 1920?

A Probably not. Right after 1920, when women gained the right to vote, the number of women voters increased, but it is unlikely that another event will take place that will make the percentage of women voters increase by that much again.

5 **Q Citizenship** If about 8 million women made up about 30 percent of all voters in 1920, how many men voted in the election?

A about 19 million
$8,000,000 = .30 \times 8,000,000 + m$,
where m is the number of men
$8,000,000 = .30(8,000,000) + .30m$
$18,666,667 \cong m$

Find Out More

Equal Representation Ask students what they would expect percentages of female and male Representatives to be, based on the percentages of female and male voters. Then have students investigate the actual gender breakdown and give possible explanations for their findings.

Fight for Your Right Ask students to investigate other groups whose right to vote was not originally protected by the Constitution, and to determine when and how they gained the right to vote.

Chapter 14 Planning Guide

Immigration

Chapter Opener

Pages 496–497

 30 minutes

Reading/Vocabulary

Chapter Reading Strategy: Monitor and Clarify, p. 495F

Resources

Grade Level Resources
Vocabulary Cards, pp. 59–66

Reaching All Learners
Challenge Activities, p. 74

Primary Sources Plus, p. 26

Big Idea Transparency 7

Interactive Transparency 7

Text & Music Audio CD

Lesson Planner & TR CD ROM

eBook

eTE

Core Lesson 1

Many New Immigrants

Pages 498–501

 40 minutes

 **Tested Objectives**

U7-1 Explain why different groups immigrated to the United States during the late 1800s and early 1900s.

U7-2 Summarize the challenges faced by immigrants in the United States at the turn of the century.

Reading/Vocabulary

Reading Skill: Compare and Contrast

persecution **tenement**
ethnic group

Cross-Curricular

Math, p. 500

Resources

Unit Resources:
Reading Skill/Strategy, p. 137
Vocabulary/Study Guide, p. 138

Assessment Options:
Lesson Test, p. 143

Extend Lesson 1

Geography

Chinatown

20–30 minutes

Pages 502–503

Focus: An old map of San Francisco introduces students to the city's famous Chinatown.

Core Lesson 2

Twentieth-Century Immigration

Pages 504–507

Tested Objectives

U7-3 Describe United States immigration policy during the first half of the twentieth century.

U7-4 Explain the results of changes in immigration policy beginning in the 1960s.

Reading/Vocabulary

Reading Skill: Cause and Effect

quota **refugee**
bracero

Cross-Curricular

Science, p. 506

Resources

Unit Resources:
Reading Skill/Strategy, p. 139
Vocabulary/Study Guide, p. 140

Assessment Options:
Lesson Test, p. 144

Extend Lesson 2

Citizenship

Changes in Immigration

20–30 minutes

Pages 508–509

Focus: How has immigration to the United States changed in the past 100 years?

National Standards

I e Importance of cultural unity and diversity
III a Use mental maps understanding of relative location, direction, size, and shape
III c Resources, data sources, and geographic tools
VI d Encourage unity and deal with diversity to maintain order and security
VI f Factors that contribute to cooperation and cause disputes
IX b Conflict, cooperation, and interdependence
X a Key ideals of the United States's form of government
X b Citizen rights and responsibilities
X h Public policies and citizen behaviors

Skillbuilder

Map and Globe Skill

Read Flow Lines on a Map

Pages 510–511

Tested Objectives

U7-5 Use flow lines on a map to interpret where people or objects come from and where tthey go.

U7-6 Gather information to make a map.

Reading/Vocabulary

flow lines

Resources

Unit Resources:
Skill Practice, p. 141

Skill Transparency 14

Core Lesson 3

The American People Today

Pages 512–515

Tested Objectives

U7-7 Describe some of the ways immigrants have contributed to the culture of the United States.

U7-8 Identify the democratic heritage that Americans share.

Reading/Vocabulary

Reading Skill: Draw Conclusions

heritage

motto

Cross-Curricular

Science, p. 514

Resources

Unit Resources:
Reading Skill/Strategy, p. 142
Vocabulary/Study Guide, p. 143

Assessment Options:
Lesson Test, p. 145

Extend Lesson 3

Literature

Poems That Go Places

40–50 minutes

Pages 516–519

Focus: Each of these three poems tells why some places are very special.

Chapter Review

Pages 520–521

30 minutes

Resources

Assessment Options:
Chapter 14 Test

Test Generator

Chapter 14 Practice Options

Lesson 1 Skill and Strategy

TEST PREP

Reading Skill and Strategy

Reading Skill: Compare and Contrast

This skill helps you understand how historical events or people are similar and different.

Read "Living in a New Country." Then fill in the Venn diagram below. Write about the lives of immigrants in the left circle and about the lives of rural Americans in the right circle. Then write anything these two groups have in common where the two circles overlap.

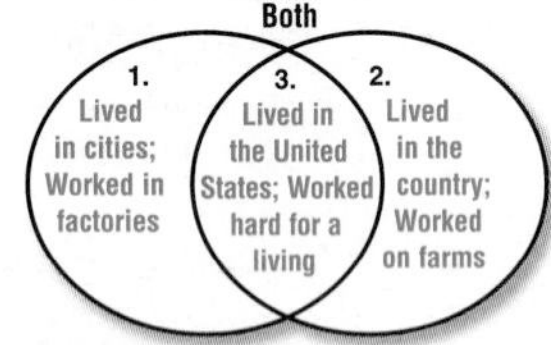

Reading Strategy: Monitor/Clarify

4. Read "Coming to America." Then check the statement that best clarifies the section.
   - ___ The new immigrants came mostly from Africa and Asia.
   - ✓ Most immigrants from Europe entered the United States on the East Coast.
   - ___ Americans welcomed immigrants from Asia more easily than immigrants from Europe.
5. Read "Living in a New Country." Then check the statement that best clarifies the section.
   - ___ Immigrants could easily afford large apartments and houses in U.S. cities.
   - ___ Many Americans disliked immigrants because of their high wages.
   - ✓ In many U.S. cities, ethnic communities provided a sense of home for new immigrants.

Unit Resources

137
Use with *United States History*, pp. 498–501

Lesson 1 Vocabulary/Study Guide

TEST PREP

Vocabulary and Study Guide

Vocabulary

Write the definition of each vocabulary word below.

1. persecution Unfair treatment that causes suffering
2. ethnic group People that share a culture, language, or national background
3. tenement A rundown, poorly maintained apartment building

Choose two words. Use each word in a sentence about the lesson.

4. Sample answer: Some immigrants had experienced persecution in their home countries.
5. Sample answer: New immigrants often liked to live among people of their own ethnic group.

Study Guide

6. Read "Coming to America." Then fill in the blanks below.

Most new immigrants to the United States between 1880 and 1920 came from southern or eastern Europe. Immigrants usually entered the country through immigration stations such as Ellis Island in New York City. Immigrants from China flocked to California to search for gold.

Read "Living in a New Country." Then fill in the classification chart below with positive and negative things about immigrating to the United States.

Positive	Negative
7. Ethnic neighborhoods; Many jobs available; Helped economy grow	8. Tenement buildings; Dangerous jobs with little pay; Some Americans disliked immigrants.

Unit Resources

138
Use with *United States History*, pp. 498–501

also in *Practice Book*, p. 82

Lesson 2 Skill and Strategy

TEST PREP

Reading Skill and Strategy

Reading Skill: Cause and Effect

This skill helps you see how one event can be related to another, either by causing it or resulting from it.

Read "A New Era of Immigration." Then fill in the chart below to show two causes for the increased immigration in the United States after 1965.

Causes	Effect
1. The government passes the Immigration and Nationality Act. 2. The United States allows more refugees into the country.	More people immigrate to the United States from many different nations.

Reading Strategy: Monitor/Clarify

3. Read "Limiting Immigration." Then check the statement that best clarifies the section.
   - ___ Quotas allowed the same number of people from each country to immigrate to the United States.
   - ___ Many Mexicans entered the United States to start their own businesses.
   - ✓ The number of immigrants able to come to the United States decreased from 1921 to 1924.
4. Read "A New Era of Immigration." Then explain where refugees to the United States came from and why.

Sample answer: Refugees from El Salvador and Vietnam escaped wars, and Cuban refugees were looking for freedom.

Unit Resources

139
Use with *United States History*, pp. 504–507

Lesson 2 Vocabulary/Study Guide

TEST PREP

Vocabulary and Study Guide

Vocabulary

Read the clue and write the answer in the blank. Then find the word in the puzzle. Look up, down, forward, and backward.

1. The maximum number of people allowed to enter a country quota
2. People fleeing danger in their home countries refugees
3. Temporary farm workers from Mexico bracero
4. A person who enters a new country to live there permanently immigrant

A	Y	I	Q	U	R	T	O
Z	C	M	B	R	E	F	G
M	N	M	O	E	X	A	H
L	M	I	B	F	R	K	U
E	S	G	T	U	S	Q	J
I	I	R	P	G	U	U	K
B	R	A	C	E	R	O	S
Q	U	N	T	E	A	T	L
E	A	T	A	S	B	A	O

Study Guide

Read "Limiting Immigration." Then fill in the sequence chart below.

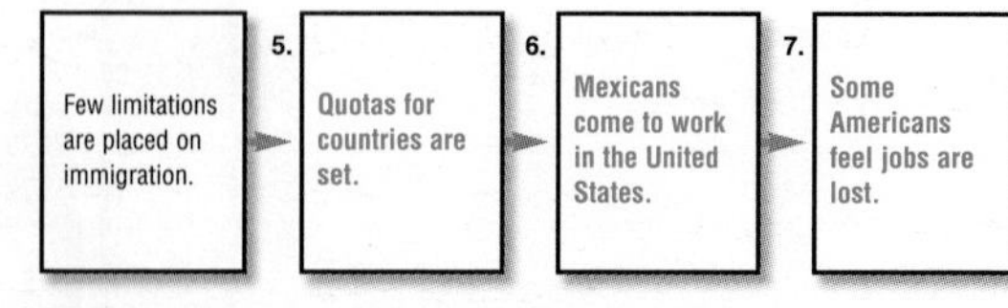

8. Read "A New Era of Immigration." Then write about the Vietnamese refugees.

Sample answer: Refugees left Vietnam because of war. They settled in large cities in Texas and California.

Unit Resources

140
Use with *United States History*, pp. 504–507

also in *Practice Book*, p. 83

Skillbuilder Practice

TEST PREP

Skillbuilder: Read Flow Lines on a Map

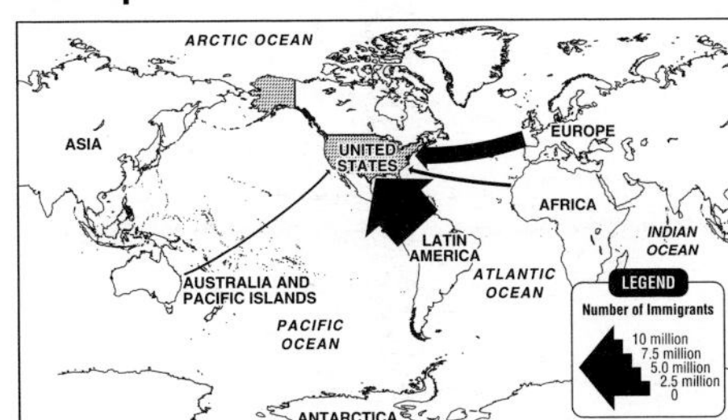

Practice

1. From what region on the map have the fewest immigrants come?
   Australia and Pacific Islands
2. Have more people immigrated to the United States from Europe or from Africa? Europe
3. About how many immigrants have come from Latin America since 1971? About 9.5 million
4. Study the widths of the flow lines and the number of people each one represents. Use the following data to draw a flow line for Asian immigration into the map.
   Asian Immigration, 1971–2000
   7,122,007

Apply

Find or create a world map. Using the data below, turn the map into a flow line map. Be sure to draw a legend for the map.

U.S. Immigration, 1850s

Ireland 160,000 **Great Britain 50,000**
Germany 80,000 **Canada 10,000**

Unit Resources

141
Use with *United States History*, pp. 510–511

also in *Practice Book*, p. 84

Lesson 3 Skill and Strategy

TEST PREP

Reading Skill and Strategy

Reading Skill: Draw Conclusions

Sometimes when you read, you have to figure out things that the writer doesn't tell you. This skill is called drawing conclusions.

Read "Our Shared Values." Then fill in the chart below. Write two sentences that support the conclusion.

Reading Strategy: Monitor/Clarify

3. Read "Many People, One Nation." Then tell how you monitored your understanding of the section.
   Sample answer: I slowly read the words and looked at the picture and the map.
4. Write any questions you had after you finished reading.
   Sample answer: How have different ethnic groups added to the culture of the United States?
5. How did you answer your questions? Answer with a complete sentence.
   Sample answer: Americans of different ethnicities share their customs, food, and languages with other Americans.

Unit Resources

142
Use with *United States History*, pp. 512–515

Lesson 3 Vocabulary/Study Guide

TEST PREP

Vocabulary and Study Guide

Vocabulary

Read the clue and unscramble the letters to write the correct word.

1. Something handed down from past generations.
   T A E H E I R G — Heritage
2. A short statement that explains an ideal.
   O M O T T — Motto
3. Unfair treatment toward a group of people.
   S M I N I A D I C O N T R I — Discrimination

Study Guide

Read "Many People, One Nation." Then choose the correct ending to each statement below.

4. Almost one-third of immigrants to the United States are from
   A. Canada. B. China. (C.) Mexico.
5. Each ethnic group adds new language, food, and
   (A.) customs. B. money. C. transportation.
6. The word *kindergarten* is originally a word in
   A. French. (B.) German. C. Japanese.

Read "Our Shared Values." Then fill in the cause in the chart below.

	Cause	Effect
7.	People fight for justice for all groups.	Rights have been extended to all Americans.

Unit Resources

143
Use with *United States History*, pp. 512–515

also in *Practice Book*, p. 85

Chapter 14

Assessment Options

Chapter 14 Test

Chapter 14 Test

Test Your Knowledge

persecution	tenement	quota	heritage

Write *T* if the statement is true or *F* if it is false.

1. __T__ Many Russian Jews immigrated to the United States to avoid religious persecution. Obj. U7–1
2. __F__ Many immigrants went to live in a dangerous tenement. Obj. U7–2
3. __F__ United States citizens learn about their heritage from future generations. Obj. U7–8
4. __T__ The government passed immigration laws that gave each country a quota. Obj. U7–3

Circle the letter of the best answer.

5. Why did thousands of Chinese people immigrate to the United States in the 1850s? Obj. U7–1
   - A. to escape persecution
   - B. to escape prejudice
   - (C.) to find gold in California
   - D. to buy land in California
6. Why did refugees from Cuba, Vietnam, and El Salvador come to the United States in the 1900s? Obj. U7–4
   - F. to find better jobs in California and Texas
   - G. to contribute their valuable skills
   - H. to meet President Jimmy Carter
   - (J.) to escape danger in their home countries
7. Why are the Constitution and the Bill of Rights part of our democratic heritage? Obj. U7–8
   - (A.) They establish the government, the rights, and the duties that all American share.
   - B. They establish where Americans are allowed to live and work.
   - C. They establish the right of a group to take power away from the people.
   - D. They establish the salaries of workers.
8. Which is part of the shared heritage in the United States? Obj. U7–8
   - F. equal housing for some
   - G. unfair job opportunities
   - (H.) democracy and equal rights
   - J. discrimination

Chapter 14 Test

TEST PREP

Apply Your Knowledge

> Many people have contributed to American English. "Yankee" is a Dutch word, and "alligator" is Spanish. "Phooey" is from German, and "prairie" is French. "Jukebox" is African, and "gung ho" is Chinese. There are hundreds more words that were originally foreign and are now part of the English language. As Abraham Lincoln said, immigrants have been "a source of national wealth and strength."
>
> —from *If Your Name Was Changed at Ellis Island*, by Ellen Levine

Use the paragraph to answer the following questions.

9. Where did the word *jukebox* come from? Obj. U7–7
   - A. Chinese immigrants
   - (B.) African immigrants
   - C. Spanish immigrants
   - D. Dutch immigrants
10. Why have immigrants been "a source of national wealth and strength" in the United States? Obj. U7–7
    - (F.) They bring new customs, talents, and diversity.
    - G. They invented architecture and parades.
    - H. They teach Americans better laws.
    - J. They can cook many foods.

Apply the Reading Skill: Compare and Contrast

Read the passage below. Then answer the question. Obj. U7–4

> Throughout the 1900s, immigrants wanted to come to the United States. In 1921 and 1924, Congress passed laws to control immigration. In 1965, the Immigration and Nationality Act allowed many more people to immigrate to the United States.

11. How were U.S. immigration laws alike? How were they different before and after 1965?
    U.S. immigration laws told how many immigrants could come to the United States. Before 1965 Congress controlled immigration. After 1965 new laws allowed more immigrants to come.

Chapter 14 Test

Test the Skill: Read Flow Lines on a Map

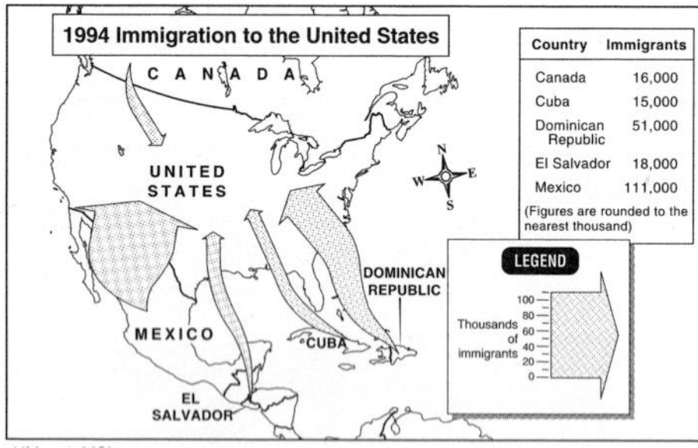

12. What is the purpose of the map?
    To show immigration numbers to the United States from five nearby countries Obj. U7–5
13. Which country had the greatest number of immigrants to the United States in 1994?
    Mexico Obj. U7–5
14. List the countries on the map from greatest to fewest numbers of immigrants in 1994.
    Mexico, Dominican Republic, El Salvador, Canada, Cuba Obj. U7–5

Apply the Skill

15. Think about the information on the immigration map. If you wanted to make a map that showed how many students at your school came from each neighborhood, what information would you need to gather? Obj. U7–5
    Names and locations of the different neighborhoods; number of students from each neighborhood

Chapter 14 Test

Think and Write

16. **Short Response:** Why were people from Mexico allowed to immigrate in the 1940s while people from other countries were not? Obj. U7–3
    Sample answers: Mexican workers were very important to the U.S. economy; there was a shortage of farm workers; Mexicans worked hard and accepted low pay.
17. **Critical Thinking: Draw Conclusions** What do you think life was like for immigrant families living in tenements in the early 1900s? Obj. U7–7
    Sample answers: It was a hard life because they had to work very hard and live in poorly built buildings that were crowded. Some tenements did not have running water.
18. **Extended Response:** Write a letter that a new immigrant in the early 1900s might have written to a family member. Describe what happened at the immigration station, where the person lives, and what he or she does for work. Explain why life in the United States is challenging. Write your letter on a separate sheet of paper. Obj. U7–2
    Letter may refer to leaving southern or eastern Europe, going through the immigration station at Ellis Island, moving to a large city, working in a factory or mill, working hard, low pay, poor living conditions.

Self-Assessment

Would I like to read more about immigration? Why or why not?

You can share the following fiction selection with students before beginning the chapter.

Activate Prior Knowledge

Ask students if they have heard of Ellis Island and the immigrants who passed through there. Then ask if they have heard of Angel Island. Students will learn about both places in this chapter. The Read-Aloud selection presents a picture of life on Angel Island.

Preview the Chapter

Have students skim the section Immigrants from Asia on page 499. Ask them how the Read-Aloud selection reflects the information in this section.

Read-Aloud Vocabulary

Explain that an **ethnic group** is made up of people from the same culture or national background. A **heritage** is a set of values or a way of life passed down from previous generations.

Preview the Reading Strategy

Monitor/Clarify Explain to students that the reading strategy they will use in this chapter is monitor/clarify. When they use this strategy, students pause during their reading and check their understanding. You may wish to use the Read Aloud to model the strategy.

Think Aloud *I've read the first paragraph, and I want to make sure I understand what's going on. Lin is in a dark building with many women and babies. She sleeps in a bunk and stands in line to wash. I don't understand why she is there, though. I'll keep reading to find out.*

Morning on Angel Island

Lin woke to the sound of chattering women and fussing babies. She climbed from her bunk and stood in line to wash her face. It was dark inside the wooden building, but she knew that outside, San Francisco Bay sparkled in the sunlight.

Lin moved forward in line, deep in thought. Would today be the day that the immigration officials would allow her family to enter America? Lin was from China. Her family had endured the long voyage over the Pacific Ocean in the hopes of finding work in America, only to be detained for weeks on Angel Island.

Lin knew that some Americans were prejudiced against her **ethnic group,** and that it was very hard to convince the officials to allow Chinese people to enter. She knew that their lives would be difficult as immigrants. But America had a **heritage** of democracy that captured her imagination. It was not a perfect place, but it was a land of possibility, even for a little girl from China.

The line moved forward, and Lin splashed cold water on her face. *We must be permitted to enter,* she thought. *We must.* She shivered, and wiped her face dry. *Maybe today.*

Begin the Chapter

Quick Look

Core Lesson 1 focuses on immigration to the United States between 1880 and 1920.

Core Lesson 2 explores immigration laws between 1921 and 2000.

Core Lesson 3 describes the background and culture of the American people today.

Vocabulary Preview

Use the vocabulary card to preview the key vocabulary words before starting the lessons and to prepare students to understand the content of the chapter.

Vocabulary Strategy

Vocabulary strategies for this chapter:

- Structural analysis, pp. 498, 504
- Word roots, p. 504
- Related words, p. 512
- Word origins, p. 498

Vocabulary Help

Vocabulary card for tenement The word *tenement* comes from a word that means "house." It has the same word root as the word *tenant*, which means "a person who is renting a house or apartment."

Vocabulary card for quota A quota refers to a maximum or minimum number. A quota can be a limit on something, such as immigration, or a goal to be reached, such as meeting a quota.

Chapter 14 Immigration

Vocabulary Preview

tenement

Immigrants came to the United States with little money to pay for food and a place to live. Most lived in crowded and unsafe buildings called **tenements.** page 500

quota

In the 1920s, the United States put a **quota** on immigrants from different countries. These numbers were set to limit immigration. page 505

Chapter Timeline

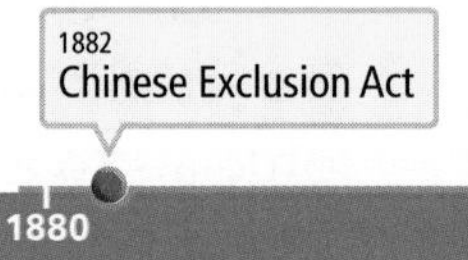

1882 Chinese Exclusion Act

1921 Immigration quotas passed

1880 — 1900 — 1920

Background

Immigrant Heritage

The United States includes people of many different ethnic groups. All these people share a heritage of laws, landmarks, symbols, and ideals. This heritage of ideals, such as the right to pursue happiness and equality before the law, allows these different groups to live together. These ideals are expressed in documents, such as the Constitution and the Bill of Rights, and monuments and objects, such as the Liberty Bell and the Lincoln Memorial.

Vocabulary

Use a graphic organizer to further student understanding of the vocabulary words.

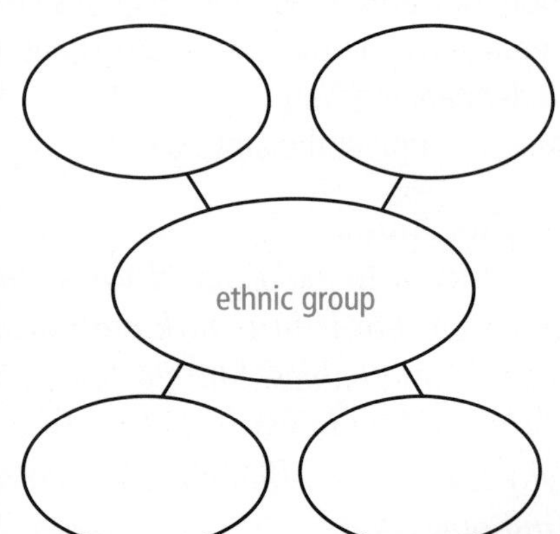

Monitor and Clarify As you read, check your understanding of the text.

Ask yourself if what you are reading makes sense. Reread, if you need to.

heritage

The ideals of democracy and human rights are part of the history of the United States. The Liberty Bell ia a symbol of this **heritage.**
page 514

motto

The short statement on the U.S. dollar means "out of many, one." This **motto** expresses one of the ideals of the United States.
page 515

1965 Immigration and Nationality Act

1940 | 1960 | 1980

Leveled Practice

Extra Support

Have students create a picture dictionary for chapter vocabulary words not pictured here. They can draw the pictures or use pictures from magazines and newspapers.
Visual-spatial

Challenge

Have students write an extended definition of heritage. Ask them to describe their *heritage*. What characteristics and ideas have they inherited, either from their family's or their nation's history?

ELL

All Proficiency Levels

- Have students play charades in small groups. Take turns acting out each of the vocabulary words, and then have the other students guess the described word.

Bodily-kinesthetic

Correct Misconceptions

If you wish, use a KWL chart to find out what students know about immigration. Write student responses on the board or on an overhead transparency.

As students read the chapter, return to the KWL chart and have students evaluate the information—did they have any misconceptions about the material?

Reading Strategy: Monitor and Clarify

To monitor and clarify, the reader reviews the material after reading and draws out important information. The reader also asks questions about the material, to determine what he or she understands or needs clarification on.

Explain to students that to monitor and clarify successfully, they should follow these steps:

- Read the passage.
- Think about what the passage says.
- Ask yourself: What is important about this passage?
- Review the passage.
- Ask yourself: Does this passage make sense? Am I learning what I think I should be learning?
- If you don't understand something, reread, read ahead, or use the headings, graphic organizers, illustrations, and captions.

Students can practice this reading strategy throughout this chapter, including on their Skill and Strategy pages in their Practice Book.

Tested Objectives

U7-1 History Explain why different groups immigrated to the United States during the late 1800s and early 1900s.

U7-2 History Summarize the challenges faced by immigrants in the United States at the turn of the century.

Quick Look

This lesson focuses on immigration to the United States in the late 1800s and early 1900s.

Teaching Option: Extend Lesson 1 is a map of San Francisco in 1878 that supports visual learning about Chinatown.

1 Get Set to Read

Preview Have students look at the photograph on page 499. Discuss what it shows.

Reading Skill: Compare and Contrast Students should consider where European and Asian immigrants arrived and what they experienced.

Build on What You Know Discuss with students the experiences they or people they know have had moving to the United States from another country.

Vocabulary

persecution *noun,* oppression or harassment of a person or group

ethnic group *noun,* a group of people who share a language, culture, or history

tenement *noun,* a rundown apartment building

Core Lesson 1

Many New Immigrants

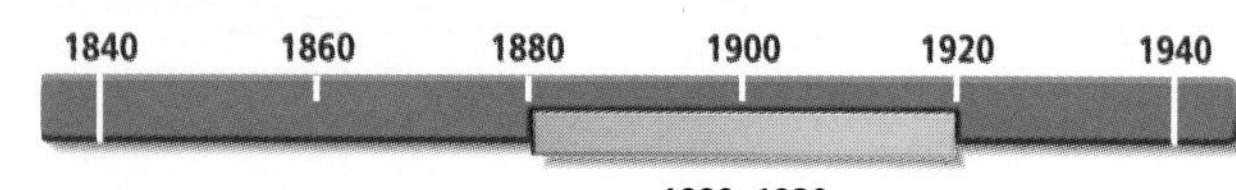

VOCABULARY

persecution
ethnic group
tenement

Vocabulary Strategy

ethnic group

Ethnic comes from a word that means nation. An **ethnic group** is a group of people from the same nation or culture.

READING SKILL

Compare and Contrast

As you read, show how European immigration and Asian immigration were alike and different.

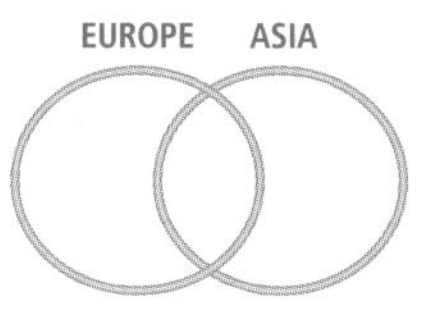

Build on What You Know You've read about thousands of immigrants coming to North America in the colonial period and after American independence. Now think of millions of immigrants from all over the world.

Coming to America

Main Idea Millions of immigrants moved to the United States in the late 1800s and early 1900s.

Immigration has been part of the story of the United States for a long time. Exploration and colonization brought people from many countries to the United States. Most of these people came by choice. They wanted to find freedom or work. Some, such as enslaved Africans, were forced to come.

Between 1880 and 1920, about 25 million immigrants moved to the United States. These new immigrants came mainly from southern or eastern European countries, such as Italy, Russia, Hungary, Greece, and Poland. Before 1 1880, most European immigrants had come from Ireland, Germany, England, Sweden, and other countries of northern or western Europe.

Immigrant Document
Every immigrant had to have an identification card like this one to enter the United States.

Skill and Strategy

Reading Skill and Strategy

Reading Skill: Compare and Contrast

This skill helps you understand how historical events or people are similar and different.

Read "Living in a New Country." Then fill in the Venn diagram below. Write about the lives of immigrants in the left circle and about the lives of rural Americans in the right circle. Then write anything these two groups have in common where the two circles overlap.

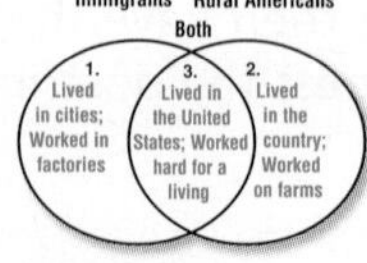

Reading Strategy: Monitor/Clarify

4. Read "Coming to America." Then check the statement that best clarifies the section.
   - ___ The new immigrants came mostly from Africa and Asia.
   - ✓ Most immigrants from Europe entered the United States on the East Coast.
   - ___ Americans welcomed immigrants from Asia more easily than immigrants from Europe.
5. Read "Living in a New Country." Then check the statement that best clarifies the section.
   - ___ Immigrants could easily afford large apartments and houses in U.S. cities.
   - ___ Many Americans disliked immigrants because of their high wages.
   - ✓ In many U.S. cities, ethnic communities provided a sense of home for new immigrants.

Unit Resources

137
Use with *United States History*, pp. 498–501

Unit Resources, p. 137

Background

Angel Island

- Angel Island in San Francisco Bay was an immigration station from 1910 to 1940.
- Today, the island is a state park and is home to an immigration museum.

New Arrivals Most ships arriving at Angel Island were from Asia. Some immigrants, however, came from Europe.

Immigrants from Europe

Immigrants left Europe for the United States because they believed they could build better lives for themselves and their families. As one immigrant from eastern Europe said,

"In America everything was possible."

Immigrants were usually poor and hoped to find work in the United States. Some came to escape persecution. **Persecution** is unfair treatment that causes suffering. In the 1880s, thousands of Jews from Russia moved to the United
2 States to escape religious persecution.

Most immigrants from Europe went through immigration stations on the East Coast. The most famous immigration station was Ellis Island in New York City's harbor. Workers at the stations asked newcomers about where they planned to live and work. Doctors made sure immigrants were healthy. Almost all European immigrants were allowed to stay.

Immigrants from Asia

The first large group of Asian immigrants came to the United States in the early 1850s. At that time, thousands of immigrants traveled from China to
California to find gold during the Gold 3
Rush. Chinese continued to arrive in large numbers until 1882. Then Congress passed a law called the Chinese Exclusion Act. This law stopped Chinese immigration for 10 years. It did not end immigration from other parts of Asia. Japanese immigrants arrived in California and filled many of the jobs that Chinese immigrants had been doing.

The largest California immigration
station was Angel Island in San Francisco 4
Bay. Prejudice against Asians made it harder for them to enter America than for Europeans. Some were there for months. Many were never let into the country.

REVIEW What was the effect of the Chinese Exclusion Act on Asian immigration? The law stopped Chinese immigration for 10 years. Immigrants from Japan, filled many of the vacant jobs.

2 Teach

Coming to America

Talk About It

1 **Q Geography** From what European countries did many immigrants come between 1880 and 1920?

A southern and eastern European countries such as Italy, Russia, Hungary, Greece, and Poland

2 **Q History** Why did many Jews from Russia come to the United States?

A to escape religious persecution

3 **Q Economics** Why did many Chinese immigrants come to the United States in the 1850s?

A to take part in the Gold Rush in California

4 **Q Citizenship** What was the largest immigration station in California?

A Angel Island

Vocabulary Strategy

persecution Point out the related word *persecute*. Explain the difference between *persecuting* (treating someone unfairly) and *prosecuting* (charging someone with a crime in a court of law).

Reading Strategy: Monitor/Clarify

Explain to students that monitoring their reading helps them make sure that they understand the information before they move on to new material.

Think Aloud *The first page of the lesson talks about millions of immigrants coming to the United States. I wonder if these immigrants kept the customs and languages of their home countries, or if they mostly gave up their home cultures when they arrived. I'll look for that information as I read.*

Leveled Practice

Extra Support

Ask students to **write a letter** that an immigrant in the 1890s might have written to his or her family. Remind them to include details about the writer's experiences in America. Verbal-lingistic

Challenge

Ask partners to research one group of immigrants that came to the United States. Have them **create a diagram** showing why they left their homes and showing the steps they took to enter the United States. Visual-spatial

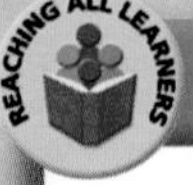

ELL

Intermediate

- Discuss with students what immigrants might have seen arriving at Ellis Island or Angel Island.
- Begin a graphic organizer on the board. Include categories such as "Other immigrants," "Buildings," and "Land and water." You may wish to include sentence stems, for example, "I can see . . ." and "I wonder if . . .".
- Have students **use these phrases** to create sentences.

Verbal-linguistic

Living in a New Country

Talk About It

5 Q Geography Why did many immigrants live in ethnic neighborhoods?

A They settled near friends, family, and others who shared their language and culture.

6 Q Economics What challenges did many immigrants find at work?

A dangerous working environments, long hours, low pay

7 Q History Why did some Americans want to limit or stop immigration?

A They feared losing their jobs to immigrants and distrusted immigrants' different customs, languages, and religions.

Vocabulary Strategy

ethnic group Point out the related word *ethnicity.* Remind students that the United States is home to a wide range of ethnic groups, and to people of many ethnicities.

tenement Contrast *tenement,* a badly maintained apartment building, and *tenant,* someone who lives in an apartment.

Critical Thinking

Decision Making If immigrants had not settled in ethnic neighborhoods, how might their experiences in America have been different?

Think Aloud *If immigrants had not settled in these neighborhoods, they might have adapted more quickly to U.S. culture. But I think they would have lost their own customs and traditions and felt lonely.*

Settling in the United States New York City was the most popular place for immigrants to settle. SKILL **Reading Maps** Which cities in the West had large numbers of immigrants? San Francisco and Los Angeles

Living in a New Country

Main Idea Immigrants usually lived in large cities and worked in factories.

5 After entering the United States, many immigrants moved to large cities such as New York and San Francisco. Immigrant communities in big cities grew quickly as people settled near friends or family. In some cities, whole neighborhoods were made up of a single religious or ethnic group. An **ethnic group** is a group of people who share a culture or language. In an ethnic neighborhood, people spoke their own language, ate the foods of their homeland, and kept many homeland customs and traditions.

Tenements were the first homes for many immigrants living in large cities. A **tenement** was a rundown, poorly maintained apartment building.

Tenements were crowded, dirty, and unsafe. Some tenements had no running water or windows. Often, several families squeezed into one small apartment.

6 Immigrants had little trouble finding jobs, but their lives were not easy. Many worked in dangerous steel mills or coal mines. Others worked in unsafe factories where they sewed clothing or made thread. In the West, Asian immigrants usually worked in small businesses, such as restaurants, or on farms. Nearly all immigrants worked long hours for very low pay. They often made so little money they could barely buy food and clothing for their families.

Immigrants supplied much of the labor that made businesses grow in the early 1900s. With the help of immigrants' hard work, the United States became one of the richest and fastest-growing countries in the world.

500 • Chapter 14

Math

Calculate Fractions

- Remind students that about 25 million immigrants moved to the United States between 1880 and 1920.
- Ask them to figure out what fraction that is of the current U.S. population of 292 million.

Logical-mathematical

Language Arts

Write a Journal Entry

Have groups write a short play about an immigrant waiting at Angel Island or Ellis Island to be admitted to the United States. Remind them to use historical details. Have groups read their plays for the class.

Verbal-linguistic

Tenements Many immigrants lived in crowded tenement buildings like the ones shown here.

Challenges for Immigrants

7 In spite of immigrants' contributions, a growing number of Americans feared and disliked these new arrivals. Some people worried about losing their jobs to immigrants because they worked for so little pay. Others distrusted immigrants because they had different customs, languages, and religions.

As more and more immigrants came to the United States, negative feelings about them grew stronger. By the 1920s, many people wanted to limit or stop new immigration.

REVIEW What kinds of jobs did new immigrants take? Immigrants worked in mills, mines, factories, small businesses, and farms.

Lesson Summary

Over 25 million immigrants moved to the United States from Europe and Asia. Many of them lived in large cities and worked in factories. The large number of immigrants made some people want to limit immigration.

Why It Matters ...

The hard work of immigrants helped to make businesses and the economy strong in the early 1900s.

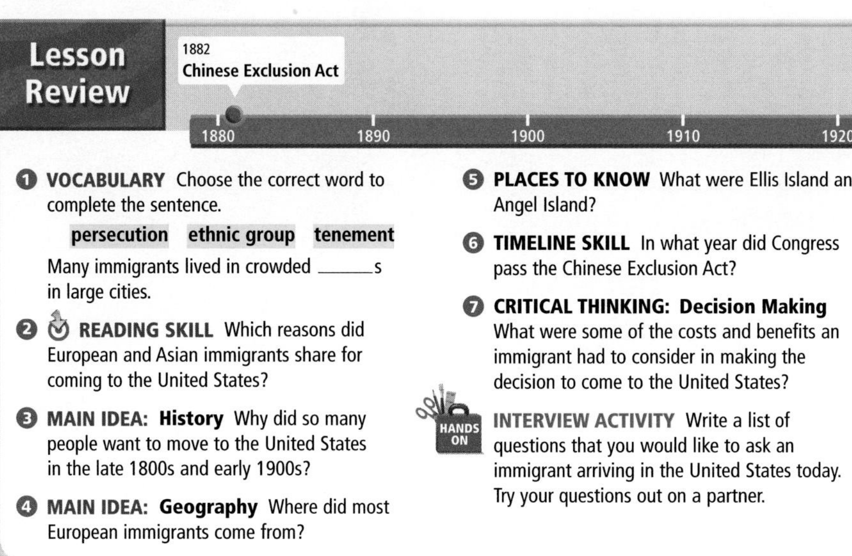

Lesson Review

1. **VOCABULARY** Choose the correct word to complete the sentence.
   persecution **ethnic group** **tenement**
   Many immigrants lived in crowded ______s in large cities.
2. **READING SKILL** Which reasons did European and Asian immigrants share for coming to the United States?
3. **MAIN IDEA: History** Why did so many people want to move to the United States in the late 1800s and early 1900s?
4. **MAIN IDEA: Geography** Where did most European immigrants come from?
5. **PLACES TO KNOW** What were Ellis Island and Angel Island?
6. **TIMELINE SKILL** In what year did Congress pass the Chinese Exclusion Act?
7. **CRITICAL THINKING: Decision Making** What were some of the costs and benefits an immigrant had to consider in making the decision to come to the United States?

HANDS ON **INTERVIEW ACTIVITY** Write a list of questions that you would like to ask an immigrant arriving in the United States today. Try your questions out on a partner.

501

3 Review/Assess

Review Tested Objectives

U7-1 Various groups immigrated to escape persecution and seek prosperity.

U7-2 Challenges included distrust by other Americans, poor pay and dangerous working conditions, and discrimination.

Lesson Review Answers

1. tenements
2. Sample answer: Both groups were searching for work and the chance to make money.
3. They saw America as a land of hope and opportunity where they could create better lives for themselves.
4. southern and eastern Europe
5. They were immigration stations that new immigrants had to pass through before being allowed into the United States; Ellis Island was in New York City harbor, and Angel Island was in San Francisco Bay.
6. 1882
7. Costs: leaving home and family; harsh living conditions in America. Benefits: potential to earn more money; escape from persecution

HANDS ON Performance Task Rubric

4	Questions are on-topic and clearly worded; partners respond thoughtfully to one another's questions.
3	Questions are mostly on-topic and clear; partners respond to one another's questions.
2	Some questions are on-topic and clear; partners do not always respond to one another's questions.
1	Most questions are off-topic and worded in a confusing way; partners do not exchange or comment on questions.

Study Guide/Homework

Vocabulary and Study Guide

Vocabulary

Write the definition of each vocabulary word below.

1. persecution Unfair treatment that causes suffering
2. ethnic group People that share a culture, language, or national background
3. tenement A rundown, poorly maintained apartment building

Choose two words. Use each word in a sentence about the lesson.

4. Sample answer: Some immigrants had experienced persecution in their home countries.
5. Sample answer: New immigrants often liked to live among people of their own ethnic group.

Study Guide

6. Read "Coming to America." Then fill in the blanks below.

Most new immigrants to the United States between 1880 and 1920 came from southern or eastern Europe. Immigrants usually entered the country through immigration stations such as Ellis Island in New York City. Immigrants from China flocked to California to search for gold.

Read "Living in a New Country." Then fill in the classification chart below with positive and negative things about immigrating to the United States.

Positive	Negative
7. Ethnic neighborhoods; Many jobs available; Helped economy grow	8. Tenement buildings; Dangerous jobs with little pay; Some Americans disliked immigrants.

Unit Resources 138 Use with United States History, pp. 498–501

Unit Resources, p. 138

Reteach Minilesson

Use a two-column chart to reteach immigration from Europe and Asia.

Europe	Asia
Escaping poverty Escaping persecution Usually allowed into the country	Joining in gold rush Chinese Exclusion Act Harder for Asians to enter America

Graphic Organizer 1

Quick Look

Connect to the Core Lesson Students have learned that thousands of immigrants traveled from China to California during the mid -1880s. In Extend Lesson 1, students will learn more about San Francisco's Chinatown and the lives of Chinese immigrants and their descendants there.

1 Teach the Extend Lesson

Connect to the Big Idea

Human Systems When large numbers of Chinese immigrated to the United States, they created communities as much like the ones they had left behind as possible. Living close together helps a group maintain common customs and aids its members economically.

Geography

CHINATOWN

Chinese immigrants lived and worked together in San Francisco, creating the first Chinatown in the United States. The view of San Francisco on these pages shows the city in 1878. At that time, Chinatown was a community covering seven narrow and crowded blocks.

By 1890, almost one-quarter of all Chinese immigrants in the United States lived in San Francisco's Chinatown. The neighborhood was the center of Chinese culture and politics. People spoke the language they learned in China. Storefront signs were in Chinese writing. The sight and smells of Chinese foods filled the markets.

Today, San Francisco's Chinatown is one of the largest in the country. Find Chinatown on a modern map of San Francisco. How big is it today?

Chinatown

Reaching All Learners

Extra Support

Compare and Contrast Photos

- Have students compare and contrast the photos on page 503 of Grant Avenue in San Francisco's Chinatown.
- What are some of the similarities and differences between the photo from 1910 and the present-day photo of the same place?

Visual-spatial

On Level

Share Recordings

- Have students use library or Internet resources to find recordings of Chinese music of a kind that might have been performed by immigrants to the United States.
- Ask students to play the music they have found in class.
- Have students display images of Chinese musical instruments.

Musical-auditory; visual-spatial

Challenge

Write a Letter

- Have students write a letter from the point of view of a Chinese immigrant to a relative living in China.
- Ask them to describe what it is like to live in the United States. Suggest that they recommend coming or not coming to the United States and explain why.

Verbal-linguistic

1910

TODAY

The photo on the left shows Grant Avenue in San Francisco's Chinatown in 1910. The photo on the right shows the same street today.

GEOGRAPHY

Activities

1. **EXPLORE IT** What details do you see on the map of 1878? What do they tell you about what life was like in San Francisco then?
2. **CHART IT** Use an atlas or almanac to find other cities that have large Chinatowns. Make a chart showing the location and population of two other Chinatown communities.

503

2 Leveled Activities

❶ **Explore It** *For Extra Support*

Sample answers: People lived very crowded together; the city is surrounded by water, so shipping was an important part of life.

❷ **Chart It** *For Challenge*

HANDS ON

Performance Task Rubric

4	Chart shows location and population of two Chinatown communities; columns have apt headings; mechanics correct.
3	Chart shows location and population of two Chinatown communities; most columns have apt headings; most mechanics correct.
2	Chart shows location and population of less than two Chinatown communities; some columns have apt headings; some mechanics correct.
1	Chart is incomplete; shows location and population of less than two Chinatown communities; headings do not make sense; many mechanical errors make chart hard to read.

ELL

Intermediate/Advanced

- Ask students to discuss what English words most Chinese immigrants would probably learn first when arriving in the United States.
- Have partners devise a short **role-play**, showing what English words Chinese immigrants would need to learn first to do a specific job.
- Have different pairs perform their role-plays for the class.

Verbal-linguistic; bodily-kinesthetic

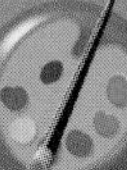

Art

Make a Diorama

Have students make a diorama of a street scene from Chinatown between the 1880s and 1910, showing adults and children in traditional clothing (including work clothing worn in the U.S.).

Bodily-kinesthetic

Graphic Organizer

Chinatown, San Francisco

- This was the first Chinatown in the United States.
- In 1890, one-quarter of all Chinese immigrants in the United States lived there.
- It is still the largest Chinatown in the country.

Graphic Organizer 8

Tested Objectives

U7-3 History Describe United States immigration policy during the first half of the twentieth century.

U7-4 History Explain the results of changes in immigration policy beginning in the 1960s.

Quick Look

This lesson focuses on twentieth-century U.S. immigration policy, which changed in major ways in the 1920s and 1960s.

Teaching Option: Extend Lesson 2 gives students a closer look at how immigration has changed from the late 1880s to the present.

1 Get Set to Read

Preview Have students look at the graph on page 505. Ask what it shows about immigration to the U.S.

Reading Skill: Cause and Effect Effects of the earlier laws included quotas and limits; later laws relaxed these.

Build on What You Know Ask students if they have ever been in a crowded room. How did they feel if more people tried to get in? Explain that some Americans wanted to limit how many people could come into the country.

Vocabulary

quota *noun,* the maximum number of people let into a country

bracero *noun,* a farm worker from Mexico temporarily working in the United States

refugee *noun,* someone who escapes dangerous conditions by leaving his or her home country

Core Lesson 2

Immigration in the 1900s

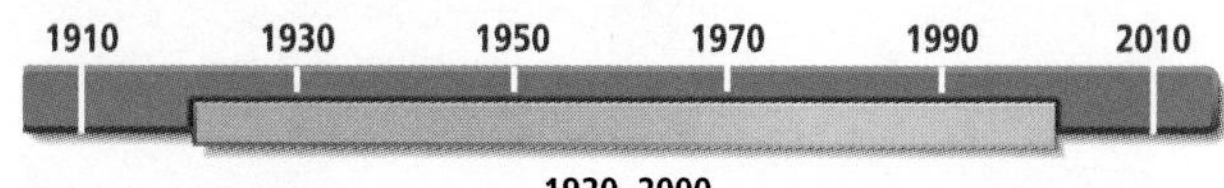

VOCABULARY

quota
bracero
refugee

Vocabulary Strategy

refugee

Find the word **refuge** in **refugee**. A refugee is someone who looks for refuge, or place of safety.

READING SKILL

Cause and Effect Note the effects that new laws had on immigration to the United States.

CAUSE	EFFECT

Build on What You Know You know that the United States has welcomed millions of immigrants from all over the world. In the 1920s, however, the country closed its doors to many immigrants.

Limiting Immigration

Main Idea In the 1920s, the United States government passed laws that limited immigration for over 40 years.

In 1921 and 1924, Congress passed laws to control immigration. These laws had two goals. The first was to limit which countries immigrants came from. The second was to limit the total number of immigrants. The government decided to use quotas to reach these goals. A **quota** is the maximum number of people allowed to enter a country. 1

New York City Immigrant neighborhoods, such as New York City's Lower East Side, grew quickly in the early 1900s.

Skill and Strategy

Reading Skill and Strategy

Reading Skill: Cause and Effect

This skill helps you see how one event can be related to another, either by causing it or resulting from it.

Read "A New Era of Immigration." Then fill in the chart below to show two causes for the increased immigration in the United States after 1965.

Causes	Effect
1. The government passes the Immigration and Nationality Act. 2. The United States allows more refugees into the country.	More people immigrate to the United States from many different nations.

Reading Strategy: Monitor/Clarify

3. Read "Limiting Immigration." Then check the statement that best clarifies the section.

___ Quotas allowed the same number of people from each country to immigrate to the United States.

___ Many Mexicans entered the United States to start their own businesses.

✔ The number of immigrants able to come to the United States decreased from 1921 to 1924.

4. Read "A New Era of Immigration." Then explain where refugees to the United States came from and why.

Sample answer: Refugees from El Salvador and Vietnam escaped wars, and Cuban refugees were looking for freedom.

Unit Resources

139

Use with *United States History*, pp. 504–507

Unit Resources, p. 139

Background

The Mexican Revolution

- One important reason that many Mexicans came to the United States between 1910 and 1920 was the Mexican Revolution, which was a time of great violence and danger for Mexicans.
- Among those who crossed the border to find work in the U.S. were soldiers, supporters of revolutionary leaders, and ordinary people who had been driven from their homes by the fighting.

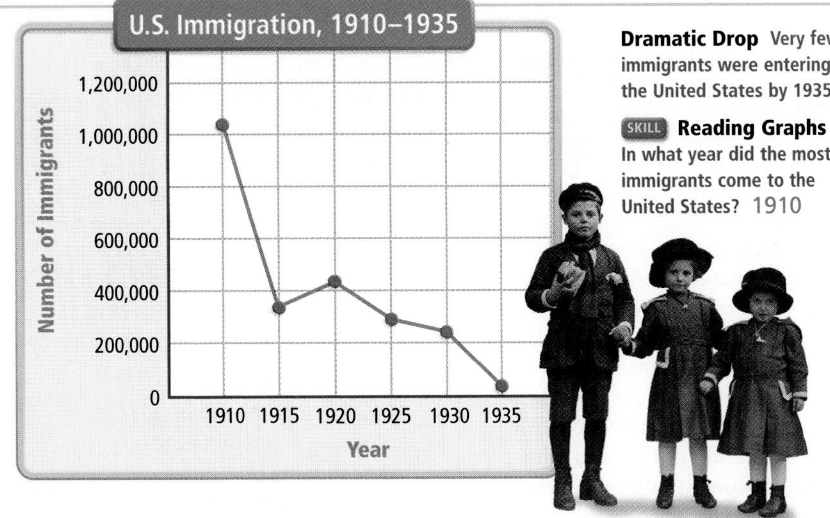

Dramatic Drop Very few immigrants were entering the United States by 1935.

SKILL **Reading Graphs** In what year did the most immigrants come to the United States? 1910

New Immigration Laws

With these new laws, each country was given a quota. Only the number of immigrants allowed by the quota could come to the United States. The new quotas did not treat all countries the same. They favored some countries, such as Great Britain and Germany. Other countries, such as Italy and Spain, had much lower quotas. Few immigrants from Asia or Africa were allowed in.

Another effect of the quotas was to lower the total number of immigrants that came each year. By 1930, the total had dropped from over one million to about 240,000 per year. The United States used these quotas until 1965.

2 The quotas did not apply to Canada or Latin America. The United States did not want to harm its neighbors. Also, workers from Latin America, and especially Mexico, had become very important to the United States economy.

Mexican Immigration

Since the late 1800s, thousands of Mexican immigrants had worked on railroads, mines, and large farms, mainly in the western United States. Between 1910 and 1920, about one million Mexicans came to the United States to work.

In the 1940s, the country faced a shortage of farm workers. To help solve the problem, many Mexicans were invited to work in the United States as temporary workers. They were called **braceros,** a Spanish word for laborer. By the 1950s, more than 200,000 braceros came to the United States almost every year.

Thousands of other Mexicans crossed the border to work without permission. They risked being arrested in order to earn more money in the United States. Employers liked to hire them because they worked hard and would accept low pay. Many people, however, felt jobs were being taken from United States citizens. 3

REVIEW What effect did quotas have on immigration? The total number of immigrants was lowered.

505

2 Teach

Limiting Immigration

Talk About It

1 **Q History** What were the goals of the new immigration laws of the 1920s?

A The laws limited how many immigrants could come from each country and what the total number of immigrants could be.

2 **Q Economics** Why did the 1920s quotas not apply to Canada or Latin America?

A The United States did not want to harm its neighbors. Workers from Latin America, and especially Mexico, had become important to the U.S. economy.

3 **Q History** Why did some Americans resent Mexican workers who came to the United States without permission?

A Mexicans often worked hard for little pay, creating job competition.

Vocabulary Strategy

quota Explain that word comes from the Latin word *quotus,* which means "of what number."

bracero This word comes from the Spanish *brazo,* arm. *Braceros* use their arms to pick fruit off trees. A farm worker in the U.S. may be called a "hired hand"; *bracero* is similar—like a "hired arm," needed to reach for fruit at harvest time.

Reading Strategy: Monitor/Clarify Have students read the first section, stopping at the end of each paragraph. Ask them to tell what the paragraph was about. If they do not understand something, review the paragraph. If the question is not answered, show them how to read on to find the answer.

Leveled Practice

Extra Support

Have students list the seven continents. Then have them **list the countries** that are mentioned in the lesson and classify them by continent. Visual-spatial; verbal-linguistic

Challenge

Ask partners to **design a board game** in which they use a map and tokens to symbolize immigration from various countries. Have students compare and play their games. Bodily-kinesthetic

ELL

Intermediate/Advanced

- Have partners **prepare for a discussion** about immigration quotas.
- Have them list reasons that quotas might be useful, harmful, fair, or unfair.
- Compare and discuss opinions as a class.

Verbal-linguistic

A New Era of Immigration

Talk About It

4 **Q History** What did the 1965 Immigration and Nationality Act do?

A It relaxed quotas, allowing people with special skills or family in the United States to immigrate.

5 **Q Geography** Where did many immigrants come from at this time?

A Asia, Latin America, and southern Europe

6 **Q History** What caused refugees to flee their home countries?

A Refugees fled from war, persecution, or hunger.

7 **Q History** Why did the United States feel a responsibility to help refugees from South Vietnam?

A The South Vietnamese government had been a wartime ally.

Vocabulary Strategy

refugee Point out the related word *refuge,* a safe place. A refugee is trying to find refuge.

Critical Thinking

Infer What reasons might government leaders have had for wanting to relax the quota laws in the 1950s and 1960s?

Think Aloud *I know that government leaders try to keep the good opinion of voters. Maybe the leaders knew that many people thought the quota laws were unfair. I can infer that the leaders thought it would make them more popular, and more likely to be re-elected, if they changed these laws to allow more people to immigrate.*

A New Era of Immigration

Main Idea After 1965, immigrants could come to the United States from all over the world.

Feelings about immigration changed during the 1950s and 1960s. The economy was doing well. Businesses needed more workers. Many government leaders did not like the old quota laws. They wanted people from every country to have the same chance to immigrate.

4 In 1965, the government passed the Immigration and Nationality Act. This law changed the old quotas and allowed many more people to immigrate. Under the new rules, relatives of people who had already immgirated to the United States were allowed to enter the country. People who had valuable skills to contribute to the nation were also let in. After
5 the 1965 law, immigration from Asia, Latin America, and southern Europe more than doubled.

Refugees Come to America

Another change in immigration laws allowed more refugees to enter the country. A **refugee** is a person who has left his or her home country to escape danger. Since 1965, millions of people have had to flee their home countries to escape 6
war, persecution, or hunger. President **Jimmy Carter** expressed the feelings of many when he said:

> **"To help them is a simple human duty. As Americans, as a people made up largely of the descendants of refugees, we feel that duty with a special keenness."**

In the 1960s, thousands of refugees left the island of Cuba. During a civil war in the 1980s, thousands of people also fled the Central American country of El Salvador. Many of them came to the United States because they saw it as a land of freedom.

Americans felt a special responsibility to help refugees from the Asian country of South Vietnam (VEE eht nahm). 7
Soldiers from the United States and South Vietnam had fought together in a long war. When the war was over, the United States wanted to help its allies. The government opened the way for thousands of Vietnamese refugees to come to the country.

New Immigrants Mexican immigrants living in Texas hold up their new citizenship papers. Almost 20 percent of all Mexican immigrants live in Texas.

Science

Make a Timeline

Ask students to find out what kinds of transportation immigrants have used to reach the United States. How has technology changed these modes of travel? Have students create a timeline showing when new technology made travel to the United States easier.

Visual-spatial

Language Arts

Write a Scene

Ask students to write a short scene in which two people discuss why refugees come to the United States. Characters might include a government leader, a refugee, or an official at Angel Island. Tell students that they may set their scene in any era from the 1880s to the present.

Bodily-kinesthetic; verbal-linguistic

Vietnamese Celebration The Los Angeles area has the largest Vietnamese community outside of Vietnam. Here, a Vietnamese American celebrates the Vietnamese New Year.

Many Vietnamese immigrants settled in California and Texas. In cities such as Los Angeles and Houston, they built communities with Vietnamese stores, schools, and places of worship.

The lives of immigrants in the United States have often been hard. Even so, immigrants have used their skills and values to contribute to the economy and culture of the United States.

REVIEW What are two ways in which immigration changed after 1965? More refugees were allowed to immigrate; more immigrants came from Asia and Latin America

Lesson Summary

- Between 1921 and 1965, immigration was limited by a system of quotas.
- Since 1965, the United States has accepted immigrants who have family members already in the United States, have special skills, or are refugees.

Why It Matters ...

After 1965, laws made it possible for immigrants from all over the world to bring new ideas, values, and skills to the United States.

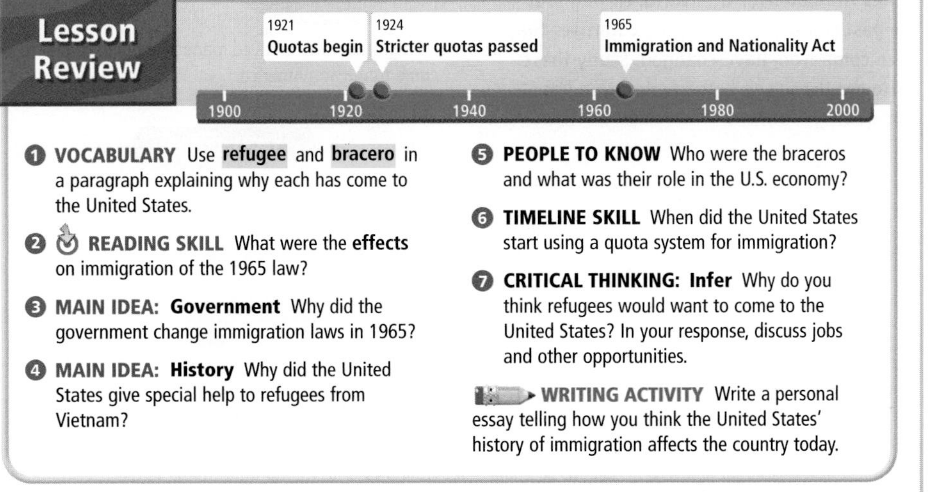

Lesson Review

1. **VOCABULARY** Use **refugee** and **bracero** in a paragraph explaining why each has come to the United States.
2. **READING SKILL** What were the **effects** on immigration of the 1965 law?
3. **MAIN IDEA: Government** Why did the government change immigration laws in 1965?
4. **MAIN IDEA: History** Why did the United States give special help to refugees from Vietnam?
5. **PEOPLE TO KNOW** Who were the braceros and what was their role in the U.S. economy?
6. **TIMELINE SKILL** When did the United States start using a quota system for immigration?
7. **CRITICAL THINKING: Infer** Why do you think refugees would want to come to the United States? In your response, discuss jobs and other opportunities.

WRITING ACTIVITY Write a personal essay telling how you think the United States' history of immigration affects the country today.

507

3 Review/Assess

Review Tested Objectives

U7-3 Quotas limited the number of immigrants who could come to the U.S. from other countries.

U7-4 After quotas were relaxed, many more immigrants came, especially from southern Europe, Latin America, and Asia.

Lesson Review Answers

1. Paragraphs might explain that refugees fled dangerous conditions, while braceros came to the United States to earn money.
2. It made it easier for people with special skills or family in the country to immigrate.
3. The government wanted to allow more immigrants into the country. Businesses needed more workers and politicians thought the old quotas were unfair.
4. They had been wartime allies of the United States.
5. The braceros were Mexican farm workers who came to the United States to fill the shortage of workers caused by World War II.
6. 1921
7. Sample Answer: The United States guarantees a lot of freedoms that other countries do not. It also has many opportunities for jobs, education, and housing.

Study Guide/Homework

Vocabulary and Study Guide

Vocabulary

Read the clue and write the answer in the blank. Then find the word in the puzzle. Look up, down, forward, and backward.

1. The maximum number of people allowed to enter a country quota
2. People fleeing danger in their home countries refugees
3. Temporary farm workers from Mexico bracero
4. A person who enters a new country to live there permanently immigrant

A	Y	I	Q	U	R	T	O
Z	C	M	B	R	E	F	G
M	N	M	O	E	X	A	H
L	M	I	B	F	R	K	U
E	S	G	T	U	S	Q	J
I	I	R	P	G	U	U	K
B	R	A	C	E	R	O	S
Q	U	N	T	E	A	T	L
E	A	T	A	S	B	A	O

Study Guide

Read "Limiting Immigration." Then fill in the sequence chart below.

Few limitations are placed on immigration. → 5. Quotas for countries are set. → 6. Mexicans come to work in the United States. → 7. Some Americans feel jobs are lost.

8. Read "A New Era of Immigration." Then write about the Vietnamese refugees.
Sample answer: Refugees left Vietnam because of war. They settled in large cities in Texas and California.

Unit Resources

140
Use with United States History, pp. 504–507

Unit Resources, p. 140

Reteach Minilesson

Use a cause-and-effect graphic organizer to reteach immigration laws.

Causes	Effects
laws of 1921, 1924	less immigration to the U.S.
1965 Immigration and Nationality Act	more immigration to the U.S.

Graphic Organizer 4

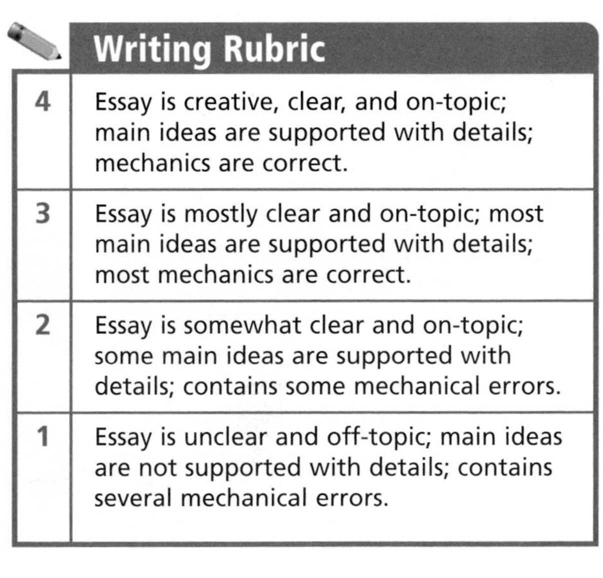

Writing Rubric

4	Essay is creative, clear, and on-topic; main ideas are supported with details; mechanics are correct.
3	Essay is mostly clear and on-topic; most main ideas are supported with details; most mechanics are correct.
2	Essay is somewhat clear and on-topic; some main ideas are supported with details; contains some mechanical errors.
1	Essay is unclear and off-topic; main ideas are not supported with details; contains several mechanical errors.

Quick Look

Connect to the Core Lesson Students have learned about immigration in the 1900s. In Extend Lesson 2, students will learn about how long it took to travel to the United States in different eras, and from which regions of the world immigrants came.

1 Teach the Extend Lesson

Connect to the Big Idea

People have immigrated to the United States from many countries and by many forms of transportation. Changes in immigration laws establishing quotas, or limits on how many people will be admitted from a given country, have greatly affected who comes to the United States.

Extend Lesson 2

Citizenship

CHANGES IN IMMIGRATION

In the last century, immigrants have come to the United States from many different countries by ship, train, car, and airplane. Before steamships became widely used in the late 1800s, it took most immigrants almost two weeks to sail from Europe by ship and almost two months from Asia. Travel by train could take several days from parts of Canada and Mexico. Now, most people can come to the United States by airplane in a day.

Immigrants have come to the United States from all over the world. Throughout the past century, however, the countries they have come from have changed. Study these circle graphs to see how immigration has changed.

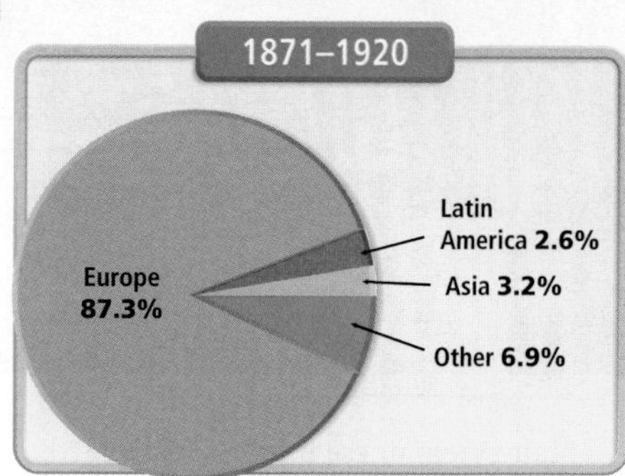

During this period, large numbers of immigrants came from Germany, Italy, and Russia.

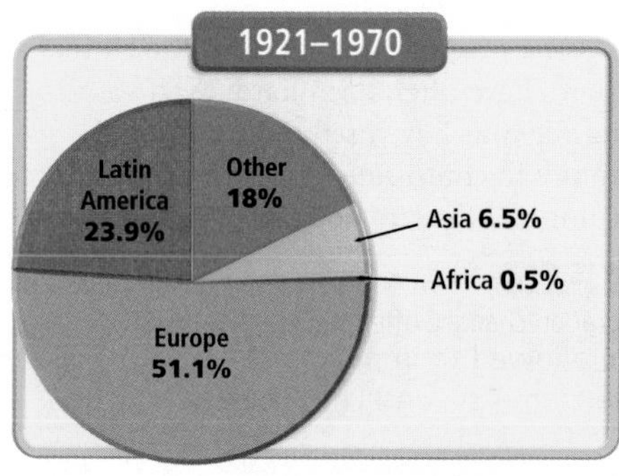

Immigration laws allowed many more immigrants to come from Latin America.

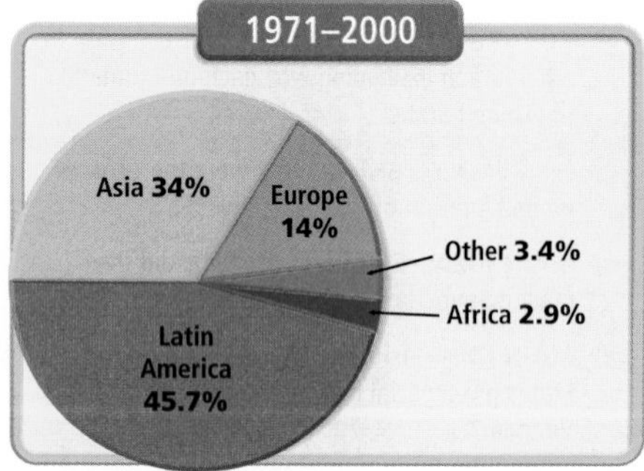

How much has immigration from Latin America and Asia increased since 1970?

Reaching All Learners

Extra Support

Use Circle Graphs

Have pairs of students use the circle graphs on page 508 to answer the following questions.

- Which period had the highest percentage of European immigrants? 1871–1920
- In the period from 1921 to 1970, what percentage of immigrants came from Latin America? 23.9%
- During which period was the percentage of immigrants from Asia higher than the percentage of immigrants from Europe? 1971–2000

Logical-mathematical; visual-spatial

On Level

Role-Play an Interview

- Have students, working in pairs, pick a decade and a country of origin and, with one member pretending to be a journalist and the other a newly arrived immigrant, make up at least three questions to ask and answer.
- Have some pairs act out their interview for the class. Permit class members to pose additional questions.

Verbal-linguistic

Challenge

Write a Journal Entry

- Have students write a journal entry from the point of view of one of the immigrants in the photo on page 509.
- Ask students to share their entries with another student.

Verbal-linguistic

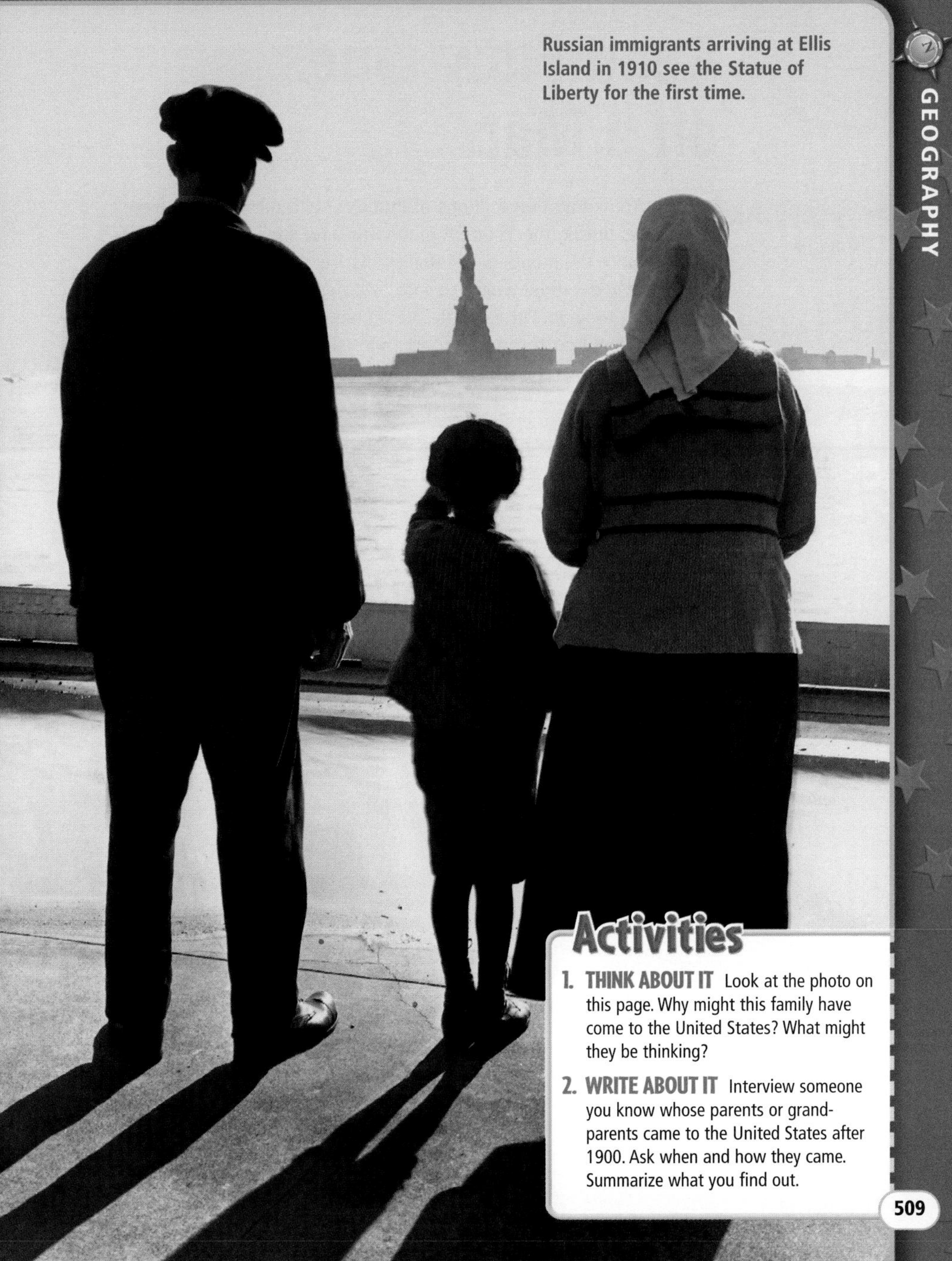

Russian immigrants arriving at Ellis Island in 1910 see the Statue of Liberty for the first time.

Activities

1. **THINK ABOUT IT** Look at the photo on this page. Why might this family have come to the United States? What might they be thinking?
2. **WRITE ABOUT IT** Interview someone you know whose parents or grandparents came to the United States after 1900. Ask when and how they came. Summarize what you find out.

509

2 Leveled Activities

❶ **Think About It** *For Extra Support*
Answers may refer to the Statue of Liberty and what it might have meant to the family when they saw it for the first time.

❷ **Write About It** *For Challenge*

Writing Rubric

4	Summary is clearly written; interviewees fit criteria; both "when" and "how" are explained; mechanics are correct.
3	Summary is adequately written; interviewees fit criteria; at least "when" or "how" is answered; few errors in mechanics.
2	Summary is written in a confused or disorganized way; interviewees may not fit criteria; some errors in mechanics.
1	Summary incomplete or confused; interviewees may not fit criteria; many errors in mechanics.

ELL

Intermediate/Advanced

- Ask students to **make cartoon strips** of immigrants arriving in the United States.
- Working in pairs, have students create word balloons for their characters, showing (in English translation) what they are saying or thinking.

Verbal-linguistic

Math

Make Tables and Graphs

- Have students make three tables, rank-ordering the origins of immigrants by continent, from highest percentage to lowest, for the three time periods shown.
- Have students make a bar graph showing immigration from Latin America during these three time periods.

Logical-mathematical

Graphic Organizer

Mode of Travel to U.S.	Travel Time
Ships from Europe, 1850	Almost two weeks
Ships from Asia, 1850	Almost two months
Steamships, 1900	One week
Airplanes, 2000	One day

Graphic Organizer 1

Tested Objectives

U7-5 Use flow lines on a map to interpret where people or objects come from and where they go.

U7-6 Gather information to make a map.

1 Teach the Skill

- Have students look at the map on page 510. Point out the flow lines.
- Ask students what they think these lines might show on this map.
- Read aloud the introductory paragraph on page 510. Make sure students understand the terms *travel routes, settlement patterns,* and *imports and exports.*
- Go through the three steps under "Learn the Skill" on page 511 with students. Answer any questions they have about flow lines.

Skillbuilder

Read Flow Lines on a Map

VOCABULARY
flow lines

You know that millions of immigrants came to the United States during the 1900s. A map with flow lines can help to compare the numbers of immigrants from different countries. **Flow lines** show where people or objects come from and where they go. For example, flow lines can show travel routes, settlement patterns, or imports and exports. The thickness of the lines shows how many have moved.

Immigration to the United States 1970–2000

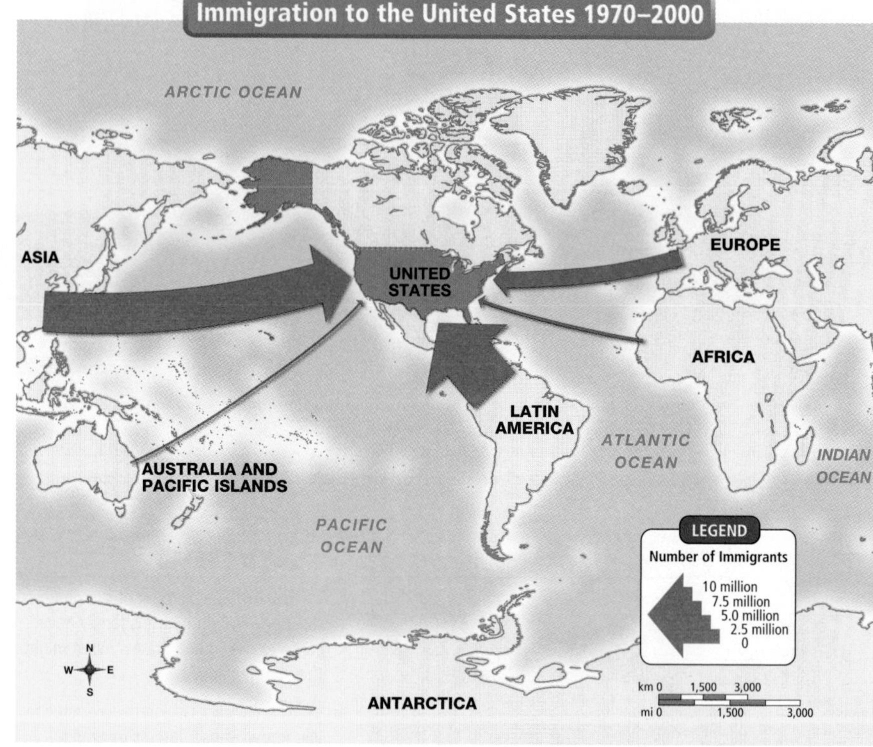

Leveled Practice

Extra Support

Have students make up sentences about the map on page 510. They may include detailed information or make general statements. Share sentences as a group. Verbal-linguistic

Challenge

Ask partners to think of a topic for a map that could include flow lines. Encourage them to choose topics from earlier chapters in the book. Have partners make sketches of their ideas. Visual-spatial

ELL

Intermediate

Point out that the words *flow* and *line* have more than one meaning. Have partners brainstorm uses of these words and create sentences or illustrations showing these uses. Compare as a group.

Verbal-linguistic

Learn the Skill

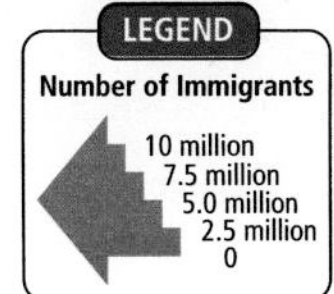

Step 1: Read the title, labels, and legend on the map. These will identify the subject and purpose of the map.

Step 2: Look at the flow lines and the direction they are pointing. Notice where the people or things come from and where they end up.

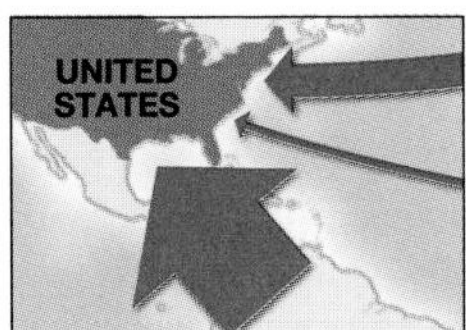

Step 3: Use a ruler to measure the widths of the lines. Compare them to the map legend to determine actual amounts.

Practice the Skill

Use the map to answer the following questions.

1. What time period does the map cover?
2. From which region of the world have the greatest number of immigrants come?
3. List the regions of the world from which immigrants have come. Begin with the country sending the most immigrants.
4. From which region did over 2.5 million immigrants come, Africa or Europe?

Apply the Skill

Find or create a map of your school. Draw flow lines from the classrooms to the library. Use the thickness of your flow lines to show the number of students from each classroom.

Skill Practice

Skillbuilder: Read Flow Lines on a Map

ARCTIC OCEAN, ASIA, UNITED STATES, EUROPE, AFRICA, INDIAN OCEAN, LATIN AMERICA, ATLANTIC OCEAN, AUSTRALIA AND PACIFIC ISLANDS, PACIFIC OCEAN, ANTARCTICA

LEGEND: Number of Immigrants — 10 million, 7.5 million, 5.0 million, 2.5 million, 0

Practice

1. From what region on the map have the fewest immigrants come? Australia and Pacific Islands
2. Have more people immigrated to the United States from Europe or from Africa? Europe
3. About how many immigrants have come from Latin America since 1971? About 9.5 million
4. Study the widths of the flow lines and the number of people each one represents. Use the following data to draw a flow line for Asian immigration into the map.

Asian Immigration, 1971–2000

7,122,007

Apply

Find or create a world map. Using the data below, turn the map into a flow line map. Be sure to draw a legend for the map.

U.S. Immigration, 1850s

Ireland 160,000	**Great Britain 50,000**
Germany 80,000	**Canada 10,000**

Unit Resources 141 Use with *United States History*, pp. 510–511

Unit Resources, p. 141

Skill Transparency

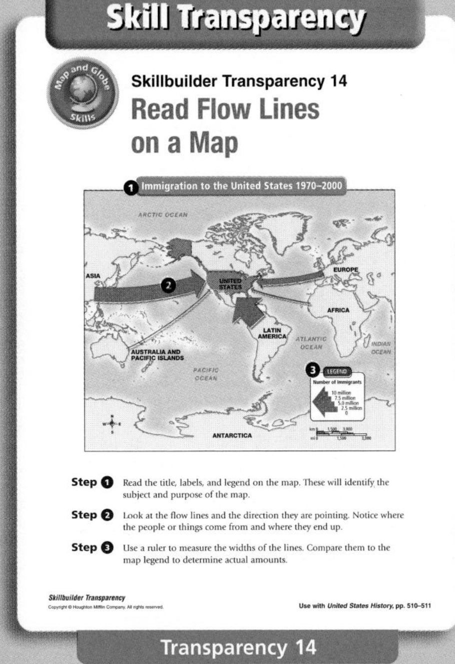

Transparency 14

2 Practice the Skill

1. 1970 to 2000
2. Latin America
3. Latin America, Asia, Europe, Africa, Australia and Pacific Islands
4. Europe

3 Apply the Skill

Ask students to find or create maps of their school, using flow lines to indicate student movement. When evaluating students' maps, consider:

- Did the student draw or find an accurate map of the school?
- Did the student draw flow lines connecting students' classrooms to the library?
- Did the student use thicker or thinner lines to show the number of students coming from each classroom?

Tested Objectives

U7-7 Culture Discuss some of the ways immigrants have contributed to the culture of the United States.

U7-8 Citizenship Identify the democratic heritage that Americans share.

Lesson Quick Look

This lesson emphasizes that many ethnic groups and cultures have contributed to the United States, where they share a common heritage of democratic values.

Teaching Option: Extend Lesson 3 features poetry about the immigrant experience in the United States.

1 Get Set to Read

Preview Have students look at the photo on page 514 and tell what it shows.

Reading Skill: Draw Conclusions Details in the chart may include languages, foods, and holidays.

Build on What You Know Ask students how they learned their special skills. Chances are someone older taught them. Explain that ideas and beliefs, like skills, can be passed down.

Vocabulary

heritage *noun,* something that is passed down through generations

motto *noun,* a brief statement that expresses an ideal or goal

Core Lesson 3

The American People Today

VOCABULARY

heritage
motto

Vocabulary Strategy

heritage

The words **heritage** and inherit are related in meaning. A heritage is something you inherit, or receive, from your family or culture.

READING SKILL

Draw Conclusions As you read, note details that support the conclusion that immigrants have strengthened the United States.

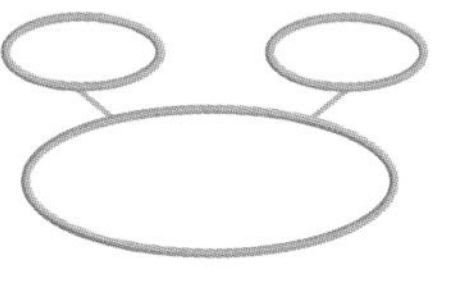

Build on What You Know Think about how each of your classmates contributes special skills and talents to your class. In a similar way, each of the over 290 million people living in the United States has something to contribute to the country.

Many People, One Nation

Main Idea The United States is made up of people from many different backgrounds and cultures.

The people of the United States come from a great number of countries and cultures. About one in every ten U.S. citizens was born in another country. Millions more are the children, grandchildren, and great-grandchildren of immigrants. 1

Each of these generations has contributed something new to the story of immigration. Today, almost one third of the people who move to the United States come from Mexico. Other Spanish-speaking immigrants are from Central and South America. One quarter of all immigrants today come from countries in Asia such as India, China, and South Korea.

Generations
Some families, such as the one shown here, have many generations in the same family.

Skill and Strategy

Reading Skill and Strategy

Reading Skill: Draw Conclusions

Sometimes when you read, you have to figure out things that the writer doesn't tell you. This skill is called drawing conclusions.

Read "Our Shared Values." Then fill in the chart below. Write two sentences that support the conclusion.

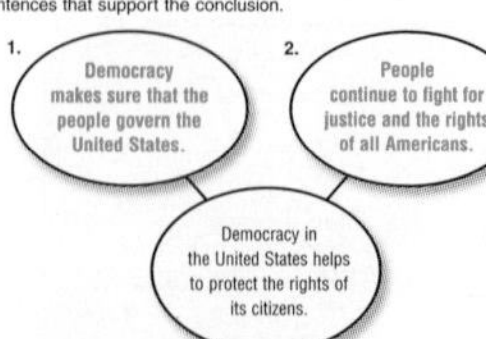

Reading Strategy: Monitor/Clarify

3. Read "Many People, One Nation." Then tell how you monitored your understanding of the section.
Sample answer: I slowly read the words and looked at the picture and the map.
4. Write any questions you had after you finished reading.
Sample answer: How have different ethnic groups added to the culture of the United States?
5. How did you answer your questions? Answer with a complete sentence.
Sample answer: Americans of different ethnicities share their customs, food, and languages with other Americans.

Unit Resources

142
Use with *United States History*, pp. 512–515

Unit Resources, p. 142

Background

The United States Today

- In the year 2000, over 170,000 Mexicans moved to the United States, making Mexico the largest source of new immigrants.
- The next five most numerous immigrant groups in 2000 came from China, the Philippines, India, Cuba, and Vietnam.
- Because of improvements in medicine, sanitation, and disease control, the average life expectancy of Americans today is about 77 years. During the colonial period, it was about 43 years.

Roberto Goizueta He led an international company with branches in over 200 countries.

Madeleine Albright She was the first woman to hold the job of Secretary of State.

I. M. Pei In 1978, he designed part of the National Gallery in Washington, D. C.

Many Ethnic Groups

Because the United States has so many ethnic groups, the nation's population is very diverse. The United States is also the most religously diverse country in the world.

Diversity of backgrounds is one of the United States' greatest strengths. Each

ethnic group adds a new language, new foods, and new customs to the culture of the United States. For example, many words we use come from different languages. The word *kindergarten* is originally a German word. *Mosquito* is Spanish. The word *skunk* comes from an American Indian language.

The culture of the United States is a mixture of traditions from around the world. Some ethnic traditions change when immigrants come to the United States. New traditions are also created. The first St. Patrick's Day parade was held in Boston, not in Ireland. The first Chinese New Year's parade with marching bands and floats was held in San Francisco. These holidays came from other countries, but the way people celebrated them in the United States was new.

Individual immigrants have also brought their knowledge and talents to the United States, making the country stronger. **Roberto Goizueta** was a refugee from Cuba who became the president of The Coca-Cola Company. **I. M. Pei** is an immigrant from China who came to the United States to go to college. Today he is a world-famous architect.

Immigrants and their children have also made important contributions to the national government. **Madeleine Albright** immigrated to the United States from eastern Europe. In 1996, President Bill Clinton chose her to be the Secretary of State. **Daniel Inouye,** the son of Japanese immigrants, is a senator from Hawaii. He is one of the longest-serving members of the Senate. 3

REVIEW What are two contributions that immigrants have made to the United States?
Sample Answer: individual knowledge and talents; new foods and customs

2 Teach

Many People, One Nation

Talk About It

1 **Q History** About what fraction of today's U.S. citizens were born in another country?
A about one in every ten citizens

2 **Q Citizenship** In what ways do various ethnic groups add to the culture of the United States?
A These people bring their customs, foods, and languages to the United States.

3 **Q Citizenship** Whom did Bill Clinton choose to be Secretary of State in 1996?
A Madeleine Albright

Reading Strategy: Monitor/Clarify As students read, suggest they pause after each paragraph and reflect on what they have read. After they think about what they've read, they should consider if anything is unclear.

Leveled Practice

Extra Support

Ask students to discuss the place or places that their families originally came from. Students may **discuss in small groups** and share what they learn with the class.
Verbal-linguistic

Challenge

Have partners **find examples of music** with roots in different countries. Have them bring in a sample to share and discuss with the class.
Musical-auditory

ELL

Beginning

- Ask students if there are words in their first language that are also used in English, or vice versa. List these words on the board.
- Ask students to make a list of words and phrases that would be useful for a new immigrant to the United States.

Verbal-linguistic

Our Shared Values

Talk About It

4 **Q Citizenship** Whose rights are protected by the Bill of Rights?

A the rights of all American citizens

5 **Q Citizenship** Which rights have ethnic groups in the United States often struggled to defend?

A the rights to equal schools, housing, and job opportunities

6 **Q Citizenship** What does the motto "E Pluribus Unum" mean, and why is it a motto of the United States?

A "E Pluribus Unum" means "out of many, one." At first, it referred to thirteen colonies becoming one country; today, it also reflects the way people of many origins form one nation.

Vocabulary Strategy

heritage Point out the related word *inherit.* People can inherit money or property when a relative passes away. They can also inherit skills, traditions, and ideas from their families and cultures.

motto Point out that a synonym for *motto* is *saying*.

Critical Thinking

Analyze If the Constitution protects the rights of all Americans, then why have Americans often had to struggle for their rights?

Think Aloud *I think that Americans' ideas about equal rights are always changing, and our laws can change with them. But bringing about change like that is not always easy. That is why Americans have often fought to protect their rights.*

The White House Many citizens go to Washington, D. C. to learn about their democratic heritage. The White House has been the home of the President since 1800.

Our Shared Values

Main Idea Americans share the belief that the government should protect citizens' rights.

All Americans share a democratic heritage. A **heritage** is something that is handed down from past generations. The values of democracy and equal rights have been an important part of the history of the United States. This democratic heritage is expressed in the Constitution and the Bill of Rights. These documents explain the government, the rights, and the duties that all Americans share.

Although the Constitution did not originally protect the rights of every American, it established a democratic form of government. The Constitution keeps any single person or group from taking power away from the people. This system has worked, and our democracy has lasted for more than 200 years.

During that time, Americans have amended the Constitution and created laws that have made the nation even more democratic and just. The Bill of
Rights guarantees all citizens the free- 4
doms of speech, religion, and assembly, or the right to gather together.

In the United States, people can hold their own opinions and discuss them. Citizens can disagree with each other and even with the government. In many countries, people are not allowed to disagree with their government.

Not every group in the United States has always enjoyed these rights. Some ethnic groups, such as African Americans and American Indians, have faced discrimination. Their rights to equal schools,
housing, and jobs have not always been 5
recognized or defended. Each new ethnic group coming to the United States has struggled for protection of their rights.

Science

Immigrant Scientists

- Many important American scientists have been first-generation immigrants.
- Ask students to choose one immigrant scientist and find out about his or her work.
- Encourage students to share their findings with the class.

Verbal-linguistic

Language Arts

State Mottos

- Have students find out the mottos of some American states. Remind them that the state motto can sometimes be seen on license plates from that state.
- Ask students to write a paragraph about one or two mottos they find interesting.
- Encourage students to design their own mottos for themselves and for the class.

Verbal-linguistic

E Pluribus Unum

Just as there have always been people who have faced unfair treatment, there have always been people who have worked for justice. The history of the United States is a story of brave people who have fought to expand the democratic principles and ideas upon which the nation was founded.

One motto of the United States is "E Pluribus Unum" (EE PLUR ih buhs
6 OON uhm). A **motto** is a short statement that explains an ideal or goal. "E Pluribus Unum" is a Latin phrase that means "out of many, one."

"E Pluribus Unum" This motto can be found on all U.S. coins.

"E pluribus unum" is written on coins and government buildings throughout the country. The motto is a reminder that the original thirteen colonies formed one country. Today, fifty states form one democratic nation with a culture that is as diverse as the people who live in it.

REVIEW What rights does the Bill of Rights guarantee? Freedom of speech, religion, and assembly

Lesson Summary

- **The American People**
  - Come from many different ethnic backgrounds
  - Share a culture that is a mix of old and new traditions
  - Share a rich democratic heritage of rights and freedoms

Why It Matters ...

The shared values and democratic heritage of the United States help people from many different backgrounds to live with and learn from each other.

Lesson Review

1. **VOCABULARY** Use the word **heritage** in a paragraph describing the background that all U.S. citizens share.
2. **READING SKILL** What immigrant contributions in this lesson support the **conclusion** that immigrants have strengthened the United States?
3. **MAIN IDEA: History** What caused the United States' population to become so diverse?
4. **MAIN IDEA: Citizenship** Explain what "E Pluribus Unum" means and how it describes the United States today.
5. **PEOPLE TO KNOW** Who is **Madeleine Albright** and what job did she hold in the government?
6. **CRITICAL THINKING: Synthesize** Why do you think the United States could be called one of the first international nations?
7. **CRITICAL THINKING: Analyze** Why is it important for the government to protect the rights of all its citizens?

HANDS ON **CITIZENSHIP ACTIVITY** Make a poster that shows what the motto "E Pluribus Unum" means to you. Use pictures from magazines and headlines from articles and newspapers.

3 Review/Assess

Review Tested Objectives

U7-7 Immigrants have enriched U.S. culture economically and also with their customs, language, and cuisines.

U7-8 Americans share a democratic heritage that is strengthened by a diverse population.

Lesson Review Answers

1. Paragraphs may include references to diversity and democracy.
2. Immigrants have brought ethnic traditions to the U.S.; they have influenced the language spoken here; some have become famous.
3. People arrived from all over the world, bringing their cultural traditions with them.
4. It means "out of many, one," and describes the many cultures that make up one diverse country.
5. Albright was Secretary of State under President Clinton; this was the highest-ranking job a woman had held in the executive branch.
6. It contains people and cultures from all over the world.
7. These rights must be protected in order to maintain a working democracy.

HANDS ON Performance Task Rubric

4	Position clearly stated; poster is persuasive; mechanics are correct.
3	Position adequately stated; poster is persuasive; few errors in mechanics.
2	Position is stated; poster is fairly persuasive; some errors in mechanics.
1	Position not stated; persuasion lacking; many errors in mechanics.

Study Guide/Homework

Vocabulary and Study Guide

Vocabulary

Read the clue and unscramble the letters to write the correct word.

1. Something handed down from past generations.
   T A E H E I R G — Heritage
2. A short statement that explains an ideal.
   O M O T T — Motto
3. Unfair treatment toward a group of people.
   S M I N I A D I C O N T R I — Discrimination

Study Guide

Read "Many People, One Nation." Then choose the correct ending to each statement below.

4. Almost one-third of immigrants to the United States are from
   A. Canada. B. China. (C.) Mexico.
5. Each ethnic group adds new language, food, and
   (A.) customs. B. money. C. transportation.
6. The word *kindergarten* is originally a word in
   A. French. (B.) German. C. Japanese.

Read "Our Shared Values." Then fill in the cause in the chart below.

	Cause	Effect
7.	People fight for justice for all groups.	Rights have been extended to all Americans.

 143 Use with United States History, pp. 512–515

Unit Resources, p. 143

Reteach Minilesson

Use a word web to review the Bill of Rights.

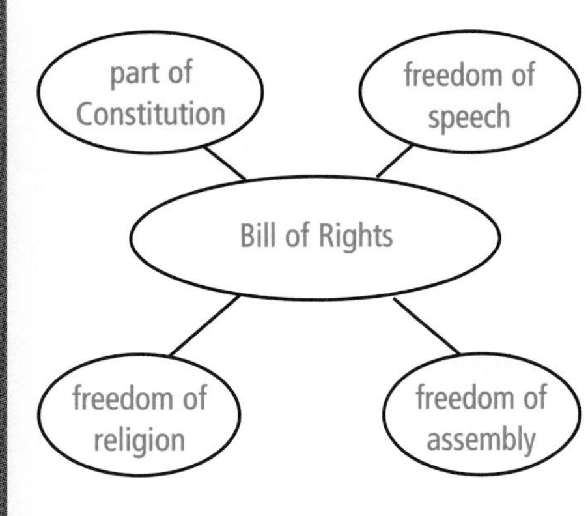

Graphic Organizer 13

Quick Look

Connect to the Core Lesson Students have learned about the diversity and shared values of the American people today. In Extend Lesson 3, three American poets write about the different places that are part of their backgrounds.

1 Preview the Extend Lesson

Connect to the Big Idea

Diversity and Identity The United States has been a nation of immigrants throughout its history. Each of the more than 280 million people living in the country today contributes to its diversity. It is the respect for differences and the desire for unity that forms the foundation of American democracy.

Extend Lesson 3

Literature

Poems That Go Places

The places in these poems may be real or imagined. They may exist in the poet's memory or outside the poet's window. The writers are from the United States, but different places are part of their backgrounds. They share these places through their poems.

516 • Chapter 14

Reaching All Learners

Background

More About the Poets

- Francisco X. Alarcon writes poetry in both English and Spanish. He grew up in the United States and in Mexico.
- Naomi Shihab Nye is the daughter of a Palestinian father and an American mother. She was raised in St. Louis, Jerusalem, and San Antonio.
- Myra Cohn Livingston published her first poem when she was eighteen.

Extra Support

Make a List

- Have students work in pairs. Ask each pair to choose one of the three poems.
- Invite students to look for geography terms in the poem they have chosen. Have students make a list of the terms they have found.
- Discuss the lists as a class.

Verbal-linguistic

On Level

Be a Poem Detective

- Read "City of Bridges," on page 517 aloud to the class.
- Ask groups of students to use clues in the poem to figure out which city Alarcon describes. San Francisco, or another bay city with streetcars, rolling hills, and bridges.
- Students may use the photograph on pages 516–517. They may also want to use a map of the United States.
- Have students explain their answers.

Verbal-linguistic; visual-spatial

Cuidad de Puentes

yo sone
una ciudad
recostada

entre alegres
colinas
y tranvias

con casas
que parecen
de muñecas

y edificios
con adornas
de pastel

yo sone
una ciudad
abierta al mar

remojandose
los pies
en una bahia

amistosa
muy alegre
y generosa

con puentes
que nos quieren
a todos abrazar

una ciudad
donde
las personas

se hacen
puentes
entre si

City of Bridges

I dreamed
a city
resting

among happy
rolling hills
and streetcars

with houses
that look like
doll houses

and buildings
decorated
like pastry

I dreamed
a city open
to the sea

soaking
her feet
in a bay

friendly
very joyful
and kind

with bridges
ready to
embrace us all

a city
where people
become

bridges
to each
other

by Francisco X. Alarcon

LITERATURE

517

2 Teach the Extend Lesson

Learning Through Poetry

Ask volunteers to read the poems aloud to the class. Discuss the poems and the different places that they describe. If these are poems that go places, where do they go? In what ways are the places similar? How are they different?

Challenge

Write a Paragraph

- Have students read "City of Bridges" on page 517.
- Discuss the poet's use of personification to describe the city. What kind of person is the city?
- Ask students to write a paragraph explaining what kind of person they think the city is and whether they would like to meet the city or live in the city.

Verbal-linguistic

ELL

Advanced

- Have a Spanish speaker read "Cuidad de Puentes" for the class. Then have an English speaker read "City of Bridges" to the class.
- Explain that Alarcon is bilingual and that he wrote both versions of the poem.
- Invite students to follow Alarcon's example and write two versions of a poem, one in their first language, and the other in English.
- Ask students to share their poems with the class.

Verbal-linguistic

Literature

Poetry

Laughing Tomatoes and Other Spring Poems, by Francisco X. Alarcon. Place this collection of poetry in your Reading Center for students who want to read more poetry by this author.

Critical Thinking

Analyze Each of the poems on pages 518 and 519 describe mountains. Have students discuss whether the mountains described are real or imaginary. Ask students to explain their answers.

Reaching All Learners

Language Arts

- Have students discuss what happens in "Torn Map" when someone tears a map by mistake and tapes it back together.
- Ask students to suppose that they could change their community by making a change to a map, globe, or chart.
- Invite students to write a fictional poem or story describing what they would do to the map, and how it would change their community.

Verbal-linguistic

Music

Write the Next Verse

- Explain that the poem on page 519 refers to the song "America the Beautiful."
- Distribute copies of the lyrics to students.
- Play a recording of the song for the class. Have them listen to the song while they read the lyrics.
- Ask students to explain the meaning of the terms "spacious skies," "amber waves of grain," and "fruited plain." Have they ever seen such things?
- Have them discuss what they think is beautiful about their part of the country.
- Invite students to write their own verse of "America the Beautiful," using plenty of details including colors, textures, sounds, tastes, and smells.

Musical-auditory

For Purple Mountains' Majesty

I saw them today.
I saw them.
So many years I have heard them in a song.
It's true. They're purple when you see them.
They rise like kings.
They are mountains.
Suddenly
I know.
I really know
What that song is all about.

by Myra Cohn Livingston

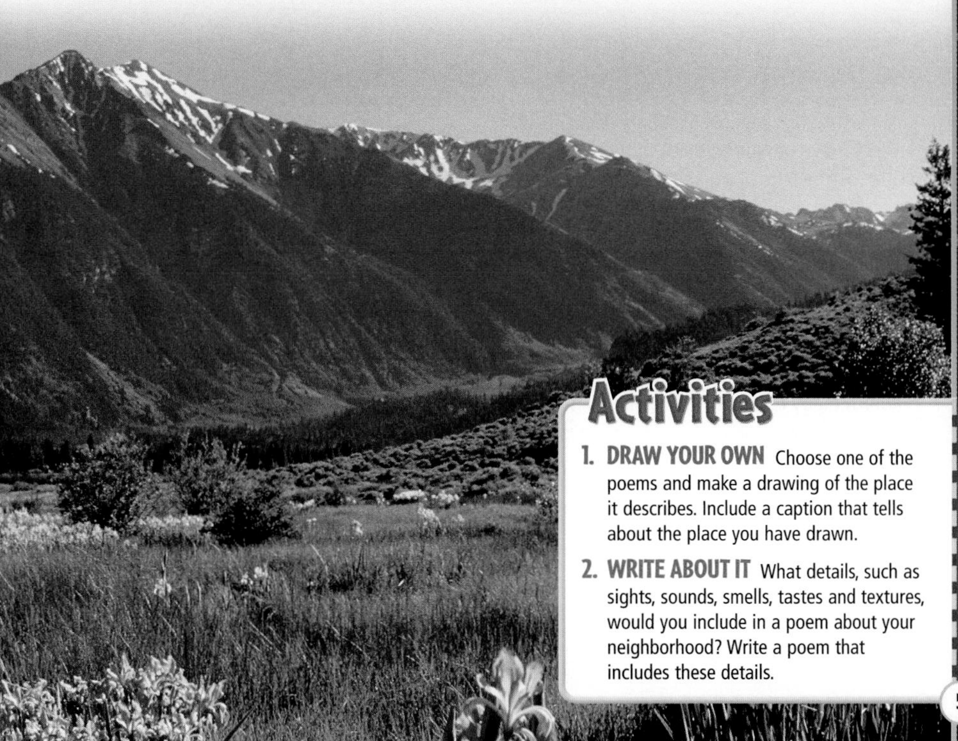

Activities

1. **DRAW YOUR OWN** Choose one of the poems and make a drawing of the place it describes. Include a caption that tells about the place you have drawn.
2. **WRITE ABOUT IT** What details, such as sights, sounds, smells, tastes and textures, would you include in a poem about your neighborhood? Write a poem that includes these details.

3 Leveled Activities

❶ **Draw Your Own** *For Extra Support*
Drawings and captions should reflect the content of one of the poems.

❷ **Write About It** *For Challenge*

Writing Rubric

4	Poem is creative; includes many sensory details; conveys a strong sense of the student's neighborhood; mechanics are correct.
3	Poem includes sensory details and conveys a sense of the student's neighborhood; most mechanics are correct.
2	Poem includes few sensory details; conveys some sense of the student's neighborhood; contains some mechanical errors.
1	Poem is incomplete; does not include sensory details; does not convey a sense of the student's neighborhood; contains many mechanical errors.

Art

Revise a Map

- Ask students to make two copies of a map from their textbook or another source.
- Have students save one copy. Have them tear, cut, paste, color, fold, and decorate the other copy to create a revision of the map.
- Ask students to compare and contrast the geography of the original map with that of the revised map.

Visual-spatial; bodily-kinesthetic

Graphic Organizer

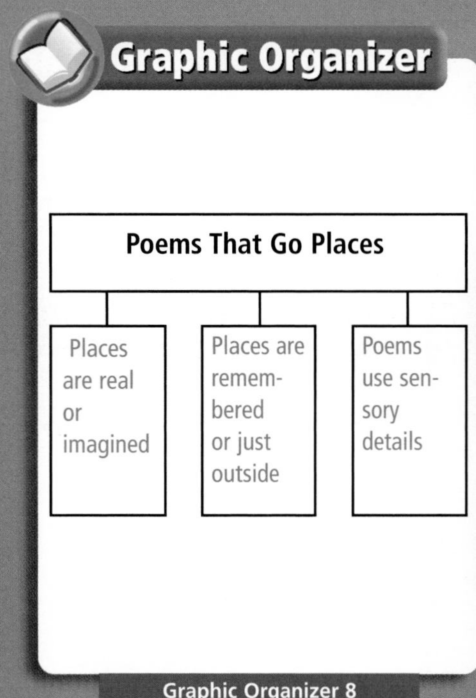

Graphic Organizer 8

Chapter Review

Tested Objectives

The lesson objective assessed by each question is shown in parentheses after the answer.

Visual Summary

1. Large numbers of immigrants came from southern and eastern Europe. The Chinese Exclusion Act stopped Chinese immigration for 10 years. *(Obj. U7-1)*
2. Quotas passed in 1921 and 1924 limited immigration. Some countries, such as England and Germany, were favored, but overall, fewer immigrants came from all countries. *(Obj. U7-1)*
3. A new immigration law passed in 1965 increased immigration from all over the world. After 1965, immigration from Asia, Latin America, and southern Europe especially increased. *(Obj. U7-4)*

Facts and Main Ideas

4. They often settled in large cities. Many immigrants formed communities with members of the same religious or ethnic group in these cities. Most new immigrants lived in tenement buildings. *(Obj. U7-2)*
5. The government passed laws that started a quota system for immigration. These quotas limited the number of immigrants who came from each country. The quotas also limited the overall number of immigrants coming into the country each year. *(Obj. U7-2)*
6. Sample answer: El Salvador, Cuba, or South Vietnam *(Obj. U7-4)*
7. The Constitution and the Bill of Rights *(Obj. U7-8)*

Vocabulary

8. **heritage** *(Obj. U7-8)*
9. **quota** *(Obj. U7-3)*
10. **persecution** *(Obj. U7-1)*
11. **ethnic group** *(Obj. U7-7)*

14 Review and Test Prep

Visual Summary

1–3. Write a description of each period of immigration named below.

Immigration to the United States	
1880 to 1920	
1920 to 1965	
1965 to Today	

Facts and Main Ideas

TEST PREP Answer each question with information from the chapter.

4. **History** Where did most immigrants settle in the late 1800s and early 1900s?
5. **Government** What did the government do to limit immigration in the 1920s?
6. **Geography** Name one country from which many refugees have come to the United States.
7. **Citizenship** Which documents express the values of equal rights and democracy on which the United States is founded?

Vocabulary

TEST PREP Choose the correct word from the list below to complete each sentence.

persecution, p. 499
ethnic group, p. 500
quota, p. 504
heritage, p. 514

8. All Americans share a democratic _____.
9. Laws in the 1920s set a _____ for how many immigrants could enter the country.
10. Thousands of Russian immigrants came to the United States to escape _____.
11. Each _____ has brought its culture and traditions to the United States.

Reading/Language Arts Wrap-Up

Reading Strategy: Monitor/Clarify

- Review with students the process of monitoring their understanding and clarifying anything they do not understand.
- Have students work in pairs, taking turns to model the process as they read.
- Partners can help each other clarify important points.

Writing Strategy

- As students write, they can apply what they have learned about monitoring and clarifying text.
- After writing a draft, students can go back and read their own writing, applying the strategy as they do. By monitoring their reading, students can find points that need clarification.

CHAPTER SUMMARY TIMELINE

1882 Chinese Exclusion Act — 1921 Quotas passed — 1924 Quotas made stricter — 1965 Immigration and Nationality Act

1880 · 1900 · 1920 · 1940 · 1960 · 1980

Apply Skills

TEST PREP **Map Skill** Look at the map below. Then use what you have learned about flow lines to answer each question.

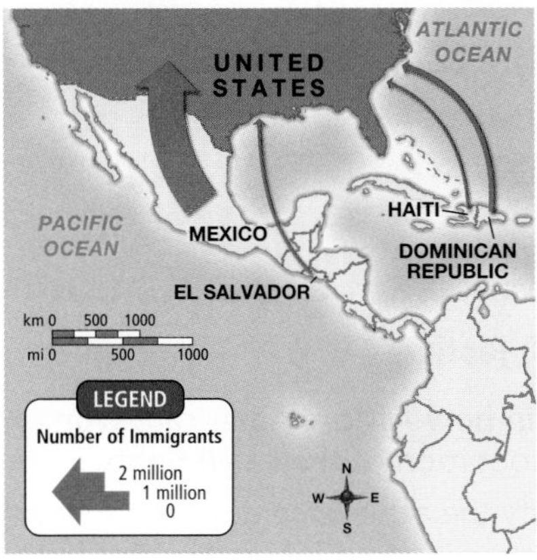

12. From which country did the most number of immigrants come?
A. Dominican Republic
B. Mexico
C. El Salvador
D. Haiti

13. About how many Mexican immigrants came to the United States between 1991 and 2000?
A. About 2 thousand
B. About 1 million
C. Under 1 million
D. About 2 million

Critical Thinking

TEST PREP Write a short paragraph to answer each question.

14. Summarize Why did lawmakers in the 1960s no longer want strict quotas?

15. Draw Conclusions Is "E Pluribus Unum" still a good motto for the United States today? Give reasons for your conclusion.

Timeline

Use the Chapter Summary Timeline above to answer the question.

16. In which decade was the Immigration and Nationality Act passed?

Activities

Research Activity Use a dictionary to find the origins of the words below.

giraffe walrus kayak
kimono shampoo llama

Writing Activity Think about a time when you had to change schools or move to a different town or country. Write a personal narrative explaining the challenges that you faced and how you overcame them.

Technology
Writing Process Tips
Get help with your essay at
www.eduplace.com/kids/hmss05/

521

Technology

Test Generator

You can generate your own version of the chapter review by using the **Test Generator CD-ROM.**

Web Link

For more ideas, visit
www.eduplace.com/ss/hmss05/

Standards

National Standards

I e Importance of cultural unity and diversity
III a Use mental maps understanding of relative location, direction, size, and shape
III c Resources, data sources, and geographic tools
VI d Encourage unity and deal with diversity to maintain order and security
VI f Factors that contribute to cooperation and cause disputes
IX b Conflict, cooperation, and interdependence
X a Key ideals of the United States's form of government
X b Citizen rights and responsibilities
X h Public policies and citizen behaviors

Apply Skills

12. B *(Obj. U7-5)*
13. D *(Obj. U7-5)*

Critical Thinking

14. The economy was doing well and businesses needed more workers. Lawmakers also wanted immigrants from all countries to have an equal opportunity to come to the United States. *(Obj. U7-4)*

15. The motto comes from the fact that the original thirteen colonies formed one country. The colonists were from several countries, but today people come from all over the world. There are many more ethnic groups in the United States. *(Obj. U7-7)*

Timeline

16. 1960s *(Obj. U7-3)*

Leveled Activities

HANDS ON Performance Task Rubric

4	Definitions are accurate and complete; mechanics are correct.
3	Definitions are generally accurate and complete; mechanics are mostly correct.
2	Definitions are partly accurate and partly complete; some errors in mechanics.
1	Definitions are absent or incomplete; many errors in mechanics.

Writing Rubric

4	Ideas clearly stated and persuasive; mechanics are correct.
3	Ideas adequately stated and mostly persuasive; few errors in mechanics.
2	Ideas are stated but confused or not persuasive; some errors in mechanics.
1	Ideas not stated and not persuasive; many errors in mechanics.

Chapter 15 Planning Guide

The Promise of America

Chapter Opener

Pages 522–523

 30 minutes

Reading/Vocabulary

Chapter Reading Strategy: Summarize, p. 521F

Resources

Grade Level Resources
- **Vocabulary Cards,** pp. 59–66

Reaching All Learners
- **Challenge Activities,** p. 75

Primary Sources Plus, p. 27

Big Idea Transparency 7

Interactive Transparency 7

Text & Music Audio CD

Lesson Planner & TR CD ROM

eBook

eTE

Core Lesson 1

Americans Work for Change

Pages 524–527

Tested Objectives

U7-9 Describe how women won recognition of their right to vote.

U7-10 Describe how the NAACP worked for African Americans' rights in the early 20th century.

Reading/Vocabulary

Reading Skill: Sequence

suffragist **activist** **prejudice**

Cross-Curricular

Drama, p. 526

Resources

Unit Resources:
- **Reading Skill/Strategy,** p. 144
- **Vocabulary/Study Guide,** p. 145

Assessment Options:
- **Lesson Test,** p. 150

Extend Lesson 1

History

Women's Rights Movement

20–30 minutes

Pages 528–529

Focus: A timeline presents important people and events in the achievement of women's rights over the past century and a half.

Core Lesson 2

The Struggle Continues

Pages 530–535

Tested Objectives

U7-11 Explain how African Americans won greater recognition of their civil rights.

U7-12 Identify the achievements of the following groups who worked for equal rights in the 20th century: women, American Indians, migrant workers, people with disabilities.

Reading/Vocabulary

Reading Skill: Predict Outcomes

civil rights **migrant worker** **nonviolent protest**

Cross-Curricular

Math, p. 532

Art, p. 534

Resources

Unit Resources:
- **Reading Skill/Strategy,** p. 146
- **Vocabulary/Study Guide,** p. 147

Assessment Options:
- **Lesson Test,** p. 151

www.eduplace.com/ss/hmss05/

Extend Lesson 2

Biographies

Champions for a Cause

20–30 minutes

Pages 536–537

Focus: Cesar Chavez and Delores Huerta worked tirelessly for the rights of migrant workers.

National Standards

I e Importance of cultural unity and diversity
ideals of a democratic republican form of government
II a How people may describe the same event differently
V d Internal conflicts
VI c How government does/does not provide for needs and wants, establish order and security, and manage conflict
VI d Encourage unity and deal with diversity to maintain order and security
VI h Tensions between the wants and needs and fairness, equity, and justice
X a Key ideals of the United States's form of government
X b Citizen rights and responsibilities
X h Public policies and citizen behaviors

Skillbuilder

Citizenship Skill

Resolve Conflicts

Pages 538–539

Tested Objectives

U7-13 Understand and apply the process of conflict resolution.

Reading/Vocabulary

conflict

Resources

Unit Resources:
Skill Practice, p. 148
Skill Transparency 15

Core Lesson 3

Democracy and Citizenship

Pages 540–543

Tested Objectives

U7-14 Explain important rights of all United States citizens, including the right to vote.

U7-15 Explain the responsibilities of United States citizens, including the responsibilities of young people.

Reading/Vocabulary

Reading Skill: Classify

naturalization, responsibility, register, volunteer

Cross-Curricular

Art, p. 542

Resources

Unit Resources:
Reading Skill/Strategy, p. 149
Vocabulary/Study Guide, p. 150
Assessment Options:
Lesson Test, p. 152

Extend Lesson 3

Citizenship

Volunteers

20–30 minutes

Pages 544–545

Focus: Helping other people is an important way to contribute to your community.

Chapter Review

Pages 546–547

30 minutes

Resources

Assessment Options:
Chapter 15 Test
Test Generator

Chapter 15 Practice Options

Lesson 1 Skill and Strategy

TEST PREP

Reading Skill and Strategy

Reading Skill: Sequence

This skill helps you understand the order in which events happened.

Read "African American Rights." Then fill in the sequence chart below to show the order in which African Americans won their rights.

1.	African Americans gained the right to vote after the Civil War.
2.	Southern states passed laws to prevent African Americans from voting.
3.	W.E.B. Du Bois and other leaders started the NAACP.
4.	The NAACP fights for equality in voting, education, and justice.

Reading Strategy: Summary

5. Read "The Fight for Women's Rights." Then check the best summary.
   - ✓ A movement for women's suffrage earned women the right to vote.
   - ___ Women could not run for national or state offices and often could not go to college.
   - ___ Jeannette Rankin became the first woman to be elected to the House of Representatives.
6. Read "African American Rights." Then check the best summary.
   - ___ Many people in southern states were prejudiced against African Americans.
   - ___ NAACP leaders held large meetings to discuss the rights of African Americans.
   - ✓ Leaders such as W.E.B. Du Bois created a movement to improve the civil rights of African Americans.

Unit Resources
 144 Use with *United States History*, pp. 524–527

Lesson 1 Vocabulary/Study Guide

TEST PREP

Vocabulary and Study Guide

Vocabulary

1. Draw a line connecting the vocabulary word to its meaning.

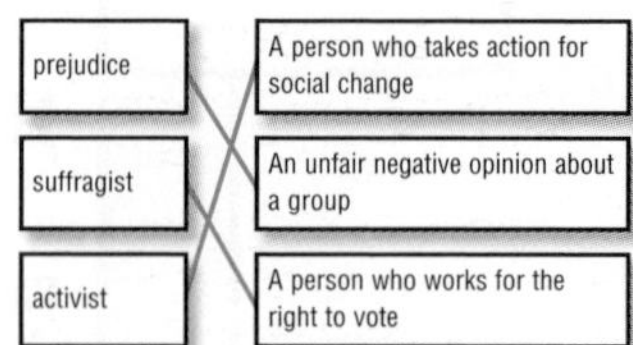

Study Guide

2. Read "The Fight for Women's Rights." Then fill in the outline below.

I. Main Idea: Women fight for their right to vote
- A. Supporting Idea: The suffrage movement
  - 1. Detail: The National American Woman Suffrage Association
  - 2. Detail: Members talk to people and Congress
- B. Supporting Idea: Women gain the right to vote
  - 1. Detail: Some states allow women to vote
  - 2. Detail: The Nineteenth Amendment gives voting rights to women

3. Read "African American Rights." Then write two methods the NAACP used to gain equality for African Americans.

Sample answers: Leaders spoke with Congress, wrote articles to educate the public, and made speeches to large groups.

Unit Resources
 145 Use with *United States History*, pp. 524–527

also in *Practice Book*, p. 86

Lesson 2 Skill and Strategy

TEST PREP

Reading Skill and Strategy

Reading Skill: Predict Outcomes

This skill allows you to think about what might happen, based on what you have read.

Read "The Civil Rights Movement." Make a prediction about the effects of the civil rights movement. Then read "Civil Rights for All." Write the actual outcome.

Prediction	1. Sample answer: Other ethnic groups enjoyed the new freedoms for which African Americans fought.
Outcome	2. Sample answer: Many other groups were inspired to protect their civil rights.

Reading Strategy: Summary

3. Read "The Civil Rights Movement." Then check the best summary.
   - ___ In the early 1950s, African American and white children went to different schools.
   - ___ Rosa Parks was arrested when she would not give up her seat on the bus.
   - ✓ African Americans used protests and the courts to protect their civil rights.
4. Read "Civil Rights for All." Then write a brief summary.

   The victories of African Americans showed other groups how to fight for their civil rights during the 1960s and 1970s.

Unit Resources
 146 Use with *United States History*, pp. 530–535

Lesson 2 Vocabulary/Study Guide

TEST PREP

Vocabulary and Study Guide

Vocabulary

As you read the lesson, fill in the word web with groups that fought for their civil rights.

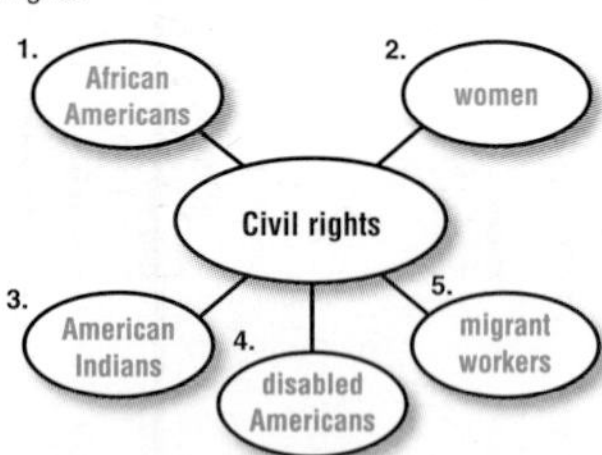

Write the definition of the term below.

6. nonviolent protest A way of bringing change without using violence

Study Guide

Read "The Struggle Continues." Then read the description. In the box, write the name of the person described.

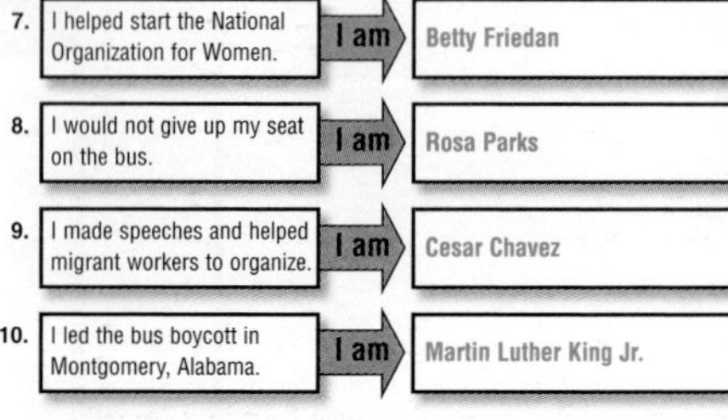

Unit Resources
 147 Use with *United States History*, pp. 530–535

also in *Practice Book*, p. 87

Skillbuilder Practice

Skillbuilder: Resolve Conflicts

In April 1963, Martin Luther King Jr. led protests against segregation in Birmingham, Alabama. More than 1,000 African American young people followed him. The Birmingham police met the protesters with snarling dogs and fire hoses that delivered painful blasts of water. Pictures of marchers getting bitten by dogs and getting knocked down by water shocked many Americans. Soon millions of Americans supported the civil rights movement. They demanded that the government take action. In May, Birmingham's leaders agreed to end segregation in the city's stores, restaurants, and workplaces. In 1964, Congress passed the Civil Rights Act, which made segregation illegal in all 50 states.

Practice

1. What did the African Americans who marched in Birmingham want? The marchers wanted equal rights.
2. Did the government of Birmingham feel the same way as the marchers? How do you know? No, because the police tried to stop the marchers.
3. What was the result of this conflict in Birmingham? The city of Birmingham agreed to end segregation in the city's stores, restaurants, and workplaces.
4. How did the U.S. government show that it agreed with the marchers' demands for civil rights? Congress passed the Civil Rights Act in 1964.

Apply

Think about a time you had a disagreement with a friend. Write a paragraph describing the disagreement you had. How did you eventually resolve the conflict? Did you both change the way you were feeling? Paragraph may refer to the two friends having different goals and resolving the conflict with a compromise.

Unit Resources

 148 Use with *United States History*, pp. 538–539

also in *Practice Book*, p. 88

Lesson 3 Skill and Strategy

Reading Skill and Strategy

Reading Skill: Classify

This skill helps you understand and remember what you have read by organizing, or classifying, facts into groups.

Read "Responsibilities of Citizens." Then fill in the classification chart below. Classify the responsibilities of adults and young people.

Adults	Young People
1. Sample answers: Obeying the law; voting; paying taxes; serving on juries	2. Sample answers: Obeying the law; protecting the environment; volunteering to help others

Reading Strategy: Summary

3. Read "Democracy and Citizenship." Then write a short summary for each section.

Section 1: Citizenship

Summary: Sample answer: Democracies give their citizens many rights.

Section 2: Responsibilities of Citizens

Summary: Sample answer: Along with their rights, citizens of democracies also have many responsibilities.

Unit Resources

 149 Use with *United States History*, pp. 540–543

Lesson 3 Vocabulary/Study Guide

Vocabulary and Study Guide

Vocabulary

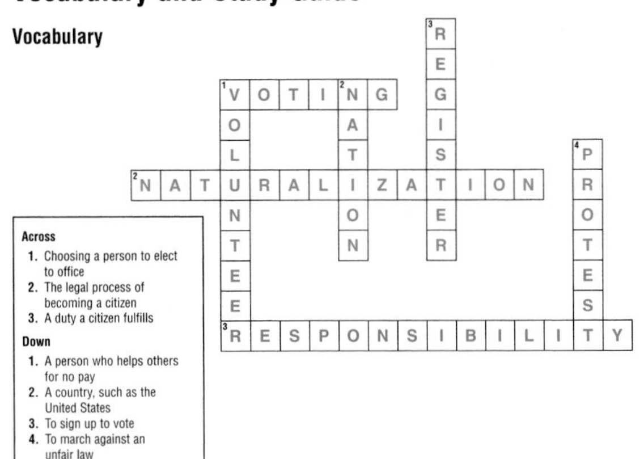

Across
1. Choosing a person to elect to office
2. The legal process of becoming a citizen
3. A duty a citizen fulfills

Down
1. A person who helps others for no pay
2. A country, such as the United States
3. To sign up to vote
4. To march against an unfair law

Study Guide

Read "Citizenship." Then fill in the chart below to explain when these three groups gained full citizenship and the right to vote.

African Americans	Women	American Indians
5. Gained citizenship and the right to vote after the Civil War	Gained right to vote in 1920	6. Gained citizenship and the right to vote in 1924

Read "Responsibilities of Citizens." Then fill in the effect in the chart below.

Cause	Effect
Organizations in Georgia need computers.	7. Free Bytes fixes old computers and donates them.

Unit Resources

 150 Use with *United States History*, pp. 540–543

also in *Practice Book*, p. 89

Chapter 15 Assessment Options

Chapter 15 Test

Chapter 15 Test

Test Your Knowledge

suffragist	prejudice	nonviolent protest	responsibility

Fill in the blank with the correct word from the box.

1. Martin Luther King Jr. believed that nonviolent protest was the best way to bring change in the civil rights movement. Obj. U7–11
2. The NAACP worked to change laws that showed prejudice against African Americans. Obj. U7–10
3. Susan B. Anthony was a suffragist and leader of the women's movement. Obj. U7–9
4. In a democracy, it is the responsibility of citizens to create an orderly society. Obj. U7–15

Circle the letter of the best answer.

5. Which of the following is an important responsibility of U.S. citizens? Obj. U7–15
   - A. to work for the government
   - B. to help lawmakers win votes
   - C. to send letters to lawmakers
   - (D.) to serve on juries
6. What does the process of naturalization do? Obj. U7–14
   - F. helps people born in the United States become citizens
   - (G.) helps immigrants become citizens
   - H. helps women keep the right to vote
   - J. helps immigrants get and keep good jobs
7. Which group did the Farm Workers Association help? Obj. U7–12
   - (A.) migrant workers
   - B. teachers
   - C. construction workers
   - D. factory workers
8. What was the main goal of the NAACP? Obj. U7–11
   - F. to help migrant workers obtain better conditions
   - G. to fight for equal rights for women
   - H. to fight against discrimination of people with disabilities
   - (J.) to get equal rights for African Americans

Chapter 15 Test

Apply Your Knowledge

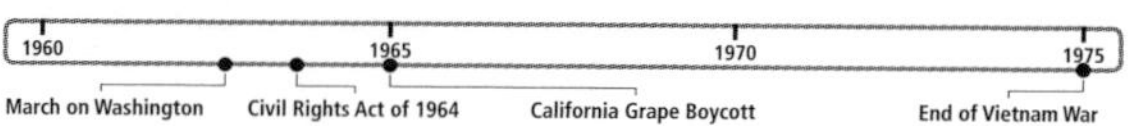

Use the timeline to answer the following questions.

9. What does the timeline show about the March on Washington and the Civil Rights Act of 1964? Obj. U7–12
   - A. The March on Washington celebrated the Civil Rights Act.
   - B. Lawmakers who passed the Civil Rights Act held the March on Washington.
   - (C.) The Civil Rights Act was passed after the March on Washington.
   - D. The Civil Rights Act was passed before the March on Washington.
10. Why might 1965 have been a good time for the California Grape Boycott? Obj. U7–12
    - (F.) Americans had become more aware of civil rights after the Civil Rights Act.
    - G. It was a good year for grapes and other crops to grow in California.
    - H. Americans were eating more grapes.
    - J. Big farm companies had made changes for their workers.

Apply the Reading Skill: Sequence

Read the paragraph below. Then answer the question. Obj. U7–12

> In the 1960s, American Indian groups began to speak out about their civil rights. The American Indian Movement asked that the U.S. government return lands that their ancestors had lived on. American Indians also held protests. Eventually, the United States returned some land in New Mexico and Alaska.

11. What two things happened before the United States returned land to the American Indians?
    The American Indian Movement asked the United States government to return lands and American Indians held protests.

Chapter 15 Test

Test the Skill: Resolve Conflicts

> In 1973, about 200 members of the American Indian Movement took over the village of Wounded Knee, South Dakota. They said they would not leave until the U.S. government looked into the treatment of American Indians. American Indians wanted more participation in deciding how they were governed. After 71 days, the government promised to consider the demands of the American Indian Movement.
>
> The United States government came up with a compromise. It returned land to many tribes. The Indian Self-Determination Act of 1975 allowed the American Indian governments to run their own health, education, and housing programs.

12. What was the American Indian Movement saying by taking over Wounded Knee? Obj. U7–13 By taking over Wounded Knee, the American Indians told the U.S. government they did not like how they were treated.
13. Describe the conflict between the American Indian Movement and the U.S. government. Obj. U7–13 Sample answer: Members of the American Indian Movement would not leave Wounded Knee until the government promised to consider their demands.
14. How did the government compromise with the American Indians? Obj. U7–13 The government compromised by letting the American Indians be in charge of their own health, education, and housing programs.

Apply the Skill

15. Compare the compromise that led to the Indian Self-Determination Act of 1975 to the compromise that led to the Civil Rights Act of 1964. How were they similar? Obj. U7–13
    Sample answer: In both cases, the government compromised to protect the rights of more people; American Indians were given power to make decisions for themselves; African Americans were given equal protection of their rights under law.

Chapter 15 Test

Think and Write

16. **Short Response:** What is women's suffrage and what law finally recognized women's right to vote? Obj. U7–9
    Women's suffrage is the right for *women* to vote. The Nineteenth Amendment to the Constitution gave women the right to vote in 1919.
17. **Critical Thinking: Synthesize** How did the Civil Rights Act and the Indian Civil Rights Act change the United States? Obj. U7–12
    Sample answer: The two acts extended full citizenship and all the rights and responsibilities to all citizens. This made the United States a more complete democracy.
18. **Extended Response:** Write a journal entry about what rights U.S. citizens have that are important to you. Think about rights that people living in other countries may not have. Write your journal entry on a separate sheet of paper. Obj. U7–14 **Journal entries should refer to rights of United States citizens, such as the right to vote and hold political office; should not confuse rights of U.S. citizens with responsibilities.**

Self-Assessment

Although I cannot yet vote, how can I be a responsible citizen of the United States?

You can share the following fiction selection with students before beginning the chapter.

Activate Prior Knowledge

Ask students if they know who Cesar Chavez was. Explain that until Cesar Chavez and his coworkers organized a union, migrant farm workers did not have basic rights such as decent pay and health care.

Preview the Chapter

Have students skim the section Migrant Workers on page 534. Ask them how the portrait of Cesar Chavez in the Read-Aloud selection compares to the information about him in this section.

Read-Aloud Vocabulary

Explain that **migrant workers** are people who move from place to place to find work, and that many work on farms. Ask students to define **civil rights** in their own words.

Preview the Reading Strategy

Summarize Explain to students that the reading strategy they will use in this chapter is summarizing, or putting something in their own words. You may wish to use the Read Aloud to model summarizing for your students.

Think Aloud *Benny and his mother are on a bus, struggling with a lot of grocery bags. A man gives Benny's mother a seat, and she gets tears in her eyes. Benny wonders why and finds out that the man is Cesar Chavez, who fought for the civil rights of migrant workers. Mr. Chavez smiles at Benny, and Benny feels as if something special has happened.*

Benny and Cesar

Benny and his mother climbed onto the bus, struggling with their grocery bags. As they stumbled down the aisle, a man with graying hair stood and offered them his seat.

"Oh no," Benny's mother protested, "I could not take your seat." But the man insisted. He stood aside, and she sat down. As Benny piled his grocery bags around his mother's feet, he noticed that she had tears in her eyes.

"Mom!" he said. "All he did was give you a place to sit."

Benny's mother had a proud look on her face. "Do you know who that man is?" she asked.

"No," said Benny.

"That man is Cesar Chavez," she said. "He has spent his life giving to others, and he is still giving."

Benny turned and looked more closely at the man. Benny had family members who were **migrant workers,** and he had heard a lot about Cesar Chavez. He never imagined that he would meet him on a bus.

As the bus started moving, Benny kept his eyes on the man who had fought so hard for the **civil rights** of others. Mr. Chavez was standing quietly, reading a book. He glanced up and caught Benny's eye. He smiled and nodded, and Benny smiled and nodded back. He felt a glow inside, as if he had been touched by something special.

Begin the Chapter

Quick Look

Core Lesson 1 focuses on movements for rights for women and African Americans between 1880 and 1920.

Core Lesson 2 explores civil rights movements between 1940 and 2000.

Core Lesson 3 describes the rights and responsibilities of U.S. citizens.

Vocabulary Preview

Use the vocabulary card to preview the key vocabulary words before starting the lessons and to prepare students to understand the content of the chapter.

Vocabulary Strategy

Vocabulary strategies for this chapter:

- Structural analysis, pp. 524, 530
- Word roots, p. 538
- Prefixes and suffixes, pp. 524, 530
- Word origins, p. 538

Vocabulary Help

Vocabulary card for activist Explain how the suffix *-ist* describes someone who takes an action or holds a belief. An activist is a person who acts for a specific cause or purpose.

Vocabulary card for nonviolent protest The American Indian Movement used nonviolent protest to reach its goals. Violent is the adjective form of the word *violence,* and the prefix *non-* means "the opposite of."

Chapter 15 The Promise of America

Technology

e • glossary

e • word games

www.eduplace.com/kids/hmss05/

Vocabulary Preview

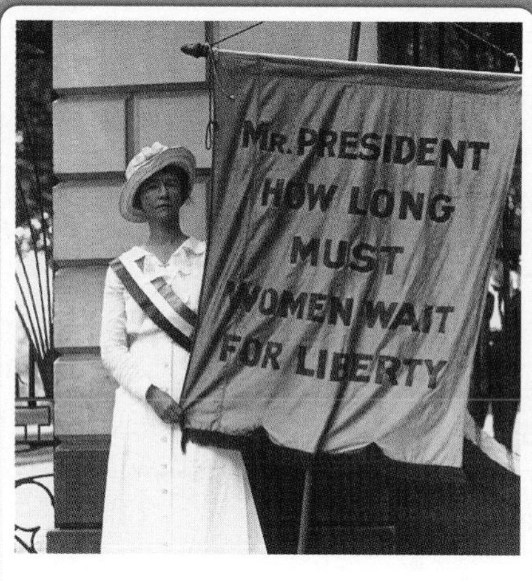

activist

A woman who fought for her right to vote was an **activist.** She might march, carry a banner, and sign petitions for this cause. **page 526**

civil rights

Dr. Martin Luther King Jr. was a leader in the fight for the **civil rights** of African Americans. These rights and freedoms are guaranteed to all citizens. **page 530**

Chapter Timeline

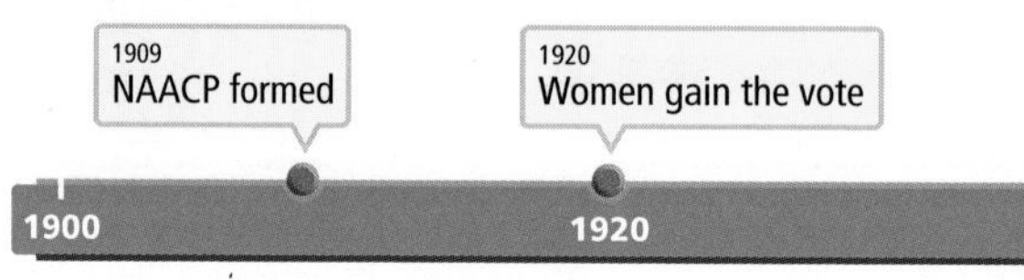

Background

Civil Rights and Criminal Rights

- Civil rights and criminal rights are related but not the same. Civil rights include freedom of speech, the right to equality in public places, and the right to vote. Discrimination violates a person's civil rights.
- Criminal rights include the right to privacy, the right to a trial by jury, and the right of people not to say things that might incriminate them. Civil rights and criminal rights are protected in different amendments of the Constitution.

Vocabulary

Use the word web graphic organizer to discuss the term *responsibility*. Write the word responsibility in the center oval. Then ask students to suggest things for which they have responsibility. Add their suggestions to surrounding ovals.

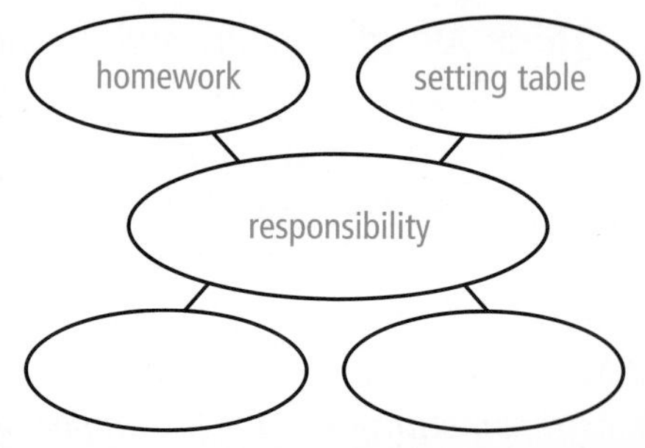

Summarize As you read, use this strategy to focus on important ideas.

Reread sections and put them in your own words.

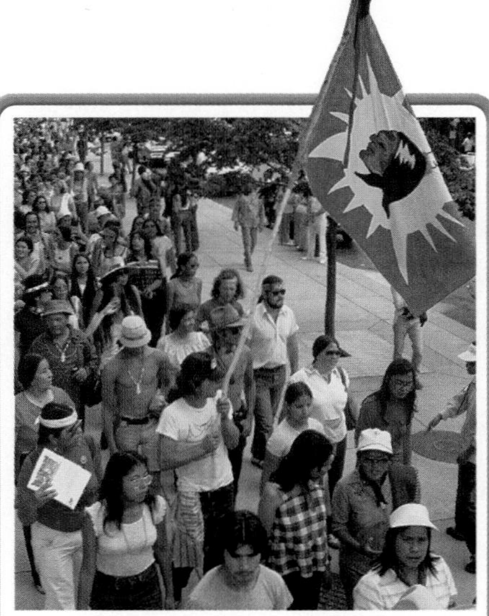

nonviolent protest

American Indians marched with flags to draw attention to injustices they faced. These marches were a form of **nonviolent protest.** page 531

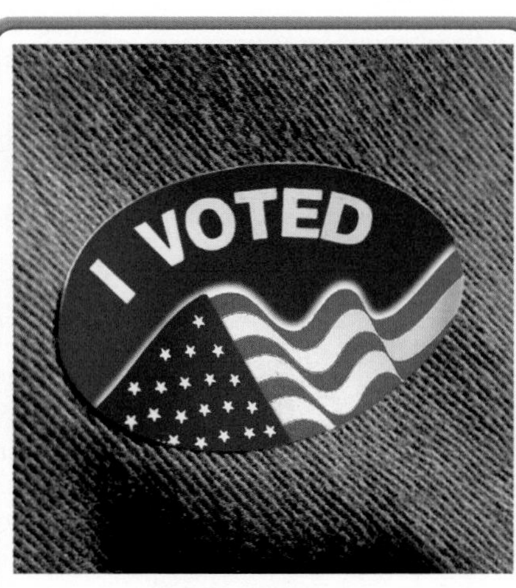

responsibility

People in the United States have many rights. They also have **responsibilities** to their country. One of these duties is to vote in elections. page 541

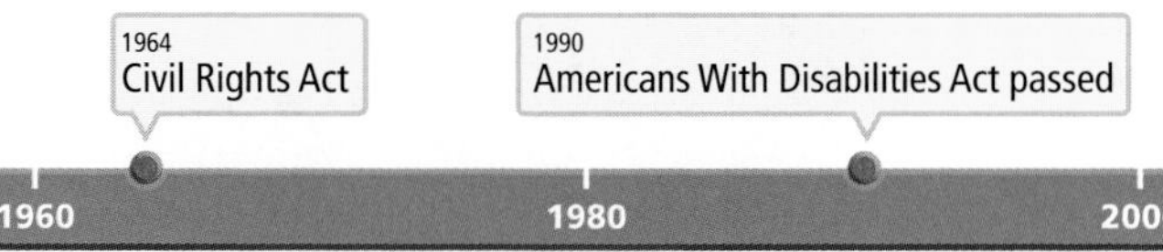

Leveled Practice

Extra Support

Have students make flash cards. Have them write the vocabulary word on one side and the definition on the other side. Have them quiz one another. Verbal-linguistic

Challenge

Have students make a list of questions they might want to ask Susan B. Anthony about her life as an activist.

ELL

All Proficiency Levels

- Have students make a list of things an activist might want to do, such as protect the environment. Have them act out some of the items on their lists to see if a partner can guess them.

Bodily-kinesthetic

Using the Timeline

Have students discuss how the events on the timeline on page 522 and 523 show progress over time. Point out the abbreviations and explain them.

Ask students if the events on the timeline are connected, and in what way. Write their responses on the board. Use the opportunity to see if they have any misconceptions about the material.

Reading Strategy: Summarize

To summarize, a reader identifies and pulls together the essential information in a longer text passage and restates that information in a condensed fashion.

Explain to students that to summarize successfully, they should follow these steps:

- Read the passage twice.
- Think about what the passage says.
- Ask yourself: What is the main topic this passage is describing?
- Find the main point of the passage. Note it down (or underline it).
- Find details that support the main point.
- Use your own words to tell what the passage means.
- Look back at the passage to check if your summary is accurate.

Students can practice this reading strategy throughout this chapter, including on their workbook Skill and Strategy pages.

Tested Objectives

U7-9 History Describe how women won recognition of their right to vote.

U7-10 History Describe how the NAACP worked for African Americans' rights in the early 20th century.

Lesson Quick Look

This lesson focuses on the women's rights movement and the African American rights movement, from the late 1800s through the early 1900s.

Teaching Option: Extend Lesson 1 features a timeline of the women's rights movement.

1 Get Set to Read

Preview Direct students' attention to the timeline and to the lesson headings on pages 524 and 526. Ask, *Which rights do you think women and African Americans were fighting for at this time?*

Reading Skill: Sequence of Events Important events include Jeannette Rankin's election in 1917 and passage of the Nineteenth Amendment in 1919.

Build on What You Know Ask students what they know about the First Amendment (free speech, freedom of religion, peaceful assembly). Ask them to share stories they've seen and heard about people exercising their First Amendment rights.

Vocabulary

suffragist *noun,* one who works to achieve the right to vote

prejudice *noun,* a judgment or opinion formed without knowledge or examination of all the facts

activist *noun,* one who believes in assertive, often militant action, such as demonstrations or strikes, as a means of opposing or supporting a cause.

Core Lesson 1

The Struggle for Equality

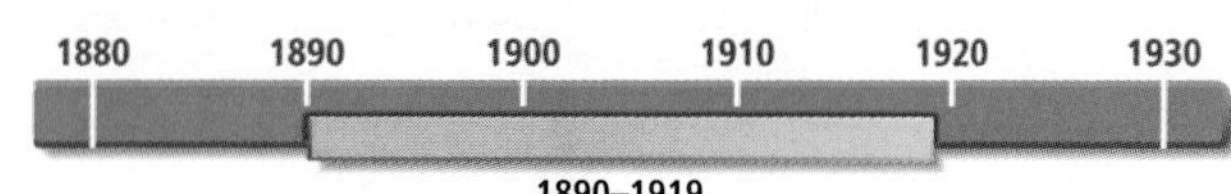

VOCABULARY

suffragist
prejudice
activist

Vocabulary Strategy

prejudice

The prefix **pre-** means "before." A **prejudice** is a prejudgment, or a judgment made before you know all the facts.

READING SKILL

Sequence As you read, list important events of the women's rights movement before World War I.

1	
2	
3	
4	

Build on What You Know The Constitution and the Bill of Rights promise democracy and freedom to all. In the early 1900s, women, African Americans, and others worked hard to make that promise a reality.

The Fight for Women's Rights

Main Idea Susan B. Anthony led a national women's rights movement.

In the 1800s, women in the United States were not guaranteed all of the same rights that men had. Women could not vote in most state or national elections. Often they could not own property, go to college, or hold certain jobs. Women began joining together to fix these inequalities. A women's rights movement was born. 1

One of the leaders of this movement was **Susan B. Anthony.** She and other women worked to improve laws that affected married women, mothers, and working women across America.

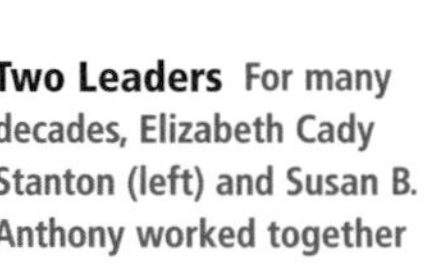

Two Leaders For many decades, Elizabeth Cady Stanton (left) and Susan B. Anthony worked together for women's rights.

Skill and Strategy

Reading Skill and Strategy

Reading Skill: Sequence

This skill helps you understand the order in which events happened.

Read "African American Rights." Then fill in the sequence chart below to show the order in which African Americans won their rights.

1.	African Americans gained the right to vote after the Civil War.
2.	Southern states passed laws to prevent African Americans from voting.
3.	W.E.B. Du Bois and other leaders started the NAACP.
4.	The NAACP fights for equality in voting, education, and justice.

Reading Strategy: Summary

5. Read "The Fight for Women's Rights." Then check the best summary.
   - ✓ A movement for women's suffrage earned women the right to vote.
   - ___ Women could not run for national or state offices and often could not go to college.
   - ___ Jeannette Rankin became the first woman to be elected to the House of Representatives.
6. Read "African American Rights." Then check the best summary.
   - ___ Many people in southern states were prejudiced against African Americans.
   - ___ NAACP leaders held large meetings to discuss the rights of African Americans.
   - ✓ Leaders such as W.E.B. Du Bois created a movement to improve the civil rights of African Americans.

Unit Resources

144
Use with *United States History*, pp. 524–527

Unit Resources, p. 144

Background

Susan B. Anthony

- In 1872, Anthony went to the New York polls with 12 other women and persuaded election officials to let them vote. All 15 were eventually arrested.
- At Anthony's trial, the judge discharged the jury and fined her $100 without even bothering to hear the case.

Suffragists People from all over the country began holding protests in the early 1900s. Here, women and children prepare for a protest on Long Island, New York.

Women's Suffrage

The women's movement fought hard for women's suffrage. In 1888, Susan B. Anthony said, "What is this little thing that we are asking for? It seems so little; it is yet everything." She believed that both men and women should vote in a democracy.

In 1890, several groups joined together to form the National American Woman Suffrage Association (NAWSA). **Elizabeth Cady Stanton,** a friend of Anthony, was its first president. To gain
 support, NAWSA members held meetings and made speeches in Congress. By the end of the century, the NAWSA was a powerful organization with members from all over the country.

Many people at the time did not like the idea of women voting. Sometimes angry mobs attacked the suffragists. A **suffragist** was a person who worked for the right to vote. The suffragists did not give up. They continued to spread their message.

By the early 1900s, a few states recognized women's right to vote in state elections. Some women were elected to state legislatures. In 1917, Jeannette Rankin of Montana became the first female member of the United States House of Representatives. 

REVIEW What were some of the inequalities the women's movement wanted to correct? Many could not hold certain jobs, vote, own property, or go to college.

2 Teach

The Fight for Women's Rights

Talk About It

1 **Q History** Who was Susan B. Anthony?
A She was a leader of the women's rights movement.

2 **Q History** What did NAWSA do to fix inequalities between men and women?
A They fought for the right to vote by holding meetings and by making speeches in Congress.

3 **Q History** Who was Jeannette Rankin?
A She was the first female member of the U.S. House of Representatives.

Vocabulary Strategy

suffragist Remind students that the suffix *-ist* can mean someone who supports a point of view. A suffragist supports *suffrage*, or the right to vote.

Reading Strategy: Summarize Explain to students that a summary is always shorter than the original text. Summarize the first paragraph of the lesson.

Think Aloud *To summarize the paragraph, I'll read it first. Then I'll try to find the main idea. In this paragraph, the main idea is that women weren't allowed to do things that men could do in the 1800s. I could also add a few more important details, however. My summary might be something like this: By the late 1800s, women grew tired of being treated unfairly and began fighting for the right to vote, buy homes, attend college, and work in business.*

Reaching All Learners: Leveled Practice

Extra Support

Have partners start a **word web** with "The Fight for Women's Rights" in the center. Tell them to fill the web with words and phrases from the lesson that are associated with this struggle. Verbal-linguistic

Challenge

Have partners **play a guessing game.** Each student should select one person, law, or event from the lesson and give hints about it until the second student can guess what is being described. Verbal-linguistic

Reaching All Learners: ELL

Beginning

Ask students to **discuss** whether they think men and women have equal rights today, either in the United States or in other countries they have lived in. Remind students to be respectful as they discuss other countries and cultures.

Verbal-linguistic

The Fight for Women's Rights *continued*

Talk About It

4 **Q History** What right did the Nineteenth Amendment guarantee women?

A the right to vote

African American Rights

Talk About It

5 **Q History** Who was W.E.B. Du Bois?

A He was an African American scholar, writer, and activist.

6 **Q History** What were some of the methods the NAACP used to meet its goals?

A Leaders spoke with members of Congress, wrote articles, led meetings and marches, and made speeches.

Critical Thinking

Compare and Contrast In what ways were women viewed differently in America before and after World War I?

The Nineteenth Amendment

The events of World War I helped the women's movement. When the United States entered World War I, women stepped in to fill the jobs of men who went to fight in the war. Women proved that they could do the jobs as well as men. Their work during the war, combined with the NAWSA's marches and speeches, convinced many people that women's right to vote should be protected by law.

By 1918, fifteen states recognized women's right to vote in state elections. Pressure was building in Congress for a national law on women's suffrage. In
4 1919, the Senate passed the Nineteenth Amendment to the Constitution. The states approved it in 1920, which meant that women could finally vote throughout the United States.

African American Rights

Main Idea W.E.B. Du Bois helped create the first national civil rights movement for African Americans.

The Fifteenth Amendment was supposed to protect the right of African American men to vote. Most southern states, however, had laws that prevented them from voting. These laws were passed because of prejudice against African Americans. **Prejudice** is an unjust negative opinion about a group of people. Prejudice against African Americans prevented them from using the rights they were guaranteed under the Constitution.

One leader who worked to improve
conditions for African Americans was 5
W.E.B. Du Bois (doo BOYS). He was an African American scholar, writer, and activist. An **activist** is a person who takes action to change social conditions or laws. Du Bois believed there should be

> **"ceaseless agitation and insistent demand for equality."**

The NAACP

In 1909, Du Bois and other black activists founded the National Association for the Advancement of Colored People, or NAACP. The NAACP's main goal was to get equal opportunity for African Americans. The members of the NAACP wanted to change laws that discriminated against African Americans in voting, education, and the legal system.

W. E. B. Du Bois From 1900 to the 1950s, Du Bois was involved in every major African American movement. He wrote 21 books and more than 100 major articles.

Drama

Panel Discussion

Have students hold a panel discussion. Assign students to argue the points of view that the following people might have, based on information in the lesson:

- Susan B. Anthony
- a woman who worked in a factory during World War I
- a senator working to pass the 19th Amendment.
- You may act as moderator or choose a student to do so.

Verbal-linguistic

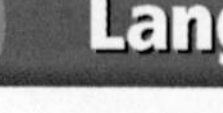

Language Arts

Write an Article

- Remind students that NAACP leaders wrote articles to educate the public about unfair treatment of African Americans.
- Have students write their own articles about this inequality.
- Share articles as a class.

Verbal-linguistic

NAACP In 1919, the NAACP led a silent march in Harlem, New York, to protest violence against African Americans.

6 NAACP leaders used different methods to gain equal treatment for African Americans. They spoke with members of Congress. They wrote articles to educate the public about the unjust treatment of African Americans. They made speeches and called supporters to large meetings and marches.

These early steps were important. They helped advance the equal rights movement for African Americans in the United States.

REVIEW What actions did the NAACP take to reduce inequalities in the United States?
They made speeches, went to court, held marches, wrote articles, and had meetings.

Lesson Summary

- Susan B. Anthony was a leader of the women's suffrage movement.
- The Nineteenth Amendment guaranteed women's right to vote.
- W.E.B. Du Bois and others created the NAACP to fight prejudice toward African Americans.

Why It Matters...

At the end of the 1800s and the beginning of the 1900s, women and African Americans organized to fight for their rights.

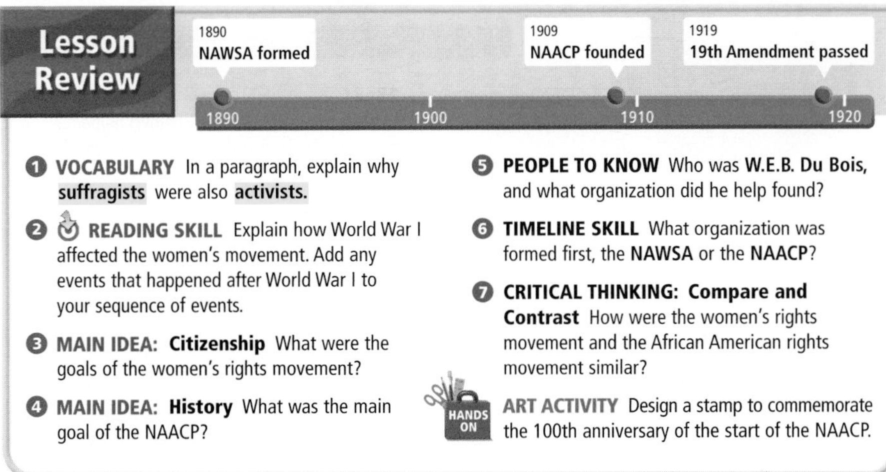

Lesson Review

1. **VOCABULARY** In a paragraph, explain why **suffragists** were also **activists.**
2. **READING SKILL** Explain how World War I affected the women's movement. Add any events that happened after World War I to your sequence of events.
3. **MAIN IDEA: Citizenship** What were the goals of the women's rights movement?
4. **MAIN IDEA: History** What was the main goal of the NAACP?
5. **PEOPLE TO KNOW** Who was **W.E.B. Du Bois,** and what organization did he help found?
6. **TIMELINE SKILL** What organization was formed first, the **NAWSA** or the **NAACP**?
7. **CRITICAL THINKING: Compare and Contrast** How were the women's rights movement and the African American rights movement similar?

HANDS ON **ART ACTIVITY** Design a stamp to commemorate the 100th anniversary of the start of the NAACP.

3 Review/Assess

Review Tested Objectives

U7-9 Women's work during World War I, along with NAWSA's marches and speeches, persuaded many people that women's right to vote should be legally protected. When states approved the Nineteenth Amendment in 1920, women's suffrage became law.

U7-10 The NAACP spoke with members of Congress, wrote articles, made speeches, and organized meetings to fight for equal voting, educational, and legal rights for African Americans.

Lesson Review Answers

1. Suffragists were activists who worked for the right to vote.
2. Women stepped in to fill men's jobs during World War I and proved that they could work as well as men.
3. to win women's right to vote, own property, attend college, and have business careers
4. to gain equality for African Americans
5. He was an African American writer, scholar, and activist; NAACP.
6. NAWSA
7. Both fought for equal treatment, formed organizations to gain support for their causes, made speeches, and talked with members of Congress.

HANDS ON Performance Task Rubric

4	Details shown are significant; picture is accurate; stamp details are all present.
3	Details shown are mostly significant; picture is generally accurate; most stamp details are present.
2	Some details shown are significant; picture contains some errors; few stamp details are present.
1	Details shown are not significant; picture is inaccurate; stamp details are absent.

Study Guide/Homework

Vocabulary and Study Guide

Vocabulary

1. Draw a line connecting the vocabulary word to its meaning.

prejudice	A person who takes action for social change
suffragist	An unfair negative opinion about a group
activist	A person who works for the right to vote

Study Guide

2. Read "The Fight for Women's Rights." Then fill in the outline below.
   I. Main Idea: Women fight for their right to vote
      A. Supporting Idea: The suffrage movement
         1. Detail: The National American Woman Suffrage Association
         2. Detail: Members talk to people and Congress
      B. Supporting Idea: Women gain the right to vote
         1. Detail: Some states allow women to vote
         2. Detail: The Nineteenth Amendment gives voting rights to women
3. Read "African American Rights." Then write two methods the NAACP used to gain equality for African Americans.
   Sample answers: Leaders spoke with Congress, wrote articles to educate the public, and made speeches to large groups.

Unit Resources

145
Use with *United States History*, pp. 524–527

Unit Resources, p. 145

Reteach Minilesson

Use a Venn diagram to reteach the women's rights movement and the African American rights movement.

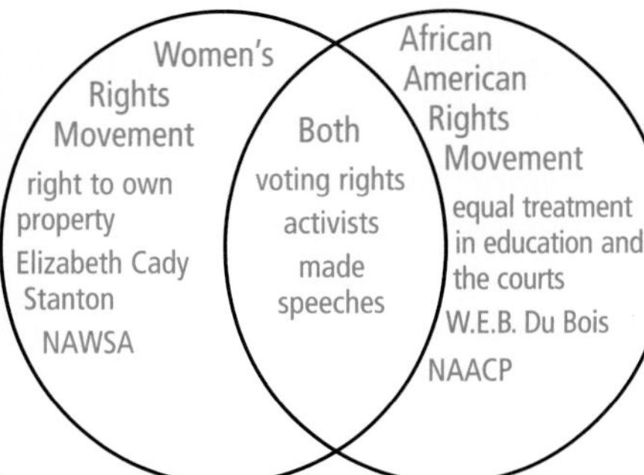

Graphic Organizer 11

Quick Look

Connect to the Core Lesson Students have learned about the struggle for equal rights in the early 1900s. In Extend Lesson 1, students will interpret events on a timeline between 1848 and 1981 to understand more about the important steps toward equal rights for women in American life.

1 Teach the Extend Lesson

Connect to the Big Idea

Democratic Values American democracy embraces certain values, including life, liberty, pursuit of happiness, common good, self-government, justice, equality of opportunity, diversity, honesty, and patriotism. The women's movement has worked to achieve many of these values.

Extend Lesson 1

History

Women's Rights Movement

For much of our history, women's rights were unprotected. In the early 1800s, they were prevented from voting or holding political office. They had far fewer chances than men to get an education. If a woman owned property, it became her husband's when she married.

People's views of women's rights have changed a great deal in the past two hundred years. Today, women vote and hold political offices. They attend college as often as men and work as doctors, lawyers, and business leaders. The changes in women's rights did not come all at once. Look at this timeline to see some of the most important steps in the march toward women's equality in American life.

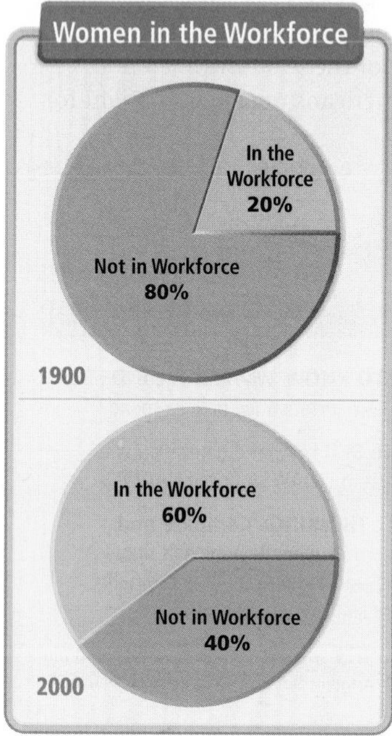

How much did the percentage of women in the workforce grow in the 20th Century?

1848
Elizabeth Cady Stanton (below) helped organize the first women's rights convention held in Seneca Falls, New York.

1878
Lawmakers defeat an amendment giving women the vote. The amendment is reintroduced in every session of Congress until 1919, when it passes.

1890
Thirty-three states protect women's right to keep their own property when they marry.

1840 1880

528 • Chapter 15

Reaching All Learners

Extra Support

Role-Play an Interview

- Have students work in small groups to prepare interview questions for a supporter of the Equal Pay Act. Have students discuss and make notes about answers to the questions based on information in the lesson.
- Then, ask students to role-play a reporter conducting a television interview with the supporter.

Bodily-kinesthetic

On Level

Write a Poem

- Explain that there have been many first steps along the path of change in women's rights. Have students work in small groups to reflect on and discuss the experience of being the first person to achieve a goal.
- Ask students to write a poem honoring someone who worked for women's rights, such as Jeanette Rankin, Sandra Day O'Connor, or the first woman admitted to a military academy.

Verbal-linguistic

Challenge

Give a Presentation

- Ask students to give an oral presentation about Elizabeth Cady Stanton or one of many others who made important contributions to the women's rights movement in the nineteenth century.
- Have students research the life and work of one of these people, including early and adult life, talents, work, and contribution to women's rights.

Verbal-linguistic; bodily-kinesthetic

1963
Betty Friedan (above) writes a book, *The Feminine Mystique*, which helps start the modern women's movement.

1920
The 19th Amendment guarantees equal voting rights for women.

1963
Congress passes the Equal Pay Act, requiring equal pay for men and women doing the same jobs.

1981
Sandra Day O'Connor (above) becomes the first woman appointed to the U.S. Supreme Court.

1920 — 1960 — 2000

1917
Jeanette Rankin (below) of Montana becomes the first woman elected to the U.S. Congress.

1976
U.S. military academies admit women.

HISTORY

Activities

1. **TALK ABOUT IT** If you were helping to pass the 19th Amendment, what would you say to leaders in Congress?
2. **ASK ABOUT IT** Interview a woman you know who remembers an event on this timeline. Ask why the event was important and what details she remembers. Write a one-page report of the interview.

529

2 Leveled Activities

❶ **Talk About It** *For Extra Support*
Students' answers should reflect an understanding that in the early 1800s, American women had few rights. They could not vote, hold public office, or own property if they married; and women had fewer chances than men to attend college.

❷ **Ask About It** *For Challenge*

Writing Rubric

4	Report includes main idea and details; is well organized; spelling, grammar, and punctuation are correct.
3	Report includes main idea and most details; is organized; spelling, grammar, and punctuation are mostly correct.
2	Report includes main idea and some details; is somewhat organized; some errors in spelling, grammar, and punctuation are present.
1	Report does not include main idea or details; is disorganized; many errors in spelling, grammar, and punctuation are present.

ELL

Intermediate/Advanced

- Have students work in pairs to **brainstorm a list** of 20 to 25 words related to the Extend topic.
- Ask partners to **sort** the words into smaller groups of words that go together for a reason. Then have students **label** the smaller lists.
- Have partners share their lists and labels with other student pairs, explaining their reasoning for categories and labels.

Verbal-linguistic

Art

Interpret Through Drawing

- Discuss with students some of their reactions to reading about events on the timeline.
- Have each student select an event on the timeline and create a drawing or cartoon to express a response to it.
- Have students reconstruct the timeline in the classroom using the drawings and date labels.

Visual-spatial

Graphic Organizer

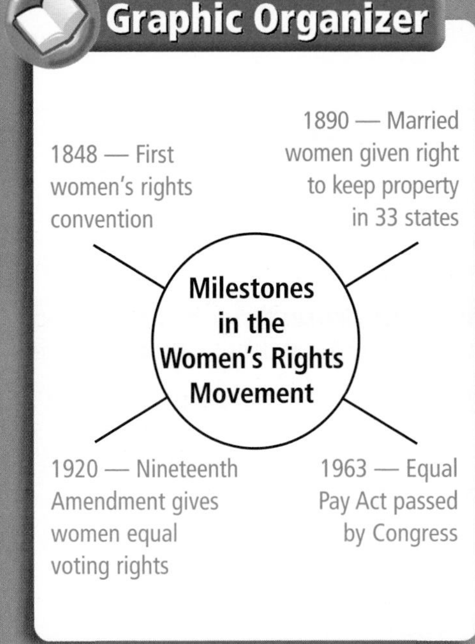

Graphic Organizer 7

Tested Objectives

U7-11 History Explain how African Americans won recognition of their civil rights in the 1950s and 1960s.

U7-12 Citizenship Identify the achievements of the following groups who worked for equal rights in the late twentieth century: women, American Indians, migrant workers, people with disabilities.

Quick Look

This lesson focuses on the fight for civil rights by African Americans, women, American Indians, migrant workers, and people with disabilities.

Teaching Option: Extend Lesson 2 presents biographies of Cesar Chavez and Dolores Huerta.

1 Get Set to Read

Preview Compare this lesson title with the title of the previous lesson. Whose struggles do you think this lesson will continue to describe?

Reading Skill: Predict Outcomes Predictions will vary, but students might consider the civil rights that Americans enjoy today.

Build on What You Know Ask students about how they have worked as part of a group to reach a goal.

Vocabulary

civil rights *noun,* the right to fair and equal treatment, guaranteed by the Constitution

nonviolent protest *noun,* a method of bringing change without using violence

migrant worker *noun,* a person who moves from place to place looking for work, particularly farm work

Core Lesson 2

The Struggle Continues

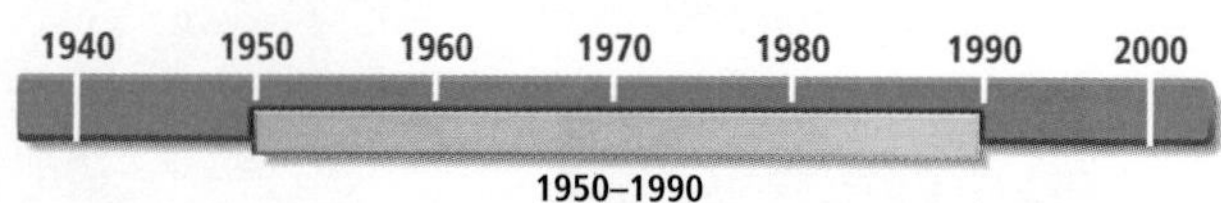

VOCABULARY

civil rights
nonviolent protest
migrant worker

Vocabulary Strategy

nonviolent protest

The prefix **non-** means "not" or "without." **Nonviolent protest** means protest without violence.

READING SKILL

Predict Outcomes Predict what you think will be the outcome of the struggle for rights by different groups.

PREDICTION

OUTCOME

Build on What You Know Sometimes, when you want to reach a goal, it helps to work with others. In the 1950s, 1960s, and 1970s, groups of people worked together to protect their rights.

The Civil Rights Movement

Main Idea Using court cases and protests, African Americans won greater recognition of their rights.

Throughout the first half of the 1900s, the U.S. government did not protect many of the civil rights of African Americans. **Civil rights** are rights and freedoms people have because they are citizens of a country. In the 1950s, African Americans and other ethnic groups made more progress. They began going to court to change laws that did not treat them the same as other citizens.

In 1954, the NAACP won a case in the Supreme Court called *Brown v. Board of Education of Topeka*. The Supreme Court said that laws allowing separate public schools for blacks and whites were not legal. The court case made segregation of public schools illegal. Segregation is the separation of people by racial or ethnic group. *Brown v. Board of Education* was the first of many important civil rights victories for African Americans and other groups in the 1950s. 1

Skill and Strategy

Reading Skill and Strategy

Reading Skill: Predict Outcomes

This skill allows you to think about what might happen, based on what you have read.

Read "The Civil Rights Movement." Make a prediction about the effects of the civil rights movement. Then read "Civil Rights for All." Write the actual outcome.

Prediction 1. Sample answer: Other ethnic groups enjoyed the new freedoms for which African Americans fought.

Outcome 2. Sample answer: Many other groups were inspired to protect their civil rights.

Reading Strategy: Summary

3. Read "The Civil Rights Movement." Then check the best summary.

___ In the early 1950s, African American and white children went to different schools.

___ Rosa Parks was arrested when she would not give up her seat on the bus.

✓ African Americans used protests and the courts to protect their civil rights.

4. Read "Civil Rights for All." Then write a brief summary.

The victories of African Americans showed other groups how to fight for their civil rights during the 1960s and 1970s.

Unit Resources

146
Use with *United States History*, pp. 530–535

Unit Resources, p. 146

Background

Voting Rights

- A 1963 march was held in Selma, Alabama to protest courthouse officials' refusal to register African Americans to vote.
- The Voting Rights Act of 1965 was passed by Congress about six months later.

March on Washington
On August 28, 1963, King (second from right) and others led this march. They protested job discrimination and prejudice toward African Americans.

Martin Luther King Jr.

In Montgomery, Alabama, buses were segregated. City law said that African Americans had to sit in their own section, usually at the back of the bus. In 1955, an African American woman named **Rosa Parks** refused to give up her seat at the front of a crowded bus and go to the back. The police arrested Parks.

Members of Parks's church organized
2 a protest. They asked everyone in the city of Montgomery to boycott the buses. A young minister named **Martin Luther King Jr.** helped lead the boycott. He inspired people with his strong faith, courage, and powerful speeches.

King believed in nonviolent protest. **Nonviolent protest** is a way of bringing change without using violence. In late 1956, the Supreme Court ruled that segragation on buses was illegal.

In 1963, Martin Luther King Jr. and other black leaders organized a march in Washington, D.C., to protest unequal protection of civil rights. Over 200,000 people marched on the nation's capital.

King gave his most famous speech at the march. He said,

> **“I have a dream that my four little children will one day live in a nation where they will not be judged by the color of their skin, but by the content of their character.”** 3

Martin Luther King Jr.'s "I Have a Dream" speech and the March on Washington caused more Americans to pay attention to the civil rights movement.

In 1964, Congress passed The Civil Rights Act. This law banned segregation in schools, work places, and public places such as restaurants and theaters. A year later, Congress passed the Voting Rights Act of 1965 to prevent discrimination in voting.

Great progress was made in the 1960s, but the decade did not end the struggle for equal rights. African Americans and other groups continued to work to end discrimination and use all their civil rights.

REVIEW What was Rosa Parks's role in the civil rights movement? Her actions started a boycott, which led to the courts saying that segregation on buses was illegal.

531

2 Teach

The Civil Rights Movement

Talk About It

1 **Q History** What big victory did the NAACP achieve in 1954? Why was this victory important?
A won *Brown v. Board of Education of Topeka* case in Supreme Court; it made segregation in public schools illegal

2 **Q History** Who helped lead the bus boycott in Montgomery, Alabama?
A Martin Luther King Jr.

3 **Q History** What does the quote from King's speech tell you about race relations in the United States in 1963?
A There was still much prejudice against African Americans.

Vocabulary Strategy

civil rights The words *civil, civic, civilian, civility,* and *civilization* all come from the Latin word that means "citizen."

nonviolent protest Synonyms for *nonviolent* are *peaceful* or *orderly.*

Reading Strategy: Summarize Ask students to read the excerpt from Martin Luther King Jr.'s famous speech. With students' help, edit the quotation to make it shorter without changing its meaning. Remind students that a summary of text is always shorter than the original text.

Leveled Practice

Extra Support

Have students find one phrase in each paragraph that best describes what that paragraph is about. Then have students **outline** the lesson using these phrases. Visual-spatial; verbal-linguistic

Challenge

Have students **interview** someone who lived during the civil rights movement about what it was like. Ask students to share what they learn with the class.
Verbal-linguistic

ELL

Intermediate/Advanced

- Remind students that Martin Luther King Jr. was an important leader. Tell each student to **describe** for the group a leader from his or her country of origin. Challenge students to explain that person's importance.

Verbal-linguistic

The Growth of Civil Rights

Talk About It

4 **Q History** What did the National Organization for Women do?

A worked for women's rights and to pass the Equal Rights Amendment

5 **Q Citizenship** What victories did the women's rights movement achieve in the 1970s and 1980s?

A more women in state legislatures; many states adopted laws guaranteeing equal pay for equal work

Vocabulary Strategy

discrimination Antonyms include *open-mindedness, tolerance,* and *fairness.*

Critical Thinking

Compare and Contrast How do you think women's lives would have been different if Congress had passed the Equal Rights Amendment?

Think Aloud *I learned that NOW proposed the amendment in the late 1960s and that by 1988 most states had passed laws requiring equal pay for men and women. I think women would have earned equal pay and been treated fairly in the workplace a lot sooner if a federal amendment had passed in the sixties.*

Civil Rights for All

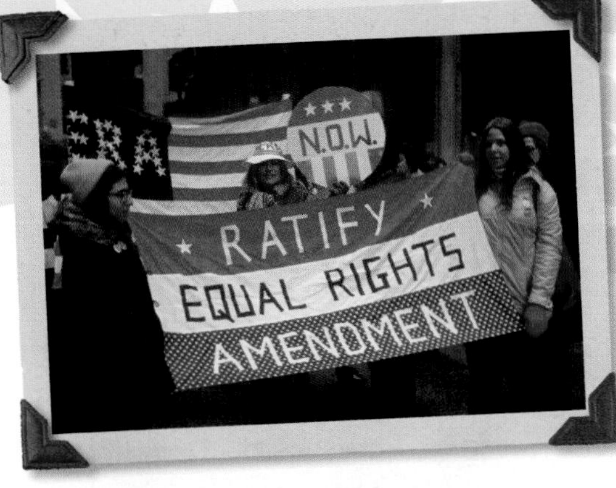

The ERA Supporters used marches, fundraisers, posters, petitions, and nonviolent protest to fight for the amendment.

Ellen Ochoa Ochoa grew up near Los Angeles, California. In 1991, she became the first Hispanic female astronaut.

The Growth of Civil Rights

Main Idea The advances of African Americans inspired other groups to fight for their rights.

Women won the right to vote in 1920. In the 1960s, however, women were still not treated as equal to men. For example, men were usually paid more than women for doing the same kind of work. Some businesses gave jobs to men instead of women, even though women were as skilled as the men.

As **Susan B. Anthony** and many others had done, women began speaking out. They wrote books with strong views about the importance of women's rights. A writer named **Betty Friedan** became a leader of a new women's rights movement.

Friedan and other women started the National Organization for Women (NOW) 4
in 1966 to fight for women's rights. The members of NOW tried to pass an amendment to the Constitution. The amendment would guarantee equal rights for women. It was called the Equal Rights Amendment (ERA).

Although the ERA failed to pass, the women's movement changed many lives in the United States. The number of women serving in state legislatures
doubled between 1975 and 1988. By the 5
late 1980s, 40 out of 50 states had laws requiring equal pay for men and women doing the same kind of work. More women have also become leaders in business, the arts, politics, and science.

532 • Chapter 15

Language Arts

Write a Play

- Use information from the lesson to write a short play about what happened to Rosa Parks in 1955.
- **Choose characters:** Include Rosa Parks and the man who demanded her seat. Consider adding the driver, other passengers, and the police officer.
- **Write the scene:** Use *dialogue* to tell what happened. Add *stage directions* that tell how characters sounded, how they spoke, and what they did.

Verbal-linguistic

Math

Make a Bar Graph

- Have students plot on a bar graph these voter registration rates for African Americans:

	1965	1988
Alabama	19.3%	68.4%
Louisiana	31.6%	77.1%
Mississippi	6.7%	74.2%

- Then, have students describe what has happened to African American voter registration rates since the passage of the Voting Rights Act.

Logical-mathematical

The Longest Walk In 1978, supporters of American Indian rights marched from California to Washington, D.C.

Ben Nighthorse Campbell A U.S. Senator from Colorado, Campbell is also a chief of the Northern Cheyenne Tribe.

Rights for American Indians

American Indians also had a difficult time having their civil rights recognized. They could not live on many of the lands that their ancestors had lived on. In the 1960s, American Indian groups began to organize and speak out. One group, called
6 the American Indian Movement, asked that the United States government return lands taken from American Indians in the past.

Just as African Americans and women had done, American Indians held protests. Sometimes they took over the land they wanted back and refused to leave, even though they risked going to jail.

In 1969, almost 100 American Indians took over the Island of Alcatraz in San Francisco Bay. They stayed for almost 18 months, demanding that land be given back to American Indian nations.

Eventually, some of these protests succeeded. The United States government returned land in New Mexico to the Taos Pueblo Indians. They also returned land 7
in Alaska to native Alaskans and land in Washington State to the Yakima Indians.

In 1968, the Indian Civil Rights Act was passed. This law stated that the governments of American Indian nations must guarantee most of the civil rights that the United States Constitution guarantees to all citizens. The Act created an Indian Bill of Rights to protect freedom of speech, of the press, and of religion.

REVIEW What was the Indian Civil Rights Act? It was a law that said American Indian governments must guarantee most of the rights guaranteed by the Constitution.

533

Extra Support

Prepare a Press Conference

- Ask students to choose one person from the lesson whom they would want to interview.
- Have students write questions they would like to ask the person about his or her experiences fighting for civil rights.
- Students can try to figure out how the person might answer, based on information in the lesson.

Verbal-linguistic

Challenge

Memorize a Speech

- Refer students to Martin Luther King Jr.'s "I Have a Dream" speech, on page R31.
- Have students use library or Internet resources to find the entire speech.
- Ask students to choose part of the speech—at least one paragraph—that they find meaningful and memorize it.
- Students can practice and then recite their passages for the class.

Verbal-linguistic

The Growth of Civil Rights *continued*

Talk About It

6 **Q History** What victories did American Indians win in the 1960s?

A The United States government returned some land to American Indian nations.

7 **Q History** What did the Indian Civil Rights Act do?

A It stated that American Indian nations' governments had to guarantee many civil rights to their citizens.

Reading Strategy: Summarize With students, write a summary of the section Rights for American Indians. Remind them to look for the main ideas in the text.

The Growth of Civil Rights *continued*

Talk About It

8 **Q Economics** Why were most migrant workers poor?

A Big farms paid very little and did not provide health care.

9 **Q History** What did Cesar Chavez and Dolores Huerta accomplish?

A started the FWA, publicized plight of migrant workers, got some companies to improve working conditions

10 **Q History** How did the Americans with Disabilities Act improve people's lives?

A It protected the rights of people with disabilities and made public spaces accessible.

Vocabulary Strategy

migrant worker Compare this word to a familiar word from an earlier lesson, *immigrant. Migrant* means someone who moves from place to place. An *immigrant* is someone who moves *into* one country from another.

Critical Thinking

Compare and Contrast Migrant workers and people with disabilities both struggled for equal treatment. Compare and contrast the goals that each group achieved.

Rights for Migrant Workers

Migrant workers were another group trying to improve their lives in the 1960s and 1970s. A **migrant worker** is a person who moves from place to place to find work. In California and Texas, large numbers of Mexican migrant workers worked on farms that grew crops such as grains, vegetables, and fruits. When they finished harvesting a crop in one area, migrant workers had to move to another area to find new work.

8 Most migrant workers were poor. The large farms they worked for paid very little and did not provide health care. Because migrant workers moved so much, it was difficult for their children to go to school. It also made it hard for workers to get any jobs other than migrant work.

In the 1960s, migrant workers in California began challenging the big farm companies. The workers wanted higher wages, better education for their children, and health care for their families.

Cesar Chavez, who was a migrant worker himself, helped the workers organize and speak out about their cause. Like Martin Luther King Jr., Chavez was an inspiring leader. His speeches attracted college students, religious leaders, and civil rights organizations to the migrant workers' cause.

In 1962, Chavez and a woman 9
named **Dolores Huerta** organized the workers into the National Farm Workers Association (NFWA). In 1966, the NFWA joined with other unions to form the United Farm Workers (UFW).

The protests of the UFW taught people about the hard conditions that farm workers and their families faced. The public began to pressure big farm companies to make changes. Finally, this pressure forced some companies to give their workers better pay and health care.

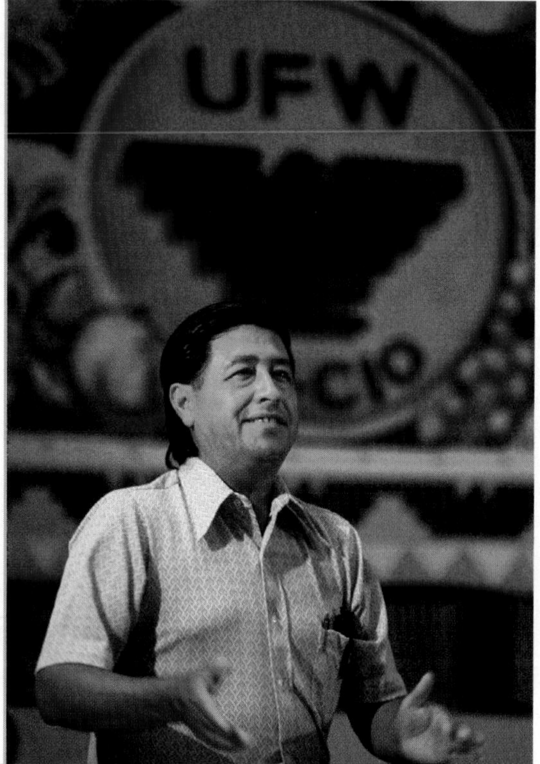

Cesar Chavez He and the United Farm Workers encouraged people to boycott products as a way to force big farm companies to change.

534 • Chapter 15

Art

Before and After Mural

- Have pairs of students choose one of these groups: women, African Americans, American Indians, migrant workers, or people with disabilities.
- Tell them to illustrate a "before" and an "after" picture for the group they choose. The "before" picture should depict life before significant civil rights gains were made. The "after" picture should depict life after their goals were achieved.
- Students can attach their illustrations to a large sheet of paper to make a mural.

Visual-spatial

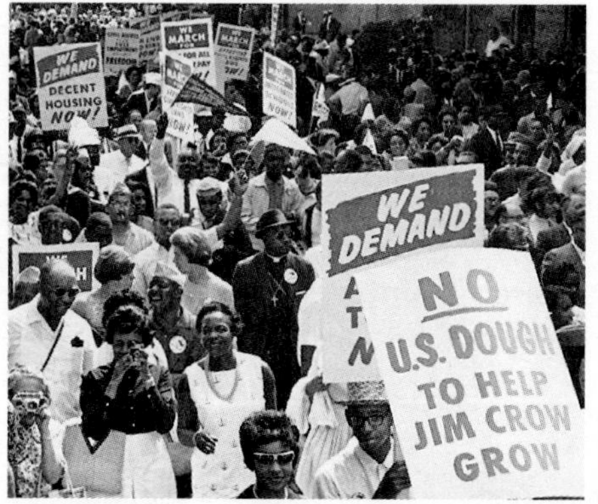

Rights for People with Disabilities

People with disabilities have also worked hard for equal treatment. People who use wheelchairs, visually impaired people, and people who have other physical or mental challenges often face discrimination. Many people fought for a law to change this, and in 1990, the
10 Americans with Disabilities Act (ADA) was passed.

A New Law George Bush was President when the ADA was signed into law.

The ADA protects the civil rights of people with disabilities. It makes it illegal to refuse to hire people because they have a disability. The ADA also says that government buildings, buses, trains, restaurants, and stores have to be built so that people can more easily enter them with wheelchairs or crutches.

REVIEW What did migrant workers fight for? They fought for higher wages, health care and schools.

Lesson Summary

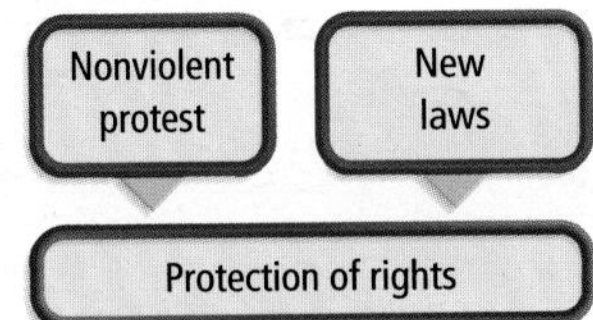

Why It Matters ...

The United States is a more democratic country because of the work and successes of civil rights groups over the last 50 years.

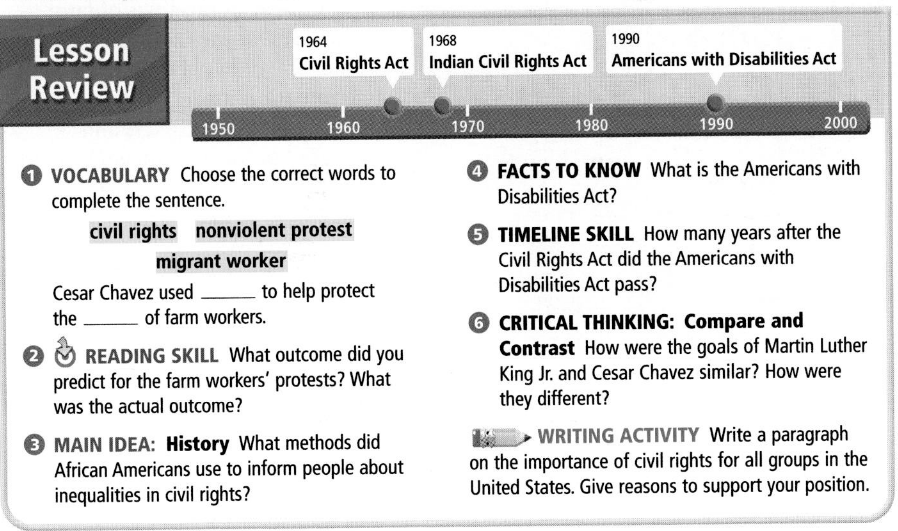

Lesson Review

1964	1968	1990
Civil Rights Act	Indian Civil Rights Act	Americans with Disabilities Act

1950 1960 1970 1980 1990 2000

1. **VOCABULARY** Choose the correct words to complete the sentence.

   civil rights **nonviolent protest** **migrant worker**

   Cesar Chavez used ______ to help protect the ______ of farm workers.

2. **READING SKILL** What outcome did you predict for the farm workers' protests? What was the actual outcome?
3. **MAIN IDEA: History** What methods did African Americans use to inform people about inequalities in civil rights?
4. **FACTS TO KNOW** What is the Americans with Disabilities Act?
5. **TIMELINE SKILL** How many years after the Civil Rights Act did the Americans with Disabilities Act pass?
6. **CRITICAL THINKING: Compare and Contrast** How were the goals of Martin Luther King Jr. and Cesar Chavez similar? How were they different?

WRITING ACTIVITY Write a paragraph on the importance of civil rights for all groups in the United States. Give reasons to support your position.

3 Review/Assess

Review Tested Objectives

U7-11 In the 1950s and 1960s, African Americans successfully protested discrimination and segregation through boycotts, marches, and court cases.

U7-12 By the late 1980s, 40 states had laws requiring equal pay for men and women doing similar work. The Indian Civil Rights Act was passed in 1968. Migrant workers received better pay and health care. The Americans with Disabilities Act was passed in 1990.

Lesson Review Answers

1. nonviolent protest; civil rights
2. predictions may vary; better pay and health care for migrant workers
3. They used nonviolent protests such as marches, boycotts, and court cases.
4. It is a law that makes it illegal for businesses to refuse to hire people just because they have a disability. It also requires public facilities to be built so that people with disabilities can more easily use them.
5. 26
6. Both used nonviolent protest to work for equal treatment. King protested discrimination against African Americans. Chavez protested against the terrible working conditions of migrant workers.

Writing Rubric

4	Position clearly stated; reasons supported by information from the text; mechanics are correct.
3	Position adequately stated; most reasons supported by information from the text; few errors in mechanics.
2	Position is stated; reasons confused or poorly supported by text information; some errors in mechanics.
1	Position not stated; reasons not supported; many errors in mechanics.

Study Guide/Homework

Vocabulary and Study Guide

Vocabulary

As you read the lesson, fill in the word web with groups that fought for their civil rights.

Civil rights: 1. African Americans 2. women 3. American Indians 4. disabled Americans 5. migrant workers

Write the definition of the term below.

6. nonviolent protest A way of bringing change without using violence

Study Guide

Read "The Struggle Continues." Then read the description. In the box, write the name of the person described.

7. I helped start the National Organization for Women. I am Betty Friedan
8. I would not give up my seat on the bus. I am Rosa Parks
9. I made speeches and helped migrant workers to organize. I am Cesar Chavez
10. I led the bus boycott in Montgomery, Alabama. I am Martin Luther King Jr.

Unit Resources 147 Use with United States History, pp. 530–535

Unit Resources, p. 147

Reteach Minilesson

Use a graphic organizer to review the struggle for equality.

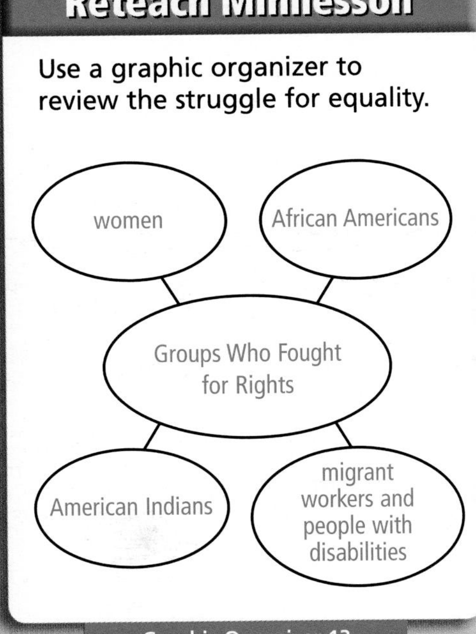

Graphic Organizer 13

Quick Look

Connect to the Core Lesson Students have just learned how different groups fought to protect their civil rights during the 1950s, 1960s, and 1970s. In Extend Lesson 2, students will hear more about how Cesar Chavez and Dolores Huerta fought to improve working conditions for migrant farm workers.

1 Teach the Extend Lesson

Connect to the Big Idea

Individuals and the Economy When Cesar Chavez and Dolores Huerta convinced consumers to stop buying grapes in the 1960s, grape growers lost money and were forced to sign bargaining agreements with the United Farm Workers Association in order to stay in business.

Extend Lesson 2

Biography

CHAMPIONS FOR A CAUSE

In the 1960s, two tireless leaders fought for the rights of the nation's migrant farm workers. Cesar Chavez and Dolores Huerta were an unbeatable team. Their efforts improved the lives of thousands.

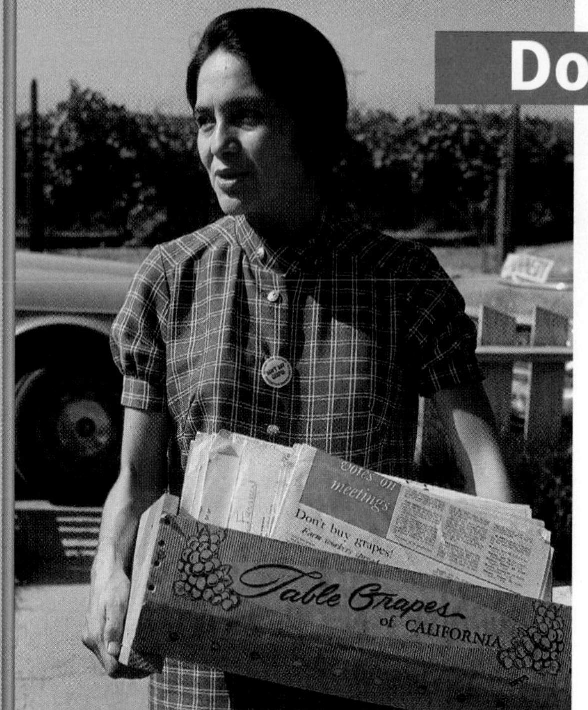

Dolores Huerta

Dolores Huerta began her career as a teacher. Many of her students were the children of **migrant workers.** They often came to class hungry or without shoes. Huerta decided to help the mothers and fathers of her students fight for higher wages and decent living conditions.

She spoke at meetings of farm workers and at the California state capital. She didn't give up. Her determination made a difference. She inspired farm workers and impressed politicians. In 1962, Huerta and Chavez founded an organization to help farm workers, later called the United Farm Workers. Their organization forced big farm companies to treat migrant workers more fairly and give them better wages.

1960 · 1965 · 1970 · 1975 · 1980

- **1962** Chavez and Huerta start Farm Workers Association
- **1965** First grape boycott begins
- **1971** United Farm Workers membership reaches 80,000 people
- **1975** California law protects rights for migrant workers

Reaching All Learners

Extra Support

Make a Sequence Chart

- Have students work in pairs to make sequence charts. Ask each pair to make one sequence chart for Dolores Huerta and one for Cesar Chavez.
- Explain to students that their charts should show the sequence of significant events in each leader's life.

Verbal-linguistic; visual-spatial

On Level

Write a News Broadcast

- Ask groups to write a script for a news broadcast about the grape boycott, including interviews with people involved in the boycott.
- Students should use information in the lesson to explain the reasons for the boycott and its effects.
- Students can perform their news broadcasts.

Verbal-linguistic

Challenge

Hold a Debate

- Remind students that there are at least two sides to every argument. An effective debater anticipates objections of opponents and is prepared to respond.
- Challenge students to think about why farm companies resisted farm workers' demands.
- Have students form two groups, farm owners and workers, and debate wages and working conditions.

Verbal-linguistic

CHARACTER TRAIT: Fairness

BIOGRAPHY

Cesar Chavez 1927-1993

From boyhood, Cesar Chavez knew firsthand about the struggles of migrant workers. He and his family spent hours working in the hot sun, bunching carrots and picking olives and grapes. Like other migrant families, they moved from farm to farm. Their house was crowded and they often had no running water. Chavez decided to fight for a better life for migrant workers when he grew up.

Chavez gave speeches and marched in demonstrations. Sometimes he went door-to-door to convince people to join him. More and more people agreed that migrant workers should be treated more fairly. In 1965, Chavez and Huerta led a nation-wide boycott against the grape growers of California. People from all over the nation refused to buy grapes from California farms. It became one of the most successful boycotts in history.

Activities

1. **LIST IT** List some of the ways that Huerta and Chavez worked for **fairness** in the treatment of migrant workers.
2. **REPORT IT** Find out more about the California Grape Growers Boycott. Write a short newspaper article as though you were a reporter for a newspaper.

Technology Read more biographies at Education Place. www.eduplace.com/kids/hmss05/

537

2 Leveled Activities

1 List It *For Extra Support*
Sample answer: gave speeches; founded the United Farm Workers Association; led nation-wide boycott against grape growers of California.

2 Report It *For Challenge*

Writing Rubric

4	Article answers the questions *who, what, where, when, why,* and *how* about the event; information is well organized; mechanics are correct.
3	Article is clear and organized, but more information is needed to give a complete picture of the boycott; mechanics are mostly correct.
2	Student focuses on the topic but doesn't give enough information; facts are mixed with opinion; errors sometimes affect understanding.
1	Article does not have a clear focus; some sentences sound as though they were copied; many mistakes make the writing difficult to understand.

Character Trait: Fairness

Ask students why Chavez and Huerta thought fairness was so important. For more information on character traits, turn to pages 584-585.

ELL

REACHING ALL LEARNERS

Advanced

- Ask students to search the article for challenges migrant farm workers faced during the 1960s. (hunger; low wages; hot sun; frequent moves; crowded living quarters; no running water)
- Tell students to **make a chart** that lists and illustrates the plight of farm workers.

Visual-spatial

Math

Take a Class Survey

- Point out that March 31st, Cesar Chavez's birthday, is a state holiday in California.
- Explain that some people believe there should be a national holiday honoring Cesar Chavez and his accomplishments.
- Have students conduct a class poll to find out how their peers feel about this issue.
- Invite them to chart or graph the results of their survey. Discuss their findings as a class.

Visual-spatial

Graphic Organizer

Dolores Huerta
- teacher of migrant workers' children
- helped students' parents

Both
- left job
- gave speeches
- founded UFWA
- led grape boycott

Cesar Chavez
- migrant farm worker
- experienced hardship
- inspired by MLK Jr.

Graphic Organizer 11

Tested Objective

U7-13 Understand and apply the process of conflict resolution.

1 Teach the Skill

- Have students read the introductory paragraph. Call on volunteers to identify two causes of conflict.
- Discuss with students the four steps under "Learn the Skill." Have students explain how these four steps could be used to resolve the conflict presented on this page over how to use the gym.
- Help students suggest solutions (Step 3) and choose the best solution (Step 4).

Citizenship Skills

Skillbuilder

Resolve Conflicts

▶ VOCABULARY
conflict

You have just read about people who worked to protect their rights. In some cases, their efforts caused conflicts. A conflict is a disagreement. Conflicts can occur when people have different goals, or similar goals but different ideas about how to reach them. To resolve, or settle, a conflict, people may need to make compromises.

Learn the Skill

Step 1: Identify the conflict.

Students are allowed to use the gymnasium for an hour after school. Different groups of students want to use it in different ways.

Step 2: State what each person or group wants and why they want it. Look for shared goals.

One group wants to play basketball. A second group wants to practice and put on a play.

Step 3: Think of possible resolutions. Look for more than one way to settle the conflict.

The students could divide the gymnasium into two sections, giving each group some space to use, or the groups could take turns, with each group using the gymnasium on different days.

Step 4: Compromise and choose one solution that will work best for the most people.

538 • Chapter 15

Leveled Practice

Extra Support

Discuss the conflict described on this page about usage of the gym. Ask if this would be an easy or difficult problem to solve, and why. Verbal-linguistic

Challenge

Have partners think of a real-life conflict and create posters illustrating the conflict and two or three potential solutions. Classmates may vote on the best solution to each problem. Visual-spatial

ELL

Beginning

To help students understand the conflict described on page 538, call on volunteers to act it out. Ask them to show what each group of students wants to do in the gym, how the two groups might react to each other, and how they will find resolution to their conflict.

Bodily-kinesthetic; verbal-linguistic

Practice the Skill

Read about a conflict among the supporters of the Americans with Disabilities Act (ADA). Then answer the questions below.

> Supporters of the ADA agreed that public buildings needed to have ramps, railings, and elevators. People did not agree about how much time businesses should have to make these changes. One group wanted the work to begin as soon as possible. Some members of Congress disagreed. They worried that the changes would be too expensive for small businesses.
>
> Supporters of the ADA compromised. They gave businesses two and a half years to make the changes. They gave even more time to businesses for which the changes would be too costly. Congress and the President then approved the ADA.

1. What was the conflict among supporters of the ADA?
2. How were the goals of the supporters alike?
3. In what way was the solution a compromise?

Apply the Skill

Use your library or Internet resources to research a conflict in the United States today. Identify the conflict and the goals of each side. Then suggest and evaluate possible solutions.

539

2 Practice the Skill

1. how much time businesses should have to make buildings accessible to people with disabilities
2. Both sides agreed that buildings should be made accessible.
3. The solution set a time limit of two and a half years for businesses to make the needed changes, with extra time for some businesses. This was probably less time than some ADA supporters wanted and longer than others were hoping for.

3 Apply the Skill

Have students research a current conflict in the United States and evaluate possible solutions. When reviewing students' application of the skill, consider:

- Did the student correctly identify the conflict?
- Did the student clearly show the goals of each side?
- Did the student suggest and evaluate solutions to the conflict?

Skill Practice

Skillbuilder: Resolve Conflicts

> In April 1963, Martin Luther King Jr. led protests against segregation in Birmingham, Alabama. More than 1,000 African American young people followed him. The Birmingham police met the protesters with snarling dogs and fire hoses that delivered painful blasts of water. Pictures of marchers getting bitten by dogs and getting knocked down by water shocked many Americans. Soon millions of Americans supported the civil rights movement. They demanded that the government take action. In May, Birmingham's leaders agreed to end segregation in the city's stores, restaurants, and workplaces. In 1964, Congress passed the Civil Rights Act, which made segregation illegal in all 50 states.

Practice

1. What did the African Americans who marched in Birmingham want? The marchers wanted equal rights.
2. Did the government of Birmingham feel the same way as the marchers? How do you know? No, because the police tried to stop the marchers.
3. What was the result of this conflict in Birmingham? The city of Birmingham agreed to end segregation in the city's stores, restaurants, and workplaces.
4. How did the U.S. government show that it agreed with the marchers' demands for civil rights? Congress passed the Civil Rights Act in 1964.

Apply

Think about a time you had a disagreement with a friend. Write a paragraph describing the disagreement you had. How did you eventually resolve the conflict? Did you both change the way you were feeling? Paragraph may refer to the two friends having different goals and resolving the conflict with a compromise.

Unit Resources

148
Use with *United States History*, pp. 538–539

Unit Resources, p. 148

Skill Transparency

Skillbuilder Transparency 15

Resolve Conflicts

> Students are allowed to use the gymnasium for an hour after school. Different groups of students want to use it in different ways. One group wants to play basketball. A second group wants to practice and put on a play.
>
> The students could divide the gymnasium into two sections, giving each group some space to use, or the groups could take turns, with each group using the gymnasium on different days.

Step 1 Identify the conflict.

Step 2 State what each person or group wants and why they want it. Look for shared goals.

Step 3 Think of possible resolutions. Look for more than one way to settle the conflict.

Step 4 Compromise and choose one solution that will work best for the most people.

Skillbuilder Transparency

Use with *United States History*, pp. 538–539

Transparency 15

Tested Objectives

U7-14 Citizenship Explain important rights of all United States citizens, including the right to vote.

U7-15 Citizenship Explain the responsibilities of United States citizens, including responsibilities of young people.

Lesson Quick Look

This lesson describes the rights and responsibilities of United States citizens.

Teaching Option: **Extend Lesson 3** features more information about volunteering.

1 Get Set to Read

Preview Look at the title, the headings, and the pictures. What aspects of citizenship do you think this lesson will focus on?

Reading Skill: Classify Rights include the right to vote and freedom of speech. Responsibilities include obeying the law, and going to school.

Build on What You Know Ask students to share what they know about democratic rights.

Vocabulary

naturalization *noun,* the legal process of acquiring full citizenship by a person of foreign birth

register *verb,* to sign up for something

responsibility *noun,* a duty or obligation; something that one is responsible for

volunteer *noun,* a person who helps other people or a cause without being paid

Core Lesson 3

Democracy and Citizenship

VOCABULARY

naturalization
register
responsibility
volunteer

Vocabulary Strategy

responsibility

Responsibility, meaning duty, is related to **respond.** Citizens in a democracy must respond to their duties.

READING SKILL

Classify Put information into these two categories: Rights and Responsibilities.

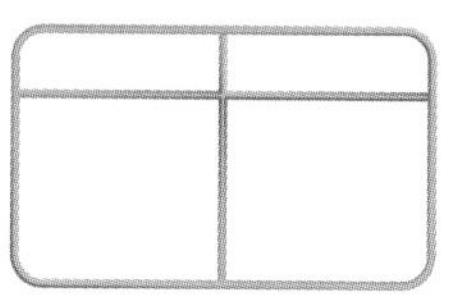

Build on What You Know You know that a car needs an engine to run. Democracy is the engine that keeps the United States running. For this engine to run smoothly, citizens need to exercise their democratic rights.

Citizenship

Main Idea Citizens in a democracy have rights.

Almost everyone in the world is a citizen of a nation. Remember that a citizen is an official member of a country. Every person born in the United States is a citizen of the United States.

Immigrants can become United States citizens through naturalization. **Naturalization** is the legal process of learning the laws, rights, and duties of being a citizen and passing a citizenship test. This process often takes two years. The last step of naturalization is a ceremony where new citizens promise to obey the Constitution. 1

Being a citizen of a democracy like the United States is special. Throughout history, ordinary people in most countries have had almost no say in their government. In a democracy, all citizens have a voice. The choices they make help shape their government.

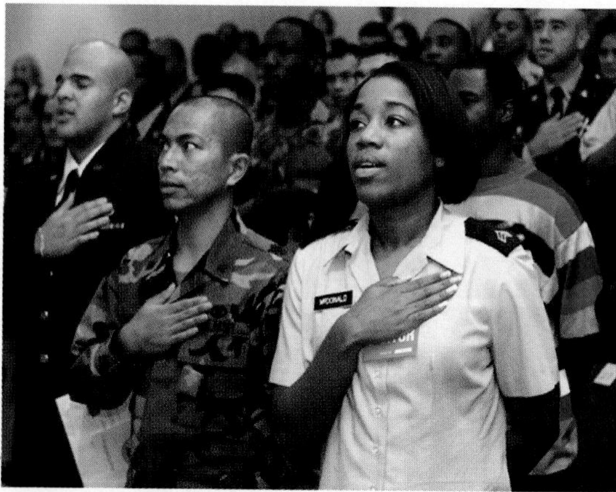

The Citizenship Pledge
Here, members of the U.S. armed forces say the pledge and become citizens.

540 • Chapter 15

Skill and Strategy

Reading Skill and Strategy

Reading Skill: Classify

This skill helps you understand and remember what you have read by organizing, or classifying, facts into groups.

Read "Responsibilities of Citizens." Then fill in the classification chart below. Classify the responsibilities of adults and young people.

Adults	Young People
1. Sample answers: Obeying the law; voting; paying taxes; serving on juries	2. Sample answers: Obeying the law; protecting the environment; volunteering to help others

Reading Strategy: Summary

3. Read "Democracy and Citizenship." Then write a short summary for each section.

Section 1: Citizenship

Summary: Sample answer: Democracies give their citizens many rights.

Section 2: Responsibilities of Citizens

Summary: Sample answer: Along with their rights, citizens of democracies also have many responsibilities.

Unit Resources

149
Use with *United States History*, pp. 540–543

Unit Resources, p. 149

Background

Requirements for Naturalization

A person must:

- be at least 18 years old (children of immigrants can get citizenship when their parents do)
- be a permanent, legal U.S. resident for five years (three if spouse has been a U.S. citizen for at least three years)
- read, write, and speak English
- demonstrate knowledge of U.S. history and government
- take an oath of allegiance.

Rights of Citizens

Vote
Join groups of your choice
Express opinions freely
Practice religion of choice
Have a fair trial
Own property and businesses
Not be discriminated against in jobs and housing

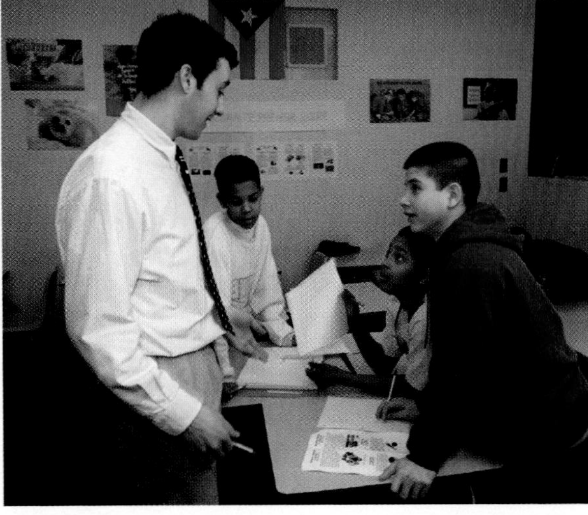

Freedom of Speech All citizens should know their rights. Here, students and their teacher discuss what they will write in their school newspaper.

Rights of United States Citizens

An important feature of democracy in the United States is that citizens have many rights. Rights are freedoms that the government must protect. One of the rights American citizens have is the right to vote. Voting lets citizens choose leaders and make decisions in their communities.
2 At age 18, a citizen can **register,** or sign up, to vote. Citizens also have the right to run for political office.

Much of the history you have read in this book has described how different groups of people have gained recognition of their rights. After the Civil War, for example, African Americans gained citizenship and the right to vote. Later, in 1920, the Nineteenth Amendment guaranteed women's right to vote. In 1924, American Indians finally gained citizenship. These changes have created a more complete democracy in the United States.

Responsibilities of Citizens

Main Idea Citizens in a democracy have important responsibilities.

Citizens have many freedoms. That doesn't mean people can do whatever they want, however. Citizens also have responsibilities to the country. A **responsibility** is a duty that someone is expected to fulfill.

In a democracy, it is the responsibility of citizens to create a safe and orderly society. Obeying the law is an important responsibility. When people obey laws, they help make a safer community.

Paying taxes is another responsibility. The government uses taxes to help pay 3
for fire and police departments, public parks, and good roads. Citizens also have responsibilities to serve on juries in law courts and to vote in elections. Men who are age 18 and over must register for the military draft.

REVIEW At what age can citizens vote?
18 years old

2 Teach

Citizenship

Talk About It

1 **Q Citizenship** How can an immigrant become a U.S. citizen?
A through naturalization, which includes learning information about citizenship and passing an exam

2 **Q Citizenship** What can United States citizens do when they reach the age of 18?
A register to vote

Responsibilities of Citizens

Talk About It

3 **Q Citizenship** What are some things that taxes pay for?
A fire and police departments, parks, roads

Vocabulary Strategy

naturalization The words *nation,* and *natural* comes from a Latin word that means "to be born." Someone who has gone through naturalization has the same rights as someone who was born a citizen.

register Synonyms for *register* are *enroll, sign up,* or *join.*

Reading Strategy: Summarize After students read the section entitled "Citizenship," ask them to write a summary of this section. Have the class share their summaries.

Leveled Practice

Extra Support

Tell pairs of students to **play a "tennis match."** Student 1 should name one thing a good citizen can do, such as *voting*. Student 2 then "returns the ball" by naming another, such as *paying taxes*.
Verbal-linguistic

Challenge

Have students find and read the *Oath of Allegiance to the United States of America,* the promise immigrants make at a citizenship ceremony. Then have them **write a summary** of the oath.
Verbal-linguistic

ELL

Beginning

- Have students **brainstorm a list** of rights that United States citizens have.
- Ask them to choose three rights that are important to them.
- They make a mural depicting the rights they chose.

Visual-spatial

Responsibilities of Citizens *continued*

Talk About It

4 Q Citizenship What was the goal of the eighth graders in Georgia? How did they achieve it?

A to provide computers for organizations that needed them; formed Free Bytes, got people to donate old computers, fixed the computers, gave them to groups in need

5 Q Citizenship What does a volunteer do?

A helps others without getting paid for it; gives time and uses talent to make his or her community a better place to live

Vocabulary Strategy

volunteer *Volunteer* comes from a Latin word that means "choice." A *volunteer chooses* to help others without getting paid.

Critical Thinking

Decision Making How can being a responsible citizen today affect people's lives in the future?

Citizen Participation

There is more to being a responsible citizen than just following the rules. Being a good citizen also means getting involved in issues that affect the community and the country. It can mean speaking out against injustice or other problems. Or it can mean taking action to change things for the better.

In California, a group of citizens started an organization called People for Trees. By planting trees in and around San Diego, they hope to contribute to a healthier environment. Since 1989, members of People for Trees have planted more than 35,000 trees for future generations.

Young people, like adults, have responsibilities as citizens. They are expected to go to school. What they learn in school helps prepare them to contribute to society and take a part in a democracy. Being informed about important issues can help young people make good choices when they become old enough to vote.

Young people can take part in government even before they can vote. When they find issues that they care about, such as protecting the environment or changing an unfair law, there are many things they can do. They can send letters to lawmakers and newspapers. They can sign petitions asking for change. They can even help a political candidate get elected.

Finding Ways to Help

In 1992, a group of eighth-graders 4
in Georgia discovered that many organizations in their state needed computers. These students started Free Bytes. This company takes old computers and fixes them. In just 10 years, Free Bytes donated over 4,000 computers to different groups.

Another way young people can help their communities is by becoming
volunteers. A **volunteer** helps other people 5
without being paid. Volunteers give their time and use their talents to make their communities better places to live.

For example, a third-grade class in Maryland collects gifts for sick children and their parents at a local hospital. In California, volunteers of all ages grow endangered plants in their own gardens when they join Adopt-A-Garden. Young people can volunteer in many other ways. All it takes is the desire to be a good citizen and to help the community.

Volunteers It is important to find an issue that you feel strongly about. These students are painting a mural for their community.

Language Arts

Write an Editorial

- Encourage students to identify issues in the school or community about which they have strong feelings.
- Tell them to write their opinions in an editorial. Remind them to give reasons for their opinion and facts and examples that explain their reasons.
- Students may wish to submit their writing for publication in the school or community newspaper.

Verbal-linguistic

Art

Make a Sign

- Have students make drawings that symbolize citizens' responsibilities.
- They can use their books for ideas, and focus on one particular responsibility.
- Display completed drawings in the classroom.

Visual-spatial

Responsibilities of Citizens

Personal	Civic
These actions improve your life and the lives of others.	These actions help make a democratic system work.
Educate yourself	Vote
Respect others	Obey laws
Help in your community	Pay taxes
Set a good example	Serve on juries

Citizens' Responsibilities As citizens, young people need to know their responsibilities, just as adults do.

The future of the United States depends on the strength of its democracy. All citizens have a responsibility to keep democracy strong and preserve the Constitution. This means protecting and respecting the rights of all Americans. It can also mean obeying laws, becoming active in politics, or working to improve your community. In big and small ways, each citizen can contribute to democracy and make the United States a better country.

REVIEW What are the responsibilities of United States citizens? create an orderly society, obey laws, pay taxes, serve on juries, vote, register for the draft, volunteer, go to school

Lesson Summary

Being a citizen of a democracy means having rights, such as freedom of speech. Citizens also have a responsibility to help create an orderly society. Young people can fulfill their responsibilities by going to school and helping others in their communities.

Why It Matters ...

Good citizenship is necessary for a better country and safer communities.

Lesson Review

1. **VOCABULARY** Choose the correct word to complete the sentence.
   register **responsibility** **volunteer**
   Many citizens believe it is their _____ to _____ to help others in their community.
2.  **READING SKILL** What duties did you **classify** as responsibilities? Explain why you did so.
3. **MAIN IDEA: Citizenship** Why is voting such an important right of citizens?
4. **MAIN IDEA: Citizenship** What are some ways that students can be good citizens?
5. **FACTS TO REMEMBER** What is the process immigrants go through to become citizens?
6. **CRITICAL THINKING: Infer** In a democracy, what qualities are important for a good leader?
7. **CRITICAL THINKING: Decision Making** What might be the costs and benefits of a student's decision to spend one afternoon each week volunteering at a local library?

HANDS ON **SPEAKING ACTIVITY** Make a list of projects your class could do to help the school or community. Pick one project, and prepare a speech telling why you think students should volunteer to help.

3 Review/Assess

Review Tested Objectives

U7-14 U.S. citizens have the right to vote, the right to run for political office, freedom of speech, and other important rights.

U7-15 U.S. citizens are responsible for obeying the law, paying taxes, serving on juries, voting in elections, and working to improve their communities. Men who are age 18 and older must register for the military draft. Young people can go to school, be informed about and involved in their communities, and volunteer.

Lesson Review Answers

1. responsibility; volunteer
2. Sample answers: obey the law, pay taxes, serve on a jury, vote, register for draft, go to school, be informed, volunteer
3. Citizens can express their opinions and vote for leaders who share their views.
4. Sample answers: go to school, send letters to lawmakers and newspapers, sign petitions, march in protest at political gatherings, volunteer to help others
5. naturalization
6. Sample answers: well informed, caring, helpful, good listener, responsible
7. Sample answer: costs might include giving up free time; working hard. Benefits might include helping the library save money so that it has more to spend on books; feeling good about helping.

Study Guide/Homework

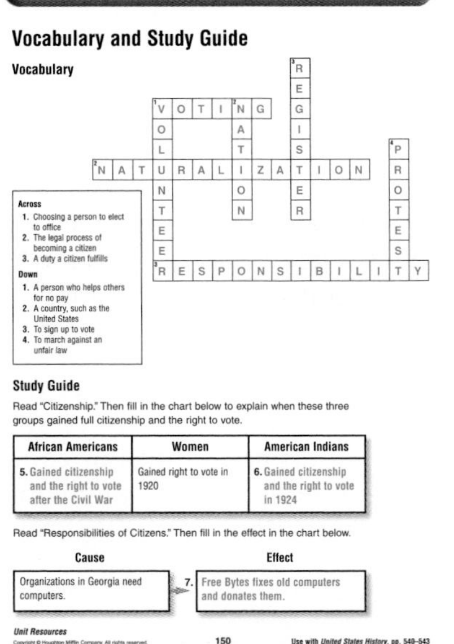

Vocabulary and Study Guide

Vocabulary

Across
1. Choosing a person to elect to office
2. The legal process of becoming a citizen
3. A duty a citizen fulfills

Down
1. A person who helps others for no pay
2. A country, such as the United States
3. To sign up to vote
4. To march against an unfair law

Study Guide

Read "Citizenship." Then fill in the chart below to explain when these three groups gained full citizenship and the right to vote.

African Americans	Women	American Indians
5. Gained citizenship and the right to vote after the Civil War	Gained right to vote in 1920	6. Gained citizenship and the right to vote in 1924

Read "Responsibilities of Citizens." Then fill in the effect in the chart below.

Cause	Effect
Organizations in Georgia need computers.	7. Free Bytes fixes old computers and donates them.

Unit Resources, p. 150

Reteach Minilesson

Use a flow chart to review the process of naturalization.

Learn laws, rights, duties of U.S. citizens
↓
Pass citizenship test
↓
Become a citizen

Graphic Organizer 6

HANDS ON Performance Task Rubric

4	Speech states position clearly; conveys ideas effectively; facts are accurate.
3	Speech states position well; conveys ideas adequately; most facts cited are accurate.
2	Speech states position in a somewhat disorganized way; conveys ideas adequately; some errors.
1	Speech states no position or one that is off topic; conveys ideas in a very general or incomprehensible way; many errors.

Extend Quick Look

Connect to the Core Lesson Students have just learned about the rights and responsibilities of United States citizens. In Extend Lesson 3, students will read about kids who demonstrate good citizenship by volunteering their time and their talents to help others.

1 Teach the Extend Lesson

Connect to the Big Idea

Nature of Culture Helping others has always been an important part of American culture and democracy. United States President John F. Kennedy articulated this sentiment in his 1961 Inaugural Address when he called upon Americans to "Ask not what your country can do for you—ask what you can do for your country."

Extend Lesson 3

Citizenship

VOLUNTEERS

Get set to build a better world! All over the United States, students your age are being good citizens by getting involved. They help their schools, their neighbors, their country, and the world. They are volunteers.

Volunteers give their time and use their talents. They learn new skills and make new friends. They show how much they care by their commitment to helping others.

Soup kitchens provide meals for people who cannot buy food. Volunteers are needed to prepare and serve food and to clean up.

TIPS ON VOLUNTEERING

- **Ask an adult for help.** An adult can help with phone calls, transportation, or making sure the volunteer project is safe.
- **Plan ahead.** Make a schedule of times when you will work on your volunteer job or project.
- **Be realistic.** Choose a job you know you can do. If the job is too big for one person, get someone to help you.
- **Be careful.** Follow safety rules.
- **Make a commitment.** Once you find a volunteer project you like, keep doing it. Others will be counting on you.

544 • Chapter 15

Reaching All Learners

Extra Support

Make a Comic Strip

- Have students choose one photo from the lesson. Suppose it is Frame 1 of a comic strip. Ask, *What might happen next?*
- Students can draw more frames to answer this question, writing a sentence for each one.
- Explain that their comic strips must include at least three of the following words: *volunteer, better world, good citizens, getting involved, satisfaction, making a difference, skills, friends.*

Visual-spatial; verbal-linguistic

On Level

Write a Short Play

- Ask students to write their own Readers' Theater.
- The play should depict a conversation between a student interested in volunteering and his or her parent(s).
- Instruct students to include or address in their dialogue each item in the "Tips on Volunteering" box on page 544.

Verbal-linguistic

Challenge

Make a Volunteer Book

- Have students make a book that lists local volunteer opportunities.
- Students can research these by speaking with school officials, reading newspapers, or calling local hospitals, nursing homes, or shelters.
- Ask students to make one page for each opportunity, including duties, hours and length of commitment, skills needed, and contact information.

Verbal-linguistic

CHARACTER TRAIT: Caring

CITIZENSHIP

Almost everyone likes a visitor with a friendly face. This girl is visiting a man who lives in a nursing home.

These students are raising money for their school. A car wash is a good way to raise money for a school or community group.

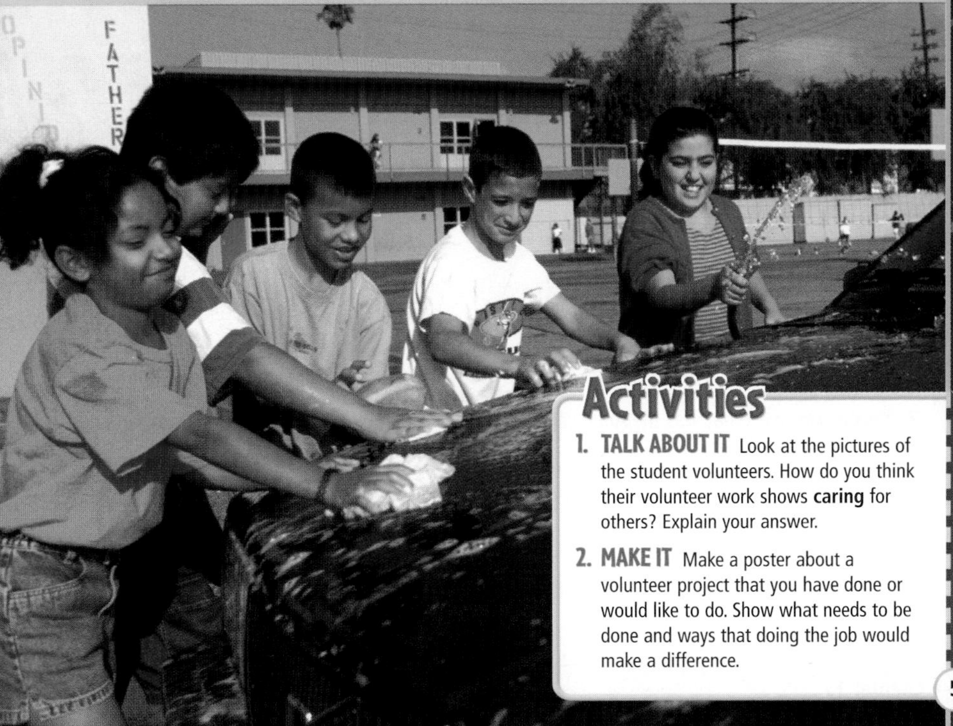

Activities

1. **TALK ABOUT IT** Look at the pictures of the student volunteers. How do you think their volunteer work shows **caring** for others? Explain your answer.
2. **MAKE IT** Make a poster about a volunteer project that you have done or would like to do. Show what needs to be done and ways that doing the job would make a difference.

545

2 Leveled Activities

1 Talk About It *For Extra Support*

Sample answers: The students show caring by preparing and serving food, cleaning, visiting someone, and raising money for their school.

2 Make It *For Challenge*

HANDS ON

	Performance Task Rubric
4	Poster focuses on one volunteer project; student uses words and pictures to convey what needed to be done and how he or she made a difference; poster is neat, clear, and attractive.
3	Poster focuses on one volunteer project; student shows what was done and how it helped; poster could have more visual interest or appeal.
2	Poster may focus on more than one project; it may not be immediately clear who was helped or how the volunteer made a difference.
1	Student does little more than list places kids could volunteer or people who need their help; poster reflects little thought or effort.

Character Trait: Caring

Ask students, Why do you think caring for others is important in a community? For more information on character traits, turn to pages 584-585.

REACHING ALL LEARNERS

ELL

Advanced

- Ask pairs of students to choose one person from the photographs on pages 544–545.
- Tell them to prepare an interview that asks the questions *who? what? where? when? why?* and *how?* about the volunteer work shown. Instruct students to use the pictures and the text to figure out what the answers might be.
- Encourage students to perform their interviews for the class.

Verbal-linguistic

Art

Create a Collage

- Help the class brainstorm a list of things kids can do to help others in school and the community.
- Challenge students to research additional volunteer opportunities for kids.
- Students can pool their findings to make a collage that shows kids volunteering. Have them think of an interesting title that calls the rest of the student body to action.
- Display the collage in a public area of the school.

Visual-spatial

Graphic Organizer

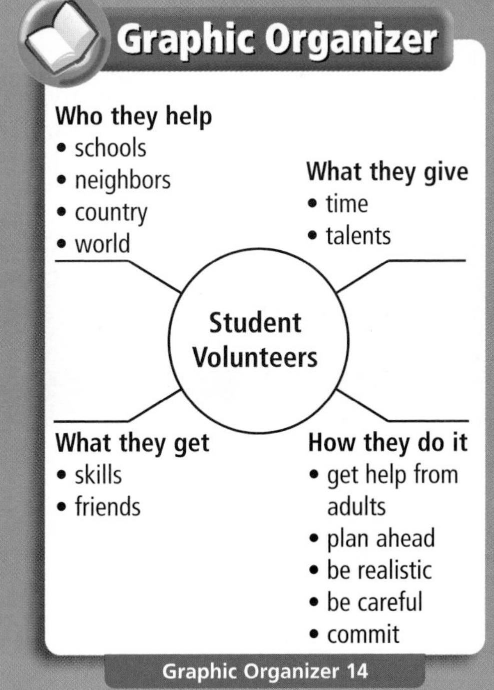

Graphic Organizer 14

Chapter Review

Tested Objectives

The lesson objective assessed by each question is shown in parentheses after the answer.

Visual Summary

1. The NAWSA was started in 1890 and worked for women's suffrage. Elizabeth Cady Stanton was the organization's first president. *(Obj. U7-9)*
2. The NAACP was started in 1910 and worked for equal treatment for African Americans. *(Obj. U7-10)*
3. The AIM worked for the return of lands taken from American Indians. *(Obj. U7-12)*
4. The UFW was started in 1966 and worked to improve conditions for migrant workers. Cesar Chavez and Dolores Huerta were important leaders of this organization. *(Obj. U7-12)*

Facts and Main Ideas

5. The Supreme Court said that segregation of public schools was illegal. It was the first major civil rights victory for African Americans at that time. *(Obj. U7-11)*
6. New Mexico, Alaska, Washington *(Obj. U7-12)*
7. It was a law that made it illegal to refuse people jobs because of a disability. It also said that all buses, trains, restaurants, stores, and government buildings must be accessible. *(Obj. U7-12)*
8. Rights: vote, run for political office; Responsibilities: Obey laws, pay taxes *(Obj. U7-14, U7-15)*

Vocabulary

9. **civil rights** *(Obj. U7-11)*
10. **nonviolent protest** *(Obj. U7-11)*
11. **responsibility** *(Obj. U7-15)*

Chapter 15 Review and Test Prep

Visual Summary

1–4. Write a description of each item named below.

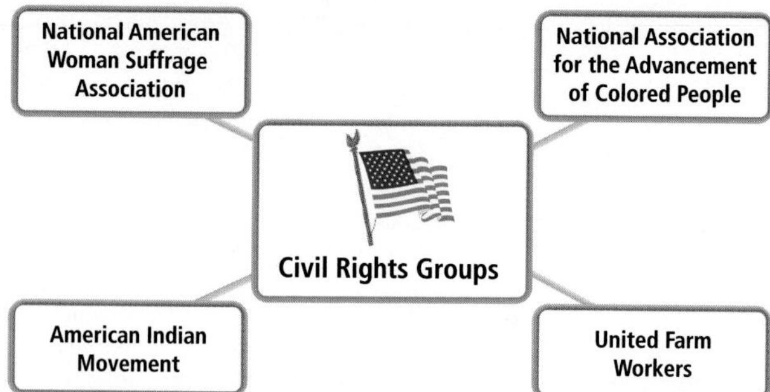

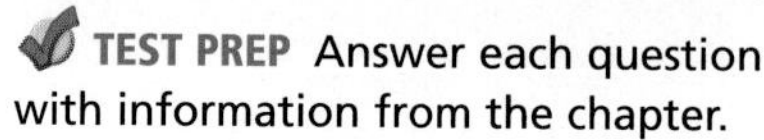

Facts and Main Ideas

TEST PREP Answer each question with information from the chapter.

5. **History** Why was *Brown v. Board of Education of Topeka* an important court case?
6. **Geography** In what three states were lands returned to American Indians during the 1960s and 1970s?
7. **Government** What was the Americans with Disabilities Act?
8. **Citizenship** Name two rights and two responsibilities of citizens.

Vocabulary

TEST PREP Choose the correct word from the list below to complete each sentence.

civil rights, p. 530
nonviolent protest, p. 531
responsibility, p. 541

9. African Americans often were denied the _____ that other U.S. citizens enjoyed.
10. Examples of _____ include boycotts and marches.
11. If you have a _____, you have a duty that you are expected to fulfill.

Reading/Language Arts Wrap-Up

Reading Strategy: Summarize

- Review with students the steps involved when they summarize a passage of text.
- Have students work in small groups. Each member of the group takes a paragraph and summarizes it for the rest of the group.
- Ask students to do a self-check: "How well did I do in summarizing?"

Writing Strategy

- Explain to students that summarizing will be a valuable tool when they need to write.
- For example, if students are taking a test in which they must write short answers to questions, they can use the summarizing strategy as they review what they know and choose the details most pertinent to the answer.

CHAPTER SUMMARY TIMELINE

1890 NAWSA formed	1920 Women gain the vote	1954 Desegregation ordered	1964 Civil Rights Act	1990 ADA passed

1880 1900 1920 1940 1960 1980 2000

Apply Skills

TEST PREP Citizenship Skill Read the paragraph. Then use what you have learned about resolving conflicts to answer each question.

Mrs. Lee's fifth-grade class wants to volunteer in the community. They all agree about the importance of volunteering, but they disagree about what to do. Some students want to visit elderly neighbors who cannot leave their homes. Others think it is more important to collect food for the food bank. Still others want to help the recycling center in town.

12. What is the first step the students should take to resolve the conflict?
    - **A.** Forget about volunteering.
    - **B.** Ask Mrs. Lee to decide what to do.
    - **C.** Identify the conflict.
    - **D.** Come up with more suggestions.
13. How can the students best resolve the conflict?
    - **A.** Compromise on a project that most students would like to do.
    - **B.** Let someone outside the class decide for them.
    - **C.** Argue until some people give up.
    - **D.** Decide not to compromise.

Critical Thinking

TEST PREP Write a short paragraph to answer each question.

14. **Fact and Opinion** Women's struggle for equal rights has been compared to the colonists' struggle for independence. Explain why you agree or disagree with the comparison.
15. **Analyze** Can citizens in a democracy have an effect on what their government does? Give reasons for your answer.

Timeline

Use the Chapter Summary Timeline above to answer the question.

16. How many years after NAWSA was formed were women allowed to vote in national elections?

Activities

Art Activity Create a brochure that explains the goals and achievements of one of the organizations mentioned in the chapter.

Writing Activity Write a personal essay about your rights and responsibilities as a citizen of the United States.

Technology
Writing Process Tips
Get help with your essay at **www.eduplace.com/kids/hmss05/**

547

Apply Skills

12. C *(Obj. U7-13)*
13. A *(Obj. U7-13)*

Critical Thinking

14. Sample answer: Disagree: Women were not like the colonists who risked their lives fighting a war for independence. Agree: Women were fighting for their independence and were just as determined and committed to their cause. *(Obj. U7-12)*

15. Sample answer: Yes, because citizens vote for government leaders. No, because leaders decide what they want to do once they are in power. *(Obj. U7-15)*

Timeline

16. 30 years *(Obj. U7-9)*

Leveled Activities

HANDS ON Performance Task Rubric

4	Information clearly stated and supported by research; brochure is very creative; mechanics are correct.
3	Information adequately stated and mostly supported by research; brochure is creative; few errors.
2	Information is stated but confused or poorly supported by research; brochure is fairly creative; some errors.
1	Information not stated and not supported by research; creativity lacking; many errors in mechanics.

Writing Rubric

4	Ideas clearly stated and accurate; mechanics are correct.
3	Ideas adequately stated and mostly accurate; few errors.
2	Ideas are confused or somewhat inaccurate; some errors.
1	Ideas not stated and not accurate; many errors.

Technology

Test Generator

- You can generate your own version of the chapter review by using the **Test Generator CD-ROM**.

Web Link

For more ideas, visit www.eduplace.com/ss/hmss05/

Standards

National Standards

I e Importance of cultural unity and diversity ideals of a democratic republican form of government
II a How people may describe the same event differently
V d Internal conflicts
VI c How government does/does not provide for needs and wants, establish order and security, and manage conflict
VI d Encourage unity and deal with diversity to maintain order and security
VI h Tensions between the wants and needs and fairness, equity, and justice
X a Key ideals of the United States's form of government
X b Citizen rights and responsibilities
X h Public policies and citizen behaviors

Unit Review

Vocabulary and Main Ideas

1. Quotas limited which countries immigrants came from and limited the total number of immigrants allowed into the United States. *(Obj. U7-3)*
2. The Constitution and Bill of Rights are the democratic heritage of everyone in the United States. This heritage helps unite the country. *(Obj. U7-8)*
3. Women held meetings and marches and made speeches to Congress. *(Obj. U7-9)*
4. It was important because Martin Luther King Jr. believed it was the best way to bring about social change. *(Obj. U7-11)*
5. By voting, people help choose leaders and make important decisions. *(Obj. U7-14, U7-15)*
6. Sample answer: Rights: vote, run for office, express opinions, practice religion, have a fair trial, own property; Responsibilities: obey the law, pay taxes, vote, serve on juries, go to school/educate yourself, respect others, help in your community, show moral behavior *(Obj. U7-14, U7-15)*

Critical Thinking

7. Sample answer: Immigrants' skills, knowledge, and talents have contributed to the economy. *(Obj. U7-7)*
8. Sample answer: No. Only citizens over the age of 18 have the responsibility of voting. *(Obj. U7-15)*

Apply Skills

9. B *(Obj. U7-13)*
10. A *(Obj. U7-13)*

UNIT 7

Review and Test Prep

Vocabulary and Main Ideas

TEST PREP Write a sentence to answer each question.

1. What effect did **quotas** have on immigration?
2. What is the **heritage** that all U.S. citizens share, and why is it important?
3. How did **suffragists** gain support for their cause?
4. Why was **nonviolent protest** an important part of the **civil rights** movement?
5. Why is it important for people to **register** to vote?
6. What rights and **responsibilities** do all U.S. citizens have?

Critical Thinking

TEST PREP Write a short paragraph to answer each question.

7. **Draw Conclusions** In what ways have immigrants strengthened the culture of the United States?
8. **Analyze** Do all citizens in a democracy have the same responsibilities? Give reasons for your answer.

Apply Skills

TEST PREP Citizenship Skill Read the paragraph below. Then use what you have learned about resolving conflicts to answer each question.

Mr. Dawson's fifth-grade class wants to go on a field trip. They all agree about the importance of seeing something outside of school, but they disagree about where they will spend their time and money. Some students want to visit a museum. Others think going to a nature center would be more valuable. Still others want to see a play.

9. What is the first step the class should take to resolve the conflict?
   - **A.** Try to convince each other that one field trip is the best.
   - **B.** Identify the conflict.
   - **C.** Ask the principal to decide.
   - **D.** Forget about going on a field trip.
10. How could the class best resolve the conflict?
    - **A.** Compromise on a field trip that most students like.
    - **B.** Argue until some people give in.
    - **C.** Let someone outside of the class decide.
    - **D.** Flip a coin.

548 • Unit 7

Technology

Test Generator

- Use the **Test Generator CD-ROM** to create tests customized to your class.
- Access hundreds of test questions and make lesson, chapter, and unit quizzes and tests.

Web Updates

Curious about new trade book titles that you can use with the program? Visit www.eduplace.com/ss/hmss05/ to update your Unit Bibliography.

Extra Support

Use an Idea Web

Have students use a idea web graphic organizer (Graphic Organizer 7) to review vocabulary words or concepts.

Unit Activity

Write a Citizen's Letter about a Problem

- Choose a problem in your community, your state, or the country. Find out more about it.
- Write a letter to the editor of your local newspaper, or to an elected leader.
- Describe your feelings about the problem and what you would like to see done.
- Send your letter.

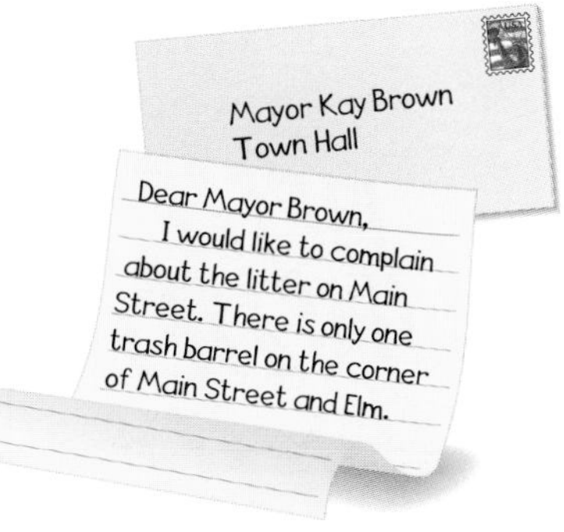

At the Library

You may find this book at your school or public library.

Remember: A Pictorial Tribute to the Brown v. Board of Education Supreme Court Decision
by Toni Morrison
Photographs and storytelling bring the history of school desegregation to life.

CURRENT EVENTS WEEKLY WR READER

Connect to Your Community

Design a volunteer project that your class can do.

- Find information about volunteer projects that kids are doing.
- Design a volunteer project to help solve a problem in your school or community. Explain how your class could work together to help.
- Present the project to your class.

Technology
Get information about volunteer projects from the Weekly Reader at **www.eduplace.com/kids/hmss05/**

Read About It

Look for these Social Studies Independent Books in your classroom.

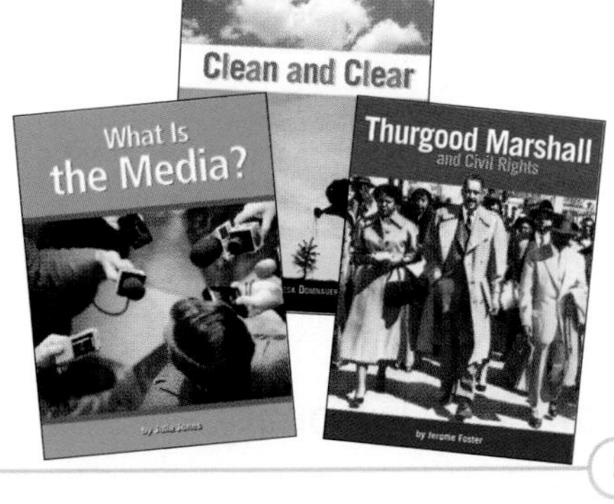

549

Unit Activity

HANDS ON Performance Task Rubric

4	Position clearly stated; reasons supported by research; letter format used correctly; mechanics are correct.
3	Position adequately stated; most reasons supported by research; letter format is used; few errors in mechanics.
2	Position is stated; reasons confused or poorly supported by research; letter format is attempted; some errors in mechanics.
1	Position not stated; reasons not supported; letter format not used; many errors in mechanics.

WEEKLY WR READER

Unit Project

- Have students present their volunteer project for class discussion. If time and resources allow, help students to plan and implement the selected projects.

At the Library

- You may wish to wrap up the unit by reading aloud from one of these suggested titles, or from one of the Read-Aloud selections included in the Unit Bibliography.

Read About It

- You may wish to provide students with the appropriate Leveled Social Studies Books for this unit. Turn to page 497B for teaching options.
- If students have written summaries or reviews of the Leveled Books or the books in the Unit Bibliography, you may wish to have them read aloud their summaries with a partner.

Language Arts

Test Taking Tip

Remind students that when they are answering a multiple choice question, they should read and consider all the possible answers before choosing one.

Standards

National Standards

I e Importance of cultural unity and diversity
II a How people may describe the same event differently
III a Use mental maps
IX b Conflict, cooperation, and interdependence
V d Internal conflicts
VI d Encourage unity and deal with diversity to maintain order and security
VI f Factors that contribute to cooperation and cause disputes
VI h Tensions between the wants and needs and fairness, equity, and justice
X a Key ideals
X b Citizen rights and responsibilities
X h Public policies and citizen behaviors

References

Citizenship Handbook

Resources

R1

Pledge of Allegiance

I pledge allegiance to the flag
of the United States of America
and to the Republic for which it stands,
one Nation under God, indivisible,
with liberty and justice for all.

Spanish

Prometo lealtad a la bandera
de los Estados Unidos de América,
y a la república que representa,
una nación bajo Diós, indivisible,
con libertad y justicia para todos.

Russian

**Я даю клятву верности флагу
Соединённых Штатов Америки
и стране, символом которой
он является, народу, единому
перед Богом, свободному
и равноправному.**

Tagalog

Ako ay nanunumpa ng katapatan
sa bandila ng Estados Unidos
ng Amerika, at sa Republikang
kanyang kinakatawan, isang
Bansang pumapailalim sa isang
Maykapal hindi nahahati, may
kalayaan at katarungan para
sa lahat.

Arabic

ادين بالولاء لعلم الولايات المتحده الامريكيه و الى

الجمهوريه التي تمثلها و دولة واحدة تؤمن باللة و

متحدة تمنح الحرية و العدالة للجميع

Chinese

忠誠誓言

我發誓忠誠于美利堅合眾國國旗
和國旗所象征的共和國，
上帝屬下之一國，不可分割，
所有眾生享有自由與正義。

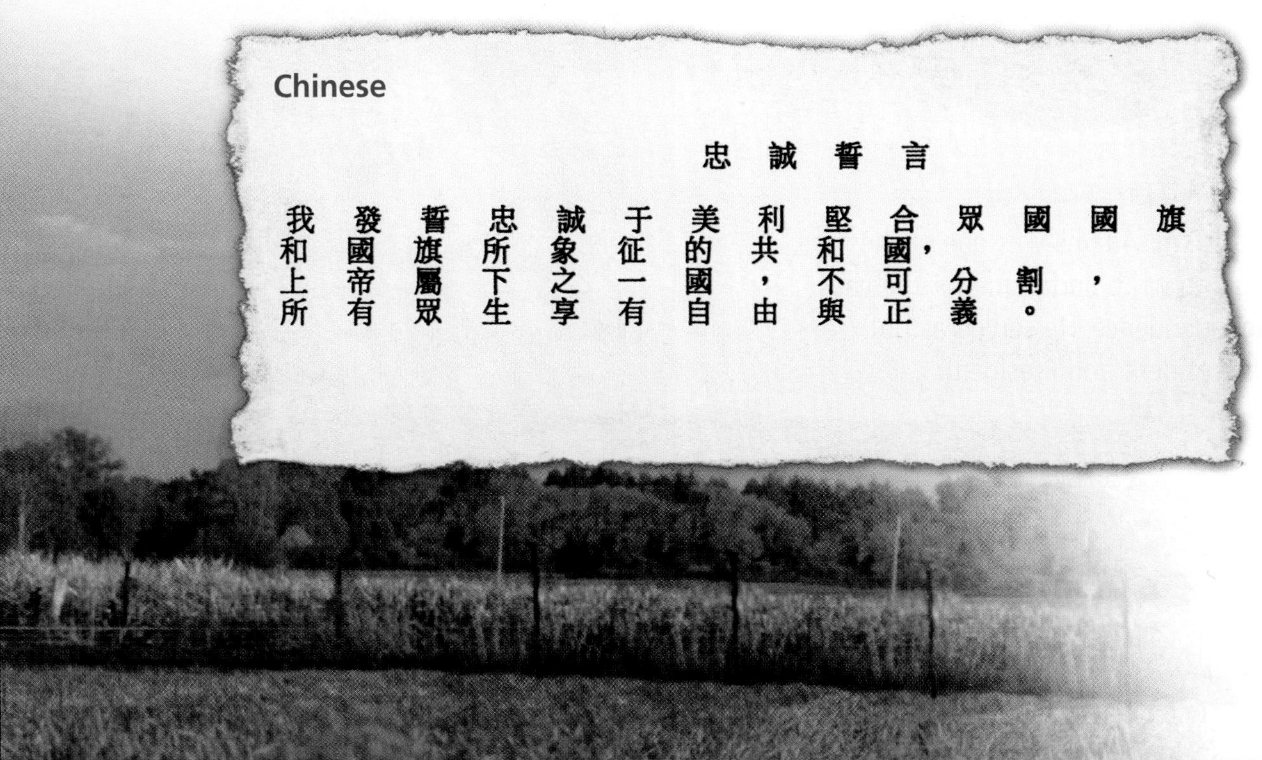

R3

Character Traits

Character includes feelings, thoughts, and behaviors. A character trait is something people show by the way they act. To act bravely shows courage, and courage is one of several character traits.

Positive character traits, such as honesty, caring, and courage, lead to positive actions. Character traits are also called "life skills." Life skills can help you do your best, and doing your best leads to reaching your goals.

Martha Washington

Responsibility During the hard years of the war, Washington helped the army and General Washington. As First Lady, her sense of responsibility toward the nation set an example.

John Adams

Patriotism Adams was one of the first people to write and argue for the cause of independence. He served as both Vice President and President.

Courage means acting bravely. Doing what you believe to be good and right, and telling the truth, requires courage.

Patriotism means working for the goals of your country. When you show national pride, you are being patriotic.

Responsibility is taking care of work that needs to be done. Responsible people are reliable and trustworthy, which means they can be counted on.

Respect means paying attention to what other people want and believe. The "golden rule," or treating others as you would like to be treated, shows thoughtfulness and respect.

Fairness means working to make things fair, or right, for everyone. Often one needs to try again and again to achieve fairness. This requires diligence, or not giving up.

Civic virtue is good citizenship. It means doing things, such as cooperating and solving problems, to help communities live and work well together.

Caring means noticing what others need and helping them get what they need. Feeling concern or compassion is another way to define caring.

R5

Historical Documents

Pilgrims are shown writing the Mayflower Compact while still aboard the ship.

The Mayflower Compact (1620)

". . . We whose names are underwritten, . . . Having undertaken, for the Glory of God, and Advancement of the Christian Faith, and Honor of our King and Country, a Voyage to plant the first Colony in the northern Parts of Virginia; Do by these Presents, solemnly and mutually, in the Presence of God and one of another, covenant and combine ourselves together into a civil Body Politick, for our better Ordering and Preservation, and Furtherance of the Ends aforesaid: And by Virtue hereof do enact, constitute, and frame such just and equal Laws, Ordinances, Acts, Constitutions, and Officers, from time to time, as shall be thought most meet and convenient for the general Good of the Colony; unto which we promise all due Submission and Obedience. . . ."

Mr. John Carver	*Mr. Samuel Fuller*	*Edward Tilly*
Mr. William Bradford	*Mr. Christopher Martin*	*John Tilly*
Mr. Edward Winslow	*Mr. William Mullins*	*Francis Cooke*
Mr. William Brewster	*Mr. William White*	*Thomas Rogers*
Isaac Allerton	*Mr. Richard Warren*	*Thomas Tinker*
Myles Standish	*John Howland*	*John Ridgdale*
John Alden	*Mr. Steven Hopkins*	*Edward Fuller*
John Turner	*Digery Priest*	*Richard Clark*
Francis Eaton	*Thomas Williams*	*Richard Gardiner*
James Chilton	*Gilbert Winslow*	*Mr. John Allerton*
John Craxton	*Edmund Margesson*	*Thomas English*
John Billington	*Peter Brown*	*Edward Doten*
Joses Fletcher	*Richard Britteridge*	*Edward Liester*
John Goodman	*George Soule*	

Pitt's Speech to Parliament on the Stamp Act (1766)

William Pitt

"The Americans have not acted in all things with prudence and temper. They have been wronged. They have been driven to madness by injustice. Will you punish them for the madness you have occasioned? Rather let prudence and temper come first from this side. I will undertake for America, that she will follow the example. . . .

Upon the whole, I will beg leave to tell the House what is really my opinion. It is, that the Stamp-Act be repealed absolutely, totally, and immediately; that the reason for the repeal should be assigned, because it was founded on an erroneous principle."

Burke's Speech to Parliament on Conciliation with America (1775)

Edmund Burke

"The proposition is peace. Not peace through the medium of war; not peace to be hunted through the labyrinth of intricate and endless negotiations . . . It is simple peace, sought in its natural course and in its ordinary haunts. . . .

Let the colonies always keep the idea of their civil rights associated with your government — they will cling and grapple to you, and no force under heaven will be of power to tear them from their allegiance. But let it be once understood that your government may be one thing and their privileges another, that these two things may exist without any mutual relation — the cement is gone, the cohesion is loosened, and everything hastens to decay and dissolution. . . .

Magnanimity in politics is not seldom the truest wisdom; and a great empire and little minds go ill together."

The Declaration of Independence

In the Declaration of Independence, the colonists explained why they were breaking away from Britain. They believed they had the right to form their own country.

In Congress, July 4, 1776

The unanimous declaration of the thirteen United States of America

Members of the Continental Congress are shown signing the Declaration of Independence.

Introduction*

When, in the course of human events, it becomes necessary for one people to dissolve the political bonds which have connected them with another, and to assume, among the powers of the earth, the separate and equal station to which the laws of nature and of nature's God entitle them, a decent respect to the opinions of mankind requires that they should declare the causes which impel them to the separation.

Basic Rights

The opening part of the Declaration is very famous. It says that all people are created equal. Everyone has certain basic rights that are "unalienable." That means that these rights cannot be taken away. Governments are formed to protect these basic rights. If a government does not do this, then the people have a right to begin a new one.

WE hold these truths to be self-evident: That all men are created equal, that they are endowed by their Creator with certain unalienable rights; that among these are life, liberty, and the pursuit of happiness; that, to secure these rights, governments are instituted among men, deriving their just powers from the consent of the governed; that whenever any form of government becomes destructive of these ends, it is the right of the people to alter or to abolish it, and to institute new government, laying its foundation on such principles, and organizing its powers in such form, as to them shall seem most likely to effect their safety and happiness. Prudence, indeed, will dictate that governments long established should not be changed for light and transient causes; and accordingly all experience hath shown that mankind are more disposed to suffer, while evils are sufferable, than to right themselves by abolishing the forms to which they are accustomed. But when a long train of abuses and usurpations, pursuing invariably the same object, evinces a design to reduce them under absolute despotism, it is their right, it is their duty, to throw off such government, and to provide new guards for their future security. Such has been the patient sufferance of these colonies; and such is now the necessity which constrains them to alter their former systems of government. The history of the present King of Great Britain is a history of repeated injuries and usurpations, all having in direct object the establishment of an absolute tyranny over these states. To prove this, let facts be submitted to a candid world.

Forming a new government meant ending the colonial ties to the king. The writers of the Declaration listed the wrongs of King George III to prove the need for their actions.

Charges Against the King

HE has refused his assent to laws, the most wholesome and necessary for the public good.

Colonists said the king had not let the colonies make their own laws. He had limited the people's representation in their assemblies.

HE has forbidden his governors to pass laws of immediate and pressing importance, unless suspended in their operation till his assent should be obtained; and, when so suspended, he has utterly neglected to attend to them.

HE has refused to pass other laws for the accommodation of large districts of people, unless those people would relinquish the right of representation in the legislature, a right inestimable to them, and formidable to tyrants only.

HE has called together legislative bodies at places unusual, uncomfortable, and distant from the depository of their public records, for the sole purpose of fatiguing them into compliance with his measures.

HE has dissolved representative houses repeatedly, for opposing, with manly firmness his invasions on the rights of the people.

*Titles have been added to the Declaration to make it easier to read. These titles are not in the original document.

HE has refused for a long time, after such dissolutions, to cause others to be elected; whereby the legislative powers, incapable of annihilation, have returned to the people at large for their exercise; the state remaining in the mean time, exposed to all the dangers of invasions from without and convulsions within.

The king had made colonial assemblies meet at unusual times and places. This made going to assembly meetings hard for colonial representatives.

In some cases the king stopped the assembly from meeting at all.

HE has endeavored to prevent the population of these states; for that purpose obstructing the laws for the naturalization of foreigners; refusing to pass others to encourage their migration hither, and raising the conditions of new appropriations of lands.

The king tried to stop people from moving to the colonies and into new western lands.

HE has obstructed the administration of justice, by refusing his assent to laws for establishing judiciary powers.

HE has made judges dependent on his will alone, for the tenure of their offices, and the amount of payment of their salaries.

The king prevented the colonies from choosing their own judges. Instead, he sent over judges who depended on him for their jobs and pay.

HE has erected a multitude of new offices, and sent hither swarms of officers to harass our people and eat out their substance.

HE has kept among us, in times of peace, standing armies, without the consent of our legislatures.

The king kept British soldiers in the colonies, even though the colonists had not asked for them.

HEhas affected to render the military independent of, and superior to, the civil power.

HE has combined with others to subject us to a Jurisdiction foreign to our constitution and unacknowledged by our laws, giving his assent to their acts of pretended legislation:

FOR quartering large bodies of armed troops among us;

FOR protecting them, by a mock trial, from punishment for any murders which they should commit on the inhabitants of these states;

FOR cutting off our trade with all parts of the world;

FOR imposing taxes on us without our consent;

FOR depriving us, in many cases, of the benefits of trial by jury;

FOR transporting us beyond seas, to be tried for pretended offenses;

King George III

FOR abolishing the free system of English laws in a neighboring province, establishing therein an arbitrary government, and enlarging its boundaries, so as to render it at once an example and fit instrument for introducing the same absolute rule into these colonies;

The king and Parliament had taxed the colonists without their consent. This was one of the most important reasons the colonists were angry at Britain.

FOR taking away our charters, abolishing our most valuable laws, and altering fundamentally the forms of our governments;

FOR suspending our own legislatures, and declaring themselves invested with power to legislate for us in all cases whatsoever.

HE has abdicated Government here, by declaring us out of his protection and waging war against us.

The colonists felt that the king had waged war on them.

HE has plundered our seas, ravaged our coasts, burned our towns, and destroyed the lives of our people.

HE is at this time transporting large armies of foreign mercenaries to complete the works of death, desolation, and tyranny, already begun with circumstances of cruelty and perfidy scarcely paralleled in the most barbarous ages, and totally unworthy the head of a civilized nation.

The king had hired German soldiers and sent them to the colonies to keep order.

HE has constrained our fellow-citizens, taken captive on the high seas, to bear arms against their country, to become the executioners of their friends and brethren, or to fall themselves by their hands.

British soldiers became a symbol of British misrule to many colonists.

HE has excited domestic insurrections amongst us, and has endeavored to bring on the inhabitants of our frontiers, the merciless Indian savages, whose known rule of warfare is an undistinguished destruction of all ages, sexes, and conditions.

The colonists said that they had asked the king to change his policies, but he had not listened to them.

Response to the King

IN every stage of these oppressions we have petitioned for redress in the most humble terms; Our repeated petitions have been answered only by repeated injury. A prince, whose character is thus marked by every act which may define a tyrant, is unfit to be the ruler of a free people.

NOR have we been wanting in our attentions to our British brethren. We have warned them from time to time, of attempts by their legislature to extend an unwarrantable jurisdiction over us. We have reminded them of the circumstances of our emigration and settlement here. We have appealed to their native justice and magnanimity; and we have conjured them, by the ties of our common kindred, to disavow these usurpations, which, would inevitably interrupt our connections and correspondence. They, too, have been deaf to the voice of justice and of consanguinity. We must, therefore, acquiesce in the necessity which denounces our separation, and hold them, as we hold the rest of mankind, enemies in war, in peace, friends.

The writers declared that the colonies were free and independent states, equal to the world's other states. They had the powers to make war and peace and to trade with other countries.

Independence

WE, therefore, the representatives of the United States of America, in General Congress Assembled, appealing to the Supreme Judge of the world for the rectitude of our intentions, do, in the name and by authority of the good people of these colonies, solemnly publish and declare, that these United Colonies are, and of right ought to be, FREE AND INDEPENDENT STATES; that they are absolved from all allegiance to the British crown, and that all political connection between them and the state of Great Britain is, and ought to be, totally dissolved; and that, as free and independent states, they have full power to levy war, conclude peace, contract alliances, establish commerce, and do all other acts and things which independent states may of right do. And for the support of this declaration, with a firm reliance on the protection of Divine Providence, we mutually pledge to each other our lives, our fortunes, and our sacred honor.

The signers pledged their lives to the support of this Declaration. The Continental Congress ordered copies of the Declaration of Independence to be sent to all the states and to the army.

Congress ordered copies of the Declaration of Independence to be sent to all the states and to the army.

NEW HAMPSHIRE
Josiah Bartlett
William Whipple
Matthew Thornton

MASSACHUSETTS
John Hancock
John Adams
Samuel Adams
Robert Treat Paine
Elbridge Gerry

NEW YORK
William Floyd
Philip Livingston
Francis Lewis
Lewis Morris

RHODE ISLAND
Stephen Hopkins
William Ellery

NEW JERSEY
Richard Stockton
John Witherspoon
Francis Hopkinson
John Hart
Abraham Clark

PENNSYLVANIA
Robert Morris
Benjamin Rush
Benjamin Franklin
John Morton
George Clymer
James Smith
George Taylor
James Wilson
George Ross

DELAWARE
Caesar Rodney
George Read
Thomas McKean

MARYLAND
Samuel Chase
William Paca
Thomas Stone
Charles Carroll of Carrollton

NORTH CAROLINA
Willam Hooper
Joseph Hewes
John Penn

VIRGINIA
George Wythe
Richard Henry Lee
Thomas Jefferson
Benjamin Harrison
Thomas Nelson, Jr.
Francis Lightfoot Lee
Carter Braxton

SOUTH CAROLINA
Edward Rutledge
Thomas Heyward, Jr.
Thomas Lynch, Jr.
Arthur Middleton

CONNECTICUT
Roger Sherman
Samuel Huntington
William Williams
Oliver Wolcott

GEORGIA
Button Gwinnett
Lyman Hall
George Walton

The Constitution of the United States

Preamble*

We the people of the United States, in order to form a more perfect Union, establish justice, insure domestic tranquility, provide for the common defense, promote the general welfare, and secure the blessings of liberty to ourselves and our posterity, do ordain and establish this Constitution for the United States of America.

Preamble The Preamble, or introduction, states the purposes of the Constitution. The writers wanted to strengthen the national government and give the nation a more solid foundation. The Preamble makes it clear that it is the people of the United States who have the power to establish or change a government.

ARTICLE I
Legislative Branch

SECTION 1. CONGRESS

All legislative powers herein granted shall be vested in a Congress of the United States, which shall consist of a Senate and House of Representatives.

Congress Section 1 gives Congress the power to make laws. Congress has two parts, the House of Representatives and the Senate.

SECTION 2. HOUSE OF REPRESENTATIVES

1. ***Election and Term of Members*** *The House of Representatives shall be composed of members chosen every second year by the people of the several States, and the electors in each State shall have the qualifications requisite for electors of the most numerous branch of the State Legislature.*

2. ***Qualifications*** *No person shall be a representative who shall not have attained to the age of twenty-five years, and been seven years a citizen of the United States, and who shall not, when elected, be an inhabitant of that State in which he shall be chosen.*

3. ***Number of Representatives per State*** *Representatives ~~and direct taxes~~** shall be apportioned among the several States which may be included within this Union, according to their respective numbers, ~~which shall be determined by adding to the whole number of free persons, including those bound to service for a term of years, and excluding Indians not taxed, three fifths of all other persons.~~ The actual enumeration shall be made within three years after the first meeting of the Congress of the United States, and within every subsequent term of ten years, in such manner as they shall by law direct. The number of representatives shall not exceed one for every thirty thousand, but each State shall have at least one representative; ~~and until such enumeration shall be made, the State of New Hampshire shall be entitled to choose three, Massachusetts eight, Rhode Island and Providence Plantations one, Connecticut five, New York six, New Jersey four, Pennsylvania eight, Delaware one, Maryland six, Virginia ten, North Carolina five, South Carolina five, and Georgia three.~~*

4. ***Vacancies*** *When vacancies happen in the representation from any State, the executive authority thereof shall issue writs of election to fill such vacancies.*

5. ***Special Powers*** *The House of Representatives shall choose their speaker and other officers; and shall have the sole power of impeachment.*

Election and Team Members Citizens elect the members of the House of Representatives every two years.

Qualifications Representatives must be at least 25 years old. They must have been United States citizens for at least seven years. They also must live in the state they represent.

Number of Representatives per State The number of representatives each state has is based on its population. The biggest states have the most representatives. Each state must have at least one representative. An enumeration, or census, must be taken every 10 years to find out a state's population. The number of representatives in the House is now fixed at 435.

George Washington watches delegates sign the Constitution.

*The titles of the Preamble, and of each article, section, clause, and amendment have been added to make the Constitution easier to read. These titles are not in the original document.

**Parts of the Constitution have been crossed out to show that they are not in force any more. They have been changed by amendments or they no longer apply.

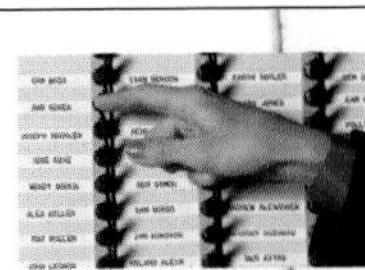

Americans often use voting machines on election day.

SECTION 3. SENATE

1. ***Number, Term, and Selection of Members*** *The Senate of the United States shall be composed of two senators from each State, chosen by the Legislature thereof, for six years; and each Senator shall have one vote.*

2. ***Overlapping Terms and Filling Vacancies*** *Immediately after they shall be assembled in consequence of the first election, they shall be divided as equally as may be into three classes. ~~The seats of the senators of the first class shall be vacated at the expiration of the second year, of the second class at the expiration of the fourth year, and of the third class at the expiration of the sixth year, so~~ that one-third may be chosen every second year; ~~and if vacancies happen by resignation, or otherwise, during the recess of the legislature of any State, the executive thereof may make temporary appointments until the next meeting of the legislature, which shall then fill such vacancies.~~*

3. ***Qualifications*** *No person shall be a senator who shall not have attained to the age of thirty years, and been nine years a citizen of the United States, and who shall not, when elected, be an inhabitant of that State for which he shall be chosen.*

4. ***President of the Senate*** *The Vice President of the United States shall be President of the Senate, but shall have no vote, unless they be equally divided.*

5. ***Other Officers*** *The Senate shall choose their other officers, and also a President pro tempore, in the absence of the Vice President, or when he shall exercise the office of the President of the United States.*

6. ***Impeachment Trials*** *The Senate shall have the sole power to try all impeachments. When sitting for that purpose, they shall be on oath or affirmation. When the President of the United States is tried, the Chief Justice shall preside: and no person shall be convicted without the concurrence of two-thirds of the members present.*

7. ***Penalties*** *Judgment in cases of impeachment shall not extend further than to removal from office, and disqualification to hold and enjoy any office of honor, trust, or profit under the United States: but the party convicted shall nevertheless be liable and subject to indictment, trial, judgement and punishment, according to law.*

Number, Term, and Selection of Members In each state, citizens elect two members of the Senate. This gives all states, whether big or small, equal power in the Senate. Senators serve six year terms. Originally, state legislatures chose the senators for their states. Today, however, people elect their senators directly. The Seventeenth Amendment made this change in 1913.

Qualifications Senators must be at least 30 years old and United States citizens for at least nine years. Like representatives, they must live in the state they represent.

President of the Senate The Vice President of the United States acts as the President, or chief officer, of the Senate. The Vice President votes only in cases of a tie.

Impeachment Trials If the House of Representatives impeaches, or charges, an official with a crime, the Senate holds a trial. If two-thirds of the senators find the official guilty, then the person is removed from office. The only President ever impeached was Andrew Johnson in 1868. He was found not guilty.

SECTION 4. ELECTIONS AND MEETINGS

1. ***Election of Congress*** *The times, places and manner of holding elections for senators and representatives, shall be prescribed in each State by the legislature thereof; but the Congress may at any time by law make or alter such regulations, except as to the places of choosing Senators.*

2. ***Annual Sessions*** *The Congress shall assemble at least once in every year, ~~and such meeting shall be on the first Monday in December,~~ unless they shall by law appoint a different day.*

SECTION 5. RULES OF PROCEDURE

1. ***Organization*** *Each house shall be the judge of the elections, returns and qualifications of its own members, and a majority of each shall constitute a quorum to do business; but a smaller number may adjourn from day to day, and may be authorized to compel the attendance of absent members, in such manner, and under such penalties as each house may provide.*

Election of Congress Each state decides where and when to hold elections. Today congressional elections are held in even-numbered years, on the Tuesday after the first Monday in November.

Annual Sessions The Constitution requires Congress to meet at least once a year. In 1933, the 20th Amendment made January 3rd the day for beginning a regular session of Congress.

Organization A quorum is the smallest number of members that must be present for an organization to hold a meeting. For each house of Congress, this number is the majority, or more than one-half, of its members.

2. ***Rules*** *Each house may determine the rules of its proceedings, punish its members for disorderly behavior, and, with the concurrence of two-thirds, expel a member.*

3. ***Journal*** *Each house shall keep a journal of its proceedings, and from time to time publish the same, excepting such parts as may in their judgement require secrecy; and the yeas and nays of the members of either house on any question shall, at the desire of one-fifth of those present, be entered on the journal.*

4. ***Adjournment*** *Neither house, during the session of Congress, shall, without the consent of the other, adjourn for more than three days, nor to any other place than that in which the two houses shall be sitting.*

Rules Each house can make rules for its members and expel a member by a two-thirds vote.

Journal The Constitution requires each house to keep a record of its proceedings. *The Congressional Record* is published every day. It includes parts of speeches made in each house and allows any person to look up the votes of his or her representative.

SECTION 6. PRIVILEGES AND RESTRICTIONS

1. ***Pay and Protection*** *The senators and representatives shall receive a compensation for their services, to be ascertained by law, and paid out of the treasury of the United States. They shall in all cases, except treason, felony and breach of the peace, be privileged from arrest during their attendance at the session of their respective houses, and in going to and returning from the same; and for any speech or debate in either house, they shall not be questioned in any other place.*

2. ***Restrictions*** *No senator or representative shall, during the time for which he was elected, be appointed to any civil office under the authority of the United States, which shall have been created, or the emoluments whereof shall have been increased during such time; and no person holding any office under the United States, shall be a member of either house during his continuance in office.*

Pay and Protection Congress sets the salaries of its members, and they are paid by the federal government. No member can be arrested for anything he or she says while in office. This protection allows members to speak freely in Congress.

Restrictions Members of Congress cannot hold other federal offices during their terms. This rule strengthens the separation of powers and protects the checks and balances system set up by the Constitution.

SECTION 7. MAKING LAWS

1. ***Tax Bills*** *All bills for raising revenue shall originate in the House of Representatives; but the Senate may propose or concur with amendments as on other bills.*

2. ***Passing a Law*** *Every bill which shall have passed the House of Representatives and the Senate, shall, before it became a law, be presented to the President of the United States; if he approve, he shall sign it, but if not, he shall return it, with his objections, to that house in which it shall have originated, who shall enter the objections at large on their journal, and proceed to reconsider it. If after such reconsideration two-thirds of that house shall agree to pass the bill, it shall be sent, together with the objections, to the other house, by which it shall likewise be reconsidered, and if approved by two-thirds of that house, it shall become a law. But in all such cases the votes of both houses shall be determined by yeas and nays, and the names of the persons voting for and against the bill shall be entered on the journal of each house respectively. If any bill shall not be returned by the president within ten days (Sundays excepted) after it shall have been presented to him, the same shall be a law, in like manner as if he had signed it, unless the Congress by their adjournment prevent its return, in which case it shall not be a law.*

3. ***Orders and Resolutions*** *Every order, resolution, or vote to which the concurrence of the Senate and House of Representatives may be necessary (except on a question of adjournment) shall be presented to the President of the United States; and before the same shall take effect, shall be approved by him, or, being disapproved by him, shall be repassed by two-thirds of the Senate and House of Representatives, according to the rules and limitations prescribed in the case of a bill.*

Tax Bills A bill is a proposed law. Only the House of Representatives can introduce bills that tax the people.

Passing a Law A bill must be passed by the majority of members in each house of Congress. Then it is sent to the President. If the President signs it, the bill becomes a law. If the President refuses to sign a bill, and Congress is in session, the bill becomes law ten days after the President receives it.

The President can also veto, or reject, a bill. However, if each house of Congress repasses the bill by a two-thirds vote, it becomes a law. Passing a law after the President vetoed it is called overriding a veto. This process is an important part of the checks and balances system set up by the Constitution.

Orders and Resolutions Congress can also pass resolutions that have the same power as laws. Such acts are also subject to the President's veto.

Historical Documents Pupil Book pp. R14–R21

SECTION 8. POWERS DELEGATED TO CONGRESS

1. ***Taxation*** *The Congress shall have the power to lay and collect taxes, duties, imposts, and excises, to pay the debts and provide for the common defense and general welfare of the United States; but all duties, imposts and excises shall be uniform throughout the United States;*

2. ***Borrowing*** *To borrow money on the credit of the United States;*

3. ***Commerce*** *To regulate commerce with foreign nations, and among the several States, and with the Indian tribes;*

4. ***Naturalization and Bankruptcy*** *To establish an uniform rule of naturalization, and uniform laws on the subject of bankruptcies throughout the United States;*

5. ***Coins and Measures*** *To coin money, regulate the value thereof, and of foreign coin, and fix the standard of weights and measures;*

6. ***Counterfeiting*** *To provide for the punishment of counterfeiting the securities and current coin of the United States;*

7. ***Post Offices*** *To establish post offices and post roads;*

8. ***Copyrights and Patents*** *To promote the progress of science and useful arts by securing for limited times to authors and inventors the exclusive right to their respective writings and discoveries;*

9. ***Courts*** *To constitute tribunals inferior to the Supreme Court;*

10. ***Piracy*** *To define and punish piracies and felonies committed on the high seas, and offenses against the law of nations;*

11. ***Declaring War*** *To declare war, ~~grant letters of marque and reprisal,~~ and make rules concerning captures on land and water;*

12. ***Army*** *To raise and support armies, but no appropriation of money to that use shall be for a longer term than two years;*

13. ***Navy*** *To provide and maintain a navy;*

14. ***Military Regulations*** *To make rules for the government and regulation of the land and naval forces;*

15. ***Militia*** *To provide for calling forth the militia to execute the laws of the Union, suppress insurrections and repel invasions;*

16. ***Militia Regulations*** *To provide for organizing, arming and disciplining the militia, and for governing such part of them as may be employed in the service of the United States, reserving to the States respectively the appointment of the officers, and the authority of training the militia according to the discipline prescribed by Congress;*

17. ***National Capital*** *To exercise exclusive legislation in all cases whatsoever, over such district (not exceeding ten miles square) as may, by cession of particular states, and the acceptance of Congress, become the seat of the government of the United States, and to exercise like authority over all places purchased by the consent of the legislature of the State in which the same shall be, for the erection of forts, magazines, arsenals, dock-yards, and other needful buildings;—and*

18. ***Necessary Laws*** *To make all laws which shall be necessary and proper for carrying into execution the foregoing powers, and all other powers vested by this Constitution in the government of the United States, or in any department or officer thereof.*

Taxation Only Congress has the power to collect taxes. Federal taxes must be the same in all parts of the country.

Commerce Congress controls both trade with foreign countries and trade among states.

Naturalization and Bankruptcy Naturalization is the process by which a person from another country becomes a United States citizen. Congress decides the requirements for this procedure.

Coins and Measures Congress has the power to coin money and set its value.

Copyrights and Patents Copyrights protect authors. Patents allow inventors to profit from their work by keeping control over it for a certain number of years. Congress grants patents to encourage scientific research.

Declaring War Only Congress can declare war on another country.

Militia Today the Militia is called the National Guard. The National Guard often helps people after floods, tornadoes, and other disasters.

National Capital Congress makes the laws for the District of Columbia, the area where the nation's capital is located.

Necessary Laws This clause allows Congress to make laws on issues, such as television and radio, that are not mentioned in the Constitution.

Historical Documents

SECTION 9. POWERS DENIED TO CONGRESS

1. ***Slave Trade*** *~~The migration or importation of such persons as any of the States now existing shall think proper to admit, shall not be prohibited by the Congress prior to the year 1808, but a tax or duty may be imposed on such importation, not exceeding ten dollars for each person.~~*

2. ***Habeas Corpus*** *The privilege of the writ of habeas corpus shall not be suspended, unless when in cases of rebellion or invasion the public safety may require it.*

3. ***Special Laws*** *No bill of attainder or ex post facto law shall be passed.*

4. ***Direct Taxes*** *~~No capitation or other direct tax shall be laid, unless in proportion to the census or enumeration herein before directed to be taken.~~*

5. ***Export Taxes*** *No tax or duty shall be laid on articles exported from any State.*

6. ***Ports*** *No preference shall be given by any regulation of commerce or revenue to the ports of one State over those of another; nor shall vessels bound to, or from, one State, be obliged to enter, clear, or pay duties in another.*

7. ***Regulations on Spending*** *No money shall be drawn from the treasury, but in consequence of appropriations made by law; and a regular statement and account of the receipts and expenditures of all public money shall be published from time to time.*

8. ***Titles of Nobility and Gifts*** *No title of nobility shall be granted by the United States: and no person holding any office or profit or trust under them, shall, without the consent of the Congress, accept of any present, emolument, office, or title, of any kind whatever, from any king, prince, or foreign state.*

SECTION 10. POWERS DENIED TO THE STATES

1. ***Complete Restrictions*** *No State shall enter into any treaty, alliance, or confederation; grant letters of marque and reprisal; coin money; emit bills of credit; make anything but gold and silver coin a tender in payment of debts; pass any bill of attainder, ex post facto law, or law impairing the obligation of contracts, or grant any title of nobility.*

2. ***Partial Restrictions*** *No State shall, without the consent of the Congress, lay any imposts or duties on imports or exports, except what may be absolutely necessary for executing its inspection laws; and the net produce of all duties and imposts, laid by any State on imports or exports, shall be for the use of the treasury of the United States; and all such laws shall be subject to the revision and control of the Congress.*

3. ***Other Restrictions*** *No State shall, without the consent of Congress, lay any duty of tonnage, keep troops, or ships of war in time of peace, enter into any agreement or compact with another State, or with a foreign power, or engage in war, unless actually invaded, or in such imminent danger as will not admit of delay.*

ARTICLE II
Executive Branch

SECTION 1. PRESIDENT AND VICE PRESIDENT

1. ***Term of Office*** *The executive power shall be vested in a President of the United States of America. He shall hold his office during the term of four years, and together with the Vice President, chosen for the same term, be elected as follows:*

2. ***Electoral College*** *Each State shall appoint, in such manner as the legislature thereof may direct, a number of electors, equal to the whole number of senators and representatives to which the State may be entitled in the Congress; but no*

Slave Trade This clause was another compromise between the North and the South. It prevented Congress from regulating the slave trade for 20 years. Congress outlawed the slave trade in 1808.

Habeas Corpus A writ of habeas corpus requires the government either to charge a person in jail with a particular crime or let the person go free. Except in emergencies, Congress cannot deny the right of a person to a writ.

Ports When regulating trade, Congress must treat all states equally. Also, states cannot tax goods traveling between states.

Regulations on Spending Congress controls the spending of public money. This clause checks the President's power.

Complete Restrictions The Constitution prevents the states from acting like individual countries. States cannot make treaties with foreign nations. They cannot issue their own money.

Partial Restrictions States cannot tax imports and exports without approval from Congress.

Other Restrictions States cannot declare war. They cannot keep their own armies.

Term of Office The President has the power to carry out the laws passed by Congress. The President and the Vice President serve four-year terms.

Electoral College A group of people called the Electoral College actually elects the President. The number of electors each state receives equals the total number of its representatives and senators.

Historical Documents

senator or representative, or person holding an office of trust or profit under the United States, shall be appointed an elector.

3. ***Election Process*** *~~The electors shall meet in their respective States, and vote by ballot for two persons, of whom one at least shall not be an inhabitant of the same State with themselves. And they shall make a list of all the persons voted for, and of the number of votes for each; which list they shall sign and certify, and transmit sealed to the seat of the government of the United States, directed to the President of the Senate. The President of the Senate shall, in the presence of the Senate and House of Representatives, open all the certificates, and the votes shall then be counted. The person having the greatest number of votes shall be the President, if such number be a majority of the whole number of electors appointed; and if there be more than one who have such majority, and have an equal number of votes, then the House of Representatives shall immediately choose by ballot one of them for President; and if no person have a majority, then from the five highest on the list the said house shall in like manner choose the President. But in choosing the President, the votes shall be taken by States, the representation from each State having one vote; a quorum for this purpose shall consist of a member or members from two thirds of the States, and a majority of all the States shall be necessary to a choice. In every case, after the choice of the President, the person having the greatest number of votes of the electors shall be the Vice President. But if there should remain two or more who have equal votes, the Senate shall choose from them by ballot the Vice President.~~*

4. ***Time of Elections*** *The Congress may determine the time of choosing the electors, and the day on which they shall give their votes; which day shall be the same throughout the United States.*

5. ***Qualifications*** *No person except a natural-born citizen, ~~or a citizen of the United States at the time of the adoption of this Constitution,~~ shall be eligible to the office of President; neither shall any person be eligible to that office who shall not have attained to the age of thirty-five years, and been fourteen years a resident within the United States.*

6. ***Vacancies*** *~~In case of the removal of the President from office, or of his death, resignation, or inability to discharge the powers and duties of the said office, the same shall devolve on the Vice President, and the Congress may by law provide for the case of removal, death, resignation, or inability, both of the President and Vice President, declaring what officer shall then act as President, and such officer shall act accordingly, until the disability be removed, or a President shall be elected.~~*

7. ***Salary*** *The President shall, at stated times, receive for his services a compensation, which shall neither be increased nor diminished during the period for which he shall have been elected, and he shall not receive within that period any other emolument from the United States, or any of them.*

8. ***Oath of Office*** *Before he enter on the execution of his office, he shall take the following oath or affirmation:—"I do solemnly swear (or affirm) that I will faithfully execute the office of President of the United States, and will to the best of my ability, preserve, protect and defend the Constitution of the United States."*

SECTION 2. POWERS OF THE PRESIDENT

1. ***Military Powers*** *The President shall be commander in chief of the army and navy of the United States, and of the militia of the several States, when called into the actual service of the United States; he may require the opinion, in writing, of the principal officer in each of the executive departments, upon any subject relating to the duties of their respective offices, and he shall have power to*

Election Process Originally, electors voted for two people. The candidate who received the majority of votes became President. The runner-up became Vice President. Problems with this system led to the 12th Amendment, which changed the electoral college system.

Today electors almost always vote for the candidate who won the popular vote in their states. In other words, the candidate who wins the popular vote in a state also wins its electoral votes.

Time of Elections Today we elect our President on the Tuesday after the first Monday in November.

Qualifications A President must be at least 35 years old, a United States citizen by birth, and a resident of the United States for at least 14 years.

Vacancies If the President resigns, dies, or is impeached and found guilty, the Vice President becomes President. The 25th Amendment replaced this clause in 1967.

Salary The President receives a yearly salary that cannot be increased or decreased during his or her term. The President cannot hold any other paid government positions while in office.

Oath of Office Every President must promise to uphold the Constitution. The Chief Justice of the Supreme Court usually administers this oath.

Military Powers The President is the leader of the country's military forces.

Historical Documents

grant reprieves and pardons for offenses against the United States, except in cases of impeachment.

2. ***Treaties and Appointments*** *He shall have power, by and with the advice and consent of the Senate, to make treaties, provided two-thirds of the Senators present concur; and he shall nominate, and by with the advice and consent of the Senate, shall appoint ambassadors, other public ministers and consuls, judges of the Supreme Court, and all other officers of the United States, whose appointments are not herein otherwise provided for, and which shall be established by law: but the Congress may by law vest the appointment of such inferior officers, as they think proper, in the President alone, in the courts of law, or in the heads of departments.*

3. ***Temporary Appointments*** *The President shall have power to fill up all vacancies that may happen during the recess of the Senate, by granting commissions which shall expire at the end of their next session.*

SECTION 3. DUTIES

He shall from time to time give to the Congress information of the State of the Union, and recommend to their consideration such measures as he shall judge necessary and expedient; he may on extraordinary occasions, convene both houses, or either of them, and in case of disagreement between them with respect to the time of adjournment, he may adjourn them to such time as he shall think proper; he shall receive ambassadors and other public ministers; he shall take care that the laws be faithfully executed, and shall commission all the officers of the United States.

SECTION 4. IMPEACHMENT

The President, Vice President, and all civil officers of the United States, shall be removed from office on impeachment for, and conviction of, treason, bribery, or other high crimes and misdemeanors.

ARTICLE III
Judicial Branch

SECTION 1. FEDERAL COURTS

The judicial power of the United States shall be vested in one Supreme Court, and in such inferior courts as the Congress may from time to time ordain and establish. The judges, both of the Supreme and inferior courts, shall hold their offices during good behaviour, and shall, at stated times, receive for their services, a compensation, which shall not be diminished during their continuance in office.

SECTION 2. AUTHORITY OF THE FEDERAL COURTS

1. ***General Jurisdiction*** *The judicial power shall extend to all cases, in law and equity, arising under this Constitution, the laws of the United States, and treaties made, or which shall be made, under their authority; to all cases affecting ambassadors, other public ministers and consuls; to all cases of admiralty and maritime jurisdiction; to controversies to which the United States shall be a party; to controversies between two or more States; between a State and citizens of another State; between citizens of different States; between citizens of the same State claiming lands under grants of different States, and between a State, or the citizens thereof, and foreign states, citizens or subjects.*

Treaties and Appointments The President can make treaties with other nations. However, treaties must be approved by a two-thirds vote of the Senate. The President also appoints Supreme Court Justices and ambassadors to foreign countries. The Senate must approve these appointments.

Duties The President must report to Congress at least once a year and make recommendations for laws. This report is known as the State of the Union address. The President delivers it each January.

Impeachment The President and other officials can be forced out of office only if found guilty of particular crimes. This clause protects government officials from being impeached for unimportant reasons.

Federal Courts The Supreme Court is the highest court in the nation. It makes the final decisions in all of the cases it hears. Congress decides the size of the Supreme Court. Today it contains nine judges. Congress also has the power to set up a system of lower federal courts. All federal judges may hold their offices for as long as they live.

General Jurisdiction Jurisdiction means the right of a court to hear a case. Federal courts have jurisdiction over such cases as those involving the Constitution, federal laws, treaties, and disagreements between states.

The President delivers the State of the Union address each year.

Historical Documents

The Supreme Court One of the Supreme Court's most important jobs is to decide whether laws that pass are constitutional. This power is another example of the checks and balances system in the federal government.

Trial by Jury The Constitution guarantees everyone the right to a trial by jury. The only exception is in impeachment cases, which are tried in the Senate.

*2. **The Supreme Court** In all cases affecting ambassadors, other public ministers and consuls, and those in which a State shall be party, the Supreme Court shall have original jurisdiction. In all the other cases before mentioned, the Supreme Court shall have appellate jurisdiction, both as to law and fact, with such exceptions, and under such regulations as the Congress shall make.*

*3. **Trial by Jury** The trial of all crimes, except in cases of impeachment, shall be by jury; and such trial shall be held in the State where the said crimes shall have been committed; but when not committed within any state, the trial shall be at such place or places as the Congress may by law have directed.*

SECTION 3. TREASON

Definition People cannot be convicted of treason in the United States for what they think or say. To be guilty of treason, a person must rebel against the government by using violence or helping enemies of the country.

*1. **Definition** Treason against the United States shall consist only in levying war against them, or in adhering to their enemies, giving them aid and comfort. No person shall be convicted of treason unless on the testimony of two witnesses to the same overt act, or on confession in open court.*

*2. **Punishment** The Congress shall have power to declare the punishment of treason, but no attainder of treason shall work corruption of blood, or forfeiture except during the life of the person attainted.*

ARTICLE IV
Relations Among the States

SECTION 1. OFFICIAL RECORDS

Official Records Each state must accept the laws, acts, and legal decisions made by other states.

Full faith and credit shall be given in each state to the public acts, records and judicial proceedings of every other State. And the Congress may by general laws prescribe the manner in which such acts, records, and proceedings shall be proved, and the effect thereof.

SECTION 2. PRIVILEGES OF THE CITIZENS

Privileges States must give the same rights to citizens of other states that they give to ther own citizens.

Return of a Person Accused of a Crime If a person charged with a crime escapes to another state, he or she must be returned to the original state to go on trial. This act of returning someone from one state to another is called extradition.

*1. **Privileges** The citizens of each State shall be entitled to all privileges and immunities of citizens in the several states.*

*2. **Return of a Person Accused of a Crime** A person charged in any State with treason, felony, or other crime, who shall flee from justice, and be found in another State, shall on demand of the executive authority of the State from which he fled, be delivered up, to be removed to the State having jurisdiction of the crime.*

*3. **Return of Fugitive Slaves** ~~No person held to service or labor in one State, under the laws thereof, escaping into another, shall, in consequence of any law or regulation therein, be discharged from such service or labor, but shall be delivered up on claim of the party to whom such service or labor may be due.~~*

Every American has a right to a trial by jury. Jurors' chairs are shown below.

SECTION 3. NEW STATES AND TERRITORIES

*1. **New States** New states may be admitted by the Congress into this Union; but no new State shall be formed or erected within the jurisdiction of any other State, nor any State be formed by the junction of two or more States, or parts of States, without the consent of the legislatures of the States concerned, as well as of the Congress.*

*2. **Federal Lands** The Congress shall have power to dispose of and make all needful rules and regulations respecting the territory or other property belonging to the United States; and nothing in this Constitution shall be so construed as to prejudice any claims of the United States, or of any particular State.*

New States Congress has the power to create new states out of the nation's territories. All new states have the same rights as the old states. This clause made it clear that the United States would not make colonies out of its new lands.

SECTION 4. GUARANTEES TO THE STATES

The United States shall guarantee to every State in this Union a republican form of government, and shall protect each of them against invasion; and on application of the legislature, or of the executive (when the legislature cannot be convened) against domestic violence.

Guarantees to the State The federal government must defend the states from rebellions and from attacks by other countries.

ARTICLE V
Amending the Constitution

The Congress, whenever two-thirds of both houses shall deem it necessary, shall propose amendments to this Constitution, or, on the application of the legislatures of two-thirds of the several States, shall call a convention for proposing amendments, which, in either case, shall be valid to all intents and purposes, as part of this Constitution, when ratified by the legislatures of three-fourths of the several States, or by conventions in three-fourths thereof, as the one or the other mode of ratification may be proposed by the Congress; provided, ~~that no amendment which may be made prior to the year 1808, shall in any manner affect the first and fourth clauses in the ninth section of the first article;~~ and that no State, without its consent, shall be deprived of its equal suffrage in the Senate.

Amending the Constitution An amendment to the Constitution may be proposed either by a two-thirds vote of each house of Congress or by a national convention called by Congress at the request of two-thirds of the state legislatures. To be ratified, or approved, an amendment must be supported by three-fourths of the state legislatures or by three-fourths of special conventions held in each state.

Once an amendment is ratified, it becomes part of the Constitution. Only a new amendment can change it. Amendments have allowed people to change the Constitution to meet the changing needs of the nation.

ARTICLE VI
General Provisions

*1. **Public Debt** All debts contracted and engagements entered into, before the adoption of this Constitution, shall be as valid against the United States under this Constitution, as under the Confederation.*

*2. **Federal Supremacy** This Constitution, and the laws of the United States which shall be made in pursuance thereof; and all treaties made, or which shall be made, under the authority of the United States, shall be the supreme law of the land; and the judges in every State shall be bound thereby, anything in the Constitution or laws of any State to the contrary notwithstanding.*

*3. **Oaths of Office** The senators and representatives before mentioned, and the members of the several State legislatures, and all executive and judicial officers, both of the United States, and of the several States, shall be bound by oath or affirmation to support this Constitution; but no religious test shall ever be required as a qualification to any office or public trust under the United States.*

Federal Supremacy The Constitution is the highest law in the nation. Whenever a state law and a federal law are different, the federal law must be obeyed.

Oaths of Office All state and federal officials must take an oath promising to obey the Constitution.

ARTICLE VII
Ratification

Ratification The Constitution went into effect as soon as nine of the 13 states approved it.

Each state held a special convention to debate the Constitution. The ninth state to approve the Constitution, New Hampshire, voted for ratification on June 21, 1788.

The ratification of the conventions of nine States shall be sufficient for the establishment of this Constitution between the States so ratifying the same.

Done in Convention by the unanimous consent of the States present the seventeenth day of September in the year of our Lord one thousand seven hundred and eighty-seven and of the independence of the United States of America the twelfth. In witness whereof we have hereunto subscribed our names.

George Washington, President and deputy from Virginia

DELAWARE
George Read
Gunning Bedford, Junior
John Dickinson
Richard Bassett
Jacob Broom

MARYLAND
James McHenry
Daniel of St. Thomas Jenifer
Daniel Carroll

VIRGINIA
John Blair
James Madison, Junior

NORTH CAROLINA
William Blount
Richard Dobbs Spaight
Hugh Williamson

SOUTH CAROLINA
John Rutledge
Charles Cotesworth Pinckney
Charles Pinckney
Pierce Butler

GEORGIA
William Few
Abraham Baldwin

NEW HAMPSHIRE
John Langdon
Nicholas Gilman

MASSACHUSETTS
Nathaniel Gorham
Rufus King

CONNECTICUT
William Samuel Johnson
Roger Sherman

NEW YORK
Alexander Hamilton

NEW JERSEY
William Livingston
David Brearley
William Paterson
Jonathan Dayton

PENNSYLVANIA
Benjamin Franklin
Thomas Mifflin
Robert Morris
George Clymer
Thomas FitzSimons
Jared Ingersoll
James Wilson
Gouverneur Morris

Delegates wait for their turn to sign the new Constitution.

AMENDMENTS TO THE CONSTITUTION

Amendments to the Constitution

AMENDMENT I (1791)*
Basic Freedoms

Congress shall make no law respecting an establishment of religion, or prohibiting the free exercise thereof; or abridging the freedom of speech, or of the press; or the right of the people peaceably to assemble, and to petition the government for a redress of grievances.

Basic Freedoms The government cannot pass laws that favor one religion over another. Nor can it stop people from saying or writing whatever they want. The people have the right to gather openly and discuss problems they have with the government.

AMENDMENT II (1791)
Weapons and the Militia

A well-regulated militia, being necessary to the security of a free State, the right of the people to keep and bear arms, shall not be infringed.

Weapons and the Militia This amendment was included to prevent the federal government from taking away guns used by members of state militias.

AMENDMENT III (1791)
Housing Soldiers

No soldier shall, in time of peace, be quartered in any house, without the consent of the owner, nor in time of war, but in a manner to be prescribed by law.

Housing Soldiers The army cannot use people's homes to house soldiers unless it is approved by law. Before the American Revolution, the British housed soldiers in private homes without permission of the owners.

AMENDMENT IV (1791)
Search and Seizure

The right of the people to be secure in their persons, houses, papers, and effects, against unreasonable searches and seizures, shall not be violated, and no warrants shall issue, but upon probable cause, supported by oath or affirmation, and particularly describing the place to be searched, and the persons or things to be seized.

Search and Seizure This amendment protects people's privacy in their homes. The government cannot search or seize anyone's property without a warrant, or a written order, from a court. A warrant must list the people and the property to be searched and give reasons for the search.

AMENDMENT V (1791)
Rights of the Accused

No person shall be held to answer for a capital, or otherwise infamous crime, unless on a presentment or indictment of a grand jury, except in cases arising in the land or naval forces, or in the militia, when in actual service in time of war or public danger; nor shall any person be subject for the same offense to be twice put in jeopardy of life or limb; nor shall be compelled in any criminal case to be a witness against himself, nor be deprived of life, liberty, or property, without due process of law; nor shall private property be taken for public use without just compensation.

Rights of the Accused A person accused of a crime has the right to a fair trial. A person cannot be tried twice for the same crime. This amendment also protects a person from self-incrimination, or having to testify against himself or herself.

AMENDMENT VI (1791)
Right to a Fair Trial

In all criminal prosecutions, the accused shall enjoy the right to a speedy and public trial, by an impartial jury of the State and district wherein the crime shall have been committed, which district shall have been previously ascertained by law, and to be informed of the nature and cause of the accusation; to be confronted with the witnesses against him; to have compulsory process for obtaining witnesses in his favor, and to have the assistance of counsel for his defense.

Right to a Fair Trial Anyone accused of a crime is entitled to a quick and fair trial by jury. This right protects people from being kept in jail without being convicted of a crime. Also, the government must provide a lawyer for anyone accused of a crime who cannot afford to hire a lawyer.

AMENDMENT VII (1791)
Jury Trial in Civil Cases

In suits at common law, where the value in controversy shall exceed twenty dollars, the right of trial by jury shall be preserved, and no fact tried by a jury shall be otherwise reexamined in any court of the United States, than according to the rules of the common law.

Jury Trial in Civil Cases Civil cases usually involve two or more people suing each other over money, property, or personal injury. A jury trial is guaranteed in large lawsuits.

*The date after each amendment indicates the year the amendment was ratified.

Historical Documents Pupil Book pp. R22–R29

AMENDMENT VIII (1791)
Bail and Punishment

Excessive bail shall not be required, nor excessive fines imposed, nor cruel and unusual punishments inflicted.

Bail and Punishment Courts cannot treat people accused of crimes in ways that are unusually harsh.

AMENDMENT IX (1791)
Powers Reserved to the People

The enumeration in the Constitution, of certain rights, shall not be construed to deny or disparage others retained by the people.

Powers Reserved to the People The people keep all rights not listed in the Constitution.

AMENDMENT X (1791)
Powers Reserved to the States

The powers not delegated to the United States by the Constitution, nor prohibited by it to the States, are reserved to the States respectively, or to the people.

Powers Reserved to the States Any rights not clearly given to the federal government by the Constitution belong to the states or the people.

AMENDMENT XI (1795)
Suits Against States

The judicial power of the United States shall not be construed to extend to any suit in law or equity, commenced or prosecuted against one of the United States by citizens of another State, or by citizens or subjects of any foreign State.

Suits Against the States A citizen from one state cannot sue the government of another state in a federal court. Such cases are decided in state courts.

AMENDMENT XII (1804)
Election of the President and Vice President

The electors shall meet in their respective States and vote by ballot for President and Vice President, one of whom, at least, shall not be an inhabitant of the same State with themselves; they shall name in their ballots the person voted for as President, and in distinct ballots the person voted for as Vice President, and they shall make distinct lists of all persons voted for as President, and of all persons voted for as Vice President, and of the number of votes for each, which lists they shall sign and certify, and transmit sealed to the seat of the government of the United States, directed to the President of the Senate; the President of the Senate shall, in the presence of the Senate and House of Representatives, open all the certificates and the votes shall then be counted; the person having the greatest number of votes for President, shall be the President, if such number be a majority of the whole number of electors appointed; and if no person have such majority, then from the persons having the highest numbers not exceeding three on the list of those voted for as President, the House of Representatives shall choose immediately, by ballot, the President. But in choosing the President, the votes shall be taken by States, the representation from each State having one vote; a quorum for this purpose shall consist of a member or members from two-thirds of the States, and a majority of all the States shall be necessary to a choice. And if the House of Representatives shall not choose a President whenever the right of choice shall devolve upon them, before the fourth day of March next following, then the Vice President shall act as President, as in case of the death or other constitutional disability of the President. The person having the greatest number of votes as Vice President, shall be the Vice President, if such number be a majority of the whole number of electors appointed, and if no person have a majority, then from the two highest numbers on the list, the Senate shall choose the Vice President; a quorum for the purpose shall consist of two-thirds of the whole number of Senators, and a majority of the whole number shall be necessary to a choice. But no person constitutionally ineligible to the office of President shall be eligible to that of Vice President of the United States.

Election of the President and Vice President Under the original Constitution, each member of the Electoral College voted for two candidates for President. The candidate with the most votes became President. The one with the second highest total became Vice President.

The 12th Amendment changed this system. Members of the electoral college distinguish between their votes for the President and Vice President. This change was an important step in the development of the two party system. It allows each party to nominate its own team of candidates.

The Twelfth Amendment allowed parties to nominate teams of candidates, as this campaign poster shows.

AMENDMENT XIII (1865)
End of Slavery

SECTION 1. ABOLITION

Neither slavery nor involuntary servitude, except as a punishment for crime whereof the party shall have been duly convicted, shall exist within the United States, or any place subject to their jurisdiction.

SECTION 2. ENFORCEMENT

Congress shall have power to enforce this article by appropriate legislation.

This etching shows a group of former slaves celebrating their emancipation.

Abolition This amendment ended slavery in the United States. It was ratified after the Civil War.

AMENDMENT XIV (1868)
Rights of Citizens

SECTION 1. CITIZENSHIP

All persons born or naturalized in the United States, and subject to the jurisdiction thereof, are citizens of the United States and of the State wherein they reside. No State shall make or enforce any law which shall abridge the privileges or immunities of citizens of the United States; nor shall any State deprive any person of life, liberty, or property, without due process of law; nor deny to any person within its jurisdiction the equal protection of the laws.

Citizenship This amendment defined citizenship in the United States. "Due process of law" means that no state can deny its citizens the rights and privileges they enjoy as United States citizens. The goal of this amendment was to protect the rights of the recently freed African Americans.

SECTION 2. NUMBER OF REPRESENTATIVES

Representatives shall be apportioned among the several States according to their respective numbers, counting the whole number of persons in each State, excluding Indians not taxed. But when the right to vote at any election for the choice of electors for President and Vice President of the United States, representatives in Congress, the executive and judicial officers of a State, or the members of the legislature thereof, is denied to any of the male inhabitants of such State, being twenty-one years of age, and citizens of the United States, or in any way abridged, except for participation in rebellion, or other crime, the basis of representation therein shall be reduced in the proportion which the number of such male citizens shall bear to the whole number of male citizens twenty-one years of age in such State.

Number of Representatives This clause replaced the Three-Fifths Clause in Article 1. Each state's representation is based on its total population. Any state denying its male citizens over the age of 21 the right to vote will have its representation in Congress decreased.

SECTION 3. PENALTY FOR REBELLION

No person shall be a senator or representative in Congress, or elector of President and Vice President, or hold any office, civil or military, under the United States, or under any State, who, having previously taken an oath, as a member of Congress, or as an officer of the United States, or as a member of any State legislature, or as an executive or judicial officer of any State, to support the Constitution of the United States, shall have engaged in insurrection or rebellion against the same, or given aid or comfort to the enemies thereof. But Congress may by a vote of two-thirds of each house, remove such disability.

Penalty of Rebellion Officials who fought against the Union in the Civil War could not hold public office in the United States. This clause tried to keep Confederate leaders out of power. In 1872, Congress removed this limit.

SECTION 4. GOVERNMENT DEBT

The validity of the public debt of the United States, authorized by law, including debts incurred for payment of pensions and bounties for services in suppressing insurrection or rebellion, shall not be questioned. But neither the United States nor any State shall assume or pay any debt or obligation incurred in aid of insurrection or rebellion against the United States, or any claim for the loss or emancipation of any slave; but all such debts, obligations and claims shall be held illegal and void.

Government Debt The United States paid all of the Union's debts from the Civil War. However, it did not pay any of the Confederacy's debts. This clause prevented the southern states from using public money to pay for the rebellion or from compensating citizens who lost their enslaved persons.

SECTION 5. ENFORCEMENT

The Congress shall have power to enforce, by appropriate legislation, the provisions of this article.

AMENDMENT XV (1870)
Voting Rights

SECTION 1. RIGHT TO VOTE

The right of citizens of the United States to vote shall not be denied or abridged by the United States or by any State on account of race, color, or previous condition of servitude.

Right to Vote No state can deny its citizens the right to vote because of their race. This amendment was designed to protect the voting rights of African Americans.

SECTION 2. ENFORCEMENT

The Congress shall have power to enforce this article by appropriate legislation.

AMENDMENT XVI (1913)
Income Tax

The Congress shall have power to lay and collect taxes on incomes, from whatever sources derived, without apportionment among the several States, and without regard to any census or enumeration.

Income Tax Congress has the power to tax personal incomes.

AMENDMENT XVII (1913)
Direct Election of Senators

SECTION 1. METHOD OF ELECTION

The Senate of the United States shall be composed of two senators from each State, elected by the people thereof, for six years; and each senator shall have one vote. The electors in each State shall have the qualifications requisite for electors of the most numerous branch of the State legislatures.

Direct Election of Senators In the original Constitution, the state legislatures elected senators. This amendment gave citizens the power to elect their senators directly. It made senators more responsible to the people they represented.

SECTION 2. VACANCIES

When vacancies happen in the representation of any State in the Senate, the executive authority of such State shall issue writs of election to fill such vacancies: Provided, that the legislature of any State may empower the executive thereof to make temporary appointments until the people fill the vacancies by election as the legislature may direct.

SECTION 3. EXCEPTION

~~*This amendment shall not be so construed as to affect the election or term of any Senator chosen before it becomes valid as part of the Constitution.*~~

The Prohibition movement used posters like this to reach the public.

AMENDMENT XVIII (1919)
Ban on Alcoholic Drinks

SECTION 1. PROHIBITION

~~*After one year from the ratification of this article the manufacture, sale, or transportation of intoxicating liquors within, the importation thereof into, or the exportation thereof from the United States and all territory subject to the jurisdiction thereof for beverage purposes is hereby prohibited.*~~

Prohibition This amendment made it against the law to make or sell alcoholic beverages in the United States. This law was called prohibition. Fourteen years later, the 21st Amendment ended Prohibition.

SECTION 2. ENFORCEMENT

~~*The Congress and the several States shall have concurrent power to enforce this article by appropriate legislation.*~~

SECTION 3. RATIFICATION

~~*This article shall be inoperative unless it shall have been ratified as an amendment to the Constitution by the legislatures of the several States, as provided in the Constitution, within seven years from the date of the submission hereof to the States by Congress.*~~

Ratification The amendment for Prohibition was the first one to include a time limit for ratification. To go into effect, the amendment had to be approved by three-fourths of the states within seven years.

AMENDMENT XIX (1920)
Women's Suffrage

SECTION 1. RIGHT TO VOTE

The right of citizens of the United States to vote shall not be denied or abridged by the United States or by any State on account of sex.

Women's Suffrage This amendment gave the right to vote to all women 21 years of age and older.

SECTION 2. ENFORCEMENT

The Congress shall have power to enforce this article by appropriate legislation.

This 1915 banner pushed the cause of women's suffrage.

AMENDMENT XX (1933)
Terms of Office

SECTION 1. BEGINNING OF TERMS

The terms of the President and Vice-President shall end at noon on the 20th day of January, and the terms of senators and representatives at noon on the 3rd day of January, of the years in which such terms would have ended if this article had not been ratified; and the terms of their successors shall then begin.

Beginning of Terms The President and Vice President's terms begin on January 20th of the year after their election. The terms for senators and representatives begin on January 3rd. Before this amendment, an official defeated in November stayed in office until March.

SECTION 2. SESSIONS OF CONGRESS

The Congress shall assemble at least once in every year, and such meeting shall begin at noon on the 3rd day of January, unless they shall by law appoint a different day.

SECTION 3. PRESIDENTIAL SUCCESSION

If, at the time fixed for the beginning of the term of the President, the President-elect shall have died, the Vice President-elect shall become President. If a President shall not have been chosen before the time fixed for the beginning of his term, or if the President-elect shall have failed to qualify, then the Vice President-elect shall act as President until a President shall have qualified; and the Congress may by law provide for the case wherein neither a President-elect nor a Vice President-elect shall have qualified, declaring who shall then act as President, or the manner in which one who is to act shall be selected, and such person shall act accordingly until a President or Vice President shall have qualified.

Presidential Succession A President who has been elected but has not yet taken office is called the President-elect. If the President-elect dies, then the Vice President-elect becomes President. If neither the President-elect nor the Vice President-elect can take office, then Congress decides who will act as President.

SECTION 4. ELECTIONS DECIDED BY CONGRESS

The Congress may by law provide for the case of the death of any of the persons from whom the House of Representatives may choose a President whenever the right of choice shall have devolved upon them, and for the case of the death of any of the persons from whom the Senate may choose a Vice President whenever the right of choice shall have devolved upon them.

President Kennedy delivers his inaugural address in 1961.

SECTION 5. EFFECTIVE DATE

~~*Sections 1 and 2 shall take effect on the 15th day of October following the ratification of this article.*~~

SECTION 6. RATIFICATION

~~This article shall be inoperative unless it shall have been ratified as an amendment to the Constitution by the legislatures of three fourths of the several States within seven years from the date of its submission.~~

End of Prohibition This amendment repealed, or ended, the 18th Amendment. It made alcoholic beverages legal once again in the United States. However, states can still control or stop the sale of alcohol within their borders.

AMENDMENT XXI (1933)
End of Prohibition

SECTION 1. REPEAL OF EIGHTEENTH AMENDMENT

The eighteenth article of amendment to the Constitution of the United States is hereby repealed.

SECTION 2. STATE LAWS

The transportation or importation into any State, territory, or possession of the United States for delivery or use therein of intoxicating liquors, in violation of the laws thereof, is hereby prohibited.

SECTION 3. RATIFICATION

~~This article shall be inoperative unless it shall have been ratified as an amendment to the Constitution by conventions in the several States, as provided in the Constitution, within seven years from the date of the submission hereof to the States by the Congress.~~

Two-Term Limit George Washington set a precedent that Presidents should not serve more than two terms in office. However, Franklin D. Roosevelt broke the precedent. He was elected President four times between 1932 and 1944. Some people feared that a President holding office for this long could become too powerful. This amendment limits Presidents to two terms in office.

AMENDMENT XXII (1951)
Limit on Presidential Terms

SECTION 1. TWO-TERM LIMIT

No person shall be elected to the office of the President more than twice, and no person who has held the office of President, or acted as President, for more that two years of a term to which some other person was elected President shall be elected to the office of the President more than once. ~~But this article shall not apply to any person holding the office of President when this article was proposed by the Congress, and shall not prevent any person who may be holding the office of President, or acting as President, during the term within which this article becomes operative from holding the office of President or acting as President during the remainder of such term.~~

SECTION 2. RATIFICATION

~~This article shall be inoperative unless it shall have been ratified as an amendment to the Constitution by the legislatures of three fourths of the several States within seven years from the date of its submission to the States by the Congress.~~

Presidential Votes for Washington, D.C. This amendment gives people who live in the nation's capital a vote for President. The electoral votes in Washington D.C., are based on its population. However, it cannot have more votes than the state with the smallest population. Today, Washington, D.C. has three electoral votes.

AMENDMENT XXIII (1961)
Presidential Votes for Washington, D.C.

SECTION 1. NUMBER OF ELECTORS

The District constituting the seat of government of the United States shall appoint in such manner as the Congress may direct:

A number of electors of President and Vice President equal to the whole number of senators and representatives in Congress to which the District would be entitled if it were a State, but in no event more than the least populous State; they shall be in addition to those appointed by the States, but they shall be considered, for the purposes of the election of President and Vice President, to be elec-

tors appointed by a State; and they shall meet in the District and perform such duties as provided by the twelfth article of amendment.

SECTION 2. ENFORCEMENT

The Congress shall have power to enforce this article by appropriate legislation.

African Americans vote in Selma, Alabama, in 1966.

AMENDMENT XXIV (1964)
Ban on Poll Taxes

SECTION 1. POLL TAXES ILLEGAL

The right of citizens of the United States to vote in any primary or other election for President or Vice President, for electors for President or Vice President, or for senator or representative in Congress, shall not be denied or abridged by the United States or any State by reason of failure to pay any poll tax or other tax.

Ban on Poll Taxes A poll tax requires a person to pay a certain amount of money to register to vote. These taxes were used to stop poor African Americans from voting. This amendment made any such taxes illegal in federal elections.

SECTION 2. ENFORCEMENT

The Congress shall have power to enforce this article by appropriate legislation.

AMENDMENT XXV (1967)
Presidential Succession

SECTION 1. VACANCY IN THE PRESIDENCY

In case of the removal of the President from office or of his death or resignation, the Vice President shall become President.

SECTION 2. VACANCY IN THE VICE PRESIDENCY

Whenever there is a vacancy in the office of the Vice President, the President shall nominate a Vice President who shall take office upon confirmation by a majority vote of both houses of Congress.

Vacancy in the Vice Presidency If the Vice President becomes President, he or she may nominate a new Vice President. This nomination must be approved by both houses of Congress.

SECTION 3. DISABILITY OF THE PRESIDENT

Whenever the President transmits to the President pro tempore of the Senate and the Speaker of the House of Representatives his written declaration that he is unable to discharge the powers and duties of his office, and until he transmits to them a written declaration to the contrary, such powers and duties shall be discharged by the Vice President as Acting President.

Disability of the President This section tells what happens if the President suddenly becomes ill or is seriously injured. The Vice President takes over as Acting President. When the President is ready to take office again, he or she must tell Congress.

SECTION 4. DETERMINING PRESIDENTIAL DISABILITY

Whenever the Vice President and a majority of either the principal officers of the executive departments or of such other body as Congress may by law provide, transmit to the President pro tempore of the Senate and the Speaker of the House of Representatives their written declaration that the President is unable to discharge the powers and duties of his office, the Vice President shall immediately assume the powers and duties of the office as Acting President.

Thereafter, when the President transmits to the President pro tempore of the Senate and the Speaker of the House of Representatives his written declaration that no inability exists, he shall resume the powers and duties of his office unless the Vice President and a majority of either the principal officers of the executive departments or of such other body as Congress may by law provide, transmit within four days to the President pro tempore of the Senate and the Speaker of the House of Representatives their written declaration that the President is unable to discharge the powers and duties of his office. Thereupon Congress shall decide

the issue, assembling within 48 hours for that purpose if not in session. If the Congress, within 21 days after receipt of the latter written declaration, or, if Congress is not in session, within 21 days after Congress is required to assemble, determines by two-thirds vote of both houses that the President is unable to discharge the powers and duties of his office, the Vice President shall continue to discharge the same as Acting President; otherwise, the President shall resume the powers and duties of his office.

AMENDMENT XXVI (1971)
Voting Age

Right to Vote This amendment gave the vote to everyone 18 years of age and older.

SECTION 1. RIGHT TO VOTE

The right of citizens of the United States, who are 18 years of age or older, to vote shall not be denied or abridged by the United States or by any state on account of age.

SECTION 2. ENFORCEMENT

The Congress shall have power to enforce this article by appropriate legislation.

AMENDMENT XXVII (1992)
Congressional Pay

Limit on Pay Raises This amendment prohibits a Congressional pay raise from taking effect during the current term of the Congress that voted for the raise.

No law, varying the compensation for the services of the senators and representatives, shall take effect, until an election of representatives shall have intervened.

The voting age was lowered to 18 in 1971.

from *The Federalist* (No. 10) (1787)

The two great points of difference between a democracy and a republic are: first, the delegation of the government, in the latter, to a small number of citizens selected by the rest; secondly, the greater number of citizens and greater sphere of country, over which the latter may be extended.

The effect of the first difference is, on the one hand, to refine and enlarge the public views, by passing them through the medium of a chosen body of citizens, whose wisdom may best discern the true interest of their country and whose patriotism and love of justice will be least likely to sacrifice it to temporary or partial considerations. . . .

By enlarging too much the number of electors, you render the representative too little acquainted with all their local circumstances and lesser interests; as by reducing it too much, you render him unduly attached to these, and too little fit to comprehend and pursue great and national objects. . . .

Extend the sphere and you take in a greater variety of parties and interests; you make it less probable that a majority of the whole will have a common motive to invade the rights of other citizens.

The Star-Spangled Banner (1814)

O say, can you see, by the dawn's early light,
What so proudly we hailed at the twilight's last gleaming,
Whose broad stripes and bright stars, through the perilous fight,
O'er the ramparts we watched were so gallantly streaming?
And the rockets' red glare, the bombs bursting in air,
Gave proof through the night that our flag was still there.
O say, does that Star-Spangled Banner yet wave
O'er the land of the free and the home of the brave?

On the shore, dimly seen through the mists of the deep,
Where the foe's haughty host in dread silence reposes,
What is that which the breeze, o'er the towering steep,
As it fitfully blows, half conceals, half discloses?
Now it catches the gleam of the morning's first beam,
In full glory reflected now shines on the stream;
'Tis the Star-Spangled Banner, O long may it wave
O'er the land of the free and the home of the brave!

O thus be it ever when free men shall stand
Between their loved homes and the war's desolation!
Blest with vict'ry and peace, may the heav'n-rescued land
Praise the Power that hath made and preserved us a nation.
then conquer we must, for our cause it is just,
And this be our motto: 'In God is our trust.'
And the Star-Spangled Banner in triumph shall wave
O'er the land of the free and the home of the brave.

Francis Scott Key wrote "The Star-Spangled Banner" in 1814 while aboard ship during the battle of Fort McHenry. The gallantry and courage displayed by his fellow countrymen that night inspired Key to pen the lyrics to the song that officially became our national anthem in 1931.

Historical Documents Pupil Book pp. R30–R31

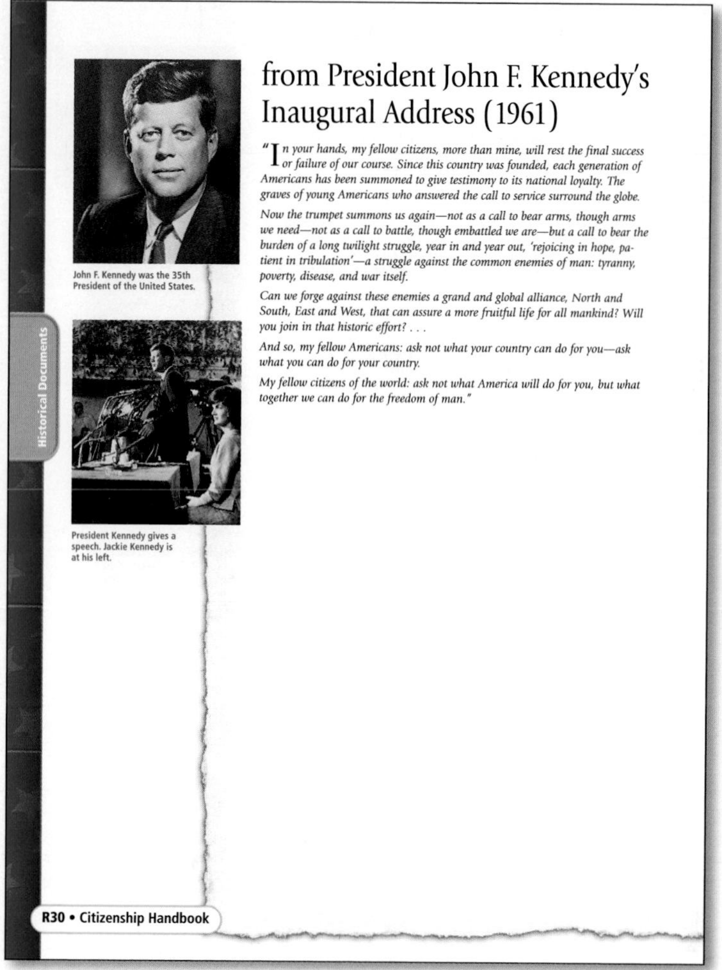

from President John F. Kennedy's Inaugural Address (1961)

"In your hands, my fellow citizens, more than mine, will rest the final success or failure of our course. Since this country was founded, each generation of Americans has been summoned to give testimony to its national loyalty. The graves of young Americans who answered the call to service surround the globe.

Now the trumpet summons us again—not as a call to bear arms, though arms we need—not as a call to battle, though embattled we are—but a call to bear the burden of a long twilight struggle, year in and year out, 'rejoicing in hope, patient in tribulation'—a struggle against the common enemies of man: tyranny, poverty, disease, and war itself.

Can we forge against these enemies a grand and global alliance, North and South, East and West, that can assure a more fruitful life for all mankind? Will you join in that historic effort? . . .

And so, my fellow Americans: ask not what your country can do for you—ask what you can do for your country.

My fellow citizens of the world: ask not what America will do for you, but what together we can do for the freedom of man."

John F. Kennedy was the 35th President of the United States.

President Kennedy gives a speech. Jackie Kennedy is at his left.

Historical Documents

R30 • Citizenship Handbook

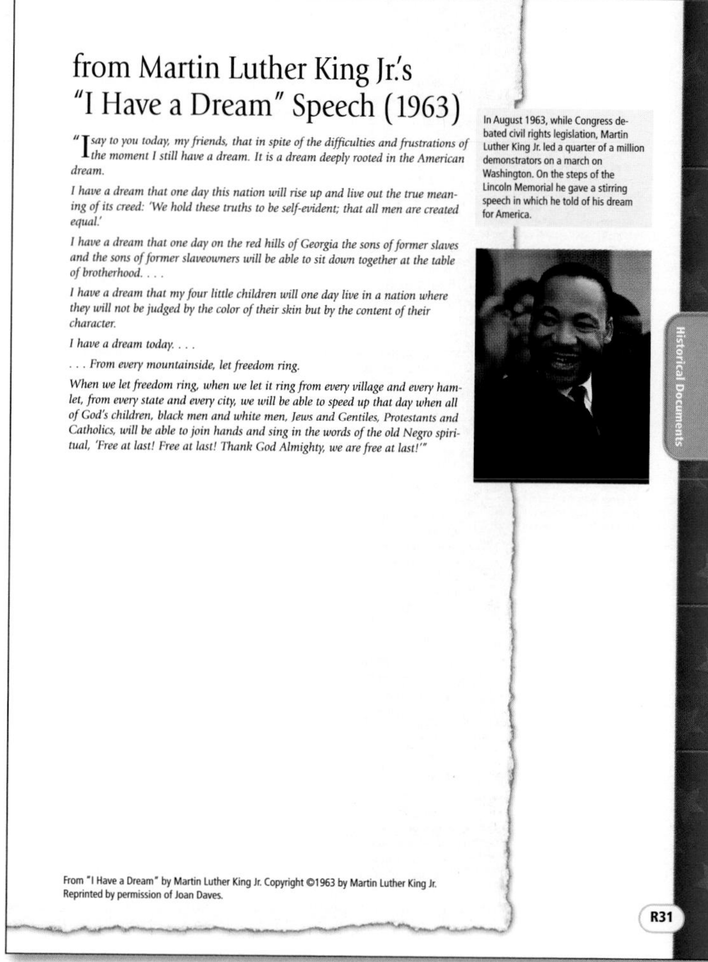

from Martin Luther King Jr.'s "I Have a Dream" Speech (1963)

"I say to you today, my friends, that in spite of the difficulties and frustrations of the moment I still have a dream. It is a dream deeply rooted in the American dream.

I have a dream that one day this nation will rise up and live out the true meaning of its creed: 'We hold these truths to be self-evident; that all men are created equal.'

I have a dream that one day on the red hills of Georgia the sons of former slaves and the sons of former slaveowners will be able to sit down together at the table of brotherhood. . . .

I have a dream that my four little children will one day live in a nation where they will not be judged by the color of their skin but by the content of their character.

I have a dream today. . . .

. . . From every mountainside, let freedom ring.

When we let freedom ring, when we let it ring from every village and every hamlet, from every state and every city, we will be able to speed up that day when all of God's children, black men and white men, Jews and Gentiles, Protestants and Catholics, will be able to join hands and sing in the words of the old Negro spiritual, 'Free at last! Free at last! Thank God Almighty, we are free at last!'"

In August 1963, while Congress debated civil rights legislation, Martin Luther King Jr. led a quarter of a million demonstrators on a march on Washington. On the steps of the Lincoln Memorial he gave a stirring speech in which he told of his dream for America.

Historical Documents

R31

Presidents of the United States

George Washington 1
(1732–1799)
President from: 1789–1797
Party: Federalist
Home state: Virginia
First Lady: Martha Dandridge Custis Washington

John Adams 2
(1735–1826)
President from: 1797–1801
Party: Federalist
Home state: Massachusetts
First Lady: Abigail Smith Adams

Thomas Jefferson 3
(1743–1826)
President from: 1801–1809
Party: Democratic-Republican
Home state: Virginia
First Lady: Martha Jefferson Randolph (daughter)

James Madison 4
(1751–1836)
President from: 1809–1817
Party: Democratic-Republican
Home state: Virginia
First Lady: Dolley Payne Todd Madison

James Monroe 5
(1758–1831)
President from: 1817–1825
Party: Democratic-Republican
Home state: Virginia
First Lady: Elizabeth Kortright Monroe

John Quincy Adams 6
(1767–1848)
President from: 1825–1829
Party: Democratic-Republican
Home state: Massachusetts
First Lady: Louisa Catherine Johnson Adams

Andrew Jackson 7
(1767–1845)
President from: 1829–1837
Party: Democratic
Home state: Tennessee
First Lady: Emily Donelson (late wife's niece)

Martin Van Buren 8
(1782–1862)
President from: 1837–1841
Party: Democratic
Home state: New York
First Lady: Angelica Singleton Van Buren (daughter-in-law)

William Henry Harrison 9
(1773–1841)
President: 1841
Party: Whig
Home state: Ohio
First Lady: Jane Irwin Harrison (daughter-in-law)

John Tyler 10
(1790–1862)
President from: 1841–1845
Party: Whig
Home state: Virginia
First Lady: Letitia Christian Tyler

U.S. Presidents

James K. Polk 11
(1795–1849)
President from: 1845–1849
Party: Democratic
Home state: Tennessee
First Lady: Sarah Childress Polk

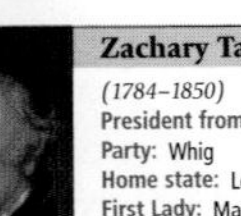

Zachary Taylor 12
(1784–1850)
President from: 1849–1850
Party: Whig
Home state: Louisiana
First Lady: Margaret Mackall Smith Taylor

Millard Fillmore 13
(1800–1874)
President from: 1850–1853
Party: Whig
Home state: New York
First Lady: Abigail Powers Fillmore

Franklin Pierce 14
(1804–1869)
President from: 1853–1857
Party: Democratic
Home state: New Hampshire
First Lady: Jane Means Appleton Pierce

James Buchanan 15
(1791–1868)
President from: 1857–1861
Party: Democratic
Home state: Pennsylvania
First Lady: Harriet Lane (niece)

Abraham Lincoln 16
(1809–1865)
President from: 1861–1865
Party: Republican
Home state: Illinois
First Lady: Mary Todd Lincoln

Andrew Johnson 17
(1808–1875)
President from: 1865–1869
Party: Democratic
Home state: Tennessee
First Lady: Eliza McCardle Johnson

Ulysses S. Grant 18
(1822–1885)
President from: 1869–1877
Party: Republican
Home state: Illinois
First Lady: Julia Dent Grant

Rutherford B. Hayes 19
(1822–1893)
President from: 1877–1881
Party: Republican
Home state: Ohio
First Lady: Lucy Ware Webb Hayes

James A. Garfield 20
(1831–1881)
President: 1881
Party: Republican
Home state: Ohio
First Lady: Lucretia Rudolph Garfield

Chester A. Arthur 21
(1830–1886)
President from: 1881–1885
Party: Republican
Home state: New York
First Lady: Mary Arthur McElroy (sister)

Grover Cleveland 22 24
(1837–1908)
President from: 1885–1889 and 1893–1897
Party: Democratic
Home state: New York
First Lady: Frances Folsom Cleveland

U.S. Presidents

Benjamin Harrison 23
(1833–1901)
President from: 1889–1893
Party: Republican
Home state: Indiana
First Lady: Caroline Lavina Scott Harrison

William McKinley 25
(1843–1901)
President from: 1897–1901
Party: Republican
Home state: Ohio
First Lady: Ida Saxton McKinley

Theodore Roosevelt 26
(1858–1919)
President from: 1901–1909
Party: Republican
Home state: New York
First Lady: Edith Kermit Carow Roosevelt

William Howard Taft 27
(1857–1930)
President from: 1909–1913
Party: Republican
Home state: Ohio
First Lady: Helen Herron Taft

Woodrow Wilson 28
(1856–1924)
President from: 1913–1921
Party: Democratic
Home state: New Jersey
First Lady: Edith Bolling Galt Wilson

Warren G. Harding 29
(1865–1923)
President from: 1921–1923
Party: Republican
Home state: Ohio
First Lady: Florence Kling Harding

Calvin Coolidge 30
(1872–1933)
President from: 1923–1929
Party: Republican
Home state: Massachusetts
First Lady: Grace Anna Goodhue Coolidge

Herbert Hoover 31
(1874–1964)
President from: 1929–1933
Party: Republican
Home state: California
First Lady: Lou Henry Hoover

Franklin Delano Roosevelt 32
(1882–1945)
President from: 1933–1945
Party: Democratic
Home state: New York
First Lady: Anna Eleanor Roosevelt Roosevelt

Harry S. Truman 33
(1884–1972)
President from: 1945–1953
Party: Democratic
Home state: Missouri
First Lady: Elizabeth Virginia Wallace Truman

Dwight D. Eisenhower 34
(1890–1969)
President from: 1953–1961
Party: Republican
Home state: New York
First Lady: Mamie Geneva Doud Eisenhower

John F. Kennedy 35
(1917–1963)
President from: 1961–1963
Party: Democratic
Home state: Massachusetts
First Lady: Jacqueline Lee Bouvier Kennedy

U.S. Presidents

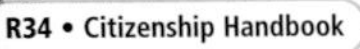

Lyndon Baines Johnson 36
(1908–1973)
President from: 1963–1969
Party: Democratic
Home state: Texas
First Lady: Claudia Alta (Lady Bird) Taylor Johnson

Richard M. Nixon 37
(1913–1994)
President from: 1969–1974
Party: Republican
Home state: New York
First Lady: Thelma Catherine (Pat) Ryan Nixon

Gerald R. Ford 38
(1913–)
President from: 1974–1977
Party: Republican
Home state: Michigan
First Lady: Elizabeth Bloomer Ford

Jimmy Carter 39
(1924–)
President from: 1977–1981
Party: Democratic
Home state: Georgia
First Lady: Rosalynn Smith Carter

Ronald Reagan 40
(1911–)
President from: 1981–1989
Party: Republican
Home state: California
First Lady: Nancy Davis Reagan

George Bush 41
(1924–)
President from: 1989–1993
Party: Republican
Home state: Texas
First Lady: Barbara Pierce Bush

William Clinton 42
(1946–)
President from: 1993–2001
Party: Democratic
Home state: Arkansas
First Lady: Hillary Rodham Clinton

George W. Bush 43
(1946–)
President from: 2001–
Party: Republican
Home state: Texas
First Lady: Laura Welch Bush

U.S. Presidents

Biographical Dictionary

The page number after each entry refers to the place where the person is first mentioned. For more complete references to people, see the Index.

A

Abigail Adams

Adams, Abigail 1744–1818, Patriot during the American Revolution (p. 266).

Adams, John 1735–1826, 2nd President of the United States, 1797–1801 (p. 241).

Adams, Samuel 1722–1803, helped inspire the American Revolution (p. 235).

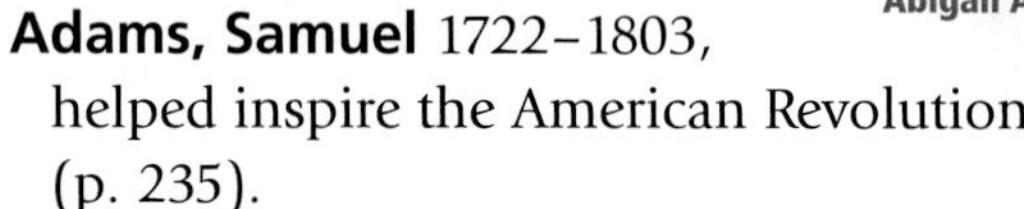

Albright, Madeleine K. 1937–, first female Secretary of State for the United States (p. 513).

Anthony, Susan B. 1820–1906, reformer who fought for women's rights (p. 391).

Arnold, Benedict 1741–1801, general in American Revolution; committed treason (p. 280).

Attucks, Crispus 1723–1770, former slave; killed in the Boston Massacre (p. 240).

B

Balboa, Vasco Núñez de 1475–1519, Spanish explorer (p. 100).

Banneker, Benjamin 1731–1806, helped survey Washington, D.C. (p. 324).

Barton, Clara 1821–1912, nurse in Civil War; began American Red Cross (p. 461).

Boone, Daniel 1734–1820, frontiersman who cut trail into Kentucky (p. 345).

Bradford, William 1590–1657, governor of Plymouth Colony (p. 138).

Brant, Joseph 1742–1807, Mohawk chief who fought for the British (p. 271).

Brown, John 1800–1859, abolitionist who led rebellion at Harpers Ferry (p. 435).

Bruce, Blanche K. 1841–1898, African American planter and politician (p. 476).

C

Cabot, John 1450–1499, English explorer; reached Newfoundland (p. 123).

Calhoun, John C. 1782–1850, politician who supported slavery and states' rights (p. 419).

Carter, Jimmy 1924–, 39th President of the United States, 1977–1981 (p. 506).

Cartier, Jacques 1491–1557, French explorer; sailed up St. Lawrence River (p. 123).

Chavez, Cesar 1927–1993, labor leader; founded the United Farm Workers (p. 534).

Dennis Chavez

Chavez, Dennis 1888–1962, first Hispanic American elected to the U.S. Senate.

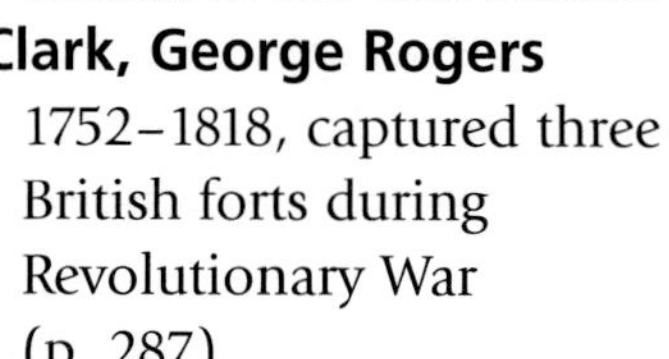

Clark, George Rogers 1752–1818, captured three British forts during Revolutionary War (p. 287).

Clark, William 1770–1838, explored Louisiana Purchase with Lewis (p. 355).

Clay, Henry 1777–1852, proposed the Missouri Compromise and the Compromise of 1850 (p. 432).

Clinton, William J. 1946–, 42nd President of the United States, 1993–2001; impeached, then acquitted (p. 513).

Columbus, Christopher 1451–1506, Italian navigator; reached the Americas (p. 96).

Cooper, James Fenimore 1789–1851, novelist and historian; wrote stories about the American frontier (p. 365).

Cornwallis, Charles 1738–1805, English general in Revolutionary War; surrendered to Americans in 1781 (p. 287).

Coronado, Francisco Vázquez de 1510–1554, Spanish conquistador (p. 106).

Cortés, Hernán 1485–1547, Spanish conquistador (p. 104).

Crockett, Davy 1786–1836, pioneer and member of Congress; died at the Alamo (p. 398).

Davis, Jefferson 1808–1889, president of Confederacy during Civil War (p. 444).

Dawes, William 1745–1799, patriot who rode with Paul Revere (p. 251).

de las Casas, Bartolomé 1474–1566, Spanish missionary opposed to slavery (p. 112).

de Soto, Hernando 1500?–1542, Spanish explorer (p. 106).

Dias, Bartholomeu 1450?–1500, Portuguese navigator (p. 93).

Dix, Dorothea 1802–1887, reformer who worked to improve care for the mentally ill (p. 393).

Douglass, Frederick 1817–1895, abolitionist and writer; escaped from slavery (p. 392).

Du Bois, W.E.B. 1868–1963, educator who helped create the NAACP (p. 526).

Edwards, Jonathan 1703–1758, preached American Puritanism (p. 178).

Elizabeth I 1533–1603, queen of England, 1558–1603; supported Walter Raleigh's colonization of Virginia (p. 124).

Equiano, Olaudah 1745–1797, West African taken into slavery; was freed and became abolitionist in England (p. 176).

Franklin, Benjamin 1706–1790, printer, writer, publisher, scientist, and inventor (p. 190).

Friedan, Betty 1921–, author of *The Feminine Mystique* and leader of women's rights movement (p. 529).

Fulton, Robert 1765–1815, civil engineer; built first profitable steamboat (p. 382).

Gálvez, Bernardo de 1746–1786, Spanish colonial administrator (p. 287).

Gama, Vasco da 1460–1524, Portuguese navigator (p. 93).

Garrison, William Lloyd 1805–1879, reformer and abolitionist (p. 425).

George III 1738–1820, king of England, 1760–1820; supported British policies that led to American Revolution (p. 204).

Goizueta, Roberto 1931–1998, immigrant from Cuba who became President of The Coca-Cola Company (p. 513).

Grant, Ulysses S. 1822–1885, 18th President of the United States, 1869–1877; Union general in Civil War (p. 454).

Greene, Nathanael 1742–1786, general in South during Revolutionary War (p. 287).

Grimke, Angelina 1805–1879, abolitionist and supporter of women's rights (p. 425).

Grimke, Sarah 1792–1873, abolitionist and supporter of women's rights (p. 425).

Hale, Nathan 1755–1776, patriot spy during Revolutionary War; hanged by British (p. 279).

Hamilton, Alexander 1755–1804, contributor to *The Federalist*; first Secretary of the Treasury (p. 306).

Hancock, John 1737–1793, first signer of Declaration of Independence (p. 265).

Henry, Patrick 1736–1799, Revolutionary leader and orator (p. 235).

Houston, Samuel 1793–1863, first president of Republic of Texas (p. 395).

Hudson, Henry ?–1611, English navigator; gave name to Hudson River (p. 124).

Huerta, Dolores 1930–, labor leader; founded United Farm Workers with Cesar Chavez (p. 534).

Hurston, Zora Neale 1891?–1960, writer during the Harlem Renaissance.

Zora Neale Hurston

Irving, Washington 1783–1859, writer of humorous tales, history, and biography (p. 365).

Isabella 1451–1504 queen of Spain, 1474–1504; supported and financed Columbus (p. 96).

R37

J

Jackson, Andrew 1767–1845, 7th President of the United States, 1829–1837; encouraged Western expansion (p. 364).

Jay, John 1745–1829, contributor to *The Federalist;* Chief Justice, U.S. Supreme Court (p. 306).

Jefferson, Thomas 1743–1826, 3rd President of the United States, 1801–1809; wrote Declaration of Independence (p. 264).

Johnson, Andrew 1808–1875, 17th President of the United States, 1865–1869; impeached, then acquitted (p. 474).

K

Key, Francis Scott 1779–1843, writer of *Star-Spangled Banner* (p. 363).

King, Martin Luther, Jr. 1929–1968, civil rights leader; assassinated (p. 531).

Knox, Henry 1750–1806, first U.S. Secretary of War (p. 255).

L

Lafayette, Marquis de 1757–1834, French; fought in American Revolution (p. 280).

Lee, Richard Henry 1732–1794, delegate to Continental Congress (p. 263).

Lee, Robert E. 1807–1870, commander of Confederacy (p. 452).

Lewis, Meriwether 1774–1809, explored Louisiana Purchase with Clark (p. 355).

Lincoln, Abraham 1809–1865, 16th President of the United States; issued Emancipation Proclamation; assassinated (p. 440).

Lowell, Francis Cabot 1775–1817, built first complete cotton spinning and weaving mill in the United States (p. 380).

Madison, Dolley 1768–1849, wife of James Madison; first lady during War of 1812 (p. 363).

Madison, James 1751–1836, 4th President of the United States (p. 303).

Magellan, Ferdinand 1480?–1521, Portuguese explorer (p. 100).

Malinche 1500?–1531, Aztec interpreter and guide for Cortés in 1519 (p. 105).

Mann, Horace 1796–1859, educator who reformed public schools (p. 393).

Marion, Francis 1732?–1795, commander in American Revolution (p. 287).

Marquette, Jacques 1637–1675, French explorer; sailed down Mississippi River (p. 147).

Marshall, John 1755–1835, Chief Justice of U.S. Supreme Court (p. 370).

Marshall, Thurgood 1908–1993, first African American appointed to U.S. Supreme Court.

Metacomet ?–1676, American Indian leader, known as King Philip to British (p. 168).

Mink, Patsy Takemoto 1927–2002, first Asian American woman elected to U.S. Congress.

Patsy Takemoto Mink

Moctezuma 1480?–1520, Aztec emperor during Spanish conquest of Mexico (p. 44).

Monroe, James 1758–1831, 5th President of the United States, 1817–1825 (p. 364).

O

O'Connor, Sandra Day 1930–, first woman appointed to U.S. Supreme Court (p. 529).

Oglethorpe, James 1696–1785, founder of Georgia (p. 204).

Oñate, Juan de 1549?–1624?, conquerer and colonizer of New Mexico (p. 111).

Osceola 1800?–1838, American Indian leader in Florida (p. 371).

Paine, Thomas 1737–1809, wrote *Common Sense,* urging a declaration of independence (p. 262).

Parks, Rosa 1913–, African American who refused to obey segregation laws in Alabama (p. 531).

Pei, I. M. 1917–, famous architect who emigrated from China (p. 513).

Penn, William 1644–1718, founder of Pennsylvania (p. 189).

Biographical Dictionary

Pinckney, Eliza Lucas 1722–1793, introduced growing of indigo (blue dye) in South (p. 211).

Pocahontas 1595?–1617, married colonist John Rolfe; converted to Christianity; American Indian name: Matoaka (p. 132).

Ponce de Léon, Juan 1460?–1521, Spanish explorer of Florida (p. 106).

Pontiac ?–1769, Ottowa chief; united several American Indian nations (p. 230).

Popé ?–1692, Pueblo leader who led a revolt against Spanish settlers in 1680 (p. 113).

R

Randolph, Edmund 1753–1813, U.S. Attorney General and Secretary of State (p. 304).

Rankin, Jeannette 1880–1973, first woman elected to U.S. Congress (p. 529).

Revels, Hiram R. 1822–1901, African American Senator during Reconstruction (p. 476).

Revere, Paul 1735–1818, rode from Boston to Lexington to warn Patriots that the British were coming (p. 241).

Rolfe, John 1585–1622, English colonist; married Pocahontas (p. 132).

Ross, Betsy 1752–1836, maker of flags during the American Revolution.

S

Sacagawea 1787?–1812, Shoshone interpreter for Lewis and Clark (p. 356).

Salem, Peter 1750–1816, patriot who fought at Battle of Bunker Hill in 1775 (p. 271).

Santa Anna, Antonio López de 1795–1876, Mexican general and president during Texas revolution (p. 395).

Scott, Dred 1795?–1858, enslaved African American who sued for his freedom (p. 434).

Sequoya 1770?–1843, Cherokee scholar (p. 370).

Shays, Daniel 1747?–1825, led a rebellion of Massachusetts farmers (p. 298).

Sherman, Roger 1721–1793, member of Constitutional Convention (p. 304).

Sherman, William Tecumseh 1820–1891, Union general in Civil War (p. 466).

Slater, Samuel 1768–1835, set up cotton mill in Rhode Island (p. 378).

Smith, John 1580–1631, leader of Jamestown colony (p. 131).

Stanton, Elizabeth Cady 1815–1902, organized first women's rights conference in Seneca Falls (p. 390).

Steuben, Baron Friedrich von 1730–1794, Prussian soldier; trained American soldiers for Revolution (p. 281).

Stowe, Harriet Beecher 1811–1896, author of *Uncle Tom's Cabin* (p. 434).

Tecumseh 1768?–1813, Shawnee chief (p. 361).

Truth, Sojourner 1797?–1883, abolitionist and supporter of women's rights (p. 392).

Tubman, Harriet 1821?–1913, helped enslaved African Americans to freedom (p. 427).

Turner, Nat 1800–1831, led rebellion of enslaved people; was captured and hanged (p. 417).

Warren, Mercy Otis 1728–1814, author of political works (p. 250).

Washington, George 1732–1799, commanded Continental armies during Revolution; first President of the United States, 1789–1797 (p. 228).

Webster, Noah 1758–1843, wrote first American dictionary (p. 365).

Wheatley, Phillis 1753?–1784, African American poet (p. 272).

Whitefield, George 1714–1770, popular Great Awakening minister (p. 178).

Whitman, Marcus 1802–1847, missionary and pioneer in Oregon territory (p. 400).

Whitney, Eli 1765–1825, inventor of the cotton gin (p. 379).

Wright, Orville 1871–1948, made first successful flight in motorized plane.

Wright, Wilbur 1867–1912, made first successful flight in motorized plane.

Orville Wright

Wilbur Wright

Young, Brigham 1801–1877, Mormon leader; settled in Utah (p. 401).

R39

FACTS TO KNOW

The 50 United States

ALABAMA

22nd
Heart of Dixie

Population: 4,500,752
Area: 52,423 square miles
Admitted: December 14, 1819

ALASKA

49th
The Last Frontier

Population: 648,818
Area: 656,424 square miles
Admitted: January 3, 1959

ARIZONA

48th
Grand Canyon State

Population: 5,580,811
Area: 114,006 square miles
Admitted: February 14, 1912

ARKANSAS

25th
The Natural State

Population: 2,725,714
Area: 53,182 square miles
Admitted: June 15, 1836

CALIFORNIA

31st
Golden State

Population: 35,484,453
Area: 163,707 square miles
Admitted: September 9, 1850

COLORADO

8th
Centennial State

Population: 4,550,688
Area: 104,100 square miles
Admitted: August 1, 1876

CONNECTICUT

5th
Constitution State

Population: 3,483,372
Area: 5,544 square miles
Admitted: January 9, 1788

DELAWARE

1st
First State

Population: 817,491
Area: 2,489 square miles
Admitted: December 7, 1787

FLORIDA

27th
Sunshine State

Population: 17,019,068
Area: 65,758 square miles
Admitted: March 3, 1845

GEORGIA

4th
Peach State

Population: 8,684,715
Area: 59,441 square miles
Admitted: January 2, 1788

HAWAII

50th
The Aloha State

Population: 1,257,608
Area: 10,932 square miles
Admitted: August 21, 1959

IDAHO

43rd
Gem State

Population: 1,366,332
Area: 83,574 square miles
Admitted: July 3, 1890

ILLINOIS

21st
The Prairie State

Population: 12,653,544
Area: 57,918 square miles
Admitted: December 3, 1818

INDIANA

19th
Hoosier State

Population: 6,195,643
Area: 36,420 square miles
Admitted: December 11, 1816

IOWA

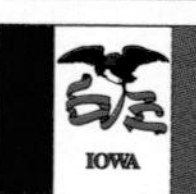

29th
Hawkeye State

Population: 2,944,062
Area: 56,276 square miles
Admitted: December 28, 1846

KANSAS

34th
Sunflower State

Population: 2,723,507
Area: 82,282 square miles
Admitted: January 29, 1861

KENTUCKY

15th
Bluegrass State

Population: 4,117,827
Area: 40,411 square miles
Admitted: June 1, 1792

LOUISIANA

18th
Pelican State

Population: 4,496,334
Area: 51,843 square miles
Admitted: April 30, 1812

MAINE

23rd
Pine Tree State

Population: 1,305,728
Area: 35,387 square miles
Admitted: March 15, 1820

MARYLAND

7th
Old Line State

Population: 5,508,909
Area: 12,407 square miles
Admitted: April 28, 1788

MASSACHUSETTS

6th
Bay State

Population: 6,433,422
Area: 10,555 square miles
Admitted: February 6, 1788

MICHIGAN

26th
Great Lakes State

Population: 10,079,985
Area: 96,810 square miles
Admitted: January 26, 1837

MINNESOTA

32nd
North Star State

Population: 5,059,375
Area: 86,943 square miles
Admitted: May 11, 1858

MISSISSIPPI

20th
Magnolia State

Population: 2,881,281
Area: 48,434 square miles
Admitted: December 10, 1817

MISSOURI

24th
Show Me State

Population: 5,704,484
Area: 69,709 square miles
Admitted: August 10, 1821

MONTANA

41st
Treasure State

Population: 917,621
Area: 147,046 square miles
Admitted: November 8, 1889

NEBRASKA

37th
Cornhusker State

Population: 1,739,291
Area: 77,358 square miles
Admitted: March 1, 1867

NEVADA

36th
Sagebrush State

Population: 2,241,154
Area: 110,567 square miles
Admitted: October 31, 1864

NEW HAMPSHIRE

9th
Granite State

Population: 1,287,687
Area: 9,351 square miles
Admitted: June 21, 1788

NEW JERSEY

3rd
Garden State

Population: 8,638,396
Area: 8,722 square miles
Admitted: December 18, 1787

NEW MEXICO

47th
Land of Enchantment

Population: 1,874,614
Area: 121,598 square miles
Admitted: January 6, 1912

NEW YORK

11th
Empire State

Population: 19,190,115
Area: 54,475 square miles
Admitted: July 26, 1788

NORTH CAROLINA

12th
Tarheel State

Population: 8,407,248
Area: 53,821 square miles
Admitted: November 21, 1789

NORTH DAKOTA

39th
Peace Garden State

Population: 633,837
Area: 70,704 square miles
Admitted: November 2, 1889

OHIO

17th
Buckeye State

Population: 11,435,798
Area: 44,828 square miles
Admitted: March 1, 1803

OKLAHOMA

46th
Sooner State

Population: 3,511,532
Area: 69,903 square miles
Admitted: November 16, 1907

OREGON

33rd
Beaver State

Population: 3,559,596
Area: 98,386 square miles
Admitted: February 14, 1859

PENNSYLVANIA

2nd
Keystone State

Population: 12,365,455
Area: 46,058 square miles
Admitted: December 12, 1787

RHODE ISLAND

13th
Ocean State

Population: 1,076,164
Area: 1,545 square miles
Admitted: May 29, 1790

SOUTH CAROLINA

8th
Palmetto State

Population: 4,147,152
Area: 32,007 square miles
Admitted: May 23, 1788

SOUTH DAKOTA

40th
Coyote State

Population: 764,309
Area: 77,121 square miles
Admitted: November 2, 1889

TENNESSEE

16th
Volunteer State

Population: 5,841,748
Area: 42,146 square miles
Admitted: June 1, 1796

TEXAS

28th
Lone Star State

Population: 22,118,509
Area: 261,914 square miles
Admitted: December 29, 1845

UTAH

45th
Beehive State

Population: 2,351,467
Area: 84,904 square miles
Admitted: January 4, 1896

VERMONT

14th
Green Mountain State

Population: 619,107
Area: 9,615 square miles
Admitted: March 4, 1791

VIRGINIA

10th
Old Dominion

Population: 7,386,330
Area: 42,769 square miles
Admitted: June 25, 1788

WASHINGTON

42nd
Evergreen State

Population: 6,131,445
Area: 71,303 square miles
Admitted: November 11, 1889

WEST VIRGINIA

35th
Mountain State

Population: 1,810,354
Area: 24,231 square miles
Admitted: June 20, 1863

WISCONSIN

30th
Badger State

Population: 5,472,299
Area: 65,503 square miles
Admitted: May 29, 1848

WYOMING

44th
Equality State

Population: 501,242
Area: 97,818 square miles
Admitted: July 10, 1890

DISTRICT OF COLUMBIA

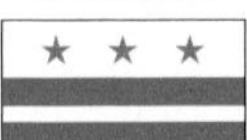

No nickname

Population: 563,384
Area: 68 square miles
Incorporated: 1802

R41

Geographic Terms

basin
a round area of land surrounded by higher land

bay
part of a lake or ocean extending into the land

coast
the land next to an ocean

coastal plain
a flat, level area of land near an ocean

delta
a triangular area of land formed by deposits at the mouth of a river

desert
a dry area where few plants grow

▲ **glacier**
a large ice mass that moves slowly down a mountain or over land

gulf
a large body of sea water partly surrounded by land

harbor
a sheltered body of water where ships can safely dock

hill
a raised area of land, smaller than a mountain

island
a body of land surrounded by water

isthmus
a narrow strip of land connecting two larger bodies of land

lake
a body of water surrounded by land

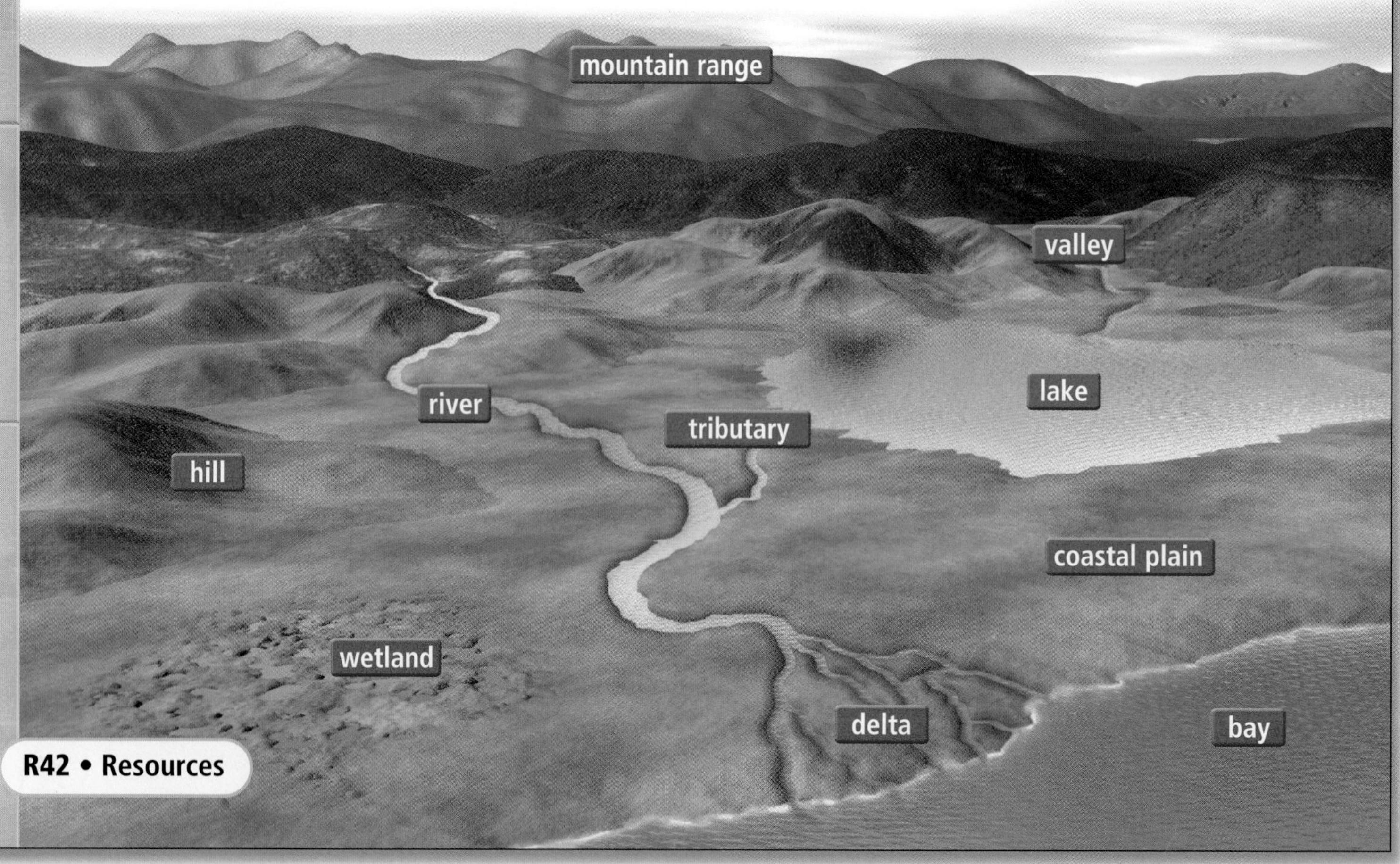

mesa
a wide flat-topped mountain with steep sides, found mostly in dry areas

mountain
a steeply raised mass of land, much higher than the surrounding country

mountain range
a row of mountains

ocean or sea
a salty body of water covering a large area of the earth

plain
a large area of flat or nearly flat land

plateau
a large area of flat land higher than the surrounding land

prairie
a large, level area of grassland with few or no trees

river
a large stream that runs into a lake, ocean, or another river

sea level
the level of the surface of the ocean

strait
a narrow channel of water connecting two larger bodies of water

tree line
the area on a mountain above which no trees grow

tributary
a river or stream that flows into a larger river

valley
low land between hills or mountains

volcano
an opening in the earth, through which lava and gases from the earth's interior escape

wetland
a low area saturated with water

Atlas

The World: Political

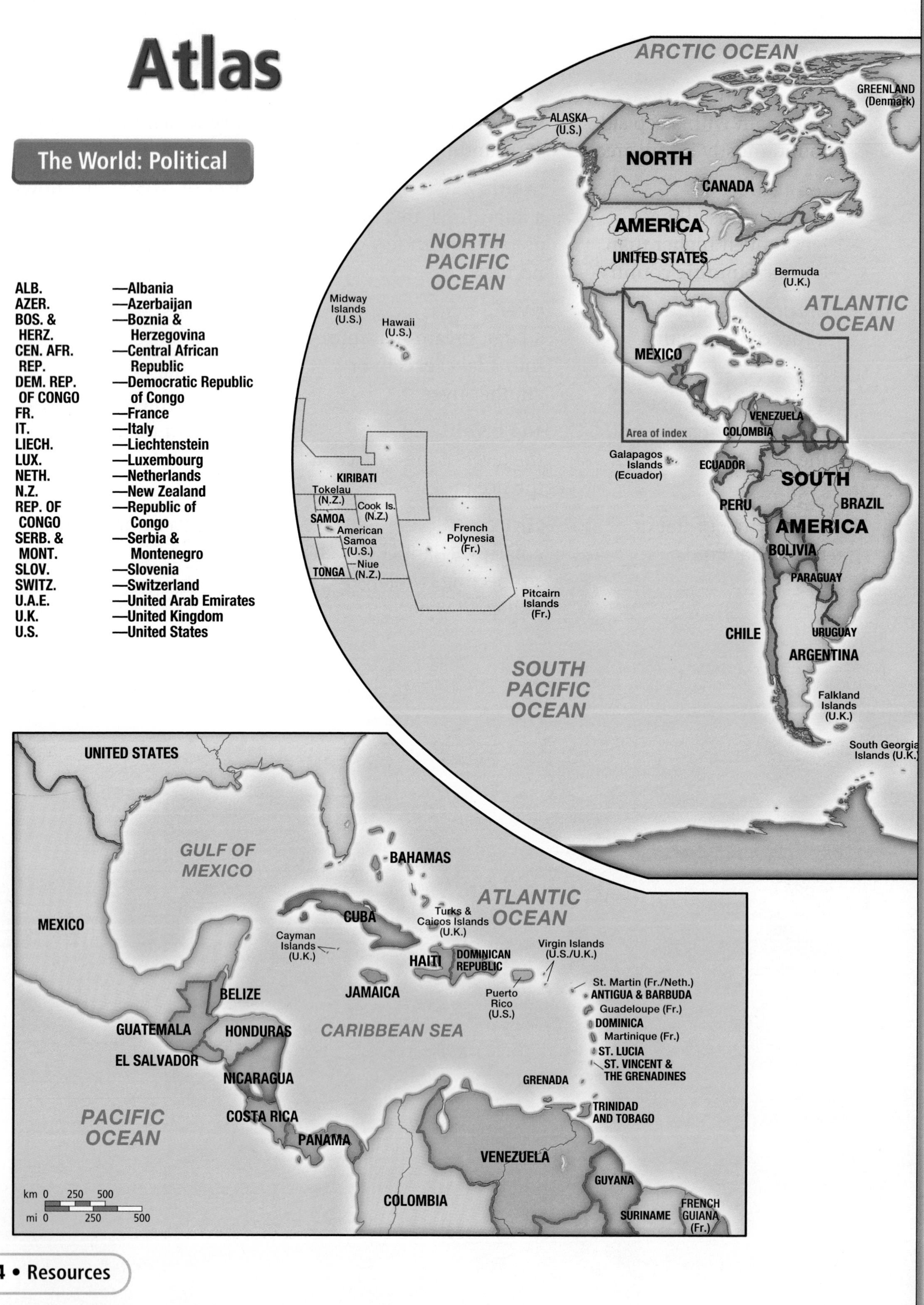

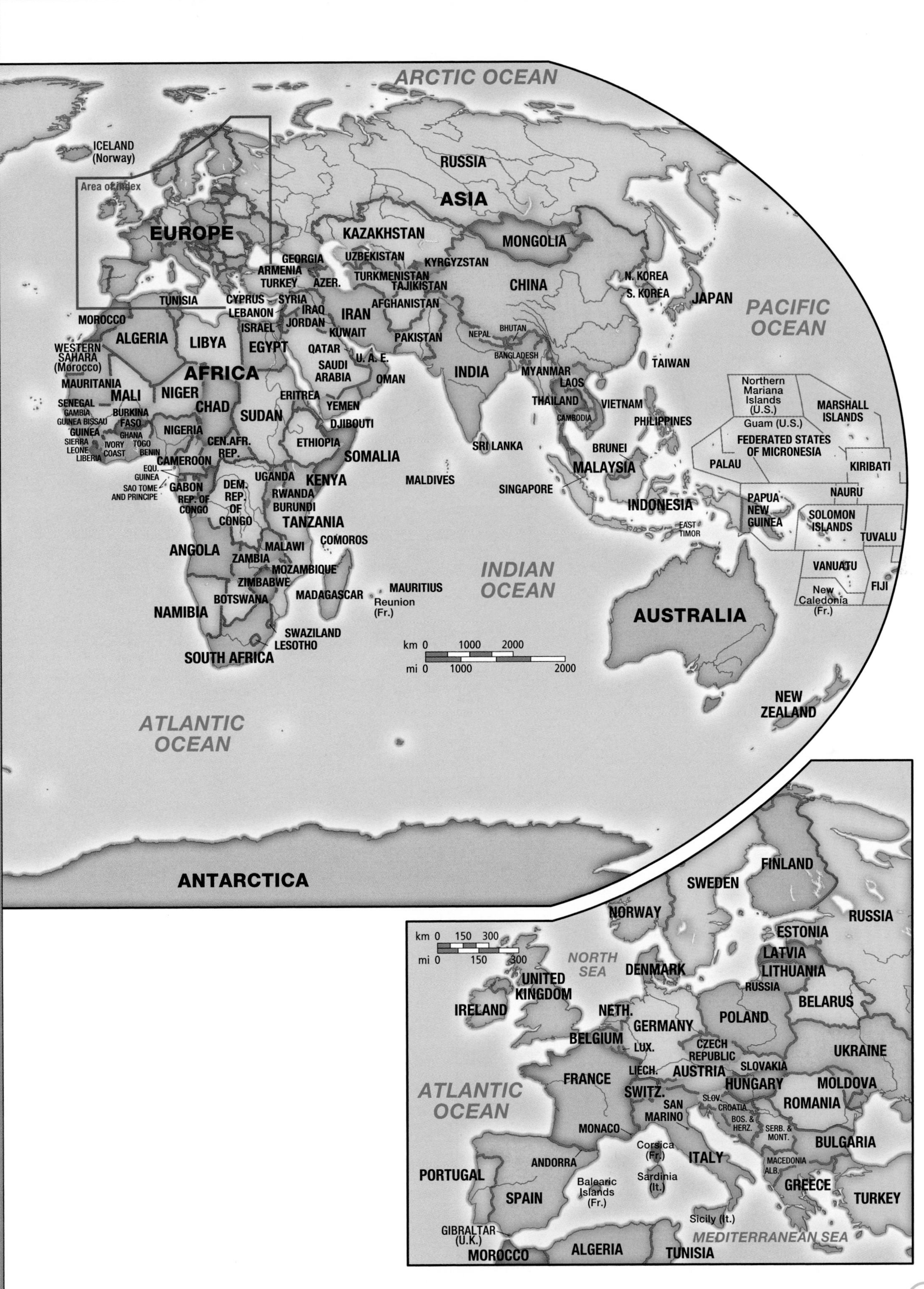

ARCTIC OCEAN
ICELAND (Norway)
Area of index
RUSSIA
ASIA
EUROPE
KAZAKHSTAN
MONGOLIA
GEORGIA
ARMENIA
TURKEY
AZER.
UZBEKISTAN
KYRGYZSTAN
TURKMENISTAN
TAJIKISTAN
CHINA
N. KOREA
S. KOREA
JAPAN
PACIFIC OCEAN
TUNISIA
CYPRUS
LEBANON
SYRIA
IRAQ
IRAN
AFGHANISTAN
MOROCCO
ISRAEL
JORDAN
KUWAIT
ALGERIA
LIBYA
EGYPT
QATAR
PAKISTAN
NEPAL
BHUTAN
WESTERN SAHARA (Morocco)
SAUDI ARABIA
U. A. E.
BANGLADESH
TAIWAN
AFRICA
MAURITANIA
OMAN
INDIA
MYANMAR
LAOS
MALI
NIGER
ERITREA
YEMEN
THAILAND
VIETNAM
Northern Mariana Islands (U.S.)
MARSHALL ISLANDS
SENEGAL
GAMBIA
GUINEA BISSAU
GUINEA
BURKINA FASO
CHAD
SUDAN
DJIBOUTI
CAMBODIA
PHILIPPINES
Guam (U.S.)
SIERRA LEONE
LIBERIA
IVORY COAST
GHANA
TOGO
BENIN
NIGERIA
CEN.AFR. REP.
ETHIOPIA
SRI LANKA
BRUNEI
FEDERATED STATES OF MICRONESIA
CAMEROON
SOMALIA
PALAU
KIRIBATI
EQU. GUINEA
SAO TOME AND PRINCIPE
GABON
REP. OF CONGO
DEM. REP. OF CONGO
UGANDA
KENYA
MALDIVES
MALAYSIA
SINGAPORE
NAURU
RWANDA
BURUNDI
INDONESIA
PAPUA NEW GUINEA
SOLOMON ISLANDS
TANZANIA
EAST TIMOR
COMOROS
TUVALU
ANGOLA
MALAWI
ZAMBIA
MOZAMBIQUE
INDIAN OCEAN
VANUATU
ZIMBABWE
FIJI
MAURITIUS
MADAGASCAR
BOTSWANA
Reunion (Fr.)
New Caledonia (Fr.)
NAMIBIA
AUSTRALIA
SWAZILAND
LESOTHO
km 0 1000 2000
mi 0 1000 2000
SOUTH AFRICA
NEW ZEALAND
ATLANTIC OCEAN
ANTARCTICA
FINLAND
SWEDEN
NORWAY
RUSSIA
ESTONIA
km 0 150 300
mi 0 150 300
NORTH SEA
LATVIA
DENMARK
LITHUANIA
UNITED KINGDOM
RUSSIA
BELARUS
IRELAND
NETH.
POLAND
GERMANY
BELGIUM
CZECH REPUBLIC
LUX.
UKRAINE
SLOVAKIA
LIECH.
AUSTRIA
FRANCE
MOLDOVA
HUNGARY
ATLANTIC OCEAN
SWITZ.
SLOV.
CROATIA
ROMANIA
SAN MARINO
BOS. & HERZ.
SERB. & MONT.
MONACO
BULGARIA
Corsica (Fr.)
ITALY
ANDORRA
MACEDONIA
ALB.
PORTUGAL
Sardinia (It.)
GREECE
Balearic Islands (Fr.)
SPAIN
TURKEY
Sicily (It.)
GIBRALTAR (U.K.)
MEDITERRANEAN SEA
ALGERIA
MOROCCO
TUNISIA

Atlas

R45

Atlas

The World: Physical

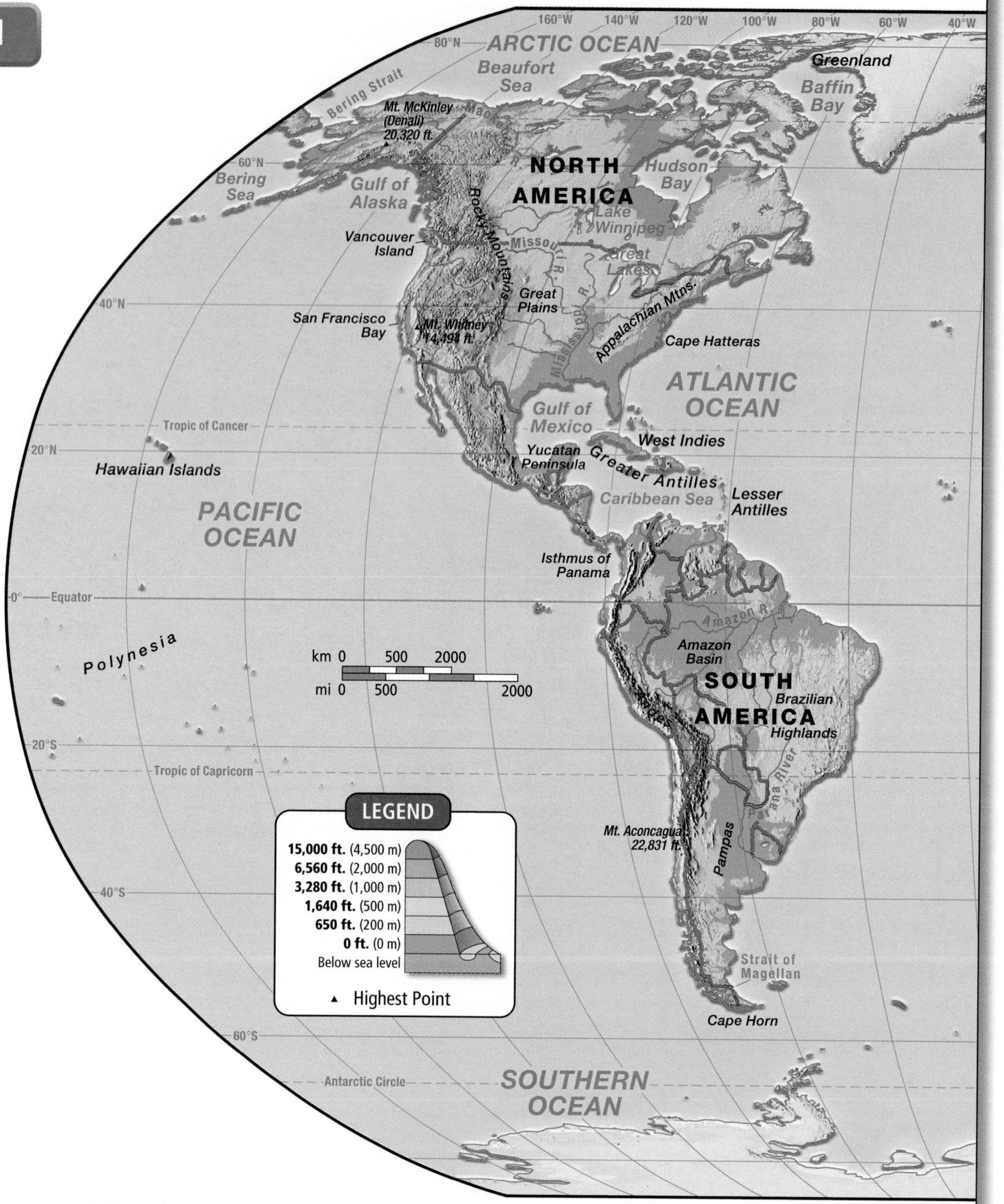

ARCTIC OCEAN
Beaufort Sea
Greenland
Baffin Bay
Bering Strait
Mt. McKinley (Denali) 20,320 ft.
NORTH AMERICA
Hudson Bay
Bering Sea
Gulf of Alaska
Rocky Mountains
Lake Winnipeg
Vancouver Island
Great Lakes
Great Plains
Appalachian Mtns.
San Francisco Bay
Mt. Whitney 14,494 ft.
Cape Hatteras
ATLANTIC OCEAN
Tropic of Cancer
Gulf of Mexico
West Indies
Yucatan Peninsula
Greater Antilles
Hawaiian Islands
Caribbean Sea
Lesser Antilles
PACIFIC OCEAN
Isthmus of Panama
Equator
Amazon R.
Amazon Basin
Polynesia
SOUTH AMERICA
Brazilian Highlands
Tropic of Capricorn
Mt. Aconcagua 22,831 ft.
Pampas
Strait of Magellan
Cape Horn
Antarctic Circle
SOUTHERN OCEAN

km 0 500 2000
mi 0 500 2000

LEGEND

15,000 ft. (4,500 m)
6,560 ft. (2,000 m)
3,280 ft. (1,000 m)
1,640 ft. (500 m)
650 ft. (200 m)
0 ft. (0 m)
Below sea level
▲ Highest Point

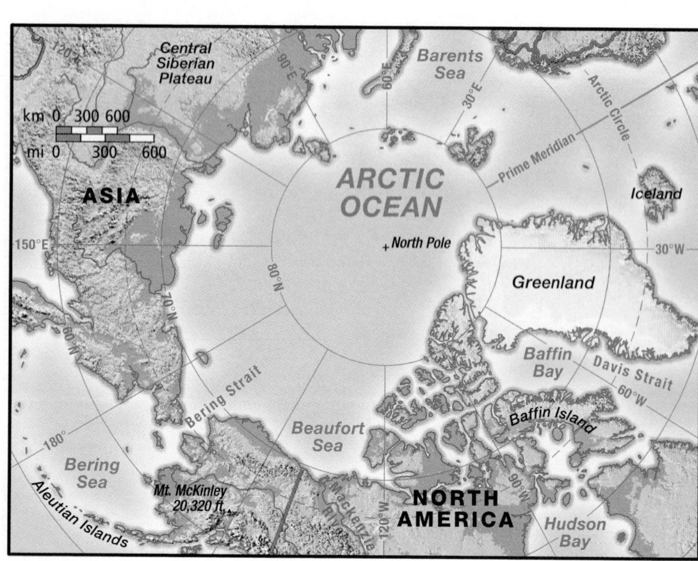

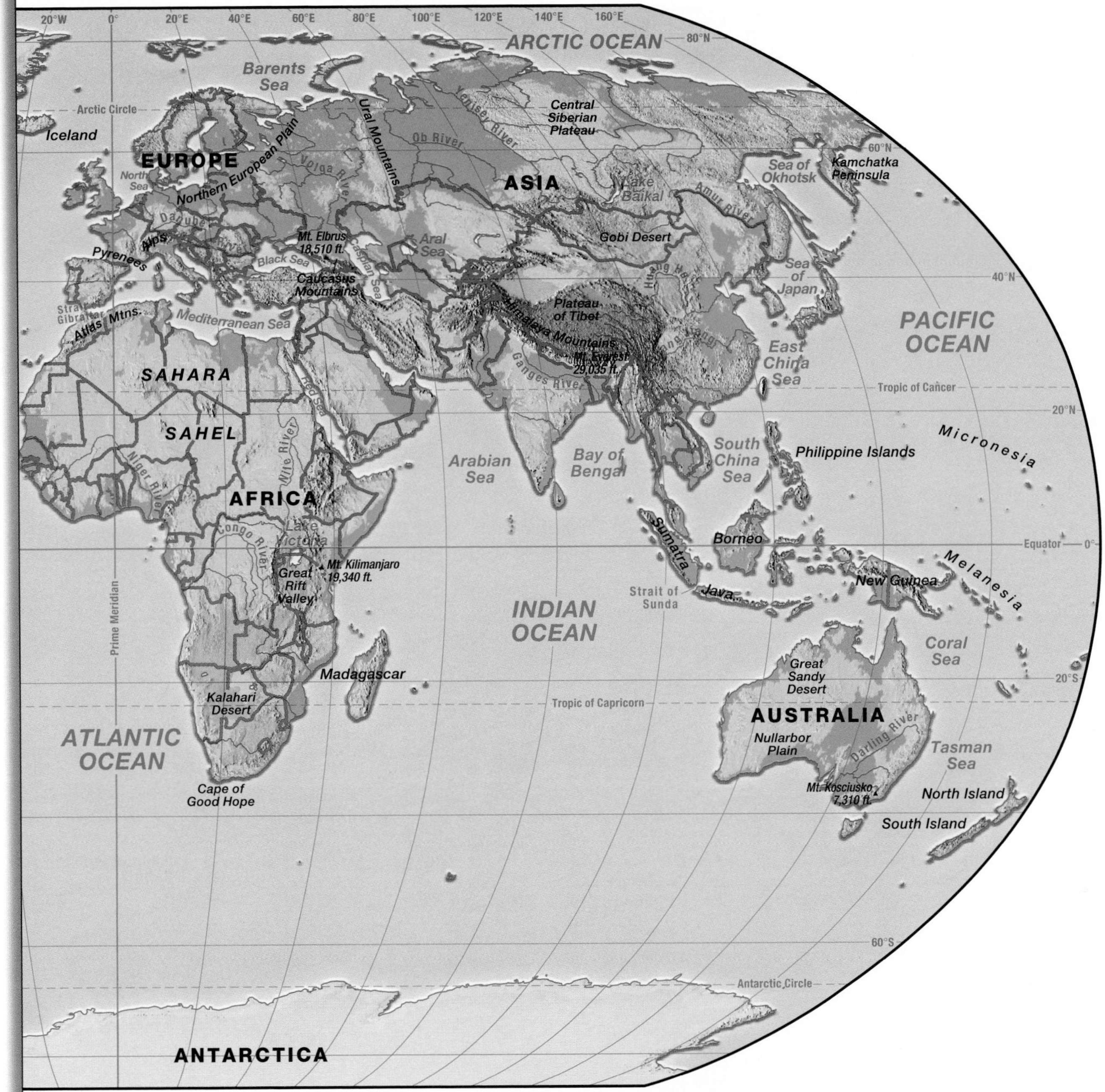

20°W 0° 20°E 40°E 60°E 80°E 100°E 120°E 140°E 160°E
ARCTIC OCEAN
80°N
Barents Sea
Arctic Circle
Iceland
EUROPE
North Sea
Northern European Plain
Ural Mountains
Central Siberian Plateau
Ob River
Yenisey River
Volga River
Danube
Alps
Pyrenees
Mt. Elbrus 18,510 ft.
Black Sea
Caucasus Mountains
Caspian Sea
Aral Sea
ASIA
Lake Baikal
Amur River
Sea of Okhotsk
Kamchatka Peninsula
60°N
Gobi Desert
Huang He
Sea of Japan
40°N
Plateau of Tibet
Himalaya Mountains
Mt. Everest 29,035 ft.
Ganges River
Chang Jiang
East China Sea
PACIFIC OCEAN
Tropic of Cancer
20°N
Strait of Gibraltar
Atlas Mtns.
Mediterranean Sea
SAHARA
SAHEL
Red Sea
Nile River
Niger River
Arabian Sea
Bay of Bengal
South China Sea
Philippine Islands
Micronesia
AFRICA
Congo River
Lake Victoria
Great Rift Valley
Mt. Kilimanjaro 19,340 ft.
Sumatra
Borneo
Equator
0°
Melanesia
New Guinea
Strait of Sunda
Java
INDIAN OCEAN
Prime Meridian
Madagascar
Coral Sea
Great Sandy Desert
20°S
Kalahari Desert
Tropic of Capricorn
AUSTRALIA
Darling River
ATLANTIC OCEAN
Nullarbor Plain
Tasman Sea
Cape of Good Hope
Mt. Kosciusko 7,310 ft.
North Island
South Island
60°S
Antarctic Circle
ANTARCTICA

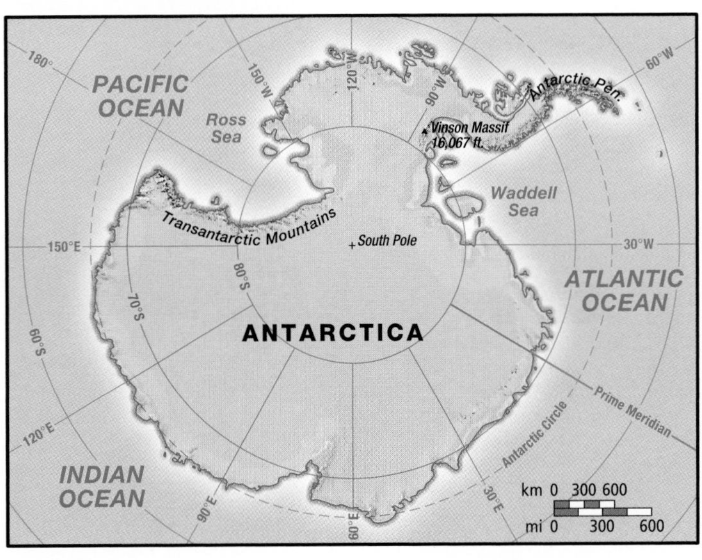

R47

Eastern Hemisphere: Political
Atlas
ARCTIC OCEAN
Beaufort Sea
Alaska (U.S.)
GREENLAND (DENMARK)
CANADA
Hudson Bay
Labrador Sea
Great Lakes
Ottawa
Great Salt Lake
UNITED STATES
Washington, D.C.
ATLANTIC OCEAN
Gulf of Mexico
BAHAMAS
Havana
CUBA
HAITI
DOMINICAN REPUBLIC
U.S. VIRGIN ISLANDS
ST. KITTS AND NEVIS
ST. LUCIA
BARBADOS
GRENADA
MEXICO
Mexico City
BELIZE
Belmopan
Kingston
JAMAICA
Santo Domingo
Port-Au-Prince
GUATEMALA
Guatemala City
Tegucigalpa
EL SALVADOR
San Salvador
Managua
San José
HONDURAS
NICARAGUA
COSTA RICA
PANAMA
Panama City
Caracas
VENEZUELA
Georgetown
Paramaribo
Cayenne
FRENCH GUIANA (FRANCE)
SURINAME
GUYANA
Bogotá
COLOMBIA
Quito
ECUADOR
Tropic of Cancer
Hawaii (U.S.)
PACIFIC OCEAN
Equator
Galápagos Is. (Ecuador)
Lima
PERU
BRAZIL
Brasilia
La Paz
BOLIVIA
Sucre
PARAGUAY
Asunción
French Polynesia (France)
Tropic of Capricorn
CHILE
Santiago
URUGUAY
Buenos Aires
Montevideo
ARGENTINA
Falkland Islands (U.K.)
South Georgia (U.K.)
N
W
E
S
LEGEND
National capital
National border
km 0 500 1000
mi 0 500 1000
140°W
120°W
100°W
80°W
60°W
40°W
60°N
40°N
20°N
0°
20°S
40°S
60°S

Eastern Hemisphere: Physical
ARCTIC OCEAN
Beaufort Sea
Bering Strait
Yukon R.
Mackenzie R.
Mt. McKinley (Denali) 20,320 ft. (6,194 m)
Bering Sea
Gulf of Alaska
GREENLAND
Baffin Bay
Davis Strait
Hudson Bay
Labrador Sea
CANADIAN SHIELD
ROCKY MOUNTAINS
Coast Mountains
NORTH AMERICA
Great Lakes
Missouri R.
Mississippi R.
APPALACHIAN MOUNTAINS
Coast Ranges
Great Salt Lake
Range and Basin
GREAT PLAINS
Death Valley -282 ft. (-86 m)
Mt. Whitney 14,495 ft. (4,418 m)
Coastal Plain
Rio Grande
ATLANTIC OCEAN
Gulf of Mexico
Bahamas
Cuba
Hispaniola
Puerto Rico
Tropic of Cancer
Hawaiian Islands
Caribbean Sea
Lake Nicaragua
Lake Maracaibo
PACIFIC OCEAN
Line Islands
Equator
Galápagos Islands
Amazon R.
AMAZON BASIN
Marquesas
ANDES
SOUTH AMERICA
Society Islands
Cook Islands
Tropic of Capricorn
Atacama Desert
N
W
E
S
Mt. Aconcagua 22,834 ft. (6,960 m)
LEGEND
15,000 ft. (4,500 m)
6,560 ft. (2,000 m)
3,280 ft. (1,000 m)
1,640 ft. (500 m)
650 ft. (200 m)
0 ft. (0 m)
Below sea level
Highest Point
Rio de la Plata
Valdés Peninsula -131 ft. (-40 m)
Falkland Islands
South Georgia
Strait of Magellan
km 0 500 1000
mi 0 500 1000
80°N
60°N
40°N
20°N
0°
20°S
40°S
60°S
160°W
140°W
120°W
100°W
80°W
60°W
40°W
Atlas
R49

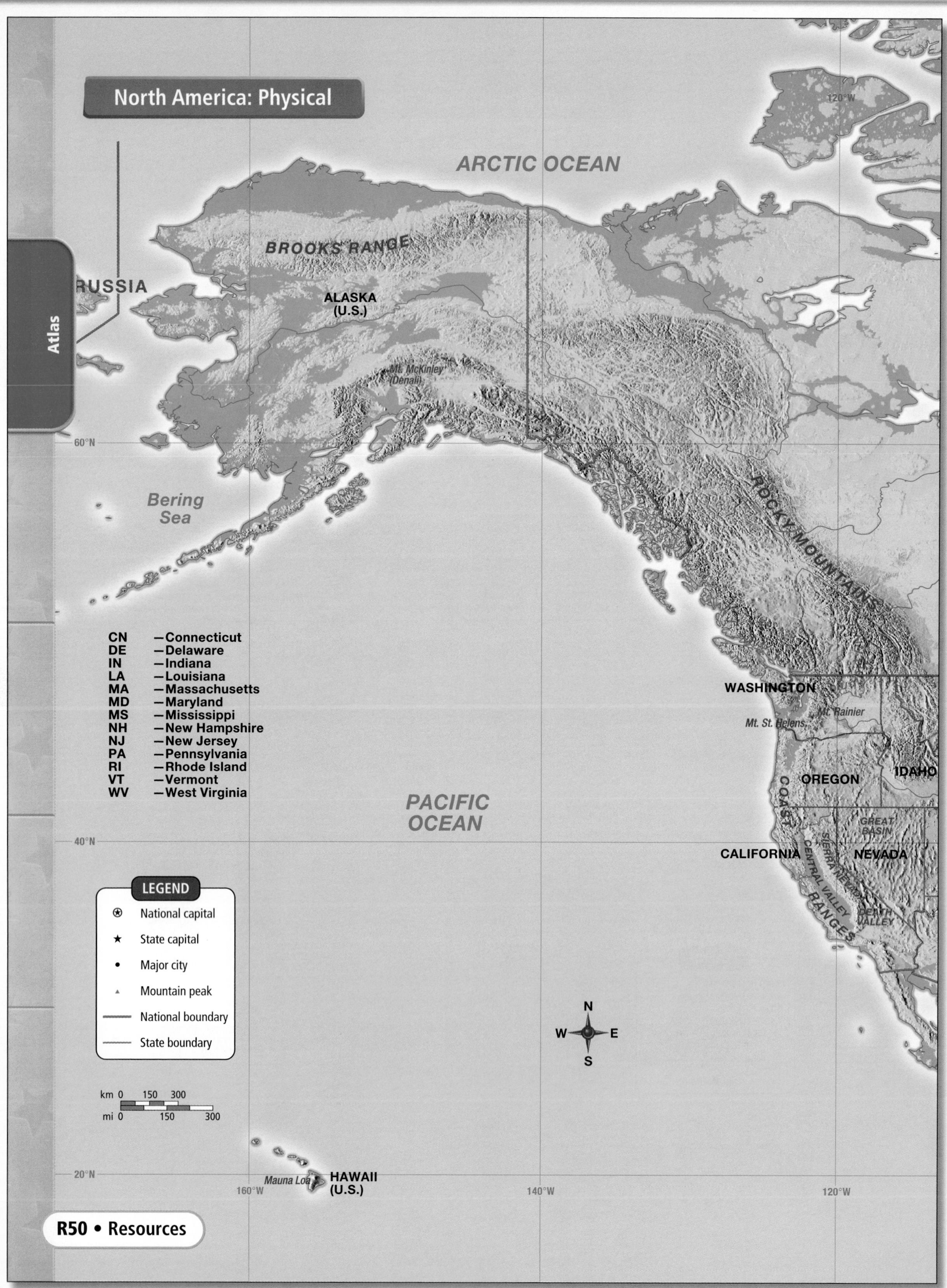
North America: Physical
ARCTIC OCEAN
BROOKS RANGE
RUSSIA
ALASKA (U.S.)
Mt. McKinley (Denali)
Atlas
60°N
Bering Sea
ROCKY MOUNTAINS
CN —Connecticut
DE —Delaware
IN —Indiana
LA —Louisiana
MA —Massachusetts
MD —Maryland
MS —Mississippi
NH —New Hampshire
NJ —New Jersey
PA —Pennsylvania
RI —Rhode Island
VT —Vermont
WV —West Virginia
WASHINGTON
Mt. Rainier
Mt. St. Helens
OREGON
IDAHO
COAST
PACIFIC OCEAN
40°N
GREAT BASIN
CALIFORNIA
NEVADA
SIERRA NEVADA
CENTRAL VALLEY
RANGES
DEATH VALLEY
LEGEND
National capital
State capital
Major city
Mountain peak
National boundary
State boundary
N
W
E
S
km 0 150 300
mi 0 150 300
Mauna Loa
HAWAII (U.S.)
20°N
160°W
140°W
120°W

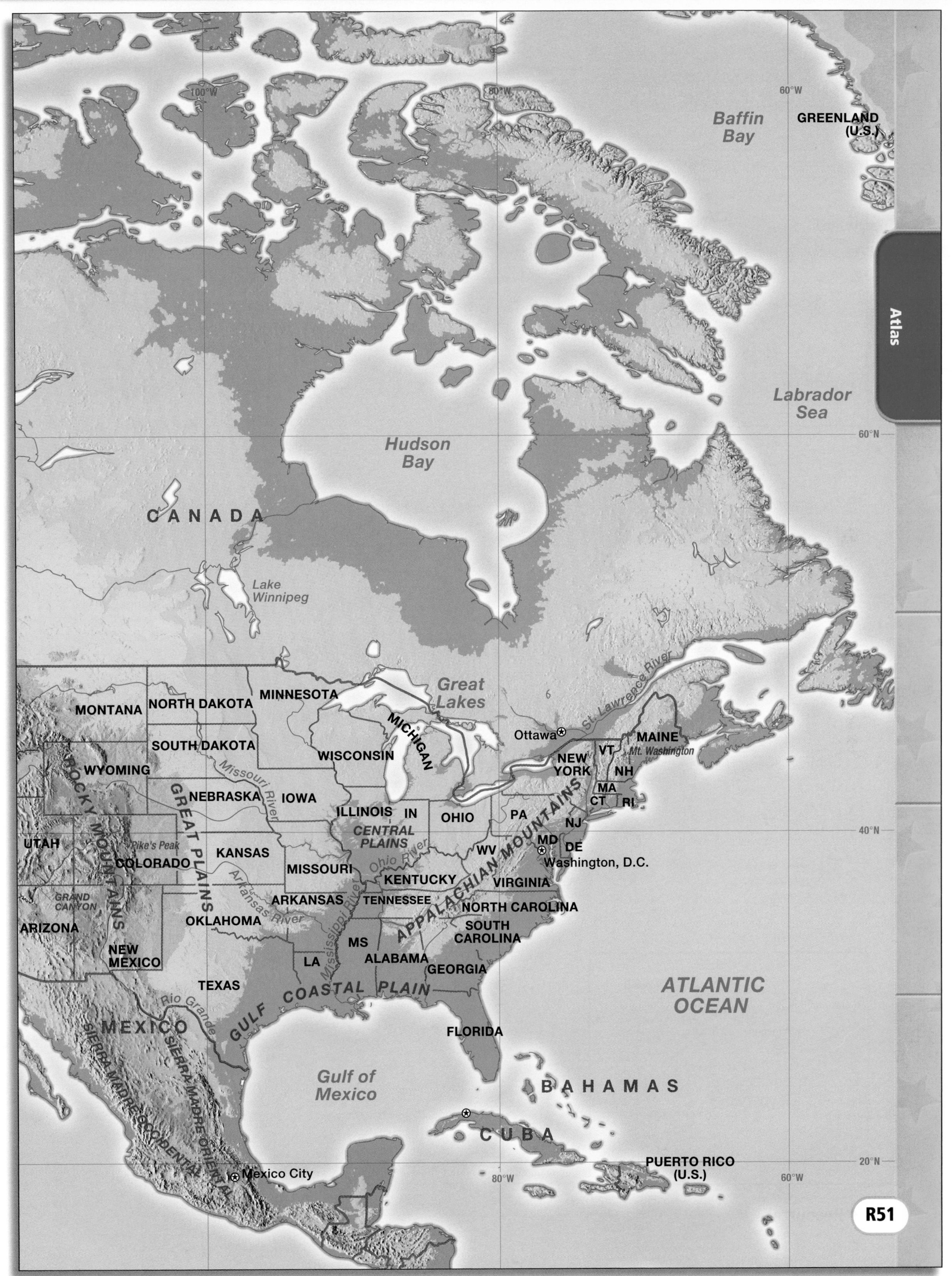
Baffin Bay
GREENLAND (U.S.)
Labrador Sea
Hudson Bay
CANADA
Lake Winnipeg
Great Lakes
St. Lawrence River
Ottawa
MAINE
Mt. Washington
VT
NH
NEW YORK
MA
CT
RI
NJ
PA
MD
DE
Washington, D.C.
MONTANA
NORTH DAKOTA
MINNESOTA
MICHIGAN
SOUTH DAKOTA
WISCONSIN
WYOMING
ROCKY MOUNTAINS
GREAT PLAINS
NEBRASKA
Missouri River
IOWA
ILLINOIS
IN
OHIO
CENTRAL PLAINS
UTAH
Pike's Peak
COLORADO
KANSAS
MISSOURI
Ohio River
KENTUCKY
WV
APPALACHIAN MOUNTAINS
VIRGINIA
GRAND CANYON
Arkansas River
ARKANSAS
TENNESSEE
NORTH CAROLINA
ARIZONA
OKLAHOMA
SOUTH CAROLINA
NEW MEXICO
MS
Mississippi River
LA
ALABAMA
GEORGIA
TEXAS
GULF COASTAL PLAIN
Rio Grande
MEXICO
SIERRA MADRE OCCIDENTAL
SIERRA MADRE ORIENTAL
FLORIDA
ATLANTIC OCEAN
Gulf of Mexico
BAHAMAS
CUBA
PUERTO RICO (U.S.)
Mexico City
100°W
80°W
60°W
60°N
40°N
20°N
R51

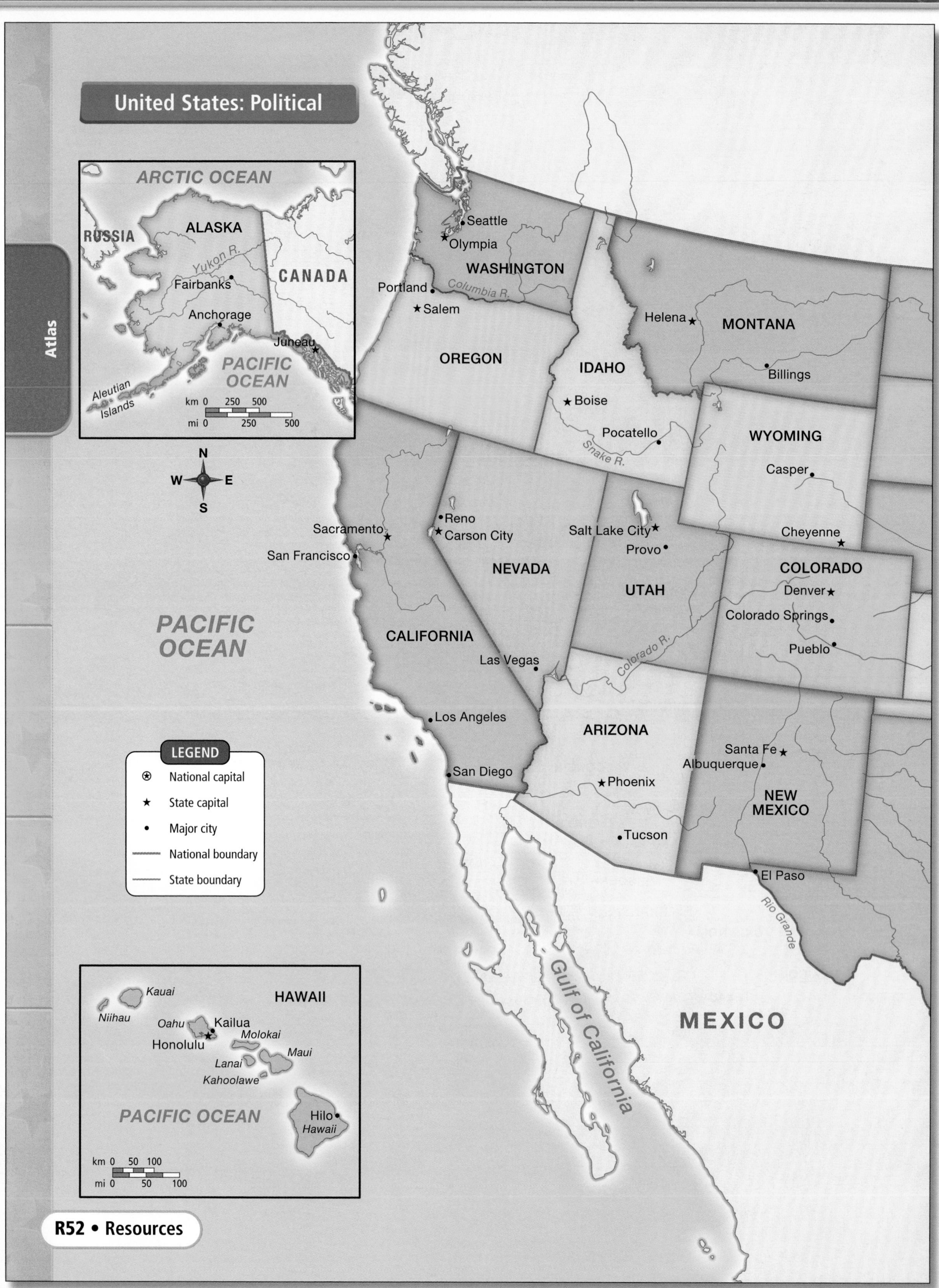

United States: Political
Atlas
ARCTIC OCEAN
RUSSIA
ALASKA
CANADA
Yukon R.
Fairbanks
Anchorage
Juneau
PACIFIC OCEAN
Aleutian Islands
km 0 250 500
mi 0 250 500
N
W
E
S
Seattle
Olympia
WASHINGTON
Portland
Columbia R.
Salem
OREGON
IDAHO
Boise
Pocatello
Snake R.
Helena
MONTANA
Billings
WYOMING
Casper
Cheyenne
Reno
Carson City
Sacramento
San Francisco
NEVADA
Salt Lake City
Provo
UTAH
COLORADO
Denver
Colorado Springs
Pueblo
PACIFIC OCEAN
CALIFORNIA
Las Vegas
Colorado R.
Los Angeles
ARIZONA
San Diego
Phoenix
Tucson
Santa Fe
Albuquerque
NEW MEXICO
El Paso
Rio Grande
Gulf of California
MEXICO
LEGEND
National capital
State capital
Major city
National boundary
State boundary
HAWAII
Kauai
Niihau
Oahu
Kailua
Honolulu
Molokai
Maui
Lanai
Kahoolawe
PACIFIC OCEAN
Hilo
Hawaii
km 0 50 100
mi 0 50 100

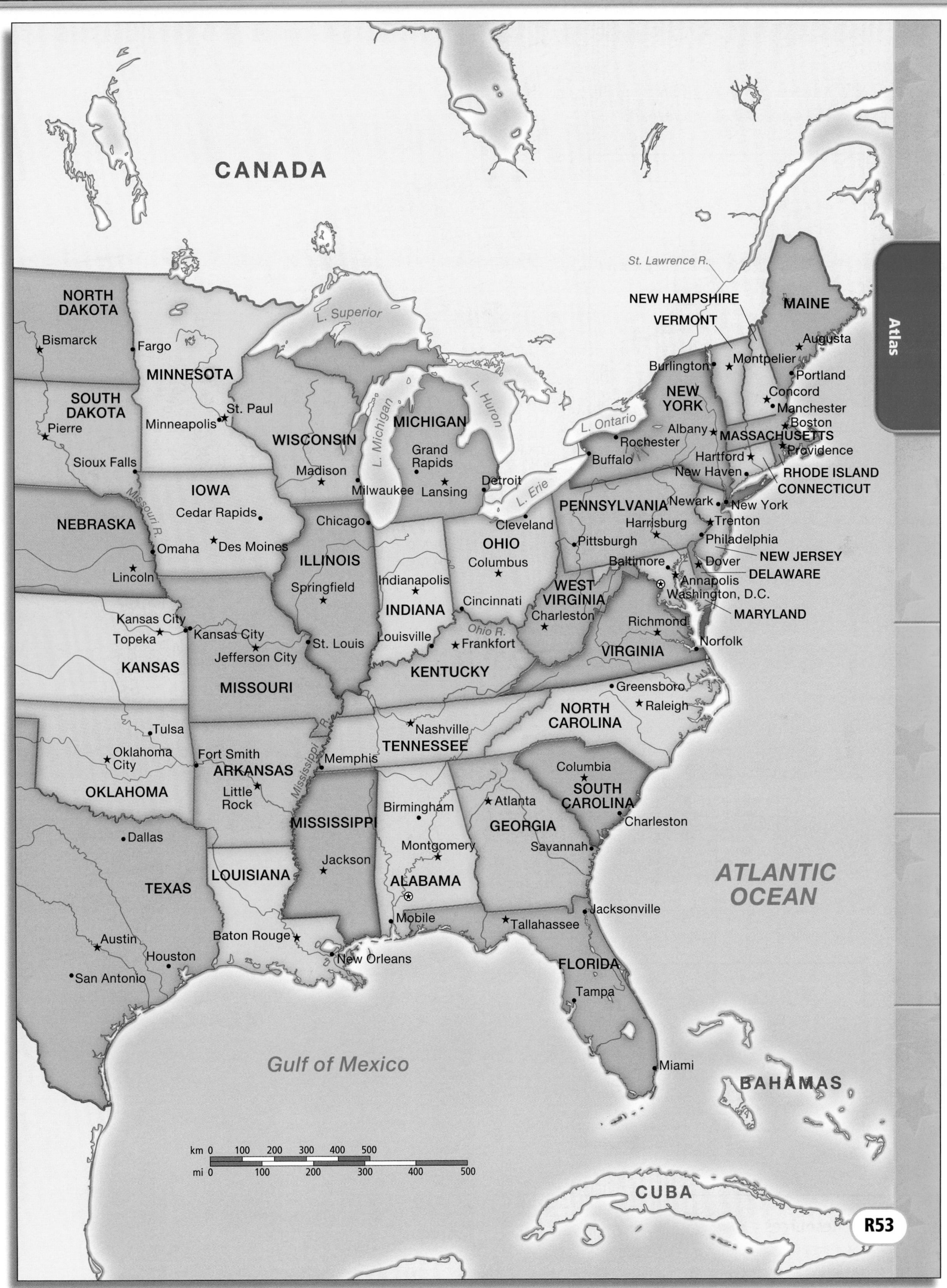
CANADA
St. Lawrence R.
L. Superior
L. Michigan
L. Huron
L. Ontario
L. Erie
NORTH DAKOTA
Bismarck
Fargo
MINNESOTA
St. Paul
Minneapolis
SOUTH DAKOTA
Pierre
Sioux Falls
WISCONSIN
Madison
Milwaukee
MICHIGAN
Grand Rapids
Lansing
Detroit
IOWA
Cedar Rapids
Des Moines
NEBRASKA
Omaha
Lincoln
Missouri R.
ILLINOIS
Chicago
Springfield
INDIANA
Indianapolis
OHIO
Cleveland
Columbus
Cincinnati
Ohio R.
PENNSYLVANIA
Pittsburgh
Harrisburg
Philadelphia
NEW YORK
Buffalo
Rochester
Albany
New York
VERMONT
Burlington
Montpelier
NEW HAMPSHIRE
Concord
Manchester
MAINE
Augusta
Portland
MASSACHUSETTS
Boston
Providence
RHODE ISLAND
CONNECTICUT
Hartford
New Haven
Newark
Trenton
NEW JERSEY
Dover
DELAWARE
Baltimore
Annapolis
Washington, D.C.
MARYLAND
WEST VIRGINIA
Charleston
VIRGINIA
Richmond
Norfolk
KANSAS
Kansas City
Topeka
MISSOURI
Kansas City
Jefferson City
St. Louis
KENTUCKY
Louisville
Frankfort
NORTH CAROLINA
Greensboro
Raleigh
TENNESSEE
Nashville
Memphis
Mississippi R.
OKLAHOMA
Tulsa
Oklahoma City
ARKANSAS
Fort Smith
Little Rock
MISSISSIPPI
Jackson
ALABAMA
Birmingham
Montgomery
Mobile
GEORGIA
Atlanta
Savannah
SOUTH CAROLINA
Columbia
Charleston
TEXAS
Dallas
Austin
Houston
San Antonio
LOUISIANA
Baton Rouge
New Orleans
FLORIDA
Tallahassee
Jacksonville
Tampa
Miami
Gulf of Mexico
ATLANTIC OCEAN
BAHAMAS
CUBA
km 0 100 200 300 400 500
mi 0 100 200 300 400 500
Atlas
R53

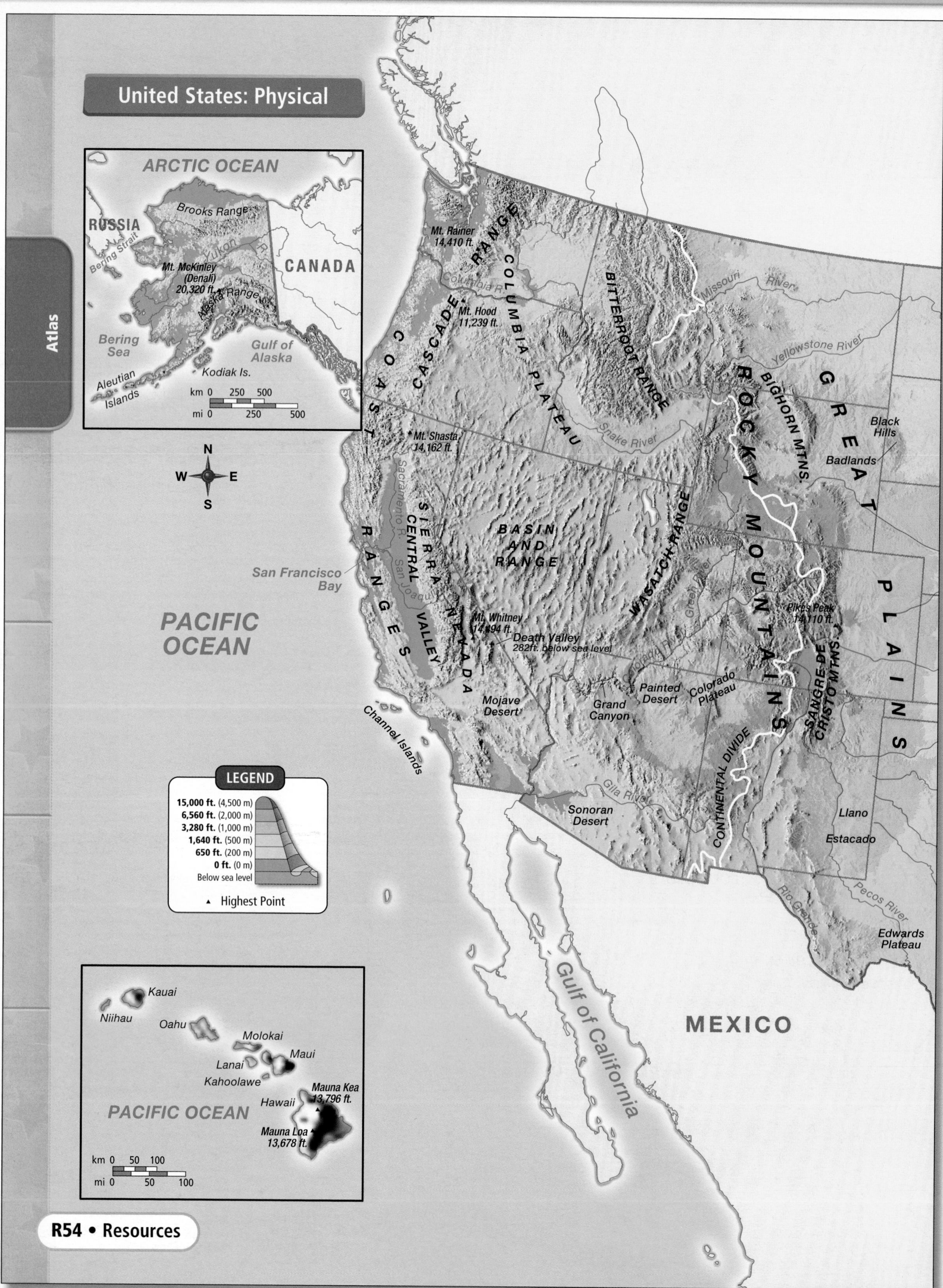

United States: Physical
ARCTIC OCEAN
RUSSIA
Brooks Range
Bering Strait
Yukon R.
CANADA
Mt. McKinley (Denali) 20,320 ft.
Alaska Range
Bering Sea
Gulf of Alaska
Aleutian Islands
Kodiak Is.
km 0 250 500
mi 0 250 500
Atlas
N
W
E
S
Mt. Rainier 14,410 ft.
CASCADE RANGE
COLUMBIA PLATEAU
Columbia R.
Mt. Hood 11,239 ft.
COAST RANGES
BITTERROOT RANGE
Missouri River
Yellowstone River
ROCKY MOUNTAINS
BIGHORN MTNS.
GREAT PLAINS
Black Hills
Badlands
Snake River
Mt. Shasta 14,162 ft.
Sacramento R.
SIERRA NEVADA
CENTRAL VALLEY
BASIN AND RANGE
WASATCH RANGE
San Joaquin R.
San Francisco Bay
PACIFIC OCEAN
Mt. Whitney 14,494 ft.
Death Valley 282ft. below sea level
Pikes Peak 14,110 ft.
SANGRE DE CRISTO MTNS.
Painted Desert
Colorado Plateau
Grand Canyon
Mojave Desert
Channel Islands
LEGEND
15,000 ft. (4,500 m)
6,560 ft. (2,000 m)
3,280 ft. (1,000 m)
1,640 ft. (500 m)
650 ft. (200 m)
0 ft. (0 m)
Below sea level
Highest Point
Gila River
Sonoran Desert
CONTINENTAL DIVIDE
Llano Estacado
Rio Grande
Pecos River
Edwards Plateau
Gulf of California
MEXICO
Kauai
Niihau
Oahu
Molokai
Maui
Lanai
Kahoolawe
Hawaii
Mauna Kea 13,796 ft.
Mauna Loa 13,678 ft.
PACIFIC OCEAN
km 0 50 100
mi 0 50 100

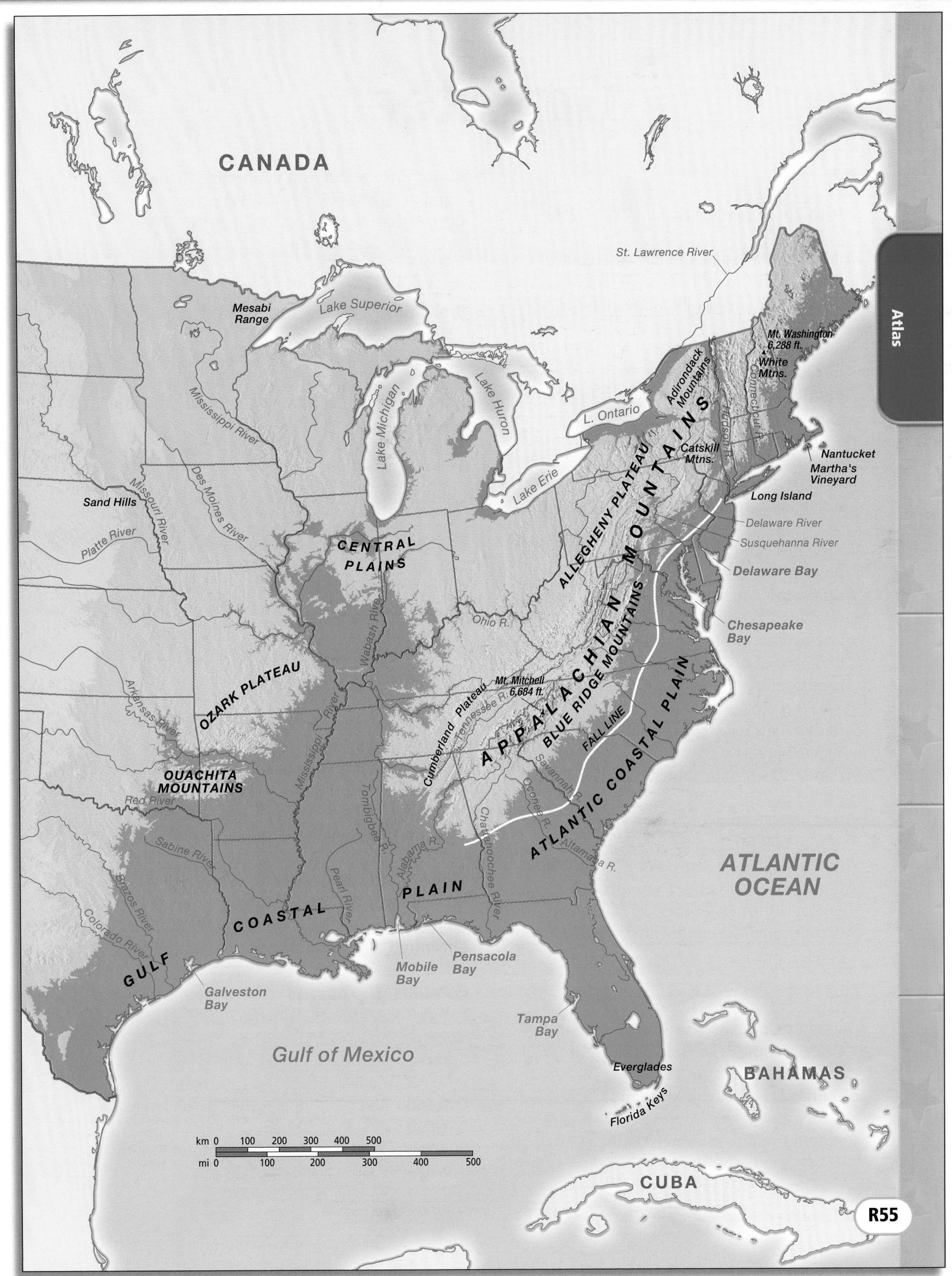
CANADA
St. Lawrence River
Lake Superior
Mesabi Range
Mt. Washington 6,288 ft.
White Mtns.
Adirondack Mountains
L. Ontario
Lake Michigan
Lake Huron
Mississippi River
Hudson R.
Connecticut R.
Catskill Mtns.
Nantucket
Martha's Vineyard
Long Island
Lake Erie
Sand Hills
Missouri River
Des Moines River
ALLEGHENY PLATEAU
APPALACHIAN MOUNTAINS
Delaware River
Susquehanna River
Platte River
CENTRAL PLAINS
Delaware Bay
Wabash River
Ohio R.
Chesapeake Bay
OZARK PLATEAU
Arkansas River
Mt. Mitchell 6,684 ft.
Cumberland Plateau
Tennessee R.
BLUE RIDGE MOUNTAINS
FALL LINE
ATLANTIC COASTAL PLAIN
Mississippi River
OUACHITA MOUNTAINS
Red River
Tombigbee R.
Savannah R.
Oconee R.
Sabine River
Alabama R.
Chattahoochee River
Altamaha R.
ATLANTIC OCEAN
Brazos River
Pearl River
PLAIN
COASTAL
GULF
Colorado River
Mobile Bay
Pensacola Bay
Galveston Bay
Tampa Bay
Gulf of Mexico
Everglades
BAHAMAS
Florida Keys
km 0 100 200 300 400 500
mi 0 100 200 300 400 500
CUBA

Gazetteer

Africa 2nd largest continent (10°N, 22°E) p. R47

Alabama 22nd state; capital: Montgomery (33°N, 88°W) p. 373

Alaska 49th state; capital: Juneau (64°N, 150°W) p. 533

Albany Capital of New York State (43°N, 74°W) p. 229

Albuquerque City in New Mexico (35°N, 106°W) p. 117

Amazon River 2nd longest river in the world; longest in South America (2°S, 53°W) p. R48

Angel Island Island in San Francisco Bay where immigrants to the United States arrived (38°N 122°W) p. 499

Antarctica Continent surrounding the South Pole, mostly covered in ice (90°S); p. R49

Antietam In Maryland; site of Civil War battle (39°N, 77°W) p. 454

Appalachian Mountains Range stretching from Canada to Alabama (37°N, 82°W) p. 164

Argentina Country in South America (36°S, 67°W) p. R46

Arizona 48th state; capital: Phoenix (34°N, 113°W) p. R54

Arkansas 25th state; capital: Little Rock (34°N, 92°W) p. R55, p. 108

Asia Largest continent in the world (50°N, 100°E) p. R47

Atlanta Capital of Georgia (34°N, 84°W) p. 467

Atlantic Ocean Extends from Arctic to Antarctic; east of United States (5°S, 25°W) p. R46

Australia Smallest continent (30°S, 151°E) p. R47

B

Bahamas Group of islands in the Atlantic Ocean; southeast of Florida (26°N, 76°W) p. 309

Baltimore Large city in Maryland (39°N, 77°W) p. R55

Belgium Country in western Europe (51°N, 3°E) p. R47

Bering Strait Waterway connecting Arctic Ocean and Bering Sea (65°N, 170°W) p. 39

Birmingham City in Alabama (34°N, 87°W) p. R55

Boston Capital of Massachusetts (42°N, 71°W) p. 190

Brazil Largest country in South America (9°S, 53°W) p. 101

Bull Run Site of two major Civil War battles (39°N, 78°W) p. 453

Bunker Hill Site of lst major battle of American Revolution (42°N, 71°W) p. 245

California 31st state; capital: Sacramento (38°N, 121°W) p. 499

Canada Country bordering United States on north (50°N, 100°W) p. R46

Cape of Good Hope Southwest extremity of Africa (34°S, 18°E) p. 93

Cape Horn Southernmost point of South America (55°S, 67°W) p. 290

Caribbean Sea North Atlantic sea (15°N, 76°W) p. 97

Charleston City in South Carolina (33°N, 80°W) p. 198

Chesapeake Bay Inlet of the Atlantic Ocean on the East Coast of the United States (37°N, 76°W) p. 134

Chicago Large city in Illinois (42°N, 88°W) p. R55

Chile Country on western coast of South America (35°S, 72°W) p. R50

China Country in East Asia (37°N, 93°E) p. R47

Cincinnati City in southwestern Ohio (39°N, 84°W) p. 348

Coast Ranges Group of mountain ranges along West Coast of North America (40°N, 123°W) p. 8

Colorado 38th state; capital: Denver (40°N, 107°W) p. R54

Colorado River 5th longest river in the United States (32°N, 115°W) p. 8

Columbia River Lewis and Clark found mouth of river in 1805 (46°N, 120°W) p. 356

Concord Site in Massachusetts of early Revolutionary War battle (42°N, 71°W) p. 251
Connecticut 5th state; capital: Hartford (42°N, 73°W) p. 202
Cuba Island nation in Caribbean Sea, south of Florida (22°N, 79°W) p. 97
Cumberland Gap Pass through the Appalachian Mountains (36°N, 83°W) p. 345

Delaware 1st state; capital: Dover (39°N, 76°W) p. 144
Delaware River Flows from New York to Delaware Bay (42°N, 75°W) p. 144
Denver Capital of Colorado (40°N, 105°W) p. R54
Detroit City in eastern Michigan (42°N, 83°W) p. 23

Egypt Country in North Africa; capital: Cairo (30°N, 31°E) p. 471
El Paso City in west Texas, on Rio Grande (32°N, 106°W) p. R54
Ellis Island Island in New York Harbor where immigrants to United States arrived (41°N, 74°W) p. 499
England Country in western Europe; part of the United Kingdom (52°N, 2°W) p. 123
Europe 6th largest continent (50°N, 15°E) p. R47

Florida 27th state; capital: Tallahassee (31°N, 85°W) p. R55
France Country in western Europe (47°N, 1°E) p. 123

Georgia 4th state; capital: Atlanta (33°N, 84°W) p. 203
Germany Country in western Europe (51°N, 10°E) p. 309
Gettysburg Site in Pennsylvania of Civil War battle (40°N, 77°W) p. 456
Grand Canyon In Arizona, deep gorge formed by the Colorado River (36°N, 112°W) p. R56
Great Lakes Five freshwater lakes between the United States and Canada (45°N, 83°W) p. R57
Great Plains In central North America, high grassland region (45°N, 104°W) p. 6
Greensboro City in North Carolina (36°N, 80°W) p. R55
Guatemala Country in Central America (16°N, 92°W) p. R50
Gulf of Mexico Body of water along southern United States and Mexico (25°N, 94°W) p. R57

Haiti Nation in the West Indies on the island of Hispaniola; capital: Port-au-Prince (18°N, 72°W) p. 290
Havana Capital of Cuba (23°N, 82°W) p. R50
Hawaii 50th state; capital: Honolulu (20°N, 158°W) p. R54
Hispaniola Island in the West Indies (18°N, 73°W) p. 97
Honolulu Capital of Hawaii (21°N, 158°W) p. R54
Houston City in Texas (30°N, 95°W) p. 507
Hudson River In New York; named for explorer Henry Hudson (43°N, 74°W) p. 124

Idaho 43rd state; capital: Boise (44°N, 115°W) p. R54
Illinois 21st state; capital: Springfield (40°N, 91°W) p. 434
India Country in south Asia (23°N, 78°E) p. 93
Indiana 19th state; capital: Indianapolis (40°N, 87°W) p. R55
Iowa 29th state; capital: Des Moines (41°N, 93°W) p. R55
Ireland Island in North Atlantic Ocean, divided between Republic of Ireland and Northern Ireland (53°N, 6°W) p. 388
Italy Country in southern Europe (44°N, 11°E) p. 471

Jamestown, Virginia First permanent English settlement in Americas (37°N, 76°W) p. 131

Gazetteer

Japan Island country off east coast of Asia (37°N, 134°E) p. 309

Kansas 34th state; capital: Topeka (39°N, 100°W) p. 433

Kentucky 15th state; capital: Frankfort (38°N, 88°W) p. 452

Lexington Site in Massachusetts of lst shots fired in Revolutionary War (42°N, 71°W) p. 251

London Capital of United Kingdom (52°N, 0°W) p. 137

Los Angeles City in California (34°N, 118°W) p. 507

Louisiana 18th state; capital: Baton Rouge (31°N, 93°W) p. 444

Madrid Capital of Spain (40°N, 3°W) p. 126

Maine 23rd state; capital: Augusta (45°N, 70°W) p. 202

Mali Country in West Africa (16°N, 0°W) p. 86

Maryland 7th state; capital: Annapolis (39°N, 76°W) p. 203

Massachusetts 6th state; capital: Boston (42°N, 73°W) p. 137

Mecca Muslim holy city (21°N, 39°E) p. 87

Mexico Country bordering the United States to the south (24°N, 104°W) p. R50

Mexico City Capital of Mexico (19°N, 99°W) p. R50

Miami City in Florida (26°N, 80°W) p. R55

Michigan 26th state; capital: Lansing (46°N, 87°W) p. R55

Milwaukee City in Wisconsin (43°N, 88°W) p. 389

Minnesota 32nd state; capital: St. Paul (45°N, 93°W) p. R55

Mississippi 20th state; capital: Jackson (33°N, 90°W) p. 444

Mississippi River Principal river of United States and North America (32°N, 92°W) p. R57

Missouri 24th state; capital: Jefferson City (38°N, 94°W) p. 433

Missouri River A major river in United States (41°N, 96°W) p. 356

Montana 41st state; capital: Helena (47°N, 112°W) p. 525

Montgomery City in Alabama (32°N, 86°W) p. 531

Montreal City in Quebec, Canada (46°N, 74°W) p. 230

Natchez City in Mississippi (32°N, 91°W) p. 287

Nebraska 37th state; capital: Lincoln (42°N, 102°W) p. 433

Netherlands Country in northwestern Europe; also called Holland (52°N, 6°E) p. 124

Nevada 36th state; capital: Carson City (40°N, 117°W) p. R54

New Hampshire 9th state; capital: Concord (44°N, 72°W) p. 202

New Jersey 3rd state; capital: Trenton (41°N, 75°W) p. 188

New Mexico 47th state; capital: Santa Fe (35°N, 107°W) p. 533

New Netherland Dutch colony in North America (41°N, 74°W) p. 144

New Orleans City in Louisiana (30°N, 90°W) p. 355

New York 11th state; capital: Albany (43°N, 78°W) p. R55

New York City Large city in New York State (41°N, 74°W) p. R55

North America Northern continent of Western Hemisphere (45°N, 100°W) pp. R52–R53

North Carolina 12th state; capital: Raleigh (36°N, 82°W) p. 203

North Dakota 39th state; capital: Bismarck (46°N, 100°W) pp. R54–R55

North Korea Country in northeast Asia; capital: Pyongyang (39°N, 125°E) p. 512

Northwest Territory Land extending from Ohio and Mississippi rivers to Great Lakes (41°N, 85°W) p. 297

Gazetteer

Ohio 17th state; capital: Columbus (41°N, 83°W) p. R55

Ohio River Flows from Pennsylvania to the Mississippi River (37°N, 88°W) p. R57

Ohio River Valley Farming region west of the Appalachian Mountains (37°N, 88°W) p. 228

Oklahoma 46th state; capital: Oklahoma City (36°N, 98°W) p. 370

Omaha Large city in Nebraska (41°N, 96°W) pp. R54–R55

Oregon 33rd state; capital: Salem (44°N, 122°W) p. 400

Oregon Territory Area from Rocky Mountains to Pacific Ocean (45°N, 120°W) p. 401

Pacific Ocean Largest ocean; west of the United States (0°, 170°W) pp. R46–R47

Panama Country in Central America (9°N, 80°W) p. 100

Paris Capital of France (49°N, 2°E) p. 324

Pennsylvania 2nd state; capital: Harrisburg (41°N, 78°W) p. 189

Peru Country on the Pacific coast of South America (10°S, 75°W) p. R50

Philadelphia Large port city in Pennsylvania (40°N, 75°W) p. 190

Philippines Island country southeast of Asia (14°N, 125°E) p. R47

Phoenix Capital of Arizona (33°N, 112°W) p. 13

Pittsburgh Manufacturing city in Pennsylvania (40°N, 80°W) p. R55

Plymouth In Massachusetts; site of first Pilgrim settlement (42°N, 71°W) p. 137

Poland Country in eastern Europe; capital: Warsaw (52°N, 21°E) p. 498

Portugal Country in western Europe; capital: Lisbon (38°N, 8°W) p. 92

Potomac River Runs from western Maryland past Washington, D.C. (38°N, 77°W) p. 322

Puerto Rico A U.S. territory in the Caribbean; capital: San Juan (18°N, 67°W) p. R50

Quebec Province of Canada; capital: Quebec City (47°N, 71°W) p. 123

Rhode Island 13th state; capital: Providence (42°N, 72°W) p. 201

Richmond Capital city of Virginia; also was Confederate capital (38°N, 78°W) p. 453

Rio Grande River forming part of the Texas–Mexico border (26°N, 97°W) p. R54

Roanoke Island Island off the coast of North Carolina; site of first English colony in the Americas (37°N, 80°W) p. 130

Rocky Mountains Mountain range in the western United States (50°N, 114°W) p. R56

Russia Formerly part of the Soviet Union; capital: Moscow (61°N, 60°E) p. 498

Sacramento Capital of California (39°N, 122°W) p. R54

St. Augustine, Florida Oldest European-founded city in U.S. (30°N, 81°W) p. 113

St. Lawrence River Links the Great Lakes to the Atlantic Ocean (49°N, 67°W) p. 123

St. Louis City in Missouri; on Mississippi River (39°N, 90°W) p. 356

Salem An early English settlement in Massachusetts (43°N, 71°W) p. 139

Salt Lake City Capital of Utah (40°N, 112°W) p. 13

San Antonio City in Texas (29°N, 98°W) p. 395

San Diego City in southern California (32°N, 117°W) p. 28

San Francisco A major port city in California (38°N, 122°W) p. 318

San Salvador Caribbean island where Columbus landed (24°N, 74°W) p. 97

Santa Fe Capital of New Mexico (35°N, 106°W) p. 13

Saratoga New York site of an important American victory against the British in 1777 (43°N, 75°W) p. 280

Savannah Oldest city in Georgia (32°N, 81°W) p. 286

R59

Seattle Large city in Washington State (48°N, 122°W) p. R54
Sierra Madre A system of mountain ranges in Mexico (27°N, 104°W) p. R53
Sierra Nevada Mountain range mainly in eastern California (39°N, 120°W) p. R56
Sonoran Desert Desert in southwestern United States (33°N, 112°W) p. 6
South Africa Nation of southern Africa; capitals: Cape Town, Pretoria, Bloemfontein (34°S, 18°E) p. 309
South America Southern continent of Western Hemisphere (10°S, 60°W) p. R50
South Carolina 8th state; capital: Columbia (34°N, 81°W) p. 203
South Dakota 40th state; capital: Pierre (44°N, 100°W) pp. R54–R55
South Korea Country in eastern Asia on Korean peninsula; capital: Seoul (37°N, 127°E) p. 512
Spain Country in Western Europe; capital: Madrid (40°N, 5°W) p. 96

Tennessee 16th state; capital: Nashville (36°N, 88°W) p. 368
Tenochtitlán Aztec city; present-day Mexico City (19°N, 99°W) p. 43
Texas 28th state; capital: Austin (31°N, 101°W) p. 394
Timbuktu City in Mali, W. Africa (17°N, 3°W) p. 86
Trenton Capital of New Jersey (40°N, 75°W) p. 279
Tucson City in Arizona (32°N, 111°W) p. R54

United Kingdom England, Scotland, and Wales (57°N, 2°W) p. R47
United States Country in central and northwest North America (38°N, 110°W) p. R46
Utah 45th state; capital: Salt Lake City (40°N, 112°W) p. 13

Valley Forge George Washington's winter camp in 1777; near Philadelphia (40°N, 75°W) p. 280
Venice City in Italy (45°N, 12°E) p. 84
Vermont 14th state; capital: Montpelier (44°N, 72°W) p. 29
Vicksburg, Mississippi Site of Civil War battle (32°N, 91°W) p. 454
Vietnam Country in southeast Asia (18°N, 107°E) p. 506
Virginia 10th state; capital: Richmond (37°N, 81°W) p. 131

Washington 42nd state; capital: Olympia (48°N, 121°W) p. 533
Washington, D.C. Capital of the U.S. (39°N, 77°W) p. R55
West Indies Islands separating the Caribbean Sea and the Atlantic (19°N, 79°W) p. 97
West Virginia 35th state; capital: Charleston (38N, 81°W) p. R55
Williamsburg Colonial capital of Virginia (37°N, 77°W) p. 206
Wisconsin 30th state; capital: Madison (40°N, 89°W) p. R55
Wyoming 44th state; capital: Cheyenne (43°N, 109°W) p. R54

Yorktown In Virginia; site of last major battle of Revolutionary War (37°N, 77°W) p. 288

Gazetteer

Glossary

A

abolitionist (ab uh LIH shuhn ist) someone who joined the movement to abolish, or end, slavery. (p. 424)

absolute location (AB suh loot loh KAY shuhn) the exact latitude and longitude of a place on the globe. (p. 116)

activist (AK tuh vihst) a person who takes action to change social conditions or unfair laws. (p. 526)

agriculture (AG rih kuhl chur) farming or growing plants. (p. 40)

ally (AL ly) a person or group that joins with another to work toward a goal. (p. 229)

amendment (uh MEND muhnt) a change to the Constitution. (p. 316)

annexation (uh nehks AY shuhn) the act of joining two countries or pieces of land together. (p. 395)

Antifederalist (an tee FEHD ur uh lihst) someone who opposed the new Constitution. (p. 306)

apprentice (uh PREHN tihs) someone who studies with a master to learn a skill or business. (p. 198)

armada (ahr MAH duh) the Spanish word for a large fleet of ships. (p. 125)

artisan (AR tih zuhn) someone who is skilled at making something by hand, such as silver spoons or wooden chairs. (p. 198)

assassination (uh SAS uh nay shuhn) the murder of an important leader. (p. 473)

astrolabe (AS truh layb) a tool that measures the height of the sun or a star above the horizon. (p. 91)

backcountry (BAK kuhn tree) the mountainous area west of where most colonists settled. (p. 163)

banish (BAN ihsh) to force someone to leave a place. (p. 167)

bar graph (bahr graf) a graph that compares amounts of things. (p. 422)

barter (BAHR tur) to exchange goods without using money. (p. 70)

benefit (BEHN uh fiht) a gain or an advantage. (p. 194)

Black Codes (blak kohds) laws that limited the rights of former enslaved people to travel, vote, and work in certain jobs. (p. 474)

boomtown (BOOM toun) a town whose population booms, or grows very quickly. (p. 402)

border state (BOHR dur stayt) a slave state that stayed in the Union. (p. 452)

boycott (BOI kaht) the refusal to buy, sell, or use certain goods. (p. 236)

braceros (brah SHE rohs) Mexicans invited to work in the United States as temporary workers. (p. 505)

Cabinet (KAB uh niht) a group chosen by the President to help run the executive branch and give advice. (p. 321)

campaign (kam PAYN) a series of actions taken toward a goal, such as winning a presidential election. (p. 369)

canal (kuh NAL) a waterway built for boat travel and shipping. (p. 346)

cape (kayp) a strip of land that stretches into a body of water. (p. 137)

capital (KAP ih tuhl) the city where the government meets. (p. 322)

capital resource (KAP ih tuhl REE sawrs) a tool, machine, or building that people use to produce goods and services. (p. 17)

caravan (KAR uh van) a group of people and animals who travel together. (p. 86)

cardinal directions (KAR dn uhl dih REHK shuhns) the main directions: north, south, east, and west. (p. 13)

cash crop (kash krahp) a crop that people grow and sell to earn money. (p. 132)

R61

casualties (KAHZ oo uhl teez) soldiers who are killed or wounded. (p. 454)

cause (kawz) an event or action that makes something else happen. (p. 248)

century (SEHN chuh ree) a period of 100 years. (p. 128)

ceremony (SEHR uh moh nee) a formal event at which people gather to express important beliefs. (p. 56)

cession (SEHSH uhn) something that is given up. (p. 397)

charter (CHAHR ter) a document giving permission to a person or group to do something. (p. 131)

checks and balances (chehks uhnd BAHL uhns ehz) a system that lets each branch of government limit the power of the other two. (p. 314)

circle graph (SUR kuhl graf) a graph that illustrates how a part compares with the whole. (p. 422)

circumnavigate (sur kuhm NAV i gayt) to sail completely around something. (p. 101)

citizen (SIHT ih zuhn) an official member of a city, state, or nation. (p. 296)

civil rights (SIHV uhl ryts) the rights that countries guarantee their citizens. (p. 530)

civil war (SIHV uhl wawr) a war between two groups or regions within a nation. (p. 445)

civilian (sih VIHL yuhn) a person who is not in the military. (p. 462)

civilization (sihv uh lih ZAY shuhn) a group of people living together who have systems of government, religion, and culture. (p. 40)

claim (klaym) something declared as one's own, especially a piece of land. (p. 124)

clan (klan) a group of related families. (p. 48)

climate (KLY miht) the type of weather a place has over a long period of time. (p. 9)

colony (KAHL uh nee) an area of land ruled by another country. (p. 110)

commander (kuh MAN dur) the officer in charge of an army. (p. 254)

compact (KAHM pakt) an agreement. (p. 137)

compass rose (KUHM puhs rohz) a part of a map that shows the cardinal and intermediate directions. (p. 13)

compromise (KAHM pruh myz) when both sides give up something they want to settle a disagreement. (p. 304)

Confederacy (kuhn FEHD ur uh see) the name for South Carolina, Mississippi, Florida, Alabama, Georgia, Louisiana, Texas, and later Arkansas, North Carolina, Tennessee, and Virginia. (p. 444)

confederation (kuhn fehd ur AY shuhn) a type of government in which separate groups of people join together, but local leaders still make many decisions for their group. (p. 70)

congress (KAHNG grihs) a group of representatives who meet to discuss a subject. (p. 229)

conquistador (kahn KEES tuh dawr) the Spanish word for conqueror. (p. 104)

conservation (kahn sur VAY shuhn) the protection and wise use of natural resources. (p. 18)

constitution (kahn stih TOO shuhn) a written plan for government. (p. 296)

consumer (kuhn SOO mur) someone who buys goods and services. (p. 25)

convert (kahn VURT) to change a religion or a belief. (p. 110)

corps (kawr) a team of people who work together. (p. 356)

correspondence (kawr ih SPAHN duhns) written communication. (p. 241)

cost (kawst) a loss or sacrifice. (p. 194)

debtor (DEHT ur) a person who owes money. (p. 204)

decade (DEHK ayd) a period of 10 years. (p. 128)

declaration (dehk luh RAY shuhn) a statement that declares, or announces, an idea. (p. 264)

delegate (DEHL ih giht) someone chosen to speak and act for others. (p. 243)

democracy (dih MAHK ruh see) a government in which the people have the power to make political decisions. (p. 312)

Glossary

desert (dih ZURT) to leave the army without permission. (p. 468)

discrimination (dih skrihm uh NAY shuhn) the unfair treatment of particular groups. (p. 425)

dissenter (dih SEHN tur) a person who does not agree with the beliefs of his or her leaders. (p. 167)

diversity (dih VUR sih tee) the variety of people in a group. (p. 145)

draft (draft) when the government chooses people who have to serve in the military. (p. 455)

economy (ih KAHN uh mee) the system people use to produce goods and services. (p. 24)

ecosystem (EH koh sihs tuhm) a community of plants and animals, along with the surrounding soil, air, and water. (p. 31)

effect (ih FEHKT) an event or action that is a result of a cause. (p. 248)

Electoral College (ih LEHK tur uhl KAH luhdj) representatives from each state who vote for the President. (p. 320)

emancipation (ih MAN suh pay shuhn) the freeing of enslaved people. (p. 456)

empire (EHM pyr) many nations or territories ruled by a single group or leader. (p. 104)

entrepreneur (ahn truh pruh NUR) a person who takes risks to start a business. (p. 380)

environment (ehn VY ruhn muhnt) the surroundings in which people, plants, and animals live. (p. 29)

epidemic (ehp ih DEHM ihk) an outbreak of disease that spreads quickly and affects many people. (p. 98)

equator (ih KWAY tur) the imaginary line around the middle of the Earth. (p. 9)

erosion (ih ROH zhuhn) the process by which water and wind wear away the land. (p. 30)

ethnic group (EHTH nihk groop) a group of people who share a language or culture. (p. 500)

executive branch (ihg ZEHK yuh tihv branch) the branch of government that suggests laws and carries out the laws made by Congress. (p. 313)

expedition (ehk spih DIHSH uhn) a journey to achieve a goal. (p. 104)

export (ihk SPAWRT) a product sent to another country and sold. (p. 175)

fall line (fahl lyn) the line where rivers from higher land flow to lower land and often form waterfalls. (p. 162)

famine (FAM ihn) a widespread shortage of food. (p. 389)

federal (FEHD ur uhl) a system in which the states share power with the central government. (p. 303)

Federalist (FEHD ur uh lihst) a supporter of the Constitution. (p. 306)

flatboat (FLAT boht) a large, rectangular boat partly covered by a roof. (p. 346)

flow lines (floh lyns) lines that show where people or objects come from and where they go. The thickness of the lines shows how many have moved. (p. 510)

foreign policy (FAWR ihn PAWL ih see) a government's actions toward other nations. (p. 364)

forty-niner (FAWR tee NY nur) a miner who went to California in 1849. (p. 402)

free enterprise (free EHN tuh pryz) the system in which people may start any business that they believe will succeed. (p. 198)

free market economy (free MAHR kiht ih KAHN uh mee) an economic system in which the people, not the government, decide what will be produced. (p. 198)

free state (free stayt) a state that did not have slavery. (p. 432)

Freedmen's Bureau (FREED mehnz BYOOR oh) an organization that provided food, clothing, medical care, and legal advice to poor blacks and whites. (p. 474)

front (fruhnt) where the fighting takes place in a war. (p. 396)

frontier (FRUHN teer) the edge of a country or settled region. (p. 345)

R63

fugitive (FYOO jih tihv) a person who is running away. (p. 434)

geography (jee AHG ruh fee) the study of the world and the people and things that live there. (p. 6)

glacier (GLAY shur) a huge, thick sheet of slowly moving ice. (p. 39)

gold rush (gohld ruhsh) when many people hurry to the same area to look for gold. (p. 402)

Great Compromise (grayt KAHM pruh myz) Roger Sherman's suggestion that the states with the largest populations send the most representatives to the House of Representatives but each state have the same number of representatives in the Senate. (p. 304)

growing season (GROH eeng SEE zuhn) the time of year when it is warm enough for plants to grow. (p. 161)

hacienda (hah see EHN duh) a large farm or ranch, often with its own village and church. (p. 112)

heritage (HEHR ih tihj) something that is passed down from one generation to the next. (p. 514)

home front (hohm fruhnt) all the people in a country who are not in the military during wartime. (p. 462)

human resources (HYOO muhn REE sohrs uhz) people and the skills and knowledge they bring to their work. (p. 17)

immigrant (IHM ih gruhnt) a person who moves to another country to live. (p. 388)

impeach (ihm PEECH) to charge a government official with a crime. (p. 475)

import (IHM pawrt) a good brought into one country from another. (p. 175)

inauguration (ihn AW gyuh ray shuhn) the official ceremony to make someone President. (p. 321)

indentured servant (ihn DEHN churd SUR vuhnt) someone who agreed to work for a number of years in exchange for the cost of a voyage to North America. (p. 132)

independence (ihn duh PEHN duhns) freedom from being ruled by someone else. (p. 262)

indigo (IHN duh goh) a plant that can be made into a dark blue dye. (p. 211)

Industrial Revolution (ihn DUHS tree uhl rehv uh LOO shuhn) a period of time marked by changes in manufacturing and transportation. (p. 378)

industry (IHN duh stree) all the businesses that make one kind of product or provide one kind of service. (p. 174)

inflation (ihn FLAY shuhn) a rise in the prices of goods. (p. 273)

injustice (ihn JUHS tihs) unfair treatment that abuses a person's rights. (p. 390)

inset map (IHN seht map) a small map within a larger one that may show a close-up of an area or provide other information about it. (p. 13)

interchangeable parts (ihn tur CHAYN juh buhl pahrts) parts made by a machine to be exactly the same in size and shape. (p. 379)

interest (IHN trihst) what people pay to borrow money. (p. 322)

intermediate directions (ihn tur MEE dee iht dih REHK shuhns) the in-between directions of northeast, southeast, southwest, and northwest. (p. 13)

interpreter (ihn TUR prih tur) someone who helps speakers of different languages understand each other. (p. 356)

invasion (ihn VAY zhuhn) an attack by an armed force to conquer another country. (p. 125)

invest (ihn VEHST) to put money into something to try to earn more money. (p. 131)

irrigation (ihr ih GAY shuhn) a way of supplying water to crops with streams, ditches, or pipes. (p. 55)

Glossary

Jim Crow (jihm kroh) laws that segregated African Americans from other Americans. (p. 484)

judicial branch (joo DISH uhl branch) the branch of government that decides the meaning of laws and whether the laws have been followed. (p. 313)

kingdom (KIHNG duhm) a place ruled by a king or queen. (p. 86)

laborer (LAY buhr ur) a person who does hard physical work. (p. 198)

landform (LAND fohrm) a feature on the surface of the land. (p. 8)

legislative branch (LEHJ ih slay tihv branch) the branch of government that makes laws for the country. (p. 313)

legislature (LEHJ ih slay chur) a group of people with the power to make and change laws. (p. 203)

liberty (LIHB uhr tee) freedom from being controlled by another government. (p. 235)

line graph (lyn graf) a graph that shows change over time. (p. 422)

lodge (lawj) a type of home that Plains Indians made using bark, earth, and grass. (p. 61)

longhouse (LAWNG hows) a large house made out of wood poles and covered with bark. (p. 69)

Loyalist (LOI uh lihst) someone who was still loyal to the king. (p. 270)

manifest destiny (MAN uh fehst DEHS tuh nee) the belief that the United States should spread across the entire North American continent, from the Atlantic Ocean to the Pacific Ocean. (p. 395)

manufacturer (man yuh FAK chuhr ur) someone who uses machines to make goods. (p. 354)

map legend (map LEHJ uhnd) a part of a map that explains any symbols or colors on a map. (p. 13)

map scale (map skayl) a part of a map that compares distance on a map to distance in the real world. (p. 13)

mass production (mas pruh DUHK shuhn) making many identical products at once. (p. 379)

massacre (MAS uh kur) the killing of many people. (p. 240)

mercenary (MUR suh nehr ee) a soldier who is paid to fight for a foreign country. (p. 279)

merchant (MUR chunt) someone who buys and sells goods to earn money. (p. 85)

meridian (muh RIHD ee uhn) a line of longitude. (p. 116)

Middle Passage (MIHD uhl PAHS ihj) the trip from Africa to the West Indies. (p. 176)

migrant worker (MY gruhnt WUR kuhr) a person who moves from place to place to find work, mostly on farms. (p. 534)

migration (MY gray shuhn) a movement from one region to another. (p. 39)

militia (muh LIHSH uh) a group of ordinary people who train for battle. (p. 250)

minutemen (MIHN iht mehn) militia with special training. They had to be ready for battle at a minute's notice. (p. 251)

mission (MIHSH uhn) a religious community where priests taught Christianity. (p. 110)

missionary (MIHSH uh nehr ee) a person who teaches his or her religion to others who have different beliefs. (p. 146)

motto (MAHT oh) a short statement that explains an ideal or a goal. (p. 515)

nationalism (NASH uh nuh lihz uhm) the belief that your country deserves more success than others. (p. 364)

natural resource (NACH ur uhl REE sawrs) a material from nature, such as soil or water. (p. 14)

naturalization (nach ur uh lihz AY shuhn) the process of becoming a citizen by learning the laws of the country and the rights and duties of its citizens. (p. 540)

navigation (nav ih GAY shuhn) the science of planning and controlling the direction of a ship. (p. 91)

R65

neutral (NOO truhl) not to take sides. (p. 270)

nomad (NOH mad) a person who moves around and does not live in one place. (p. 61)

nonrenewable resource (nahn rih NOO uh buhl REE sawrs) a natural resource that cannot be replaced once it is used, such as oil. (p. 15)

nonviolent protest (nahn VY uh luhnt PROH test) a way of bringing change without using violence. (p. 531)

Northwest Passage (nawrth WEHST PAS ihj) the water route that explorers were hoping to find. (p. 123)

opportunity cost (ahp ur TOO nih tee kahst) the thing you give up when you decide to do or have something else. (p. 18)

ordinance (AWR dn uhns) a law. (p. 297)

outline (OWT lyn) text that identifies the main ideas and supporting details of a topic. (p. 352)

overseer (OH vuhr see uhr) a person who watches and directs the work of other people. (p. 214)

parallel (PAR uh lehl) a line of latitude. (p. 116)

parallel timelines (PAR uh lehl TYM lynz) two or more timelines grouped together. (p. 128)

Patriot (PAY tree uht) a colonist who opposed British rule. (p. 250)

persecution (pur sih KYOO shuhn) unfair treatment that causes suffering. (p. 499)

petition (puh TIHSH uhn) a written request from a number of people. (p. 254)

physical map (FIHZ ih kuhl map) a map that shows the location of physical features, such as landforms, bodies of water, or resources. (p. 12)

pilgrim (PIHL gruhm) a person who makes a long journey for religious reasons. (p. 136)

pioneer (py uh NEER) one of the first of a group of people to enter or settle a region. (p. 345)

plantation (plan TAY shuhn) a large farm on which crops are raised by workers who live on the farm. (p. 202)

plateau (pla TOH) a high, steep-sided area rising above the surrounding land. (p. 8)

point of view (poynt uhv vyoo) the way someone thinks about an issue, an event, or a person. (p. 310)

political map (puh LIHT ih kuhl map) a map that shows cities, states, and countries. (p. 12)

political party (puh LIHT ih kuhl PAHR tee) an organized group of people who share similar ideas about government. (p. 322)

pollution (puh LOO shuhn) anything that makes the soil, air, or water dirty and unhealthy. (p. 30)

popular sovereignty (PAHP yuh luhr SAHV uhr ihn tee) an idea that the people who live in a place make decisions for themselves. (p. 433)

potlatch (PAHT lach) a large feast that could last for several days. (p. 47)

prejudice (PREHJ uh dihs) an unfair, negative opinion that can lead to unjust treatment. (p. 526)

presidio (prih SEE dee oh) a fort built by the Spanish to protect their claims and guard themselves against attack. (p. 111)

primary source (PRY mehr ee sawrs) firsthand information about an event, a place, or a time period. (p. 480)

prime meridian (prym muh RIHD ee uhn) the main line of longitude located at zero degrees. (p. 116)

proclamation (prahk luh MAY shuhn) an official public statement. (p. 230)

productivity (proh duhk TIHV ih tee) the amount of goods and services produced by workers in a certain amount of time. (p. 379)

profit (PRAHF iht) the money a business has left over after all expenses have been paid. (p. 92)

proprietor (pruh PRY ih tur) a person who owned and controlled all the land of a colony. (p. 188)

prosperity (prah SPEHR ih tee) economic success and security. (p. 364)

protest (PROH tehst) an event at which people speak out about an issue. (p. 235)

pueblo (PWEH bloh) the Spanish word for town. (p. 42)

quarter (KWAWR tur) to give people food and shelter. (p. 242)

quota (KWOH tur) the maximum number of people allowed to enter a country. (p. 504)

ratify (RAT uh fy) to accept. (p. 306)

rebellion (rih BEHL yun) a fight against a government (p. 230)

Reconstruction (ree kuhn STRUHK shuhn) the period when the South rejoined the Union. (p. 472)

reform (rih FOWRM) an action that makes something better. (p. 390)

refuge (REHF yooj) a safe place. (p. 203)

refugee (REHF yoo jee) a person who escapes war or other danger and seeks safety in another country. (p. 506)

region (REE jehn) an area that has one or more features in common. (p. 22)

register (REHJ ih stur) to sign up to vote. (p. 541)

renewable resource (rih NOO uh buhl REE sawrs) a natural resource that can be replaced, such as wood. (p. 15)

repeal (rih PEEL) to cancel something, such as a law. (p. 236)

representative (rehp rih ZEHN tuh tihv) someone who is chosen to speak and act for others. (p. 189)

republic (rih PUHB lihk) a government in which the citizens elect leaders to represent them. (p. 303)

responsibility (rih sphahn suh BIHL ih tee) a duty that someone is expected to fulfill. (p. 541)

retreat (rih TREET) to move away from the enemy. (p. 279)

revolt (reh VUHLT) a violent uprising against a ruler. (p. 113)

rights (ryts) freedoms that are protected by a government's laws. (p. 264)

ruling (ROO lihng) an official decision. (p. 370)

scarcity (SKAIR sih tee) not having as much of something as people would like. (p. 18)

secession (sih SEHSH uhn) when a part of a country leaves or breaks off from the rest. (p. 440)

secondary source (SEHK uhn dehr ee sawrs) information from someone who did not witness an event. (p. 480)

sectionalism (SEHK shuh nuh lihz uhm) loyalty to one part of the country. (p. 419)

segregation (sehg rih GAY shuhn) the forced separation of the races. (p. 484)

self-government (sehlf GUHV urn muhnt) when the people who live in a place make laws for themselves. (p. 167)

settlement (SEHT uhl muhnt) a small community of people living in a new place. (p. 98)

sharecropping (SHAIR krahp ihng) when landowners let poor farmers use small areas of their land. In return, the sharecropper gave the landowner a share of the crop. (p. 483)

Silk Road (sihlk rohd) several trade routes connecting China and Europe. (p. 85)

slave state (slayv stayt) a state that permitted slavery. (p. 432)

slave trade (slayv trayd) the business of buying and selling human beings. (p. 176)

slavery (SLAY vuh ree) a cruel system in which people are bought and sold and made to work without pay. (p. 93)

smuggling (SMUHG lihng) to import goods illegally. (p. 235)

source (sawrs) the place where a river begins. (p. 357)

specialization (spehsh uh lih ZAY shuhn) when people make the goods they are best able to produce with the resources they have. (p. 24)

spiritual (SPIHR ih choo uhl) a religious song. (p. 215)

staple (STAY puhl) a main crop that is used for food. (p. 56)

R67

states' rights (stayts ryts) the idea that states, not the federal government, should make the final decisions about matters that affect them. (p. 419)

stock (stahk) a share of ownership in a company. (p. 131)

strategy (STRAT uh jee) a plan of action. (p. 286)

suffrage (SUHF rihj) the right to vote. (p. 368)

suffragist (SUHF ruh jihst) a woman who worked to gain the right to vote. (p. 525)

summary (SUHM uh ree) a short description of the main points in a piece of writing. (p. 66)

surplus (SUHR pluhs) extra. (p. 47)

surrender (suh REHN dur) to give up. (p. 288)

tariff (TAR ihf) a tax on imported goods. (p. 418)

tax (taks) money that people pay to their government in return for services. (p. 234)

technology (tehk NAHL uh jee) the use of scientific knowledge and tools to do things better and more rapidly. (p. 90)

telegraph (TEHL ih graf) a machine that sends electric signals over wires. (p. 467)

temperance (TEHM pur uhns) controlling or cutting back on the drinking of alcohol. (p. 390)

tenement (TEHN uh muhnt) a poorly built apartment building. (p. 500)

territory (TEHR ih tawr ee) land ruled by a national government but which has no representatives in the government. (p. 297)

textile (TEHKS tyl) cloth or fabric. (p. 378)

tidewater (TYD wah tur) where the water in rivers and streams rises and falls with the ocean's tides. (p. 162)

tolerance (TAHL ur uhns) the respect for beliefs that are different from one's own. (p. 145)

total war (TOHT uhl wawr) the strategy of destroying an enemy's resources. (p. 467)

town meeting (town MEET ihng) a gathering where colonists held elections and voted on the laws for their towns. (p. 166)

trade (trayd) the buying and selling of goods. (p. 25)

traitor (TRAY tur) someone who is not loyal. (p. 286)

travois (truh VOY) equipment similar to a sled that was made from two long poles and usually pulled by a dog. (p. 61)

treason (TREE zuhn) the crime of fighting against one's own government. (p. 266)

treaty (TREE tee) an official agreement between nations or groups. (p. 190)

unconstitutional (uhn kahn stih TOO shuh nuhl) when a law does not agree with the Constitution. (p. 314)

Underground Railroad (UHN dur ground RAYL rohd) a series of escape routes and hiding places to bring slaves out of the South. (p. 426)

Union (YOON yuhn) another name for the United States. (p. 433)

veto (VEE toh) to reject. (p. 314)

victory (VIHK tuh ree) success in battle against an enemy. (p. 279)

volunteer (vahl uhn TEER) someone who helps other people without being paid. (p. 543)

wagon train (WAG uhn trayn) a line of covered wagons that moved together. (p. 401)

wampum (WAHM puhm) pieces of carefully shaped and cut seashell. (p. 70)

Glossary

Index

Page numbers with *m* after them refer to maps. Page numbers that are in italics refer to pictures.

R69

Index

R71

Index

K

Index

Index

R75

Z

Index

Acknowledgments

Permissioned Literature Selections

Excerpt from *Ann's Story: 1747,* by Joan Lowery Nixon. Copyright © 2000 by Joan Lowery Nixon and The Colonial Williamsburg Foundation. Used by permission of Random House Children's Books, a division of Random House, Inc. and Daniel Weiss Associates, Inc. Excerpt from *"Chinook Wind Wrestles Cold Wind,"* from *They Dance in the Sky: Native American Star Myths,* by Jean Guard Monroe and Ray A. Williamson. Text copyright © 1987 by Jean Guard Monroe and Ray A. Williamson. Reprinted by permission of Houghton Mifflin Company. *"City of Bridges"/"Ciudad de pientes,"* from *Iguanas in the Snow and Other Poems / Iguanas en la nieve y otros poemas de invierno,* by Francisco X. Alarcon. Poem copyright © 2001 by Francisco X. Alarcon. Reprinted with the permission of the publisher, Children's Book Press, San Francisco, CA. *"Dream Variation,"* from *The Collected Poems of Langston Hughes,* by Langston Hughes. Copyright © 1994 by The Estate of Langston Hughes. Used by permission of Alfred A. Knopf, a division of Random House, Inc. and Harold Ober Associates Incorporated. Excerpt from *Emma's Journal: The Story Of A Colonial Girl,* by Marissa Moss. Copyright © 1999 by Marissa Moss. Reprinted by permission of Harcourt, Inc. and the author. Excerpt from *First In Peace: George Washington, the Constitution, and the Presidency,* by John Rosenburg. Copyright © 1998 by John Rosenburg. Reprinted by permission of The Millbrook Press, Inc. *"For Purple Mountains' Majesty,"* from *The Malibu and Other Poems,* by Myra Cohn Livingston. Copyright © 1972 by Myra Cohn Livingston. Reprinted by permission of Marian Reiner. *"Green Card Fever"* from *We The People,* by Bobbi Katz. Text copyright © 2000 by Bobbi Katz. Used by permission of HarperCollins Publishers. Excerpt from the Speech, *"I Have a Dream,"* by Dr. Martin Luther King Jr. Copyright © 1963 by Dr. Martin Luther King Jr., copyright renewed © 1991 by Coretta Scott King. Reprinted by arrangement with the Estate of Martin Luther King Jr., c/o Writers House as agent for the proprietor New York, NY. Excerpt from *In the Days of the Vaqueros: America's First True Cowboys,* by Russell Freedman. Text copyright © 2001 by Russell Freedman. Reprinted by permission of Houghton Mifflin Company. Excerpt from *"Juan Ponce de Leon,"* from *Around the World In A Hundred Years: From Henry The Navigator To Magellan,* by Jean Fritz. Text copyright © 1994 by Jean Frtiz. Used by permission of G.P. Putnam's Sons, a division of Penguin Young Readers Group, a member of Penguin Group (USA) Inc., 345 Hudson Street, New York, NY 10014. All rights reserved. Excerpt from *"Our Friend Squanto,"* from *This New Land,* by G. Clifton Wisler. Copyright © 1987 by G. Clifton Wisler. Published by arrangement with Walker & Co. Excerpt from *Remember Me,* by Irene N. Watts, published by Tundra Books of Northern New York. Copyright © 2000 by Irene N. Watts. Permission to reproduce work must be sought from originating publisher. Reprinted by permission. *"Speak Up,"* from *Good Luck Gold and Other Poems,* by Janet S. Wong. Copyright © 1994 by Janet S. Wong. Reprinted with the permission of Margaret K. McElderry Books, an imprint of Simon & Schuster Children's Publishing Division. All rights reserved. Excerpt from *Stealing Freedom,* by Elisa Carbone. Text copyright © 1998 by Elisa Carbone. Reprinted by arrangement with Random House Children's Boosk, a division of Random House, Inc., New York, New York. *"Torn Map,"* from *Come With Me: Poems For A Journey,* by Naomi Shihab Nye. Text copyright © 2000 by Naomi Shihab Nye, Reprinted by permission of HarperCollins Publishers.

Photography

COVER (Lincoln Memorial) © Dennis Brack. (Capitol) © Royalty Free/CORBIS. (map) © Granger Collection, New York. (compass) HMCo./Michael Indresano. (spine Lincoln memorial) © Peter Gridley/Getty Images. (back cover statue) © Connie Ricca/CORBIS. (back cover nickel) Courtesy of the United States Mint. **vi-vii** © Neil Rabinowitz/CORBIS **vii** (t) The Art Archive/ National Anthropological Museum Mexico/Dagli Orti. **viii** (t) Photodisc/Getty Images. (b) © National Portrait Gallery, Smithsonian Institution/Art Resource, NY. **ix** (t) Royal Albert Memorial Museum, Exeter, Devon, UK/ Bridgeman Art Library. (b) Colonial Williamsburg Foundation. **x** (t) Courtesy Bostonian Society/Old State House. **x-xi** © Private Collection/Art Resource, NY. **xi** (t) © Andrea Pistolesi/Getty Images. **xii** (t) The Granger Collection, New York. (b) © D. Robert & Lorri Franz/ CORBIS. **xiii** (t) Courtesy Don Troiani, Historical Military Image Bank. (b) © Bettmann/Corbis. **xiv** (t) Brown Brothers. (b) NASA. xv © Yann Arthus-Bertrand/CORBIS. **xx-xxi** The Granger Collection, New York. **1** Terry Donnelly/Getty Images **2** (l) © David Muench.(m) The Granger Collection, New York. (r) © Archivo Iconografico, S.A./CORBIS. **3** (r) Smithsonian American Art Museum, Washington, DC/Art Resource, NY. **4** (l) Bill Strode/ Woodfin Camp.(r) © E. R. Degginger. **5** (l) © Grant Heilman/Grant Heilman Photography, Inc. Alan Kearny/ Getty Images. **10** (b) © Warren Faidley/ Weatherstock. **10-11** Laboratory for Atmospheres at NASA Goddard Space Flight Center. **14-15** Grant Heilman/Grant Heilman Photography, Inc. **16** (l, m) Grant Heilman/Grant Heilman Photography, Inc. (r) Debra Ferguson/AgStockUSA. **17** (l, ml) Arthur C. Smith III/Grant Heilman Photography, Inc. **18** © Russell Curtis/Photo Researchers, Inc. **19** © Adamsmith/ SuperStock **20-21** Stefano Paltera/American Solar Challenge **22** Paul McCormick/Getty Images **24** (l) © Larry Lefever/Grant Heilman Photography, Inc. (r) © Grant Heilman/Grant Heilman Photography, Inc. **26** Courtesy Dawn Wright. **27** (l) Courtesy Mei-Po Kwan. (r) Courtesy Dr. William Wood, Photo: Ray Isawa. **28** D. Megna/Raw Talent Photo. **30** (l) David R. Frazier. (r) Mine-engineer.com, Long Beach, California. **32** Library Of Congress, LCZ62-114352. **36** (l) Art Archive/Museo Cuidad Mexico/Nicolas Sapieha. (r) Jeff Greenberg/Photo Researchers, Inc. **37** (l) Garry D. McMichael/Photo Researchers, Inc. (r) NativeStock **38** Bill Varie/CORBIS. **39** Jonathan Blair/CORBIS. **40-41** Cahokia Mounds State Historic Site, painting by Michael Hampshire. **41** (t) Richard A. Cooke/CORBIS. (b) Ohio Historical Society. **42** (t) © J.C. Leacock/Network Aspen. (b) © David Muench. **43** The Art Archive/National Anthropological Museum Mexico/Dagli Orti. **44-45** The Art Archive/Mireille Vautier. **46** © David Muench. **49** © 1997 Clark James Mishler. **54** © David Muench. **57** © Suzi Moore/Woodfin Camp & Associates, Inc. **58** Courtesy Victor Mesayesva Jr. **58-59** Courtesy Leslie Marmon Silko. **59** (t) Los Alamos National Laboratory, Public Affairs Office. Photo: Leroy Sanchez. **60** © Tom Bean. **62** Smithsonian American Art Museum, Washington, DC/Art Resource, NY. **63** © Marilyn Angel Wynn/Nativestock.com. **64** Cincinatti Art Museum, Gift of General M. F. Force, Photo: T. Walsh. **64-65** University of Pennsylvania Museum, T4-3061. **68** © E. R. Degginger/Photo Researchers, Inc. **70** (l) The Granger Collection, New York. (r) Hiawatha Wampum Belt, NYSM Ref. #E-37309; now curated at The Onondaga Nation. Photo courtesy of New York State Museum, used with permission of The Council of Chiefs, Onondaga Nation. **71** Ray Ellis/Photo Researchers, Inc. **78** (t) Musée National de la Renaissance, Ecouen, France/Bridgeman Art Library. (b) Archivo Iconografico, S.A./CORBIS. **79** (tl) National Museum of Fine Arts, Madrid. (tr) © SuperStock. (bl) Granada Cathedral Photo: Oronoz. (br) The Art Archive/ National Anthropological Museum Mexico/Dagli Orti. **80** (l) Metropolitan Museum of Art, New York/Bridgeman Art Library. (m) © Giraudon/Art Resource, NY. (r) © Schalkwijk/ Art Resource, NY. **81** (t) Higgins Amory Museum, Worcester, MA, (HAM #13), Photo: Don Eaton. (bl) North Wind Picture Archives. (br) Photodisc/Getty Images. **82** (l) Time Life Pictures/Getty Images. (r) Stockbyte/PictureQuest **83** (l) Private Collection/ Bridgeman Art Library. (r) Wood Ronsaville Harlin, Inc. **85** (t) British Library,London, UK/Bridgeman Art library. (b) © China Stock. **87** The Art Archive/John Webb. **89** AP Wide World Photo. **90** © SPL/ Photo Researchers, Inc. **91** Bibliothéque Nationale, Paris, France/Bridgeman Art Library **92** © Stapleton Collection/ CORBIS. **95** (t) © Giraudon/Art Resource, NY. (b) © Victoria & Albert Museum, London/Art Resource, NY. **96** Metropolitan Museum of Art, New York/Bridgeman Art Library. **98** (t) © Giraudon/Art Resource, NY. **98-99** Royalty-Free/CORBIS. **101** The Art Archive/General Archive of the Indies Seville/Dagli Orti. **102-3** Library Of Congress. **104** © Archivo Iconografico, S.A./CORBIS. **105** © Giraudon/ Art Resource, NY. **106** Higgins Amory Museum, Worcester, MA, (HAM #13), Photo: Don Eaton. **107** © Ron Watts/ CORBIS. **108** (l, m) The Granger Collection, New York. (r) © Bettmann/CORBIS. **109** (bkgd) © Library of Congress/ Geography and Map Division. (l, r) The Granger Collection, New York. **110** © Schalkwijk/Art Resource, NY. **111** The Granger Collection, New York. **112** (t) North Wind Picture Archives. (b) © A. Ramey/Photo Edit. **114** Mithra-Index/ Bridgeman Art Library. **115** © Nancy Carter/North Wind Picture Archives. **120** (l) Erich Lessing/Art Resource, NY. (r) Library Of Congress. **121** (l) Pilgrim Society, Plymouth, Massachusetts. (r) New York Public Library/Art Resource, NY. **122** Bristol City Museum and Art Gallery, UK/Bridgeman Art Library. **124** © Erich Lessing/Art Resource, NY. **126** The Granger Collection, New York. **127** Private Collection/Bridgeman Art Library. **128** © Jeffrey L. Rotman/CORBIS. **129** © Giraudon/Art Resource, NY. **130** The Granger Collection, New York. **131** © Susan M. Glascock. **132** (l) © Marilyn Angel Wynn/Nativestock.com. (r) Ashmolean Museum, Oxford, UK/Bridgeman Art Library. **133** © National Portrait Gallery, Smithsonian Institution/Art Resource, NY. **134** (t) © North Wind Picture Archives. **134-5** Sidney King, National Park Service, Colonial National Historic Park, Jamestown Collection. **136** Photodisc/Getty Images. **137** Pilgrim Society, Plymouth, Massachusetts. **139** The Granger Collection, New York. **141** © Dorothy Littell Greco/Stock, Boston Inc./PictureQuest. **143** © Joseph Sohm;ChromoSohm Inc./CORBIS. **144** © CORBIS. **145** The Granger Collection, New York. **147** The Granger Collection, New York. **154** (t) © Bettmann/CORBIS. (b) © Photodisc/Getty Images. **155** (tl) The Granger Collection, New York. (tr) The Granger Collection, New York. (bl) North Wind Picture Archives. (br) Photodisc/Getty Images. **156** (l) The Granger Collection, New York. (m) The Granger Collection, New York. (r) © Shelburne Museum, Shelburne, Vermont. **157** (l) The Granger Collection, New York. (r) Private Collection/ Bridgeman Art Library. **158** (l) David Parnes/Index Stock Imagery. (r) Private Collection/Bridgeman Art Library. **159** (l) The Granger Collection, New York. (r) Archives Charmet/ Bridgeman Art Library. **160-1** © Neil Rabinowitz/CORBIS **162** (l) © Robert Estall/CORBIS. (r) © Jason Hawkes/ CORBIS. **163** © Phil Degginger. **165** © Alex S. MacLean/ Landslides. **166** Private Collection/Bridgeman Art Library. **167** (l) The Granger Collection, New York. (r) © Kindra Clineff. **169** © Shelburne Museum, Shelburne, Vermont. **174** Archives Charmet/Bridgeman Art Library. **176** (l) Royal Albert Memorial Museum, Exeter, Devon, UK/ Bridgeman Art Library. **176-7** Addison Gallery of American Art, Phillips Academy, Andover, Massachusetts. All Rights Reserved. **178** (l) North Wind Picture Archives. (r) Stock Montage. **179** Private Collection/Bridgeman Art Library. **180-1** Dorset Museum, Dorchester, England. **180** (l) © Stapleton Collection/CORBIS. **186** (l) The Granger Collection, New York. (r) Colonial Williamsburg Foundation. **187** (l) © Andre Jenny/Focus Group/Picture

R77

Quest. (r) © Alan Detrick/Photo Researchers, Inc. **188** The Granger Collection, New York. **190** (t) © Bettmann/ CORBIS. (b) The Granger Collection, New York. **191** Courtesy, CIGNA Museum and Art Collection. **192** (t) © National Portrait Gallery, Smithsonian Institution/Art Resource, NY. (b) American Philosophical Society Library. **193** (t, m, mr) Franklin Institute. (ml) Digital Stock. (b) The Granger Collection, New York. **196** North Wind Picture Archives. **198** (l) New York Public Library/Art Resource, NY. (r) Colonial Williamsburg Foundation. **199** Colonial Williamsburg Foundation. **202-3** © Andre Jenny/Focus Group/Picture Quest. **203** (r) The Granger Collection, New York. **205** Corpus Christi College, Oxford, UK/Bridgeman Art Library. **210** Hulton/Archive/Getty Images. **211** (l) Glen Allison/Stone/Getty Images. (m) ©Photo Edit. (r) ©Alan Detrick/Photo Researchers, Inc. **212** (t) Kaminski House Museum. (b) © Joseph Sohm: Visions of America/CORBIS. **213** (l) North Carolina Museum of History. (r) Colonial Williamsburg Foundation. **214** "View of Mulberry, House and Street", 1805, by Thomas Coram (1756-1811), oil on paper, Gibbes Museum of Art/Carolina Art Association, 68.18.01. **215** (l) Abby Aldrich Rockefeller Folk Art Center, Williamsburg, Virigina 35.301.3. (r) Collection of the Blue Ridge Institute & Museums, Ferrum College. **216-7** Colonial Williamsburg Foundation. **217** © Farrell Grehan/CORBIS. **222** (t) Museum of Fine Arts, Boston: Gift of Joseph W. Revere, William B. Revere and Edward H. R. Revere 30.781. (b) Concord Museum. **223** (tl) Museum of Fine Arts, Boston: Bequest of Winslow Warren 31.212. (tr) © New-York Historical Society, New York, USA/Bridgeman Art Library. (bl) Photodisc/Getty Images (digital composite). (br) The Daughters of the American Revolution Museum, Washington, D.C. **224** (l) Courtesy Colonial Williamsburg Foundation. (m) © Kevin Fleming/CORBIS. (r) © Henryk Kaiser/Index Stock Imagery. **225** (bl) The Granger Collection, New York. (br) Lauros/Giraudon/Bridgeman Art Library. (tr) © Bettmann/CORBIS. (br) Antony Edwards/ Getty Images. **226** (l) Architect of the Capitol. (r) The Granger Collection, New York. **227** (l) Courtesy of the Trustees of the Boston Public Library: George Washington at Dorchester Heights, by Emmanuel Luetze. (r) Hulton Archive/Getty Images. **229** (t) The Granger Collection, New York. (b) © Stock Montage. **231** The Granger Collection, New York. **232** (l) © CORBIS. **233** (t) © Bettmann/CORBIS. (b) © New-York Historical Society, New York, USA/Bridgeman Art Library. **234** Giraudon/ Bridgeman Art Library. **235** (l) © Bettmann/CORBIS. (m) © North Wind Picture Archives. (r) The Granger Collection, New York. **236** © North Wind Picture Archives. **237** American Philosophical Society. **240** © Stock Montage. **241** The Granger Collection, New York. **242** The Granger Collection, New York. **250** © Lee Snider/CORBIS. **252** (l) Massachusetts State House Art Collection, Courtesy Mass. Art Commission. (m) Photo from the collection of the Lexington, Massachusetts Historical Society. (r) © Bettmann/CORBIS. **253** (l) Massachusetts State House Art Collection, Courtesy Mass. Art Commission. (r) Courtesy Don Troiani, Historical Military Image Bank. **254** (l) Courtesy of the Trustees of the Boston Public Library: George Washington at Dorchester Heights, by Emmanuel Luetze. (r) National Museum of American History by Shirley Abbott (Harry N. Abrams, Inc.), ©Smithsonian Institution. **255** Tom Lovell, "The Noble Train of Artillery", Fort Ticonderoga Museum. **260** (l) © Pete Saloutos/CORBIS. (r) The Granger Collection, New York. **261** (tl) Reproduced from the original held by the Department of Special Collections of the University Libraries of Notre Dame. (bl, mt, mb, r) The Granger Collection, New York. **262** The Granger Collection, New York. **263** (l) Lilly Library, Indiana University. (r) © Bettmann/CORBIS. **264** (t) SuperStock. (b) Rhode Island Historical Society. **265** (b) Photodisc/Getty Images (digital composite). **266** The Granger Collection, New York. **267** Michael Herron/Take Stock. **268** (t) Independence National Historical Park. (bl) © Royalty-Free/CORBIS. (bm) © Ted Spiegel/CORBIS. (br) Monticello/ Thomas Jefferson Foundation, Inc. **269** (t) Library of Congress. (b) National Museum of American History, Smithsonian Institution, Behring Center, Neg #83-4689. **270-1** (bkgd) © Christie's Images/CORBIS. **271** (t) The Granger Collection, New York. (b) Fenimore Art Museum, Cooperstown, New York. Photo: Richard Walker. **272** (t) The Fraunces Tavern Museum. (m) The Granger Collection, New York. (b) Library of Congress, LC-USZC4-5316DLC. **273** (t) The Granger Collection, New York. (bl) Reproduced from the original held by the Department of Special Collections of the University Libraries of Notre Dame. (br) The Granger Collection, New York. **274** (r) Photodisc/Getty Images. **278** Courtesy Bostonian Society/Old State House. **279** The Metropolitan Museum of Art, Gift of John Stewart Kennedy, 1897 (97.34) Photograph © 1992 the Metropolitan Museum of Art. **282** (ml, r) Courtesy National Park Service, Museum Management Program and Morristown National Historical Park. (mr) Courtesy National Park Service, Museum Management Program and Valley Forge National Historical Park. **282-3** SuperStock. **285** Comstock KLIPS. **286** The Granger Collection, New York. **287** The Granger Collection, New York. **288** The Senate of the Commonwealth of Virginia, Courtesy of the Library of Virginia. **289** National Archives. **290** (t) © Academy of Natural Sciences of Philadelphia/CORBIS. (m) The Granger Collection, New York. (b) The Granger Collection, New York. **291** (tm) © Erich Lessing/Art Resource, NY.(tr) © Bettmann/CORBIS. (bl) The Art Archive/ Dagli Orti. (br) The Granger Collection, New York. **294** (r) The Granger Collection, New York. **295** (r) New York Historical Society/Bridgeman Art Library. **297** © Alex S. MacLean/Landslides. 298 (l) © North Wind Picture Archives. (r) The Granger Collection, New York. **299** Virginia Historical Society, Richmond, Virginia. **302-3** Independence National Historical Park. **303** (l) Courtesy of National Constitution Center (Scott Frances, Ltd.). (r) © Reunion des Musées Nationaux/Art Resource, NY. **306** (t) © Art Resource. NY. (b) © Joseph Sohm; ChromoSohm Inc./CORBIS. **308** © Dennis Brack. **310** (t) The Granger Collection, New York. (b) © Reunion des Musées Nationaux/Art Resource, NY. **313** (l) © Reuters New Media Inc.CORBIS. (r) © Joseph Sohm/Visions of America, LLC/Picture Quest. **316** © Bob Daemmrich/The Image Works. **317** © Bettmann/CORBIS. **318** (l) © Bettmann/CORBIS. (r) Independence National Historical Park. **318-9** Independence National Historical Park. **320** National Museum of American History, Smithsonian Institution, Behring Center, Neg #s 97-7908 and 97-7917. **321** New York Historical Society/Bridgeman Art Library. **322** (l) White House Historical Association. (r) © National Portrait Gallery, Smithsonian Institution/Art Resource, NY. **324** (t) (detail) Abigail Smith Adams (Mrs. John Adams), by Gilbert Stuart Gift of Mrs. Robert Homans, Image © 2003 Boar of Trustees, National Gallery of Art, Washington. (b) The Granger Collection, New York. **324-5** The Granger Collection, New York. **325** (t) (detail) William Thornton, by Gilbert Stuart, Andrew Mellon Collection, Image © 2003 Board of Trustees, National Gallery of Art, Washington. **328-9** Photodisc/Getty Images. **331** (t) Peter Gridley/Getty Images. (m) Andrea Pistolesi/Getty Images. (b) Photodisc/ Getty Images. **332** (b) © Dennis Brack/Black Star Publishing/PictureQuest. **333** (bl) © SW Productions/Brand X Pictures/PictureQuest. (br)Photodisc/Getty Images. **338**(t) Independence National Historical Park. (b) National Museum of American History, Smithsonian Institution, Behring Center, Neg# 95-3550. **339** (tl) Stock Montage. (tr) The Granger Collection, New York. (bl) National Museum of American History, Smithsonian Institution, Print/Neg # 73-11287. (br) Artville. **341** © Steve Vidler/ SuperStock. **340** (l) National Museum of American History, Smithsonian Institution 89-6712. (m) Monticello/Thomas Jefferson Foundation, Inc. **342** (l) Albany Institute of History & Art. (r) Montana Historical Society. **343** (l, r) The Granger Collection, New York. **344** George Caleb Bingham, Daniel Boone Escorting Settlers through the Cumberland Gap, 1851-52. Oil on canvas, 36 1/2 X 50 1/4". Washington University Gallery of Art, St. Louis. Gift of Nathaniel Phillips, 1890. **346** The Granger Collection, New York. **347** (detail) Robert Griffing, "Logan's Revenge" **354** © Burstein Collection/ CORBIS. (frame) Image Farm. **356** John Ford Clymer, "Up the Jerfferson", Courtesy Mrs. John F. Clymer and The Clymer Museum. **358** (l) © John Warden/SuperStock. (r) Jack Olson. **359** (l) © Shan Cunningham. (r) Jack Olson. **360** © Bettman/CORBIS. **361** (t) The Granger Collection, New York. (b) Library of Congress. **363** New York Historical Society/Bridgeman Art Library. (frame)Image Farm. **365** The Granger Collection, New York. **367** © Bettmann/CORBIS. **368** Architect of the Capitol. **370** (l) © National Portrait Gallery, Smithsonian Institution/Art Resource, NY. (r) Library of Congress. **371** Private Collection/Bridgeman Art Library. (frame) Image Farm. **376** (l) The Granger Collection, New York. (r) © Bettmann/ CORBIS. **377** (l) Star of the Republic Museum. (r) North Wind Picture Archives. **379** National Museum of American History, Smithsonian Institution Neg # 89-6712. **380** (t) The Granger Collection, New York. (b) American Textile History Museum, Lowell, Massachusetts. **381** (l) The Granger Collection, New York. (r) Courtesy of PictureHistory. **383** The Granger Collection, New York. **389** © CORBIS. **390** © Bettmann/CORBIS. **391** The Granger Collection, New York. **393** (t) The Granger Collection, New York. (ml, mr) © Bettmann/CORBIS. (bl) © National Portrait Gallery, Smithsonian Institution/Art Resource, NY. (br) Library of Congress - May Wright Sewall Collection, LC-USZ61-790DLC. **394** Yale University, Beinecke Rare Book & Manuscript Library, WAMSS S498 Box 1/File 13. **395** © Steve Vidler/SuperStock. **396** Star of the Republic Museum. **398** (t) State Preservation Board (Austin, Texas). (b) The San Jacinto Museum of History, Houston (detail). **399** (t) The Daughters of the Republic of Texas Library at the Alamo. (b) Texas State Library and Archives Commission. **400** Whitman Mission National Historic Site. **401** Culver Pictures. **403** California State Library. **404** Rick Egan. **410** (t) © CORBIS. **411** (tl) Library of Congress, LCUSZ62-984. (tr) Library of Congress.(bl) National Museum of American History, Smithsonian Institution, Behring Center, Neg # 95-5528. (br) Photodisc/Getty Images. **412** (l) The Granger Collection, New York. (m) © National Portrait Gallery, Smithsonian Institution/Art Resource, NY. (r) © Scala/Art Resource, NY. **413** (l) © Bettman/CORBIS. **414** (l) © National Portrait Gallery, Smithsonian Institution/Art Resource, NY. (r) © Bettman/CORBIS. **415** (l) Picture Research Consultants, Inc. (r) The Granger Collection, New York. **416-7** Private Collection/Bridgeman Art Library. **418** The Granger Collection, New York. **419** (frame) Image Farm. **419** © National Portrait Gallery, Smithsonian Institution/Art Resource, NY. **421** © Burke/Triolo/Brand X Pictures/PictureQuest. **424** South Carolina Confederate Relic Room and Museum. **425** (l) © National Portrait Gallery, Smithsonian Institution/Art Resource, NY. (m) © National Portrait Gallery, Smithsonian Institution/Art Resource, NY. (r) © Bettman/CORBIS. **427** © Bettman/ CORBIS. **432** The Granger Collection, New York. **434** (tl) Picture Research Consultants Archives.(tr) Schlesinger Library, Radcliffe Institute, Harvard University. (b) The Granger Collection, New York. **435** The Granger Collection, New York. **440** © Bettman/CORBIS. **441** (t) Robertstock. (b) Library of Congress. **442-3** State Historical Society of Illinois, Chicago, IL, USA/Bridgeman Art Library. **443** (t) Courtesy PictureHistory (digital composite). (b) Stanley King Collection. **444** National Archives. **445** © Scala/Art Resource, NY. **450** (l) Library of Congress, USZCN4-49, G01231. (r) © Medford Historical Society Collection/CORBIS . **451** Electricity Collection, NMAH, Smithsonian Institution, Neg # 74-2491. (r) Brown Brothers. **452** Cook Collection, Valentine Museum. **456** Library of Congress, USZCN4- 49, G01231. **457** Gettysburg National Military Park. **458** The Granger Collection, New York. **460** The Granger Collection, New York. **461** (l) Library of Congress. (r) Paragon Light, Inc. **462** The Granger Collection, New York. **463** Larry Kolvoord/The Image Works. **464** National Archives. **465** (t) The Granger Collection, New York. (b) © Private Collection/Art Resource, NY. **466** Library of Congress. **467** National Archives, 77-F-194-6-56. **468** (l) Tom Lovell/ National Geographic. (r) National Museum of American History, Smithsonian Institution Neg #95-5515-7. **470** (l) Fort Loreto Museum, Puebla. (r) Electricity Collection, NMAH, Smithsonian Institution, Neg # 74-2491. **471** (tl)

The Granger Collection, New York. (tr) Hulton Archive/Getty Images. (bl) The Granger Collection, New York. (br) © Polak Matthew/CORBIS SYGMA. **472** The Meserve Collection. **473** (l) Courtesy of the New York Historical Society, NYC, Neg#21185. (r) New York Historical Society/Bridgeman Art Library. **477** © CORBIS. (frame) Image Farm. **478** (t) © Medford Historical Society Collection/CORBIS. **478-9** Charleston Museum. **482-3** Brown Brothers. **484** (l) The Granger Collection, New York. (r) © Dhimitri/Folio Inc. **485** Brown Brothers. **486** © CORBIS. **486-7** © CORBIS **492** (t) AP Wide World Photos. (b) Photodisc/Getty Images. **493** (tl) Mario Tama/Getty Images. (tr) © 1976 George Balthis/ Take Stock. (bl) Courtesy State Department. (br) Hulton Archive/Getty Images. **494** (l) © Bettmann/CORBIS. (m) Hulton/Archive/ Getty Images. (r) Carl Iwasaki/Time Life Pictures/Getty Images. **495** (l) Robert E. Daemmrich/Getty Images. (r) AP Wide World Photos. **496** (l) © Laurie Platt Winfrey Inc. (r) New York Public Library. **497** (r) (detail) Independence National Historical Park. **498** Photographs taken by MetaForm Incorporated/Karen Yamauchi of artifacts in the National Park Service Collection, Statue of Liberty National Monument, Ellis Island Immigration Museum. **499** California State Museum. **501** © Laurie Platt Winfrey Inc. **502-3** The Granger Collection, New York. **503** (l) Brown Brothers. (r) © Yoshio Tomii/SuperStock. **504** Library of Congress. **505** Brown Brothers. **506** Robert E. Daemmrich/Getty Images. **507** © Tony Freeman/ PhotoEdit. **509** Brown Brothers. **512** © Lawrence Midgale/Photo Researchers, Inc. **513** (l) Carl Mydans/Time Life Pictures/Getty Images. (m) © AFP/CORBIS. (r) © Maroon/FOLIO, Inc. **514** © Richard T. Nowitz/Photo Researchers, Inc. **516-7** Bill Losh/Getty Images. **518-9** David Lawrence/Panoramic Images. **522** (l) © Bettmann/CORBIS. (r) Michael Herron/Take Stock. **523** (l) © Wally McNamee/CORBIS. (r) © Tony Freeman/ PhotoEdit. **524** © Bettmann/CORBIS. **525** Hulton Archive/Getty Images. **526** © Bettmann/CORBIS. **527** © Bettmann/CORBIS. **531** Robert W. Kelley/Time Life Pictures/Getty Images. **532** (l) © Charles Gatewood/The Image Works. (r) NASA. **533** (l) © Wally McNamee/ CORBIS. (r) AP Wide World Photos. **534** © Bob Fitch/Take Stock. **535** AP Wide World Photos. **536** Arthur Schatz/Time Life Pictures/Getty Images. **537** Arthur Schatz/Time Life Pictures/Getty Images. **538** AP Wide World Photos. **539** © Syracuse Newspapers/The Image Works. **540** © Jim West/The Image Works. **544** © Myrleen Ferguson Cate/PhotoEdit. **545** (t) © Ellen Senisi/The Image Works. (b) © Michael Newman/ PhotoEdit.

Assignment Photography

All Photography © HMCo./Angela Coppola. 539 © HMCo./Allan Landau.

Illustration

21 (t) Joel Dubin. **32-33** Matthew Pippin. **72-73** Karen Minot. **48** Will Williams. **50-53** David Diaz. **56** Wood Ronsaville Harlin, Inc ©. **148-149** Wood Ronsaville Harlin, Inc. **149** (t) Joel Dubin. **200-201** Inklink. **207-209** David Soman. **238-239** Wood Ronsaville Harlin, Inc. **274-277** Steve Patricia. **300-301** Will Williams. **348-351** Steve Patricia. **372-373** Wood Ronsaville Harlin, Inc. **404-405** Wood Ronsaville Harlin, Inc ©. **420-421** Inklink. **429-430** Beth Peck. **436-439** Will Williams. **474-475** Barbara Higgins Bond. **512-513** Pat Rossi Calkin. **585** William Brinkley. **668** Matthew Pippin. **702-705** Dave Klug.
Charts and Graphs by Pronk&Associates

R79

Using Videotapes to Teach Social Studies

Overview

Videotapes on social studies topics are an excellent way to enhance, extend, and reinforce social studies concepts and content. They provide students an opportunity to hear and see the people, places, and events they read about in their texts. Students and teachers have few chances to travel outside the classroom to different places and time periods; videos can provide the "field trip" experience without permission slips and bus rentals.

As with real field trips, however, videos are most useful when they are integrated into the curriculum. Houghton Mifflin Social Studies provides the opportunity to use a video that is correlated to the unit. They have been specifically chosen to interest students in the contents of the unit. These videos can be used to

- Provide an alternate instructional mode to meet individual needs
- Generate interest in the unit
- Supplement existing classroom teaching
- Review and wrap up the unit
- Offer opportunities for extending activities and collaborative learning

Using the Unit Video

Videos can be shown as an introduction to the unit; as a means of reinforcing a concept taught in the unit; and/or as a way to wrap-up the unit. You may wish to choose one of the following models throughout the year or vary your approach unit by unit.

Introducing the Unit

Begin by having students look at the Unit Opener and discuss the Big Idea presented there. You may enhance the discussion through the use of the Big Idea Transparency.

Once students have begun to explore their ideas about what they will be learning in the unit, show them the Unit Video.

- Practice listening and viewing skills by having them jot down notes as they watch. Suggest that they write only the most important ideas and information that they have learned.
- After viewing, ask students to write one sentence that describes the main idea of the video. You may wish to ask volunteers to read aloud their sentences as a starting point for class discussion: do other students agree? Would they modify the sentence at all?
- You may wish to discuss point of view with your class. What feelings were expressed in the video and who expressed them? How did the students themselves feel after they watched it?
- Next, talk about the unit in the text. Ask students to predict what they think it will be about.

Reinforcing a Concept

Before teaching a specific lesson that is connected to the content of the Unit Video, build background by showing the video to the class.

- Create a KWL chart: ask students what they know about the topic and what they want to learn about the topic. Use the video as a springboard to their brainstorming. After teaching the lesson, complete the chart with what students have learned about the topic.
- If students seem unsure about the concepts or people covered in the lesson, reshow the video to review.

Unit Wrap-Up

After completing the unit, give students a chance to review what they remember. Ask them to suggest ideas, people, and events from the unit that they think are important and to explain why. Before assessing their understanding, show the class the unit video.

- Encourage students to be active listeners by taking notes while viewing the video.
- Discuss what ideas, people, and/or events th video focused on and how that compares with their list of important ideas, people, an events.
- Use the video as a jumping off point for a unit activity, by having students create a screenplay for a unit video that they would like to show. If your school has the equipment, you may encourage one or more groups to produce and film their unit videos

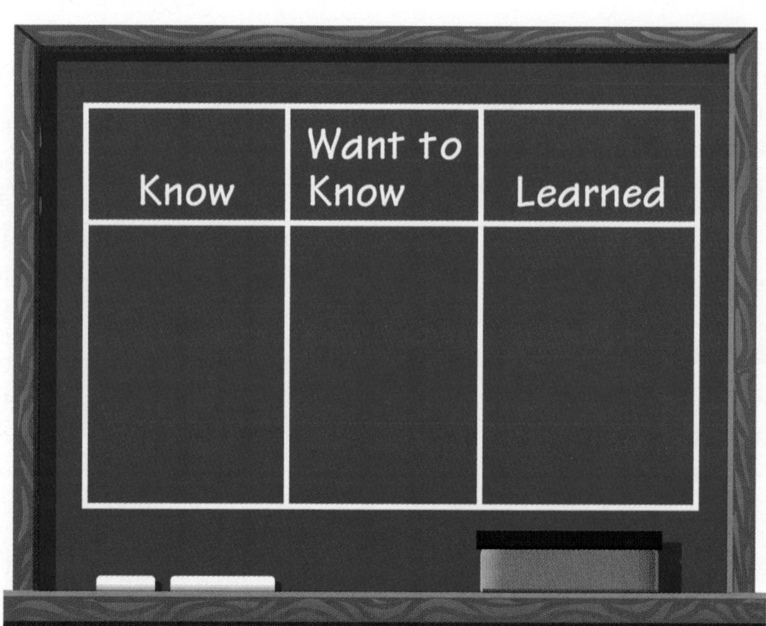

Family Newsletter for Unit 5

The New Nation

Learn About It

In this unit, your child will learn:

- how settlers moved across the frontier and how the nation expanded
- what the Industrial Revolution meant for the people of the United States

Here are some ways that you can help your child learn:

Read to Learn More About It

How We Crossed the West: The Adventures of Lewis and Clark, by Rosalyn Schanzer. Readers are introduced to the adventures of Lewis and Clark through actual letters and journal entries.

My Name Is York, by Elizabeth Van Steenwyck. York, an enslaved African American who traveled with Lewis and Clark on their expedition, tells his story.

Washington City Is Burning, by Harriet Gillem Robinet. Set during the War of 1812, this historical novel tells the story of an enslaved girl who devises a plan to free other enslaved people while the British occupy and burn Washington.

Talk About It

Chapter 10: The Early Republic

Exploring new places Discuss with your child what it feels like to be in a new place. Talk about how people adapt to new situations and the fun of seeing something new. What would you do to feel more comfortable in a new place?

Chapter 11: A Growing Country

New technology Many inventions were made during the Industrial Revolution. Many inventions are still being made today. Discuss with your child the technologies in your home, such as the television, radio, computer, and so on. Talk about how people came up with these ideas. Ask your child what ideas he or she has for new inventions.

Make It

A park map Lewis and Clark explored the West and made maps as they explored. Working together, map a nearby park or playground. Draw a map for someone who does not know the land. The person should be able to use the map to find a specific part of the park, such as a special tree or a bench.

Technology
Check out **www.eduplace.com/parents/hmss05/** for more information.

Carta a la familia: Unidad 5

La nueva nación

Investíguenlo

En esta unidad, su niño aprenderá:

- acerca de cómo los pioneros se movieron a través de la frontera y de cómo se expandió la nación
- de lo que significó la Revolución Industrial para los habitantes de los Estados Unidos

Aquí tiene algunas formas de ayudar a que su niño aprenda:

Lean para aprender más

Como los perros de la praderas (Prairie Dog Pioneers) por Josephine Harper Mae Dean y su familia viajan hacia el estado de Texas para empezar allí una nueva vida.

Un caballo llamado Libertad (Riding Freedom) por Pam Muñoz Ryan En esta vívida novela histórica, la autora relata la historia real de Charlotte Parkhurst.

Coméntenlo

Capítulo 10: La joven república

Explorar nuevos lugares Hablen de cómo se siente estar en un lugar por primera vez. Luego hablen de cómo la gente se adapta a situaciones nuevas y de lo divertido que puede ser ver algo nuevo. ¿Qué harían para sentirse más cómodos en un nuevo lugar?

Capítulo 11: Un país en crecimiento

Una nueva tecnología Hubo muchos inventos durante la Revolución Industrial. Hoy en día, también hay muchos inventos. Hablen de las tecnologías que hay en su propia casa como, por ejemplo, la televisión, la radio y el computador. Luego hablen de cómo se produjeron esos inventos. Pida a su niño que comparta con usted ideas sobre nuevos inventos.

Háganlo

Un mapa del parque Lewis y Clark exploraron el Oeste de los Estados Unidos e hicieron mapas durante su exploración. Hagan juntos un mapa de un parque cercano, para una persona que no conozca el área del parque. La persona debería poder usar el mapa para encontrar cualquier área específica del parque como, por ejemplo, un árbol o una banca en particular.

Tecnología
Para obtener más información, visite **www.eduplace.com/parents/hmss05/**

Family Newsletter for Unit 6

The Civil War

Learn About It

In this unit, your child will learn:

- the causes of the Civil War and the important battles that took place during the war
- how the reunified United States reconstructed the South after the war

Here are some ways that you can help your child learn:

Read to Learn More About It

If You Lived at the Time of the Civil War, by Kay Moore. The Civil War is seen from the perspectives of both the North and the South.

The Long Road to Gettysburg, by Jim Murphy. An account of the Battle of Gettysburg in text, photos, and drawings.

Never Were Men So Brave: The Irish Brigade During the Civil War, by Susan Provost Beller. Thomas Francis Meagher founded the Irish Brigade, 535 fearless men who fought for the Union and to whom a monument was dedicated at Gettysburg.

Talk About It

Chapter 12: Causes of the Civil War

Resolving conflict The North and the South had many differences. Many people thought that fighting was the only way to solve the problems. What are some ways to resolve conflict without fighting?

Chapter 13: The Civil War and Reconstruction

Turning points The Civil War was decided by a series of turning points. But what is a turning point? Play a game with your child to demonstrate this concept. Explain that during a game, one team or player may win by gaining an advantage at a certain point in the game.

Make It

Reconstruction After the war, the South had to be rebuilt. Work together to make a plan for reconstructing something in your town that needs repair, such as an old statue or a building destroyed by fire. Together, make a list of the steps you would take for reconstruction. Then have your child construct the finished product using craft supplies.

Technology
Check out
www.eduplace.com/parents/hmss05/
for more information.

Carta a la familia: Unidad 6

La Guerra Civil

Investíguenlo

En esta unidad, su niño aprenderá:

- acerca de las causas de la Guerra Civil y de la importancia de las batallas que se llevaron a cabo durante la guerra
- de cómo los Estados Unidos unificados reconstruyeron el Sur después de la guerra

Aquí tiene algunas formas de ayudar a que su niño aprenda:

Lean para aprender más

Pink y Say (Pink and Say) por Patricia Polacco
Narración real que relata la amistad entre dos soldados de la Guerra Civil.

Abraham Lincoln: El niño y el hombre (Abraham Lincoln: The Boy and the Man) por Lloyd Ostendorf
El autor ofrece detalles de la vida de un gran héroe norteamericano.

Coméntenlo

Capítulo 12: Las causas de la Guerra Civil

Resolución de conflictos Había muchas diferencias entre el Norte y el Sur. Muchas personas pensaban que la única manera de resolver las diferencias era peleando. ¿Qué otras maneras hay de resolver conflictos sin necesidad de pelear?

Capítulo 13: Guerra Civil y Reconstrucción

Puntos claves La Guerra Civil fue decidida por una serie de puntos claves que le dieron giro a la guerra. ¿Pero en qué consiste un punto clave? Jueguen juntos un juego que demuestre este concepto. Expliquen que durante un juego un equipo o jugador puede ganar al obtener una ventaja durante un determinado punto del juego.

Háganlo

Una reconstrucción Después de la guerra, el Sur tuvo que ser reconstruido. Trabajen juntos para hacer un plan para reconstruir algo en su ciudad que lo necesite, tal como una estatua o un edificio que haya sido destruido en un incendio. Hagan juntos una lista de los pasos que llevarían a cabo para la reconstrucción. Luego pida a su niño que use materiales de arte para hacer un modelo de lo que van a reconstruir.

Tecnología
Para obtener más información, visite **www.eduplace.com/parents/hmss05/**

Family Newsletter for Unit 7

Linking to Today

Learn About It

In this unit, your child will learn:

- the factors that led to the large numbers of immigrants from Europe, Asia, and Mexico
- the different struggles that took place in the early 20th century for women, African Americans, American Indians, and others

Here are some ways that you can help your child learn:

Read to Learn More About It

The Harlem Renaissance, by James Haskins. Haskins introduces the African American men and women of literature, painting, sculpture, and music who were part of the cultural period called the Harlem Renaissance.

Red Tail Angels: The Story of the Tuskegee Airmen, by Patricia and Fredrick McKissack. Recounts the true story of the Red Tail Angels, African American pilots who won the respect and admiration of their peers as well as a hundred and fifty Distinguished Flying Crosses and Legions of Merit.

You Want Women to Vote, Lizzie Stanton?, by Jean Fritz. A biography of the leader in the fight for women's suffrage.

Talk About It

Chapter 14: Immigration

Where we come from Over the course of American history, there have been several waves of immigration. From what country does your family originally come? If you know, discuss how your ancestors first came to the United States and where they settled. Or you can talk about the many different cultures from which Americans come.

Chapter 15: The Promise of America

Rights for all Together, read the Bill of Rights. Discuss how these rights have affected women, African Americans, American Indians, and others. How do they affect your daily life? What is being done today to make sure everyone has the same rights?

Make It

Family trees Many Americans can trace their heritage to another country. Work together to create a family tree. Try to go back as far into the past as you can. When did your family come to the United States? If your ancestors lived in another country, write it under their names.

Carta a la familia: Unidad 7

Conexión con el presente

Investíguenlo

En esta unidad, su niño aprenderá:

- acerca de los factores por los cuales ha habido una gran inmigración de Europa, Asia y México
- acerca de las dificultades que las mujeres, los afroamericanos y los grupos indígenas tuvieron al comienzo del siglo XX

Lean para aprender más

El vuelo de los colibríes (The Flight of the Hummingbirds) por Alma Flor Ada Una familia relata sus experiencias al mudarse de México a California.

Compañeros de equipo (Teammates) por Peter Golenbock En una época de desigualdad racial, dos hombres superan barreras y aprenden que son hermanos a pesar del color de su piel.

Aquí tiene algunas formas de ayudar a que su niño aprenda:

Coméntenlo

Capítulo 14: Inmigración

De dónde provenimos A través de la historia de los Estados Unidos, ha habido varias olas de inmigración. ¿De qué país proviene su familia? Si lo saben, hablen acerca de cómo llegaron sus ancestros a los Estados Unidos y dónde vivieron. También pueden hablar de las muchas culturas de las que provienen los estadounidenses.

Capítulo 15: La promesa de Estados Unidos

Derechos para todos Lean juntos el *Bill of Rights* (Enmiendas sobre Derechos Civiles). Hablen de cómo esos derechos han afectado a las mujeres, a los afroamericanos y a los grupos indígenas. ¿Cómo afectan esos derechos su diario vivir?

Háganlo

Árboles de familia Muchos estadounidenses tienen ancestros en otros países. Trabajen juntos para crear un árbol genealógico de la familia. Traten de llegar tan atrás en la historia de la familia como les sea posible. ¿Cuándo llegó su familia a los Estados Unidos? Si sus ancestros vivieron en otro país, escriban el nombre del país debajo de sus nombres.

Tecnología
Para obtener más información, visite **www.eduplace.com/parents/hmss05/**

Name ____________________ Date ____________

Two-Column Chart

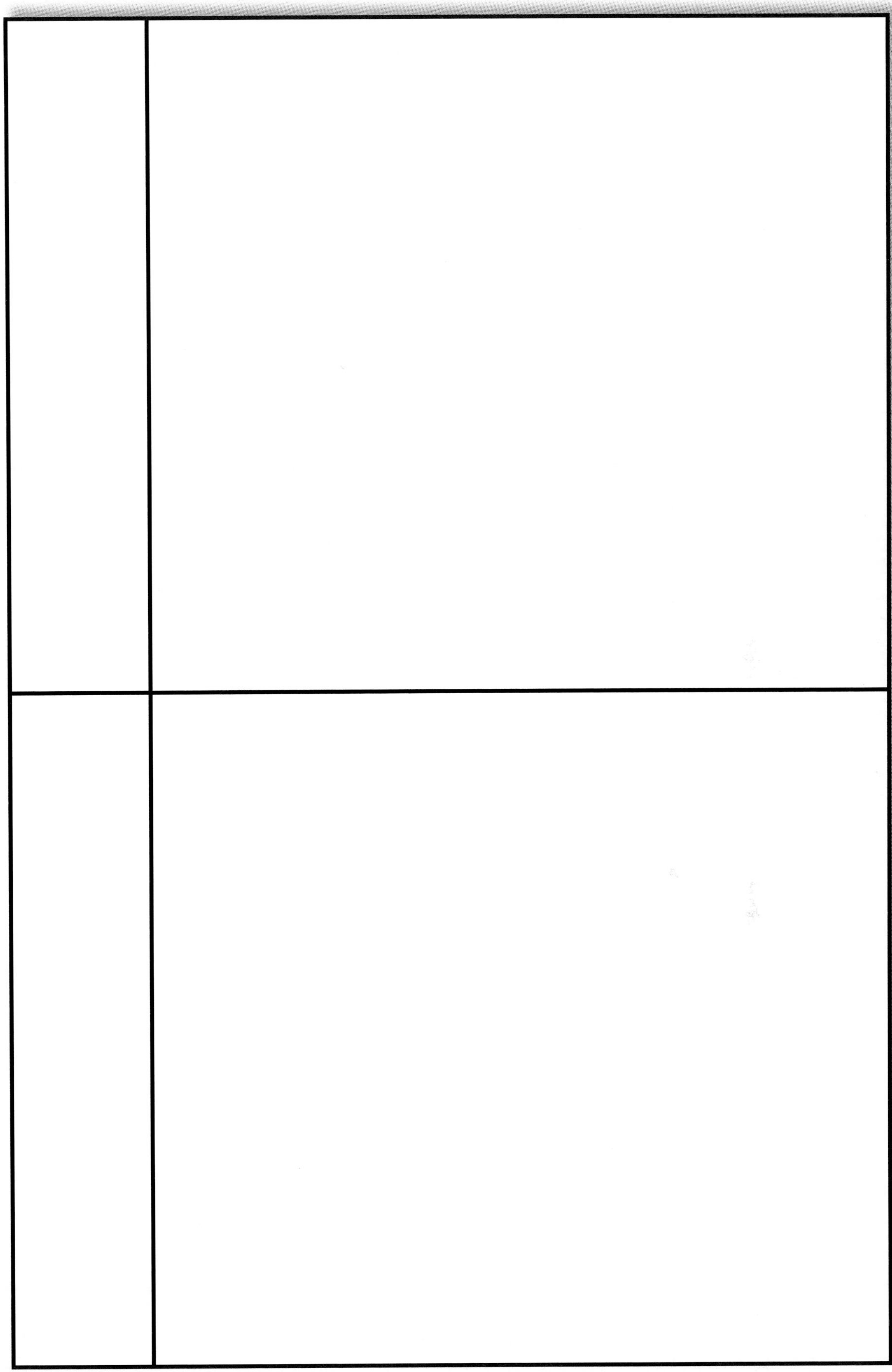

Name ______________________ Date ______________

Three-Column Chart

Name ______________________________ Date ____________________

Two-Step Flow Chart

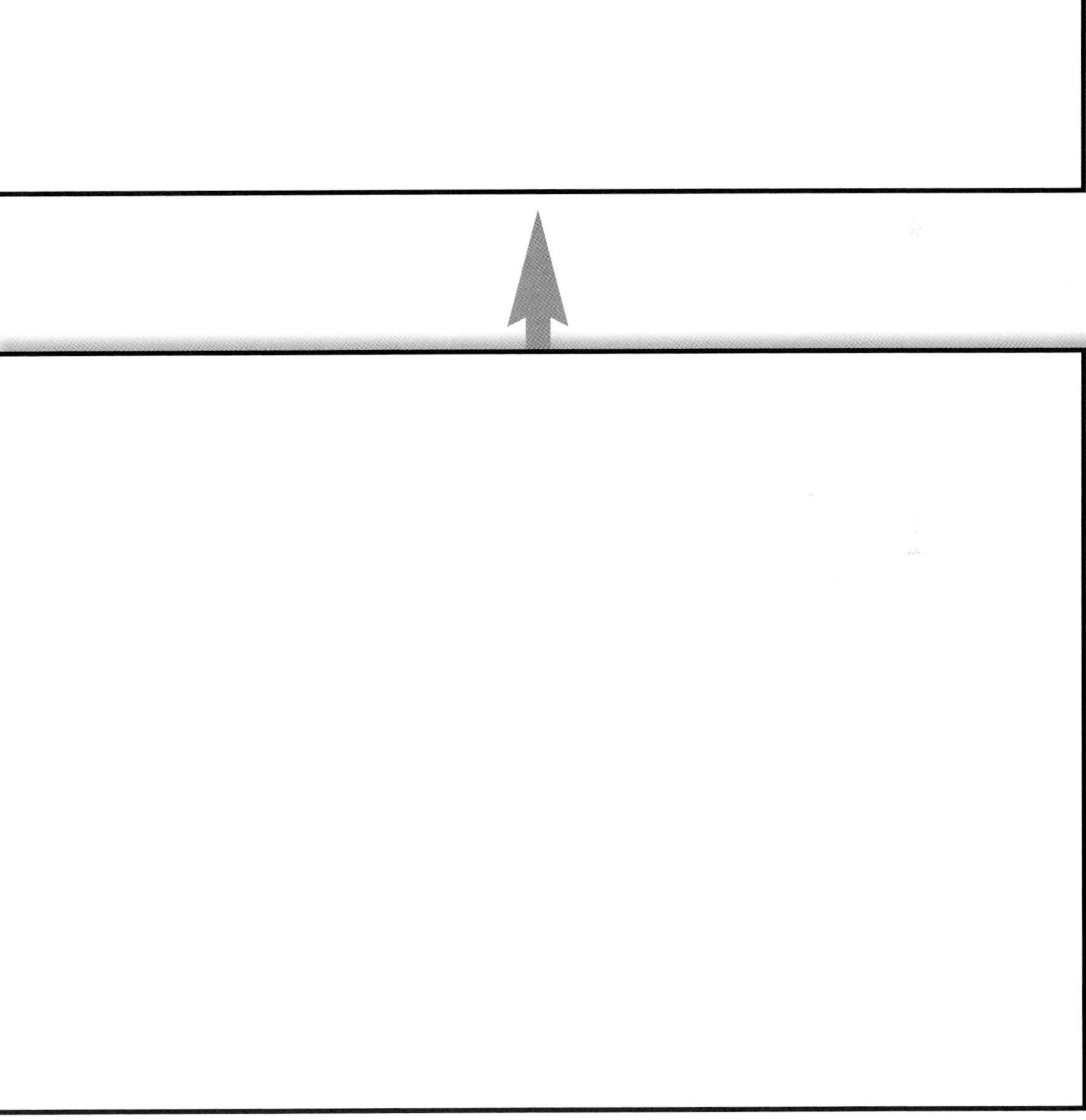

Name ______________________ Date ______________

Two-Part Flow Chart

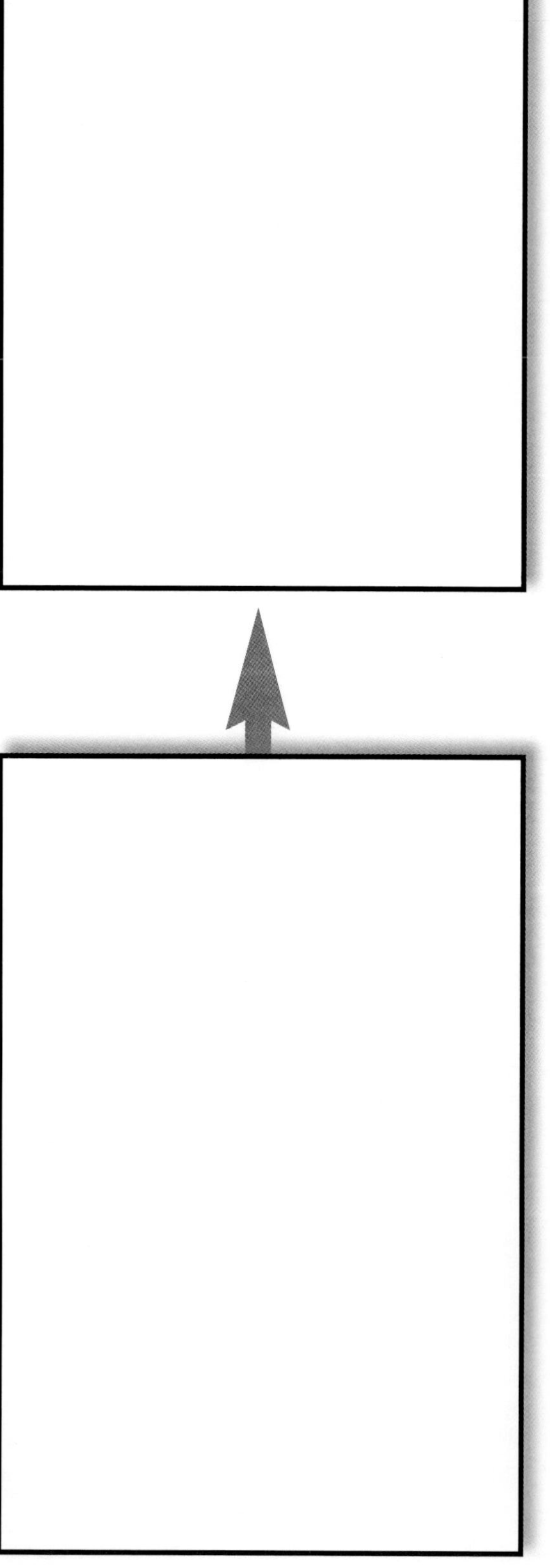

Name ______________________ Date ______________

Three-Step Flow Chart

Name ______________________ Date ______________

Three-Level Flow Chart

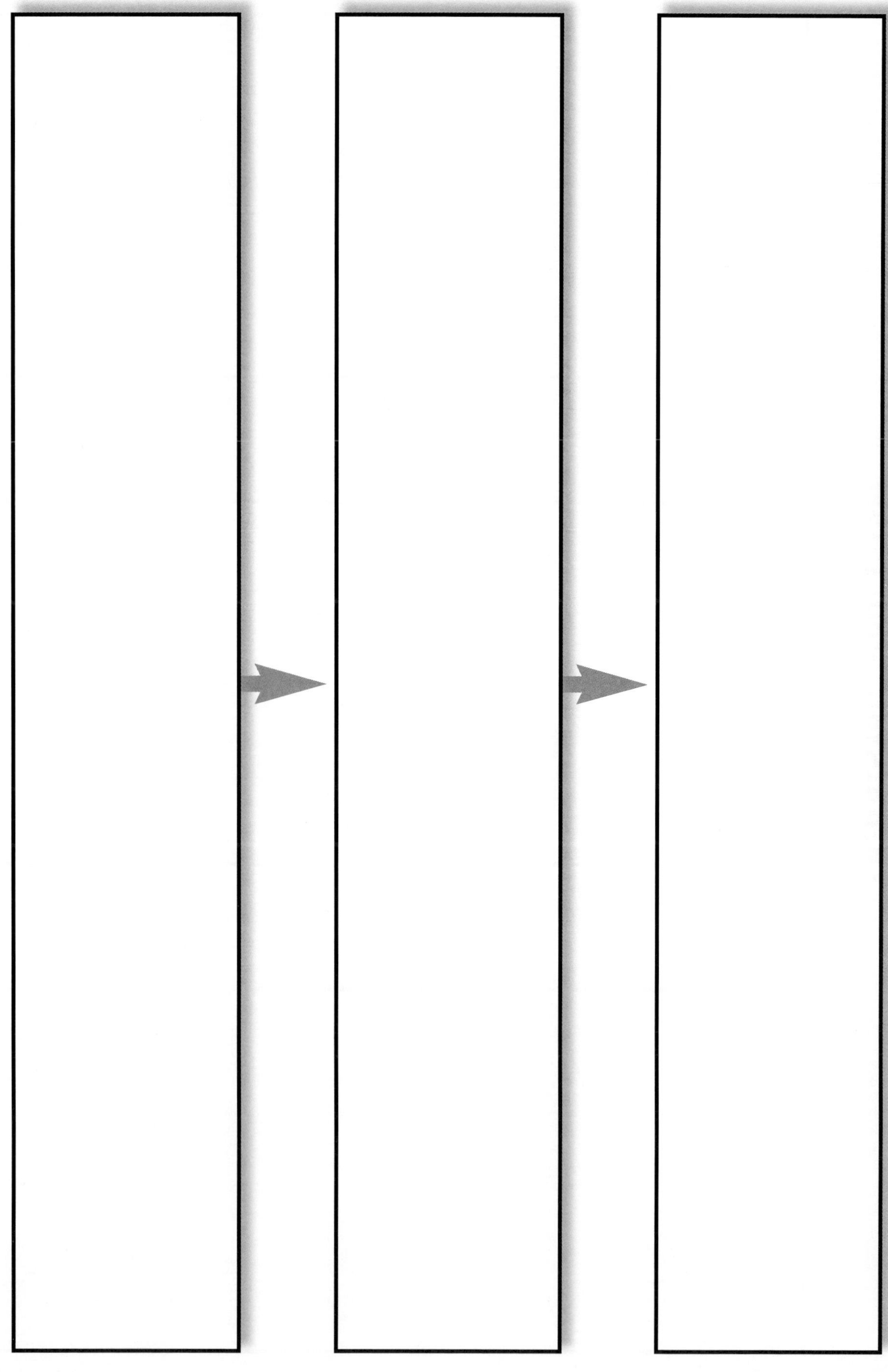

Name ______________________ Date ______________

Idea Web

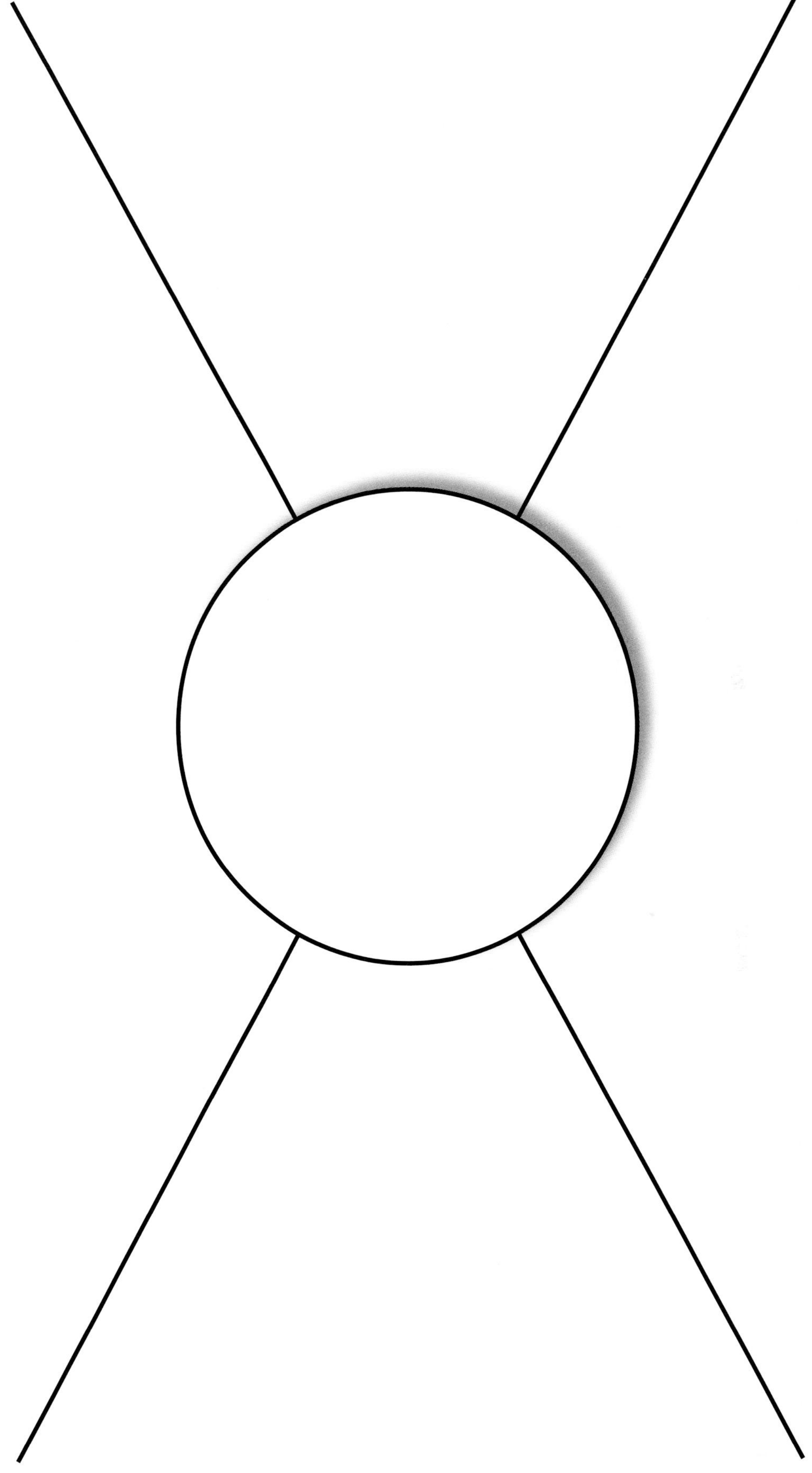

Name ______________________ Date ______________

Organizer 1

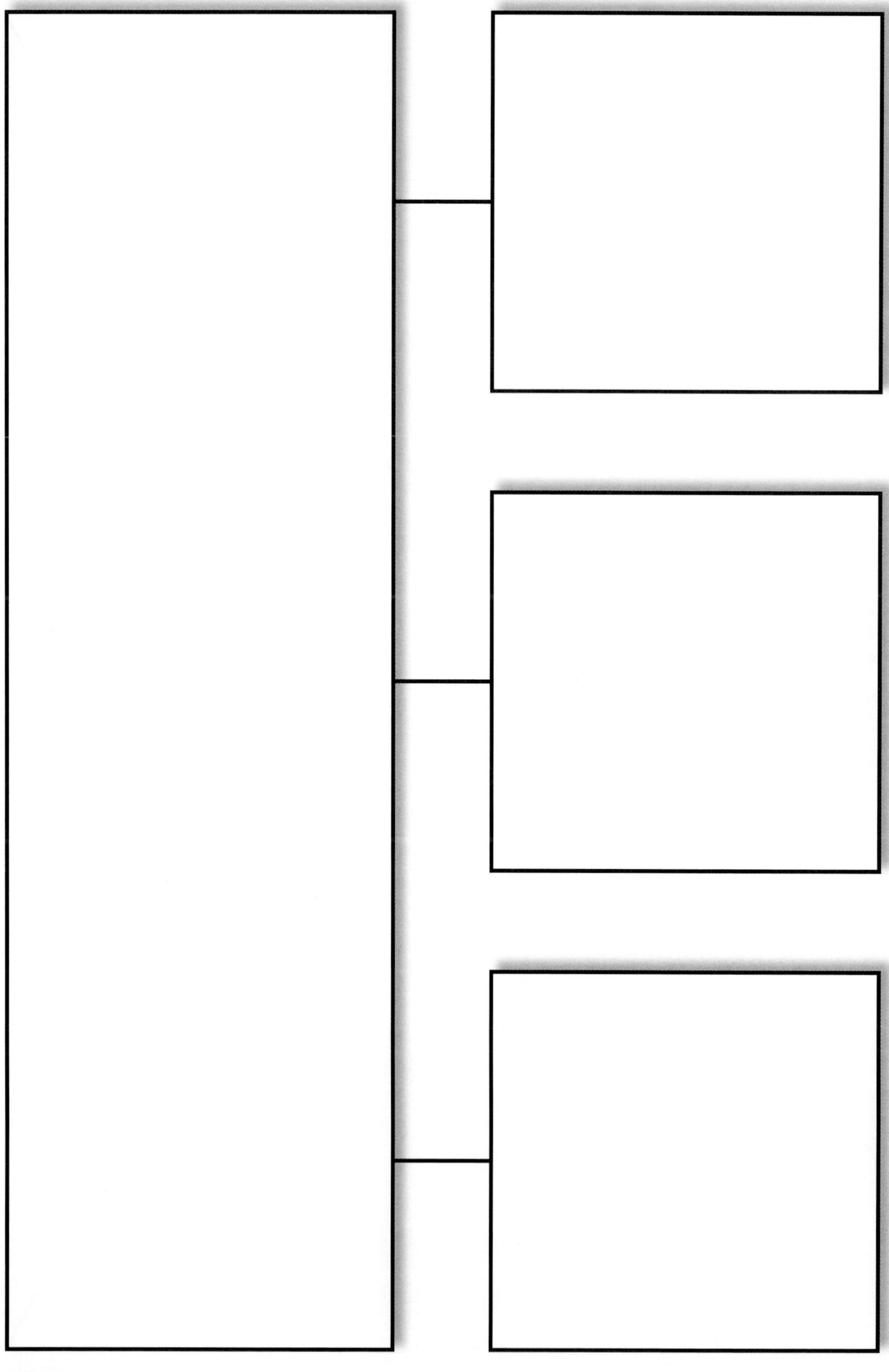

Name ________________________ Date ________________

Organizer 2

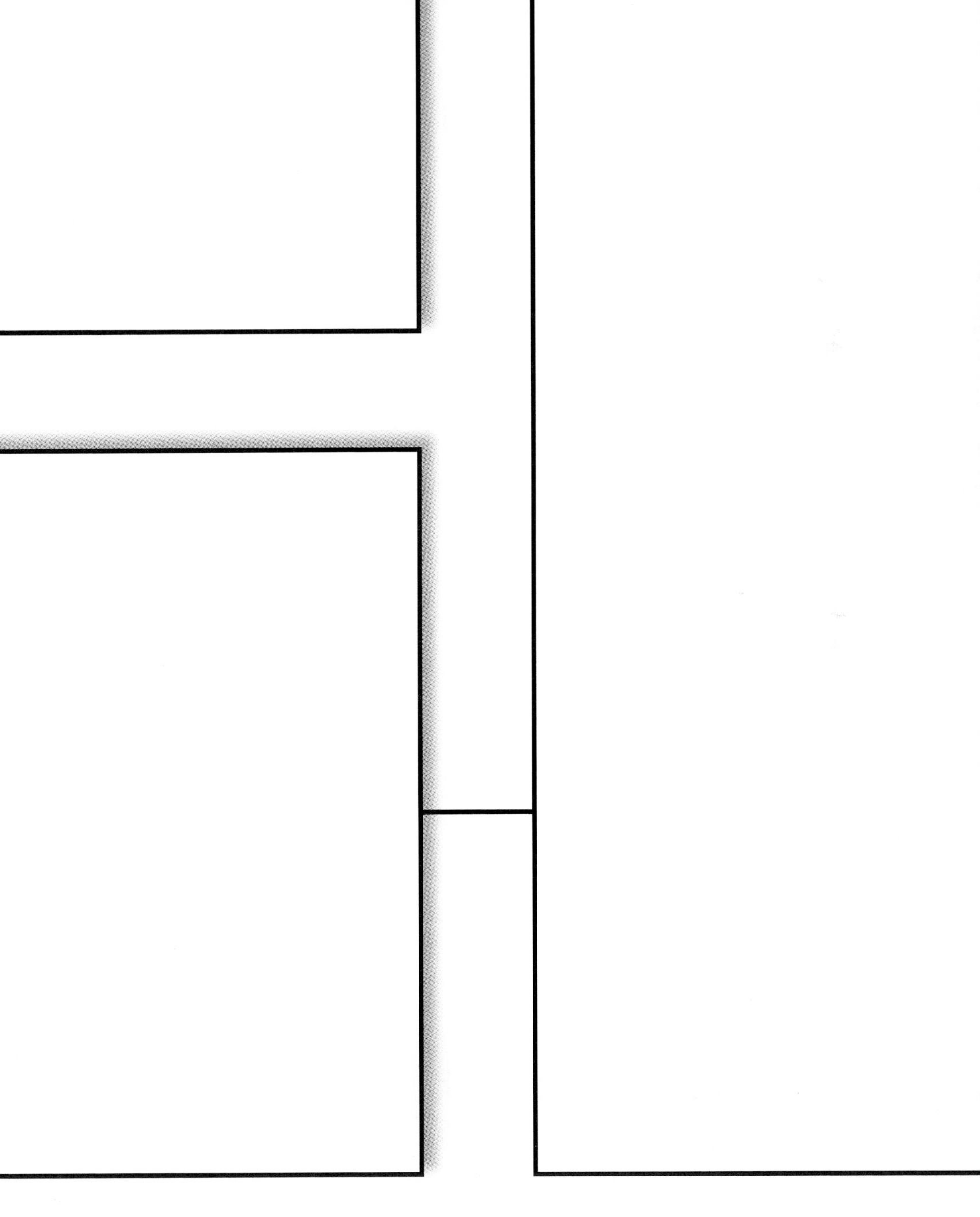

Name ______________________ Date ______________

Organizer 3

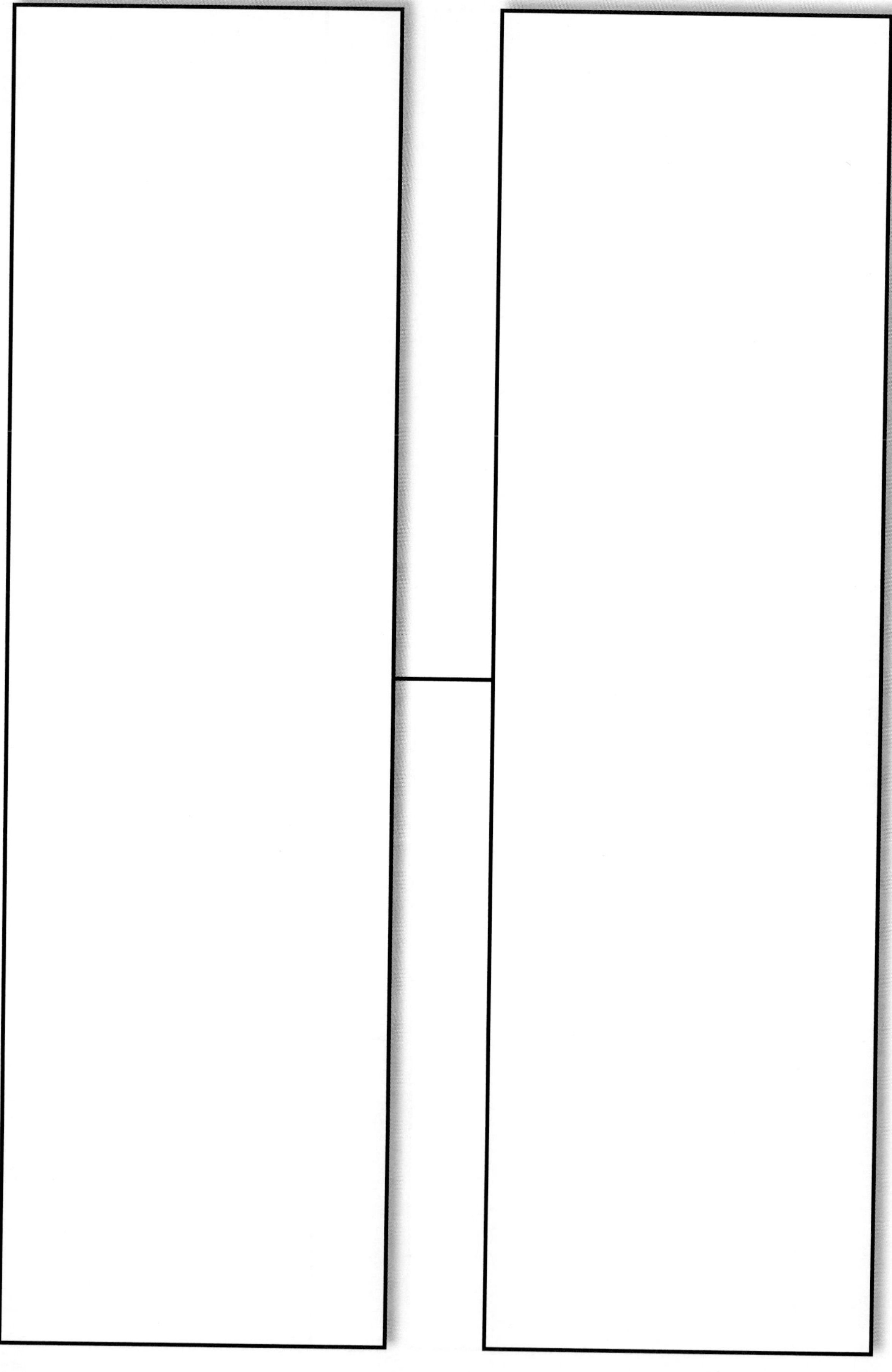

Venn Diagram

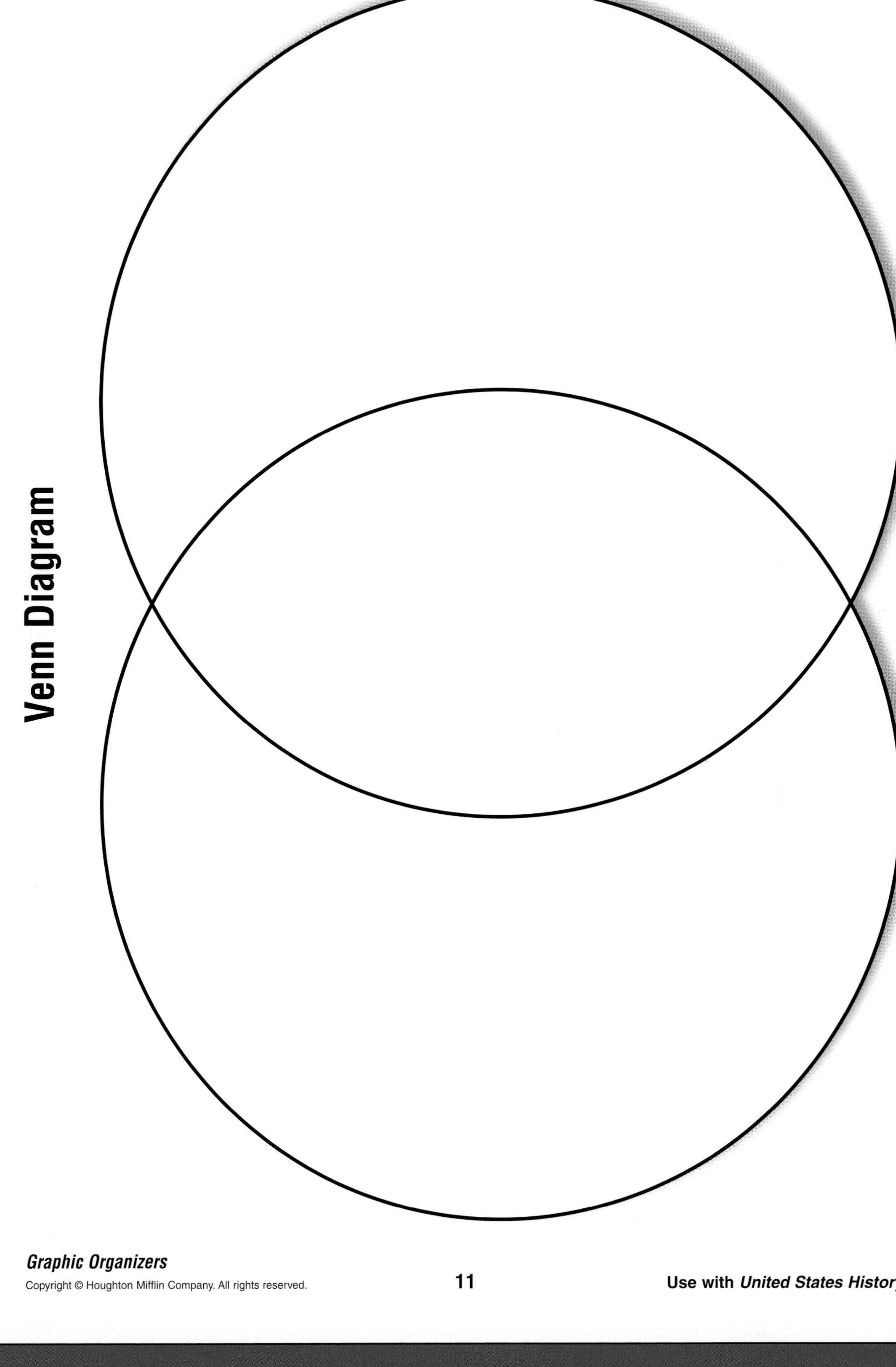

Frame Game

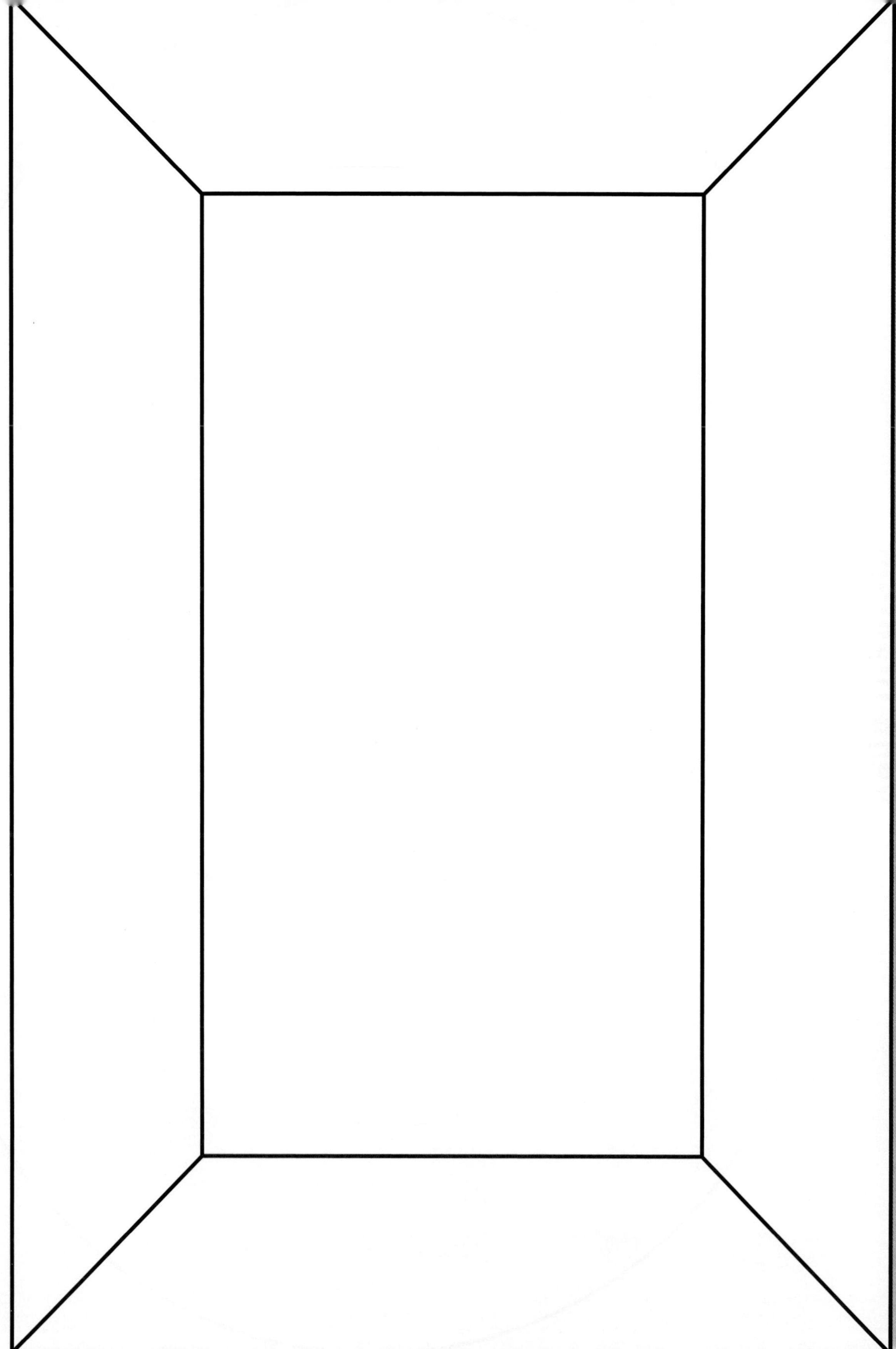

Name ______________________________ Date ____________________

Word Web

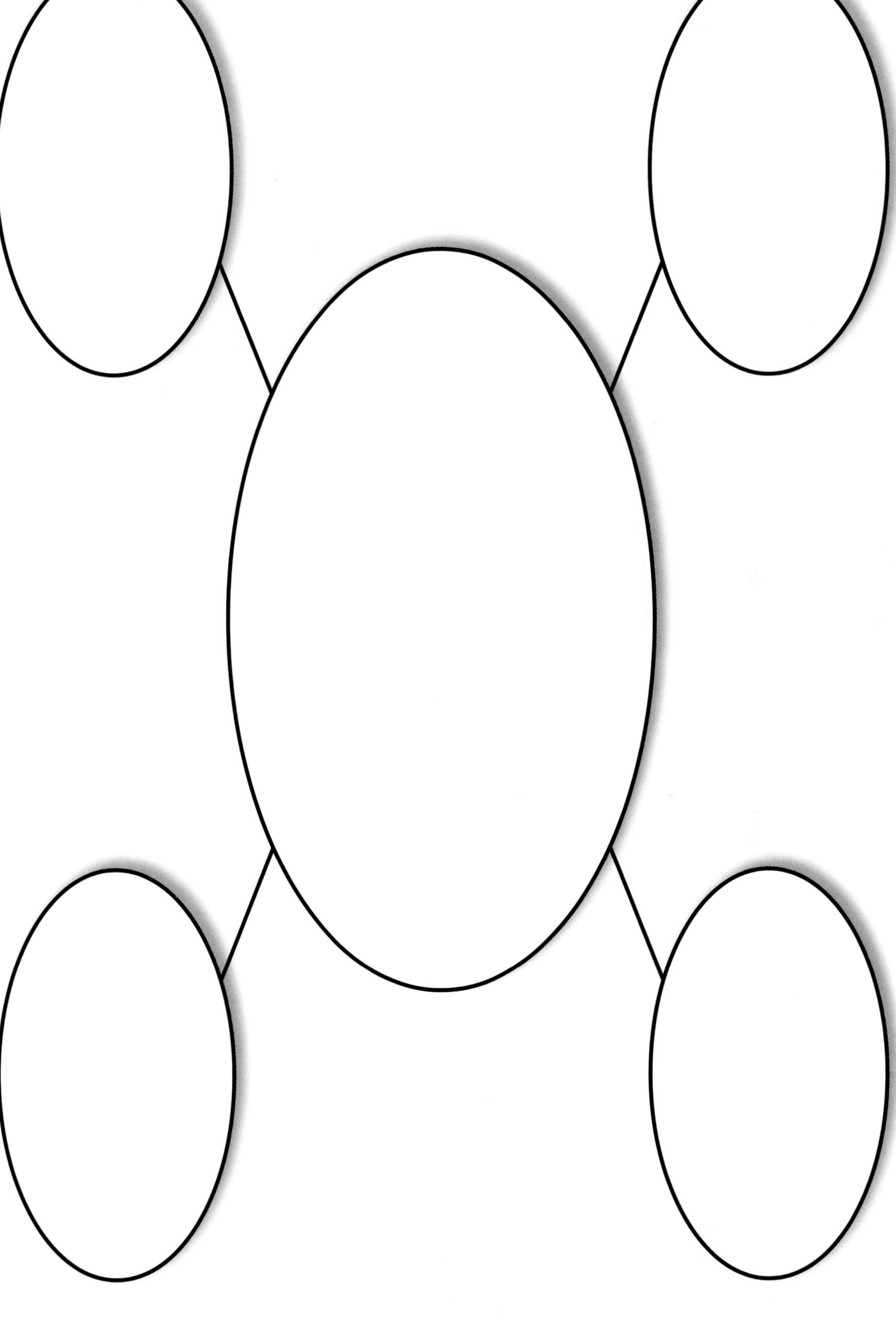

Name ______________________ Date ______________

Spider Map

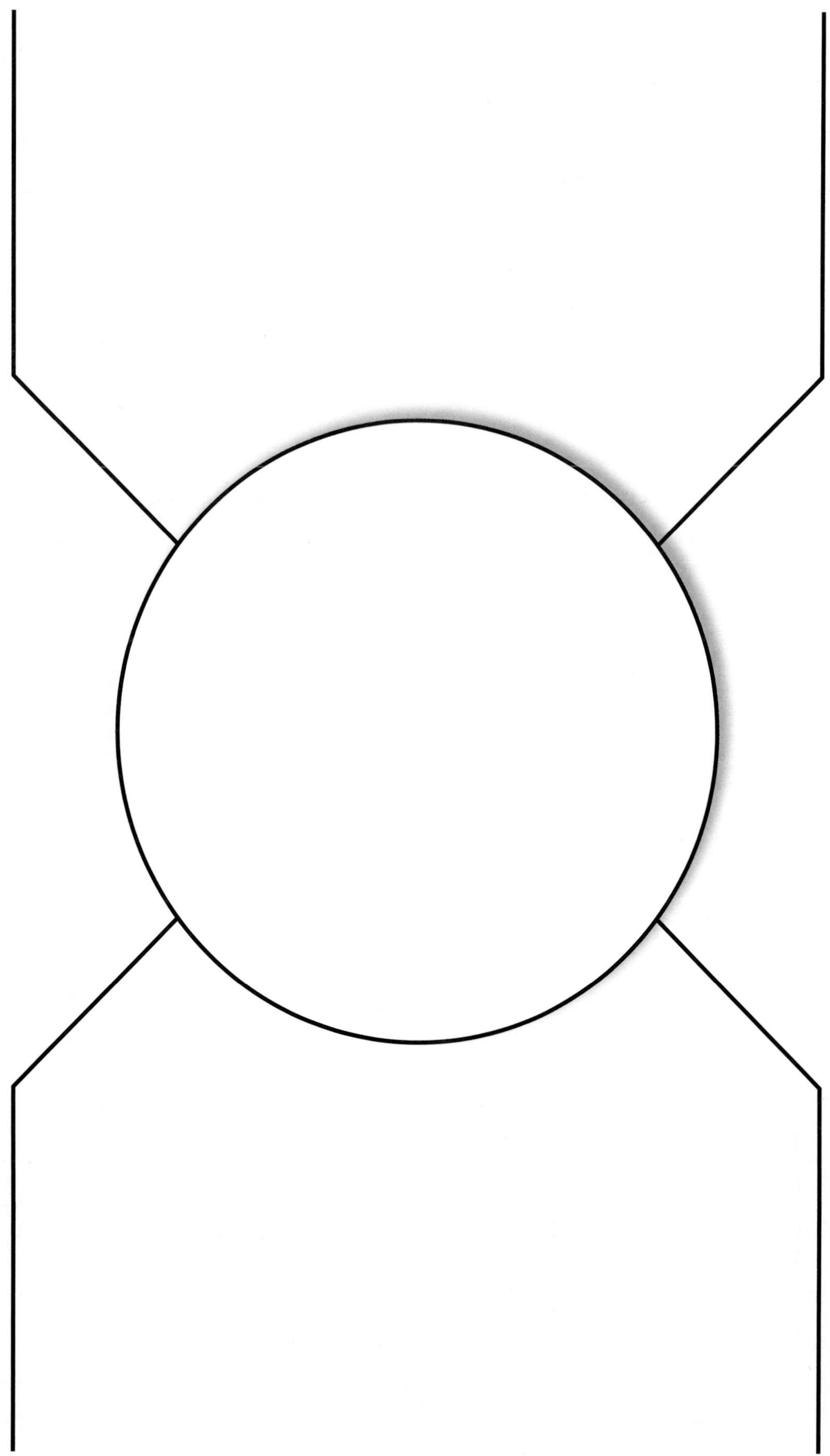

Name ______________________ Date ______________

Sequence Chart

1	
2	
3	
4	

Name ______________________________ Date ______________________

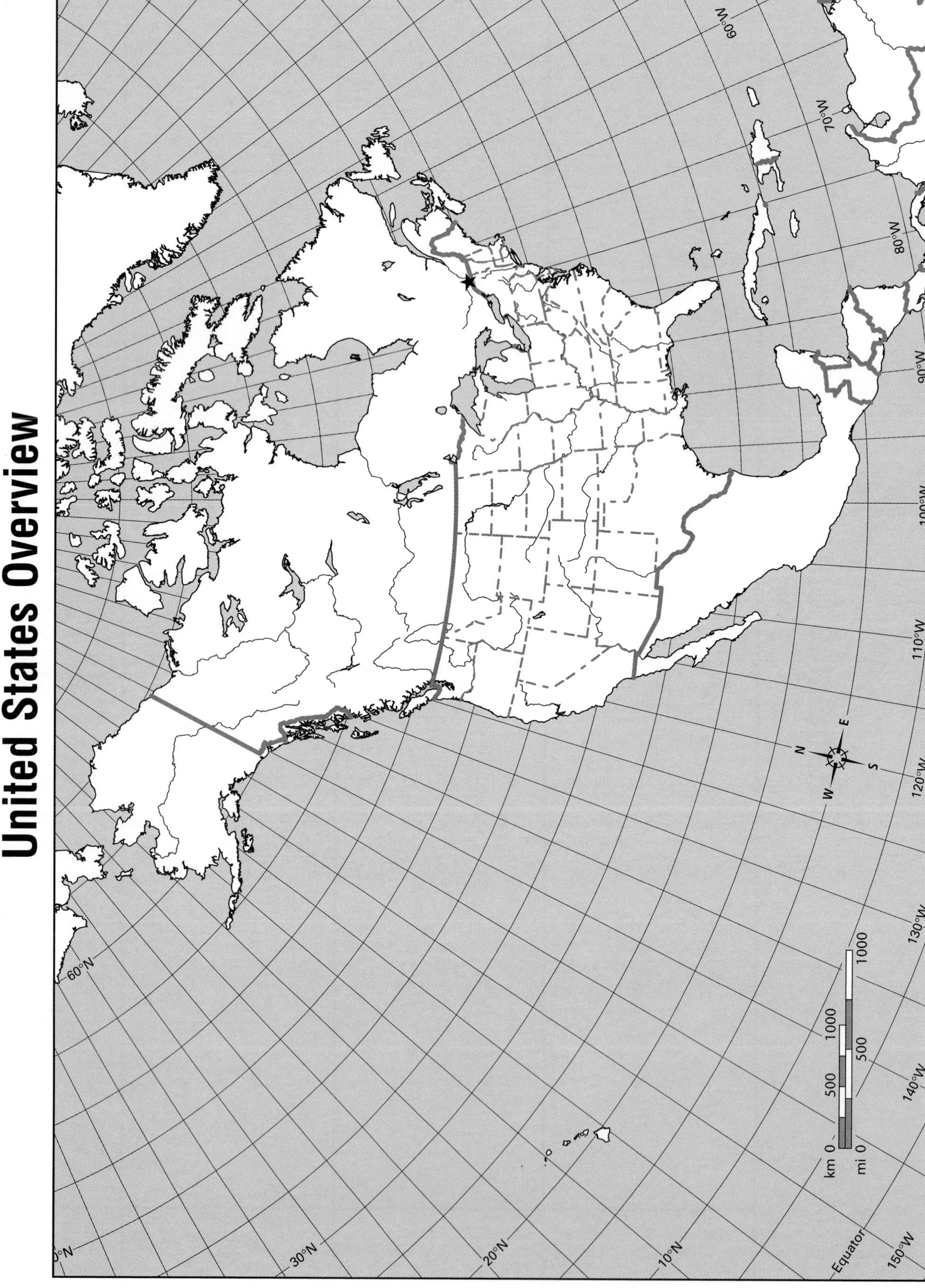
United States Overview
60°W
70°W
80°W
90°W
100°W
110°W
120°W
130°W
140°W
150°W
60°N
30°N
20°N
10°N
Equator
N
E
S
W
km 0
500
1000
mi 0
500
1000

Name ______________________________ Date ________________

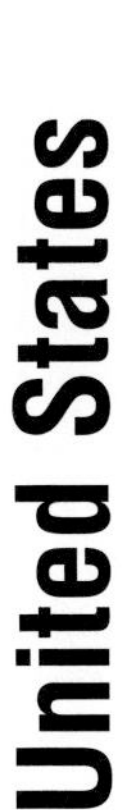

United States

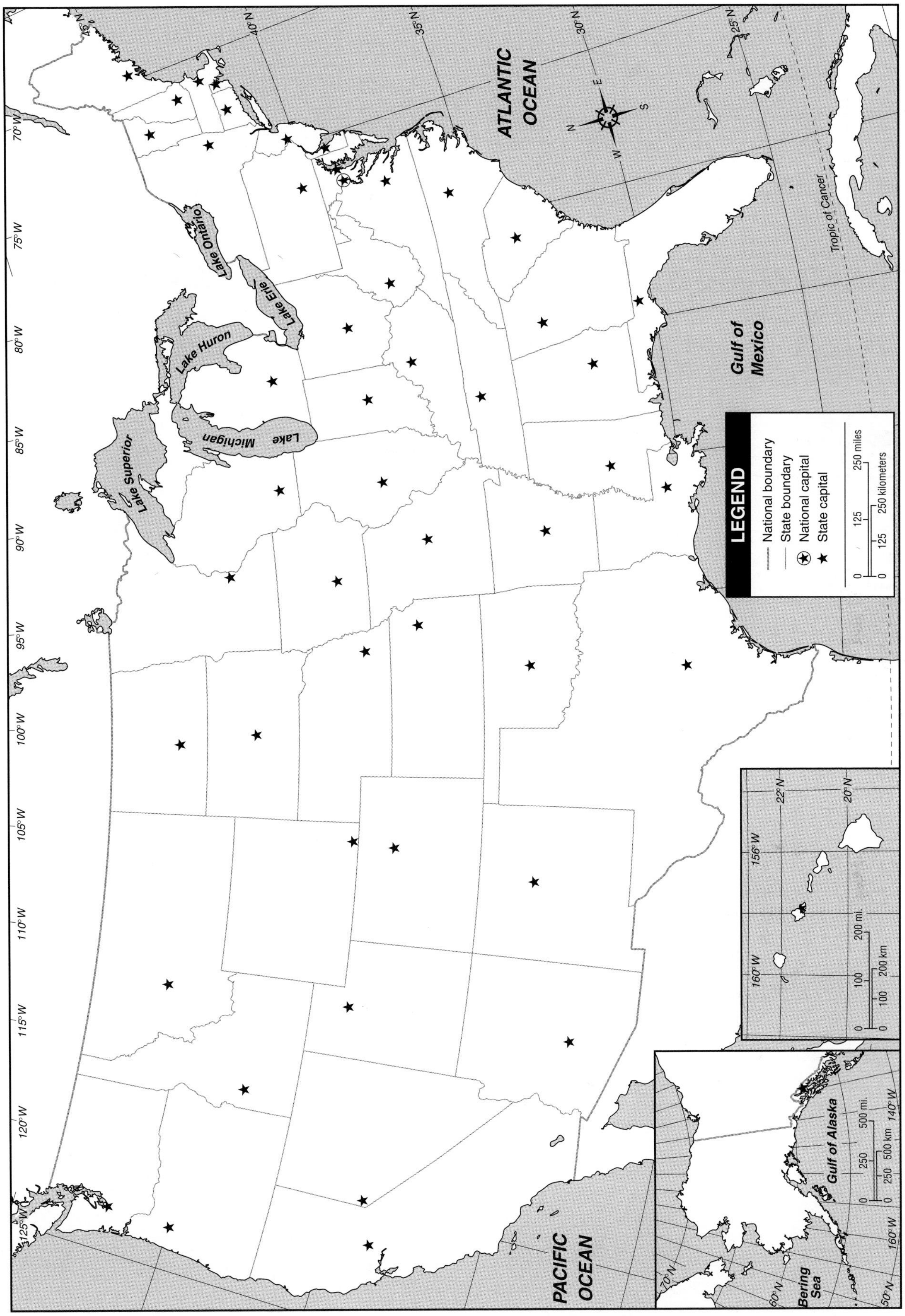
ATLANTIC OCEAN
Gulf of Mexico
PACIFIC OCEAN
Lake Ontario
Lake Erie
Lake Huron
Lake Michigan
Lake Superior
Tropic of Cancer
N E S W
45° N
40° N
35° N
30° N
25° N
70° W
75° W
80° W
85° W
90° W
95° W
100° W
105° W
110° W
115° W
120° W
125° W
LEGEND
National boundary
State boundary
National capital
State capital
0 125 250 miles
0 125 250 kilometers
22° N
20° N
156° W
160° W
0 100 200 mi.
0 100 200 km
Gulf of Alaska
Bering Sea
70° N
60° N
50° N
140° W
160° W
0 250 500 mi.
0 250 500 km

Name ______________________________ Date ____________________

States and Major Cities

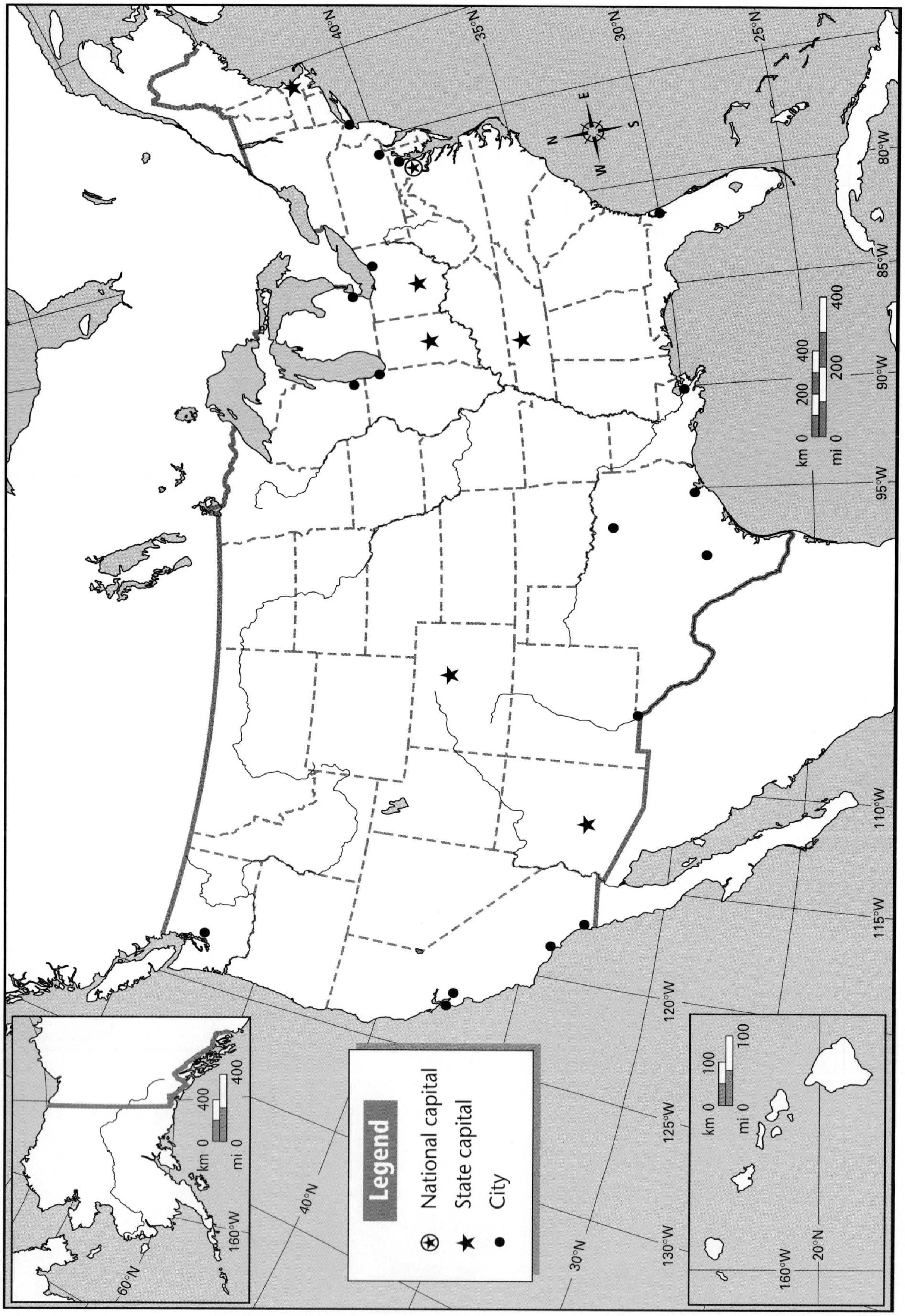

Legend
- ⊛ National capital
- ★ State capital
- ● City

N E S W

km 0 200 400
mi 0 200 400

km 0 400
mi 0 400

km 0 100
mi 0 100

40°N 35°N 30°N 25°N 20°N 60°N
80°W 85°W 90°W 95°W 110°W 115°W 120°W 125°W 130°W 160°W

Name ______________________________ Date ______________________

United States Landforms

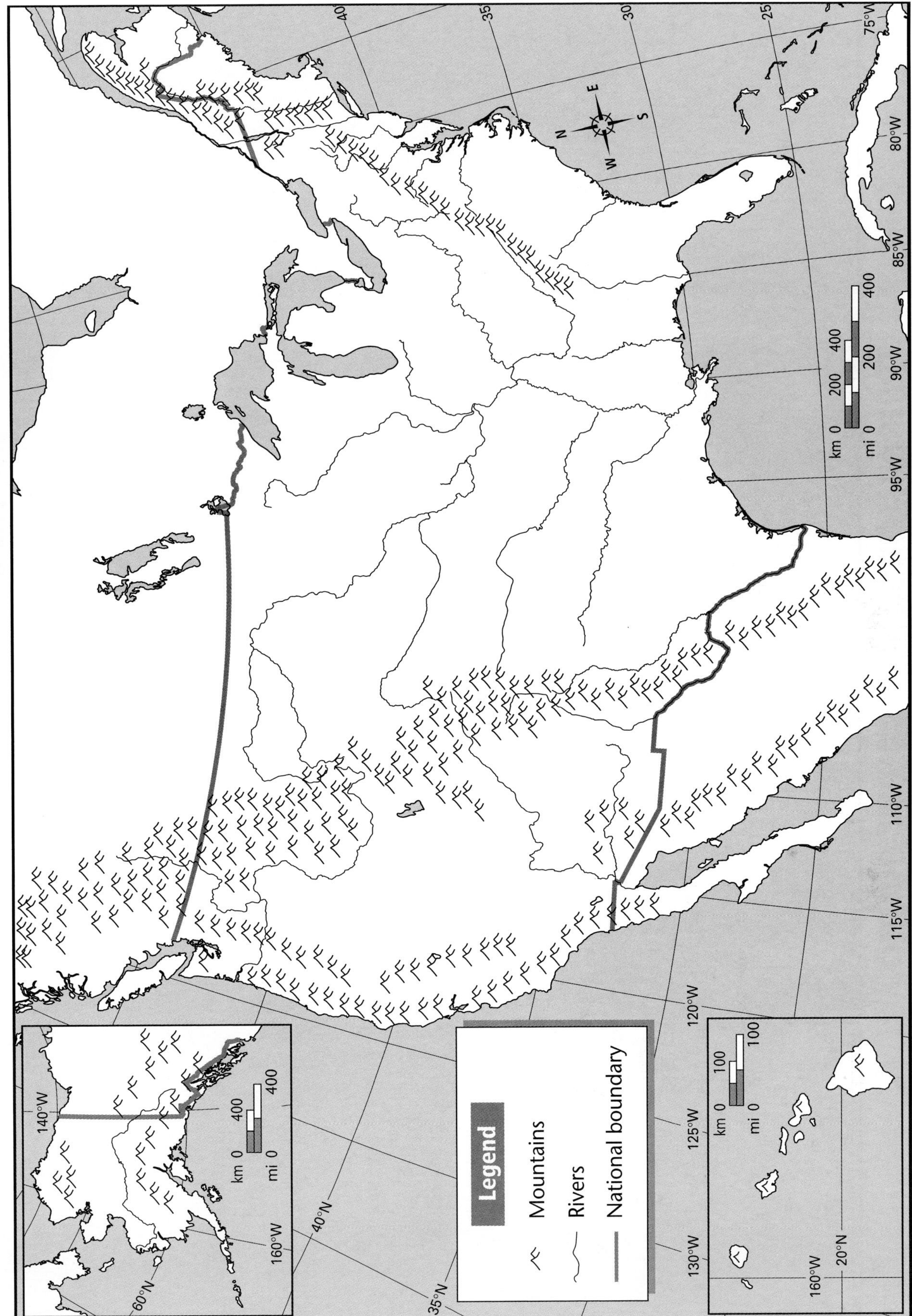

Name ______________________________ Date ______________________

United States Political/Physical

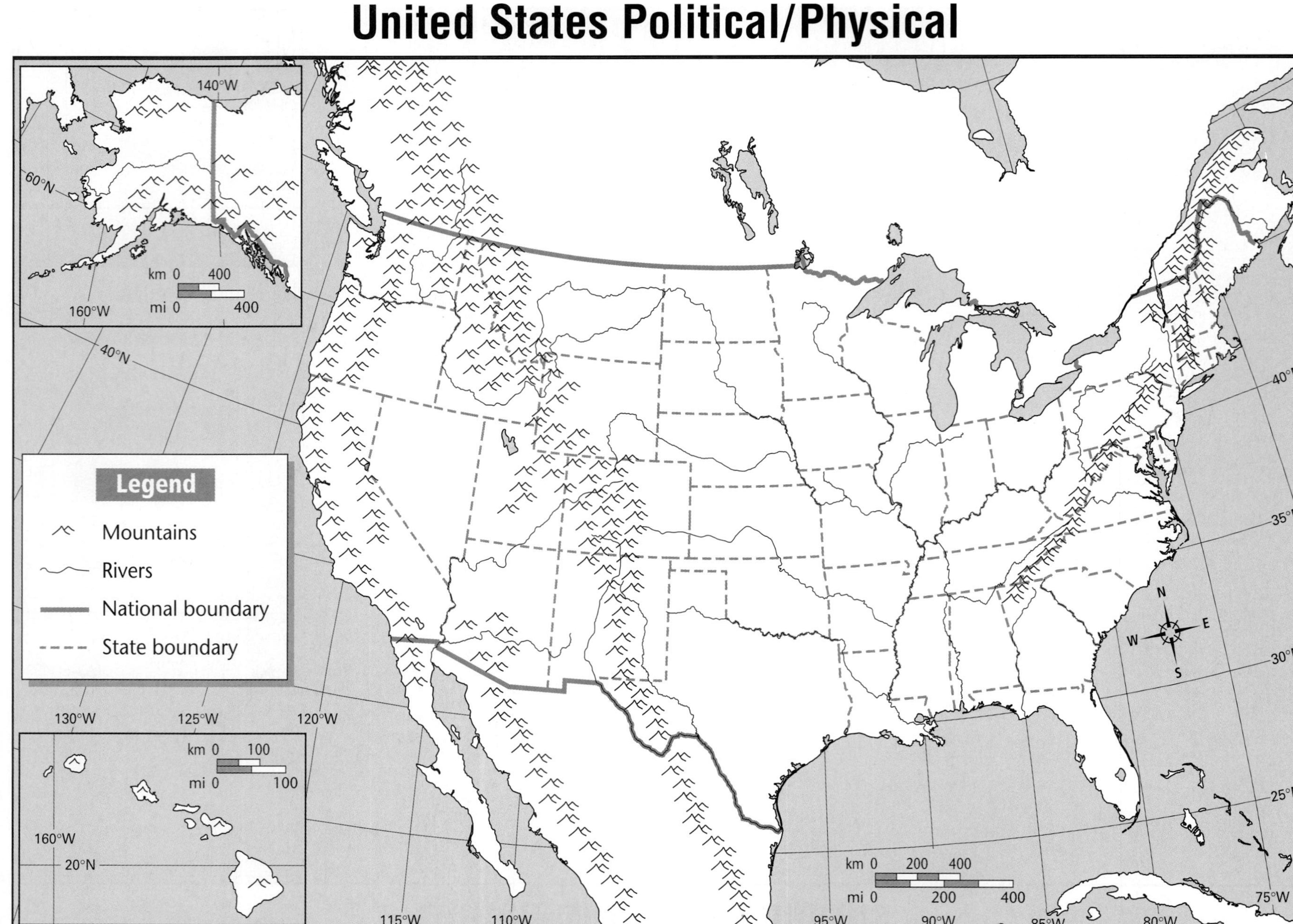

Name ______________________________ Date ____________________

United States Regions

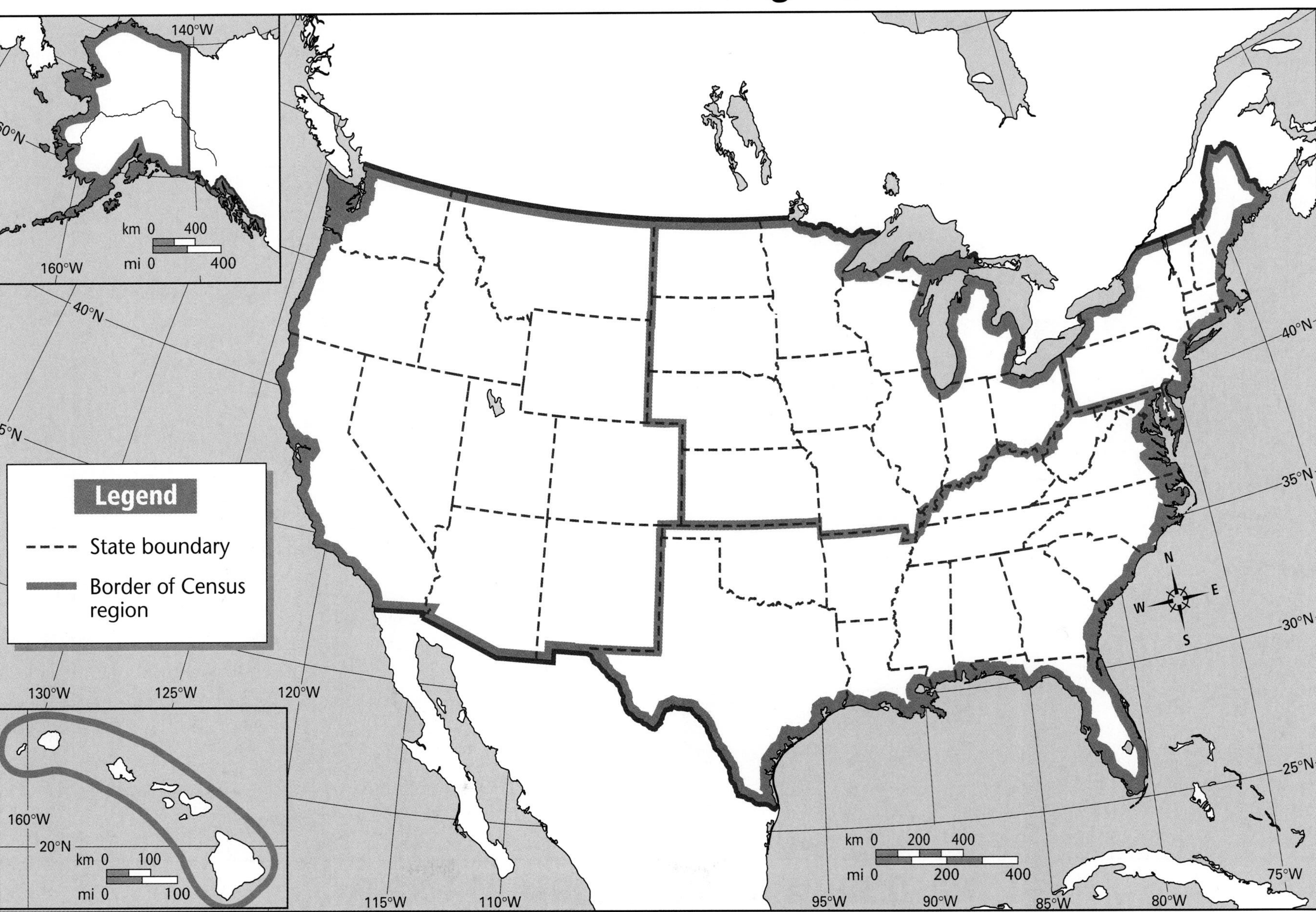

Name ______________________ Date ______________

Western Hemisphere: Countries

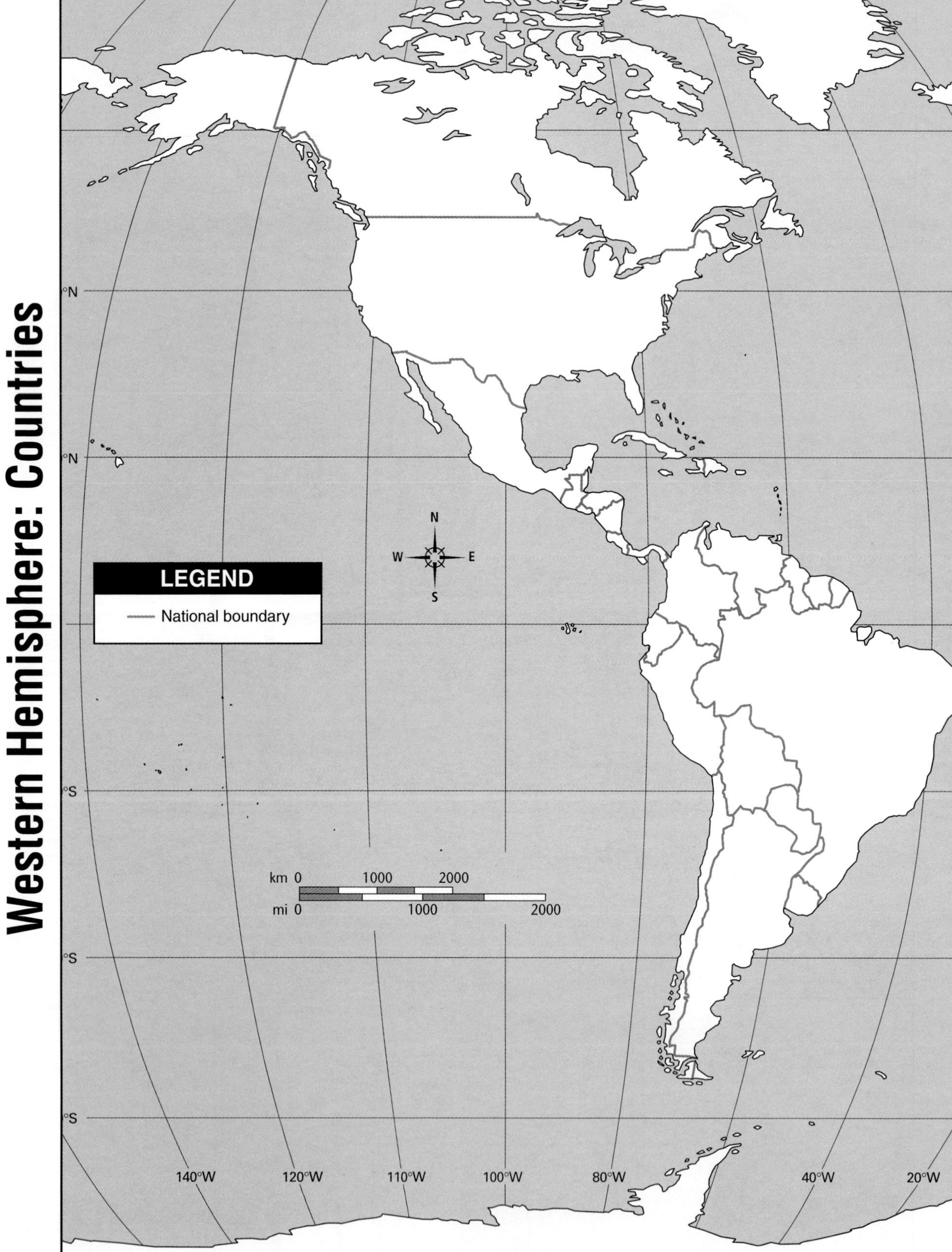

Name ______________________________ Date ____________________

World Continents

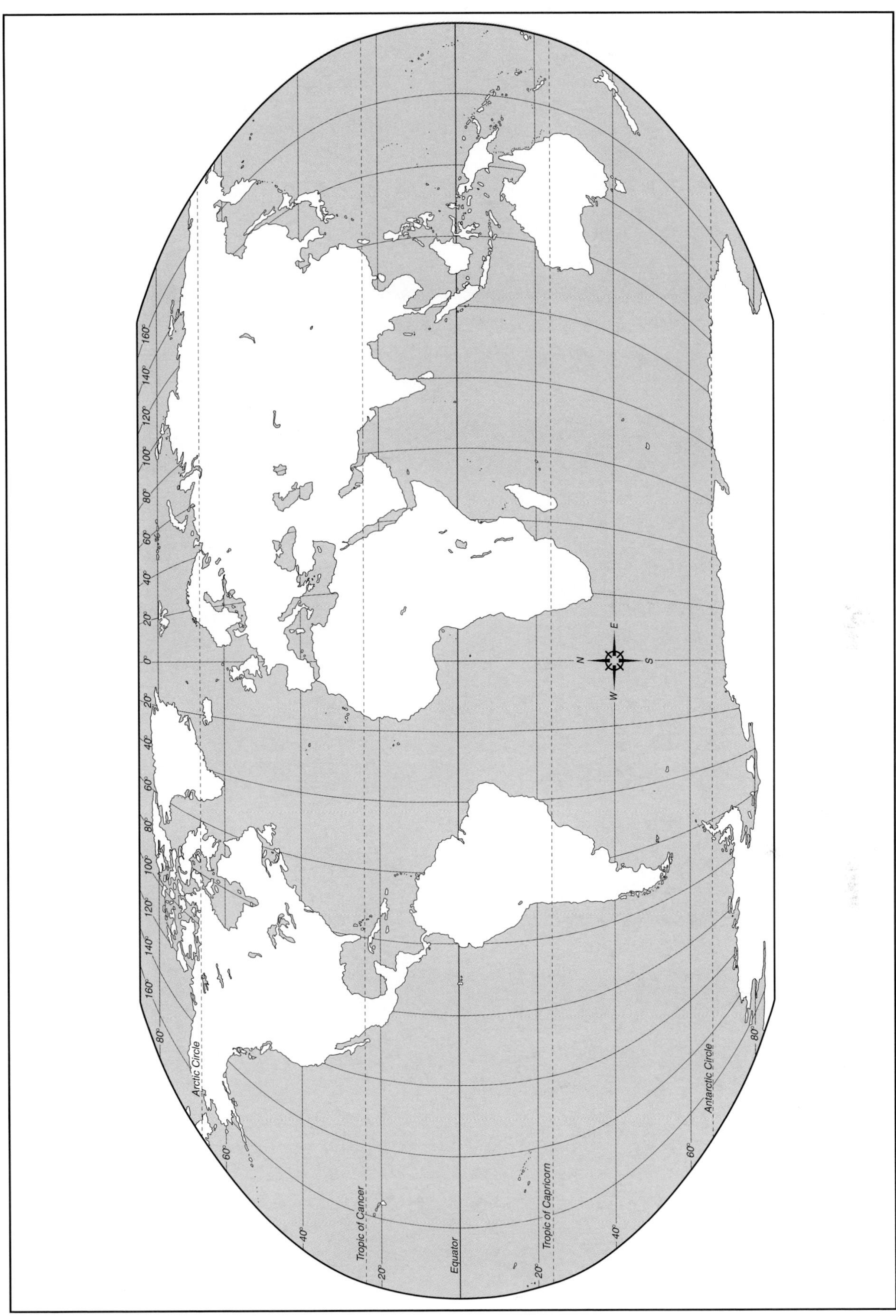

Name ______________________________ Date ____________________

World Countries

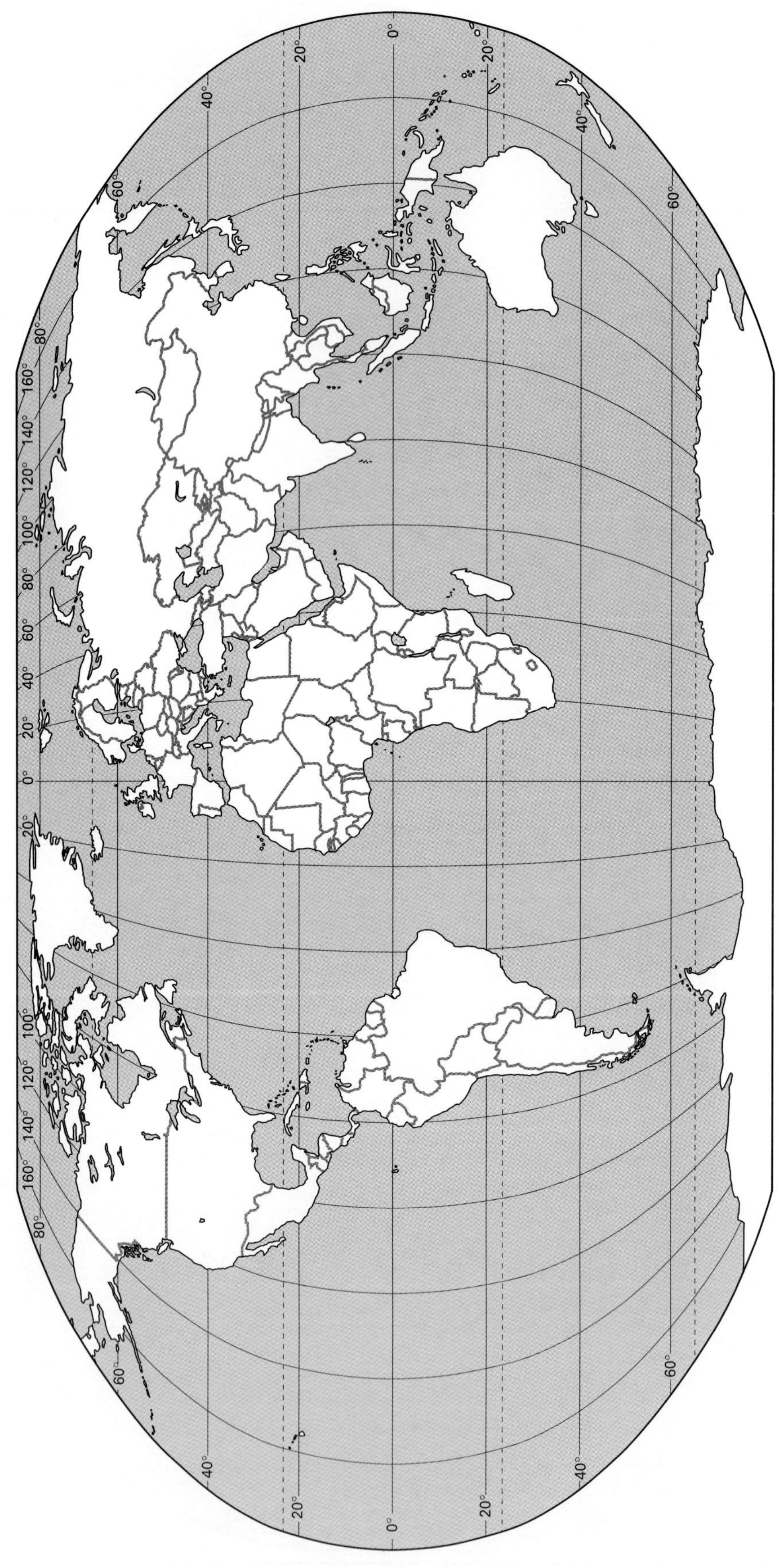

Name ______________________________ Date ____________________

World Landforms

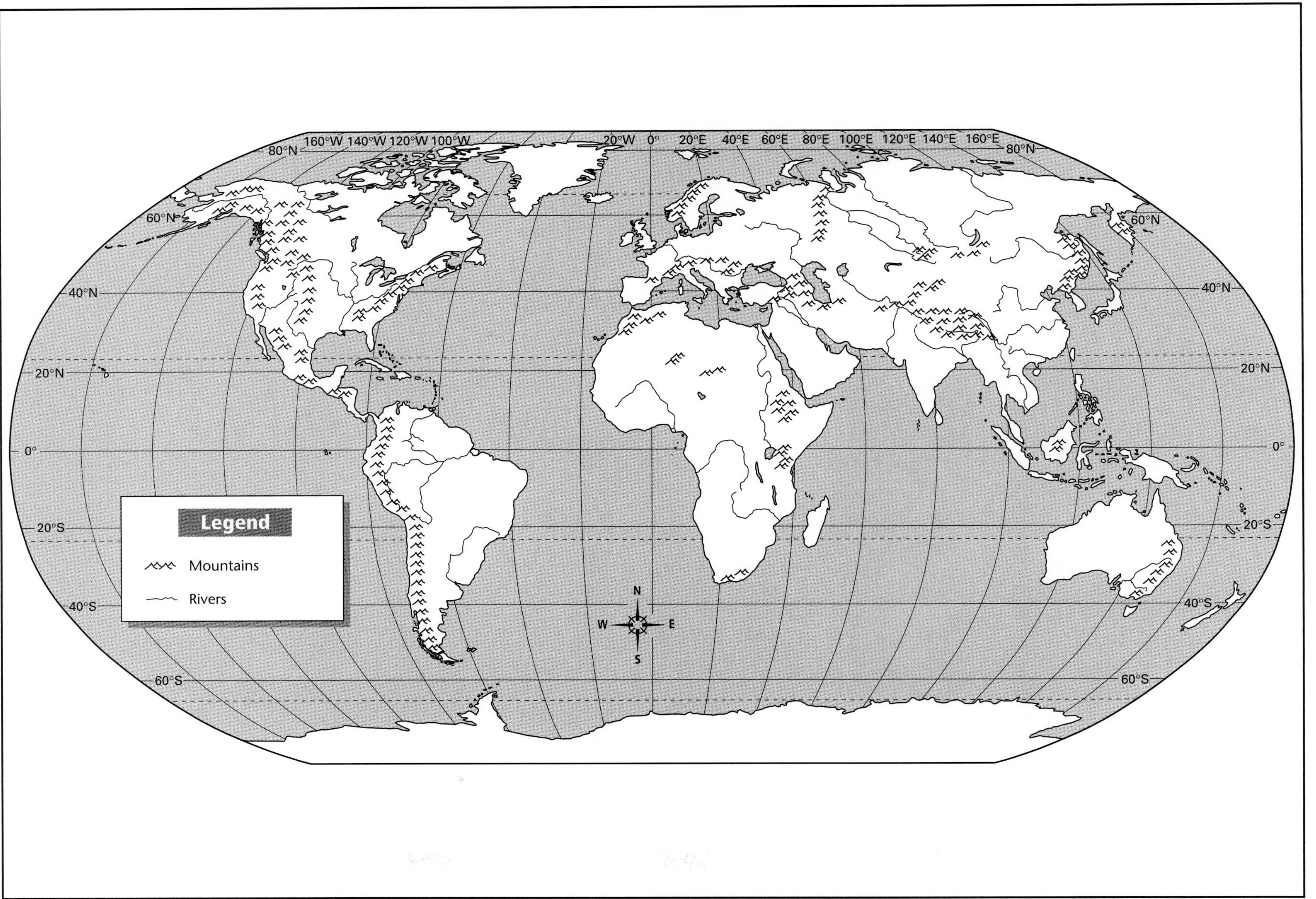

Name ______________________ Date ______________

Colonial America 1776

Name ______________________ Date ______________

United States 1790

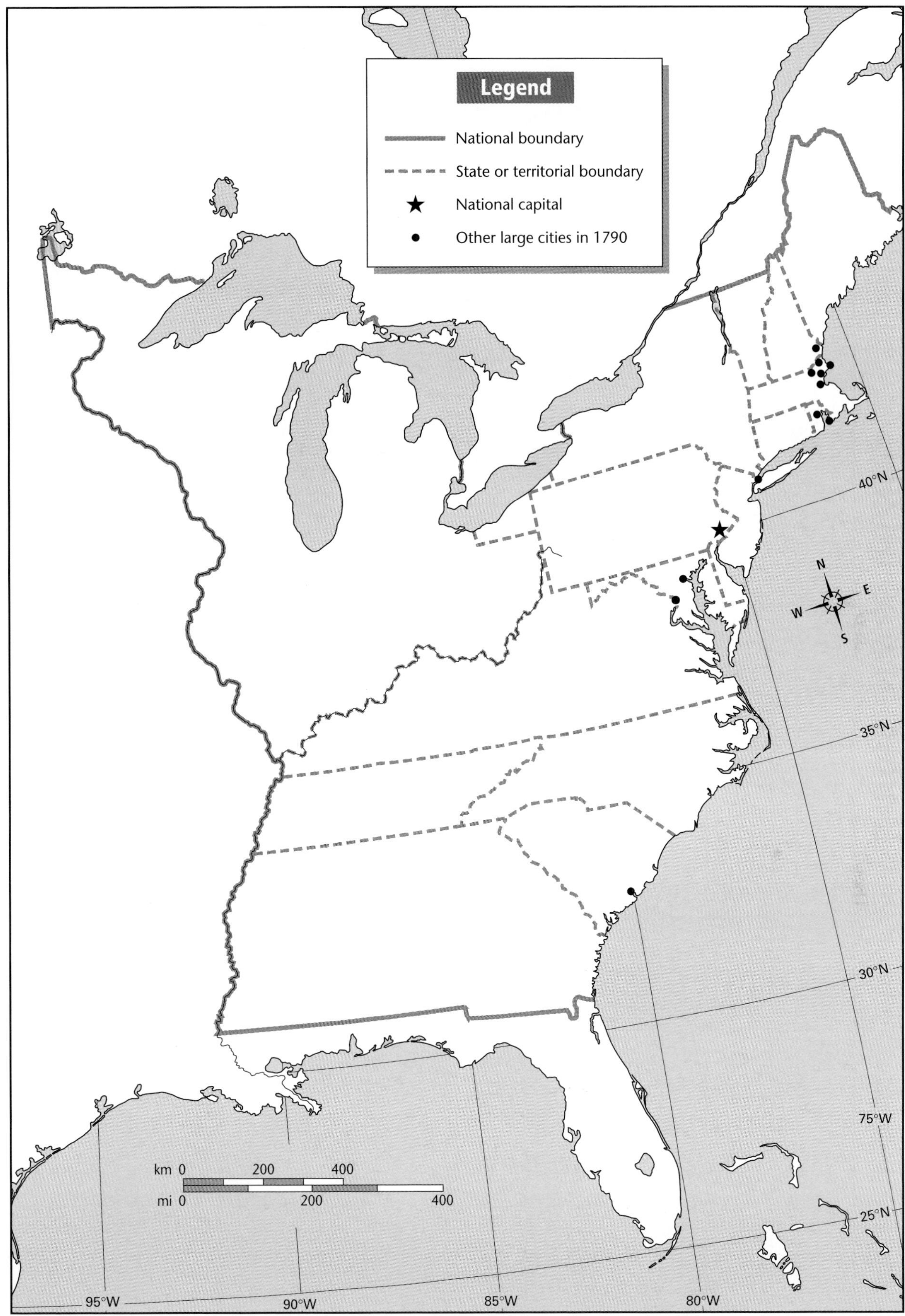

Name ______________________ Date ______________

United States 1820

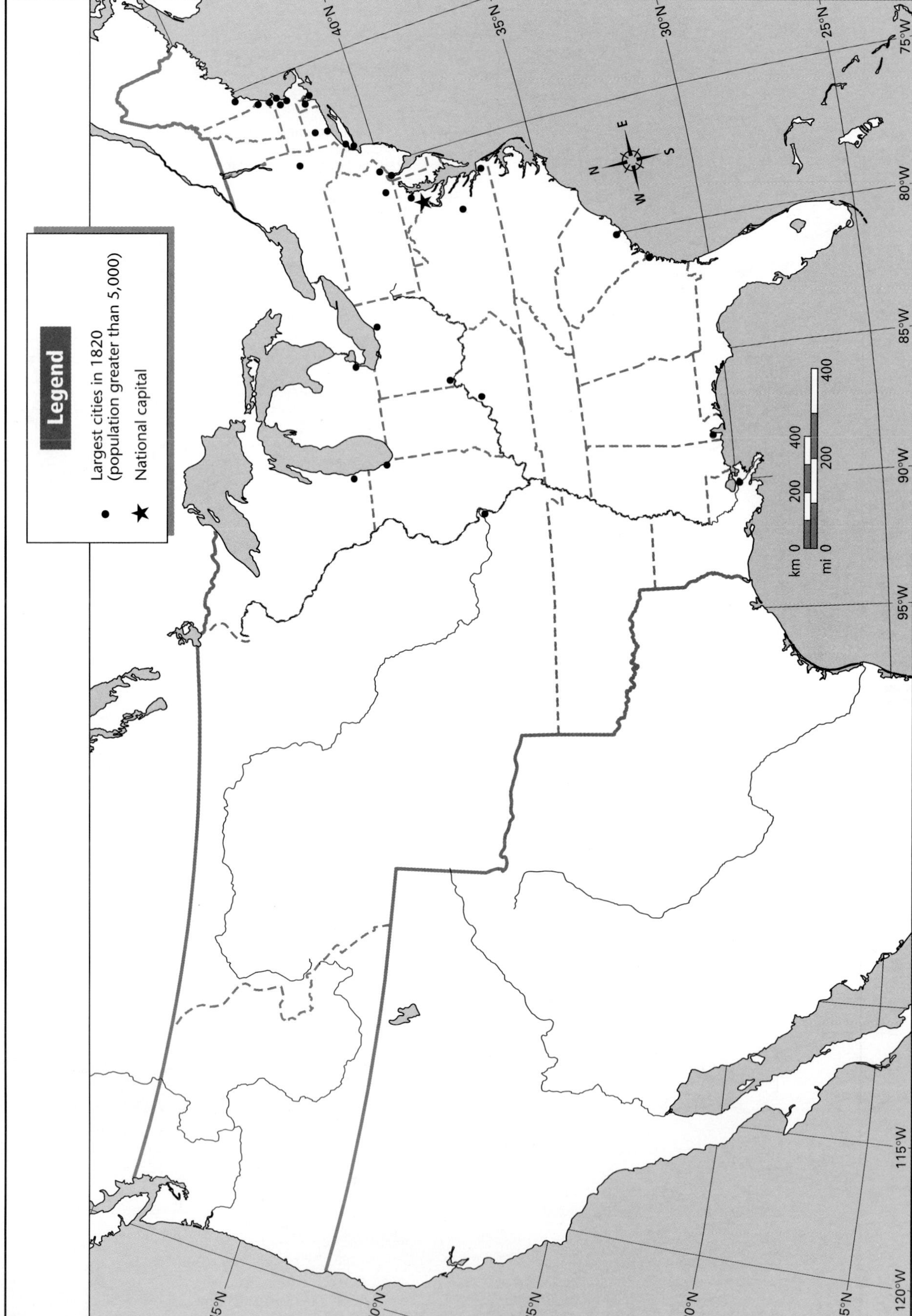

Name ______________________________ Date ____________________

United States 1860

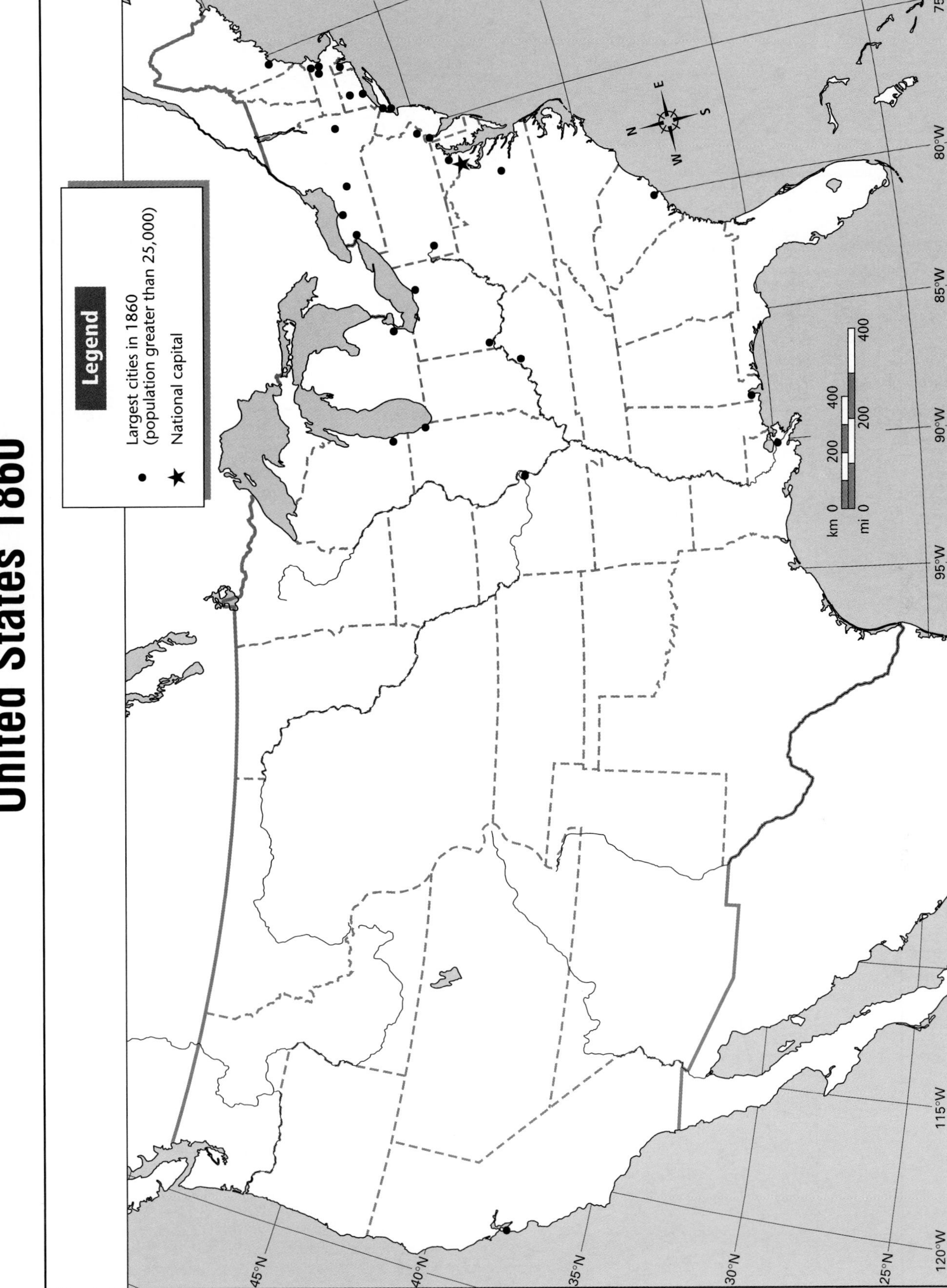

Name ______________________ Date ______________

United States 1900

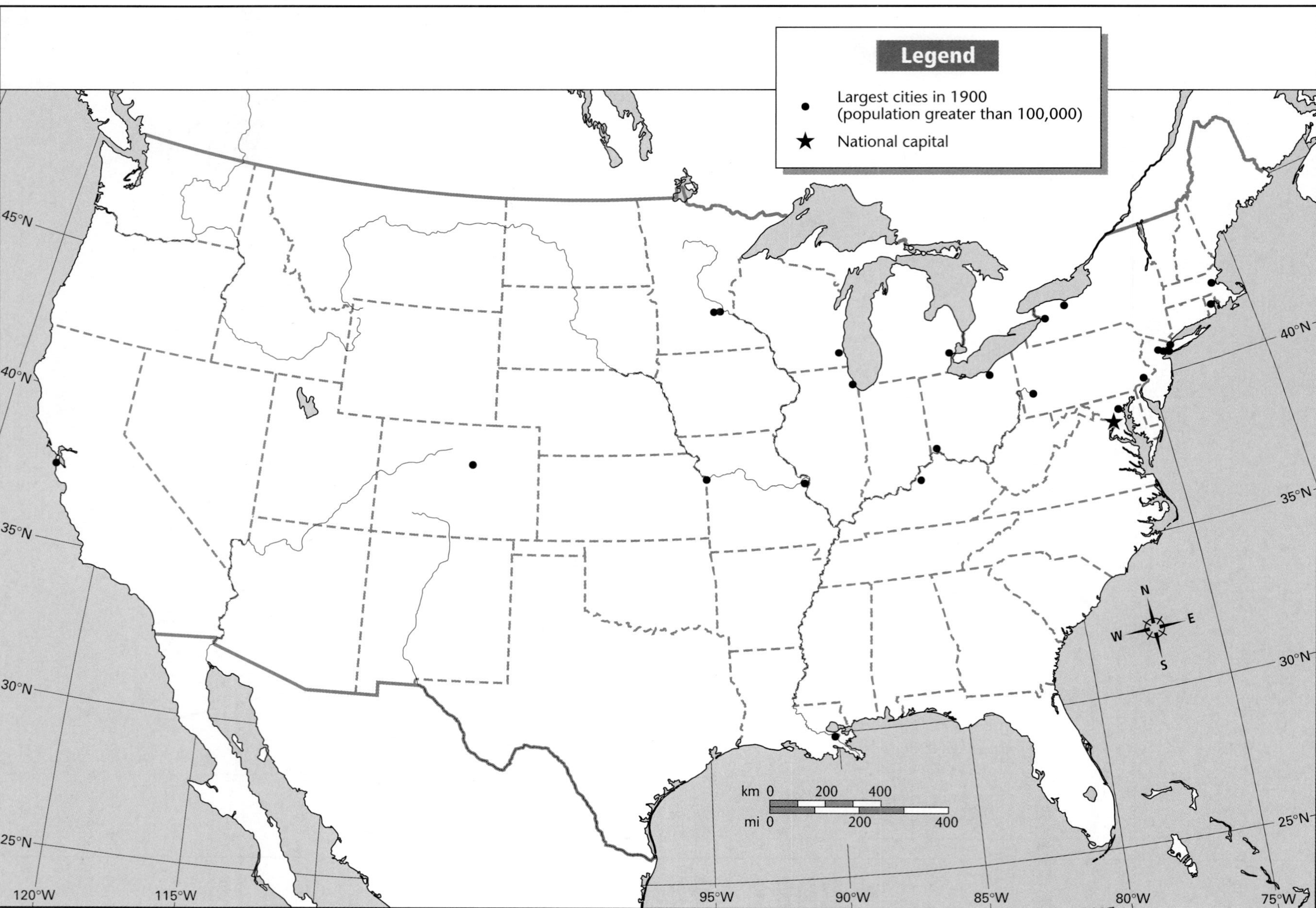

Name ______________________________ Date ____________________

North America: Countries

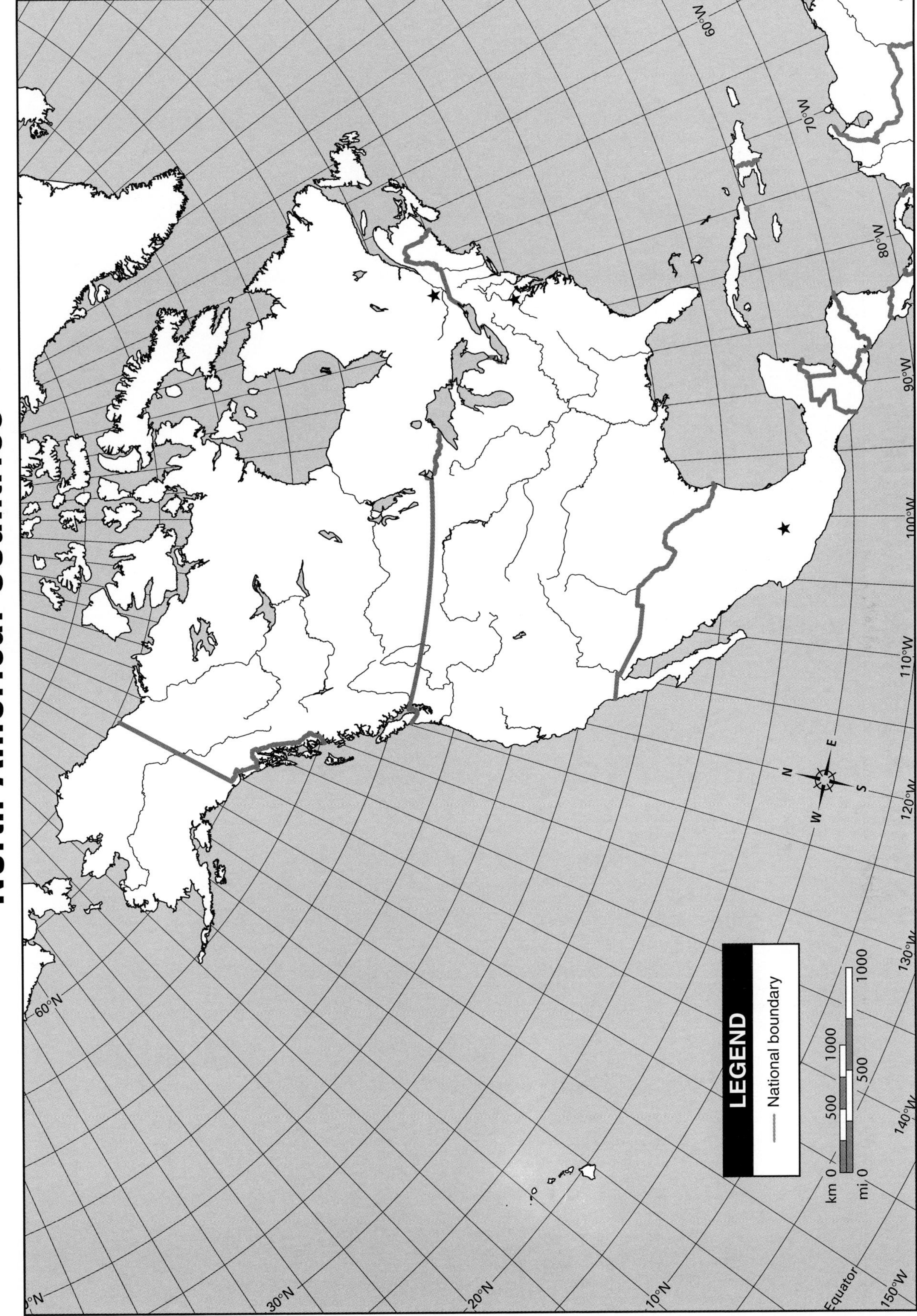

Name ______________________ Date ______________

South America: Countries

Name ______________________ Date ______________________

Africa: Countries

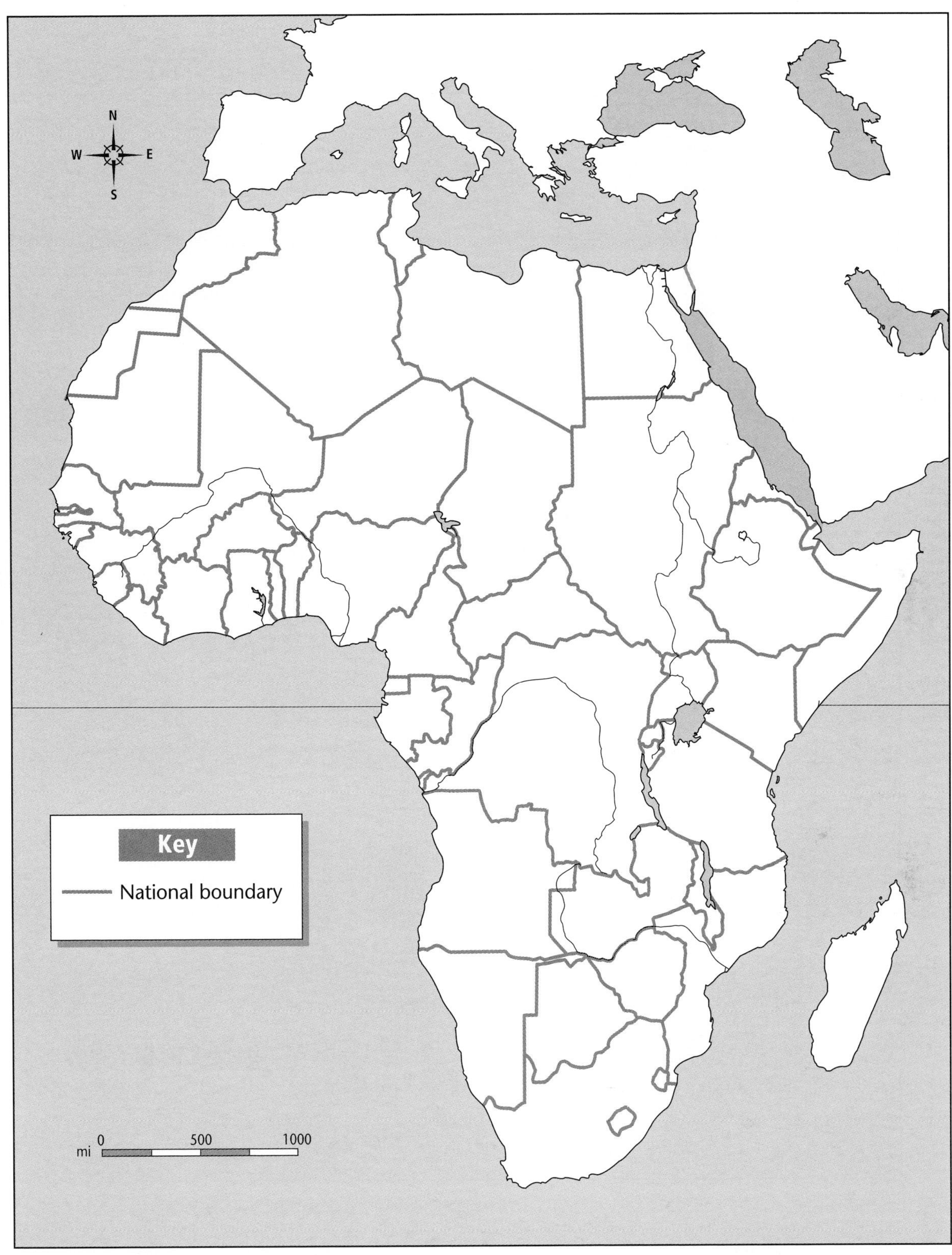

Name ______________________________ Date ____________________

Europe: Countries

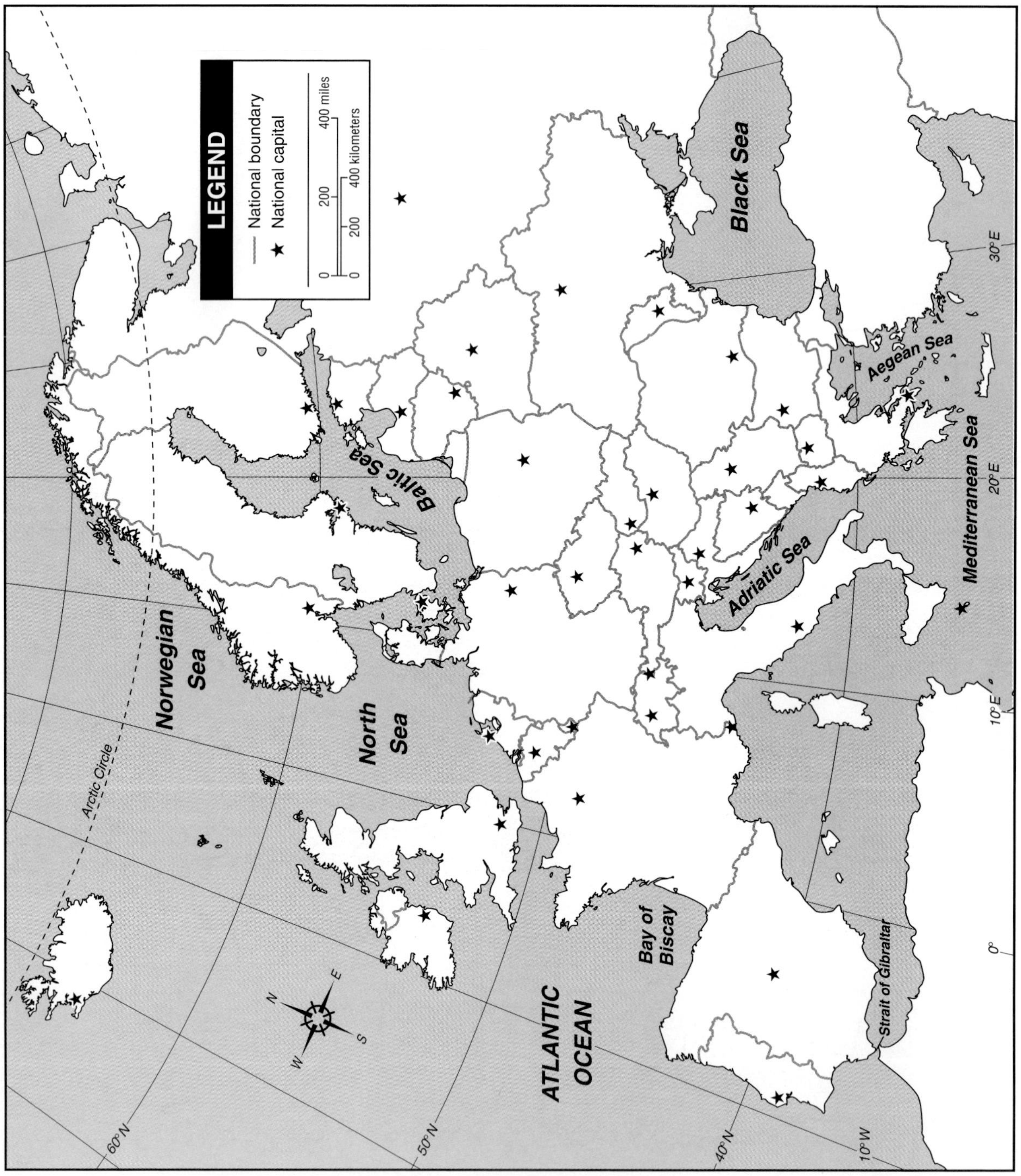

LEGEND
— National boundary
★ National capital
0 200 400 miles
0 200 400 kilometers

Norwegian Sea
North Sea
Baltic Sea
Black Sea
Aegean Sea
Adriatic Sea
Mediterranean Sea
Bay of Biscay
ATLANTIC OCEAN
Strait of Gibraltar
Arctic Circle
60°N
50°N
40°N
10°W
0°
10°E
20°E
30°E
N
E
S
W

Name ______________________________ Date ____________________

Asia and the South Pacific: Countries

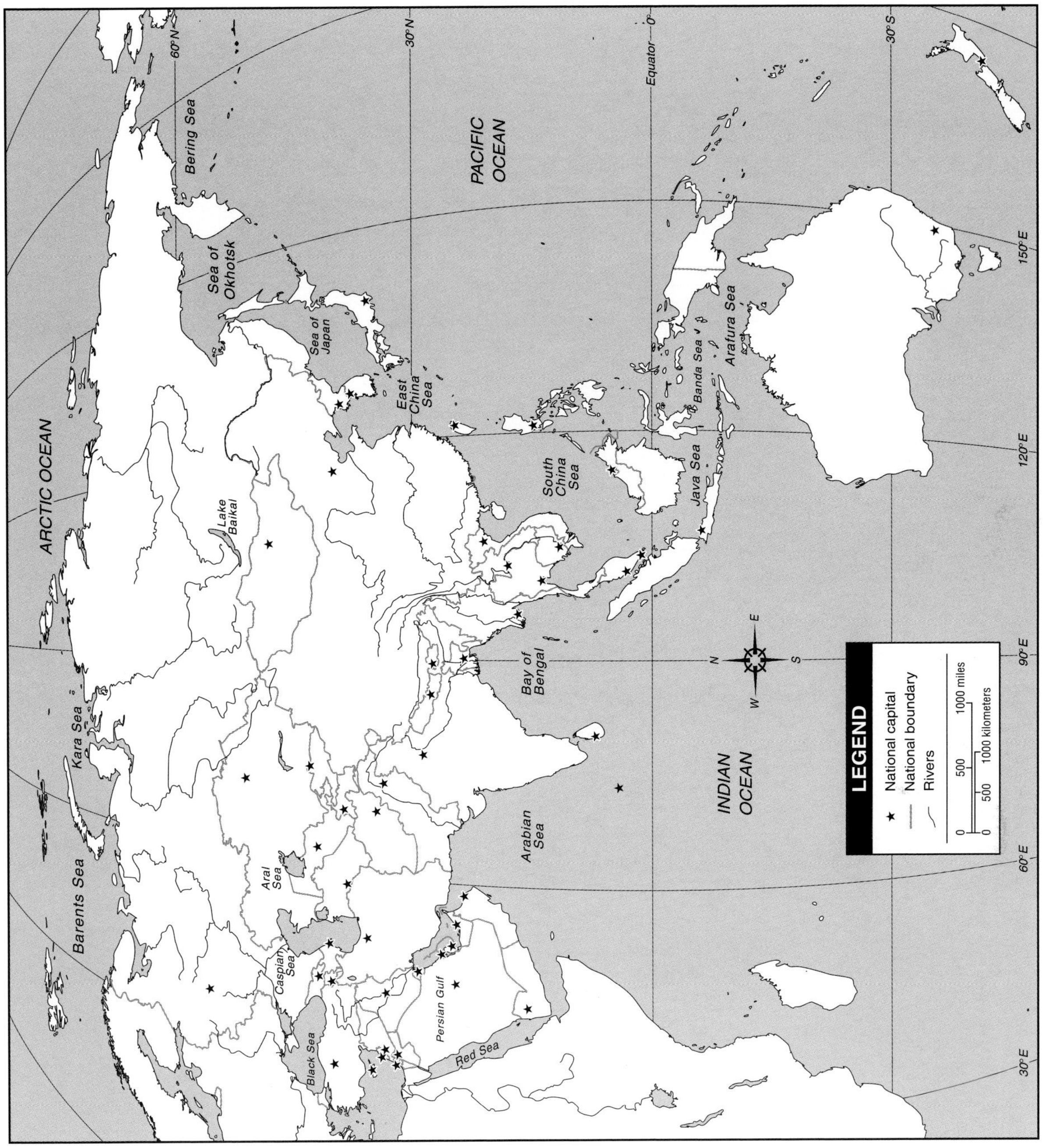

LEGEND

★ National capital

— National boundary

~ Rivers

0 500 1000 miles

0 500 1000 kilometers

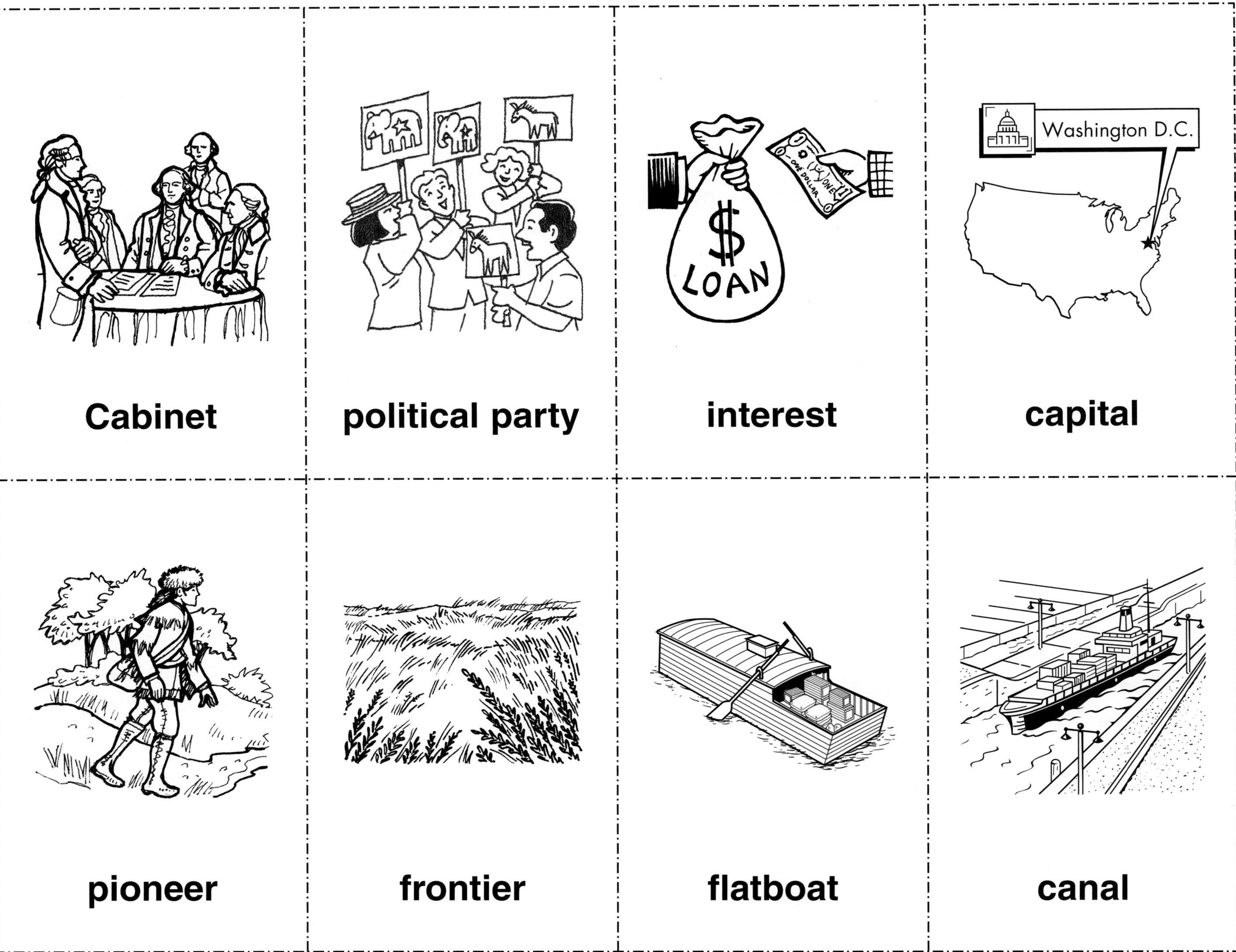
Cabinet
political party
LOAN
ONE DOLLAR
interest
Washington D.C.
capital
pioneer
frontier
flatboat
canal

Noun
A city where the government meets.

(Chapter 9, Lesson 4)

Noun
What people pay to borrow money.

(Chapter 9, Lesson 4)

Noun
A group of people who share similar ideas about government.

(Chapter 9, Lesson 4)

Noun
A group chosen by the President to help run the executive branch and give advice.

(Chapter 9, Lesson 4)

Noun
A waterway built for boat travel and shipping.

(Chapter 10, Lesson 1)

Noun
A large, rectangular boat partly covered by a roof.

(Chapter 10, Lesson 1)

Noun
The edge of a country or settled region.

(Chapter 10, Lesson 1)

Noun
One of the first of a group of people to enter or settle a region.

(Chapter 10, Lesson 1)

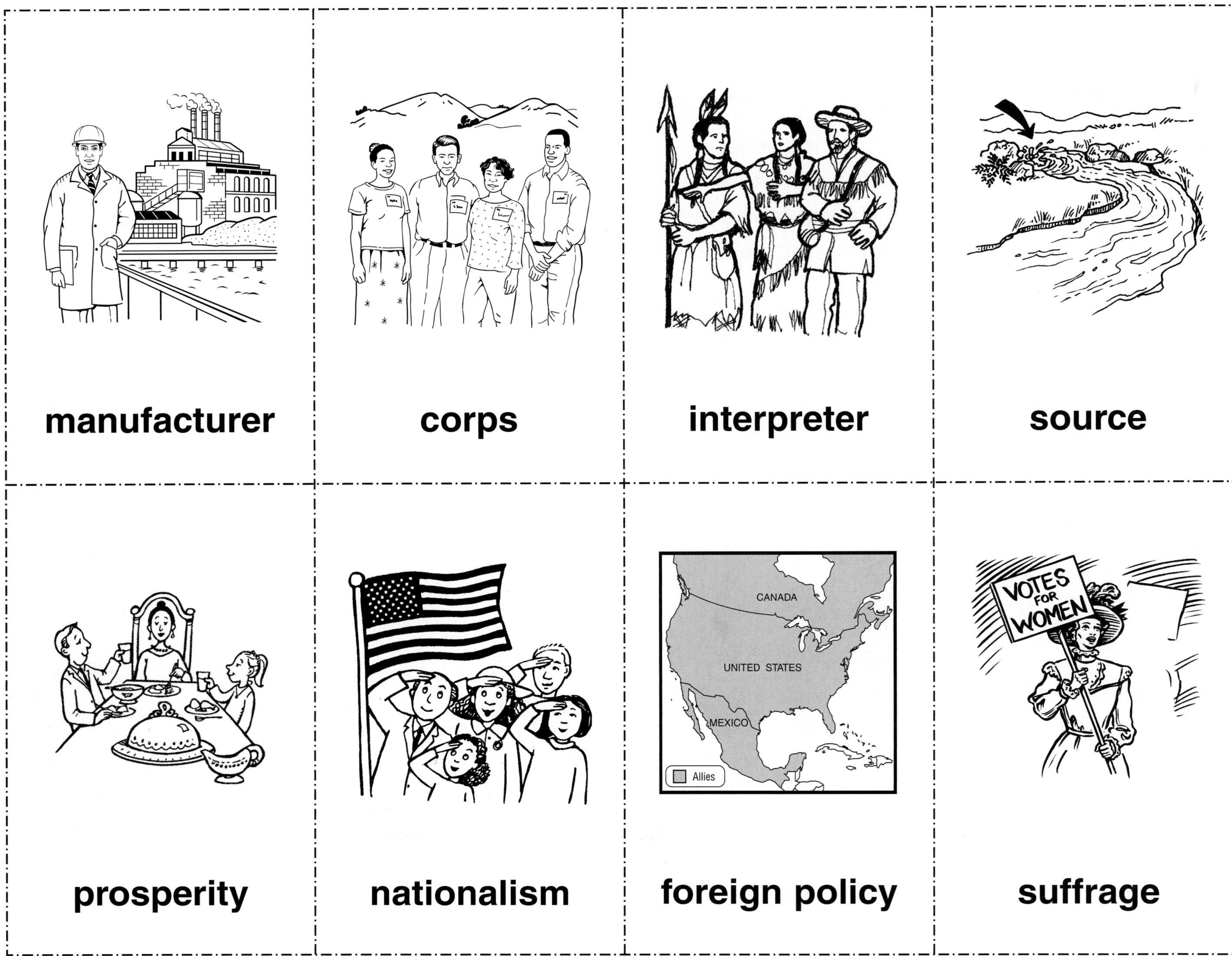
manufacturer
corps
interpreter
source
prosperity
nationalism
CANADA
UNITED STATES
MEXICO
Allies
foreign policy
VOTES FOR WOMEN
suffrage

Noun **The place where a river begins.** (Chapter 10, Lesson 2)	*Noun* **Someone who helps speakers of different languages understand each other.** (Chapter 10, Lesson 2)	*Noun* **A team of people who work together.** (Chapter 10, Lesson 2)	*Noun* **Someone who uses machines to make goods.** (Chapter 10, Lesson 2)
Noun **The right to vote.** (Chapter 10, Lesson 4)	*Noun* **A government's actions toward other nations.** (Chapter 10, Lesson 3)	*Noun* **Devotion to one's country.** (Chapter 10, Lesson 3)	*Noun* **Economic success and security.** (Chapter 10, Lesson 3)

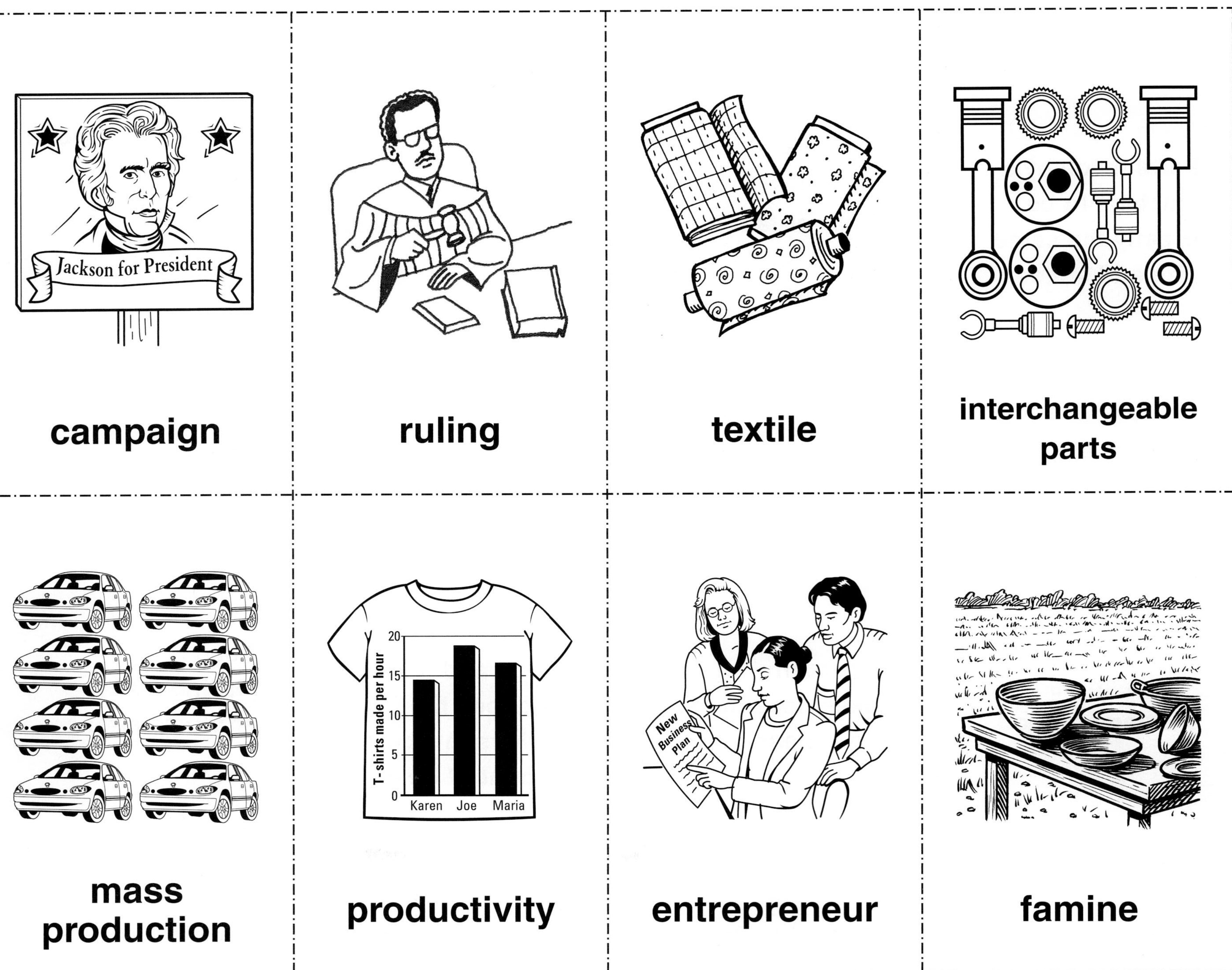

Jackson for President
campaign
ruling
textile
interchangeable parts
mass production
20
15
10
5
0
T-shirts made per hour
Karen
Joe
Maria
productivity
New Business Plan
entrepreneur
famine

Noun
Parts made by a machine to be exactly the same size and shape.

(Chapter 11, Lesson 1)

Noun
Cloth or fabric.

(Chapter 11, Lesson 1)

Noun
An official decision.

(Chapter 10, Lesson 4)

Noun
A series of actions taken toward a goal, such as winning a presidential election.

(Chapter 10, Lesson 4)

Noun
A widespread shortage of food.

(Chapter 11, Lesson 2)

Noun
A person who takes risks to start a business.

(Chapter 11, Lesson 1)

Noun
The amount of goods and services produced by workers in a certain amount of time.

(Chapter 11, Lesson 1)

Noun
Making many products at once.

(Chapter 11, Lesson 1)

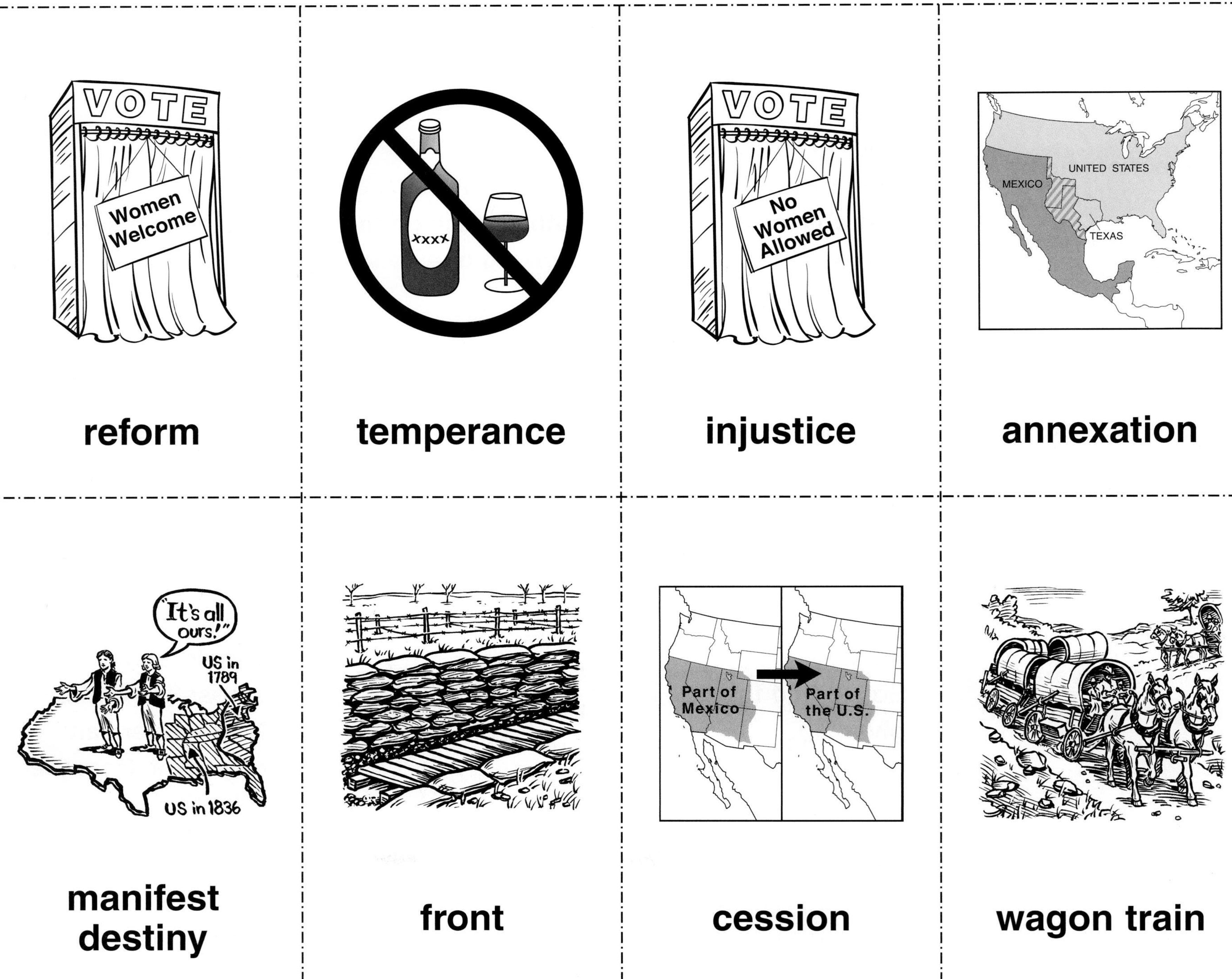
VOTE
Women Welcome
reform
temperance
VOTE
No Women Allowed
injustice
UNITED STATES
MEXICO
TEXAS
annexation
"It's all ours!"
US in 1789
US in 1836
manifest destiny
front
Part of Mexico
Part of the U.S.
cession
wagon train

Noun
The act of joining two countries or pieces of land together.

(Chapter 11, Lesson 3)

Noun
Unfair treatment that abuses a person's rights.

(Chapter 11, Lesson 2)

Noun
Controlling or cutting back on the drinking of alcohol.

(Chapter 11, Lesson 2)

Noun
An action that makes something better.

(Chapter 11, Lesson 2)

Noun
A line of covered wagons that moved together.

(Chapter 11, Lesson 4)

Noun
Something that is given up.

(Chapter 11, Lesson 3)

Noun
Where the fighting takes place in a war.

(Chapter 11, Lesson 3)

Noun
The belief that the United States should spread across the entire North American continent, from the Atlantic Ocean to the Pacific Ocean.

(Chapter 11, Lesson 3)

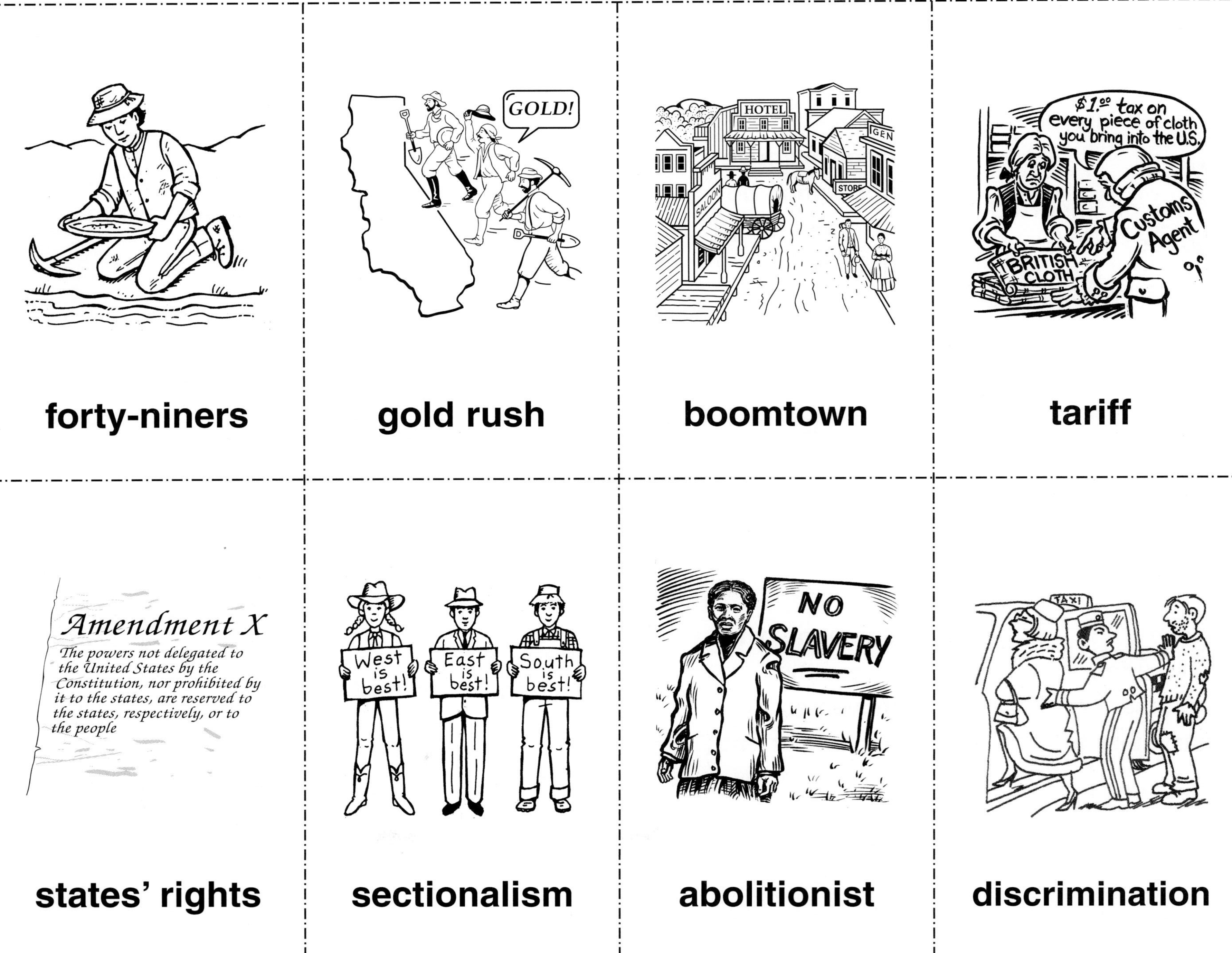

forty-niners

gold rush

boomtown

tariff

states' rights

sectionalism

abolitionist

discrimination

Noun
A tax on imported goods.

(Chapter 12, Lesson 1)

Noun
A town whose population booms, or grows very quickly.

(Chapter 11, Lesson 4)

Noun
When many people hurry to the same area to look for gold.

(Chapter 11, Lesson 4)

Noun
A miner who went to California in 1849.

(Chapter 11, Lesson 4)

Noun
The unfair treatment of particular groups.

(Chapter 12, Lesson 2)

Noun
Someone who joined the movement to abolish, or end, slavery.

(Chapter 12, Lesson 2)

Noun
Loyalty to one part of the country.

(Chapter 12, Lesson 1)

Noun
The idea that states, not the federal government, should make the final decisions about matters that affect them.

(Chapter 12, Lesson 1)

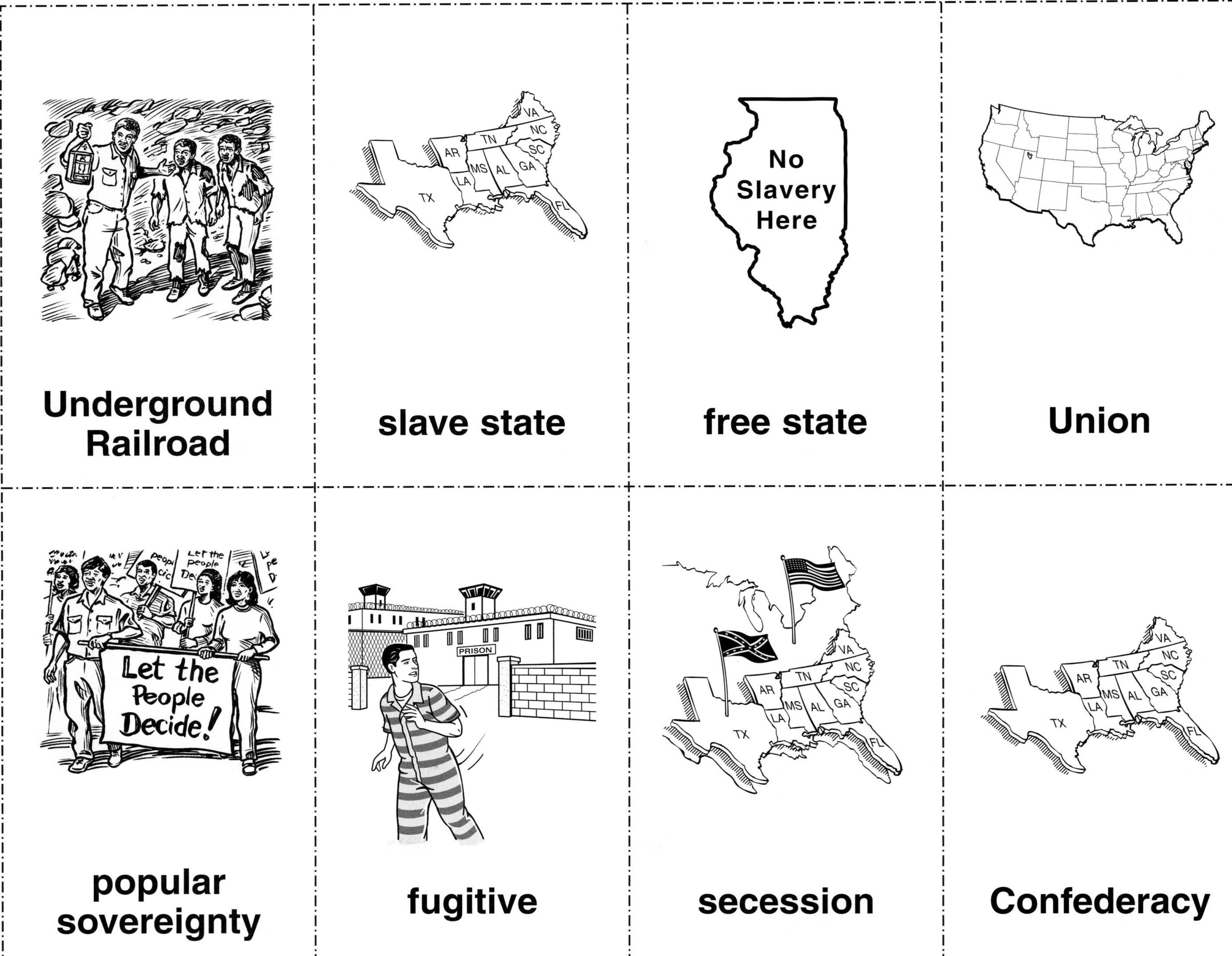
Underground Railroad
slave state
No Slavery Here
free state
Union
Let the People Decide!
popular sovereignty
PRISON
fugitive
secession
Confederacy

Noun
Another name for the United States.

(Chapter 12, Lesson 3)

Noun
A state that did not have slavery.

(Chapter 12, Lesson 3)

Noun
A state that permitted slavery.

(Chapter 12, Lesson 3)

Noun
A series of escape routes and hiding places to bring slaves out of the South.

(Chapter 12, Lesson 2)

Noun
The name for South Carolina, Mississippi, Florida, Alabama, Georgia, Louisiana, Texas, and later Arkansas, North Carolina, Tennessee, and Virginia.

(Chapter 12, Lesson 4)

Noun
When a part of a country leaves or breaks off from the rest.

(Chapter 12, Lesson 4)

Noun
A person who is running away.

(Chapter 12, Lesson 3)

Noun
The idea that the people who live in a place make decisions for themselves.

(Chapter 12, Lesson 3)

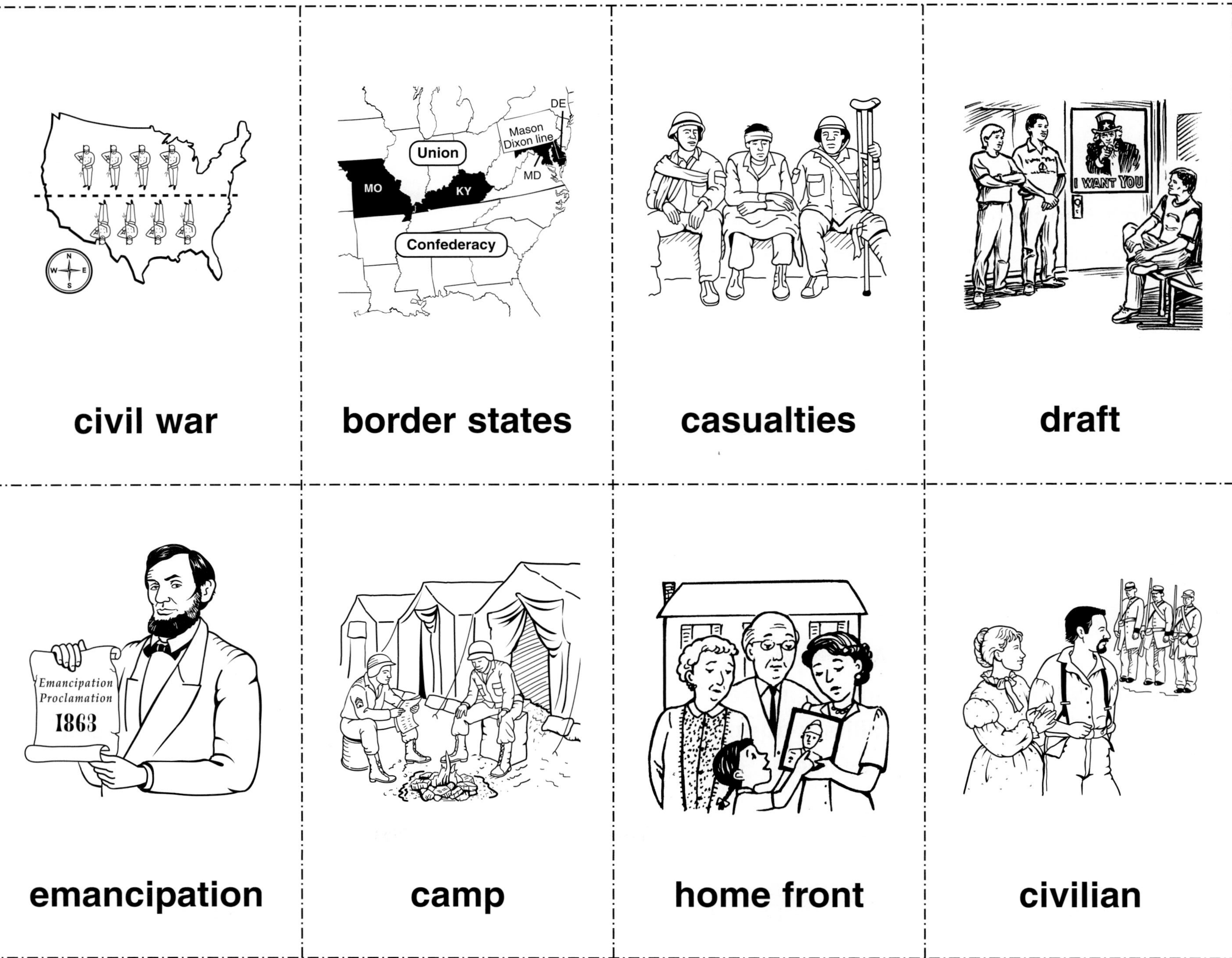
N
E
S
W
civil war
Union
Confederacy
MO
KY
MD
DE
Mason
Dixon line
border states
casualties
I WANT YOU
draft
Emancipation
Proclamation
1863
emancipation
camp
home front
civilian

Verb **To force people to be soldiers.** (Chapter 13, Lesson 1)	*Noun* **Soldiers who are killed or wounded.** (Chapter 13, Lesson 1)	*Noun* **Slave states that stayed in the Union.** (Chapter 13, Lesson 1)	*Noun* **A war between two groups or regions within a nation.** (Chapter 12, Lesson 4)
Noun **A person who is not in the military.** (Chapter 13, Lesson 2)	*Noun* **All the people who are not in the military during wartime.** (Chapter 13, Lesson 2)	*Noun* **A group of temporary shelters, such as tents.** (Chapter 13, Lesson 2)	*Noun* **The freeing of enslaved people.** (Chapter 13, Lesson 1)

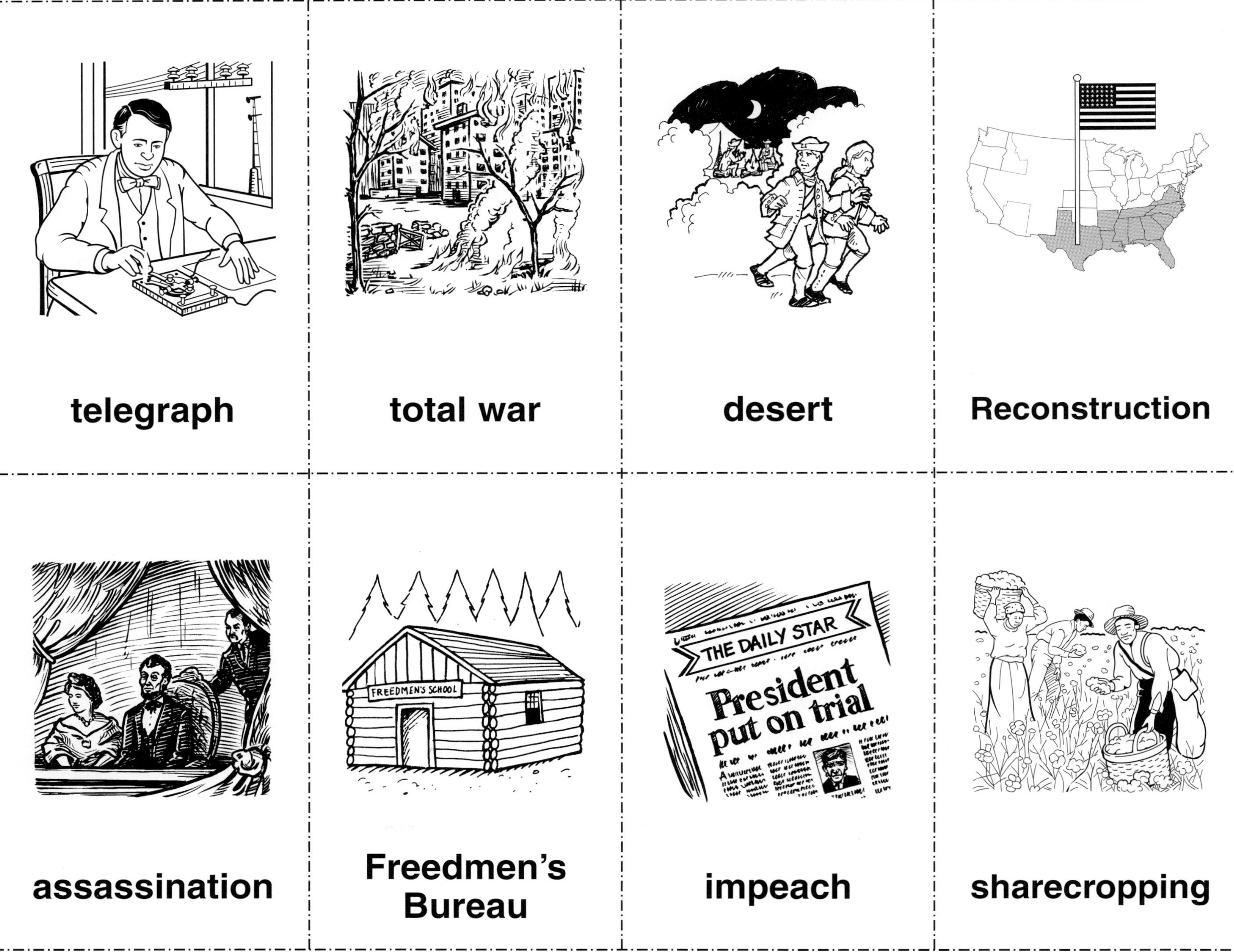

telegraph
total war
desert
Reconstruction
FREEDMEN'S SCHOOL
THE DAILY STAR
President put on trial
assassination
Freedmen's Bureau
impeach
sharecropping

Noun
The period when the South rejoined the Union.

(Chapter 13, Lesson 4)

Verb
To leave the army without permission.

(Chapter 13, Lesson 3)

Noun
The strategy of destroying an enemy's resources.

(Chapter 13, Lesson 3)

Noun
A machine that sends electric signals over wires.

(Chapter 13, Lesson 3)

Noun
When landowners let poor farmers use small areas of their land. In return, the sharecropper gave the landowner a share of the crop.

(Chapter 13, Lesson 5)

Verb
To charge a government official with a crime.

(Chapter 13, Lesson 4)

Noun
An organization that provided food, clothing, medical care, and legal advice to poor blacks and whites.

(Chapter 13, Lesson 4)

Noun
The murder of an important leader.

(Chapter 13, Lesson 4)

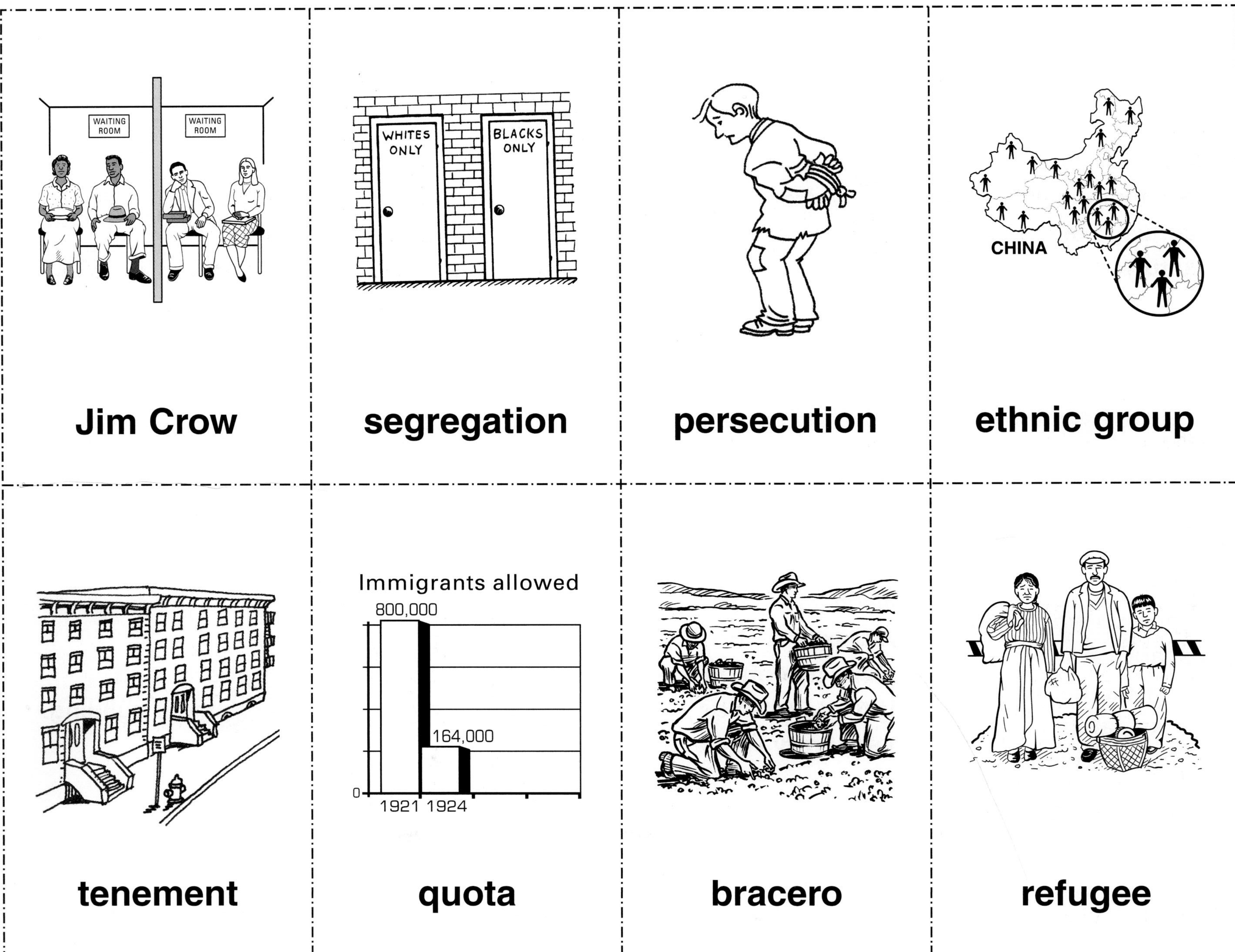

WAITING ROOM
WAITING ROOM
Jim Crow
WHITES ONLY
BLACKS ONLY
segregation
persecution
CHINA
ethnic group
tenement
Immigrants allowed
800,000
164,000
0
1921 1924
quota
bracero
refugee

Noun **A group of people who share a language or culture.** (Chapter 14, Lesson 1)	*Noun* **Unfair treatment or punishment.** (Chapter 14, Lesson 1)	*Noun* **The forced separation of the races.** (Chapter 13, Lesson 5)	*Noun* **Laws that segregated African Americans from other Americans.** (Chapter 13, Lesson 5)
Noun **A person who escapes war or other danger and seeks safety in another country.** (Chapter 14, Lesson 2)	*Noun* **A Mexican who came to work in the United States as a temporary worker.** (Chapter 14, Lesson 2)	*Noun* **The maximum number of people allowed to enter a country.** (Chapter 14, Lesson 2)	*Noun* **A poorly built apartment building.** (Chapter 14, Lesson 1)

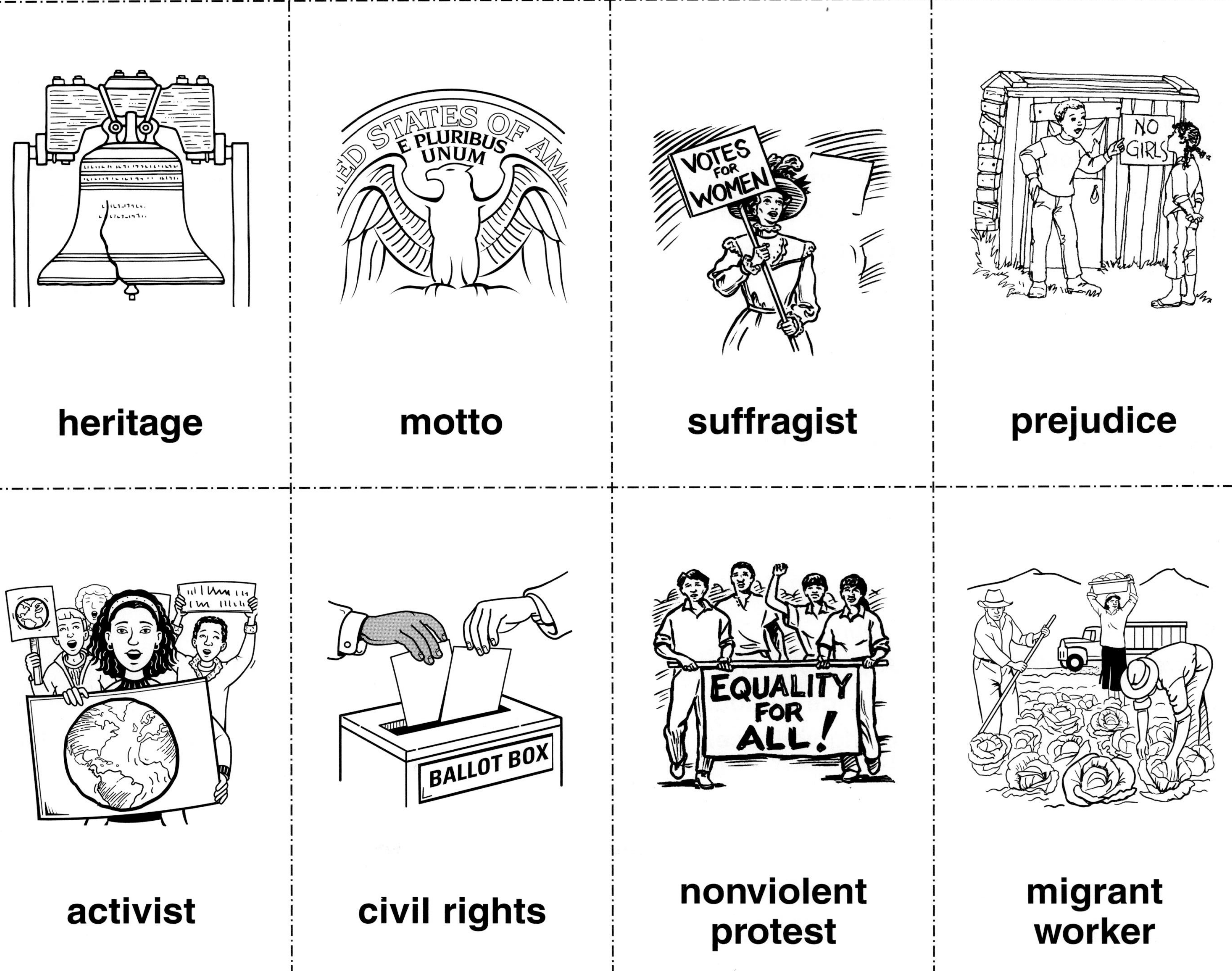
heritage
STATES OF AM
E PLURIBUS UNUM
motto
VOTES FOR WOMEN
suffragist
NO GIRLS
prejudice
activist
BALLOT BOX
civil rights
EQUALITY FOR ALL!
nonviolent protest
migrant worker

Noun
An unfair, negative opinion that can lead to unjust treatment.

(Chapter 15, Lesson 1)

Noun
A woman who worked to gain the right to vote.

(Chapter 15, Lesson 1)

Noun
A short statement that explains an ideal or a goal.

(Chapter 14, Lesson 3)

Noun
Something that is passed down from one generation to the next.

(Chapter 14, Lesson 3)

Noun
A person who moves from place to place to find work, mostly on farms.

(Chapter 15, Lesson 2)

Noun
A way of bringing change without using violence.

(Chapter 15, Lesson 2)

Noun
The rights that countries guarantee their citizens.

(Chapter 15, Lesson 2)

Noun
A person who takes action to change social conditions or unfair laws.

(Chapter 15, Lesson 1)

naturalization
Freedom
Equality
Rights
BILL OF RIGHTS
register
Sign Up to VOTE
responsibility
volunteer

Noun
Someone who helps other people without being paid.

(Chapter 15, Lesson 3)

Noun
A duty that someone is expected to fulfill.

(Chapter 15, Lesson 3)

Verb
To sign up to vote.

(Chapter 15, Lesson 3)

Noun
The process of becoming a citizen.

(Chapter 15, Lesson 3)